D1373649

Access™ 2007 Guidebook

6th Edition

Access™ 2007 Guidebook

6th Edition

MAGGIE TRIGG

PHYLLIS DOBSON

Colorado Community Colleges Online

PEARSON

Addison
Wesley

Boston San Francisco New York
London Toronto Sydney Tokyo Singapore Madrid
Mexico City Munich Paris Cape Town Hong Kong Montreal

Publisher	Greg Tobin
Executive Editor	Michael Hirsch
Acquisitions Editor	Matt Goldstein
Editorial Assistant	Maurene Goo
Associate Managing Editor	Jeffrey Holcomb
Cover Designer	Joyce Cosentino Wells
Digital Assets Manager	Marianne Groth
Senior Media Producer	Bethany Tidd
Marketing Assistant	Sarah Milmore
Senior Author Support/Technology Specialist	Joe Vetere
Senior Manufacturing Buyer	Carol Melville
Production Coordination	Shelley Creager, Aptara
Text Design, Composition, and Illustrations	Aptara, Inc.
Cover Image	© AGE Fotostock America Inc.

Many of the designations used by manufacturers and sellers to distinguish their products are claimed as trademarks. Where those designations appear in this book, and Addison-Wesley was aware of a trademark claim, the designations have been printed in initial caps or all caps.

The interior of this book was composed in QuarkXpress using ETM v2.

Library of Congress Cataloging-in-Publication Data

Trigg, Maggie.
    Access 2007 guidebook / Maggie Trigg, Phyllis Dobson. — 6th ed.
        p. cm.
    Includes index.
    ISBN-13: 978-0-321-51701-2
    ISBN-10: 0-321-51701-6
    1. Microsoft Access.   2. Database management.   I. Dobson, Phyllis.   II. Title.

QA76.9.D3T6954 2004
005.75'65—dc22

2007027860

Copyright © 2008 Pearson Education, Inc. All rights reserved. No part of this publication may be reproduced, stored in a retrieval system, or transmitted, in any form or by any means, electronic, mechanical, photocopying, recording, or otherwise, without the prior written permission of the publisher. Printed in the United States of America. For information on obtaining permission for use of material in this work, please submit a written request to Pearson Education, Inc., Rights and Contracts Department, 501 Boylston Street, Suite 900, Boston, MA 02116, fax (617) 671-3447, or online at http://www.pearsoned.com/legal/permissions.htm.

ISBN-13: 978-0-321-51701-2
ISBN-10: 0-321-51701-6
1 2 3 4 5 6 7 8 9 10—EB—11 10 09 08 07

Contents

Preface

WHAT THIS BOOK DOES

We have been teaching courses in database software products for microcomputers for many years. It has often been difficult to find the right textbook—one that combines clearly written instructions, good reference materials, and challenging exercises. That shouldn't be a problem anymore! We hope you find this book helpful in teaching and learning Access 2007.

The book is intended for a three- or four-credit introductory Access course that focuses on skill building and application. It is suitable for a traditional classroom or lab environment, a self-paced class, or an online Internet-based class.

The book teaches the concepts and procedures needed to become a designer, developer, and informed user of simple Access databases. It provides extensive coverage of the tasks you need to perform in Access, with enough theory to provide understanding of important terms and ideas.

HOW THIS BOOK DOES IT

The book is designed for hands-on learning and encourages you to try out the new material as you learn it. It is also designed to be a good reference after you have completed the course.

Reference

This book provides outstanding reference materials and features the following:

- Easy-to-use glossaries at the beginning of each chapter and a master glossary of all terms in Appendix C.

- Step-by-step end-of-chapter procedures, called the Fast Track.

- A complete summary of the built-in Access functions in Appendix B.

Hands On

This text offers extensive, varied, and challenging exercises containing both practice activities and reflective questions. There are opportunities to both rehearse new procedures and increase knowledge by answering questions that require experimentation, analysis, and discussion. More practice develops smoother skills and makes you more comfortable when tackling new problems, while reflection and experimentation help you put this new knowledge into context.

Transfer of Knowledge

One of our most enduring teaching problems has been the discovery that our students often can only perform exercises that exactly resemble those presented in the book. This book seeks to avoid that result. Unlike other hands-on books, this book does not list every keystroke or button needed to complete a practice activity. The generalized procedure contains the list of keystrokes and clicks required, but the practice activities require you to carry out those steps from within the context of the task at hand. In addition, many different types of problems, databases, and projects are included in the examples and exercises.

COURSE STRUCTURE, BOOK OUTLINE

There are twelve chapters in the book. The first six introduce database design and the simpler component objects—tables, queries, forms, and reports. Chapter 7 takes an in-depth look at database design, including entity–relationship diagrams and table normalization. Chapters 8 through 11 tackle the more advanced objects and aspects of Access, including macros, complex queries, SQL, and custom forms and reports. Chapter 12 deals with customizing Access applications.

Use the diagram below to help determine the sequence for covering the material.

- Chapter 1 and Chapter 2 must be covered before any of the other chapters; however, Chapter 7 can be done in conjunction with Chapters 1 and 2.

- Chapters 3–7 can be done in any sequence.

- Chapter 8 must follow Chapter 4; Chapter 9 must follow Chapter 5; and Chapter 10 must follow Chapter 6.

- Chapter 11 requires that you cover Chapters 1–6 first.

- Chapter 9 should be done before Chapter 12.

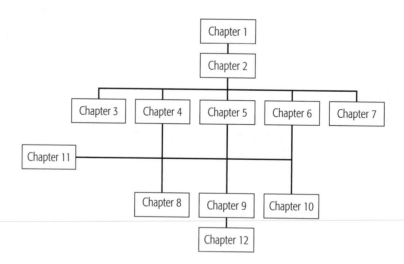

BOOK PREREQUISITES

The book assumes no previous experience with Access or any other database product and begins with introductory database terms and concepts. The language used is direct and simple and doesn't require advanced reading skills, nor is a knowledge of math beyond simple calculations required. The book does assume familiarity with Windows as far as basic usage.

Hardware and Software Assumptions

You will need to use a computer that is already configured with Windows Vista or XP and Access 2007. The computer configuration used in the book is fairly typical and includes a hard disk drive, C:, and a CD-ROM drive, D:.

The desktop, windows, dialog boxes, folders, and so forth shown in the figures may vary slightly from what you see on your screen; however, this should not change the steps needed to perform procedures. If buttons referred to in the text don't show on the toolbar or specific features or commands are unavailable to you, check with your instructor or lab assistant.

If you are working in a networked environment, ask your instructor about file storage, printer sharing, or any other related issues of concern.

When you begin an Access class or lab session, the computer will display the main desktop. To start Access, click on the desktop icon or on the listing for Access on the Start menu. If the desktop isn't displayed, check with your instructor or lab assistant.

When you end an Access class or lab session, you should save the database file you have been working on, then close the Access window. The screen will display the main desktop. If you have been using a floppy disk, don't forget to take it with you. Ask your instructor or lab assistant if they have any additional requirements such as removing files from the hard drive or shutting down the computer.

USING THE DATA FILES

The student data set that comes with this book contains all the data files needed to complete the exercises, examples, and case studies. These files are organized by chapter, and each chapter database has a new set of objects provided so no data set is dependent on completing the previous chapters' exercises. The data files are available at:

www.aw.com/trigg_dobson

The files may be installed in multiple locations, and can be copied from the hard drive to flash drives or CDs as needed. Putting the data set onto a flash drive would allow you to work at school or at home.

Each chapter provides a new set of database objects, so no data set is dependent on completing previous chapters' exercises. Some of the case studies, however, use objects created in the case study of a previous chapter.

FEATURES OF THIS BOOK

This book has several features designed to enhance its use as a reference or to increase its effectiveness as a hands-on tutorial.

Reference

Objectives

Read these before starting the chapter to see the scope of what you will learn, then again after completing the chapter to review new knowledge and skills.

Appendix B Access Functions

Refer to this list of all Access's built-in functions for descriptions, syntax, and an example of usage.

Dictionary

Skim through terms before reading the chapter and note those that are new to you. Use this as a reference while reading if you encounter an unfamiliar term. Appendix C, the Glossary, contains all the terms for all chapters.

Q: Question
A: Answer

Refer to these hints to avoid common mistakes or to troubleshoot problems encountered while doing the exercises.

Fast Track

Use these to look up procedures while working on the exercises or after class is finished. This list of procedures provides a fast reference to the material in the chapter where the procedure is introduced.

Hands-On Tutorial

How to...

Read these while sitting at the computer using Access.

Try It Yourself

Follow the instructions while using the computer and apply the procedure learned in the corresponding "How To" steps. Notice that in many cases, the accompanying figure(s) show the results of various steps. In a self-paced environment, you should complete these activities before proceeding to the next section.

Review Questions

Answer these while reading, practicing, or as a review at the end of the chapter. In a self-paced environment, you should answer these questions before proceeding to the next section.

Exercises

Complete these as determined by your instructor. Answers to the first exercise in each chapter are included in Appendix A.

Professional Tip

Read these for additional information about a topic. The tips come from working professionals and cover concepts, design ideas, maintenance suggestions, and potential problems.

Case Studies

Complete these as determined by your instructor or for extra practice on your own. Each case study uses skills learned in a chapter to complete another step in the development of a business application. Hints are included to help you solve the more complex problems.

BOOK CONVENTIONS

The book uses italics for database object names, such as the *tblMusic* table. Tables are used to summarize possible values, selections, properties, and settings of objects. Figures show how screens are laid out, how sample documents and objects look, and other visual aids that illustrate a concept or complete a procedure.

The term *click* refers to pointing at an object and clicking the left mouse button. Clicking the right mouse button is sometimes referred to as a *right click*.

EXERCISES

All end-of-chapter exercises are hands-on, except the discussion questions. Many exercises are a combination of hands-on and reflective discussion. Answer any questions by writing the answers on your printouts or a separate piece of paper. You should complete the work, then save and print as directed in the exercise.

The first exercise in each chapter is a **review activity** that lets you practice all or most of the procedures learned in a chapter. Hints are sometimes included.

The second exercise in each chapter is also a practice activity. It's a little more difficult than the first exercise.

In addition, each chapter has a group activity that can be used in class. Also, other exercises are included that explore more difficult topics and require activity and reflection.

The last exercise in each chapter is a set of **discussion questions** that can be done in small groups, as a whole-class discussion, or written as individual papers.

The answers are provided to all Review Questions and to all questions in Exercise 1 of each chapter. You will find these answers and partial solutions in Appendix A.

CASE STUDIES

Three case studies are provided at the end of each chapter. These case studies follow three different businesses, build from chapter to chapter, and present three different levels of challenge. In most instances, each case study requires the completion of the corresponding case studies in previous chapters. For example, you should complete Case Study A in Chapters 1, 2, and 3 before beginning Case Study A for Chapter 4.

The tables and database objects used in the case studies are not provided; they are created in the Chapter 1 and 2 case studies. Any other necessary data files are included on the student CD.

Hints labeled *Need More Help?* are given in many of the case studies. It's best to complete as much of the work as you can, then use the hints to complete the more complex tasks, if help is needed.

The case studies usually require the prior completion of the corresponding case studies in previous chapters. Case Study C is the most complex case study and in some instances may be easier to complete if a data set is provided to students. These databases have been included on the instructor's data set, but not the student data set, because they are often the solution database for the previous chapter's case study. It is suggested that instructors provide these files to students as they are needed, and only after the previous case study has been completed.

INSTRUCTOR RESOURCES

This text has extensive instructors' materials:

- Test bank
- Exercise solutions
- Case Study data and solution files
- Chapter PowerPoint® presentations
- Chapter outlines

WHAT'S DIFFERENT IN THIS EDITION?

The 6th edition is one of the most extensive updates ever of *The Access Guidebook*. Not only have changes been made to reflect the changes to Access 2007, but most of the examples and case studies are new, and over half the exercises have been replaced or rewritten. There are 95% new screen shots showing updated windows, commands, and operations. Graphic elements have been redesigned for easier reference.

The examples and exercises are now more oriented to business, yet still retain the simplicity necessary for their use as learning tools. Some databases have more records, so students have the experience of working with larger sets of data. Case Study B has been rewritten and Case Study C is all new. Case Study C is still the most challenging of the case studies, but it's easier than old Case Study C. Chapters 1 and 7 now have additional examples that show how to develop and normalize database tables.

ACKNOWLEDGMENTS

We would like to thank the following faculty for their feedback and suggestions. Their insightful comments helped shape this book into the useful tool we had hoped it would be.

Reviewers of the Various Editions

John Avitable
College of Saint Rose

Kris Chandler
Pikes Peak Community College

Fred Clark
Peninsula College

Robert Coleman
Pima Community College

Janet Collins
Lamar University

Art Dearing
Tarleton State University

Gretchen Douglas
State University of New York at Cortland

Maureen Duncan
Vista College

Timothy J. Fullam
University of Alaska Southeast

Fred Hills
McLennan Community College

Dennis Hipp
Guilford Technical Community College

Larry Holder
The University of Tennessee at Martin

Laura Hunt
Tulsa Community College

Jerry Isaacs
Carroll College

Kathy Jesiolowski
Milwaukee Area Technical College

Holly L. Johnson
Central Community College—
Columbus Circle

Mary Johnson
Mt. San Antonio College

Mozelle Johnson
Pima Community College

Patricia Kelly
College of Charleston

Ramesh Kumar
California State University, Fullerton

Cathie LeBlanc
Keene State College

Stanley Leja
Del Mar College, Corpus Christi, Texas

Harry Lichtbach
Alamedan Unlimited

Melissa Browning Lizmi
Montgomery College, Maryland

John Longstreet
Harold Washington College

Luis Lopez
Saint Phillips College

Jackie Lou
Lake Tahoe Community College

John L. May
Oklahoma State University, Olkmulgee

Patricia Milligan
Baylor University

Phillip L. Morrison
Aiken Technical College

Cathy Moore
Brookhaven College

Ed Mott
Central Texas College

Mary Myers
Edison Community College

Ladimer Nagurney
University of Hartford

Brenda Nielsen
Mesa Community College

Connie O'Neill
Sinclair Community College

David Paradice
Texas A&M University

Merrill Parker
Chattanooga Technical Community
College

Virginia Phillips
Youngstown State University

Judy Richardson
Fox Valley Technical College

John Russo
Wentworth Institute of Technology

Ruby Sanhga
Orange Coast College

Patty Santoianni
Sinclair Community College

Werner Schenk
University of Rochester

Elaine Silber
Southern Ohio College

BJ Sineath
Forsyth Technical Community College

Debi Smith
University of Alaska, Anchorage

Richard Stearns
Parkland College

Vickee Stedham
St. Petersburg College

Cherie Stevens
South Florida Community College

Arta Szathmary
Bucks County Community College

Khanh Vu
Northern Virginia Community College

Ken Wade
Champlain College

Reggie White
Black Hawk College

Victor Wright
Chapman University, California State
University, Fullerton

Beth Whiting
Kennesaw State College

Lenard Wittlake
Walla Walla College

We'd also like to thank those faculty and students who made this book a more
effective teaching tool.

Faculty

Dave Williams
California State University, Fullerton

Trevis Hicks
Tri-County Community College

Chester Barkan
Long Island University

Students

Dennis Gauci

Pam Drummond
California State University, Fullerton

Mark May

Sherry Anderson

Peggy Anderson

Judy Davenport

Tracey Payne

Jackie Blount

James Patterson

Ed Young
Tri-County Community College

Chapter 1

Access and Data Basics

Objectives

After completing this chapter you will be able to

Understand basic database concepts:

- Know how data is organized.
- Know how data is changed into information.
- Understand databases.
- Identify the objects in a database.
- Know how a computer can aid in organizing large quantities of data.
- Define a relational database.
- Understand the function of Access.

Design a database before using the computer:

- Know which fields to include in a database.

- Construct tables that minimize storage and editing time.
- Know how to identify key and common fields.
- Recognize some of the factors that affect database design.

Start and navigate through Access:

- Launch Access from multiple locations within Windows.
- Identify the components of the Access window.
- Use the online help functions.
- End an Access session.

Dictionary

Application software	A group of files that, when running, can focus the computer on a specific task or set of tasks.
Bit	The smallest unit of data on a computer—a one or a zero.
Byte	A string of eight bits representing one character.
Data	Raw facts, numbers, or names that are input into the computer for processing.
Data organization	How data is arranged in the computer—from bits to a database.
Database	A large collection of related data files, forms, queries, reports, and so forth.
Database management system (DBMS)	A computerized method for managing, organizing, and using a database.
Field	The smallest unit of data in a database.
File	Data or programs stored on a disk.

Foreign key	Field(s) containing the same values as those in the primary key of another table.
Form	A special screen used for data display and editing.
Information	Useful processed data.
Macro	An automated sequence of commands.
Module	A group of Visual Basic programs that work with an Access database.
Navigation pane	The left side of the Access window containing a list of database objects.
Normalization	The process of making a table match a relational database design standard called a normal form.
Office button	A button in the upper left corner that opens the office menu that provides database level commands.
Primary key	A field or fields that uniquely identify a record.
Query	Processed database information displayed on the screen, or used as input for other objects.
Quick Access toolbar	A small customizable toolbar for frequently used commands.
Record	A collection of related fields that describes one member of the group represented by a table.
Relational database	A type of database that stores information in tables that can be related, or cross-referenced. Access is a relational database.
Report	Printed output from the database containing organized information.
Ribbon	An area in the upper part of the window containing buttons for database commands.
Table	The Access object that contains data about a specific group or entity.

1.1 Introducing Data

This book will teach you about an application software package called Access. Computers can perform many different tasks, or applications, by obeying a series of instructions we call software. When the software allows you to do something specific— play a game, write a document, or draw a picture—it's called application software.

Access is an application that belongs to the family of database management products. Databases are used for record-keeping functions, such as tracking your courses and grades or remembering the birthdays and anniversaries of family and friends. Databases are collections of data, and stored specifications on how to organize and retrieve the data. Database managers are tools that make it easy for you, the user, to handle databases. They help you create places to store data; allow you to add, change, or delete data; organize it in dozens of different ways; and view it on the screen, on paper, or even as a Web page.

What is Data?

The reason that computers have become so prevalent in our world is that they can provide us with useful information extremely quickly. Computers take data in and rearrange it into useful information. Data is simply the raw material or facts used as input for processing. When data is processed by the computer, it becomes information. Processing can mean that the data is organized—grouped or sorted—or it can mean that data is transformed by mathematics—numbers added or multiplied, and so forth. Information is useful processed data.

Information is usually viewed or printed, but can be stored and eventually processed again, perhaps in a different format, to become new information. Information is useful within a particular context or situation—one user's information can be another user's data.

A database, therefore, is a collection of related pieces of data that can be processed into information useful for a specific purpose. Databases in Access also include stored instructions on how to process, view, print, and store the data. For example, a database might

Q: What is data?

A: Data is raw facts. When it is processed, organized or transformed, it becomes information.

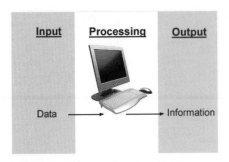

Figure 1.1 The information cycle

contain payroll data about employees and the time each one spent on each job during a pay period. It would also contain instructions for calculating and printing paychecks.

What is a Database Management System?

Data is a valuable resource for any company or business and managing this data effectively is extremely important. Data is useless if it can't be retrieved easily and in appropriate formats for different users. Think again about the payroll database example. The time that employees spend on jobs is the raw data. This data needs to be processed into paychecks for the employees, but it can also be reorganized or sorted into groups of jobs, so that customers can be billed.

Databases help manage data for people. A variety of databases are used in everyday life without the help of a computer. Telephone directories, cookbooks, and encyclopedias are noncomputer databases.

The computer, however, can make organizing, locating, and retrieving data much easier and faster than is possible by the "old-fashioned" method. To manage large quantities of data on the computer, database management system software is necessary. A database management system (DBMS) defines the data and provides a structure to enter the data into records. These records can then be edited or retrieved in various formats. Data entry forms and different types of reports can be created within a DBMS. Access is such a system. A computerized database management system is an invaluable tool for business, but there are many practical home uses for this type of software as well.

How is Data Organized?

Because database management systems are concerned with organizing data, it's important to know how the computer uses a hierarchy of data organization.

At the lowest or machine level, data is stored in bits, short for binary digits. A binary number system contains two numbers: zero and one. A bit can be either on, 1, or off, 0. Back in the early days of computers, the internal components of a computer were made up of a series of switches and vacuum tubes, as opposed to the circuit boards and chips of today. These switches physically turned the tubes either on or off.

Bits aren't very useful by themselves, as they can only represent two things—a zero or a one. Strings of eight bits are put together into bytes—one byte represents one character, or key, on the keyboard. The standard code ASCII (American Standard Code for Information Interchange) governs what string of bits represents which character, so that data is always represented the same way on every computer. For example, the letter a is represented by the byte 01100001 and $ is 00100100.

When bytes are grouped into meaningful words, phrases, paragraphs, and numbers in a database, they are called fields. This is the beginning point of data organization in a database management system. Fields are the smallest units of data in a database. Figure 1.2 shows how a field is composed of a series of bytes.

Q: What is a database?

A: A database is a collection of related pieces of data that can be processed into information useful for a specific purpose.

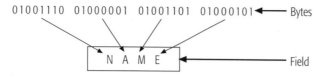

Figure 1.2 Bytes make up data-fields

A collection of related fields is called a record. A record holds all the information about one person or thing. Records play an important part in data organization because the values in the records are the raw data. Figure 1.3 shows a record with the names of the fields—*Name, Address,* and so forth—on the left side of the box, with the actual data following each colon.

> *Name:* Luke Warm
> *Address:* 7996 S. Pinewood
> *City:* Hillridge
> *State:* CO
> *Zip Code:* 80999

Figure 1.3 Related fields in one record

A table is a collection of related records. The fields, or data items, needed for a project can be organized into any number of related tables. These tables are stored together with other data objects, as one database file on a disk. A file is any data or program stored on a disk. We'll discuss later how to decide which fields belong in which table.

Tables are almost always represented by matrices or grids, similar to the layout of a spreadsheet. Let's assume that the table shown in Figure 1.4 represents a group of students taking an Access class. Because these students are in the same class, they have something in common and they form a group. All the data about one student, or one row in the table, is a record. One column, representing one attribute of the students, such as name or address, is a field. Looking down a column shows all the data values stored in one field—the field names are shown on the top row.

Field

Student ID	First Name	Last Name	Address	City	State	Zip Code
3214	Luke	Warm	7996 S. Pinewood	Hillridge	CO	80999
3897	Justin	Case	14760 Meadow Rd.	Jordan City	CO	81374
4355	Anne	Aconda	2344 E. Rustic Dr.	Nighthawk	CO	84123

Record →

Figure 1.4 Records in a *Students* table

Another table, like the one in Figure 1.5, might consist of all the courses offered at the college.

Course Number	Name	Credits	Textbook
CIS 110	Introduction to Computers	2	*The World of Computers*
BUS 200	Business Ethics	3	*Ethics in Business*
CIS 140	Introduction to Database	2	*The Access Guidebook*
MAT 201	Calculus I	4	*Introducing Calculus*
CIS 138	Introduction to Windows	2	*The Windows Guidebook*

Figure 1.5 Fields and records in a *Courses* table

These two tables, *Students* and *Courses,* are the beginning of a college records database. Other tables might include faculty members, degree programs, and class schedules by semester or quarter.

Hierarchy of Data Organization

The pyramid in Figure 1.6 shows the way data is organized, from the smallest bit to an entire database. Each unit of data is made up of a group of the data items listed above it. For example, a byte is a collection of related bits; a field is a collection of related bytes; a record is a collection of related fields; a table is a collection of related records; and a database is a collection of related tables.

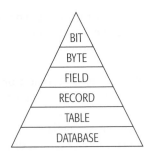

Figure 1.6 Hierarchy of data organization

1.2 Introducing Other Database Objects

A complete database file in Access contains more than just data tables. Databases also include instructions for how you'd like to organize and retrieve the data. In the college records example, the database might include course schedules, individual student schedules, rosters of students in a class, and so forth.

Access objects include forms, reports, queries, macros, and modules. These objects allow users to input, process, and output the data.

Queries

Queries are questions, or inquiries, about the data in a database. For example, you might want to know how many students are enrolled in a course, how many more credits a student needs to graduate, or if there are any night sections of a particular course. These questions are translated into sets of conditions placed upon the data contained in a table, multiple tables, or another query. The output from a query is a set of records that match the given specifications.

Queries are used for many different purposes. The set of records produced by a query can be used as input into other database objects, such as forms and reports. Some queries

Q: What objects are found in
a database?

A: Data tables, reports, queries,
forms, macros, and modules.

can update data in tables or even create new tables. Other queries can summarize data by calculating totals, averages, and other statistics about the included data.

Queries are stored with the database and can be used whenever you need an answer to the question posed by the query. As the data in the table or tables used by the query changes, the answer given by the query will adjust to reflect the current data.

Forms

Forms are special screens designed for data display, data entry, and data editing. Forms can display data from single or multiple tables and/or queries. Using a form rather than a table or query to display and edit data makes it easier to interpret the data. When a form is used for data entry and editing, you can include rules that control the data being added or changed.

Forms are one of the most widely used database objects. They often have macros and Visual Basic programs attached to them so that they can process data and open other forms. Some special forms are not attached to a data source such as a table or query. These forms are used to display menu selections and other text and graphic information.

Reports

A report is a printed document produced by the database. Reports can print all or only part of the information in a table or query, or they can combine data from multiple tables or queries. Report data can be grouped and sorted in many different ways, and reports make it easy to summarize and subtotal data.

There are a number of different formats you can choose for report printing. The format, or design layout, is stored as part of the database and used whenever you need to print the report. Each time you produce the report, the data printed shows the most current data in the database.

Many reports are printed on a regular schedule. For example, a printed roster of all the students in a class would be printed at the beginning of the semester or quarter. Other reports may be printed on demand, such as a student's transcript of courses.

Access can also print specialized reports or reports containing specialized objects. You can create mailing labels of various sizes and use them to print names and addresses from any table or query. You can also create a report that is a graph or chart, or embed a graph or chart in another report.

Macros

Macros allow you to automate sequences of commands that are frequently used, difficult to remember, or intended to run when a specified event occurs. They are really programs that contain only a limited number of commands, called actions. For example, an Access macro might run a query when data is entered or changed on a form, so additional data in another table can be updated.

Access macros can be quite useful, and are easier to learn than Visual Basic programming. Macros are often attached to customized menus and ribbons so they run whenever the menu command is selected or a button is clicked. Other macros are attached to command buttons and run when the button is clicked. Access macros have some characteristics of a programming language, such as the ability to conditionally branch and the ability to contain several submacros.

Modules

Modules are groups of Visual Basic programs or procedures. If you need to do a lot of programming or if you want to automate a task that doesn't have a corresponding macro action, you can create a Visual Basic procedure.

Modules may be attached to a specific form or report. The procedures in these modules are executed when an event occurs within the form or report. For example, a procedure may update a table after a report is printed or it might calculate and display values on a form after certain data is entered.

Other modules, called standard modules, are attached to the entire database. These modules contain procedures that are shared by all the objects in a database. For example, a procedure in a standard module might display address data in a block format—something that is useful on several different forms and reports in the database.

1.3 Starting Access

Access is one of the major program components of the Microsoft Office software package. It was written to be totally compatible with the other programs in this software suite. Files can be easily imported or exported into other applications, giving the user the major advantages of time savings and data accessibility. Some of the other applications in the Microsoft Office software package are:

- Word
- Excel
- PowerPoint
- Publisher
- Outlook

Different combinations of these applications are offered in the various Office suites—Access is part of the Professional suite and the Ultimate suite. Depending on how Access was installed and your particular computer, there can be several methods for starting this program. If there is an Access shortcut on the desktop, double-click it to start Access. If there's an Access button on the taskbar, click it to begin. Otherwise, use one of the other techniques as described below.

How to Start Access

From the Windows Start button:

1. Press the Start button, and click All Programs on the Start menu.

Figure 1.7 All Programs item on the Windows Vista Start menu

2. Choose the Microsoft Access option from the list of available programs. You may have to click on the Microsoft Office menu item first.

Figure 1.8 Access 2007 icon on the All Programs menu

From the Windows Start button, alternate method:

1. Click the Start button.
2. Click the MS-Office Access 2007 icon.

Figure 1.9 Access 2007 icon on the Windows Start menu

From the Explorer menu:

1. Choose the Windows Explorer option from the list of available programs on the Start menu. You may first need to select Accessories from the menu and then locate Explorer.

Figure 1.10 Windows Explorer icon on the Start menu

2. From the Explorer screen, open the MS Office folder by clicking its icon or name. Open the Office 12 folder.

3. Double-click on the Access icon in the right window pane. The screen shown in Figure 1.11 may look a little different—it depends on the software that's stored on your computer.

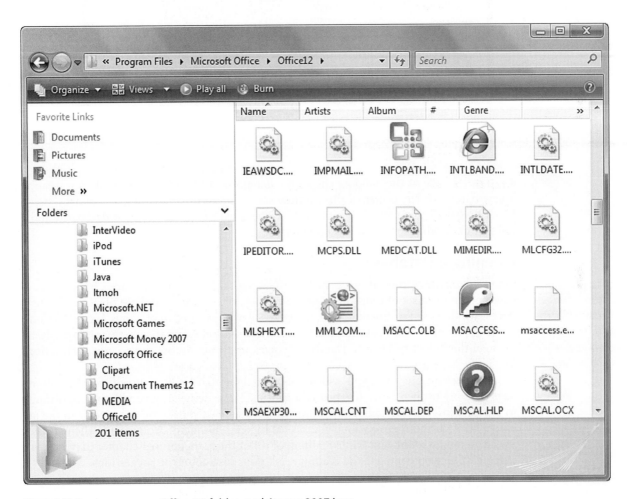

Figure 1.11 Explorer screen, Office 12 folder, and Access 2007 icon

1.4 / Recognizing Screen Layout

When Access 2007 is opened, a window appears displaying an informational Getting Started page (see Figure 1.12). This page is set up like a Web page, with navigation links that open databases with one click. You can create a new database either from scratch or from a template, or you can open an existing database.

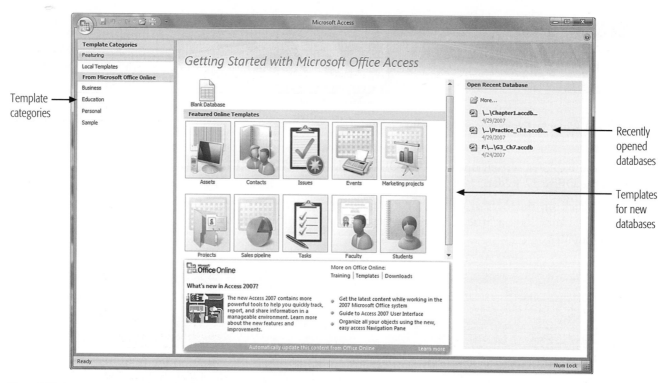

Template categories →

← Recently opened databases

← Templates for new databases

Figure 1.12 Access 2007 window displaying the Getting Started page

The left side of the window shows the categories of templates available for creating a new database. The center of the window shows options for creating a new database—blank or specific template. The right side shows a list of recently opened databases and a link, More ..., that shows all available databases.

Opening a Database

Once a database is created or opened, the Getting Started page is replaced by a database page containing a set of tools for creating, editing, and viewing database objects. This new Access window is very different than the database window used in previous Access versions.

To open your first database, use the information following the next paragraph. Read through the "How to Open a Database" steps, and then follow the specific instructions in "Try It Yourself 1.4.2."

Throughout the book you will see sections labeled "Try It Yourself" in the column next to many of the "How To" procedure steps. These activities give you the opportunity to try the procedure described on your computer. They can be done at home or in the lab before class, or they may be done in class led by your instructor. You may do them as they are encountered in the text while reading, or all of the activities in a chapter may be done together after you complete the reading. Ask your instructor for suggestions.

How to Open a Database

From the Access window:

1. Click on one of the database names in the Open Recent Database list (see Figure 1.12).

   OR

   Choose the More ... option (under the Open Recent Database heading) on the right side of the window (see Figure 1.12).

   The Open dialog box appears as shown in Figure 1.13.

2. Locate the folder containing the database file in the Look in text box (see Figure 1.13).

TRY IT YOURSELF 1.4.1

A. Download data files as instructed in the Preface.

B. Copy the files to a folder as instructed by your teacher.

TRY IT YOURSELF 1.4.2

A. Open the *Practice_CH1* database from the student data set. The screen should be similar to that shown in Figure 1.14.

B. Examine the navigation pane to see the list of database objects. There are four tables, one query, three forms, one report, and one macro in the database.

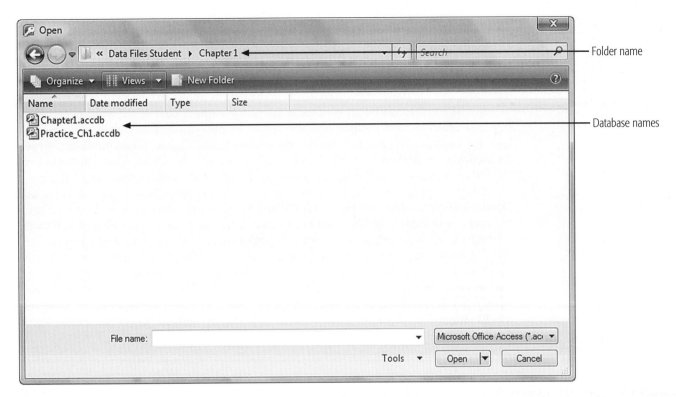

Figure 1.13 The Open dialog box

3. Select the database name from the list of files displayed.

4. Click on the Open button in the lower right corner, or double-click on the file name.

5. The Access window appears as shown in Figure 1.14. Note the security warning message. To allow macros and programs to work, click on the Options button, choose "Enable this content," and click the OK button.

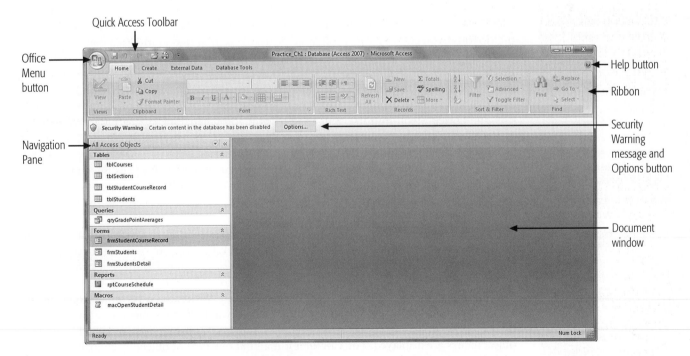

Figure 1.14 The Access window with an open database

The Access Window

Once a database is opened, the Access window takes on a completely new look, as shown in Figure 1.14. The window is divided into three main areas. The top of the window has controls and commands, the lower left shows a list of objects in the currently opened database, and the lower right area displays the details about any selected object.

Access has three different command areas in the upper part of the window—the ribbon, the Quick Access toolbar, and the Office Menu button. The ribbon contains buttons for commanding the various database objects, the Quick Access toolbar contains frequently used commands such as copy and print, and the Office Menu button opens the Office menu which provides database level commands such as open and backup.

Ribbon commands are grouped on tabbed pages—Home, Create, External Data, and Database Tools, as shown in Figure 1.15. These tabs can vary when certain database objects are opened—new tab names will always appear on the right side of the ribbon. Click on the tab name to view the commands on the tab, and then click on the command button to activate the command. Command buttons are clustered into functional groups on a tab, with the group name appearing below the buttons. When you rest the mouse over a command button, its name and function appear next to the button. Ribbon commands can also be activated from the keyboard by pressing the Alt key and a letter key simultaneously. To see the letters assigned to these commands, press the Alt key and the keystroke letters, called KeyTips, appear beside the commands.

Figure 1.15 The ribbon and the Quick Access toolbar

TRY IT YOURSELF 1.4.3

A. With the *Practice_CH1* database open, verify that the Navigation pane resembles Figure 1.17.

B. Open the View menu, and arrange the objects in order by Created Date. See how the filtering changes to time based criteria in the lower part of the View menu.

C. Arrange by Object Type and filter out all but the forms in the database.

D. Try arranging the objects by Tables and Related Views. You will see objects listed by the table that supplies data to the object.

E. Go back to the default view by choosing the menu options shown in Figure 1.17.

The Quick Access toolbar is positioned above the ribbon, but can be moved below the ribbon if you choose. This toolbar is meant to contain frequently used commands that can be quickly activated without switching to a different tab. When you first use Access, this toolbar contains only the commands to save, undo, and redo, but it's easy to change these buttons. There's a customization arrow on the right edge of the toolbar which allows you to add and remove command buttons, and also to move the toolbar.

The Office Menu button opens the Office menu when clicked (see Figure 1.16). The Office menu contains commands for creating, opening, and saving database files, as well as commands for printing and sharing information. Notice the Recent Documents list on the right side of the menu. Clicking on a database name in this list opens the named database. The Access Options button in the lower right corner allows you to customize various options such as screen display, command behavior, and file security. In the same area, there's a button to exit Access.

The Navigation Pane, in the lower left area of the window, provides a list of all the objects in the current database. It's shown in Figure 1.17. You can open one specific database object for use or for editing by clicking on the object name. Double-click to view and use the object; right-click and choose Design View from the menu to edit the object.

The Navigation Pane contents can be viewed in a variety of ways by clicking on the View Menu button, and then choosing the view you want from the menu (see Figure 1.17). By default, objects are grouped by type—tables, queries, forms, reports, and macros, and all object names are displayed. You can filter out all but one type of object by choosing the type in the lower part of the menu. For example, clicking on Forms shows only the forms in the

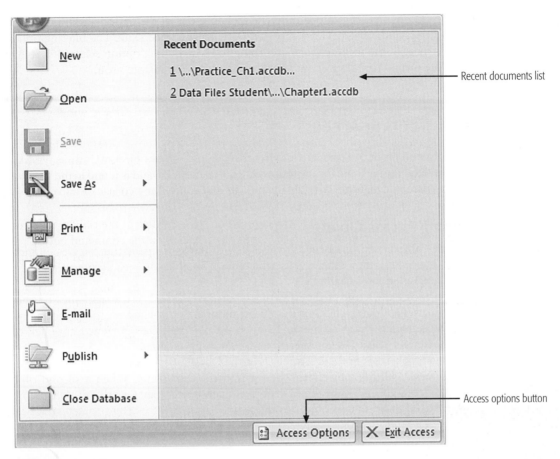

Figure 1.16 The Office menu

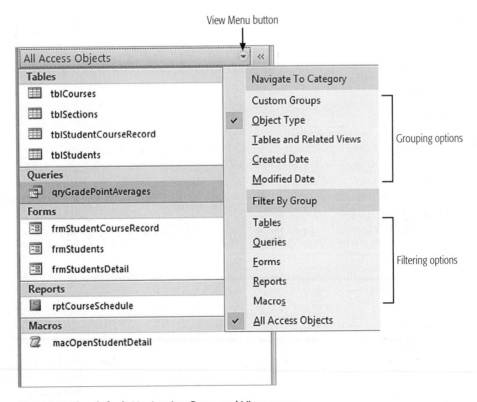

Figure 1.17 The default Navigation Pane and View menu

database. To see objects grouped differently, choose one of the options from the top of the menu—Tables and Related Views, Created Date, or Modified Date. The filtering options in the lower part of the menu change according to the grouping option selected in the upper part of the menu. You can also define your own rules for custom groups.

1.5 Touring Access

Let's take a quick tour of Access and briefly examine some of the objects found in a typical database. The database we'll use for the tour is called *Practice_Ch1* and is found in the student data files. This database manages data about students and courses at a college or university.

Opening Access Objects

All Access objects can be opened for usage with data, or opened in the Design view for editing. There are a few other views which are available for specific object types. These will be covered in later chapters.

First, locate the name of the object to be opened in the Navigation Pane. To open the object for usage, double-click on the object name or right-click on the object name and select Open from the pop-up menu. To open the object in Design view, right-click on the object name and select Design View from the pop-up menu.

When an object is opened, it appears in the Document window in the lower right area of the screen. Multiple objects can be open at the same time. When a second object is opened, it's placed on top of the first object. Each object has a small tab on the top that can be clicked to bring that object to the front.

Tables

When you open a table, Access adds a Datasheet tab to the ribbon, and colors the ribbon buttons to show those commands appropriate for an opened table. If you open the table in Design view, a new Design tab is added to the ribbon with commands suitable for editing tables.

Figure 1.18 shows the opened *tblStudents* table. Look at the figure and notice that the data is displayed in a grid or matrix. Each row in the display corresponds to one

TRY IT YOURSELF 1.5.1

Using the Practice_CH1 database

A. Open the *tblStudents* table and view the data. Your screen should look similar to Figure 1.18.

B. Close the table.

C. Open the *tblStudents* table in Design view (see Figure 1.19).

D. Close the table.

Student	Last name	First name	Address	City	State	Zip	Phone	Enrollment date	Certficate progra
0103	O'Casey	Harriet	4088 Ottumwa Way	Mentira	CO	81788	(303) 417-4438	8/25/2005	☑
0122	Logan	Janet	860 Charleston St.	Oxalys	CO	84133	(712) 441-3321	1/19/2006	☐
0123	Hernandez	Greg	6065 Rainbow Falls Rd.	Roselle	CO	87203	(712) 472-0398	6/10/2005	☑
0139	Carroll	Pat	4018 Landers Lane	Lafayette	CO	84548	(303) 476-2718	8/25/2005	☑
0148	Wolf	Bee	1775 Bear Trail	Outcropping	CO	84345	(303) 443-4863	1/19/2006	☑
0167	Krumple	Scott	580 E Main St.	La Garita	CO	88413	(303) 444-1324	8/25/2005	☐
0171	Harvey	Elliot	34 Kerry Dr	El Mano	CO	80646	(712) 406-4647	8/25/2005	☑
0181	Zygote	Carrie	8607 Ferndale St	Grenoble	CO	80631	(303) 406-3104	8/25/2005	☑
0194	Loftus	Abner	8077 Montana Place	Big Fish Bay	CO	86505	(303) 468-0858	1/19/2006	☑
0251	Grainger	John	2256 N Sante Fe Dr.	Iliase	CO	84847	(303) 444-4757	1/19/2006	☑
0276	Snide	Steve	39430 Big Rock Road	Flame Thrower	CO	82012	(712) 420-1216	1/19/2006	☐
0385	Stocking	David	291-A Gorgonzola	Cleo	CO	81029	(303) 410-2990	1/19/2006	☑
0629	Wheeler	Frank	2225 Iola Ave	Cartuchi	CO	81804	(712) 414-0404	6/10/2005	☑
1022	Fox	Brittany	297-B Gorgonzola	Cleo	CO	81029	(303) 410-2942	8/25/2005	☐
1123	McCoy	Fran	1440 Manchester Way	Mountain View	CO	87757	(712) 477-8783	1/19/2006	☐
2011	Thomas	Joan	67438 E. 91st St.	Baseboard	CO	85493	(303) 484-9384	1/19/2006	☑
2345	Stiggle	Ted	12920 Workers Rd.	Scraggy View	CO	82191	(303) 421-9147	8/25/2005	☑
3456	Farrell	Dean	121 Highway 80	Excelsior	CO	85331	(303) 483-3111	8/25/2005	☑
3465	Waltz	Marsha	1900 Industrial Way	Fargone	CO	81923	(712) 419-2349	6/10/2005	☐

tblStudents

Navigation buttons → Record: ◄ 4 of 25 ► ►◄ No Filter Search

Figure 1.18 Open *tblStudents* table

record in the table, and each column represents a field. You can scroll through the records using the window scroll bars or the intelligent mouse wheel. You can also jump to different records using the navigation buttons at the bottom of the screen (see Figure 1.18). The navigation buttons are arrows that allow you to jump to the next, previous, first, and last records in the table.

When a table is open, data can be added, edited, and deleted. You can also sort data on any field(s), and apply filters that mask out records you don't want to see. At the bottom of the window near the navigation buttons, are buttons for filtering and sorting data.

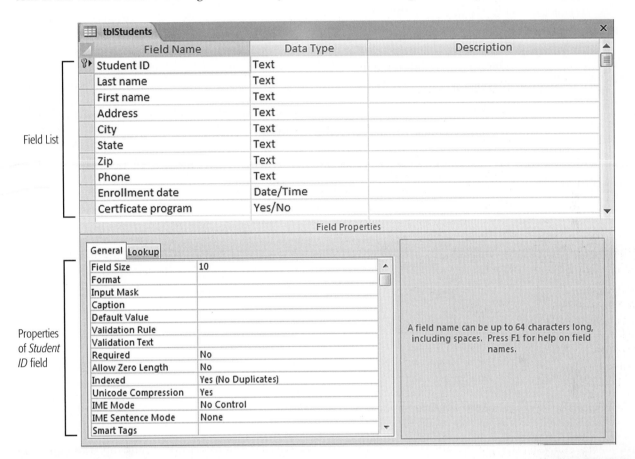

Figure 1.19 Table *tblStudents* in Design view

The plus sign to the left of the Student ID field in each record indicates that the table has a subdatasheet (see Figure 1.18). A subdatasheet displays related data that is stored in another table in the database. Figure 1.20 shows the subdatasheet for the *tblStudents* table, which shows a list of courses taken by the student shown in the main record. The subdatasheet gets its data from the *tblStudentCourseRecord* table.

	Student ▾	Last name ▾	First name ▾	Address ▾	City ▾	St:
⊟	0103	O'Casey	Harriet	4088 Ottumwa Way	Mentira	CC
	CoursePrefi: ▾	CourseNuml ▾	Grade ▾	SemesterTal ▾	GradePoints ▾	
	CIS	118	C	07FALL	4	
	CIS	138	B	07FALL	5	
	CIS	139	C	06FALL	4	
	CIS	140	A	06FALL	6	
✱	CIS				0	

Close subdatasheet

Figure 1.20 Table *tblStudents* displaying a subdatasheet

TRY IT YOURSELF 1.5.2

Using the *Practice_CH1* database:

A. Open the *tblStudents* table.

B. Go to the last record in the table using the navigation buttons.

C. Go to the first record in the table.

D. Click on the plus sign to the left of the *Student ID* field and view the subdatasheet (see Figure 1.20).

E. Click on the minus sign to the left of the *Student ID* field to close the subdatasheet.

F. Close the *tblStudents* table by closing the window.

Tables can also be opened in Design view to see the underlying structure—what fields are called, what type of data they contain, and other properties of the fields in the table. Figure 1.19 shows the *tblStudents* table in Design view. The field list is shown at the top of the screen, and detailed properties of the fields are shown at the bottom of the screen. To switch to Design view, click on the View button on the left edge of the ribbon.

When a table is open in Design view, its structure can be changed. In other words, you can add, edit, and remove fields; you can change the properties of any field; and you can designate indices and primary keys for the table. Primary keys are discussed later in this chapter in Section 1.8.

Queries

Queries create information from table data to answer questions about the database. A question is translated into a set of conditions and input into the query. The output from a query is a set of records that matches the specifications given. When a query is opened, this set of records is shown (unless the query has been designated to update or create a table).

An open query looks the same as an open table with data arranged into rows and columns. Figure 1.21 shows the records in an open query named *qryGradePointAverages* that calculates students' grade point averages. Data edited in an open query will be changed in the source table that supplies the data.

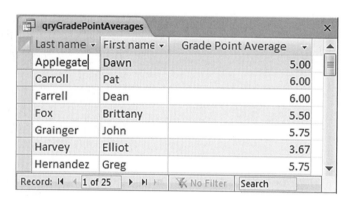

Figure 1.21 Open *qryGradePointAverages* query

To see the rules used to create the set of query records, you must open the query in Design view. This view shows the source tables (where the data comes from) in the upper part of the screen. The lower screen area shows the conditions used to select the record and the fields to be included. New fields can be created in a query by placing an expression (a calculation) in one of the field columns.

Figure 1.22 shows how the records in Figure 1.21 were produced. The data comes from two tables—*tblStudents* and *tblStudentCourseRecord*. The students' last and first names are taken from the *tblStudents* table, and their grades are averaged from the *tblStudentCourseRecord* table.

Forms

Forms are customized screens that allow the data from tables and queries to be viewed and updated. Forms can show data from one or more sources, and can display one record at a time or a list of multiple records. Some forms are not tied to any data source and are used mainly as menus, selections, lists, or splash screens (company or product logos).

Figure 1.23 shows the opened *frmStudents* form. This form contains data from multiple tables—data from the *tblStudents* table is shown in the upper part of the form, while the courses taken by that student are shown below. The course data comes from the

TRY IT YOURSELF 1.5.3

Using the *Practice_CH1* database:

A. Click on the View button to open the *tblStudents* table in Design view.

B. Note the properties available to the *Student ID* field (see Figure 1.19).

C. Click on the field *Enrollment date* and note the properties available. Each type of data (text, numbers, dates, and so forth) has its own group of properties.

D. Close the *tblStudents* table by closing the window.

TRY IT YOURSELF 1.5.4

Using the *Practice_CH1* database:

A. Open the *qryGradePoint Averages* query and view the data. It should resemble Figure 1.21.

B. Click on the View button to open the *qryGradePoint Averages* query in Design view.

C. Note the two tables used to supply the data and fields selected (see Figure 1.22)

D. Note the fields that are used to sort the data (last and first name).

E. Note the calculation used to produce the GPA (average).

F. Close the query.

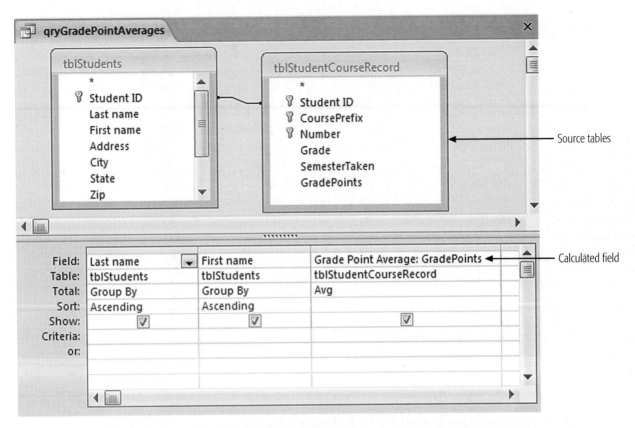

Figure 1.22 *qryGradePointAverages* query open in Design view

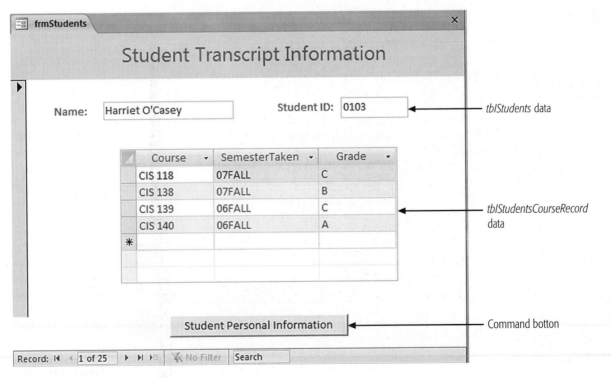

Figure 1.23 Open *frmStudents* form

TRY IT YOURSELF 1.5.5

Using the *Practice_CH1* database:

A. Open the *frmStudents* form and view the data. It should resemble Figure 1.23.

B. Click on the navigation buttons at the bottom of the form to see other student records. Note that when a new student is displayed, the list of classes is updated to the new student's classes.

C. Click on the button at the bottom of the screen that says "Student Personal Information," and view the detailed student data.

D. Close both forms.

E. Open the *frmStudents* form in Design view. It should resemble Figure 1.24.

F. Close the form

tblStudentCourseRecord table. This form is really two forms—the course list form is embedded in the student data form. The command button at the bottom of the form opens a more detailed student data form when clicked.

Figure 1.24 shows the same form in the Design view. You can clearly see the embedded course list form in this view. While in Design view, any object on the form can be edited, formatted, or deleted; and new objects can be added.

Reports

Reports are printed pages of information. Reports can be either previewed or opened in the Design view. When a report is previewed on the screen, a button is available for printing the report. Reports are very similar to forms in the way they are laid out and in the way they contain data from tables and/or queries, but reports can contain multiple levels of grouping and subtotaling. For example, a report showing sales for a nationwide company might print dollar and volume subtotals at the end of each product line grouping, at the end of each territory listing, and a grand total at the end of the report.

Figure 1.25 shows a preview of the *rptCourseSchedule* report. The data is grouped by course number and each course is sorted by section number, but no subtotals are printed, as they are not appropriate for this report. When you click the mouse on the report it zooms in and out so that you can see either the data detail or the entire page layout.

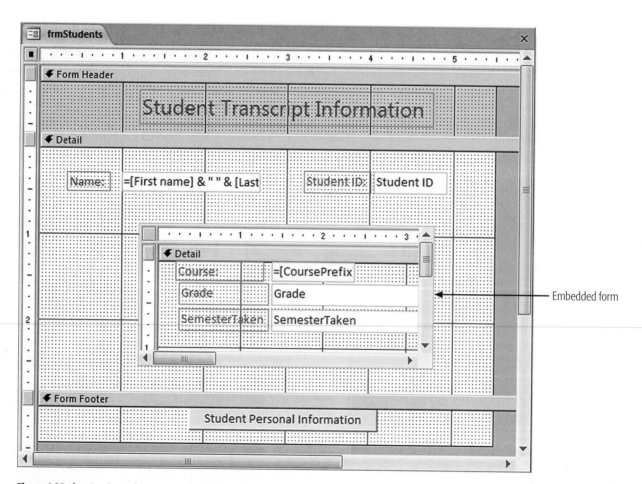

Figure 1.24 *frmStudents* form open in Design view

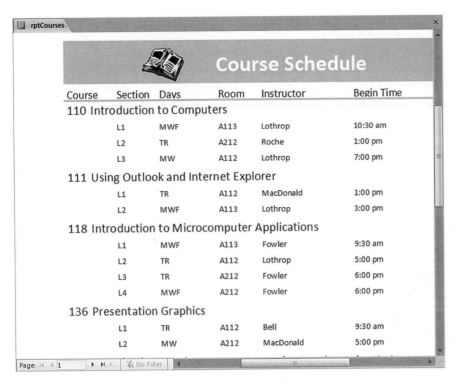

Figure 1.25 Report *rptCourseSchedule* in Preview mode

TRY IT YOURSELF 1.5.6

Using the *Practice_CH1* database:

A. Preview the report *rptCourseSchedule*. It should look similar to Figure 1.25.

B. Click the mouse on the report a couple of times to zoom in and out.

C. Close the report.

D. Open the report *rptCourseSchedule* in Design view. It should look similar to Figure 1.26.

E. Point at the picture in the report header, click and drag with your mouse. Objects on both forms and reports can be moved in this way.

F. Close the report (and don't save the changes).

Figure 1.26 shows the same report in Design view. Notice how the objects on the report are very similar to a form seen in Design view (see Figure 1.24). Report objects are resized, moved, and edited in much the same way as form objects are.

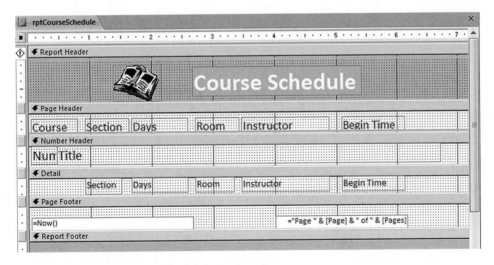

Figure 1.26 Report *rptCourseSchedule* in Design view

TRY IT YOURSELF 1.5.7

Using the *Practice_CH1* database:

A. Open the macro named *macOpenStudentDetail* in Design view.

B. Click on the empty row below the OpenForm action. Notice that the Action Arguments area at the bottom of the screen clears, because no macro action is specified. Click back on the OpenForm row and the Action Arguments return. Note that the Where Condition specifies only data where the student ID fields match (see Figure 1.27).

C. Close the Zoom window and the macro.

D. Open the *frmStudents* form and click on the button at the bottom of the screen that says "Student Personal Information." The macro opens the form and puts the correct student data in the form (see Figure 1.28).

E. Close both forms.

Macros

Access macros are programs that operate on a database, but use only a limited number of actions, or commands. For example, an Access macro can open a form, place a piece of data on a form, run a query, print a report, and so forth. Macros are easier to write than Visual Basic programs, so are often the first encounter that people have with programming their database. From the Database window, macros can either be opened in the Design view or run (although most macros are created to run from a form or report.)

Access macros are sequences of actions that interact with various objects in the database to perform a designated task. For example, a macro might open a form and display a specific record, or it might display a screen to select one of two label sizes and then print labels of the chosen size. The actions are listed in the upper portion of the window, and additional information, called arguments, is shown in the lower area.

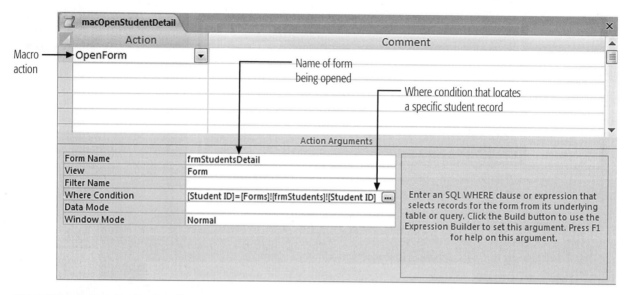

Figure 1.27 *macOpenStudentDetail* macro in Design view

Figure 1.27 shows the macro named *macOpenStudentDetail* open in Design view. This macro is run from the *frmStudents* form when the "View Student Personal Data" button at the bottom of the screen is clicked (see Figure 1.23). It opens the form called *frmStudentsDetail* and displays data about the student shown on the *frmStudents* form. The action executed by this macro is "OpenForm." The arguments tell the macro to open the form called *frmStudentsDetail*, and how to match data on the two forms so the same student appears on both.

Student Personal Information

Student ID:	0103	Zip:	81788
Last name:	O'Casey	Phone:	(303) 417-4438
First name:	Harriet	Enrollment date:	8/25/2005
Address:	4088 Ottumwa Way	Certficate program	☑
City:	Mentira		
State:	CO		

Figure 1.28 Open *frmStudentsDetail* form

1.6 Using Access Help

Getting help in Access 2007 is very straightforward. Click on the Help button—the small question mark on the far right end of the ribbon (see Figure 1.29).

Help button

Figure 1.29 Help button

The Help window that opens is essentially a Web page. Clicking on the Help button connects you to the online Office Help site. Figure 1.30 shows the Help window. Help topics can be browsed by clicking on one of the links in the center area of the window. If you don't see the topic you're interested in, type it into the Search box in the upper part of the window, and click on the Search button. The lower part of the Help window contains links to other online content of interest.

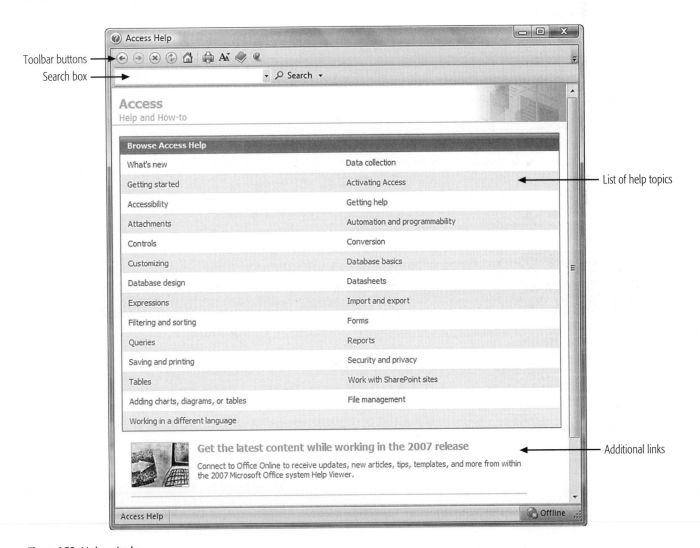

Toolbar buttons

Search box

List of help topics

Additional links

Figure 1.30 Help window

Whether you browse from a listed topic, or type in your own word or words to search for, the result is a list of articles to choose from. Just click on an article title to open it and read it. You can move back and forth between Help pages by clicking on the arrow buttons on the toolbar (see Figure 1.30). Other buttons on this toolbar let you print a Help page, go back to the home or first Help page, and do several other useful things.

Reading an article is the same as reading information on any Web page. The article has an index listed at the top of the page with links to topics, and the bottom of the page has links to other related topics. The Help window can be moved, resized, and kept open while you work in Access. Figures 1.31 and 1.32 show two different Help articles.

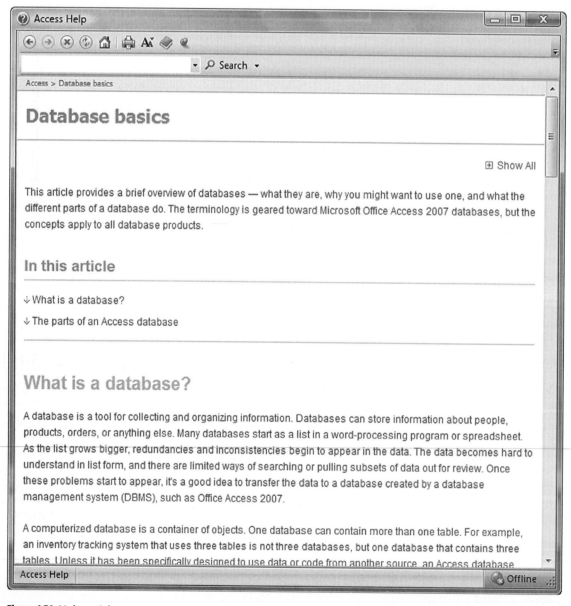

Figure 1.31 Help article

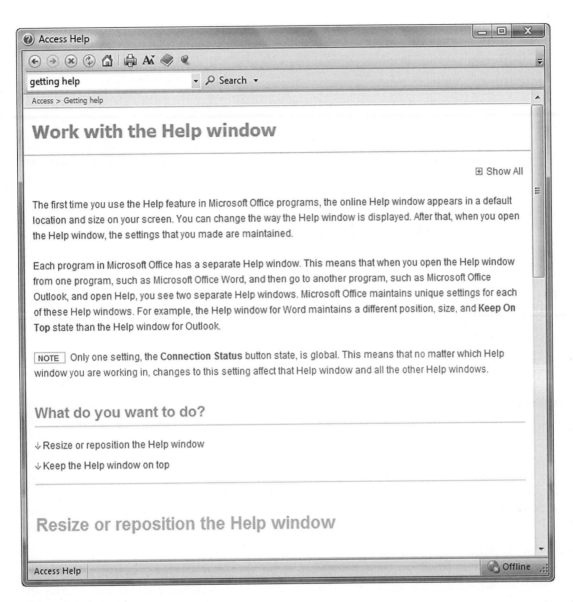

Figure 1.32 Help article

How To Use Access Help

1. Click on the Help button on the far right of the ribbon.
2. Pick a topic from the list shown by clicking on it.

   OR

   Type a topic into the Search box and click on the Search button.

   Another list of topics is displayed.
3. Click on any article title to open it.

1.7 / Exiting Access

Access is exited in the same way as all other Office applications. When you leave Access, the open database is automatically closed.

TRY IT YOURSELF 1.6.1

Using the *Practice_CH1* database:

A. Open the Help window.

B. Click on the topic "Getting started."

C. Open the article "Database basics"; as shown in Figure 1.31.

D. Search for articles on the topic "Getting help."

E. Open the article "Work with the Help window" as shown in Figure 1.32, and read through the information.

F. Close the Help window.

How to Exit Access

1. Click on the close box (X) in the upper right corner of the window.

   OR

   Click on the Office button and click on the Exit Access button in the lower right corner of the Office window.

   Access only allows one database file to be open at once, and will automatically close the database in use if a new one is opened. If you are closing from the Datasheet view or the Design view, you may be prompted to save any changes you may have made an open object.

How to Close a Database File

1. Click on the Office button and choose the Close Database command in the lower left.

   OR

   Open another database.

   OR

   Exit Access.

1.8 Defining a Relational Database

Access is a relational database because it organizes data in a collection of related tables. A relational database allows information to be stored in tables that can be easily related, or cross-referenced. A nonrelational database, sometimes called a "flat file" system, stores all data together in one table or file. This design uses excessive storage, encourages errors, and makes retrieving and updating data difficult. It should only be used in the simplest applications such as a mailing list or telephone directory.

Tables can be related to each other when they share a common field. This allows you to store information only once and link it to associated tables when you need it. You can use Access without employing relational database techniques, but this will increase the disk storage required, and affect data accuracy and redundancy.

Data is easily rearranged and updated. Records and fields can appear in any order, either when viewed on the screen or when printed in a report. New records don't need to be inserted in a specific location because the records can be sorted in any order. New fields can be added anywhere in the list of fields—the position of the field doesn't affect where the field appears on the screen or on paper.

Relational Database Rules

There are a number of rules that should be followed when you are designing and creating the tables in a relational database. These rules ensure the integrity of the data—how the data contributes to the accuracy and performance of the system. The rules apply to how the tables, fields, records, and table joins are constructed.

Relational database tables should be designed to meet standards called normal forms. When tables are normalized—that is, when they meet the standards of normal form—the entire database contains no redundant data and is easy to maintain and change. Normalization will be discussed in detail in Chapter 7; however, the rules for establishing relational tables prior to normalizing is described in this section and the next.

By following a few basic rules, tables can be designed so that data maintenance, storage, and retrieval are more accurate and efficient. These rules are applied to the first draft of tables in a database. The rules are as follows:

1. Each record in a table should be unique.

2. No field in a record should have more than one possible value.

3. Data should appear in only one table.

Each record in a table should be unique—no two records should be exactly the same. This ties into the concept of a primary key, which will be discussed later. When each record is unique, it ensures that specific records are easy to locate, examine, or edit.

No field in a record should have more than one possible value. When this happens it's called a repeating group, and it affects data storage and integrity. Removing a repeating group is sometimes called flattening a table, because repeating groups add the effect of depth to a field—as if the fields were stacked on top of each other. Removing the repeating groups flattens out the stack. For example, if the *tblStudents* table contains a field for all the courses taken by a student, there will be multiple values in the field because one student can take several courses. The data appears to be stacked in the *Course Number* field as shown in Figure 1.33.

tblStudents Table

Student ID	First Name	Last Name	Address	Course Number
3214	Luke	Warm	7996 S. Pinewood	BUS 200
3897	Justin	Case	14760 Meadow Rd.	CIS 110 CIS 120 CIS 150
4355	Anne	Aconda	2344 E. Rustic Dr.	BUS 200 CIS 100

Figure 1.33 Multiple occurrences of a value in a field

The data shown in Figure 1.33 should be split into two tables, as shown in Figure 1.34. The repeating group, *Course Number*, has been moved into its own table to eliminate the repeating data group.

Data should appear in only one table, unless it is stored in the common field shared by two tables enabling them to be linked or joined. Storing the same data in several places

tblStudents Table

Student ID	First Name	Last Name	Address
3214	Luke	Warm	7996 S. Pinewood
3897	Justin	Case	14760 Meadow Rd.
4355	Anne	O'Malley	2344 E. Rustic Dr.

tblCourses Taken by Student Table

Student ID	First Name	Last Name	Course Number
3214	Luke	Warm	BUS 200
3897	Justin	Case	CIS 110
3897	Justin	Case	CIS 120
3897	Justin	Case	CIS 150
4355	Anne	O'Malley	BUS 200
4355	Anne	Aconda	CIS 100

Figure 1.34 Tables with the repeating group removed

wastes disk storage and invites mistakes. For example, if a person's name is stored in more than one table, you will have to edit all occurrences when a name changes or data accuracy is lost. It's easy to forget to make the change to all the occurrences of a field. Figure 1.34 shows the tables *tblStudents* and *tblCourses Taken by Student*. "Anne Aconda" has been changed to "Anne O'Malley" in the *tblStudents* table but not in all the records of the *tblCourses Taken by Student* table, making this database inaccurate.

A better way to design these tables would be to remove the *First Name* and *Last Name* fields from the *tblCourses Taken by Student* table, leaving only the *Student ID* and *Course Number* fields (see Figure 1.35). When student names are needed, the two tables can be joined on the *Student ID* field. In addition, the first three letters of the *Course Number* field are the prefix, and they repeat from record to record. This field should be split into *Course Number* and *Course Prefix*.

Q: What are the minimal requirements for a relational database?

A: 1. Each record in a table should be unique.
    2. No field in a record should have more than one possible value.
    3. Generally, a data field should appear in only one table, unless it is the link used to join two tables.

tblStudents Table

Student ID	First Name	Last Name
3214	Luke	Warm
3897	Justin	Case
4355	Anne	O'Malley

tblCourses Taken by Student Table

Course Prefix	Course Number	Student ID
BUS	200	4355
CIS	100	4355
CIS	110	3897

Figure 1.35 Student names removed from *tblCourses Taken by Student* table

There are many more rules to follow if you want to design a truly relational database. Once you are more experienced with Access, you may want to learn more about proper data design, including all levels of data normalization.

Primary Key Fields

The primary key in a table is the field or fields that represent a unique identifier for a record. Keys are used to locate specific records for displaying, printing, or editing. For example, a Social Security Number could be a key because it is unique for each person in a table. Using a proper key for a *tblStudent* table ensures that a student will be enrolled for the right classes and will receive the correct grades.

Primary keys must have two properties—they must exist in every record and each record must have a unique value in the key field or fields. The field must exist in every record—there should be no blanks in the key field in any record. The field must be unique—each record should have a different value in the key field. If either of these conditions is not met, the key can't be used to retrieve records in the table. Figure 1.35 shows that the *Student ID* would make a good key for the *tblStudent* table, because it is unique and is present in every record.

When determining the primary key, list all possibilities by asking if each field occurs in every record and is unique in each record. Eliminate fields that have lengthy data values. Ideally, keys should contain short strings of characters and/or numbers. Usually, one field will emerge as the best choice.

Sometimes there is no single field that is unique in each record, but there is a combination of fields that is unique. Key fields can be a combination of two or more fields. Refer back to Figure 1.35 to verify that neither the *Course Number* nor the *Student ID* alone uniquely identifies a record in the *tblCourses Taken by Student* table. However, the combination of the two fields meets the criteria for a key.

If a primary key can't be determined, create one. Credit card numbers are good examples of keys that were created to uniquely identify accounts—even last and first name combinations aren't unique in large groups of people.

Primary keys play an important role in joining tables. Tables are frequently joined to provide data for queries, forms, and reports. Two tables must have a common field (the same field containing the values) to be joined. Primary keys are often used as the common field; therefore they are added to other tables to enable a join. When a primary key from one table appears in a second table, it is called a foreign key in the second table. For example, the field *Student ID* is the primary key in *tblStudents* and a foreign key in *tblCourses Taken by Student*, as shown in Figure 1.35.

Professional Tip: Getting Started in Database Design

Drawing a rough diagram can help determine the tables, fields, and table joins needed in a database. Let's say that a database needs to be designed that will track the faculty, departments, and degrees at a college. Start by drawing circles that represent each data group or entity that will be used by the database, as shown.

Now, determine which groups interact with each other and draw a line between them. It can be helpful to write a verb describing the interaction on the connecting line. Once this has been done, the table joins in the database become obvious. The diagram below represents our example, and shows that each table in the database needs to be able to join with each of the other tables.

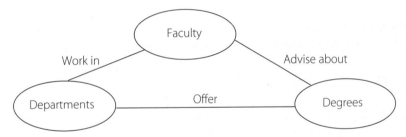

The last step is to include the fields needed by each group. Fields can be written inside the group circles, or added to lines outside the group circles. The diagram below shows some of the fields used in our example.

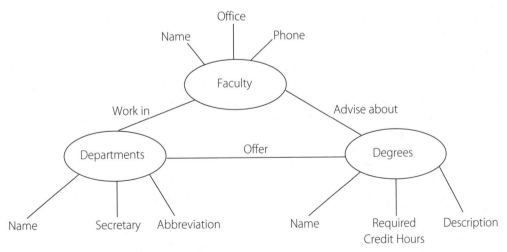

Fields will need to be added to tables to facilitate joins. For example, to join the Faculty and Departments tables, a department field should be added to the Faculty table. This will identify the department in which a faculty member works.

The diagrams can be drawn with pencil and paper, and are really the first step in creating Entity-Relationship diagrams. Entity-Relationship diagrams are discussed in detail in Chapter 7.

1.9 / Designing a Database

The design of the database is an extremely important step in ensuring good data management. It is better to take the time and effort to sit down and think through the design of the database using paper and pencil, than to end up with tables that need to be restructured and mountains of data that can't be accessed.

It is easiest to visualize the final output first and work backward when designing a database. Look at the reports, letters, and other documents that will be generated by the database. If no reports exist, have the end user draw a picture of what he or she wants.

Design Questions

The following questions will help you design a database. The first eight general questions guide you in determining the tables in your database. Queries and reports are based on the responses to question 2. The last question controls the way the forms in the database look and act, and the way the user interacts with the interface (screens and controls).

1. What is the main goal of the entire database?
   A. What is the purpose of the database?
   B. What is its most important function?

2. What types of reports, forms, and queries must be generated from the data to meet the needs of the end users?
   A. Are existing printed materials OK or do they need to be changed?
   B. Do you need to produce additional new documents? If so, have the users draw pictures of what they would like to see on a printed page or screen.

3. What data will be stored in tables?
   A. What fields are necessary to produce the output (reports, forms, queries, and so forth) identified in step 2? Examine the output you have, and list the fields on paper.
   B. Do any fields appear more than once? If so, cross out repeats.
   C. Are there fields that can be derived from other fields, such as a total and each item in the total?
      I. Can you produce any field by performing arithmetic on some other fields? If so, eliminate the end result field.
      II. Do you see any places where the same text is used more than once? If so, eliminate the text that is a subset of the larger phrase.
   D. What are the common fields throughout all output objects? These fields will define the core tables in the system, and many will become key fields.

4. How can these fields be grouped together so that each group describes an entity such as a student, a payment made, or a book in the library? These groups, or entities, will become the tables in the database. Make a new list putting them in groups.
   A. What name describes each group? The names you select for these data groups can be used to name your tables.

5. This step helps create a database in first normal form (see Chapter 7). As a new user, you can skip it if you want.
   A. Does any table have a group of fields that you've labeled item1, item2, and so forth? Are there any repeating groups? Can any field have more than one value in some records? These fields should be moved into another table.

6. Can any fields be broken down into several smaller fields? *Name* is a good example of a field that is usually best broken down into *Last Name* and *First Name,* or *Address* into *Street Address, City, State,* and *Zip Code.* It's easier to combine fields than it is to take them apart.

7. Which field is the primary key field for each table?

    A. Does the key field have a unique value for each record and does it exist in each record?

8. What type of data will be contained in each field (text, dates, numbers, etc.)? This will help determine the actual structure or design of the table.

    A. What will be the longest name or largest amount stored in the field? Think about the biggest example you've seen of each field. This will help determine the length of each field.

9. Who will use this database?

    A. Will it serve one user or many users?

        I. Will the database be used on a network?

    B. Who will input the data, run reports, and generate queries?

        I. What is their level of competence?

            a. How easy should the use of this database be?

            b. How much control should you give the user?

Let's go through a couple of examples of this process. Remember that the actual procedure would be more complex and require more work than we can do here.

Example 1: Online Auction Business

The first scenario to be developed into a database is that of selling goods on the online auction site Going, Going, Gone. The auction site will be called G3 for short from now on. The database user or client is selling vintage household goods that she inherited from her great aunts.

Mainly, the client needs to track the items that she sold on G3. She'd like to be able to see how many items she sold each month, how much profit she made each month, which items are sold but not paid for, whether or not invoices have been sent to customers, which items are paid for and ready to ship, and she'd like to print address labels for shipping. She also would like to be able to see what kinds of items sell best on G3, and has organized her items into four groups—books, clothing, kitchen wares, and miscellaneous.

G3 charges each seller a fee when a new item is listed for auction. The fee varies based on the starting price and length of auction. G3 also charges the seller 5.25% of the ending or selling price for an item. When an item sells, the buyer pays the ending price plus a shipping charge. The actual shipping cost for an item can be different from the estimated shipping charge. Our client accepts payment by check, money order, cash, or Pay Friend—an online payment service.

Based on this information, the following data will be recorded: G3 auction number, item name, item category, item starting price, item ending price, G3 fees, invoiced/not invoiced, paid/not paid, payment type, payment date, shipped/not shipped, shipping date, shipping cost estimate, actual shipping amount, date listed, date sold, buyer name, email address, and mailing address. In addition, the status of an item—for sale, sold, or not sold—will be important.

Now, the data needs to be organized. Are there any repeating groups within the table? Well, if a buyer bought more than one item, the buyer data would be repeated. There really is data about two entities, sales and buyers, so two tables are needed, as shown in Figure 1.36. The Buyers table will contain the fields buyer name, buyer email address, and buyer mailing address. The Sales table will hold all the rest of the fields. Now that the buyer information has been moved into a separate table and there are no repeating groups, the data is in first normal form.

Can any of the fields be broken down into two or more fields? The buyer's mailing address can be split into street address, city, state, and zip code. Doing this makes the data more flexible for printing labels or viewing address information on the screen. The buyer's name could be split into first name and last name fields, although at the moment it doesn't seem to serve a specific purpose.

```
┌─────────────────────┐  ┌─────────────────────────────┐
│ BUYERS              │  │ SALES                       │
│ Name                │  │ Item name                   │
│ Email address       │  │ Item category               │
│ Mailing address     │  │ Starting price              │
└─────────────────────┘  │ Ending price                │
                         │ G3 fees                     │
                         │ Invoiced/Not Invoiced       │
                         │ Paid/Not Paid               │
                         │ Payment type                │
                         │ Payment date                │
                         │ Shipping date               │
                         │ Shipping estimate           │
                         │ Actual shipping amount      │
                         │ Date listed                 │
                         │ Date sold                   │
                         │ Item Status                 │
                         └─────────────────────────────┘
```

Figure 1.36 Tables for G3 auction database after design step 5

Now, a primary key needs to be selected for each table. When an item is listed for auction, G3 assigns a unique auction number to it. This will be ideal for the primary key for the Sales table. The Buyers table primary key could be the unique user name chosen by every buyer and seller on G3.

The last step is to make sure the data from all the tables can be connected into one form or report as needed by our client. Move the Buyer ID into the Sales table, so there's a way to know who bought each item. This will connect the two tables together. The final tables for the G3 auction buying database are shown in Figure 1.37, with the primary keys underlined.

```
┌─────────────────────┐  ┌─────────────────────────────┐
│ BUYERS              │  │ SALES                       │
│ G3 user ID          │  │ G3 Auction number           │
│ Name                │  │ Item name                   │
│ Email address       │  │ Item category               │
│ Street address      │  │ Starting price              │
│ City                │  │ Ending price                │
│ State               │  │ G3 fees                     │
│ Zip code            │  │ Invoiced/Not Invoiced       │
└─────────────────────┘  │ Paid/Not Paid               │
                         │ Payment type                │
                         │ Payment date                │
                         │ Shipping date               │
                         │ Shipping estimate           │
                         │ Actual shipping amount      │
                         │ Date listed                 │
                         │ Date sold                   │
                         │ Item Status                 │
                         │ Buyer ID                    │
                         └─────────────────────────────┘
```

Figure 1.37 Final tables for G3 auction database

Example 2: College Database Example

1. What is the main goal of the entire database?

To manage the data needed to produce course-related reports for college-wide distribution. We are doing one piece of a large, college-wide database system.

2. What type of reports, forms, and queries must be generated from the data to meet the needs of the end users?

- *Class rosters for instructors*
- *Student transcripts*
- *Class schedules for each semester*
- *College course catalog*
- *Information sheets showing degree requirements*

    See the samples shown in Figure 1.38.

3. What data will be stored in tables?

    A. What fields are necessary to produce the output?

    From "Class Roster":

    Course prefix, Course number, Section, Instructor, Location, Day, Time, Student name, Student number

    From "Student Transcript":

    Student name, Student Address, Student number, Student course taken, Student course grade, Semester course taken

---

Class Roster

Class: CIS 140
Section: 01
Instructor: Dobson
Location: J102
Day & Time: MW 10:00

Name		Student Number
Stan	Dupp	16283
Jen	Ettick	17269
Clara	Fye	17342

Student Transcript

Name: Dupp, Stan
Address: 3672 N. Oak
           Glenisle, CO 89171
Student #: 16283

Course	Grade	Semester
CIS 140	A	Fall 04
MAT 150	B	Fall 04
CIS 120	B	Spring 05
ENG 201	A	Spring 05

Semester Class Schedule

Course: CIS 140
Introduction to Access

Section	Day	Time	Location	Instructor
01	M	8:00	J130	Trigg
02	MW	11:00	J102	Dobson
03	T R	1:00	J102	Gateau
04	F	5:00	J102	Dobson

Course: CIS 150
Introduction to Excel

Section	Day	Time	Location	Instructor

Course Catalog

Course: CIS 140
Introduction to Access
Credits: 2
Description: This course introduces database concepts. Access is used in the lab to learn the process of creating and maintaining a database system.

Course: CIS 150
Introduction to Excel

Degree Requirements

Program Name: Computer Information Systems
Total Hours: 56

Required Course		Hours
CIS 140	Introduction to Access	2
CIS 115	Introduction to Computers	3
BUS 100	Introduction to Business	3
MAT 150	Algebra II	3
MAT 200	Business Statistics	3

Figure 1.38 College database sample reports

From "Semester Class Schedule":

Course prefix, Course number, Course title, Section, Day, Time, Location, Instructor

From "Course Catalog":

Course prefix, Course number, Course title, Course credits, Course description

From "Degree Requirements":

Degree name, Degree total hours, Course number in degree, Course name in degree, Course hours in degree

B. Do any fields appear more than once?

Yes; with duplicates removed, the fields are:

Course prefix, Course number, Course title, Section, Instructor, Location, Day, Time, Student name, Student number, Student address, Student course taken, Student course grade, Semester course taken, Course credits, Course description, Degree name, Degree total hours, Course number in degree, Course name in degree, Course hours in degree

C. Are there fields that can be derived from other fields, such as a total and each item in the total?

Yes—degree total hours. (You can add all individual course hours in the degree to arrive at this number.)

D. What are the common fields throughout all output objects?

There are many. Course prefix, Course number, Student number, and Student name are most frequent.

4. How can these fields be grouped together to form a logical organization in a table? Make a new list putting them in groups (see Figure 1.39).

COURSES	STUDENTS	DEGREES
Course prefix	Student name	Degree name
Course number	Student number	Degree total hours
Course title	Student address	Required course number 1
Section	Student course taken 1	Required course name 1
Instructor	Student course grade 1	Required course number 2
Location	Semester course taken 1	Required course name 2
Day	Student course taken 2	etc.
Time	Student course grade 2	
Course credits	Semester course taken 2	
Course description	etc.	
Student name 1		
Student number 1		
Student name 2		
Student number 2		
etc.		

Figure 1.39 Organized lists of fields

5. Does any table have a group of fields that you've labeled item1, item2, etc.?

Yes, they are listed below.

COURSES: *Student name in a class, Student number in a class*

STUDENTS: *Course taken, Course grade*

DEGREES: *Required course number, Required course name*

Repetitively occurring fields should be moved to separate tables. So your tables now are:

COURSES
Course prefix
Course number
Course title
Section
Instructor
Location
Day
Time
Course credits
Course description

STUDENTS
Student name
Student number
Student address

DEGREES
Degree name
Degree total hours

COURSES IN DEGREE
Degree name
Course number
Course name

COURSES TAKEN BY STUDENT
Student number
Course taken
Grade
Semester taken

STUDENTS IN COURSE
Course prefix
Course number
Section number
Student name
Student number

Figure 1.40 Tables with repeating groups removed

As you examine these tables you'll notice that they can be reorganized according to the following criteria.

- *COURSES table*
  Course prefix, Course number, and Course title are repeated in every section of the same course, so you can separate the table into COURSES and SECTIONS with the Course prefix and number as the common fields.

COURSES
Course prefix
Course number
Course title
Course credits
Course description

SECTIONS
Course prefix
Course number
Section
Instructor
Location
Day
Time

Figure 1.41 Courses and Sections tables

- *COURSES IN DEGREE table*
  Course name can be found by looking in the COURSES table if Course number and prefix are known, so this field can be removed.

COURSES IN DEGREE
Degree name
Course prefix
Course number

Figure 1.42 Courses in Degree table

- *The tables STUDENTS IN COURSE and COURSES TAKEN BY STUDENT are very similar. Combine them into*

STUDENT RECORD
Student number
Course prefix
Course number
Section
Grade
Semester taken

Figure 1.43 Student Record table

6. Can any fields be broken down into several smaller fields?

   Student name in the STUDENTS table can become Last name and First name. The same could be done for Instructor in the SECTIONS table. However, this field could be best represented by an Instructor ID number. Split Student address into Street address. City, State, and Zip code. STUDENTS table now has the following fields.

STUDENTS
Last name
First name
Student number
Street address
City
State
Zip code

Figure 1.44 Students table

7. Which field is the key field for each table?

   COURSES: Course prefix and Course number (together)

   SECTIONS: Course prefix, Course number, and Section (together)

   STUDENTS: Student number

   DEGREES: Degree ID number (created key)

   COURSES IN DEGREE: Degree ID number, Course prefix, and Course number (together)

   STUDENT RECORD: Student number, Course prefix, Course number, and Section (together)

   The completed tables in the college database are shown in Figure 1.45.

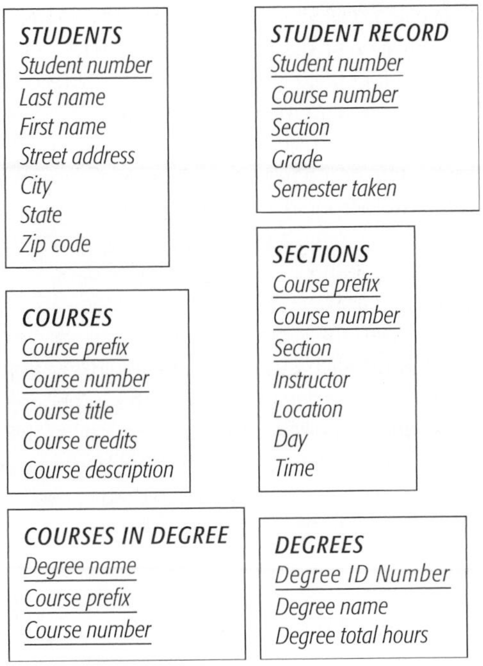

Figure 1.45 Completed table design (primary keys are underlined)

8. What type of data will be contained in each field (text, dates, numbers, etc.)? This will help determine the actual structure or design of the table.

   Text fields: Course prefix, Course title, Course description, Instructor, Location, Day, Student name, Student address, Grade, Semester taken, Degree name

   Number fields: Course number, Course credits, Section, Time, Student number, Degree ID number, Degree total hours

9. Who will use this database?

   The system will reside on a network. Faculty and administrators will need output right now. Ultimately, parts of the system will be available for students to browse. The system should be easy to use and have very tight controls because of its widespread use. Administrators and clerical personnel will update the tables.

Professional Tip: Beginning Normalization

This tip comes from Jeff Putnam, who has been a practicing Database Architect (DBA) since soon after the dawn of time. He has worked with dBase, Access, Paradox, Sybase, and MS SQL Server. He currently manages a widespread implementation of SQL Server 7.0 databases at Careerbuilder, Inc. The full article can be found online at http://databasejournal.com/sqletc/article.php/1443021.

If you're a DBA who has never managed the data itself, or a new database architect, you'll need to know the ins and outs of normalization. For those who aren't comfortable with the concept, **normalization** is the process of structuring tables for maximum efficiency of joins, while assuring minimum duplication of data and maximum data integrity.

Why normalize? Yes, building a database that isn't normalized is quicker. If you're the one in charge of maintaining it, though, you'll pay later: Explosion in the size of your database, convoluted coding, duplication of data, and even contradictory data aren't uncommon. There are often good reasons NOT to normalize, too: If your database is largely a reporting platform, you may want to retain duplicated data to avoid unnecessary joins.

Okay, you may have heard of the "normal forms." The forms are a set of standards that state how well a database is normalized. They aren't rules; nobody will come to your office and slap you if you violate them. Different developers go to different lengths to implement them—most folks I know don't go above 3rd normal form on a regular basis. Here are the quick and dirty definitions in English.

1st Normal Form (1NF): All 1NF says is that you don't repeat groups of data as separate fields. An example of this is having a customer table with three phone number fields (home, work, and fax). To avoid violating 1NF, you'd need a separate phone numbers table.

2nd Normal Form (2NF): Okay, now each column in the table must be dependent on the ENTIRE key. Using the example above (the primary key is two fields combined—Customer ID and Phone number), you wouldn't want to keep the customer name in the phone numbers table. Since there would be 0–3 records for each customer, you could say that the number itself is dependent on the key (i.e., there is just one record for each key/phone combination) but the customer name is NOT dependent (the key/name combination has the possibility of duplication). Basically, the customer name applies to lots of different kinds of records (invoices, addresses, etc.) and therefore should be stored separately and related to each different record using a key. Now, if you add "Phone type" to the key, you're not in violation.

For a complete explanation of normalization, see Chapter 7.

Fast Track   A quick guide to procedures learned in this chapter

Starting Access

From the Windows Start button:

1. Press the Start button, and click All Programs on the Start menu.

2. Choose the Microsoft Access option from the list of available programs. You may have to click on the Microsoft Office menu item first.

From the Windows Start button, alternate method:

1. Click the Start button.

2. Click the MS Office Access 2007 icon.

From the Explorer menu:

1. Choose the Windows Explorer option from the list of available programs on the Start menu. You may first need to select Accessories from the menu and then locate Explorer.

2. From the Explorer screen, open the MS Office folder by clicking its icon or name. Open the Office 12 folder.

3. Double-click on the Access icon in the right window pane.

Opening a Database

1. Click on one of the database names in the Open Recent Database list.

   OR

   Select the More ... option (under the Open Recent Database heading) on the right side of the window.

2. Locate the folder containing the database in the Look in drop-down list.

3. Select the database name from the list of files.

4. Click on the Open button in the lower right corner, or double-click on the database name.

Opening an Object for Use

1. Select the name of the object to be opened from the Object list in the Navigation Pane.

2. Double-click on the name of the object to be opened.

Opening an Object in Design View

1. Select the name of the object to be edited. From the Object list in the Navigation Pane.

2. Right-click on the object name and select Design View from the pop-up menu.

Opening Access Help

1. Click the Help button on the far right end of the ribbon.

Using the Help Window

1. Pick a topic from the list shown, by clicking on it.

OR

Type a topic into the Search box and click on the Search button.

2. Click on any article title to open it.

Exiting Access

1. Click on the close box (X) in the upper right corner of the window.

OR

Click on the Office button and click on the Exit Access button in the lower right corner of the Office window.

Closing a Database File

1. Click on the Office button and choose the Close Database command in the lower left.

OR

Open another database.

OR

Exit Access.

Review Questions

1. What is the difference between data and information?

2. What is a database?

3. Is a record in a table represented by a row or a column?

4. What fields might be included in a *Classroom* table in the college records database?

5. List four different objects found in an Access database.

6. What is the function of a macro?

7. Give an example of a form that could be used to enter data into the college records database. What is the function of the form? Who uses the form?

8. Would you create a report or a query to produce a list of all classes being taught during the current term, grouped by faculty?

9. Describe one method for starting Access.

10. What icon is used to represent Access?

11. What is the area containing the object list called? Is it on the left side or right side of the Access window?

12. Is the ribbon located in the upper or the lower area of the screen? What are the tabs on the ribbon for?

13. What's the easiest way to open a database object?

14. What is the Design view used for?

15. List two ways to exit Access.

16. What is a relational database?

17. Why is it advantageous to follow the rules for designing a relational database?

18. Give an example of a table containing a repeating group.

19. What is a key field?

20. How do you begin designing a database? Why is it helpful to examine the reports you'd like to have printed from a new database?

21. (T/F) Queries can include calculated fields based on data stored in a table or another query.

22. (T/F) Forms are used for both input and output.

23. (T/F) Forms are edited in a very different way from reports.

24. (T/F) Most macros are run from within queries.

25. (T/F) The objects in the Navigation Pane are always listed in date order.

26. Which field would make the best key in Table 1.1? Why? Would you recommend creating an ID Number as a key?

Table 1.1 Art Inventory

Title of Piece	Artist	Type	Media	Value
Elvis in Vegas	Elbrin	Painting	Oil on velvet	$ 400
First Glance	McIntyre	Sculpture	Bronze	$1200
Summer Dreams	Jessup	Painting	Watercolor	$ 250
Hands Across the Sea	Jessup	Painting	Watercolor	$ 400

27. What problems do you see with Table 1.2?

Table 1.2 Ski Rentals

Customer Name	Ability	Ski Size	Boot Size	Rental Date
Russell Wright	Beginner	155	10	11-30-08
				12-15-08
Lynne Vanore	Beginner	150	8	12-22-08
Rick Rycker	Intermediate	165	9	1-18-09
				1-25-09
				2-12-09
Patsy Flood	Advanced	170	7	2-1-09

Exercises

Exercise 1—Review and Guided Practice

1. Sir Dance-A-Lot is a small music store specializing in music from the 1950s, 60s and 70s. They sell vinyl albums, cassettes, CDs, and even 8-track tapes. They would like to keep track of the recordings they have in inventory—the name of the album, the artist, the record label, media type, price, how many are in the store, and the type of music—rock, jazz, country, etc. Here's a list of fields in the table *Recordings:* Artist, Title, Music Category, Record Label, Media Type, Quantity on Hand, and Price.

2. Here are some sample data in the table *Recordings*.

Artist	Title	Music Category	Record Label	Media Type	Quantity on Hand	Price
BeeGees	The Very Best Of	Rock	Decca	Compact Disk	4	11.99
BeeGees	The Very Best Of	Rock	Decca	Long Playing Vinyl	1	15.99
Perry Como	Catch a Falling Star	Easy Listening	Decca	Compact Disk	3	11.99
Bob Dylan	Blonde on Blonde	Rock	A & M	Compact Disk	3	11.99
Bob Dylan	Blonde on Blonde	Rock	A & M	Long Playing Vinyl	1	9.99
Bob Dylan	Highway 61 Revisited	Rock	A & M	Cassette	1	10.99

The fields Artist, Title, Music Category, and Record Label are repeated whenever there are multiple media types of one recording in the store. Put a piece of paper below this line to cover the solution, and try separating the *Recordings* table into two tables: *Recordings* and *Inventory*.

3. Here's the two tables *Recordings* and *Inventory*.

Recordings

Music ID	Artist	Title	Music Category	Record Label
1	BeeGees	The Very Best of	Rock	Decca
2	Perry Como	Catch a Falling Star	Easy Listening	Decca
3	Bob Dylan	Blonde on Blonde	Rock	A & M
4	Bob Dylan	Highway 61 Revisited	Rock	A & M

Inventory

Music ID	Media Type	Quantity	Price
1	Compact Disk	4	11.99
1	Long Playing Vinyl	1	15.99
2	Compact Disk	3	11.99
3	Compact Disk	3	11.99
3	Long Playing Vinyl	1	9.99
4	Cassette	1	10.99

4. Now, look at the *Recordings* table. Which fields are repeated? Put a piece of paper below this line to cover the solution, and try separating the *Recordings* table into four tables: *Recordings* and three others.

5. Here's the four tables *Recordings*, *Artists*, *Category*, and *Label*.

Recordings

Music ID	Artist	Title	Category	Label
1	11	The Very Best of	21	31
2	12	Catch a Falling Star	22	31
3	13	Blonde on Blonde	21	32
4	13	Highway 61 Revisited	21	32

Artists

Artist ID	Name
11	BeeGees
12	Perry Como
13	Bob Dylan

Category

Category ID	Music Category
21	Rock
22	Easy Listening

Label

Label ID	Record Label
31	Decca
32	A & M

Just the ID numbers are repeated in the *Recordings* table now, and that's alright. Each category name appears only once in the *Category* table, each artist name appears only once in the *Artists* table, and each label name appears only once in the *Label* table.

6. Now, look back at step 3 at the *Inventory* table. Which field is repeated (besides Music ID)? Put a piece of paper below this line to cover the solution, and try separating the *Inventory* table into two tables.

7. Here are the two tables *Inventory* and *Media*.

Inventory

Music ID	Media ID	Quantity	Price
1	31	4	11.99
1	32	1	15.99
2	31	3	11.99
3	31	3	11.99
3	32	1	9.99

Media

Media ID	Media Type
31	Compact Disk
32	Long Playing Vinyl

8. At the beginning there was only one table, but after following the steps to normalize or remove the repeating groups, six tables are needed to contain the data. This may seem more cumbersome, but it really isn't. The database will be more accurate and efficient because of this process.

Exercise 2—Practicing New Procedures

ACTIVITY AND REFLECTION

Exercise 2A: Becoming Familiar with Access

1. Start Access and open the *Practice_CH1* database.

2. Sort the object list in the Navigation Pane by date modified. Which object appears to have been modified the most recently?

3. Right-click in the background (white space) in the Navigation Pane, and select View By, Details from the pop-up menu. Now you can see the creation and modification dates for each object. What date was *tblStudents* modified?

4. Open *tblStudents* in the Design view. Save the table by clicking on the Save button in the Quick Access toolbar. Close the table. What is the date modified for *tblStudents* now?

5. Change the view back to List by right-clicking on the background and choosing View By, List from the pop-up menu. Change the sort order back to object type.

6. On which tab of the ribbon, do you find the following commands?

   a. Switchboard Manager

   b. Macro

   c. Clipboard

   d. Relationships

   e. Excel

   f. Spelling

   g. Create Email

   h. Table Templates

7. Click on the Office button and select Save As. What two types of things can the Save As command be applied to? Can this command be used to save a database for usage with a previous version of Access?

8. Under which command in the Office window will you find the instruction to back up the database?

9. Click on the downward pointing arrow on the right end of the Quick Access toolbar. Add the QuickPrint command to the toolbar.

10. Choose More Commands... from the Customize Quick Access Toolbar menu. What is the title of the window that opens? What other action opens this same window?

Exercise 2B: Using Help

1. Using Access Help, search for the phrase "create a database." Open the article "Create a new database."

   a. What are two ways to create a database in Access?

2. Locate this information: What are the specifications of a database? Answer the following questions:

   a. What is the maximum size of an Access database file?

   b. How many characters are allowed in a table name?

   c. How many fields are allowed in a table?

   d. How many actions can be recorded in a macro?

   e. How many objects can be contained in a database?

   f. How many tables can be included in a query?

   g. What is the maximum number of printed pages allowed in a report?

Exercise 2C: Designing a Database

1. List all the fields needed to track fundraising efforts by your local charitable organization, given that
   a. You will be sending donors a thank-you note, so you'll need mailing labels;

   b. You will need to print monthly and annual totals of the donations received; and

   c. You will need to keep a record of how much was donated by each individual donor, and when.

2. Can one person donate more than one time?

3. What does that tell you about the fields that contain the donated amount and the donation date?

4. Can you put all these fields into one table?

5. Create names for your tables and list the fields in each.

6. What field occurs in both tables?

7. What are the key fields in both tables?

ACTIVITY AND REFLECTION

Exercise 3—In-Class Group Practice

Softball League Database Design

Divide into groups of three or four, as determined by your instructor. Each group will do the problem below.

You are in charge of keeping track of an amateur softball league for the summer. You know the following facts:

- The league is comprised of eight teams.

- Each team has 10 team members, who are employees of a local company that sponsors the team.

- Each team chooses a team name and a manager, who is responsible for making team arrangements.

- The games are played in two locations: Municipal Field and Babe Ruth Park. Each Friday night, two games are played in each location, one at 6:00 p.m. and one at 9:00 p.m.

- The season lasts from May 1 through June 30.

Three reports will be needed for the league. Examples are shown in Figure 1.46.

LEAGUE SUMMER SCHEDULE			
Schedule for team: Lugnuts			
Date	Time	Location	Opponent
5/1	6:00	Municipal Field	Artichokes
5/8	9:00	Babe Ruth Park	Spiders

LEAGUE TEAM ROSTER		
Team Name: Lugnuts		
Manager: Allan Rentch		
Player Name	Position	Batting Avg.
Harry Veneer	Pitcher	.390
Sally Pixel	Catcher	.420

LEAGUE TEAM DIRECTORY			
Company Name	Team Name	Manager's Name	Phone Number
Larry's Garage	Lugnuts	Allan Rentch	545-9182
Tri-County Bank	Artichokes	Joe King	545-0743

Figure 1.46 League reports

1. List all the fields you need.

2. Eliminate fields that can be derived from other fields, such as a total when each item in the total is also a field.

3. Make a new list grouping the fields into tables.

4. Does any table have a group of fields that you've labeled item1, item2, and so forth? Repetitively occurring fields should be put into a separate table.

5. Which field is a unique or key field in each table?

6. What type of data will be contained in each field (text, dates, numbers, etc.)?

7. The first group to answer the first six questions will write their design for database tables on the board.

8. Members of other groups may now question the first group as to why they designed the tables as they did. Suggested changes can be discussed, if they occur.

9. All groups should come to a consensus as to the best design for the project.

10. How would you change the tables to accommodate keeping track of which team has the most wins at the end of the season?

Exercise 4—Critical Thinking: Designing an Airline Reservation Database

ACTIVITY AND REFLECTION

1. All the fields needed to create an airline reservation system are listed below:

   Airline name, Flight number, City of origin, Destination city, Date, Time, Seat number, Passenger name, Passenger address, Passenger phone number, Special meal (yes or no).

2. If all these fields are put into one table, what data must be entered for every passenger added?

Data that is entered over and over wastes time and storage space, and opens the door to mistakes. (Will you always type the flight number correctly?)

3. Put these repetitively occurring fields into a separate table.

4. Which table is the *tblFlight* table, and which is the *tblPassenger* table?

5. Which field or fields connect(s) the *tblFlight* table and the *tblPassenger* table?

6. Which field is a unique or key field in each table?

7. What type of data will be contained in each field (text, dates, numbers, etc.)?

ACTIVITY AND REFLECTION

Exercise 5—Challenge: Designing a Recipe Database.

1. List all the fields needed to create a database for your recipes, so that you can print:

   a. Each recipe, both the ingredients and the cooking process; and

   b. A shopping list of ingredients needed for each recipe.

2. Make a new list putting the fields into tables. Name each table.

3. Put repetitively occurring fields into separate tables.

4. Which field is a unique or key field in each table?

5. What type of data will be contained in each field (text, dates, numbers, etc.)?

ACTIVITY AND REFLECTION

Exercise 6—Challenge: Designing a Consignment Sales Database

1. Your cousin is opening a used clothing store, where items are sold on consignment. He needs a database to track the store inventory items. When an item is sold, the amount of the consignment (25% of sales price) and the person to whom it should be paid will be recorded. List all the fields needed to create the database.

2. Make a new list putting the fields into tables. Name each table.

3. Put repetitively occurring fields into a separate table.

4. Which field is a unique or key field in each table?

5. What types of data will be contained in each field (text, dates, numbers, etc.)?

REFLECTION

Exercise 7—Discussion Questions

1. How do the parts of an Access database—tables, records, fields, reports, and forms—relate to the parts of a manual record-keeping system—file cabinets, file folders, and so forth?

2. If you have a database running on a network with multiple users, why is it important to allow only one user to edit a specific record? Are there other actions that should be restricted?

3. What software application packages besides Access have you used or heard of?

4. Is Windows an application software package?

5. If you are sitting at a computer, run another Microsoft application. Ask your instructor for help if you need it. What features on the screen are the same as they are in Access? Why is this helpful?

CASE STUDY A: MRS. SUGARBAKER'S COOKIES

Mrs. Sugarbaker owns a small home-based business—baking, packaging, and selling gourmet cookies. She has several types of cookies that she sells in boxed assortments. Previously, all her inventory, customer lists, and sales transactions were done the old-fashioned way—with a ledger, index cards, paper, and pencil. Now, since her business is booming, she has decided to computerize.

Mrs. Sugarbaker bought a new computer with Windows and Microsoft Office software. She has begun by learning to use MS Office—Word, Excel, and Access. She has created a letter in Word that she wants to send to her customers, and she has tried to enter her orders into Excel, but she can't keep up with baking, shipping, and setting up the business on the computer. You have been hired to create a computerized record-keeping database. Here are some of her requirements:

- The system must be easy to run.

- Data must be kept accurate by trapping errors during data entry.

- All data must be easy to enter and retrieve.

- Letters and labels for mass mailings, as well as various reports, must be generated.

Access will be used to develop the database, and you will try to use as much of the existing data as possible to eliminate re-entering data. The following sample documents have been provided for you to use in planning and designing the database:

- Marketing letter showing a product list

- Customer address and phone list on index cards

- Customer statement

- Picture of an order form

Part 1: Planning the Database

The best way to start any database project is to collect and examine existing sample documents. You should also check with the user to get samples of any new documents that should be added to the database products.

Examining Sample Documents

Mrs. Sugarbaker has provided you with some samples of output she has been using. These were either typed manually or are stored as Word documents.

Marketing Letter

The marketing letter shown in Figure 1.47 is from the CD, is called *Valued Customer.doc,* and is stored in the *Case Study A* folder. It's a letter that Mrs. Sugarbaker recently sent to all her customers.

Mrs. Sugarbaker's
1275 Appleberry Lane
Rocky Ridge, CO 80808
1-800-COO-KIES

Customer name and address

Dear Valued Customer:

Because you have enjoyed Mrs. Sugarbaker's Cookies in the past, we are inviting you to review our new line of gift boxes.

BonBon Box	Melt-in-your mouth delicacies including French Vanilla BonBons, Chocolate Truffles, Black Forest Truffles, and Cherry BonBons	$24.95
Brownie Mini Bites	All-brownie bonanza including Caramel Nut, German Chocolate, Chocolate Swirl, and Double Dutch brownies	$27.95
Cappuccino Companion Collection	Taste treats to accompany your favorite java. Includes Strawberry Thumbprints, Milk Chocolate Chip Cookies, and Biscotti	$24.95
Citrus Cooler Gift Box	Refreshing citrus cookies including Orange Chiffon Meltaways, Key Lime Bars, Lemon Coolers, and Tangerine Coconut Smoothies	$27.95
Chocolate Indulgence Collection	A chocolate lover's dream—Milk Chocolate Chip and White Chocolate Chip, as well as an assortment of brownies: German Chocolate, Chocolate Swirl, and Double Dutch	$32.95
Fruit Jewels Assortment	Fruity Favorites including Apricot Jewels, Cherry BonBons, Coconut Patties, and Strawberry Thumbprints	$24.95
Holiday Gift Assortment	Traditional holiday favorites—Gingerbread Elves, German Spritz, Apricot Jewels, and beautifully decorated Sugar Christmas Trees	$28.95
Old World Assortment	Old World favorites including German Spritz, Raspberry Rugelah, Scottish Shortbread, and Polish Keifle	$26.95

Call our toll-free order line and place your orders soon. We appreciate your continued support.

Sincerely,

Martha P. Sugarbaker

Figure 1.47 Marketing letter showing a product list (*Valued Customer.doc*)

Customer Index Cards

Mrs. Sugarbaker has been keeping customer addresses and phone numbers in a card file reproduced in Figure 1.48. This data is not available on the computer—you'll have to enter it yourself. In the past, Mrs. Sugarbaker has typed mailing labels using the first three lines of the cards.

Chessmen, Geneva
126 Rich Lane
Richland, WA 98001
(816) 555-1612

Bordeaux, Lacy
11487 Glengary Rd.
Bismark, SD 67543
(602) 555-1991

Savoy, Desdemona
887 Tower Road
Denver, CO 80222
(303) 555-6545

Winters, Madeline
303 Hunter Lane
Denver, CO 80222
(303) 555-9922

Curry, George
6759 Milano Court
Littleton, CO 80123
(303) 777-8943

Sanders, Colonel
87 Kentucky Road
Wingding, WY 92458
(515) 777-9682

Twist, Cinnamon
222 Pepperidge Lane
Stollen, CO 80654
(303) 555-8586

Buckle, Theodosia
68 Plum Court
Hollis, WY 92761
(515) 666-9001

Nutt, Macadamia
6011 Truffle Circle
Marshall, CO 80765
(303) 555-5224

Peppermint, Patty
777 Rocky Road
Praline, WA 98378
(816) 555-7112

Figure 1.48 Customer index cards

Customer Statements

Statements have been sent out to customers each month. A sample statement typed manually is shown in Figure 1.49. Some of the data is available in an Excel spreadsheet named *Orders.xls* in the *Case Study A* folder. The rest of the data is available in a dBase database file named *Payments.dbf.* in the *Case Study A* folder.

Statement   29-Apr-07

Name   Lacy   Bordeaux

Address   11487 Glengarry Rd.

              Bismark   SD   67543

Date	Description	Amount
11/15/2008	Order #3	$61.00
12/2/2008	Payment	($61.00)
	Balance Due:	$0.00

Figure 1.49 Customer statement

Orders

A manually typed order is shown in Figure 1.50. The data shown is available in an Excel spreadsheet named *Orders.xls*. Mrs. Sugarbaker would like to have a data entry screen for adding orders that is similar to this layout.

Order ID: 1

Date: 11/11/08

Name: Geneva Chessmen

Quantity	Product Name	Unit Price	Amount
1	Brownie Mini Bites	$27.95	$27.95
2	Old World Assortment	$26.95	$53.90
		Item Total:	$81.85
		Shipping:	$ 6.95
		Order Total:	$88.80

Figure 1.50 Order form

1. Make a list containing all fields needed for the *Mrs. Sugarbaker's Cookies* database based on the sample documents.

2. Group the fields into tables and name each table.

Need More Help?

1. Look at Figure 1.47, the marketing letter. What customer data is needed for the letter? What product information is listed? Is there any other data shown in the letter that you'll need to store in tables?

2. Examine the customer cards. What pieces of information are found on all cards?

3. Look at the customer statement (Figure 1.49). Is there any customer information here that wasn't shown in the customer card file (Figure 1.48)? If so, list it. Write down each piece of information shown about each order.

4. Examine the order form (Figure 1.50) and list any information you see that isn't on the customer statement.

5. Take the fields in your list and place each one in the appropriate group below. Don't list a field twice unless you think it's a common field used to link two tables.

    CUSTOMERS   PRODUCTS   ORDERS

Be sure that the *tblOrders* table doesn't contain data that can be found elsewhere, such as a customer's address or the price of a box of cookies.

Part 2: Making Relational Tables

Designing relational tables correctly helps keep data accurate and current and helps save storage space by eliminating redundant data. Check and revise the tables created in Part 1 as follows:

1. Check to see that tables have no repeating values in fields. If you see the same data occurring over and over, pull that data out into a table of its own and add an ID number to tie the new table to the old. For example, are there multiple groups of item fields (item name, quantity, and so forth) in the *tblOrders* table? Are there multiple payments for some customers?

2. Check to see that data is not duplicated in two or more tables. For example, does a customer's address appear in both the *tblCustomers* and *tblOrders* tables?

3. Define primary keys for each table and set their properties. A primary key should be unique—there should be a different value in every record. A primary key is also a required field—no record has a blank (no data) in this field. If no key naturally occurs, add an auto-number or other ID code.

4. Verify that common-field links are in place. Look at tables that must be joined in order to create the required query, form, or report. Make sure these tables have a field in common. Common fields are often primary keys in the "one" table of a one-to-many relationship.

CASE STUDY B: SANDY FEET RENTAL COMPANY

Part 1: Planning the Database

The Sandy Feet Rental Company rents condominiums at the Sandy Feet oceanside resort. There are two buildings, each of which has condos with two or three bedrooms and two bathrooms. In The Shores building, condos are either oceanview (with a view of the ocean) or oceanfront, which means they have a balcony facing the ocean but not directly on the shore. The ocean-front condos rent for more than the oceanview properties. The Outrigger building is away from the beach, back in the resort property. These properties do not have a view of the ocean and the beach is a short walk through the resort.

All the properties rent per week and do not take daily rates. The rate schedule varies by location, number of bedrooms, and season of the year. Some properties have high-speed Internet access and some properties accept pets. Renters pay a $150 deposit per pet if they want to bring their cat or dog with them on vacation. All properties have the following amenities on the property:

- Outoor pool
- Indoor pool
- Water slide
- Hot tub
- Fitness center
- Playground
- Dog park

Sandy Feet Rental Company wants to keep their records in a database. The company deals with customers, owners, transactions, and housekeeping charges, among other information. They take in all rental amounts, pay housekeeping per unit and disperse rental funds to the property owners while keeping 25% of the rental fee for their services. The cleaning crew charges between $50 (for two bedrooms) and $60 (for three bedrooms).

Examining Sample Documents and Other Data

Sandy Feet would like to be able to run reports, use forms for data entry, and query the database. They would like to use other automated functions of Access. The data for Sandy Feet Rental Company (SFRC) is scattered among several sources. The rate schedule for different condos and locations is displayed in Table 1.3.

Table 1.3 Rate schedule per week

Condo Type	1/01–3/31	4/01–5/31	6/01–8/31	9/01–10/31	11/01–12/31
ShoresOF2BR	375	450	575	450	375
ShoresOF3BR	425	500	625	500	425
ShoresOV2BR	350	400	550	400	350
ShoresOV3BR	400	450	600	450	400
Outrigger2BR	325	350	400	350	325
Outrigger3BR	350	375	450	375	350

The Property Report contains information about the condos in SFRC's property database (see Figure 1.51).

The Owners form shows the data entry form for information on the condo owners (see Figure 1.52).

Properties Report

Property Number	Property Address	Condo Type	Accepts Pets	High Speed Internet	Amenities Code
P1	301S	ShoresOF3BR	☑	☑	1
P10	1005S	ShoresOV3BR	☐	☑	1
P2	207S	ShoresOF2BR	☐	☐	1
P3	11000	Outrigger3BR	☐	☑	1
P4	1201S	ShoresOF2BR	☐	☑	1
P5	317O	Outrigger2BR	☐	☑	1
P6	110S	ShoresOV2BR	☐	☐	1
P7	1010S	ShoresOF2BR	☑	☑	1
P8	409O	Outrigger2BR	☑	☐	1
P9	5050	Outrigger3BR	☐	☑	1
P11	656S	ShoresOV2BR	☑	☐	1
P12	942S	ShoresOF3BR	☐	☐	1

Figure 1.51 Property report

Owners Form

Owner Number:	1
Property Number:	P1
Last Name:	Claus
First Name:	Sandy
Address:	123 North Pole Drive
City:	Snowshoe
State:	PA
Zip Code:	23987-
Phone Number:	(404) 678-0909
Phone Number 2:	
Fax Number:	
Email Address:	SandyClaus@net.com
Notes:	

Figure 1.52 Owners form

Client information is gathered on a form similar to this (see Figure 1.53).

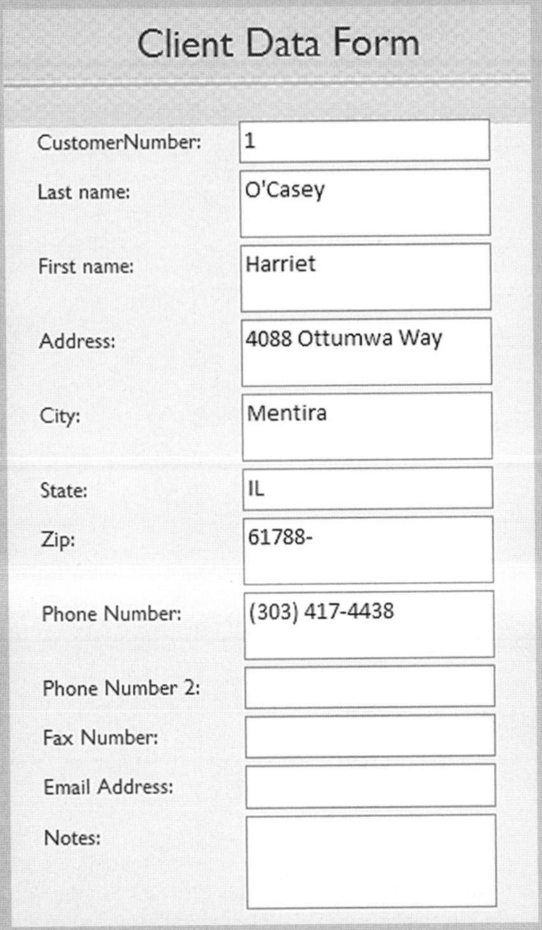

Client Data Form

CustomerNumber:	1
Last name:	O'Casey
First name:	Harriet
Address:	4088 Ottumwa Way
City:	Mentira
State:	IL
Zip:	61788-
Phone Number:	(303) 417-4438
Phone Number 2:	
Fax Number:	
Email Address:	
Notes:	

Figure 1.53 Client data form

Housekeeping data is reflected in the report that is generated from this data once a month (see Figure 1.54). Rental transactions are input through a data entry form (see Figure 1.55).

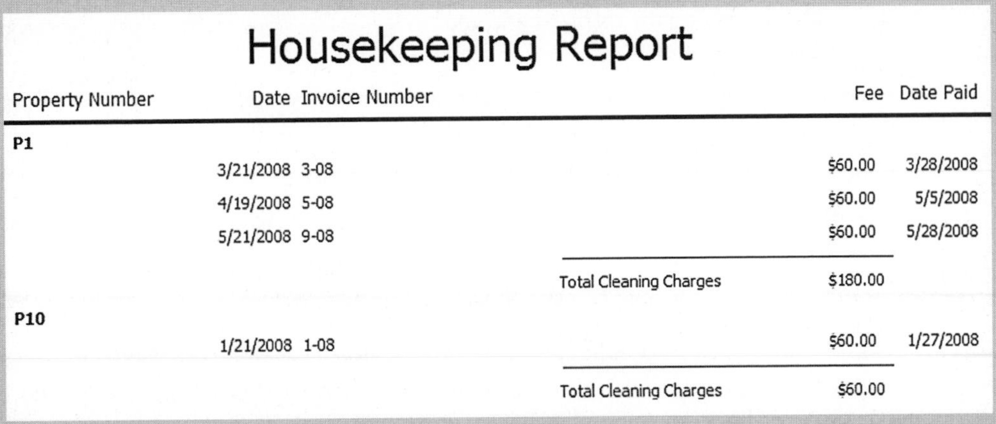

Housekeeping Report

Property Number	Date	Invoice Number	Fee	Date Paid
P1				
	3/21/2008	3-08	$60.00	3/28/2008
	4/19/2008	5-08	$60.00	5/5/2008
	5/21/2008	9-08	$60.00	5/28/2008
		Total Cleaning Charges	$180.00	
P10				
	1/21/2008	1-08	$60.00	1/27/2008
		Total Cleaning Charges	$60.00	

Figure 1.54 Housekeeping report

Rental Transactions Data Entry Form

Rental Number:	5
Property Number:	P1
Customer Number:	1
Date Arrive:	5/14/2008
Date Depart:	5/21/2008
Deposit Amount:	$300.00
Method of Payment:	Visa
Pet Deposit:	$150.00
Number of pets:	1
Notes:	small dog

Figure 1.55 Rental transaction data entry form

Part 2: Designing the Tables

After carefully examining all the data, begin to design the tables for this database on paper (not in Access). All fields must be included in the tables. Record data will be provided in the next chapter.

1. List all the fields that can be identified through the information given. Identify the type of data that will be in each field. Example: Currency, Date, etc. Make sure all the data is included in a table.

2. Group the fields into tables. Consider all the data that is presented to be sure that all necessary tables will be created.

3. Move any repeating groups of fields to their own separate table.

4. Name the tables using the *tbl* prefix and with a clearly descriptive name. Example: *tblOwners* for the Owners table.

5. Make sure each field is broken down into its smallest unit of data. Example: Name should be broken down into *FirstName* and *LastName* fields.

6. Underline the key field in each table.

7. Identify the fields by which the tables are joined together. Which tables should be joined to each other?

8. List other reports that could be generated from this data for SFRC.

9. Describe three forms that will be used to retrieve and enter data in the database.

10. Think of three questions that the management company will want answered by this database. These will become potential queries.

CASE STUDY C: PENGUINS SKI CLUB

The Penguins Ski Club is a nonprofit organization funded by several of the ski areas in Colorado. Its purpose is to promote skiing among children 7–11 years old. Penguins Ski Club provides ski rentals, discounted ski passes, organized activities, and transportation to and from ski areas for its members.

About 100 children belong to Penguins each year. Membership is $200 per year and covers everything except ski equipment rental, which is an additional $50 per year per member. Payments can be made all at once or in two installments.

Members may rent more than one set of equipment in a season. Shoe sizes and abilities change, so the database has to allow for the return of one set of equipment and the rental of another. This database only needs to record the equipment package number, not detailed information about sizes or kinds of equipment.

The membership year runs from November through March, in which time there are eight planned events. Events are always on Saturdays, and are always held in the mountains at a ski area, but not always the same ski area. Buses take the Penguins to and from the events. Each year there are two race days, two lesson days, and four recreational skiing days.

Here's a list of the tasks that Penguins would like their database to perform:

- Print a membership directory with names, addresses, and phone numbers of members.

- Print statements for fees due, and labels to send them to parents.

- Print a roster of attendees for each event.

- View, enter, and edit member and parent data.

- View, enter, and edit event information including name, location, and type and date of event, plus the names of attendees.

- View and print member lists grouped by ability levels and ages.

- View and print a list of members who are currently renting equipment, and which equipment package they are renting.

- View and print a list of events attended by each member.

- View and print a list of members with outstanding amounts due.

Design the tables for the Penguins Ski Club database on paper. Name each table, and make a list of fields in each table below the table name.

1. Begin by designing a table to hold member data. The parent who is responsible for the billing may not always live at the same address as the member, so put the parent's name and address in a separate table and join the two tables with the member ID number. Parent data doesn't have to be separate, but it makes looking at member records easier when there aren't a lot of fields in the table. Also, parent data will only be used for billing purposes, so it doesn't need to always be available when a membership record is opened. Include a field in the parent table for the amount due (membership fees plus rental fee, if applicable).

2. Design a table to hold rental equipment information. It should indicate the rental package number and the date the package was rented and returned.

3. Design a table to hold payment data.

4. Design one or more tables for event and attendance data.

5. Check each table to make sure there are no repeating data groups. If so, move the repeating data to its own table.

6. Check each table to make sure that each field has been broken down into the smallest piece of data appropriate for the task.

7. Be sure each table has a candidate for a primary key.

8. Be sure each table contains the fields needed to join it to other tables where appropriate.

9. Underline the name of the primary key in each table.

Chapter 2

Creating a Database

Objectives

After completing this chapter you will be able to

Create a new database:

- Create a database using templates, or from scratch.
- Follow appropriate naming conventions for database objects.

Create and maintain tables:

- Build a table from the Design view, or from Datasheet view.
- Use field templates and the field list pane.
- Select the appropriate data type for a field.
- Enter simple field properties.
- Understand a primary key, its use, and how to set one.
- Modify a table's design.
- Add records to a table and edit existing records.

Set controls to maintain data integrity:

- Mask and validate input.
- Create lookup fields to control data entry.

- Ensure the uniqueness and validity of the primary key.
- Use the Table Analyzer to split tables.

Control screen display:

- Move between the Design view and Datasheet view on the screen.
- Resize columns and rows in Datasheet view.
- Retrieve and open a completed table in both Datasheet and Design view.
- Change color schemes, fonts, and more in Datasheet view.
- Modify the Access environment by customizing options.

Store on disk:

- Create a database file, name it, and save it to disk.

Print information:

- Print both table records and table design.

Dictionary

Column	The vertical strip of data representing a field in Datasheet view. Each column shows all the data in one field.
Data type	The kind of data contained in a field, such as numeric or text. There are eight basic data types.
Database file	Stored file that includes all related objects in a database.
Database window	The main screen for Access. It displays all objects created for a particular database file.
Datasheet view	A view of the table data organized into columns and rows.
Design view	A view of the structure or organization of the table, showing all field properties.

Field	The smallest unit of data, such as someone's last name or phone number. One column in the table.
Field properties	The descriptive attributes of fields, such as a size specification or an automatically assigned value (default value).
Lookup field	A field that displays data from a list or from another table.
Naming conventions	Accepted standards for naming database objects using a three-letter prefix (ex: tbl for an Access table).
Objects	Individual parts of a database file, such as tables, queries, reports, forms, or macros.
Primary key	A field or group of fields that uniquely identifies a record.
Record	All of the data about one member of a group or table. One row in the table.
Row	The horizontal strip of data representing a record in Datasheet view.
Table	All the data collected about a group of related items.
Total row	A row that can be added to the bottom of a table displayed in Datasheet view. Simple statistical calculations can be a shown on this row.
Template	A predesigned Access database file.
Wizard	A feature in Access to assist in database and object creation.

2.1 Introducing Database Files

The database file in Access is the umbrella file that includes all the data and related objects in a database project. The Access icon (a document page with a key) preceding the file name will identify an Access file. The database file has an .accdb extension automatically assigned to it by Access. This extension may not display on a directory listing of files on your disk if you are viewing it in the Windows Explorer. (Some versions of Access (network) may show the .accdb extension when you create the database, however.) A file's extension gives you information about the file's type—.accdb indicates to other software packages that the file is an Access database.

An object is not a file that can stand by itself, but is part of the database file and is stored under the database file name. Examples of objects are tables, queries, forms, reports, macros, and modules. Each one of these objects has an identifying name but is not stored individually on your disk. The size of the database file will increase as new objects are created and as data is entered into tables.

Creating a database file is always the first thing you do on a new project. Try to use a descriptive name for your database—one that characterizes the overall project or is inclusive of all groups of data you are using. For example, the database containing information about sales on the online auction site G3 (Going, Going, Gone) could be called G3.

After creating the database file, you can begin adding objects to the database. Tables are created first in order to hold the necessary data. Remember to use the tables and fields you have already developed during the design phase. Other objects—forms, queries, reports, and so forth—are added as needed.

Q: How can you identify an Access database in a file list, say, when you are using Windows Explorer?

A: Look for an icon depicting a key on top of a page or for a file extension .accdb.

2.2 Creating Database Files

There are two ways to create a new database file: design it yourself or use a template. When you create a new database by designing it yourself, you start with a blank database and add each object (table, form, query, etc.) one at a time. The template, which is a predesigned Access database, is downloaded from a Microsoft Web site to your computer. Using a template will create all the objects in one procedure. You will just insert the data into the tables. Remember that a database can be modified at any time, regardless of the method used to create it.

First, let's examine the manual process of creating a blank database file.

Q: What's the easiest way to create a database?

A: Use one of the templates. A Database Wizard will help you create the database and objects.

How to Create a Blank Database File

1. Start the Access program.

2. From the Getting Started window, click on the Blank Database icon (see Figure 2.1).

   OR

   Click on the Office button and click on the New button. The Blank Database pane opens on the right side of the screen (see Figure 2.1).

3. Type the name of the database into the File Name box, and click on the folder icon to specify a location for your database (see Figure 2.1).

TRY IT YOURSELF 2.2.1

A. Create a new database file called *G3* (see Figures 2.1–2.3).

B. Close Access when finished.

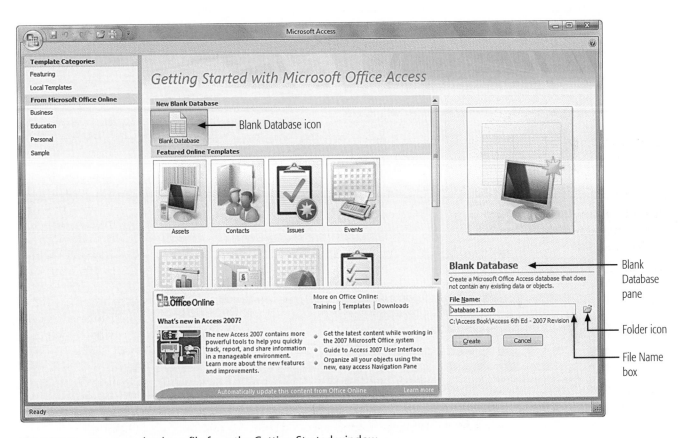

Figure 2.1 Create a new database file from the Getting Started window

4. The File New Database dialog box opens. Use the Navigation pane on the left to select the correct folder (see Figure 2.2). Click the OK button.

5. Click the Create button. An Access database file is created and saved. A window is opened for the first new table (see Figure 2.3).

6. You may continue by creating a new table, or close the table Datasheet view by clicking on the X button (see Figure 2.3).

Using Templates

A template is a database file that contains pre-designed Access objects, such as tables, reports, forms, etc. You will need to enter the data, and you can edit any object in the database. There are several different types of templates, and each is downloaded from the Internet automatically.

Q: How do you create a new database?

A: You can design it yourself or use a template.

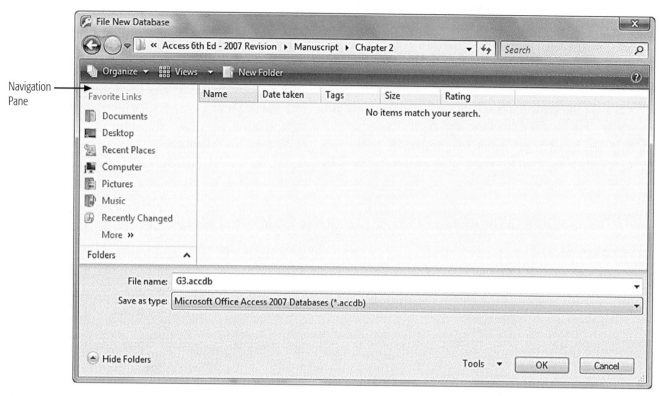

Navigation
Pane

Figure 2.2 File New Database dialog box

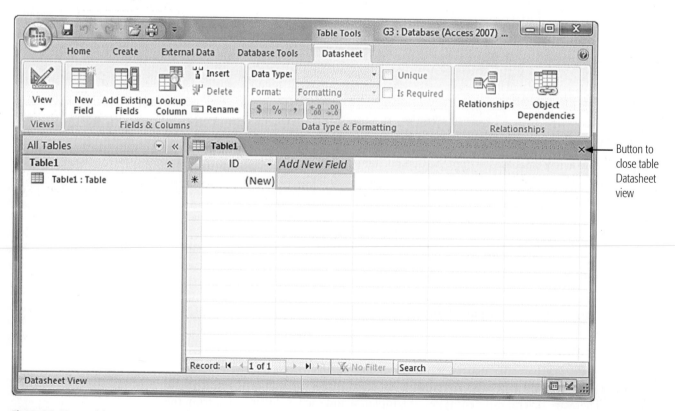

Button to
close table
Datasheet
view

Figure 2.3 New table in Datasheet view

How to Use a Template

1. Start the Access program, and be sure you are connected to the Internet.

2. From the Getting Started window, click on the template button for the database you want to create (see Figure 2.4).

3. Type the database name into the File Name box. Specify a location for the database by clicking on the folder icon.

4. Click on the Download button and wait for the template to load on your computer.

5. Once the template has loaded, the new database opens, showing one of the tables in Datasheet view (see Figure 2.5).

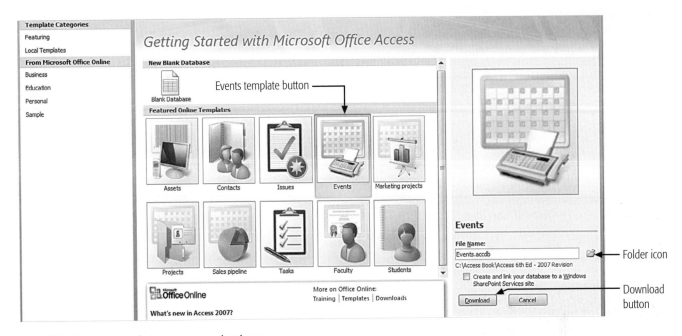

Figure 2.4 Using a template to create a database

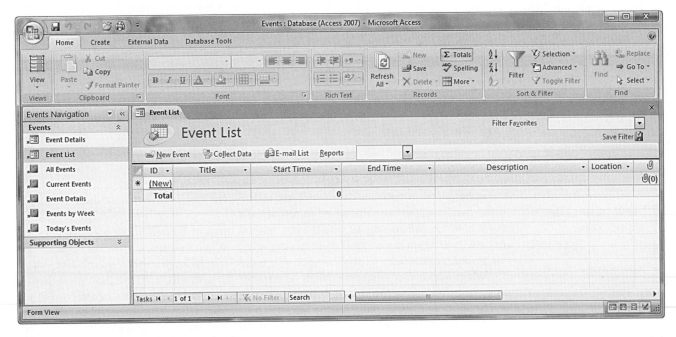

Figure 2.5 The first table in the Events database

TRY IT YOURSELF 2.2.2

Using the templates, create a new database.

A. Start Access, and be sure you're connected to the Internet.

B. Create a new database using the Events template.

C. Follow the steps shown in Figures 2.4–2.6, and display a list of the objects in the Events database.

D. Close the database using the Office menu.

6. You can begin entering data into this table, or work with any other object in the database (see Figure 2.6).

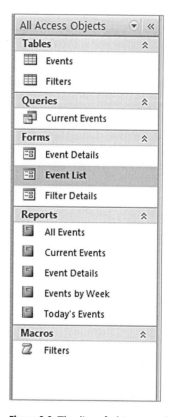

Figure 2.6 The list of objects in the Events database

Examining the Main Access Window

Once you have created a database, the main Access window opens. This window is the launching point for creating and using all objects in the database file.

Object names are listed on the left side of the screen in the Navigation Pane. Double-click on an object name to open it (see Figure 2.7). When an object is opened, it's displayed in the center area of the screen, called the document window. Multiple objects can be opened at one time and are stacked on top of each other in the document window. Small tabs on the top of the object title bars allow you to switch from one object to another (see Figure 2.8). Close an object by clicking on the X in the upper right corner of the object window.

Saving and Copying a Database

A database is automatically saved as soon as it is created. As objects and data are added to the database, they too are saved automatically.

When you are editing an object (you have it open in Design view) you can click on the Save button on the toolbar to save your work. When you try to close an object without saving, Access asks whether or not you would like to keep the changes.

When you are editing data in the Datasheet view, the data is saved as soon as you move to a different record or close the table. You can also save the data in a record while you are editing it by clicking on the Save button in the Records group on the ribbon.

You don't often lose data in Access. However, it is still wise to create backup copies of your database. From within Access, click on the Office button and use the Save As

Q: How do you make a copy of a database file?

A: You can use the Office button and use the Save As command to make a copy, or use Windows Explorer instead.

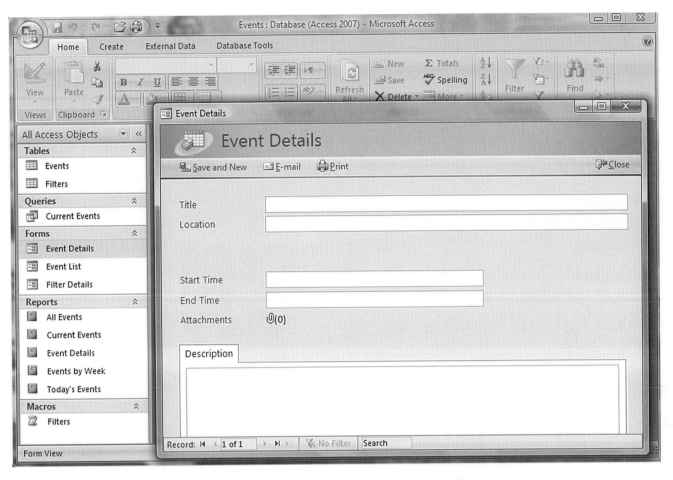

Figure 2.7 The opened Event Details form

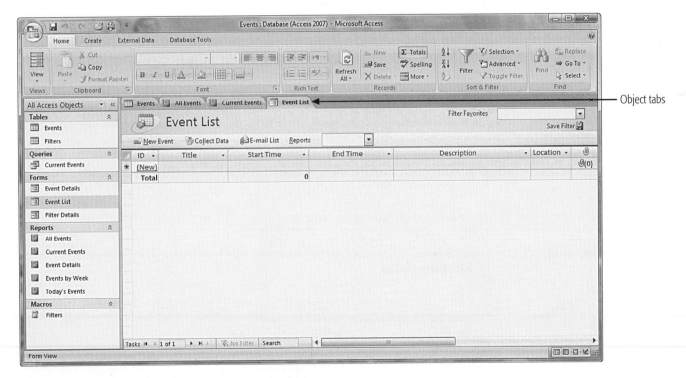

Figure 2.8 Multiple objects opened in the Events database

command to save the database with a different name. Using Windows Explorer, copy the database file by right-clicking on the file and then pasting it into a new location. You can also rename the file by right-clicking on the new copy and using the Rename command.

You can also make copies of individual objects in a database file. It is helpful to make a copy of an object before making significant changes so that the original can be restored if needed.

TRY IT YOURSELF 2.2.3

A. Open the *Events* database created in Try it yourself 2.2.2.

B. Open the table *Events*, the report *All Events*, the query *Current Events,* and the form *Event List.* Your screen should resemble Figure 2.8.

C. Close the objects opened in Step B.

D. Make a copy of the query *Current Events* (see Figures 2.9, 2.10, and 2.11).

E. Close the database.

How to Copy a Database Object

1. Open a database file.

2. Right-click on the name of the object that will be copied.

3. Click on the Copy command from the pop-up menu (see Figure 2.9).

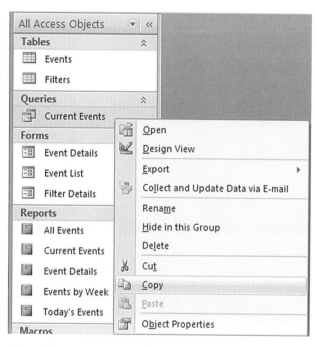

Figure 2.9 Copying a database object

4. On the background of the Navigation Pane, right-click to display the pop-up menu.

5. Click on the Paste command.

6. The Paste As dialog box appears. Enter the new table name. Click the OK button to finish (see Figure 2.10).

Figure 2.10 Past As dialog box

7. The copied object is now displayed in the list of available objects (see Figure 2.11).

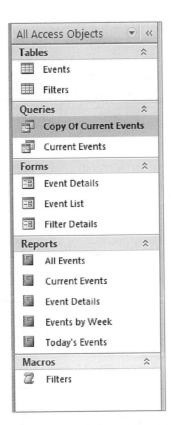

Figure 2.11 Copied query in object list

Professional Tip: **Free Database Templates**

This tip comes from Tony D'Ambra, an independent developer in Sydney, Australia. His company, AAD Consulting, has completed Access projects for companies such as Compaq Australia and Qantas Airways. The AAD Consulting Web site is full of Access tips and tools. There are free downloadable Access templates including the following ready-to-run business applications. You can download these applications at http://www.aadconsulting.com/dbases.html.

Program Manager
A complete business solution. Manages Clients, Contacts, and Client Programs. Allows multiple contacts for each client, and individual address and contact details for each contact. Nominate separate client program and invoicing contacts.

Project Manager
Tracks and controls projects in a business unit.

Sales Manager
Comprehensive reporting and product-costing functionality.

Client Manager
Covers clients and contacts, data import from MS Outlook, mailmerge, and more. Source code is included.

Document Tracker
Document management system with automatic document referencing and creation.

Contractor Tracker
The ultimate contractor tracking and control application. Remove sample data before using.

2.3 / Creating a Table

Tables are the first objects created when building a new database. Tables contain all the data about a group of related items. All other objects are just ways of looking at or using the data stored in tables. Tables can be created using a template, by entering data into the Datasheet view, or by defining fields in Design view. These commands are all found under the Create tab on the ribbon.

Naming Conventions

Names of Access objects and fields can contain up to 64 characters, and can include all letters, all numbers, and most special characters. It's acceptable to use a space in an object name, but later on you will have to enclose the name in square brackets [ ] when you use it in an expression or formula.

Names cannot start with a space, nor can they include the characters period (.), exclamation point (!), accent grave (e.g., è), or brackets ([ ]). Names should not be the same as any Access reserved words, such as Date. If a field is named Date, it may cause errors when used in expressions because Date is an Access function that provides the current date.

You may name an object anything you like, but there are rules and guidelines that you can follow. Use descriptive names for objects so it's easy to remember the object's function. An accepted standard for naming database objects is to use a three-letter prefix for each object name. Implementing this practice makes it easy to refer to objects in queries, macros, and Visual Basic modules. Table 2.1 shows the standard prefix for each type of Access object. For example, when implementing these standards, *tblStudents* would be the name of a table and *frmStudentDetail* would be the name of a form.

Table 2.1   Access Object Name Prefixes

Object	Prefix
Table	tbl
Query	qry
Form	frm
Report	rpt
Macro	mcr

In general, the plural form of a word is used as a table name. For example, a table containing the degrees offered by a college would be named *tblDegrees* rather than *tblDegree*. If a table contains information that joins two tables, use both table names in the third table name. For example, *tblFacultyDegrees* is a table with data showing which faculty members advise about which degrees. The table *tblFacultyDegrees* contains data from both the *tblFaculty* table and the *tblDegrees* table. Field names are usually singular, such as *Description* and *Address*. Most professionals recommend that lowercase letters be used with a leading capital letter, and names composed of multiple words have no spaces, with each word capitalized, as in *LastName* and *ZipCode*.

Using Table Templates

Table templates are similar to database templates, they are predefined structures that you can modify or use as is. There are only five table templates available—Contacts, Tasks, Issues, Events, and Assets. If you need other templates, consider using a database template to create a database full of tables. Then, create a new database and import only the tables you want from the template database.

How to Use a Table Template

1. Click on the Create tab on the ribbon (see Figure 2.12).

2. Click on the Table Templates button, and chose a template from the list that appears. The table is created and displayed in Datasheet view (see Figure 2.13).

3. Enter data into the table, or modify its fields.

4. Close and save the table with an appropriate name.

TRY IT YOURSELF 2.3.1

A. Create a new database called *G3*. If a new table called *Table1* opens automatically, close it and don't save it.

B. Create a table from the Contacts table template.

C. Close the table and name it *tblBuyers*.

D. Close the *G3* database.

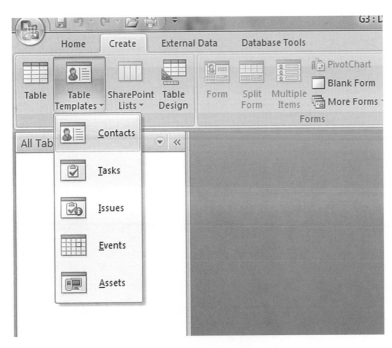

Figure 2.12 Table Templates list

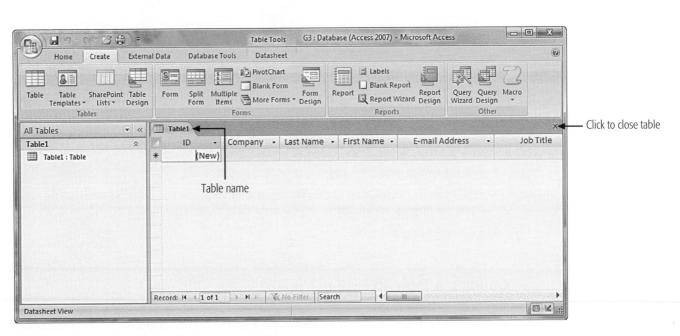

Figure 2.13 *Table1* created from the Contacts template

TRY IT YOURSELF 2.3.2

A. Using the *G3* database make a new table in Datasheet view. Refer to Figures 2.14–2.19.

B. Type the first two records as shown in Figure 2.16.

C. Rename the field *ID* as *CategoryID*, and *Field1* as *CategoryName*.

D. Save the table and name it *tblCategory*.

E. Change the Navigation pane to show all objects. It should resemble Figure 2.19.

F. Close the *G3* database.

Creating a Table in Datasheet View

The Datasheet view shows a table in a grid layout, with field names at the tops of the columns and records in rows below. This view is used for adding and editing data, but it also provides a quick way to create a table.

How to Create a Table in Datasheet View

1. Click on the Create tab on the ribbon.

2. Click on the Table button (see Figure 2.14). A new table appears temporarily named *Table1* (see Figure 2.15).

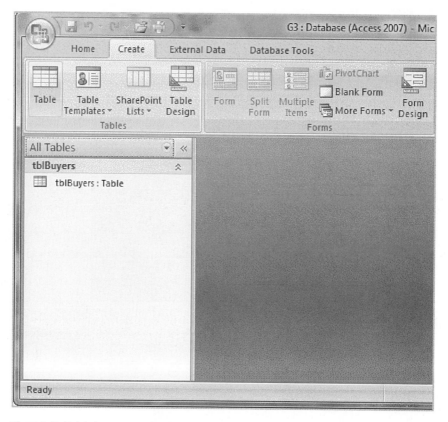

Figure 2.14 Table button under the Create tab

3. Fields will be automatically named as you type data into the first empty row (see Figure 2.16). Data cannot be entered into an ID field, it's an autonumber field and will be discussed in the next section. Press the enter key at the end of a field.

4. Use the mouse or arrow key to go to the next record.

5. Fields can be renamed by right-clicking on the field name, choosing Rename Column from the pop-up menu, and type the new field name (see Figure 2.17).

6. Save and name the table.

Building a Table in Design View

Building a table in the Design view gives you more control over the fields included in the table. You can determine the field names, data types, field descriptions, and various other properties for each field.

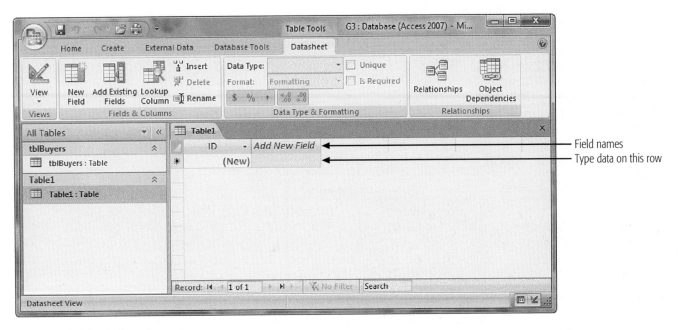

Figure 2.15 *Table 1* in Datasheet view

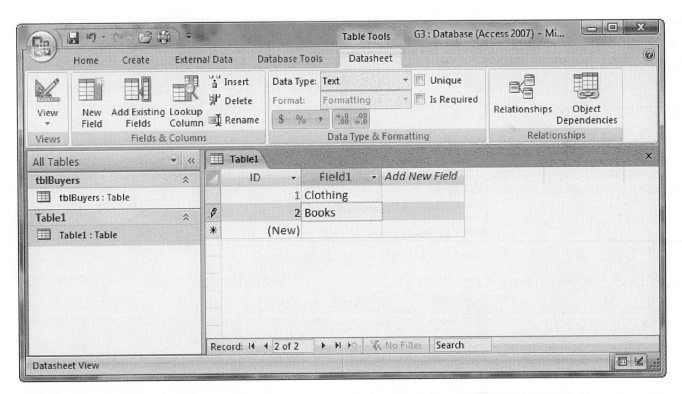

Figure 2.16 Defining fields in Datasheet view

How to Create a Table in Design View

Before creating a table, you must have a database file opened.

1. Select the Create tab on the ribbon, and click on the Table Design button (see Figure 2.20).

2. The new table opens in Design view as shown in Figure 2.22.

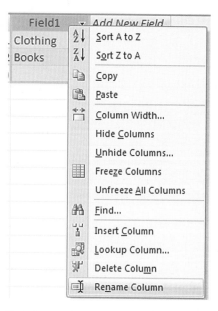

Figure 2.17 Renaming fields in Datasheet view

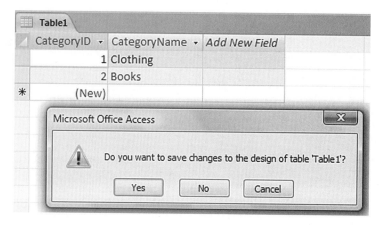

Figure 2.18 Saving a table

Figure 2.19 The new table name in the object list

Figure 2.20 The Table Design button in the Create tab

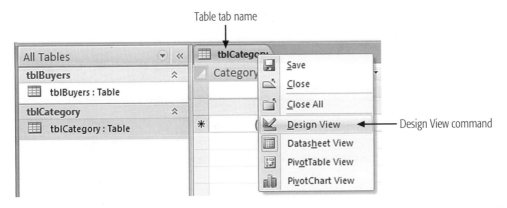

Figure 2.21 Moving from the Datasheet view to the Design view

You can also open an existing table in Design view using two different methods. You can right-click on the table name in the Navigation pane, and then select Design view from the pop-up menu. If a table is already open in Datasheet view, you can switch to the Design view by right-clicking on the tab name of the table, then choosing Design view from the pop-up menu (see Figure 2.21).

Design View Window

The Design view window is divided into two parts: the Field List area at the top of the screen where the name, data type, and an optional description are entered, and the Field Properties area below where specific characteristics are chosen for each field.

The Design tab contains several buttons that help in the table design process. You can move between Design and Datasheet view using the View button at the far left. There are buttons for inserting and deleting rows, setting a primary key, building a numeric expression, and other useful actions. Take a moment to look at the buttons shown in Figure 2.22.

Field Entry Area

The Field entry area contains three columns and many rows where you can build a table by entering field names, data types, and descriptions. Enter a field name and data type in each row and a new field is created. The description is optional, but useful for documentation.

TRY IT YOURSELF 2.3.3

A. Using the *G3* database, open the table *tblBuyers* in the Design view.

B. Close the table *tblBuyers*.

C. Open the table *tblCategory* in Datasheet view.

D. Change to the Design view using the example shown in Figure 2.21.

E. Close the *G3* database, or continue on.

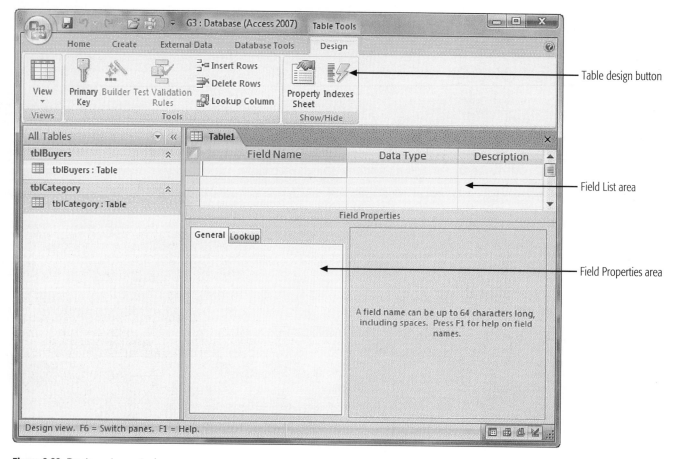

Figure 2.22 Design view window

TRY IT YOURSELF 2.3.4

A. Open the *G3* database, if it's not already open.

B. Create a new table in Design view. Your screen should resemble Figure 2.22.

C. Add two text fields to the table: *G3Number* and *ItemName*. Refer to Figure 2.23.

D. Continue with Try It Yourself 2.3.4 and finish creating the table.

Field Names

The field name identifies the field for both Access and for users. There are a few rules governing field names:

- They can be 1–64 characters in length. They should be descriptive but not too long.
- They can include letters, numbers, and some special characters.
- They cannot include the following special characters:.! []
- They cannot begin with a blank space but can include spaces.
- They can be entered in uppercase, lowercase, or mixed case.

Data Types

You must identify the type of data that a field contains. There are eleven types of data that can be entered. Some types have different options available. They are described in Table 2.2.

How to Enter Field Names, Data Types, and Descriptions

1. Place the pointer in the Field Name column.

2. Type the field name.

3. Press the ENTER or TAB key or use the mouse pointer to move to the Data Type column. Select the appropriate type from the drop-down list as shown in Figure 2.24.

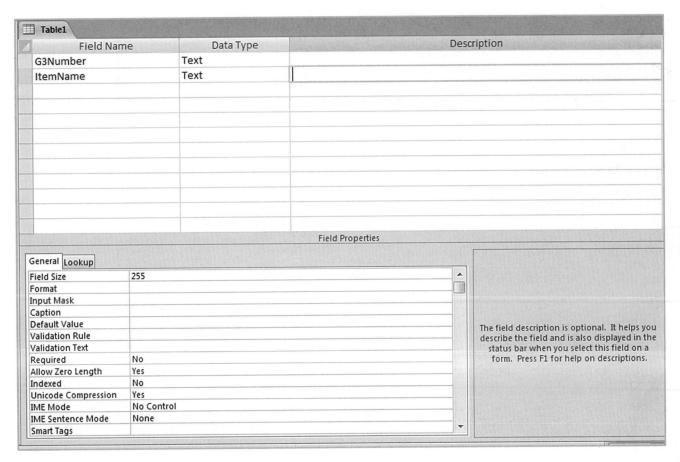

Figure 2.23 New table with two fields defined

Table 2.2 Data Types

Data Type	Description
Text	Any type of data that contains words or characters. Some numeric data should be considered text if the numbers will not be used in calculations (address, phone number, social security number, zip code). A text field has a limit of 255 characters.
Memo	Can contain a variable amount of data up to 65,535 characters for each record. Useful for notations when field size cannot be determined. Rich text with a limited amount of formatting can be stored in a memo field. Set the Text Format property of the field to "Rich Text".
Number	Allows for numeric data entry that can be used in calculations.
Date/Time	Can store dates, times, or both. There are several display formats for this data type.
Currency	Can store numeric data up to 15 digits to the left of a decimal point and 4 digits to the right of the decimal point.
AutoNumber	Automatically enters a unique number (counter) for each record.
Yes/No	Allows the user to enter only one of two values. The format can be changed to display Yes/No, True/False, or On/Off.
OLE Object	Allows the user to store the image of an object in an OLE server file. Graphics, documents, and other Office files are some of the objects that can be stored in this type of field.
Hyperlink	Allows the user to store Internet addresses of file locations.
Attachment	Attaches external data such as graphics, audio files, and Office documents to a field. Attachment fields are better than OLE object fields because they use storage space more efficiently.
Look Up Wizard	Allows the user to create a field that can be linked to a field in another table. The values displayed in the field are actually stored in the other table, eliminating redundant storage.

4. Press the ENTER or TAB key or use the mouse pointer to move to the Description column, if you want to add a description (it's optional). Use a description to clarify or provide more documentation about the field, if necessary. Use the ENTER or TAB key, or the mouse pointer to move to the next field name row.

TRY IT YOURSELF 2.3.5

A. Using the new table from Try It Yourself 2.3.4, add the fields *StartDate, StartPrice,* and *Paid* with the data types shown in Figure 2.24.

B. Save the table as *tblSales,* and don't define a primary key yet.

C. Close the *G3* database, or continue on.

Field Name	Data Type
G3Number	Text
ItemName	Text
StartDate	Date/Time
StartPrice	Currency
Paid	Yes/No

Text
Memo
Number
Date/Time
Currency
AutoNumber
Yes/No
OLE Object
Hyperlink
Attachment
Lookup Wizard...

General Lookup

| Format | Yes/No |
| Caption | |

Figure 2.24 Design view showing the data type drop-down list

5. Continue until all field names, types, and descriptions are entered. To select a data type other than text, move to the Data Type column, click the drop-down list, and select the appropriate data type.

Creating a lookup field is a little different from creating other types of fields. Lookup fields display data from another source—another table or a typed list. The most common use of a lookup field is to display data that is stored in another table. By putting the primary key from the second table into the field, the field can display any data from the second table. The value of the primary key is actually stored in the first table, but the user sees the linked data from the second table.

Consider the example of the G3 database. In the table *tblCategory*, there are two fields—*Category ID* (a unique ID number) and *CategoryName*. Each item in *tblSales* will be categorized, so a lookup field can be added to *tblSales* that links to the *CategoryName* field in *tblCategory*. The *CategoryID* will actually be stored in *tblSales*, but the user will see the *CategoryName*.

By picking Lookup Wizard from the data type list, you start the wizard that links the tables together and displays the correct data in the field. You must specify the name of the table containing the data to be displayed, the key field in this table, and the field to be displayed. Figure 2.25 shows how the *Category* field in *tblSales* looks when it looks values up in *tblCategory*. A complete discussion of this topic is found in Chapter 7.

TRY IT YOURSELF 2.3.6

A. Open *tblSales* in Design view and add a new field called *Category*. Make it a lookup field that displays the *CategoryName* from *tblCategory*.

B. Switch to Datasheet view and compare your result to Figure 2.25.

C. Close the *G3* database, or continue on.

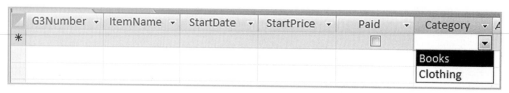

Figure 2.25 Datasheet view of *tblSales* showing *Category* as a lookpu field

Defining Data Types in Datasheet View

New to Access 2007 is the ability to define field data types in Datasheet view. You can now pick field names and data using field templates, or create lookup fields by picking fields from other tables shown in the field list.

How to Define a Field Using a Field Template

1. Create or open a table in Datasheet view.

2. Click on the Datasheet tab on the ribbon, and click on the New Field button (see Figure 2.26). The Field Templates pane appears.

3. Double-click on the field name shown in the list in the Field Templates pane. The new field appears as a column in the table.

A field added from a field template will have the name and data type assigned. These can be changed most easily by going into the Design view and editing the name or data type.

TRY IT YOURSELF 2.3.7

A. Open *tblSales* in Datasheet view.

B. Using a field template, add a new field called *PurchasePrice* as shown in Figure 2.26.

C. Save *tblSales*.

C. Close the *G3* database, or continue on.

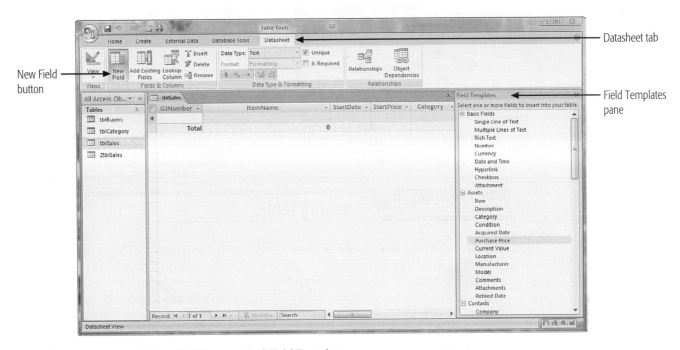

Figure 2.26 Datasheet tab, New Field button, and Field Templates pane

How to Define a Lookup Field Using the Field List

1. Create or open a table in Datasheet view.

2. Click on the Datasheet tab on the ribbon, and click on the Add Existing Fields button (see Figure 2.27). The Field List pane appears.

3. Double-click on the field name shown in the list in the Field List pane. The Lookup Wizard begins as shown in Figure 2.27.

4. Select the field to be displayed in the table, and complete the steps in the Lookup Wizard. The new field appears as a column in the table. The new field will display a drop-down list of values from the other table when clicked.

How to Save the Table Design

Press the Save button on the Quick Access toolbar, or close the table to save. If you are saving the table for the first time, Access will ask for a table name (up to 64 characters). You will also be asked to specify a primary key—press the No button for now. Defining a primary key is discussed in the next section. Remember to add the *tbl* prefix to the table name.

TRY IT YOURSELF 2.3.8

A. Open *tblSales* in Datasheet view.

B. Using the field list, add a lookup field for *BuyerID* as shown in Figure 2.27.

C. Save *tblSales*.

D. Close the *G3* database.

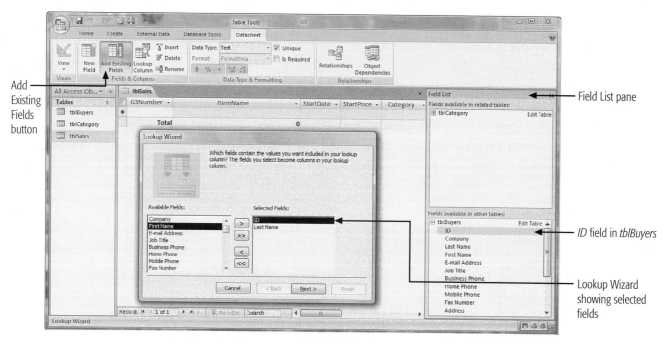

Figure 2.27 Add Existing Fields button, Field List pane, and Lookup Wizard

---

Professional Tip: **Creating Tables**

Design and create your tables right the first time, as changing the fields in a table can cause problems. If a query is based on a table and one field is deleted or renamed in the table, the query still refers to the old field and will not run. If the query is run by a macro or program, it may not be obvious that it didn't run correctly and errors may go undetected for some time.

Changing tables can be especially difficult if the database is networked (has multiple people using the same data). Tables in a networked database must be locked to make changes in the Design view. When a table is locked, users are prevented from accessing the data in the table, which disrupts business operations. On a busy network, the developer may have to make table changes during off-business hours.

2.4 Setting Field Properties

Field properties can further define fields. They are used to control the validity and accuracy of data input into the field, and the output display of the data in a form. Field properties can be simple, such as setting the field size—or very complex, such as restricting field values to a range of numbers or words. Every field has properties; either user-defined properties or default properties that are automatically determined when the field is created. These properties are different for each data type, and are grouped into two categories: General and Lookup (see Figure 2.28).

How to Set Properties

1. Position the pointer on the desired field in the Design view.

2. Use the F6 or the mouse pointer to switch between the Field entry area and the Field Properties area.

General tab

Lookup tab

Properties values

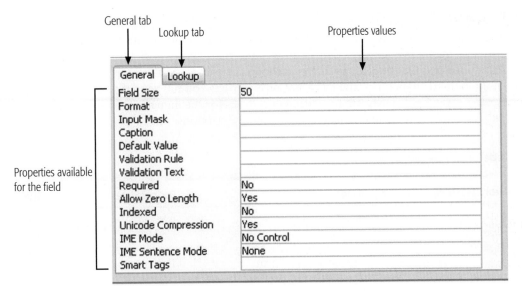

Properties available for the field

Figure 2.28 Design view window, Field Properties area

3. Move the mouse pointer to the line of the property you want to change.

4. Delete the default value, if necessary, and enter the new values, or use the drop-down list arrow to display predefined values.

5. The property list is saved with the field structure when the table is saved, so be sure to save the table after changing property values.

General Properties

These properties may affect the way the data in a field looks on the screen, how it's entered into a table, and how it's stored on disk. The General Properties are displayed when you click on the General tab as shown in Figure 2.28. See Table 2.3 for brief descriptions of general properties.

Table 2.3 General Properties

Screen Display	
Format	Affects the style in such matters as displaying text in all caps or numbers as currency.
Caption	Changes the name of the field on the screen; good for complicated or long names.
Data Entry	
Input mask	Allows only certain characters to be typed in a field.
Validation rule	Allows only specific letters or numbers to be typed in a field.
Validation text	Displays message regarding data validation rules.
Required	Does not allow the field to be left blank.
Allow zero length.	Allows nothing to be typed in a text field.
Indexed	Speeds up searches, joins, and queries involving the field.
IME mode and IME sentence mode	Interpret Asian characters.
Smart tags	Links to data and actions in other applications.
Storage	
Field size	Restricts the length of the field.
Default value	Puts an automatic value in the field when a record is added.
Decimal places	Determines the number of digits to the right of the decimal point in a numeric field.
Unicode compression	Allows text and memo fields to take up less storage space.

TRY IT YOURSELF 2.4.1

A. Open the *G3*, database, and open *tblBuyers* in Design view.

B. Change the size of the *State* field to 2 characters.

C. Save the table of switch to Datasheet view.

D. Type "abc" into the *State* field of the first record. Note you're not permitted to type more than 2 characters.

E. Close the *G3* database, or continue.

Field Size

The Field Size property works differently for text and numeric data types. The text field size determines storage size, that is, how large the maximum field length can be. The default for text fields is 50 characters, although this and other defaults are customizable.

In numeric data types, the Field Size property lets you further define the type of number in a given field. There are five different settings for the numeric field size property. See Table 2.4 below for numeric field settings and descriptions.

Table 2.4   Numeric Field Settings

Field Size Setting	Range	Decimal Places	Size
Byte	0 to 255	None	1 byte
Integer	−32,768 to 32,767	None	2 bytes
Long Integer	−2,147,483,648 to 2,147,483,647	None	4 bytes
Double	−1.797 x E308 to 1.797 x E308	15	8 bytes
Single	−3.4 x E38 to 3.4 x E38	7	4 bytes
Replication ID	N/A	N/A	16 bytes
Decimal	$-10^{\wedge}38$ to $10^{\wedge}38$	28	12 bytes

For example, you could create a State field and set the size property to two letters. This would allow people to enter the two-letter state abbreviation for each state, but prevents state names from being spelled out completely. You might also use the size property to set up a field to contain a grade point average. A student's GPA is generally a real number (a number containing a fraction) between zero and four (sometimes the upper limit of the scale is six or some other number less than ten). To represent GPA correctly, you would create a numeric field with a size property set at Single. (Setting the property to Byte allows only integers to be entered.)

TRY IT YOURSELF 2.4.2

A. Using *tblBuyers* from the previous Try it yourself, open the table in Design view.

B. Change the Default Value property for the field *Job Title* to "Buyer" (see Figure 2.29).

C. Go to the Datasheet view and note that the word "Buyer" applies in the *Job Title* field in the new record row.

D. Close *G3* or continue.

Default Value

This property automatically assigns an initial value to a field when a new record is added. You can change the value if you want. Use this property if the field has the same value most of the time. For example, if most courses are three credit hours, 3 would be a good default value for the *Credit Hours* field. It's often useful to set the default value of a date to date(), a function that places today's date in a fields.

Decimal Places

This property applies only to numeric data. It allows you to select the number of digits to the right of the decimal point. If you leave it at Auto, Access will adjust the number of decimal places automatically for each value in the field.

Format

The Format property allows you to customize the data display according to your needs. It affects the way data is displayed, not how it is stored in the table or how it is entered. There are several formats available for each data type. See Table 2.5 for a listing and a brief description of various formats.

The format property can be used effectively in many situations. For example, a two-letter state abbreviation could have a format property of ">" to force all letters in the field to appear as uppercase. An amount field could have the format property set to Currency so all numbers entered appear with dollar signs and two decimal places. In other words, you could type "123" and it would appear as "$123.00." Remember that data only appears formatted, it is not actually stored in the table with the formatting.

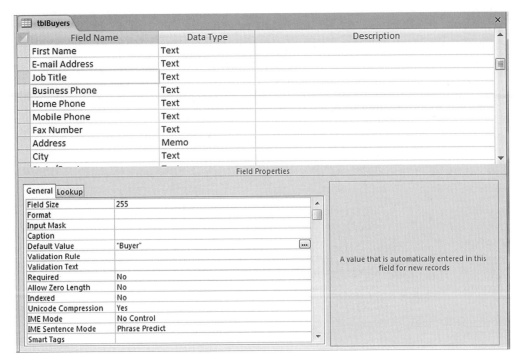

Figure 2.29 Changing the Default Value property in Design view

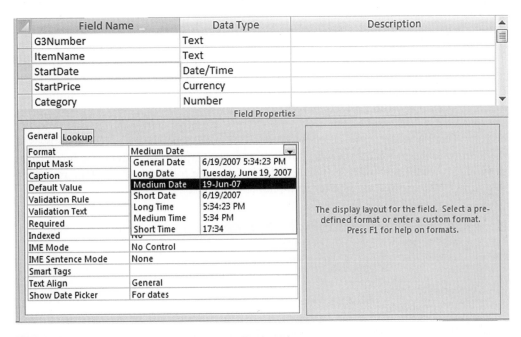

Figure 2.30 Changing the Format property in Design view

Q: What is the small grid that appears to the right of a date field?

A: It's an automatic calendar that pops up when clicked, and allows you to select a date value for the field.

TRY IT YOURSELF 2.4.3

A. Open *tblSales* in the *G3* database in Design view.

B. Change the format of field *StartDate* to Medium Date as shown in Figure 2.30.

C. Save the table as *tblSales*, and go to Datasheet view.

D. Type today's date into the *StartDate* field on the bottom row, or pick the date from the automatic calendar that appears to the right of the field. Note that the format changes as soon as you move the cursor from that record.

E. Close the *G3* database, or continue on.

Caption

The Caption property allows the user to display a different name for a given field. This caption can be more or less descriptive than the original field name. A caption is not required.

TRY IT YOURSELF 2.4.4

A. Using *tblBuyers,* change the caption of the *E-mail Address* field to "Email".

B. Go to the Datasheet view and note the column heading change for the field.

C. Return to Design view.

D. Close the *G3* database or continue.

Table 2.5 Formats

Formats	Description
Text	
>	Makes all text in the field uppercase.
<	Makes all text in the field lowercase.
@	Displays either a character or a space in the field.
&	Default text format.
Number	
General	Default number format.
Currency	Shows dollar sign and two decimals.
Fixed	Provides a specific number of decimal points.
Standard	Displays a thousands separator.
Percent	Displays percent sign and decimals, if needed.
Date/Time	
General Date	Default date format. Display depends on value entered.
Long Date	Displays day of week and complete date information.
Medium Date	Displays date-month-year.
Short Date	Displays date in numeric format.
Long Time	Displays hour, minute, seconds, AM/PM.
Medium Time	Displays hour, minutes, AM/PM.
Short Time	Displays 24-hour clock time.
Yes/No	
Yes/No	Default displays Yes or No.
True/False	Displays True or False.
On/Off	Displays On or Off.

TRY IT YOURSELF 2.4.5

A. Using *tblBuyers,* change the Input Mask property of the field *State* to force only two uppercase letters to be entered, as shown in Figure 2.31.

B. Save the table and go to Datasheet view.

C. Type two lowercase letters into the *State* field on the bottom row. Note that the letters appear in uppercase.

D. Close the *G3* database, or continue on.

Input Mask

The Input Mask property lets you define filters that only certain data can pass through if it is to be entered into that field. This property gives you more control over the type of data entered in a particular field. For example, an Input Mask can prohibit entering numbers in a text field, or it can force all letters to be uppercase. It is very important to know exactly the type of data that will be entered in the field, as all other data entered will be locked out. The Input Mask must be entered in the form of predefined codes shown in Table 2.6.

For example, to force data in a state field to be two uppercase letters, the Input Mask property would be set to > LL. The > indicates that the following characters are uppercase, and each L represents a letter or alphabetic character.

Figure 2.31 Changing the Input Mask property

Table 2.6 Input Mask Characters

Character	Description
0	Digit (0–9) required with no + or − signs
9	Digit or space with no + or − signs
#	Digit or space with + or − signs allowed
L	Letter (A–Z) required
?	Letter (A–Z) optional
A	Letter or digit required
a	Letter or digit optional
&	Any character or space required
C	Any character or space optional
<	Convert characters to lowercase
>	Convert characters to uppercase
!	Fill input mask from right to left
\	Character that follows to be displayed literally
.,:;-/	Decimal placeholder, thousands, and date and time separator

An input mask can be created for a text field that contains a leading capital letter with all other letters lowercase, such as a name. Set the Field Size property to the total number of letters allowed, and use the symbols > and < in the Input Mask property. Using the example of a field *LastName*, the Field Size property could be set to 15 and the input mask would be: >L<?????????????? (14 question marks). In the input mask, the character ">" indicates the following character must be uppercase, the "L" indicates a required letter, the "<" means that all characters following are lowercase, and the "?" indicates an optional letter. You must account for all characters indicated by the field size, so in this example there must be 15 characters as placeholders in the input mask (plus the two symbols for upper- and lowercase). Using the "?" makes a character optional, so that a name of less than 15 characters is accepted.

Running the Input Mask Wizard is by far the easiest way to create or modify an Input Mask. The wizard contains templates for most common masks—a phone number, a social security number, and so forth. To start the Input Mask Wizard, click on the button with an ellipsis (...) to the right of the Input Mask property line (see Figure 2.32).

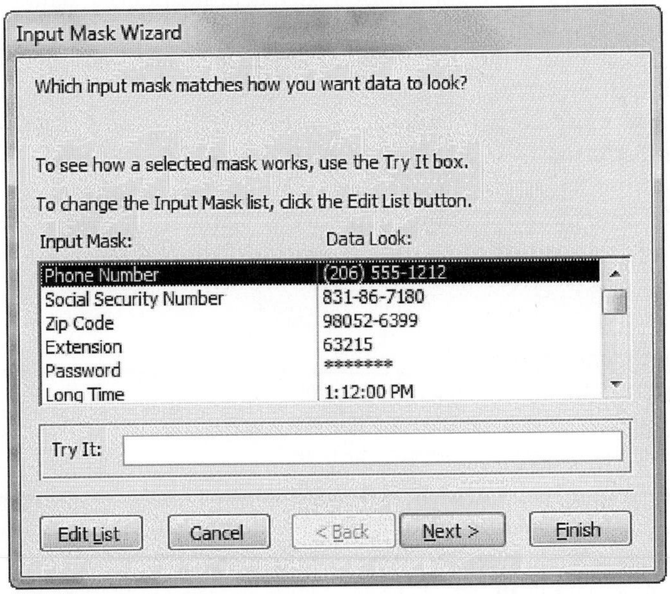

Figure 2.32 Input Mask Wizard

TRY IT YOURSELF 2.4.6

A. Using *tblSales*, set the Valida-tion Rule property for the field *StartPrice* to > = .99, and set the Validation Text to "Start Price must be 99 cents or greater." Refer to Figure 2.33 for help.

B. Go to the Datasheet view.

C. Type .5 into the *StartPrice* field and observe the error message. Press OK to clear the error message.

D. Type 1 into the *StartPrice* field.

E. Return to Design view, and continue.

Validation Rule and Validation Text

The Validation Rule property allows you to limit the actual data values that are entered in a particular field. This helps eliminate many data entry errors. An error message can be displayed to help the user enter the correct value.

Validation rules can be very useful when tight data entry controls are necessary, but they can also become very complicated and cumbersome. Keep any rules you use very simple at first.

AND and OR operators can be used in the Validation Rule. With AND, both parts of the Validation Rule must be true. With OR, only one part of the Validation Rule needs to be true.

Field Name	Data Type
G3Number	Text
ItemName	Text
StartDate	Date/Time
StartPrice	Currency
Category	Number

Field Properties

General | Lookup

Format	Currency
Decimal Places	Auto
Input Mask	
Caption	
Default Value	
Validation Rule	>=0.99
Validation Text	Start Price must 99 cents or greater
Required	No
Indexed	No
Smart Tags	
Text Align	General

Figure 2.33 Validation Rule and Validation Text properties

The Validation Text line allows you to enter a message to assist the user in entering the correct data. This text is displayed when the Validation Rule is broken during data entry.

The Validation Rule and Validation Text properties could be used to allow a number between one and five to be entered into the *Credit Hours* field. To do this, you would type the following Validation Rule: < 6 And > 0. The "And" indicates both conditions must be true, so a number must be less than six and greater than zero. The same Validation Rule could be expressed by typing: 1 Or 2 Or 3 Or 4 Or 5. The "Or" indicates any one of the values in the list may be used. An appropriate Validation Rule for this field could be: "Credit hours must be a number between 1 and 5." If a user were to type a zero or a number larger than five, the message in the Validation Text property would be displayed.

Required, Allow Zero Length, and Indexed

The Required property line allows you to set this field as a required field; that is, data must be entered in this field.

The Allow Zero Length property allows you to specify a zero length string that can be entered in this field. For display purposes, the field will appear blank.

The Indexed property line lets you create an index entry for this field. Indexing a field is similar to adding a word to a book index in that it promotes fast searching, but it will take longer to update a table if data is added or changed in an indexed field. The Yes, No Duplicates choice from the drop-down list will prohibit duplicate data from being entered in the field. This property is automatically set on a primary key along with the required property.

Lookup Properties

Lookup properties are displayed when you click on the Lookup tab as shown in Figure 2.34. The Lookup property window shows the Display Control line. This line shows a drop-down list that displays several control type choices—text box, list box, combo box, and check box—depending on the data type of the field. This choice will determine the type of control used for this field in a Form view. Fields created with the Lookup Wizard and Yes/No type fields have Lookup properties.

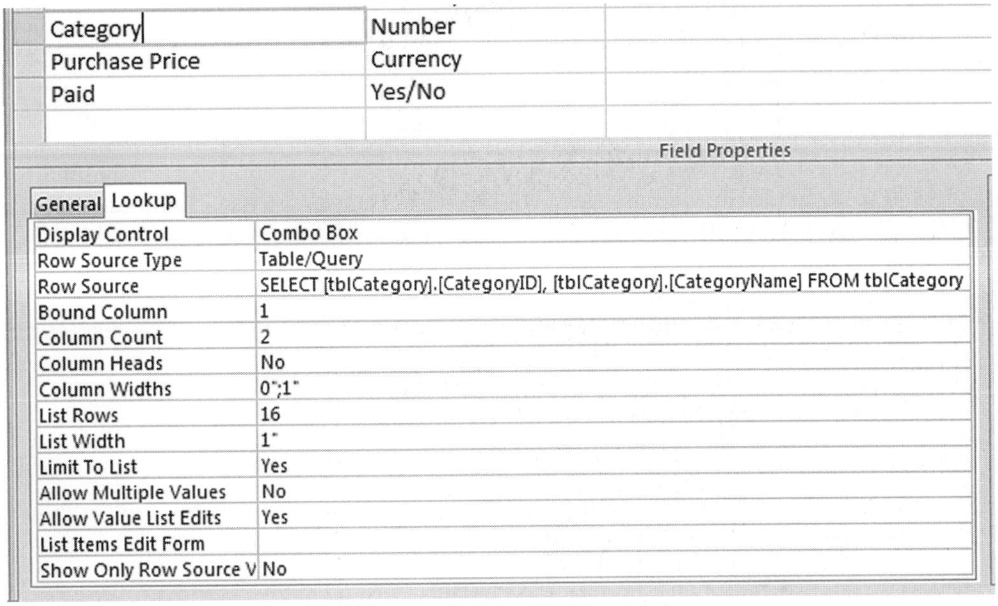

Category	Number	
Purchase Price	Currency	
Paid	Yes/No	

Field Properties

General | **Lookup**

Display Control	Combo Box
Row Source Type	Table/Query
Row Source	SELECT [tblCategory].[CategoryID], [tblCategory].[CategoryName] FROM tblCategory
Bound Column	1
Column Count	2
Column Heads	No
Column Widths	0";1"
List Rows	16
List Width	1"
Limit To List	Yes
Allow Multiple Values	No
Allow Value List Edits	Yes
List Items Edit Form	
Show Only Row Source V	No

Figure 2.34 Lookup tab properties for the *Category* field in *tblSales*

The default value is a text box—a rectangle that displays one value. Other choices depend on the data type of the field. You can select a text, list, or combo box to control text and numeric fields. List and combo boxes display a list of choices for you to pick from, instead of typing a value into the field. Yes/No fields can be represented by check boxes that show a check mark in a box representing a yes value.

Remember that a lookup field looks up field values in another table. The Lookup properties for a lookup field include a query that is used to obtain the values from the second table. For example, the table *tblSales* has two lookup fields—*Category* and *BuyerID*. Although *tblSales* stores the ID codes in the records, the user sees the Category name and the buyer's name that have been looked up in their respective tables. In this case, a number of additional properties will be displayed under the Lookup properties tab (see Figure 2.34). These properties describe the query that obtains the data, how many columns of the query to display, how wide the columns should be, and other formatting considerations. This type of Lookup will be discussed in Chapter 7, Section 3.

Establishing a Primary Key

The primary key is a record's unique identifier, just as a license plate is a car's unique identifier. Only one car can have a specific license plate number, and only one record

Q: What is a primary key?

A: A primary key is like the license plate on a car — it uniquely identifies a record.

Q: Why use an AutoNumber data type?

A: To create a primary key when one doesn't occur naturally.

TRY IT YOURSELF 2.4.7

A. Using the table *tblSales*, make *G3Number* the primary key (see Figure 2.35).

B. Save the table and close it.

C. Close the *G3* database, or continue.

can have a specific value in the primary key field. The data in the primary key is unique within that table. Also, just as every car must have a license plate, every record must contain a value in the primary key field. If no primary key is specified in a table, it may negatively affect searching for records within the table and linking the table to other tables.

If no field meets the requirements for a primary key, you can create an AutoNumber data type field and make it the primary key. AutoNumber fields contain incremental integers that are automatically assigned by Access, so they exist in every record and are unique. For example, the first record in a table would be assigned an AutoNumber value of 1, the second record a 2, and so forth.

When entering records into the table, Access will display the data in the order of the primary key, and check for duplicate data in the primary key. Duplicate data is not allowed in a key field, and an error message is displayed to warn of duplicate data.

Q: When I save a table, I get an error or message saying "Index or primary key cannot contain a Null value". What should I do?

A: Click OK, then turn off the primary key. The error occurs because some records have no data values in the primary key field. Add data to these records, then turn the primary key on again.

How to Set a Primary Key

There are two ways to create a primary key (see Figure 2.35).

1. In the table Design view, click on the Design tab on the ribbon. Select the field or fields to be made the primary key. Multiple fields can be selected by holding down the CTRL key while clicking on the row selector to the left of the field name.

2. Designate the primary key by doing one of the following:

   Click the Primary Key button on the ribbon

   OR

   Right-click the mouse to display the shortcut menu and select Primary Key

   OR

   Save the table without designating a primary key and Access will ask to create one. This happens only the first time you save the table.

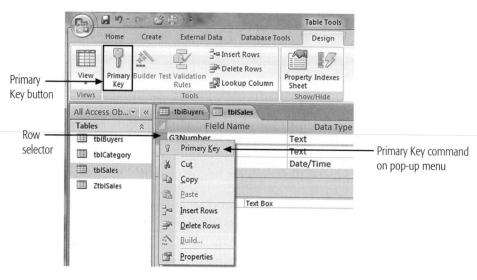

Figure 2.35 Table Design view, Primary Key options

Professional Tip: Primary Keys and Autonumbers

This tip comes from Jon Sanders, Ringmaster of the Microsoft Access Web ring found at http://a.webring.com/t/Microsoft-Access. He also hosts a Web site, containing tips and tutorials on using Access, that can be found at http://www.applecore99.com. Jon is a Computing Support Officer for a large UK charity, and has been using Microsoft Access for several years developing desktop applications and Web pages using Active Server Pages. Jon is an active participant in the various Internet newsgroups that support Microsoft Access.

When creating a table, I prefer to have the primary key as the first field, followed by any foreign keys, and then the rest of the fields. I normally try to use descriptive field names, made up of two or more words joined together without spaces. Normally, I prefer to end any primary/foreign key name with "ID."

If there is a natural key for the table, then that may be used. However, there might be the problem that although there is a unique value for each object, at the time of entry this value isn't known. Therefore, you must use an artificial key. Access supplies its own built-in unique field, in the shape of an Auto-Number. However, there are various problems with using an AutoNumber:

First, you shouldn't be revealing the AutoNumber field to the user in a database, and expect it to have any meaning. The AutoNumber should really only be used internally by Access to relate records in relationships. AutoNumbers are not guaranteed to be consecutive. If the entry of a new record is interrupted, the primary key will already have been allocated, and therefore when the next record is added successfully, it is not given the value of the uncommitted record, but the one after that. Once an AutoNumber has been created and then deleted, there is no way to reuse that number.

A question that is often asked is how to reset the AutoNumber back, so that it starts incrementing from 1 again. To reset the AutoNumber, delete all of the data from the table, and then compact your database. Now the first record that you enter into this table will start off at 1.

Author's Note—Of course, copy the table before deleting all the records, then add the records back into the empty table. And, don't do this if the AutoNumber is used as a foreign key (see Chapter 7 for more information).

2.5 Printing the Table Design

Access will generate a Table Design report showing the fields, properties, and so forth of the selected table.

How to Print the Table Design

1. Click on the Database Tools tab on the ribbon, and click on the Database Documenter button as shown in Figure 2.36.

Figure 2.36 Printing the table design

Q: What if the Documenter
Wizard is not installed?

A: Insert your Office CD-ROM in
the drive and follow the
prompts on the screen.

2. Click the Tables tab to display all tables in the database file. Click on the desired table, then press the Select All button, as shown in Figure 2.37. The Select All button will select all tables to analyze.

Tables tab →

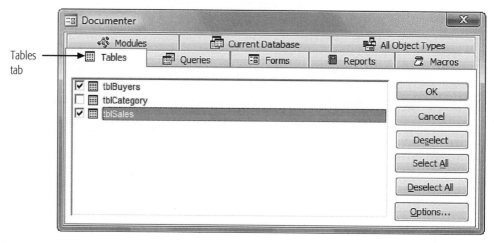

Figure 2.37 Documenter screen

TRY IT YOURSELF 2.5.1

A. Generate the table design report for the tables *tblBuyers* and *tblSales* using the Print Table Definition selections as shown in Figure 2.38.

B. View the information, then close the Object Definition window.

C. Close the *G3* database, or continue on.

3. Click the Options button. The Print Table Definition screen appears (see Figure 2.38).

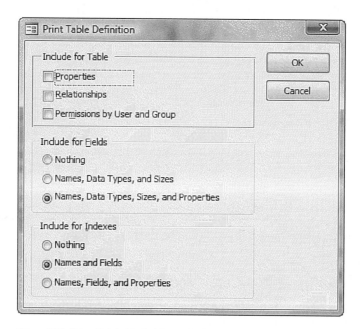

Figure 2.38 Print Table Definition window

4. Select the desired options, then click the OK button to move back to the Documenter screen, as shown in Figure 2.37. Click the OK button to generate the report. (This may take a few moments.) You will see an Object Definition window showing a preview of the report (see Figure 2.39).

5. Press the Quick Print button on the Quick Access toolbar as shown in Figure 2.40.

   OR

   Click on the Office button and choose the Print command. Select Print or Quick Print.

6. Close the Object Definition window.

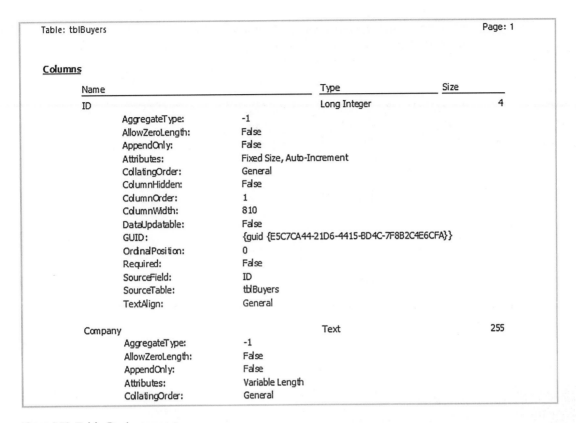

Figure 2.39 Table Design report

Figure 2.40 Quick Print button on the Quick Access toolbar

Modifying Table Design

The table design can be changed at any time after creation. Open the table in the Design view from the main Database window. Edit existing field names, data types, properties, and descriptions from this screen. You may also add new fields, delete old ones, or move fields to different locations.

How to Edit Fields in an Existing Table

1. Open the table in Design view.

2. To insert a new field in the field list:

   Click where the new field will be inserted. The new field will appear above the selected field.

   Click the right mouse button and choose Insert Rows from the shortcut menu

   OR

   Click the Insert Rows button in the Tools group on the ribbon Design tab.

Q: What if I forget to include a field, or assign the wrong data type to a field?

A: You can always change the table design even after records have been added to the table.

Q: What happens to the data in a field when the field is deleted?

A: If you are deleting a field in which data has been entered, the data will also be deleted.

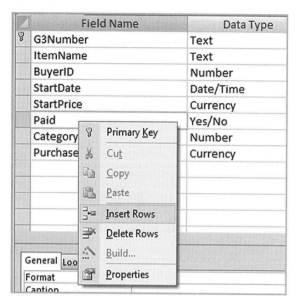

Figure 2.41 Insert Rows command on shortcut menu

TRY IT YOURSELF 2.6.1

A. Open the table *tblSales* in Design view and insert a new field above the field *Paid* (see Figure 2.41).

B. Name the new field *Listing Cost* and make it a currency field. Give it a default value of $1.50.

C. Save and close the table.

3. To delete a field from the field list:

Click on the field to be deleted.

Click the right mouse button and choose Delete Rows from the shortcut menu

OR

Click the Delete Rows button in the Tools group on the ribbon Design tab.

Don't make too many changes in the table design at one time. Be sure to save each new change individually to ensure that the design will not be compromised or corrupted. Changing the name and data type of a field at the same time may result in some data loss. Also, changing the primary key after data has been added may cause you to lose records with duplicate values in the new primary key field. It's wise to create backup files of important databases before making any major changes to the table design.

In previous versions of Access, if you renamed a field in a table, you had to find all the objects that used that field (forms, reports, and so forth) and change the field name in those objects also. Access automatically corrects field names (and other objects with changed names) whenever an object is opened that refers to the old name. This feature is called Name AutoCorrect. The only exceptions are Visual Basic modules that refer to the old object—these must be manually corrected.

To use Name AutoCorrect, you must be sure the feature is turned on. Click on the Office button and click the Access Options button. Choose the Current Database page from the list on the left. Name AutoCorrect is on by default and affects all Access databases. When you convert a database from a previous version of Access, you must turn on the Name AutoCorrect feature for that database (see Figure 2.42).

2.7 Entering Data in the Datasheet View

The Datasheet view shows the records in the table in rows. It's used for viewing and editing the actual data in the table. The Datasheet view can be displayed by double-clicking on the table name in the Navigation pane.

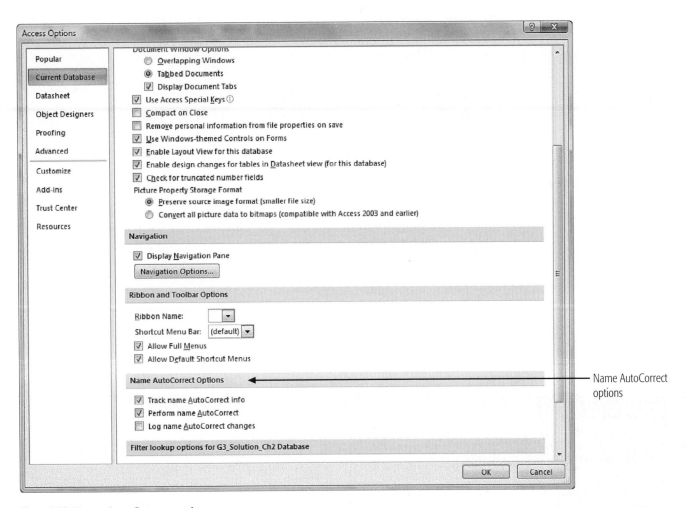

Figure 2.42 Name AutoCorrect options

Comparing Datasheet and Design View

The Design view displays table design information, such as field names, types, and properties, so they can be viewed or changed. This view can be accessed from the main Database window by selecting the table name and then clicking the Design button.

From either view, you can toggle to the other view. Use the View button on the Home tab of the ribbon, or right click on the table name in the Navigation pane or on the Object tab to switch views.

Table 2.7   Comparison of Views

View	Use
Datasheet view	Easy data entry or record editing. Quick table creation.
Design view	Checking or modifying field names, types, and properties. In-depth table creation.

Interpreting the Screen

When a table is opened in Datasheet view, different command buttons are displayed in the Home tab of the ribbon. These buttons are for formatting and organizing data (see Figure 2.43).

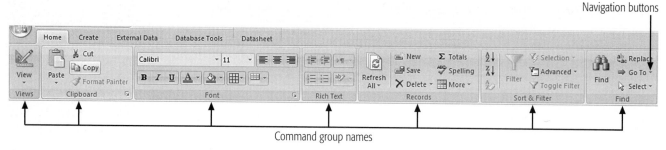

Figure 2.43 Home tab on the ribbon

The document window on the right side of the screen shows data displayed in rows and columns. The field names from the table design are the column headings. Each row contains one record. Each column shows all the data in one field. The record indicator at the left side of each record shows the current record position (see Figure 2.44).

Figure 2.44 Records displayed in Datasheet view

The status bar at the bottom of the screen shows error messages, field descriptions, and other messages. Navigation buttons that help you move easily between records are also located on the status bar. Click the buttons to move from record to record (see Figure 2.45).

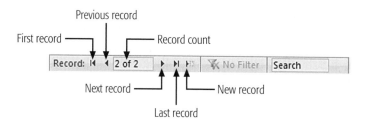

Figure 2.45 Navigation buttons on the status bar

Q: How do you save a record?

A: As records are entered, they are automatically saved. To activate a save, use the Save button on the Quick Access toolbar or choose the Save command from the Office window.

Multiple tables or other objects can be opened at the same time. Each object has its own document window. Click on the object tab to switch to another object window (see Figure 2.44).

Entering Records

When a table is opened in the Datasheet view, all the records are displayed. If this is a newly created table, there are no records to show—only the field names will appear on the screen at the top of an empty datasheet.

How to Add New Records to an Existing Table

1. Open your table in Datasheet view.

2. Enter the data. Data is automatically saved when records are entered.

How to Enter Data

1. Position the pointer in the correct field column of the bottom blank row of the table, and type the data.

2. Position the pointer in the next field, or use the ENTER key, TAB key, or the arrow keys to move to the next field.

Pressing the New Record button on the status bar will move you quickly to the bottom row of the table, so you can add records. You can also use the navigation buttons on the right end of the Home tab of the ribbon. Refer to Figures 2.43 and 2.45 for the location of the navigation buttons.

The ENTER or TAB key will move to the next record, after the last field of the current record is entered.

How to Edit Existing Records

1. Select the field you want to edit using the mouse.

2. To delete your selection, press the DELETE key

   OR

   To change your selection, position the mouse pointer anywhere in the selection and type the appropriate characters.

You can add characters to a field by typing the characters after positioning the cursor. You can also type over characters by selecting data first. Using the TAB key to move between fields automatically selects the entire field. Use the Undo button on the Quick Access toolbar to undo the most recent changes to your work.

Resizing Columns

The field columns can easily be resized in the Datasheet view. Remember, however, this can be a permanent change that you see every time you use the table in this view.

How to Resize Columns

1. In the Datasheet view, position the mouse pointer on the right borderline of the field to resize it. The pointer will change to a double arrow.

2. Click and drag the borderline to its desired location

   OR

   Double-click on the borderline to automatically resize the column width to the longest entry.

3. Save the table layout changes if you want to keep these changes.

Rearranging Columns

Columns can easily be moved to different locations in the Datasheet view. You will be prompted to save these changes to the layout as you close the Datasheet window. Even though columns can be moved and resized, these actions change only the appearance of

TRY IT YOURSELF 2.7.1

A. Open *tblBuyers* and add two records as shown in Figure 2.44.

B. Check that Input Masks and other properties are working properly to control the fields.

C. Continue with Try It 2.7.2.

Q: When entering or editing data in a date field, what is the small icon that appears to the right of the field?

A: This icon represents a calendar. Click on it to use a pop-up calendar for selecting a date value for the field.

TRY IT YOURSELF 2.7.2

A. Using *tblBuyers*, widen the columns for the fields *Email* and *Address*.

B. Continue with Try It 2.7.3.

TRY IT YOURSELF 2.7.3

A. Using *tblBuyers*, rearrange the columns so that your screen resembles the one shown in Figure 2.44.

B. View the table in Design view. It should look like Figure 2.46.

C. Close the table, saving the changes to the layout.

the table in Datasheet view, and do not affect the table design. When you view the table in Design view, the fields will still be in their original order. If you save the layout changes, the table will appear in the same order the next time you open it.

How to Rearrange Columns

1. Click anywhere inside the top square of the column you want to move. The square is darkened and contains the name of a field. The mouse pointer should have a small rectangle attached to it when you click, which means the whole column will be selected.

2. Click and drag the column to the left or right until it is in the correct position.

Field Name	Data Type
ID	AutoNumber
Company	Text
Last Name	Text
First Name	Text
E-mail Address	Text
Job Title	Text
Business Phone	Text
Home Phone	Text
Mobile Phone	Text

	ID	Company	Last Name	First Name	Email	Address	City	State/	ZIP/Po:
⊞	3	Baby Needs	Walker	Jadyn	babyneeds@msn.com	P.O. Box 711	Whoville	CO	83614
⊞	5	Boomer Baby	Warren	Nina	bommeroo@aol.com	351 Johnson Road	Carmel	CA	93921

Figure 2.46 Columns moved in Datasheet view, but not in Design view

Freezing Columns

If a table has many fields, it may be difficult to view the data in Datasheet view. You may want certain fields or columns to be visible all the time regardless of how far to the right you might scroll to see all the data. To make certain columns stay on the screen, they can be frozen so they become the leftmost columns in the Datasheet view. Even if a column doesn't appear at the left side of the screen, it will move there once it has been frozen.

TRY IT YOURSELF 2.7.4

A. Open the table *tblBuyers* in Datasheet view.

B. Freeze the three columns: *Company*, *LastName*, and *FirstName* as shown in Figure 2.47.

C. Scroll all the way to the right and observe that these three columns remain on the screen.

D. Unfreeze the columns.

E. Close the table or continue.

How to Freeze a Column

1. Open a table in Datasheet view.

2. Select the column or columns you want to freeze.

3. Point to the selected column or columns and right-click to display the shortcut menu. Choose the Freeze Columns command as shown in Figure 2.47.

Once a column is frozen, it remains on the screen no matter how far right you scroll. When you close the Datasheet view, you will be asked whether or not you'd like to save changes to the layout. If you select "Yes," the frozen column or columns will remain frozen when the table is reopened in Datasheet view. To unfreeze columns, choose the Format, Unfreeze All Columns command from the menu (see Figure 2.47).

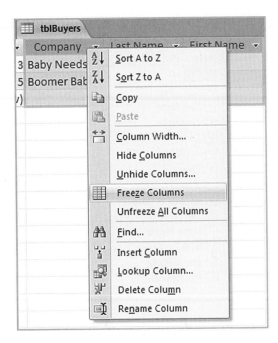

Figure 2.47 Freeze Columns and Hide Columns commands

Hiding Columns

At times, you may want to hide columns of data in the Datasheet view if certain fields don't need to be seen at the moment, or if certain fields contain sensitive data and shouldn't be viewed by all people. Of course, the hidden fields will show when you display the Design view of the table.

How to Hide a Column

1. Open a table in Datasheet view.

2. Select the column or columns you want to hide.

3. Right-click on the selected column and choose the Hide Columns command as shown in Figure 2.47.

When you close the Datasheet view, you will be asked whether or not you'd like to save changes to the layout. If you select "Yes," the hidden column or columns will remain hidden when the table is reopened in Datasheet view. To unhide columns, right-click on any column header, choose the Unhide Columns command, and select the names of the columns that you want to show (see Figure 2.48). Be cautious about hiding columns; it's easy to forget they exist.

Displaying Total Rows

A new feature of Access 2007 is the ability to display a Total row at the bottom of the Datasheet window. Any selection from the following list of simple statistical calculations can be displayed: sum, average, count, maximum, minimum, standard deviation, and variance. All the values in one field are included in the calculation. Only numeric fields—those with a number or currency data type—can have all the calculations displayed on the Total row. Values of any data type can be counted.

TRY IT YOURSELF 2.7.5

A. Open the *tblBuyers* table in Datasheet view.

B. Hide the *ID* field and observe its disappearance.

C. Unhide the field (see Figure 2.48).

D. Close the table.

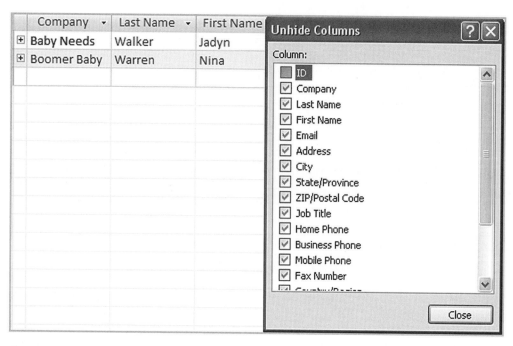

Figure 2.48 Unhide Columns dialog box with *ID* field hidden

TRY IT YOURSELF 2.7.6

A. Open *tblSales* in Datasheet view.

B. Enter two data records as shown in Figure 2.49.

C. Add a total row, and sum the field *PurchasePrice*. Again, refer to Figure 2.49.

D. Save *tblSales* and close the *G3* database, or continue on.

How to Add a Total Row

1. Click on the Home tab of the ribbon.

2. In the Records group, click the Totals button (see Figure 2.49). A new row appears below the last record with the word Total in the first column.

3. Click in any column on the Total row, and select a calculation from the dropdown list as shown in Figure 2.49. The result of the calculation appears in the cell.

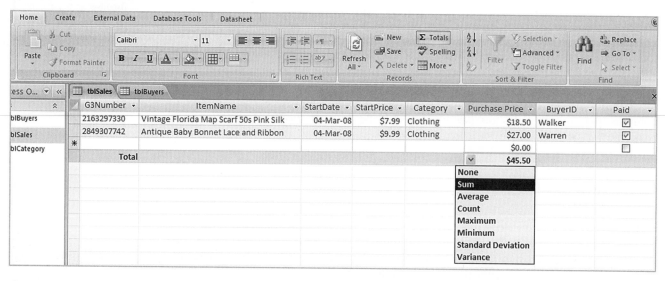

Figure 2.49 *tblSales* in Datasheet view with a Total row

2.8 / Formatting and Setting Access Options

Access gives you a lot of control over the appearance and behavior of a database and its environment. Not only can you change the properties and settings of each object, you can also the set parameters that affect Access globally.

Formatting the Datasheet View

When a table is open in Datasheet view, the Home tab of the ribbon has a group of command buttons that change fonts, background colors, and text alignment (see Figure 2.50). If a format setting is changed, it will only affect the open table. These settings are automatically saved for the table, and will be in effect again when you close and re-open the table. If a different table is opened, its Datasheet view will revert back to the default settings.

Changing the formatting is only a matter of clicking on the command button, and in some cases, making a selection from a secondary menu. Figure 2.50 shows the color menu that pops up when the button is clicked to change alternate row colors. The records in the database can be displayed with a different background color, or with rows in alternating colors. The type face, font size and font color can be changed, as well as text enhancements—bold, italics, and underline, and text alignment—left, center, and right.

TRY IT YOURSELF 2.8.1

A. Open *tblBuyers* in Datasheet view.

B. Change the alternate row color to Aqua Blue 2 as shown in Figure 2.50.

C. Change the font color and type face.

D. Now, open *tblSales* in Datasheet view, and note that the default settings are in effect.

E. Change the settings back to the default for *tblBuyers*.

F. Close both tables and close the *G3* database, or continue on.

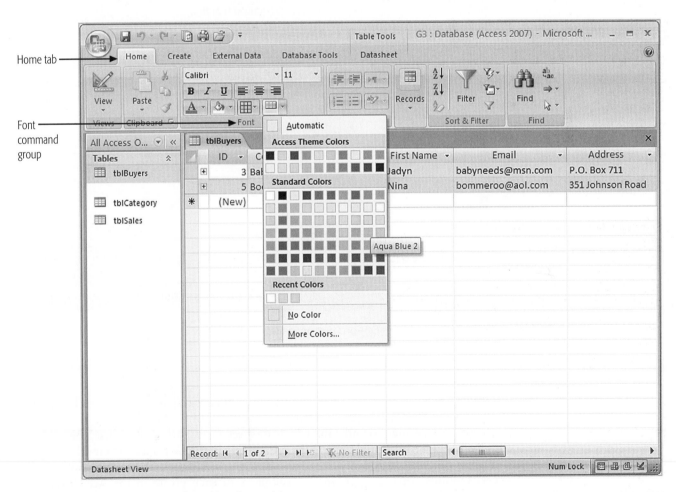

Figure 2.50 Formatting the Datasheet view for a table

Changing Access Options

The Access environment is the set of properties that controls how Access looks and behaves. It includes screen settings, typing behavior, file locations, security permissions, and other options used to create and modify databases and their objects.

The Access Options button in the Office window allows you to customize the Access environment. Click on the Office button to open the Office window, and then click on the Access Options button (see Figure 2.51) to open the Access Options window. The Access Options window has a navigation pane on the left side containing a list of ten groups. The document window on the right displays the various options and settings available in the selected group. Once you've made the appropriate changes, click on the OK button to save the changes and close the window.

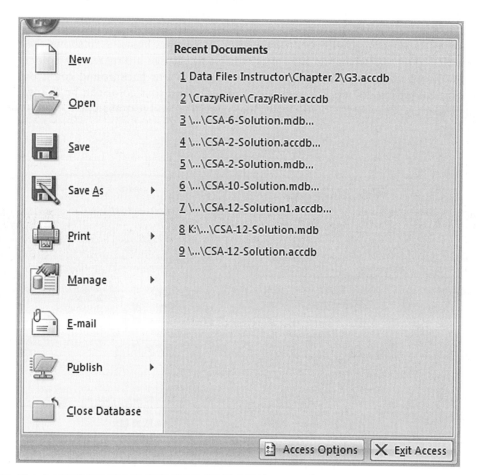

Figure 2.51 The Access Options button in the office window

Many of the changes you can make to individual database objects can be applied to all objects of the same type by changing Access Options. For example, if you'd like to change the settings for all tables in Datasheet view, rather than just one table as described above, you would change the parameters in the Datasheet group. If you want to change where Access looks for database files, you'll find these commands under Access Options. Table 2.7 provides a summary of each group in the Access Options window.

Table 2.7 Groups of Access Option commands

Group Name	Contains Settings *For:*
Popular	Commonly used preferences such as overall color scheme and default file folder name
Current Database	Database window, navigation pane, ribbon and other specifications
Datasheet	Font and color choices for all datasheets
Object Designers	Defaults used when creating new database objects
Proofing	Spelling and text correction options
Advanced	Editing—mouse and keyboard behavior, print margins, display, and locking/sharing actions
Customize	Adding and removing command buttons on the Quick Access toolbar
Add-ins	Managing add-in programs that extend or enhance Access features
Trust Center	Security issues. Allow or disallow databases to be opened based on the database location or author
Resources	Additional online articles, updates, and services

TRY IT YOURSELF 2.8.2

A. Using the *G3* database, open the Access Options window.

B. Add a title of "Going, Going, Gone" to the database as shown in Figure 2.52.

C. Change the Document Window Options to Overlapping Windows, again refer to Figure 2.52.

D. Click OK to activate the settings. Close and reopen the database for them to take effect.

E. Open *tblBuyers* and *tblSales*. Compare the database window to Figure 2.53.

F. Close both tables and change the settings back to the defaults.

G. Close the *G3* database, or continue on.

When you're working in a classroom or lab at school, you should not change these settings because these settings will remain in effect after you close Access and leave. Most schools have set the options for their specific requirements, and changing them can create confusion and errors for other students. Check with your instructor or lab assistant to learn the rules for your location.

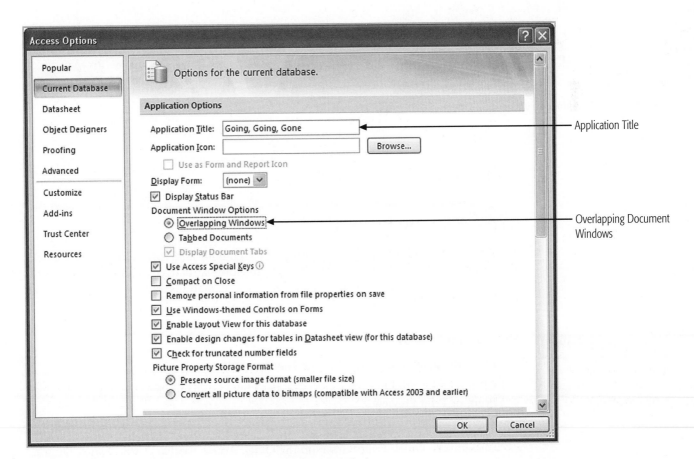

Figure 2.52 The Current Database group in the Access Options window

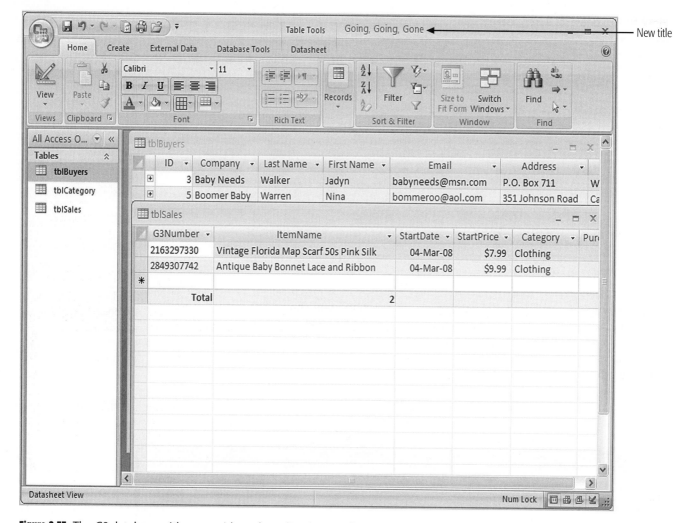

Figure 2.53 The *G3* database with a new title and overlapping windows

2.9 Printing Records

All the records in the table can be printed in a column and row layout similar to the Datasheet view. There is also a Print Preview function so that you can view the records before they are printed. Print-related changes such as margins and page orientation can be made in Print Preview mode.

How to Print Records

1. Select the table to be printed in the Navigation Pane.

2. Click on the Office button and choose the Print command. Select either Print, Quick Print, or Print Preview

   OR

   Click on the Quick Print button on the Quick Access toolbar.

TRY YOURSELF 2.9.1

A. Print all the records in the *tblSales* table.

B. Close the table.

How to Change the Page Layout

1. Follow the instructions above to open the Print Preview window.

2. Click on the appropriate command button in the Page Layout group of the ribbon to change page size, orientation, or margins. Refer to Figure 2.54.

3. Click on the Page Setup button to display the Page Setup dialog box, if needed. Choose settings on either the Margins or Page tabs, and click the OK button when finished. Refer to Figure 2.55.

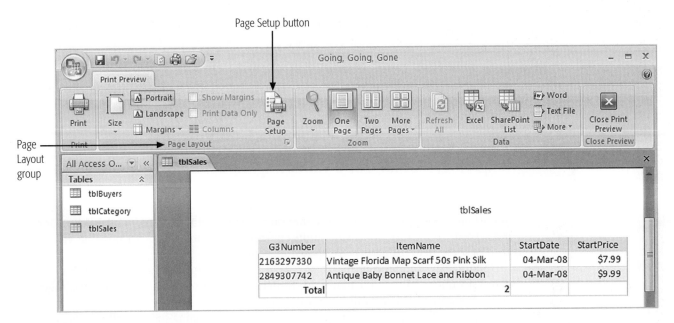

Figure 2.54 Print Preview window for *tblSales*

Figure 2.55 Print Setup dialog box

2.10 / Maintaining Data Integrity

The most important function of both the database developer and the database administrator is to maintain data integrity. Data integrity is the accuracy and reliability of the data in a database, and is achieved through proper table design, data validation, and correct table joins. The four different types of data integrity are:

- User-defined integrity—the data complies with specific business and user rules.
- Entity integrity—no duplicate records exist in any table.
- Domain integrity—the values in any given field are within an accepted range.
- Referential integrity—all foreign keys have values that correspond to records in the referenced table (the table in which the value is the primary key).

An in-depth discussion of data integrity can be found in Chapter 7, and an introduction to referential integrity is included at the end of Chapter 3. Some of the first steps for assuring data integrity are described below.

Requiring, Masking, and Validating Input

Protecting the table from erroneous data will make subsequent searches and queries easier and more accurate. Requiring data in a field prevents blank values from occurring in important fields. You can make sure that only correct data is entered while adding or editing records, by setting data validation controls or input masks. All possible values for each of these field properties are shown in Table 2.6.

Setting the Required property of a field to Yes means that a record won't be saved unless a value is entered for that field. Primary key fields, fields that join tables together, and other critical fields should be required.

Input masks are used to require specific kinds of data, such as all numbers, to be entered in a field. You can also require a specific layout, such as three numbers, a hyphen, and four more numbers—a telephone number. Use the Input Mask Wizard to easily create an input mask for a telephone number, zip code, or other common data item.

Data validation requires that only specific data be allowed in the field. For example, only a number between ten and twenty can be entered, or only the letters A, B, C, or D. The properties Validation Rule and Validate Text control this function.

Ensuring Existence of Primary Keys

You will recall that primary keys are used to uniquely identify records, just as license plates uniquely identify cars. It is extremely important that every table have a primary key. Primary keys are usually a single field, but may be a composite key made from two or more fields. You can make sure a table has a primary key by opening it in Design view. The primary key field or fields will have a key icon to the left of the field name.

Primary key fields should always be indexed. Activating the Index property speeds up searches, joins, sorts, and filters associated with the field, and these operations are frequently performed on primary keys. When a single field is designated as a primary key, its Indexed property is changed automatically from "No" to "Yes (No Duplicates)."

If a table has a composite primary key, the Indexed property is not automatically set on any of the fields in the key. It should be set to "Yes (Duplicates OK)" for all of the key fields because in most cases any single field in the key will have the same value in multiple records. It's the combination of the fields that's unique in each record.

The primary key should always contain a value. The key is always checked when a record is added to make certain that a value has been entered in the field, even though the Required property of the key field is still set to "No." If no data is entered in the primary key of a record, an error message is generated when you try to exit the record. The Required property need not be changed to "Yes" for primary keys, although setting it to "Yes" will not affect the table.

Analyzing Tables

It's often challenging for database beginners to have the tables in a database structured correctly. Perhaps there are repetitive records, redundant fields, or no primary key. Any one of these situations can cause data errors and threaten the integrity of the database. (Refer to the discussion in Chapter 1, Section 1.8 regarding Defining a Relational Database). Access's Table Analyzer command can make restructuring your tables a little easier.

The Table Analyzer examines a single table and makes suggestions for splitting the data into multiple related tables. It sets or creates a primary key and even corrects spelling if any typos are detected. You can let the Table Analyzer Wizard make decisions or you can decide yourself how your table will be split and which field(s) will become the primary key. The wizard contains examples that demonstrate how and why tables should be split. You can view these examples by clicking on the buttons displayed on the wizard screens.

The wizard will generate a Lookup field if one or more fields are useful to both new tables. The data is stored in only one table, but is displayed in the second table. Lookup fields will be discussed in a later chapter.

The wizard gives you the option to create a query using the fields found in your original table. (Queries will be discussed in a later chapter.) If you create a query, you will still be able to use any form or reports that were created with the original table.

You can revise the table structure, field properties, and relationships of the new tables using any of the methods previously discussed in this chapter.

How to Use the Table Analyzer

1. Select the name of the table to be analyzed in the Navigation Pane, and click on the Analyze Table button in the Analyze group of the Database Tools tab on the ribbon (see Figure 2.56).

2. When the wizard begins, click the Next button to move past the first two screens, which are informational, unless you want to view the optional examples.

3. Select the table you wish to analyze on the third screen of the wizard (see Figure 2.57).

4. Click the Next button to move to the next screen.

5. Click on one of the option buttons to select if you want the wizard to decide how to split the table or if you want to make the decisions yourself. Let the wizard decide if you are not sure.

TRY IT YOURSELF 2.10.1

A. Open the database *Practice_Ch2*.

B. Using the Table Analyzer, split the table *tblAllSales* into two tables—sales information and buyer information. Refer to Figures 2.56–2.61 as a guide.

C. Close the *Practice_Ch2* database.

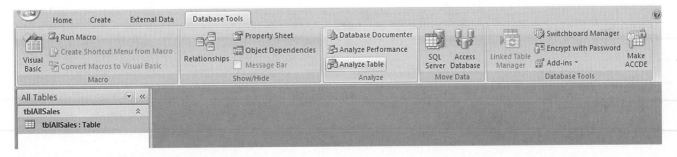

Figure 2.56 Starting the Table Analyzer

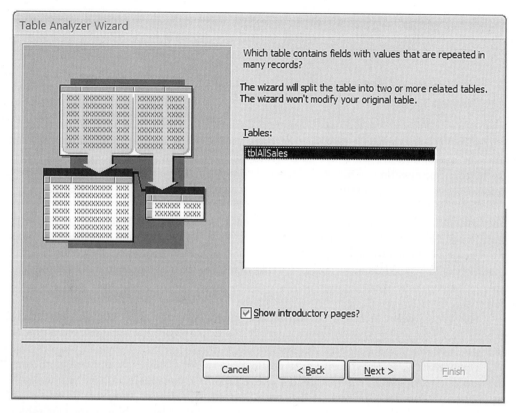

Figure 2.57 Selecting the table to analyze

6. Click the Next button to move on to the next screen, the Relationships screen appears (see Figure 3.21).

7. Drag and drop the fields from one table to another, if the tables have been created by the wizard. If you chose to split the tables yourself (step 5), drag and drop the fields that you want in a new table into the space to the right of the original table. You may make as many tables as necessary from the original table. Click on the Tips button for additional help (see Figure 2.58).

8. Rename the tables to more appropriate names using the Rename Table button (see Figure 2.58. If you chose to split the tables yourself (step 5), a new table box containing the dropped fields appears along with a dialog box asking for a new table name. In either case, type the new table name and click the OK button (see Figure 2.59).

9. Click on the Next button to go to the next screen.

10. Determine a primary key. You will notice that Access creates a generated unique ID to be the new primary key, if an appropriate key field is not found. This field produces a consecutively numbered ID field. If you realize that you already have a key field and want to eliminate the Access-generated key field, select the field you wish to make your key field and click on the Set Unique Identifier button. The Access-generated field will be deleted and your new tables will be linked on the new primary key field (see Figure 2.60).

11. Click on the Next button, and Access will ask if you'd like to create a query that reproduces the original table. In most cases, Choose "No, don't create the query." as shown in Figure 2.61.

12. Click on the Finish button to complete the process.

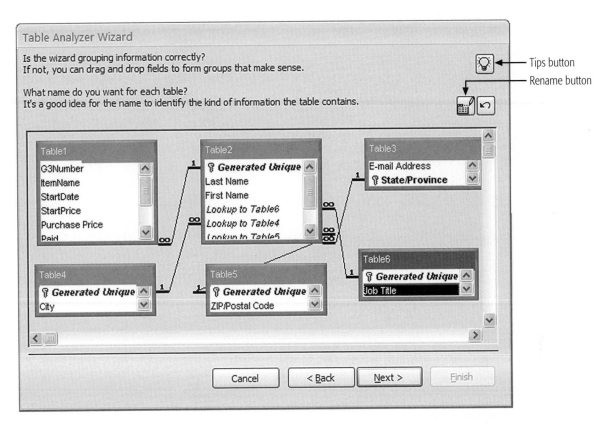

Figure 2.58 Table Analyzer Wizard showing split tables

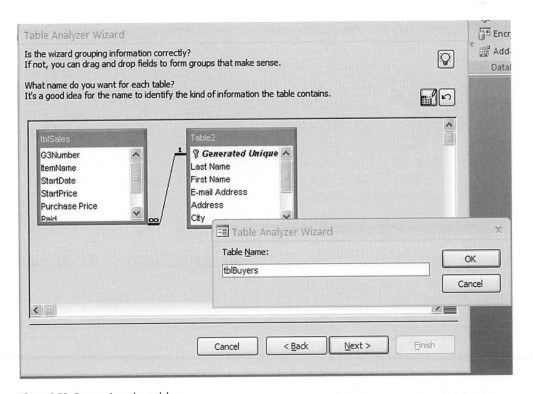

Figure 2.59 Renaming the tables

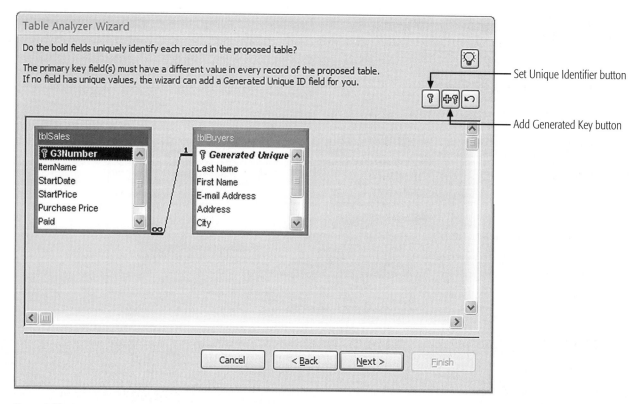

Figure 2.60 Creating primary keys

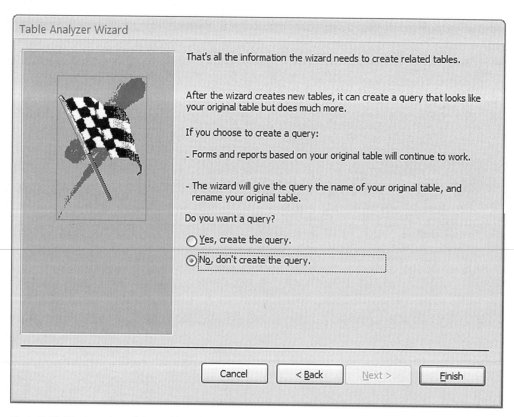

Figure 2.61 Final screen of the Table Analyzer Wizard

Creating a Blank Database

1. Start the Access program.
2. From the Getting Started window, click on the Blank Database icon.

   OR

   Click on the Office button and click on the New button. The Blank Database pane opens on the right side of the screen.
3. Type the name of the database into the File Name box, and select a folder in which to store the database.
4. The File New Database dialog box opens. Use the Navigation Pane on the left to select the correct folder. Click the OK button.
5. Click the Create button.

Creating a New Database Using a Template

1. Start the Access program and be sure you're connected to the Internet.
2. From the Getting Started window, click on the template button for the database you want to create.
3. Type the database name into the File Name box. Specify a location for the database by clicking on the folder icon.
4. Click on the Download button and wait for the template to load on your computer.
5. Once the template has loaded, the new database opens, showing one of the tables in the Datasheet view.

Copying a Database Object

1. Open a database file.
2. Right-click on the name of the object that will be copied.
3. Click on the Copy command from the pop-up menu.
4. On the background of the Navigation Pane, right-click to display the pop-up menu.
5. Click on the Paste command.
6. The Paste As dialog box appears. Enter the new table name. Click the OK button to finish.
7. The copied object is now displayed in the list of available objects.

Creating a New Table with a Template

1. Click on the Create tab on the ribbon.
2. Click on the Table Templates button, and chose a template from the list that appears. The table is created and displayed in Datasheet view.
3. Enter data into the table, or modify its fields.
4. Close and save the table with an appropriate name.

Creating a New Table in Design View

1. Select the Create tab on the ribbon, and click on the Table Design button.
2. The new table opens in Design view.

Entering Field Names, Data Types, and Descriptions

1. Place the pointer in the Field Name column.
2. Type the field name.
3. Press the [ENTER] or [TAB] key, or use the mouse pointer to move to the Data Type column. Select the appropriate type from the drop-down list.
4. Press the [ENTER] or [TAB] key or use the mouse pointer to move to the Description column, if you want to add a description (it's optional). Use a description to clarify or provide more documentation about the field, if necessary. Use the [ENTER] or [TAB] key, or the mouse pointer to move to the next field name row.
5. Continue until all field names, types, and descriptions are entered. To select a data type other than text, move to the Data Type column, click the drop-down list, and select the appropriate data type.

Saving the Table Design

1. Close the table and click the Yes button for saving.

   OR

   Click the Save button on the Quick Access toolbar.

Defining a Field Using a Field Template

1. Create or open a table in Datasheet view.
2. Click on the Datasheet tab on the ribbon, and click on the New Field button. The Field Templates pane appears.
3. Double-click on the field name shown in the list in the Field Templates pane. The new field appears as a column in the table.

Defining a Lookup Field Using the Field List

1. Create or open a table in Datasheet view.
2. Click on the Datasheet tab on the ribbon, and click on the Add Existing Fields button. The Field List pane appears.
3. Double-click on the field name shown in the list in the Field List pane. The Lookup Wizard begins.
4. Select the field to be displayed in the table, and complete the steps in the Lookup Wizard. The new field appears as a column in the table. The new field will display a drop-down list of values from the other table when clicked.

Setting Properties

1. Position the pointer on the desired field in the Design view.
2. Use the [F6] key or the mouse pointer to switch between the Field entry area and the Field Properties area.

3. Move the mouse pointer to the line containing the property you want to change.

4. Delete the default value, if necessary, and enter the new values, or use the drop-down list arrow to display predefined values.

5. The property list is saved with the field structure when the table is saved, so be sure to save the table after changing property values.

Setting a Primary Key

1. In the table Design view, click on the Design tab on the ribbon. Select the field to be made the primary key by doing one of the following:

   Click the Primary Key button on the ribbon

   OR

   Right-click the mouse to display the shortcut menu and select Primary Key

   OR

   Save the table without designating a primary key and Access will ask to create one.

Printing the Table Design

1. Click on the Database Tools tab on the ribbon, and then click on the Database Documenter button.

2. Click the Tables tab to display all tables in the database file. click on the desired table, then press the Select All button. The Select All button will select all tables to analyze.

3. Click the Options button. The Print Table Definition screen appears.

4. Select the desired options, then click the OK button to move back to the Documenter screen. Click the OK button to generate the report. (This may take a few moments.) You will see an Object Definition window showing a preview of the report.

5. Press the Quick Print button on the Quick Access toolbar.

   OR

   Click on the Office button and Choose the Print Command. Select Print or Quick Print.

6. Close the Object Definition window.

Editing Fields in an Existing Table

1. Open the table in Design view.

2. To insert a new field in the field list:

   A. Click where the new field will be inserted. The new field will appear above the selected field.

   B. Right-click and choose Insert Rows from the shortcut menu

      OR

      Click the Insert Rows button on the ribbon.

3. To delete a field from the field list:

   A. Click on the field to be deleted.

B. Right-click and choose Delete Rows from the shortcut menu

OR

Click the Delete Rows button on the ribbon.

Adding New Records to an Existing Table

1. Open your table in Datasheet view.

2. Enter the data. Data is automatically saved when records are entered.

Entering Data

1. Position the pointer in the correct field column of the bottom blank row of the table, and type the data.

2. Position the pointer in the next field, or use the ENTER key, TAB key, or the arrow keys to move to the next field.

Editing Existing Records

1. Select the field you want to edit using the mouse.

2. To delete your selection, press the DELETE key

OR

To change your selection, position the mouse pointer anywhere in the selection and type the appropriate characters.

Resizing Columns

1. In the Datasheet view, position the mouse pointer on the right borderline of the field to resize it. The pointer will change to a double arrow.

2. Click and drag the borderline to its desired location

OR

Double-click on the borderline to automatically resize the column width to the longest entry.

3. Save the table layout changes if you want to keep these changes.

Rearranging Columns

1. Click anywhere inside the top square of the column you want to move. The square is darkened and contains the name of a field. The mouse pointer should have a small rectangle attached to it when you click, which means the whole column will be selected.

2. Click and drag the column to the left or right until it is in the correct position.

Freezing Columns

1. Open a table in Datasheet view.
2. Select the column or columns you want to freeze.
3. Right-click on the selected columns. Choose the Freeze Columns command.

Hiding Columns

1. Open a table in Datasheet view.
2. Select the column or columns you want to hide.
3. Right-click on the selected column. Choose the Hide Columns command.

Adding a Total Row in Datasheet View

1. Click on the Home tab of the ribbon.
2. In the Records group, click the Totals button. A new row appears below the last record with the word Total in the first column.
3. Click in any column on the Total row, and select a calculation from the drop-down list. The result of the calculation appears in the cell.

Formatting the Datasheet View

1. Click on a formatting command button on the Home tab of the ribbon.
2. Make the appropriate selection to change fonts, background colors, and text alignment.

Changing Access Options

1. Click on the Office button.
2. Click on the Access Options button to open the Access Options window.
3. Choose one of the command groups listed in the Navigation pane on the left.
4. Change the appropriate setting in the document window on the right.
5. Click on the OK button to save the changes and close the window.

Printing Records

1. Select the table to be printed in the Navigation Pane.
2. Click on the Office button and choose the Print command. Select either Print, Quick Print, or Print Preview.

   OR

   Click on the Quick Print button on the Quick Access toolbar.

Changing the Page Setup

1. Select the table to be printed in the Navigation Pane.
2. Click on the Office button and choose the Print command. Select Print Preview.

3. Click on the appropriate command button in the Page Layout group of the ribbon to change page size, orientation, or margins.

4. Click on the Page Setup button to display the Page Setup dialog box, if needed. Choose settings on either the Margins or Page tab, and click the OK button when finished.

Using the Table Analyzer

1. Select the name of the table to be analyzed from the list in the Navigation Pane, and click on the Analyze Table button in the Analyze group of the Database Tools tab on the ribbon.

2. When the wizard begins, click the Next button to move forward past the first two screens.

3. On the third screen of the wizard, select the table you wish to analyze.

4. Click the Next button to move to the next screen.

5. The next screen will ask you if you want Access to decide how to split the table and make the decisions for you or whether you want to make the decisions. Select the No, I want to decide bullet.

6. Click the Next button to move on. The Relationships screen appears.

7. Drag and drop fields from one table to another. Click on the Tips button for additional help.

8. Rename the tables, if necessary. Click on a table window and click the Rename Table button to enter other names for these tables. Or, if you have chosen to make all the decisions yourself, a new table box with the dropped fields will appear. Then, a dialog box will appear, asking for a new table name. Enter the new name and click the OK button. Continue to drag fields from the original table to the new table window.

9. Click on the Next button to go to the next screen.

10. Determine a primary key. Access may have generated a unique ID field to be the key. This field will be an autonumber field. To select another field for the key field and eliminate the Access-generated key field, click on the Set Unique Identifier button.

11. Click on the Next button and Access will ask if you'd like to create a query that reproduces the original table. Choose either the Yes or No button.

12. Click the Finish button to complete the process.

Review Questions

1. Describe the function of a database file.

2. What objects can be included in a database file?

3. Name two different ways that you can create a database file.

4. When would you use a lookup field?

5. How is an Access file identified in a list of filenames?

6. How do you open the Field Templates pane?

7. List two ways to switch a table to Design view.

8. List three calculations that can be displayed on the Total row of a datasheet.

9. Which type of data can have an entry on the Total row?

10. What is the benefit of creating a table in Design view?

11. Identify the parts of the Design view window.

12. Name five different data types for fields.

13. What is the function of field properties?

14. Name three different field properties and describe their purposes.

15. What two qualities must each primary key have?

16. What icon is used to represent the Primary Key on the ribbon?

17. If you delete a field in a table, what happens to the data in that field?

18. Can a primary key be changed without impact to the data in the table?

19. Can all field properties be changed after data has been added to a table?

20. Under which ribbon tab will you find the button to begin the process of printing the table design?

21. Which view—Datasheet or Design—is used for adding new records to a table?

22. Which tab on the ribbon contains command for formatting the Datasheet view?

23. Must records be saved individually after each one is entered?

24. Does rearranging a column in the Datasheet view affect the table design?

25. Which row of the datasheet is used for adding new records to the table?

26. What is the difference between hiding a column and freezing a column?

27. List two methods for printing records from the Datasheet view.

Exercises

Exercise 1—Review and Guided Practice

ACTIVITY

It's time to create the tables for the Sir Dance-A-Lot music store. Here's a recap of the tables designed in Chapter 1, Exercise 1.

Table Name	Fields
tblRecordings	Music ID, Artist, Title, Category, Label
tblInventory	Inventory ID, Music ID, Media Type, Quantity On Hand, Price
tblArtists	Artist ID, Name
tblCategory	Category ID, Music Category
tblRecordLabels	Label ID, Record Label
tblMedia	Media ID, Media Type

1. Create a new database called SDAL, an abbreviation for Sir Dance-A-Lot.

2. Create six new tables in the database, based on the specifications above. Use an autonumber data field for ID fields whenever there is no naturally occurring ID field.

3. Create a primary key in each table.

4. Create lookup fields as follows: *tblRecordings* should look up *Artist* in *tblArtists*, *tblRecordings* should look up *Category* in *tblCategory*, *tblRecordings* should look up *Label* in *tblRecordLabels*, *tblInventory* should look up *MusicID* in *tblRecordings*, and *tblInventory* should look up *MediaID* in *tblMedia*.

5. Print the Table Definition. Include the names, data types, and sizes, for all fields in all tables (no properties). Don't print anything for indexes or other table information.

ACTIVITY

Exercise 2—Practicing New Procedures

Exercise 2A: Creating a Database

You are working for a travel agent who needs you to design a database and tables for holding cruise information.

The following data will become records in three different tables. An asterisk (*) indicates that airfare is included with that cruise.

Create the database and tables using the following steps:

1. Break the data into tables that can be related on a common field(s). You should have 3 tables: Cruises, Ships, and Cruise Lines.

2. Create each table by entering appropriate field names and data types.

3. Create a primary key field for each table. The tables *tblCruises* and *tblShips* have AutoNumber keys, and *tblCruiseLines* has an ID number that is 3 text characters in length. ID number is the first of the Cruise Line name and the digits 01.

4. Decide which fields will be used to join tables, and be sure to include the common field in both tables that will be joined.

3 Marvel Cruise Line	Departs 5/15/09 To: Puerto Rico From: Miami	Ship: Delfina First class: $2600, 24 tickets available Regular class: $1800, 39 tickets available	Length: 7 days
4 *Marvel Cruise Line	Departs 5/02/09 To: Cabo San Lucas From: Los Angeles	Ship: Mermaid First class: $1900, 8 available Regular class: $1100, 4 available	Length: 3 days
5 Marvel Cruise Line	Departs 5/31/09 To: Jamaica From: Miami	Ship: Delfina First class: $2450, 17 available Regular class: $1400, 9 available	Length: 5 days
6 *Adventure Cruises	Departs 5/15/09 To: Acapulco From: San Diego	Ship: Coral Queen First class: $3300, 15 available Regular class: $2400, 19 available	Length: 7 days
7 *Adventure Cruises	Departs 5/15/09 To: Cozumel From: Miami	Ship: Sun Goddess First class: $3750, 8 available Regular class: $2800, 9 available	Length: 10 days
8 *Getaway Cruises	Departs 5/05/09 To: Alaska From: Seattle	Ship: Chinook First class: $4600, 7 available Regular class: $3550, 3 available	Length: 14 days
9 *Getaway Cruises	Departs 5/20/09 To: Aruba From: Miami	Ship: Bahia First class: $3200, 15 available Regular class: $2450, 10 available	Length: 7 days
10 Getaway Cruises	Departs 5/30/09 To: Tobago/Trinidad From: Miami	Ship: Bahia First class: $4600, 9 available Regular class: $3800, 12 available	Length: 14 days

Exercise 2B: Creating an Input Mask

Create an input mask on the *CruiseLineID* field in *tblCruiseLines*. It should restrict input to three characters: one uppercase letter that is the first letter of the cruise line name, and two digits. For example, "Getaway Cruises" would have a value of "G01" in the field *CruiseLineID*.

Exercise 2C: Entering Data into Tables

Enter the records into the tables

Exercise 3—In-Class Group Practice

1. Choose a partner to work with according to your instructor's instructions.

2. One member of the pair is going to create a table using the Table Wizard, and the other person is going to do it manually, using the Design view. Decide on your task assignments.

3. You will each create a new table called *tblStudents* and store it in a new *College Records* database file. You will have two separate but similar tables when you're finished. Use the following fields, and add one more of your own choosing:

   Name, address, phone, gender, major/ degree program, grade point average, date of birth, and full-time/part-time student designation.

4. Add yourself to the table.

5. Swap seats and add yourself to your partner's table.

6. Go back to your own table and print the table design.

7. Now compare your table design with that of your partner, and answer the following questions:

   a. Which method of table creation was faster, using a template or the Design view?

   b. Were all the fields available in the template, or did you have to add some yourself?

   c. What data type did you use for phone? For gender? For full-time/part-time student designation? If you made different choices, discuss why you chose the types you did.

   d. What field(s) of your own choosing did you create? Why?

   e. Which field would be the primary key? Does this field meet the requirements for a primary key?

   f. Was it easy to add data to your partner's table? Was it obvious by the field name what data to type in each field?

8. Find other pairs in the class, and add yourselves to their tables. Update six to eight other tables, then go back to your own computer.

9. Look at the data that has been entered into your table.

   a. Did everyone type information the same way, or did some type data in all caps and some in all lowercase?

   b. Are names entered consistently (Jones, Pat or Pat Jones)?

   c. Discuss the importance of consistent data entry with your partner. Could sloppy data entry cause problems later on? What can you do to prevent inconsistent data from being typed into the table?

10. Print both the table design and the list of records in your table, and attach them to your answer sheet.

ACTIVITY AND
REFLECTION

Exercise 4—Critical Thinking: Table Design

Design a table for each of the following situations.

1. You would like to keep track of family and friends' addresses, phone numbers, and important dates.

2. You are the secretary for a professional organization and need to send mailings to members and record their dues payments each year.

3. You have to create a computerized list of books for the library where you work.

4. You are planning a conference where presenters each have two hours for their individual workshops and seminars. The facility has several different conference rooms, and presentations can occur simultaneously. You are paying each presenter a fee, and you need to know if each needs audio or video equipment.

5. You want to keep your list of potential customers up to date, including when you last talked to them and what was said.

ACTIVITY AND
REFLECTION

Exercise 5—Challenge: Database Creation

1. Create a new database named *Lottery* containing tables to hold data about people who have won prizes in the state lottery. Include the following fields:

   - Name
   - Address
   - City
   - State
   - Zip code
   - Phone number
   - Age
   - Social security number
   - Amount of prize
   - Date of win
   - A field to indicate whether this person has won before

2. Set the primary key for each table. All keys can be AutoNumbers except the key to the winners table, which should be the winner's social security number.

3. Change the properties of the following fields:

   - State—2 characters in length. Only uppercase letters permitted. Should default to your home state.

   - Date of win—Must be after 12/31/07. An appropriate error message should be displayed if an incorrect date is entered.

   - Amount of prize—Format as currency.

   - Zip code—Should have an appropriate input mask.

   - Phone number—Should have an appropriate input mask that includes area code.

   - Social security number—Should have an appropriate input mask.

4. Add five records each to these tables.

5. Print the table records and the table designs.

Exercise 6—Challenge: Database Design and Creation

You are going to create a database file for your mother-in-law's video rental business. You must do a good job!

1. Create a new database file on your disk. What name did you choose?

2. Create a table to hold information about the videotape collection. You will want to record the movie title, major stars' names, length of the movie in hours, a subject or category for the video, and a field to hold a brief description of the movie. The categories of videos are: Drama, Comedy, Action, Horror, Cartoon, and Musical. What other fields are needed?

3. Add your five favorite movies to the table.

4. Print both the table design and the list of records in the table.

5. What is the primary key in the table?

6. What properties might you change to improve the screen display, data entry, and storage processes?

7. What other tables will be needed to manage the business? Write both the suggested table name and the major fields to be included. Indicate primary key fields.

8. Will you need to locate specific movies for customers? What fields might you search to meet your customers' requests?

9. What other information might you need to display to the screen on a daily basis? Should this information be sorted in a particular sequence?

10. What printed reports might be required to run the business? List the report name and the major fields that should be included in the report.

CASE STUDY A: MRS. SUGARBAKER'S COOKIES

1. Create a database named *Sugarbaker.*

2. Create all necessary tables to hold the data previously described in Chapter 1. Follow these steps:

a. Using the field list you previously made, eliminate any repeating fields in any of the tables.

b. Identify the primary keys in each of the tables. Look for the unique field in each table. If you cannot readily identify that field, create an AutoNumber ID field.

c. Identify the common fields on which to relate the tables. Make sure the fields are the same in all related tables.

d. *tblOrderItems* has a multiple-field primary key. Which fields are used? To create a multiple-field primary key, select all fields before clicking on the Primary Key button.

e. Do any other tables need a multiple-field primary key?

3. Add one record to each table based on the data shown in the figures for Case Study A in Chapter 1.

4. Print the table design and records for each table.

CASE STUDY B: SANDY FEET RENTAL COMPANY (SFRC)

1. Create a database file named *SFRC.accdb*.

2. Based on the designs you created previously, create the tables for SFRC.

3. Name each table with the *tbl* prefix.

4. Enter each field into the appropriate table. Choose the correct data type based on the type of data to be entered into that field.

Rental Rates

Condo Type:	Outrigger2BR
1/01-3/31:	325
4/01-5/31:	350
6/01-8/31:	400
9/01-10/31:	350
11/01-12/31:	325

Figure 2.62 Rental Rates Information Sample Data

Housekeeping Report

Invoice Number	Date	Property Number	Fee	Date Paid
1-08	1/21/2008	P10	$60.00	1/27/2008
10-08	5/10/2008	P8	$50.00	5/17/2008
2-08	2/14/2008	P9	$60.00	2/21/2008
3-08	3/21/2008	P1	$60.00	3/28/2008
4-08	4/27/2008	P4	$50.00	5/5/2008
5-08	4/19/2008	P1	$60.00	5/5/2008
6-08	5/19/2008	P4	$50.00	
7-08	2/19/2008	P2	$50.00	
8-08	2/14/2008	P6	$50.00	2/28/2008
9-08	5/21/2008	P1	$60.00	5/28/2008
11-08	4/15/2008	P12	$60.00	4/25/2008
12-08	5/31/2008	P11	$50.00	

Figure 2.63 Housekeeping data

5. Identify and create the key field for each table.

6. Identify the common fields on which to relate the tables. Make sure the fields and the data are the same in each related table.

7. Enter as much data as possible from the following reports, forms, tables or figures. Other data will be given to you in Chapter 3 to complete the database.

8. For the tables that have no records at this time, design the structure of the table. Check Case Study B in Chapter 1 for more data.

tblProperties					
Property Number	Property Address	Condo Type	Accepts Pets	High Speed Internet	Amenities Code
P1	301S	ShoresOF3BR	Yes	Yes	1
P10	1005S	ShoresOV3BR	No	Yes	1

Figure 2.64 Property sample data

Client Data Form

CustomerNumber: 1

Last name: O'Casey

First name: Harriet

Address: 4088 Ottumwa Way

City: Mentira

State: IL

Zip: 61788-

Phone Number: (303) 417-4438

Phone Number 2:

Fax Number:

Email Address:

Notes:

Figure 2.65 Client sample data

Rental Transactions

Rental Number: 3

Property Number: P1

Customer Number: 14

Date Arrive: 3/12/2008

Date Depart: 3/19/2008

Deposit Amount: $200.00

Method of Payment: Visa

Pet Deposit:

Number of pets:

Notes:

Figure 2.66 Rental Transactions sample data

Owners Data Form

Owner Number:	1
Property Number:	P1
Last Name:	Claus
First Name:	Sandy
Address:	123 North Pole Drive
City:	Snowshoe
State:	PA
Zip Code:	23987-
Phone Number:	(404) 678-0909
Phone Number 2:	
Fax Number:	
Email Address:	SandyClaus@net.com
Notes:	

Figure 2.67 Owners sample data

CASE STUDY C: PENGUINS SKI CLUB

1. Create a new database and name it *Penguins*.

2. Using the table design developed in Case Study A in Chapter 1, create the tables in the *Penguins* database. You should have either four or five tables, as data about parents can be stored in the member table or in a separate table.

3. Create lookup fields wherever possible. When you look up the MemberID, display the member's last name; when you look up an Event ID, display the name of the event.

4. Designate a primary key for each table.

5. Set a default value of $200 for the membership fee due. Set a validation rule on age, so it must be between ages 7 and 11.

6. Either print the table definitions for your instructor, or turn in the completed database.

Chapter 3

Using a Table

Objectives

After completing this chapter you will be able to

Perform basic data maintenance operations to keep data current:
- Add records to a table.
- Edit records.
- Delete records.
- Use the Search, Find, and Find and Replace functions.
- Check the spelling of table data.

Create information from data:
- Sort records.
- Create and apply a filter.
- Calculate simple statistics such as totals, counts, and averages.

Perform operations for restructuring table design:
- Insert and delete fields.
- Move fields.
- Set captions.

Import data from an external data source:
- Bring in data from other Access databases, Excel spreadsheets, and other sources.
- Link tables from other databases.

Set and remove simple relationships between tables in a database:
- Use subdatasheets.
- Set relationships in the Relationships window.
- Delete relationships.
- Print relationships.
- Understand the concept of referential integrity.

Perform table housekeeping operations:
- Rename a table.
- Delete a table.

Dictionary

Caption	An alternate heading used to identify a field.
Composite key	A primary key consisting of more than one field.
Data integrity	The reliability and accuracy of the data.
Delimited Text File	A file with commas, tabs, or other characters separating data items from each other.
Edit	To make basic changes to a record.
External source	Another data source outside of the original table, such as another database file, a spreadsheet file, or other data.

Filter	A command to selectively choose records based on certain criteria.
Find	A command to locate certain records.
Foreign key	A field that is used as a primary key in another table.
Import	A command to bring in data from an external source.
Index	A field property that speeds up searches, joins, sorts, and filters associated with the field, when the property is set to Yes.
Input mask	A control that restricts data entry to specified characters, such as only numbers or capital letters.
Linked table	A pointer to another table in a different database.
Many-to-many join	A join where many records in both tables relate to many records in another table.
One-to-many join	A join where one record in the first table relates to many records in the second table.
One-to-one join	A join where one record in the first table relates to one record in the second table.
Referential integrity	A set of rules that ensures that data in joined tables remains accurate.
Refresh All	A command button that refreshes the data in all opened database objects when clicked.
Relationship	Joining of tables on related fields.
Replace	Command to assist in editing records by locating and replacing data in fields.
Restructuring	Changing the structure of the table by adding, removing, or changing a field; or by altering the properties of a field.
Rich text	Text that has some limited formatting attached, such as font and line justification.
Sort	Reordering the records of a table according to ascending or descending order of values in a field.
Subdatasheet	A datasheet that displays data from a joined table.
Undo	A command to cancel a previous operation.
Validation	A control that restricts data entry to specified values, such as data with a value of either 1 or 2.
Wildcards	Used in searching to represent specific characters in the search string.

3.1 Performing Basic Data Maintenance

While working in the Datasheet view, it is simple to update the table data. Figure 3.1 shows the controls used to move from record to record in the table. The current record is identified by darker shading and an outline. The status bar at the bottom of the window

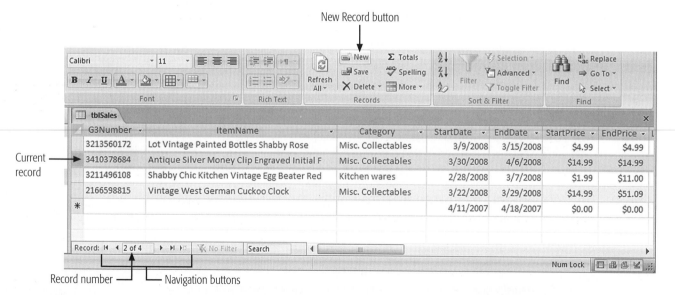

Figure 3.1 Navigation buttons in Datasheet view

shows the current record number, and the total number of records in the table. You can move from record to record by using the navigation buttons on the status bar. These buttons will take you to the first, previous, next, last, and new record in the table. You can also add a new record by clicking on the New Record button in the Records group of the Home tab on the ribbon.

Adding Records to a Table

It doesn't matter where records are added in a relational database table—they can be ordered (sorted) in any sequence you choose. In Access, data is always added to the last record, or bottom row in the Datasheet view. When you move to the bottom row, the new record indicator—an asterisk—appears to the left of the new record.

How to Add Records to a Table

1. Position the cursor using one of the following ways:

   Click the mouse on the first field of a new record at the bottom of the table

   OR

   Use the navigation buttons at the bottom of the screen to position the cursor to the last record, then press the [ENTER] or [TAB] key to move to a new record

   OR

   Press the New Record button located in the Records group of the Home tab on the ribbon.

   The New Record indicator shows the location of the next new record.

2. Enter the new data in the appropriate fields.

3. Press the [TAB] key to move to the next field or move the mouse pointer to the next field.

4. Continue to enter as many new records as necessary. New records are automatically saved when the next new record is created or when the table is closed. If in doubt, you can save the table by pressing the Save button on the Quick Access toolbar.

   Entering data into fields with data types other than text is slightly different. Yes/No fields require only that you click the check box to change data. Data is entered into a lookup field by making a selection from a drop-down list of values. Each time you move the cursor

TRY IT YOURSELF 3.1.1

A. Open the database *G3_Ch3*.
B. Open *tblSales* and add the four records shown in Table 3.1 below.
C. Close *tblSales* or continue on.

Q: How do you change data in an AutoNumber field?

A: You can't change data in AutoNumber fields–use the [TAB] key to move to the next field.

Table 3.1 The four records to be added to *tblSales*

G3Number	Item Name	Category	StartDate	EndDate	StartPrice	EndPrice	ListingCost
3213560172	Lot Vintage Painted Bottles Shabby Rose	Misc. Collectables	3/9/2008	3/10/2008	$ 4.99	$ 4.99	$0.70
3410378684	Antique Silver Money Clip Engraved Initial F	Clothing	3/30/2008	4/6/2008	$14.99	$14.99	$1.90
3211496108	Shabby Chic Kitchen Vintage Egg Beater Red	Kitchen wares	2/28/2008	3/7/2008	$ 1.99	$11.00	$0.55
2166598815	Vintage West German Cuckoo Clock	Misc. Collectables	3/22/2008	3/29/2008	$14.99	$51.09	$0.95

Shipping Charge	BuyerID	Payment Type	Payment Date	Status	Actual Shipping	G3Percentage	Shipping Date	Invoiced	Paid	Shipped
$ 6.00	Babyneeds$	Pay Friend	3/16/2008	Sold	$ 6.00	5.25%	3/17/2008	Yes	Yes	Yes
$ 3.85	bigDigree	Cash	4/13/2008	Sold	$ 3.85	5.25%	4/15/2008	Yes	Yes	Yes
$ 3.85	blueangles	Money Order	3/25/2008	Sold	$ 4.90	5.25%	3/27/2008	Yes	Yes	Yes
$11.30	boomerbaby	Pay Friend	3/30/2008	Sold	$11.30	5.25%	3/31/2008	Yes	Yes	Yes

to a date field, a small calendar icon appears to its right. Clicking on the icon opens a calendar so you can select a date to enter into the field. Figure 3.2 shows the calendar control.

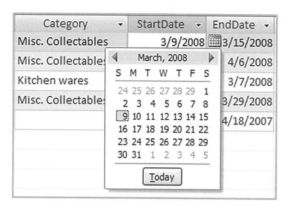

Figure 3.2 Calendar control for entering data into a date field

Memo fields are just like text fields, unless they are formatted as rich text. Rich text is text that can be formatted, but only in a limited way. If a memo field is rich text, a mini toolbar with formatting commands appears above the text when text in the field is selected. You can change fonts, add emphasis such as bold or italics, justify or center text lines, and more. To format a memo field as rich text, change the Text Format property of the field from plain to rich text.

Editing Records

Records can be edited by changing entire fields or only parts of fields. Large numbers of records can be changed all at once by using the Replace button on the Home tab of the ribbon.

TRY IT YOURSELF 3.1.2

Using *tblSales:*

A. Change the *Category* of the second record to "Misc. Collectables."

B. Change the *EndDate* of the first record to 3/15/08.

C. Change the *Payment Type* in record three to "Check."

D. Close *tblSales* or continue on.

How to Edit Records

1. Position the data entry point by doing one of the following:

    Move the cursor to the field you want to edit either with keyboard movements (TAB or arrow keys) or by using the mouse to position the pointer in the field you want to edit.

2. Type in the new data value, if the field has no value entered in it. If the field already contains data, select the entire value and press the DELETE key to delete it—then type in the new data.

    To select an entire field:

    Click to the left of the value when the cursor changes to a large plus sign (+)

    OR

    Click to the left of the value and drag the mouse pointer over the whole field.

    To edit only a portion of the data in a field, use the mouse to position the pointer in front of any character in that field. The insert mode is then activated, enabling the user to insert new text at that point. The DELETE and BACKSPACE keys are also useful in editing a small portion of data entered in a field.

    Some fields cannot be edited. Table 3.2 describes each one. Remember too, that data validation rules and input masks can restrict data entry to specific characters or types of characters. See Chapter 2 for specific settings.

Table 3.2 Fields That Cannot Be Edited

Type of Field	Description
AutoNumber fields	Access number records automatically as new records are created.
Calculated fields	Calculated fields are created from formulas in forms or queries and cannot be edited in the Datasheet view.
Locked or Disabled fields	Certain properties can be set to lock entry for a specific field. Data cannot be edited unless this field is unlocked.

Using Undo and Refresh

When a record is being edited, the Undo function becomes available to undo mistakes (see Figure 3.3). The Undo function can be activated from the

Undo button on the Quick Access toolbar

OR

The [ESC] key on the keyboard.

The [ESC] key will cancel a changed value or a previously changed field. The Undo button will undo changes made to the value in a particular field. You can undo several previous changes, if you wish.

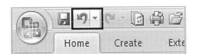

Figure 3.3 Undo button

If you mistakenly delete a table, or other database object, the Undo botton will restore the object. The Undo button will not, however, restore a deleted data record.

When two related tables are open, and data is changed in one, it will not be reflected in the second table unless the Datasheet views are refreshed. For example, say a new value is added to *tblBuyers* or *tblCategory* in the *G3* database while *tblSales* is open. If you click on *BuyerID* or *Category* field in *tblSales*, you won't see the new value in the drop-down list. The data needs to be refreshed so that the new value can be read and added to the list. Click on the Refresh All button in the Records group on the ribbon Home tab to refresh the data in all the open database objects (see Figure 3.4).

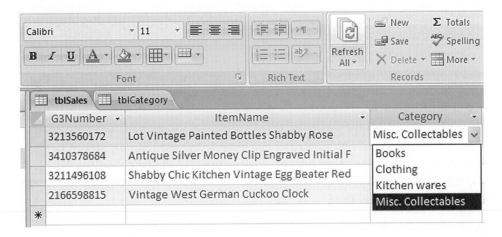

Figure 3.4 The Refresh All button

Q: Can I undo everything?

A: No, you can't undo record deletions.

Q: How many actions can I undo?

A: The Undo function will only work for your edits in the current field.

TRY IT YOURSELF 3.1.3

A. Using the database *G3_Ch3*, open *tblSales* and *tblCategory*.

B. Add a new category "Fabrics" to *tblCategory*.

C. View the *Category* field in any record of *tblSales*. Note that "Fabrics" doesn't appear in the list (see Figure 3.4).

D. Refresh all the open database objects, and check the *Category* field again. The new value should appear in the drop-down list now.

E. Close the tables, or continue on.

Moving and Copying Data

Sometimes parts of one table need to be moved or copied to another table. Moving data means you need to cut it from one location and paste it to another. This might happen when you redesign a database and split one table into two, or when you archive old data into another table. Copying data involves using the Copy and Paste commands. Copying helps to eliminate extra work when entering new records that are very similar to old ones.

The Clipboard is a temporary storage area that can hold up to 24 pieces of information at a time. Data can be cut or copied to the Clipboard and then pasted into another field or record in a table. Data can also be cut, copied, and pasted between tables, database files, or other applications such as Word or Excel. The Clipboard works with the Cut, Copy, and Paste commands. Copy or cut items to the Clipboard and then paste them to a new location.

The Clipboard must be displayed before it can be used. If the Clipboard is not displayed, you can only cut/copy and paste one item at a time. The Clipboard will display all the items collected on it and display them in the Clipboard gallery. These collected items stay on the Clipboard until you exit all Office applications. You can choose to paste all the items or only selected items from the Clipboard.

How to Display the Clipboard

1. Click on the arrow in the lower right corner of the Clipboard group on the ribbon Home tab (see Figure 3.5).

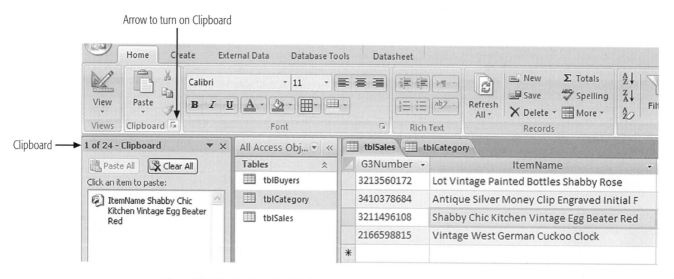

Figure 3.5 Displaying the Clipboard

The Clipboard can be cleared by clicking on the Clear All button. It can be closed by clicking on the Close button in the upper right corner of the Clipboard.

How to Move and Copy Data

1. Select the data you want to move or copy by using the mouse as described in Table 3.3.

2. Click the Cut or Copy button in the Clipboard group on the ribbon (see Figure 3.6).

OR

Click the right mouse button to display the shortcut menu and choose Cut or Copy.

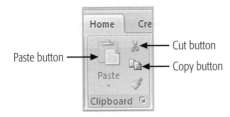

Paste button — Cut button

Copy button

Figure 3.6 Cut, Copy, and Paste buttons

3. Position the cursor on the new record location.

4. Paste the data in the new location by using the Paste button on the ribbon.

Table 3.3 summarizes the various ways you can select data so it can be cut or copied, then pasted.

TRY IT YOURSELF 3.1.4

A. Using *tblSales*, open the Clipboard and copy the value in field *ItemName* in the third record as shown in Figure 3.5.

B. Go to a new record and paste in *ItemName*.

C. Fill in data in this record as you want.

D. Close *tblSales* or continue on.

Table 3.3 Selecting Data

Area to Select	Mouse Action
All or part of a field in one record	Click and drag. Double-click selects one word.
One record	Click in the gray box on the far left edge of record.
All records	Click in the box in the upper left corner of table. It contains two triangles, one dark and one light gray.
Contiguous records	Click on the first record of the group with the left mouse button. Move to the end of the record list to be deleted and hold the SHIFT key down while clicking the left mouse button. *OR* Click in the gray box on the far left edge of first record and drag down to the last record.
One field in all records	Click in field name area at the top of the table.
Contiguous fields in all records	Click in field name area of first field and drag across to the last field.

Deleting Records

Data records can be permanently deleted from a table using the Delete command. One record or several records can be deleted at a time.

How to Delete Records

1. Select the record or records you want to delete.

2. Press the DELETE key on the keyboard

OR

Click the Delete button in the Records group of the ribbon Home tab (see Figure 3.7)

OR

Click the right mouse button to bring up the shortcut menu. Choose the Delete Record command (see Figure 3.7).

TRY IT YOURSELF 3.1.5

A. Using *tblSales*, delete the record you just added in Try It Yourself 3.1.4.

B. Close the table, or continue on.

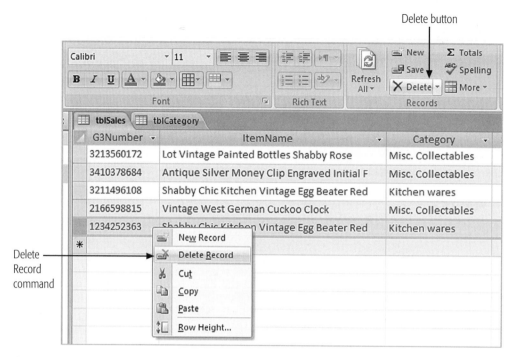

Figure 3.7 Delete record command on shortcut menu with record selected

3. The Delete dialog box (see Figure 3.8) will appear, asking for confirmation of the delete operation. The Yes option permanently removes the records from your database file. You cannot undo such an operation. The No option will cancel the delete operation. Click the Yes button to delete the selected records.

Figure 3.8 Delete dialog box

Finding and Searching for Data

The Find and Search functions simply locate a data value within a table. They do not make any changes to the record containing the data value. The user must complete the editing process.

How to Find Data

1. Position the cursor in the field where you want to find the data.

2. Activate the Find command by doing one of the following:

Click on the Find button in the Find group of the ribbon Home tab (see Figure 3.9)

OR

Press the CTRL key and F key together to activate the Find command.

Figure 3.9 Find button

The Find dialog box appears (see Figure 3.10).

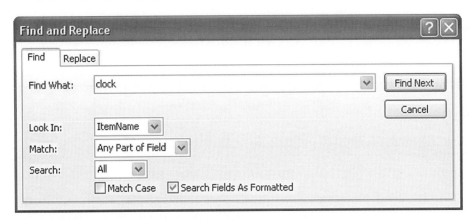

Figure 3.10 Find dialog box

3. Fill in the Find What text box with the value you want to search for. Enter the entire value as it appears in the field or use the available wildcard characters. See Table 3.4 for a summary of wildcard characters and their uses.

4. Select the appropriate choice from the Match drop-down list as shown in Table 3.5. Unless the data value you're finding is the entire field, choose "Any Part of Field."

Q: What if Find doesn't find data that I know is in the table?

A: Be sure that the option "Whole Field" or "Any Part of Field" is correctly selected.

Table 3.4 Summary of Wildcard Characters

Wildcard Characters	Uses
*	Replaces any number of characters.
?	Replaces any one character.
#	Replaces any one number.

Examples of Wildcard Characters

*XYZ will find values that begin with any letter(s) but end with XYZ.

X* will find values that begin with X followed by any number of others characters.

SM*TH will find values that begin with SM and end with TH but have any other characters between those two strings.

#th will search for any one number value that ends with th. *th will also produce this result (but will also include letters as well as numbers).

Table 3.5 Match Options

Option	Effect
Whole Field	Finds the string when it is an entire field. Example: Finds the whole word FORD, if FORD is the entire last name.
Any Part of Field	Finds the string included within any entries in the field. Example: Finds FORD included in BLACKFORD and FORDSON.
Start of Field	Finds the string at the beginning of the field. Example: Finds FORD at the beginning of the word as in FORDSON.

TRY IT YOURSELF 3.1.6

A. Using *tblSales*, find the word "clock" in the *ItemName* field (see Figure 3.10).

B. Close *tblSales* or continue on.

5. Select how to conduct the search from the drop-down list in the Search option. You can choose to search all the records, or only the records above or below the current record.

6. Choose from other Find options as shown in Table 3.6.

Table 3.6 Other Search Options

Option	Effect
Search: text box with drop-down list	Will search all records, or from current record down or up.
Match Case check box	Determines if it's necessary to match the case—uppercase or lowercase letter pattern—of the entry. If the box is checked, the search will be case sensitive and the search string must be entered in the exact case pattern of the field value.
Search Fields As Formatted check box	Limits the search to the exact values displayed in the table. (This option is useful for fields that have specific formats such as currency.)

7. Click the Find Next button to proceed through the datasheet and locate the requested values. The Find dialog box will stay on the screen to allow for further searching.

8. Click the Close button to close the dialog box when the process is complete.

Quick search is also available in Datasheet view (and when viewing a form). Quick search looks through every field in every record until it finds the data you're looking for, and it will find only the first occurrence of the data. Just type the data into the Search box on the status bar (see Figure 3.11).

Replacing Data

Another useful editing tool available in Access is the Replace command. This command directs Access to find certain data and replace it with other data. Data can be replaced automatically or with user confirmation. This feature can be very helpful when it is necessary to make multiple changes in a large table.

Although it is not necessary, it is a good idea to position your cursor at the beginning of the datasheet records when you start the Replace command. To limit the search to a specific field, position the cursor in that particular field. Only the selected field will be searched when the corresponding box is checked in the Replace dialog box. You can specify whether to search all the records or only those below or above the current record in the table, by changing the selection in the Search box (see Figure 3.12).

The Replace command cannot be undone, however, you are given the opportunity to confirm or cancel the command. You can always repeat the replace, and reverse the find and replace data values, if you make a mistake.

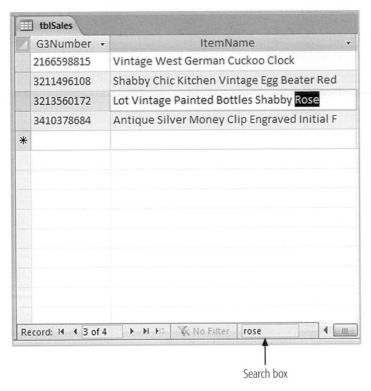

Figure 3.11 Using the Search box to locate text

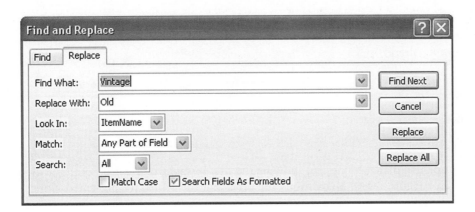

Figure 3.12 Replace dialog box

How to Replace Data

1. Click on the Replace button in the Find group of the ribbon Home tab.

2. Enter the Find What data.

3. Enter the Replace With data.

4. Make selections from options listed in Tables 3.5 and 3.6 as necessary.

5. Click the Find Next button or use the ENTER key to activate the find and replace. The first matching data will be highlighted.

6. Select Replace to replace that data and then press the Find Next button. This option will give you the opportunity to confirm each replacement

TRY IT YOURSELF 3.1.7

Using *tblSales:*

A. Replace all occurrences of "Vintage" with "Old" in the *ItemName* field (see Figure 3.12).

B. Close *tblSales* or continue on.

OR

Choose the Replace All button to replace all occurrences of matching data globally without individual user confirmation (see Figure 3.12).

As with any computer operation, it is important to be accurate in keying in the correct data. Any misspellings will result in an incomplete or incorrect operation.

Checking Spelling

The Spelling command checks your table for spelling mistakes. To check the spelling of an entire table, you may start the Spelling command from the Datasheet view or from the Database window. As with any spelling checker, some proper nouns or unusual spellings will be highlighted as misspelled when they are simply not in the spelling dictionary. If you have common words with unique spellings, it would be wise to add them to the custom dictionary.

How to Use the Spelling Command

1. Open the table in Datasheet view, and position the cursor in the first field of the first record

   OR

   Select the table name in the Navigation Pane.

2. Click the Spelling button in the Records group of the Home tab of the ribbon (see Figure 3.13).

Figure 3.13 Spelling button on the ribbon

The Spelling dialog box open, showing the first instance of a word not in the dictionary (see Figure 3.14). Suggestions for replacing the word are presented along with

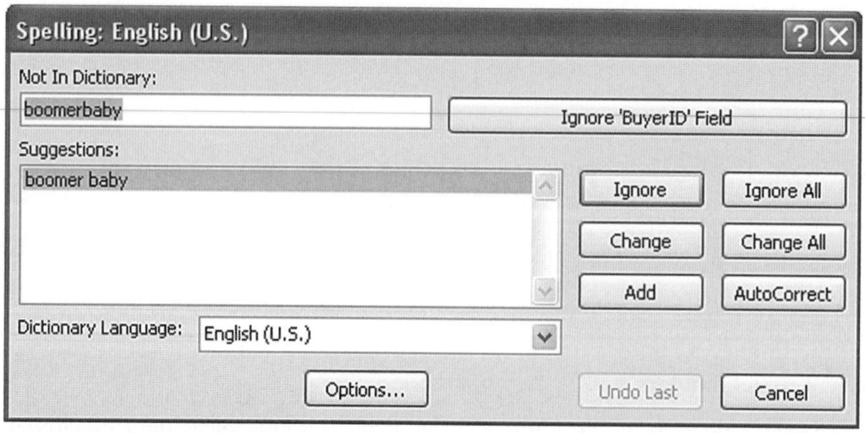

TRY IT YOURSELF 3.1.8

A. Using *tblSales*, check the spelling of the data.
B. The first misspelled word is shown in Figure 3.14. Click on the Ignore 'BuyerID' Field button so that the whole field is ignored.
C. Close *tblSales* or continue on.

Figure 3.14 Spelling dialog box

buttons to ignore the word or field, change the word, add it to the dictionary, or auto-correct. Autocorrect uses the first suggested correction to change the word.

3. Click on the word or button of your choice.

4. Continue checking the spelling of all words in the table. Access will tell you when it has completed the process.

5. Click on the OK button to close the information box.

Professional Tip: Restoring the Default Value

This tip comes from Jim Stiles, the Network Administrator for his local sheriff's office and a teacher and developer of Microsoft Office applications for over twelve years. Jim is a certified Internet Web master and designer, and has 18 years of experience in law enforcement and corrections. Jim hosts "Uncle Jim's Microsoft Access Tutorial" for Access 2000 located at http://www.jdstiles.com/mso2k/access/.

You can use a field or control's Default Value property to enter data automatically. This is especially helpful when you repeat one entry often from record to record. When the default entry isn't appropriate for the current record, you can simply overwrite it by typing a new entry. If you change your mind, you can return to the default value by pressing CTRL ALT SPACE, which overwrites the current entry with the default value.

3.2 Importing and Linking Data

Importing and linking data are ways of referencing or copying data in other databases or tables. Data can be imported from a variety of sources, or it can be linked to tables in another database.

Linking to tables in other databases allows you to add and update records in those tables, but you're not allowed to change the table structure. When a database is used on a network, one set of tables can be used for many users by linking the users to the tables. Each user can have a different set of database objects that work with the tables, so each user's view of the data is customized for his or her own usage.

Importing data is necessary when a database is being converted from an old to a new system. Data may be in an old Access database, or in any of several different formats. Importing is also necessary if data must be brought in from elsewhere on an ongoing basis. This could be data collected on a Web site, or created in another application. Usually, data can be converted to a text file as an interim measure, and then imported into Access if conversion is more than a one-click process.

Importing Data from Other Access Databases

One method for adding records to a table is to import the data from an external source. The external source can be another Access database file, an Excel spreadsheet, or another application program such as Paradox, FoxPro, dBase, or Lotus 1-2-3. You can also import SQL database files, XML and HTML files, delimited text files, and fixed-width text files into a table.

All data types can be imported to new tables, but only spreadsheet files, text files, and other Access tables can be imported to existing tables. This may mean that you have to import data into a new table temporarily, then move it from the temporary table to the end of an existing table in a second step.

TRY IT YOURSELF   3.2.1

A. Import the table *tblSalesData* from the *Practice_Ch3* database to the *G3_Ch3* database.

B. Verify the table imported correctly.

C. Close the table, or continue on.

Figures 3.15, 3.16, and 3.17 show how the screen should look during this process.

If the data you want to import isn't one of those types listed above, remember that any data that you can copy to the Clipboard can be pasted into Access. It's easy to convert a Word table to an Access table via the Clipboard. You can also export data from Access to other applications this way. Besides tables, other Access objects such as queries, reports, forms, macros, or modules can also be imported.

How to Import Data from Another Access Database

1. Open the database file into which the data will be imported, or create a new one.

2. Click on the External tab of the ribbon, and then click on the Access button in the Import group. The Get External Data dialog box opens (see Figure 3.15).

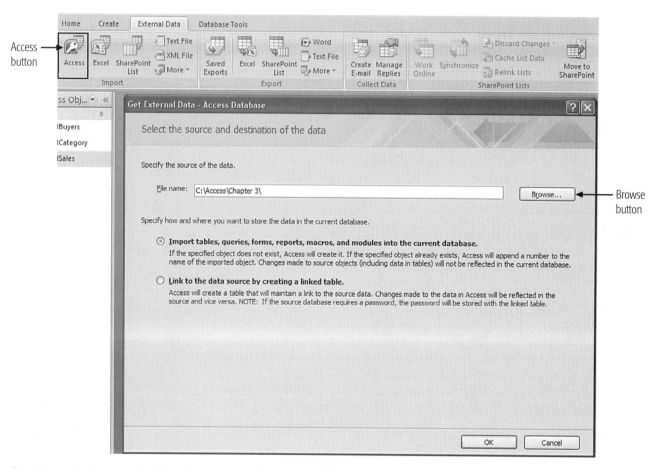

Figure 3.15 Get External Data dialog box for importing Access objects

3. Specify the data source by clicking on the Browse button and finding the correct folder in the File Open dialog box (see Figure 3.16).

4. Verify that the Files of type box says "Microsoft Office Access" (see Figure 3.16). Select the name of the database, and make sure the name appears in the File name box.

5. Click on the Open button. The File Open dialog box closes.

6. Click on the OK button in the Get External Data dialog box. The Import Objects dialog box opens (see Figure 3.17).

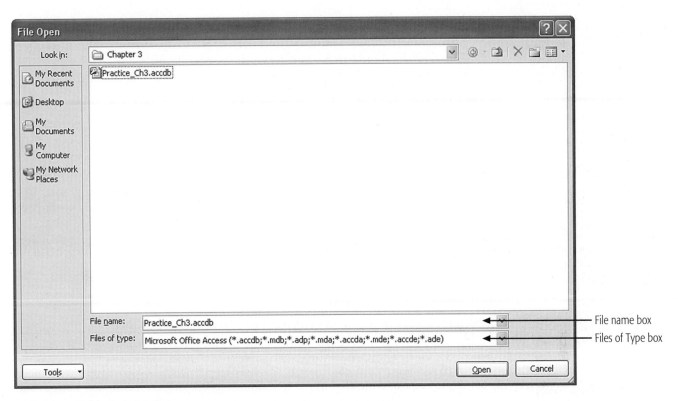

Figure 3.16 File Open dialog box

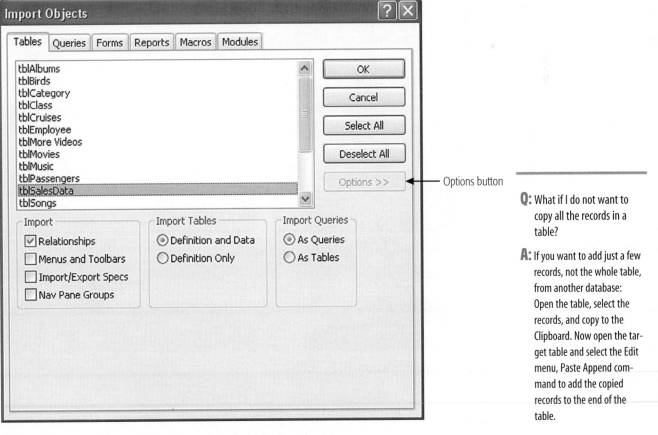

Figure 3.17 Import Objects dialog box with options displayed

Q: What if I do not want to copy all the records in a table?

A: If you want to add just a few records, not the whole table, from another database: Open the table, select the records, and copy to the Clipboard. Now open the target table and select the Edit menu, Paste Append command to add the copied records to the end of the table.

7. Select the table to import or use the Select All button to choose all objects in a specific category.

8. Use the Options button to further define the importing procedure if necessary. The table can be imported with its design or just the data can be imported.

9. Click the OK button to import, then click Close to finish the process. The imported object will be displayed in the object list.

Importing Data from Other Sources

Access gives you the capability of importing data from other software programs, Web pages, and text files. Data stored in Excel is the easiest to import. All buttons for importing data are found in the External Data tab of the ribbon. If the data source you have is not listed on any of the import command buttons, try to convert the data to a delimited text file first, and then import it into Access.

How to Import Data from Excel

1. Open the database into which you want to import the spreadsheet.

2. Select the External tab on the ribbon, and click on the Excel button in the Import group (see Figure 3.18).

3. Select the name and location of the spreadsheet by clicking on the Browse button, and choosing the folder and file name in the File Open dialog box. Click Open to return to the Get External Data dialog box (see Figure 3.18).

Excel button in Import group

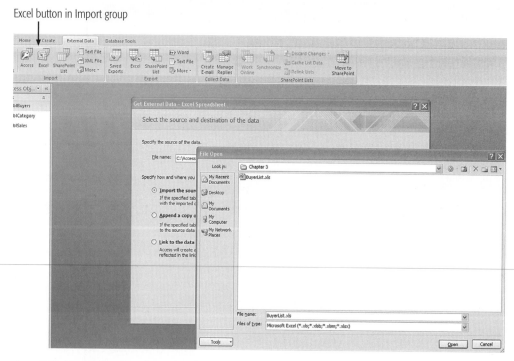

Figure 3.18 Importing data from Excel

4. Click on the OK button. The Import Spreadsheet wizard opens (see Figure 3.19).

5. Choose the worksheet name, and then click on the Next button (see Figure 3.19).

TRY IT YOURSELF 3.2.2

Using the *G3_Ch3* database, and referring to Figures 3.18–3.22:

A. Import the Excel spreadsheet *BuyersList.xls*.

B. Make *BuyerID* the primary key.

C. Name the table *tblBuyersList*.

D. Open the table and verify that it contains 30 records.

E. Close the database, or continue on.

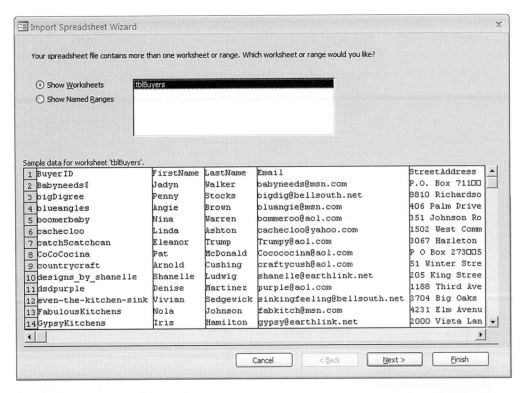

Figure 3.19 Import Spreadsheet wizard

6. The second page of the wizard opens. If the spreadsheet has column headings that can be used for field names, select the check box for First Row Contains Column Headings. If not, leave it unchecked. Refer to Figure 3.20.

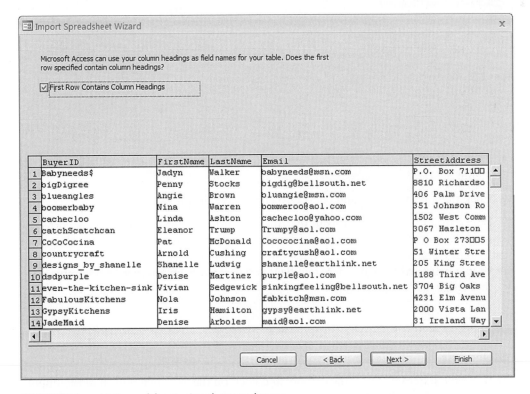

Figure 3.20 Import Spreadsheet wizard, second page

7. Click the Next button. The upper area of the window changes. If you want to change the name or data type of a column, change the selections in the Field Options area.

8. Click the Next button. The next screen appears for selecting the primary key (see Figure 3.21). Click on the button to either let Access add a primary key, choose your own primary key, or not designate a primary key.

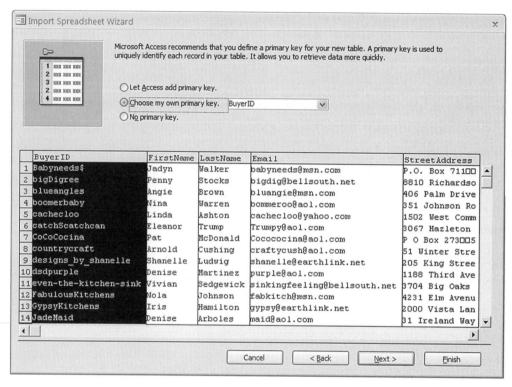

Figure 3.21 Import Spreadsheet wizard, primary key selection

TRY IT YOURSELF 3.2.3

Using the *G3* database, and referring to Figures 3.23–3.25:

A. Import the text file *MoreBuyers.txt.*

B. Append the data to the table *tblBuyersList* from the previous Try It Yourself. The text file is delimited with commas.

C. Open the table and verify it now contains 35 records.

D. Close the database, or continue on.

9. Click the Next button. The last screen appears. Specify the name of the table (see Figure 3.22).

10. Click the Finish button, and choose to either save or not save the steps.

Data can also be imported from text files. In order to put data into fields correctly, Access needs to know how the data is formatted in the text file. The data can either be in fixed width columns where shorter data values are padded with blanks on the end, or it can be in a delimited format where one field is separated from another by a comma, tab, or other character.

How to Import Data from a Text File

1. Open the database into which you want to import the text.

2. Select the External tab on the ribbon, and click on the Text File button in the Import group (see Figure 3.23).

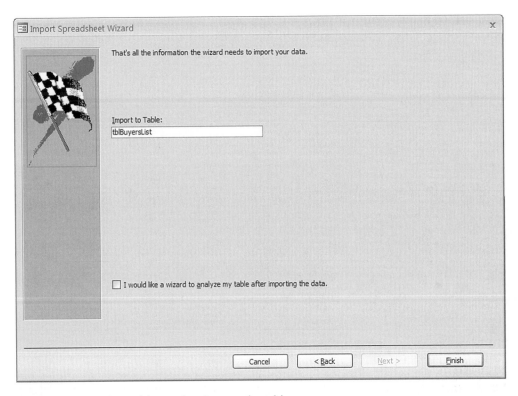

Figure 3.22 Import Spreadsheet wizard, name the table

3. Select the name and location of the file by clicking on the Browse button, and choosing the folder and file name in the File Open dialog box. Click Open to return to the Get External Data dialog box (see Figure 3.23).

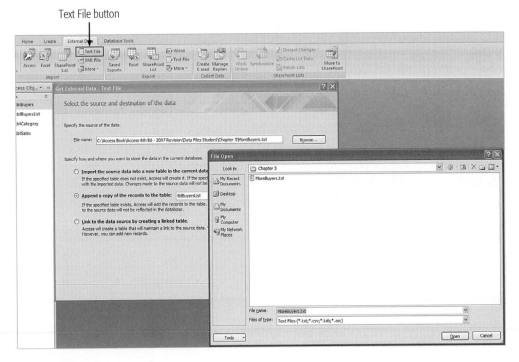

Figure 3.23 Importing text data

4. Click on the OK button. The Import Text wizard opens (see Figure 3.24).

5. Choose the format, Delimited or Fixed Width, and then click on the Next button (see Figure 3.24).

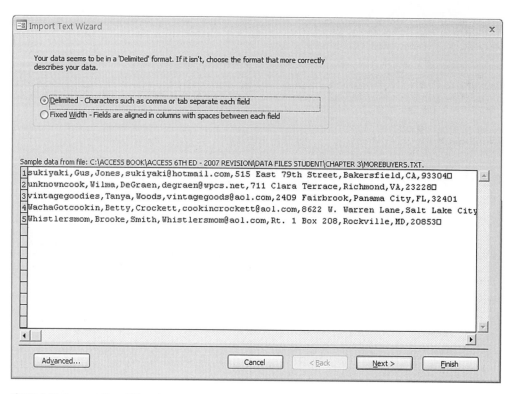

Figure 3.24 Import Text Wizard

6. The second page of the wizard opens. If the text file is delimited, select the delimiter (see Figure 3.25). If it's fixed width, adjust the field widths.

7. If you are appending data to an existing table, skip to step 9

    OR

    Click the Next button. The data is shown in columns. If you want to change the name or data type of a column, change the selections in the Field Options area.

8. Click the Next button. The next screen appears for selecting the primary key (see Figure 3.21). Click on the button to either let Access add a primary key, choose your own primary key, or not designate a primary key.

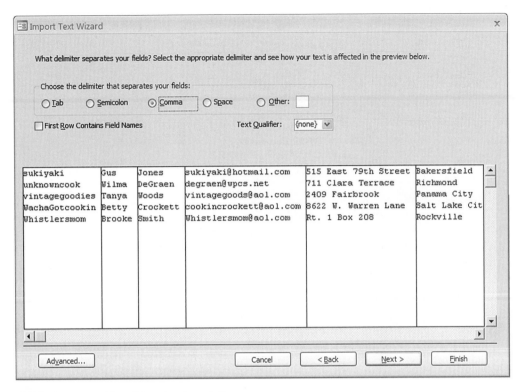

Figure 3.25 Import Text Wizard, select delimeter

9. Click the Next button. The last screen appears. Specify the name of the table (see Figure 3.22).

10. Click the Finish button, and choose to either save or not save the steps.

How To Import Data From Other File Types

1. Open the database into which you want to import the file.

2. Select the External tab on the ribbon, and click on the More button in the Import group (see Figure 3.26).

3. Choose the file type from the list (see Figure 3.26).

4. Select the name and location of the file by clicking on the Browse button, and choosing the folder and file name in the File Open dialog box. Click Open to return to the Get External Data dialog box.

5. Click on the OK button. Click the Finish button, and choose to either save or not save the steps. The new table will have the same name as the data source file.

TRY IT YOURSELF 3.2.4

Using the *G3* database, and referring to Figure 3.26:

A. Import the dBase file *Categori.dbf*.

B. Open the table and verify it contains five records.

C. Close the database, or continue on.

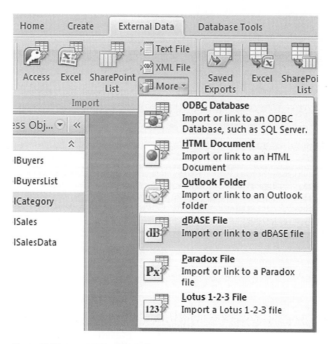

Figure 3.26 Importing data from dBase

Linking Data

Q: Why would I want to link tables?

A: To enable multiple users on a network to share the same set of data tables.

Instead of importing data, you can link it into a database from tables in another database. When tables are linked, they are actually stored in only one location called the source database. You may insert a link into a second database, so that all (or only some of) the tables in the source database can be used in the second database. The second database contains a pointer for each linked table that tells where the source table is stored, on what disk and in which folder.

Linking tables has several advantages and a couple of disadvantages. Linked tables work well when a database needs to be shared among many people over a network. Each user has links to the source data, which is stored on a central file server. This ensures that everyone is using the same data set.

Many database developers like using linked tables because it's easier to update users to new versions of database objects, such as new forms, reports, and queries. All the objects are in a separate database from the data tables, so only the objects database needs to be replaced. Links to the data tables can easily be refreshed in the new objects database.

Linking tables can also help when transporting a database because it reduces the size of the objects database file. Smaller file sizes mean it's easier to copy databases to floppy disks or attach them to email.

A disadvantage to using linked tables is that the linked tables can't be edited in Design view (except in the source database). This means that field names and properties can't be changed outside the source database, which can be cumbersome during development of the database. In some situations, the inability to edit the table structures is considered an advantage as unsophisticated users are prevented from making accidental changes.

How to Link Tables

1. Open the database file into which you want to place the linked table.

2. Select the External tab on the ribbon, and click on the Access button in the Import group.

3. Select the source database file name and location containing the table to link, by clicking on the Browse button.

4. Select the option to "Link to the data source by creating a linked table" as shown in Figure 3.27. Click OK. The Link Tables dialog box opeans as shown in Figure 3.28.

5. Select the table you wish to link and click the OK button (see Figure 3.28). The linked table from the external source will be displayed as a table in the destination database, with an arrow before the table name to show that it is an external linked object (see Figure 3.29).

TRY IT YOURSELF 3.2.5

A. Open the *Practice_Ch3* database.

B. Link in the *tblCourses* table from the *Chapter1* database. See Figures 3.27, 3.28, and 3.29 for samples of how your screens should look during the process.

C. Open the *tblCourses* table in Datasheet view and observe the data.

D. Open the table in Design view (you will not be permitted to edit).

E. Close the *tblCourses* table.

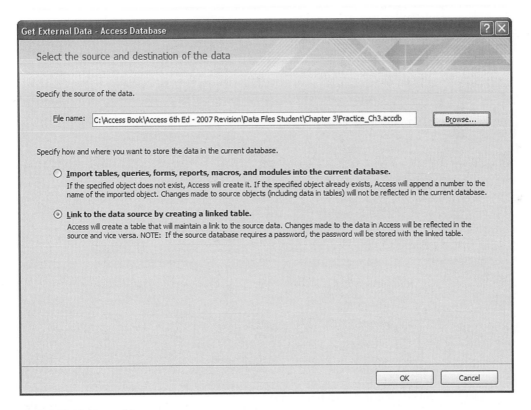

Figure 3.27 Linking tables

If the source database is moved or other changes are made to the physical locations of either of the linked databases, the table links will need to be refreshed. You can refresh links by using the Linked Table Manager.

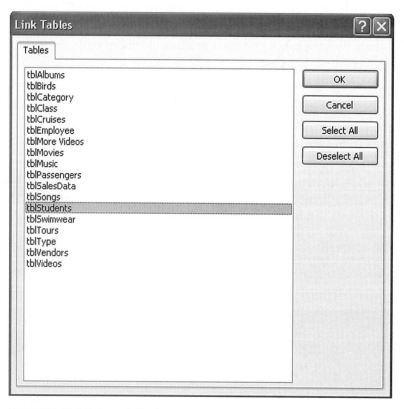

Figure 3.28 Link Tables dialog box

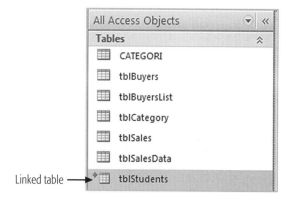

Figure 3.29 Linked table in Navigation pane

How to Refresh Table Links

1. Open the database file containing the links.

2. Select the Database Tools tab on the ribbon and click on the Linked Table Manager button (see Figure 3.30). The Linked Table Manager dialog box opens.

3. Click in the check box preceding each table name that needs to be refreshed, and click on the OK button as shown in Figure 3.30. A window opens for you to select the location.

Linked Table Manager button

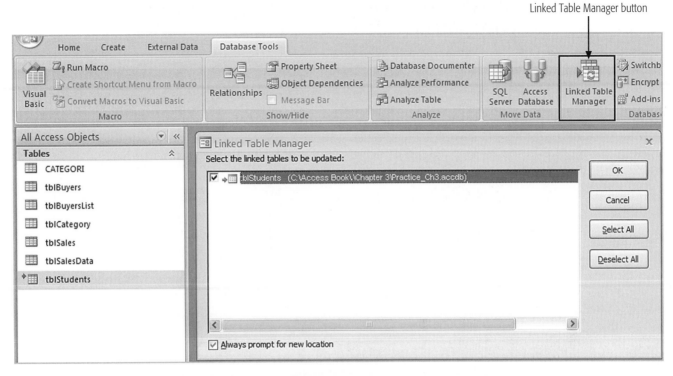

Figure 3.30 Refreshing links with the Linked Table Manager

4. Select the location and database file name, then click the Open button. A message appears confirming that the links were refreshed.
5. Close the Linked Table Manager window.

3.3 Creating Information from Data

Once data is entered into a table, it must be processed or organized in order to become information. Records in a table can be sorted so that they appear in any order you specify. You can also suppress the display of specific records in a table by setting a filter. Both sorting and filtering allow you to browse the information in a format that meets your immediate needs.

Sorting Records

The data records in a table are ordered by the primary key as they are entered. Table data can be quickly sorted for other purposes on one or more fields using the Sort Ascending/Sort Descending buttons in the Sort & Filter group on the Home tab of the ribbon. The records can be sorted in ascending or descending order, either alphabetically or numerically, depending on the type of data in that field. Ascending sorts are usually used for text, so that information appears listed from A to Z. Descending sorts are often used for numbers, so that the numbers appear in order from the largest to the smallest value.

Q: Is this the only way to sort data?

A: It's the easiest way to sort an entire table; however, you can also sort the data in a query, form, or report. We'll look at these objects in later chapters.

TRY IT YOURSELF 3.3.1

A. Using the *G3_Ch3* database, open the table *tblSalesData* in Datasheet view.
B. Sort on the *ItemName* field in ascending order (see Figure 3.31).
C. Close the table or continue on.

How to Sort on One Field

1. Open the table in the Datasheet view.
2. Click in the field to be sorted.
3. Click on the ascending or descending Sort button in the Sort & Filter group on the Home tab of the ribbon.

   OR

   Right-click and select either Sort A to Z or Sort Z to A from the shortcut menu (see Figure 3.31). The records are sorted in the specified order.

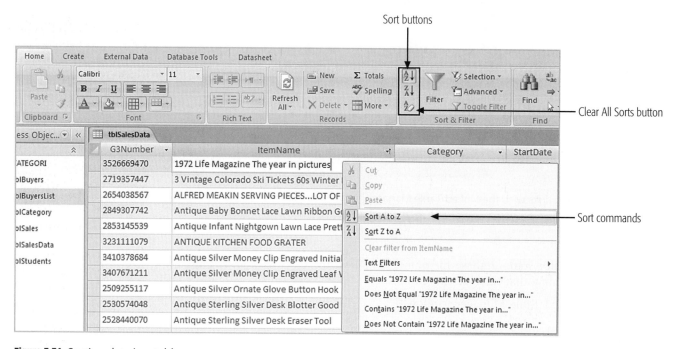

Figure 3.31 Sorting data in a table

The Undo button will return the records to their order prior to the last sort. If several sorts have been performed, click on the Clear All Sorts button (see Figure 3.31) and the records will return to their original sequence before all sorts.

Sometimes records have the same data in one field, so you may further sort by specifying a secondary level. For example, if a table containing people's names is sorted by last name, many records could have the same data value—for example, Smith. To organize the names better, specify the first name as the secondary sort field so that names appear the way they do in the telephone book—Aaron Smith, Carol Smith, Don Smith, etc. To sort on multiple fields, you must first be able to move fields, as sort columns must be next to each other.

Moving Fields

There are two methods for moving fields in the Design view or in the Datasheet view. When fields are moved in Design view and saved, they are permanently changed. When fields are moved in Datasheet view, it doesn't affect the field sequence in Design view. However, when the Datasheet view of the table is opened it will reflect the changes in field order if they were saved.

How to Move a Field in Design View

1. Open the table in Design view.
2. Click the left mouse button in the gray row selector box to select the field you want to move (see Figure 3.32).
3. Click the left mouse button and drag the field to the new location. A faint outline of a rectangle will move with the cursor arrow (see Figure 3.32). Release the mouse button.
4. Save the table with the changes. The Datasheet view will also reflect these changes.

Q: How do I un-move a field?

A: If you wish to undo this move, you can use the undo Move command from the Edit menu or the Undo button on the toolbar before saving the table.

TRY IT YOURSELF 3.3.2

Using the *tblSalesData* table:

A. In Design view, move the *Status* field below the *ItemName* field. Save the changes (see Figure 3.32).
B. In Datasheet view, move the *BuyerID* field to the right of the *Status* field. Save the changes (see Figure 3.33).
C. Close the table, or continue on.

Field Name	Data Type
G3Number	Text
ItemName	Text
Category	Number
StartDate	Date/Time
EndDate	Date/Time
StartPrice	Currency
EndPrice	Currency
ListingCost	Currency
ShippingCharge	Currency
BuyerID	Text
PaymentType	Text
PaymentDate	Date/Time
Status	Text
ActualShipping	Currency

Cursor

Row selector box

Figure 3.32 Moving a field in Design view

Q: When I move a field in Datasheet view, does it stay in the new position?

A: If you make changes to the field order in Datasheet view, it will not affect the order of the fields in the table design. They will remain as they were originally set in the table design. However, if you save these changes in Datasheet view, when you reopen the table the changes will remain.

How to Move a Field in Datasheet View

1. Open the table in Datasheet view.
2. Select the entire field by clicking the left mouse button on the field name. The entire column will be highlighted.
3. Click on the field name and drag the field (column) to the new location. A faint outline of a rectangle will follow the cursor arrow. A heavy dark line will appear on the side of the column to indicate where the moved column will be inserted (see Figure 3.33).
4. Release the mouse button to drop the field in the new location.
5. Close the table. A prompt appears that asks if you want to save changes to the structure. Choose Yes if you want to make this arrangement a permanent change.

Status	Category	StartDate	EndDate	StartP	EndPr	ListingC	Shippin	BuyerID
Not Sold	Misc. Collectables	2/8/2008	2/15/2008	$7.95	$0.00	$0.70	$0.00	
Sold	Misc. Collectables	2/21/2008	2/28/2008	$4.78	$5.53	$0.46	$6.30	Whistlersmom
Sold	Clothing	3/4/2008	3/9/2008	$7.99	$10.19	$0.55	$3.30	catchScatchcan
Sold	Misc. Collectables	3/9/2008	3/15/2008	$2.99	$8.00	$1.41	$3.50	Letradingpost
Sold	Misc. Collectables	3/22/2008	3/29/2008	$14.99	$51.09	$0.95	$11.30	boomerbaby
Sold	Clothing	3/23/2008	3/30/2008	$3.99	$8.83	$1.40	$1.50	princessqueen

Figure 3.33 Moving a field in Datasheet view

Q: Will records stay sorted?

A: If you save the changes when you close a table, the sort order wil be preserved.

How to Sort on Multiple Fields

1. Open the table in the Datasheet view. The primary sort field must appear to the left of the secondary sort field. If this is not the case, move the primary sort field to the left of the secondary sort field.

2. Select the fields for the multiple sort by clicking on the top row of the table—the row containing the names of the fields. Drag the mouse pointer across both the primary sort field and the secondary sort field names.

3. Click the Sort button (ascending or descending). Both levels of sorting are done simultaneously.

G3Number	Category	ItemName
3526669470	Books	1972 Life Magazine The year in pictures
3525014678	Books	B.H.&G. Cookbook 1949
3505984948	Books	Kitchen Digest Vintage Book Homemaking Dakota
3526670158	Books	LOT Vintage Life Magazines featuring LBJ
3526669868	Books	LOT VINTAGE LIFE MAGAZINES JULY 1964
3526670033	Books	LOT VINTAGE LIFE MAGAZNES 1965
2849307742	Clothing	Antique Baby Bonnet Lace Lawn Ribbon Gorgeous
2853145539	Clothing	Antique Infant Nightgown Lawn Lace Pretty
2509255117	Clothing	Antique Silver Ornate Glove Button Hook
2825761008	Clothing	Vintage 60's Satin Beaded Clutch Purse

Figure 3.34 *tblSalesData* sorted by *Category* and *ItemName*

TRY IT YOURSELF 3.3.3

A. Using *tblSalesData*, sort by the fields *Category* and *ItemName* in ascending order (see Figure 3.34).

B. Close the table without saving the changes, or continue on.

Creating and Applying a Filter

The filter commands allow the user to display a set of records that match certain criteria. Only those records that match the prescribed criteria are displayed. For example, a filter could be applied to the *tblSales* table that shows only the sold items. In this case, the criteria you would use in the filter is *Status* = "Sold." Filters can be quite complex and can be based on multiple fields, such as a filter on the *tblSales* table that shows only clothing that sold for more than $20 in August. Filters can be applied to tables in the Datasheet view, or when displayed in forms and queries.

There are three types of filter commands: Filter By Form, Filter By Selection, and Advanced Filter/Sort. (Advanced Filter/Sort will not be covered in this chapter as the command creates a query.) Filter commands are found on the Home tab of the ribbon, or can be accessed by clicking on the triangle to the right of a field name or right clicking in any field. Refer to Figure 3.35. There are three ways to apply a filter—by selection, by form, and by advanced filter/sort.

Q: What does a filter do?

A: It allows you to view only records that meet your specifications.

Filter By Selection

Filter By Selection lets you select records based on the value in the currently selected or highlighted field. You can select the value to be matched from the table in Datasheet view, and then set the filter to display only those records that match that value. You can also produce a display of all records that do not match the criteria, or filter based on values greater than or less than numbers or dates.

Q: Can I use Filter By Selection on more than one field?

A: Yes. Select a record field within the results of the first filter, and click on the Filter By Selection button again.

How to Filter By Selection

1. Open the table in the Datasheet view.

2. Select the value to be matched. It can either be a whole field or any part of a field.

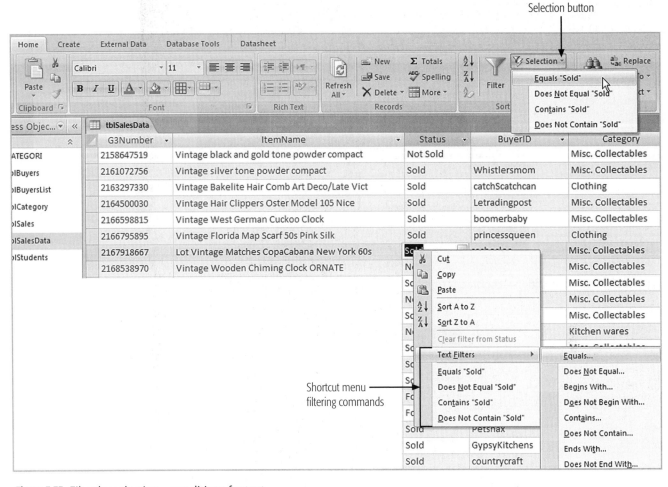

Figure 3.35 Filter by selection—conditions for text

3. Select the Home tab on the ribbon. Click the Selection button in the Sort & Filter group (see Figure 3.35)

   OR

   Click the right mouse button and choose one of the filtering options from the lower portion of the shortcut menu.

   Only records matching the criteria are displayed.

   Filter by selection is a very fast way to filter, and there are so many variations built into the command that it is adequate for creating most filters. Figure 3.35 shows the different filter settings available for a text field; most of them are found on the shortcut menu. You can view only the records which match the selected text, those which don't match it, those which contain it (or not), or those which begin or end with it. Other data types have even more options available. Figure 3.36 shows the options available for filtering numeric data. These include equals, does not equal, less than, greater than, and between two values.

   Date fields have the most built-in filter conditions. Figure 3.37 shows the available date filters. Not only are the numeric options listed, but there are also filters based on a variety of time periods—days, weeks, months, quarters, years, future, and past. Prior to the 2007 release of Access, working with dates was difficult. By providing such an extensive list from which to select, working with dates has now become very easy.

TRY IT YOURSELF 3.4.4

A. Using *tblSalesData*, apply a filter by selection to show only the items with a "Sold" status. Refer to Figure 3.35.

B. Apply a second filter to show only the items that sold for $10 or more. The *EndPrice* field contains the selling price. Refer to Figure 3.36.

C. Apply a third filter to see only those items sold in August. The *EndDate* field contains the date the item sold. Refer to Figure 3.37.

D. After applying all three filters, there should be five records displayed.

E. Close *tblSalesData*, or continue on.

Category	StartDate	EndDate	StartP	EndPrice	ListingC	Shippin	PaymentType	PaymentDat
Misc. Collectables	5/23/2008	5/30/2008	$7.50	$7.50	$0.55	$5.00	Check	6/3/20
Misc. Collectables	6/6/2008	6/13/2008	$6.50	$6.50	$0.55	$3.00	Pay Friend	6/13/20
Kitchen wares	8/17/2008	8/24/2008	$4.50	$10.00	$0.55	$5.00		
Kitchen wares	9/11/2008		$3.75					
Kitchen wares	9/11/2008		$4.75					
Clothing	2/16/2008	2/23/2008	$7.99	$22.				3/1/20
Misc. Collectables	3/9/2008	3/17/2008	$19.99	$19.				3/20/20
Misc. Collectables	4/6/2008	4/13/2008	$7.99	$36.				4/14/20
Misc. Collectables	4/13/2008	4/20/2008	$9.99	$19.				4/21/20
Misc. Collectables	4/27/2008	5/2/2008	$19.99	$19.				
Misc. Collectables	5/2/2008	5/9/2008	$16.00	$17.				
Misc. Collectables	5/9/2008	5/18/2008	$19.99	$25.				

Right-click menu:
- Cut
- Copy
- Paste
- Sort Smallest to Largest
- Sort Largest to Smallest
- Clear filter from EndPrice
- Number Filters ▶
  - Equals...
  - Does Not Equal...
  - Less Than...
  - Greater Than...
  - Between...
- Equals $10.00
- Does Not Equal $10.00
- Less Than or Equal To $10.00
- Greater Than or Equal To $10.00

Record: 15 of 59   ☒ Unfiltered   Search

Figure 3.36 Filter by selection—conditions for numbers

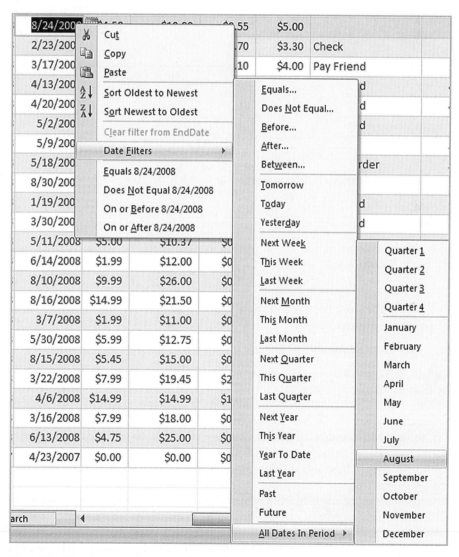

Figure 3.37 Filter by selection—conditions for dates

When a filter has been applied to a table, Access gives you several visual indicators. These are depicted in Figure 3.38. In the Sort & Filter group on the ribbon, the Toggle Filter button is highlighted. In the status bar, the Filtered icon is highlighted. Also, each field that is filtered shows a tiny filter icon (a funnel) to the right of the field name.

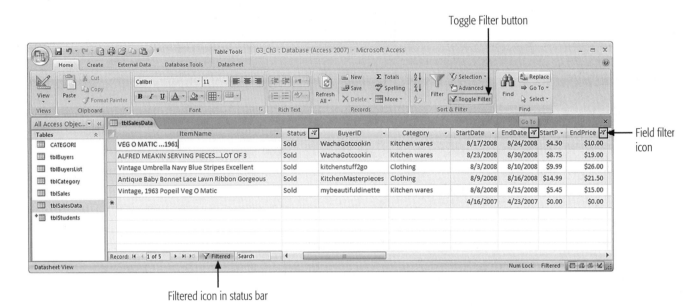

Figure 3.38 Filter-on indicators

How to Remove All Filters

1. In the Sort & Filter group on the ribbon, click on the Toggle Filter button

OR

In the status bar, click on the Filtered icon.

Once the filter is turned off, all the records should reappear and the filter buttons should no longer be highlighted. You can toggle the filter back on by pressing the Toggle Filter button again.

You can also turn filtering off for only one field in a multiple-field filter.

How to Remove The Filter From One Field

1. Click on the field filter icon to the right of the field name to clear

OR

Right-click on any data in the field filter to clear.

2. Select the Clear Filter From Field command from the shortcut menu. Figure 3.39 shows the Clear Filter From StartDate command for *tblSalesData*.

To permanently clear all filters, click on the Advanced button in the Sort & Filter group, and choose Clear All Filters from the menu. Figure 3.40 shows this command right above the Filter By Form command.

TRY IT YOURSELF 3.4.5

A. Use *tblSalesData*, with the filter set as specified in Try It Yourself 3.4.4.

B. Turn off the filter to see only those items sold in August. Refer to Figure 3.39.

C. Turn off all filters. Refer to Figure 3.38.

D. Close *tblSalesData*, or continue on.

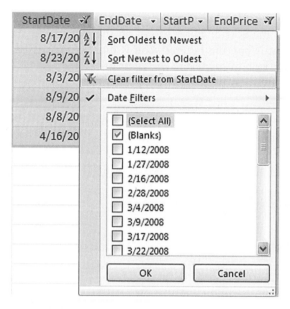

Figure 3.39 Turning off a filter on one field

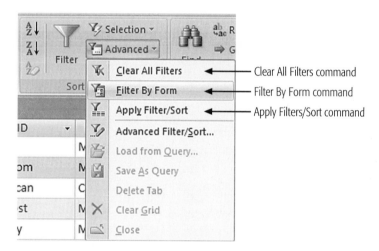

Figure 3.40 Advanced Filter commands

Filter By Form

Because Filter By Selection allows you to select only one criterion at a time, Filter By Form is better for selecting records based on multiple criteria. Filter By Form displays an empty record into which you can enter data values for filtering. Multiple criteria can be constructed two different ways, as described next.

- The criteria are joined by an AND condition, which means for a record to be included in the filter, both criteria must be true. For example, "all people who live in Utah and own a computer" includes only Utah residents with a computer.

- The criteria are joined by an OR condition, which means for a record to be included in the filter, either criterion can be true. For example, "all people who live in Utah or own a computer" includes all Utah residents with or without a computer, and all computer owners regardless of where they live.

When criteria are joined with an AND, the resulting group is smaller than that obtained by filtering with an OR criteria.

How to Filter By Form

1. Open the table in Datasheet view.

2. Display an empty record by clicking on the Advanced button in the Sort & Filter group on the ribbon, and selecting Filter By Form as shown in Figure 3.40.

The Filter By Form window opens on a separate tab (see Figure 3.41).

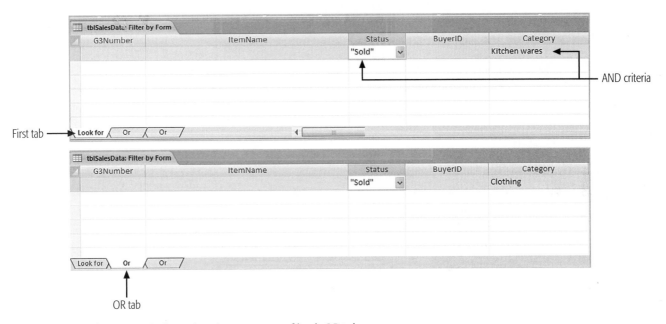

Figure 3.41 Filter by Form window, showing contents of both OR tabs

3. Click on the field to enter the filter criteria (see Figure 3.41).

4. Specify the criteria:

Select from the drop-down list

OR

Type in the criteria.

- To create a multiple-criteria filter based on an AND condition, put criteria into more than one field box.

- To create a multiple-criteria filter based on an OR condition, click on the OR tab located at the bottom of the screen and specify multiple conditions for a single field. Refer to Figure 3.41.

5. Click on the Toggle Filter button on the ribbon, or select Apply Filter/Sort from the Advanced menu as shown in Figure 3.40. Records matching the criteria are displayed.

You can select Clear All Filters from the Advanced menu as shown in Figure 3.40 to remove all filters. To delete a single entry, highlight that entry and press the DELETE key to remove it from the grid.

Adding a total row to filtered data can give you valuable information. You can display statistics such as sums or averages about groups of data in your tables.

TRY IT YOURSELF 3.3.4

A. Using *tblSalesData* and Filter By Form, display all items sold in either the Clothing or Kitchen wares categories.

B. Print the list of filtered records. Refer to Figure 3.42.

How to Print Filter Results

1. Click the Print button on the Quick Access toolbar after the filter has been applied and the results are displayed on the screen

   OR

   Select the Print command from the Office menu after the results are displayed.

G3Number	ItemName	Status	BuyerID	Category
2163297330	Vintage Bakelite Hair Comb Art Deco/Late Vict	Sold	catchScatchcan	Clothing
2166795895	Vintage Florida Map Scarf 50s Pink Silk	Sold	princessqueen	Clothing
2341299043	VEG O MATIC ...1961	Sold	WachaGotcookin	Kitchen wares
2509255117	Antique Silver Ornate Glove Button Hook	Sold	Petsnax	Clothing
2628581918	Japanese Lusterware Salt and Pepper Set	Sold	even-the-kitchen-sink	Kitchen wares
2654038567	ALFRED MEAKIN SERVING PIECES...LOT OF 3	Sold	WachaGotcookin	Kitchen wares
2825761008	Vintage 60's Satin Beaded Clutch Purse	Sold	vintagegoodies	Clothing
2836698359	Vintage Handheld Fan	Sold	mybeautifuldinette	Clothing
2848166699	Vintage Umbrella Navy Blue Stripes Excellent	Sold	kitchenstuff2go	Clothing
2849307742	Antique Baby Bonnet Lace Lawn Ribbon Gorgeous	Sold	KitchenMasterpieces	Clothing
2853145539	Antique Infant Nightgown Lawn Lace Pretty	Sold	CoCoCocina	Clothing
3211496108	Shabby Chic Kitchen Vintage Egg Beater Red	Sold	blueangles	Kitchen wares
3225719382	Lot 2 Canisters 40s Ransburg Black Floral VG	Sold	FabulousKitchens	Kitchen wares
3231111079	ANTIQUE KITCHEN FOOD GRATER	Sold	kitchenbelle	Kitchen wares
3237063659	Vintage, 1963 Popeil Veg O Matic	Sold	mybeautifuldinette	Kitchen wares

Record: 1 of 15   Filtered   Search

Figure 3.42 Filter by Form result showing items sold in either the Clothing or Kitchen wares category

3.4 Restructuring Table Design

Although it's very important, initially, to design your table structure with care, it is also possible to make changes to the table design after data has been entered. Changes such as adding a new field, deleting a field, changing the field order, switching primary keys, and changing field properties are possible. However, be forewarned that some changes can be dangerous to the health of your database—they can result in loss of data or corruption of the database file. Be particularly careful about creating a new primary key in a table or changing the data type of a field. Designating a new primary key will affect any joins to other tables (see Section 3.7) and changing data types could result in losing data that can't be converted. Access automatically updates objects that refer to renamed fields, when the Name AutoCorrect feature is turned on (it's on by default). If fields are moved to other tables, you will have to manually change any objects that refer to those fields.

Q: What if I make a mistake while changing the table design?

A: Before changing the structure of a table, it is a good idea to make a backup copy of your database file or of the table in case of problems.

Inserting and Deleting Fields

How to Add a Field in Design View

1. Open the table in the Design view.

2. Click in the field below where the new field will be. The new field will be inserted above this field.

3. Click the right mouse button to display the shortcut menu, then select Insert Rows from the shortcut menu (see Figure 3.43)

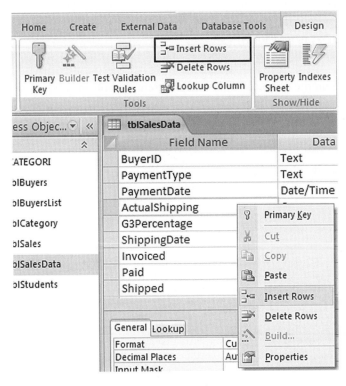

Figure 3.43 Inserting a row in Design view

OR

Select the Design tab on the ribbon, and click on the Insert Rows button in the Tools group.

A new blank field appears above the selected row.

4. Add the field name, data type, description (optional), and any field properties.

5. Save the table again to make sure the changes are saved. If you try to leave this screen without saving first, Access will prompt you to save the changes.

The table is now ready for data to be entered in the new field.

How to Add a Field in Datasheet View

1. Open the table in Datasheet view.

2. Select the entire column to the right of the location where the new field will be inserted.

3. Select the Datasheet tab on the ribbon, and click on the Insert button in the Fields & Columns group

OR

Click the right mouse button to bring up the shortcut menu. Choose the Insert Column command.

The new field column will appear to the left of the selected column.

Modifying Fields

When fields are added in Datasheet view, they should be modified to include a new field name and other appropriate field properties. The default name for a new field is *Field1*

Q: What happens if I designate a new primary key on a table containing data?

A: Access will check to make sure the key field doesn't have duplicate values in more than one record. If it does, the key can't be created.

TRY IT YOURSELF 3.4.1

A. Using *tblSalesData*, add a new field called *PaymentAmount* below the *PaymentDate* field (see Figure 3.43).

B. Save the table.

C. Close the table, or continue on.

Q: Will I lose data if I change a field name?

A: No, the data remains in the field. If you change the data type, Access will try to convert the existing data. Also, any other objects (forms, reports, etc.) that use the field are updated with the new name.

with other newly added fields numbered consecutively. The default properties for this field are text data type and a field size of 50. It's much easier to modify fields in Design view (see Chapter 2); however, some changes can be made in Datasheet view.

How to Rename a Field in Datasheet View

1. Select the entire field.

2. Select the Datasheet tab on the ribbon and click on the Rename button (see Figure 3.44)

   OR

   Right-click on the field and from the shortcut menu, choose the Rename Column command (see Figure 3.44).

3. Type in the new field name.

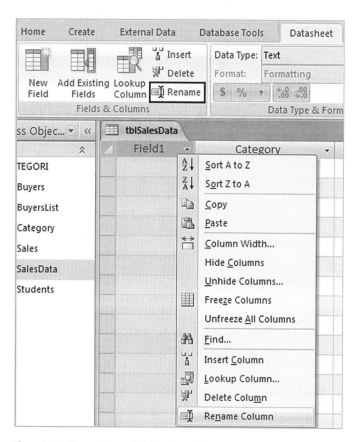

Figure 3.44 Renaming a field in Datasheet view

TRY IT YOURSELF 3.4.2

Using the *tblSalesData* table:

A. Rename the field *EndPrice* as *SalesPrice*.

B. Change to Datasheet view and verify the field name change.

C. Close the table when you're finished but don't save the changes.

You can easily change the name, data type, and other properties of a field in the Design view. Open the table in Design view and select the item to be changed. Type or select the new name or property and save the table.

Deleting a Field

Deleting a field results in deleting all the data associated with that field. Be sure this is what you want before proceeding.

How to Delete a Field in Design View

1. Open the table in Design view.

2. Click in the field selector area to the left of the field you want to delete.

3. Select the Design tab on the ribbon, and click on the Delete Rows button in the Tools group (see Figure 3.45)

   OR

   Click the right mouse button to open the shortcut menu, then choose the Delete Rows command (see Figure 3.45)

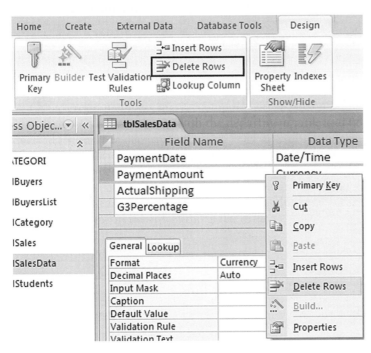

Figure 3.45 Deleting a field in Design view

   OR

   Press the [DELETE] key on the keyboard.

4. A dialog box will appear on the screen asking for confirmation of the delete operation. Choose the Yes button to confirm this operation or the No button to cancel the operation. The deletion can be reversed at this point by using the Undo Delete command from the Edit menu.

5. Save the file again to make the changes permanent.

How to Delete a Field in Datasheet View

1. Open the table in Datasheet view.

2. Select the column to delete by clicking the field name at the top of the column.

3. Select the Datasheet tab on the ribbon and click on the Delete button in Fields & Columns group

   OR

   Use the right mouse button to display the shortcut menu, then choose the Delete Column command

Q: Can I un-delete a field?

A: Yes, you can click the Undo button and get the field back. Remember, you can only undo the last delete—previous deletions are lost.

Q: Can I un-delete a field after closing the table?

A: No, once the table is saved with the changes, the delete process cannot be reversed. Any deleted data is lost.

OR

Press the ⎡DELETE⎤ key on the keyboard.

4. Confirm the deletion by clicking on the Yes button in the confirmation dialog box. The new column will disappear from the table. The data associated with this column (field) will also be deleted.

5. Save these new changes to the design of the table.

Setting Captions

At times, the field name given in the table design is inappropriate for display in Datasheet view. Using the Caption property in Design view will allow the user to name the field appropriately for the structure, but display another descriptive name in Datasheet view.

How to Set Field Captions

1. Open the table in Design view.
2. Click on the field to be assigned a caption.
3. Click on the Caption line in the Field Properties window (see Figure 3.46).
4. Add text for the caption.
5. Save changes to the table.

Remember that you can change other field properties at any time.

TRY IT YOURSELF 3.4.3

Using the *tblSalesData* table:
A. Delete the field *PaymentAmount* (see Figure 3.45)
B. Close the table, or continue on.

TRY IT YOURSELF 3.4.4

A. Using *tblSales Data,* add the caption "BuyerName" to the field *BuyerID*.
B. View the caption in Datasheet view.
C. Close the table, or continue on.

Field Name	Data Type
StartPrice	Currency
SalesPrice	Currency
ListingCost	Currency
ShippingCharge	Currency
BuyerID	Text
PaymentType	Text

General	Lookup	
Field Size	50
Format	
Input Mask	
Caption	Buyer Name	← Caption property
Default Value	

Figure 3.46 Changing the Caption property

Renaming and Deleting Tables

It is sometimes necessary to delete entire tables or other objects from the database file. Also, any Access object can easily be renamed, but no two objects of the same type can have the same name. It's a good idea to make a backup copy of a database before you delete it, in case you change your mind.

How to Delete a Table

1. In the Navigation pane, click on the name of table to delete.
2. Using the right mouse button, choose the Delete command from the shortcut menu

Q: How do I delete other database objects, such as queries and forms?

A: You can use the same procedure to delete any object created in the database.

OR

Press the DELETE key on the keyboard.

3. Confirm the deletion.

The table is then deleted from the database file. You can undo this command and restore the table to the database.

How to Rename a Table

1. Select the table you want to rename, in the Navigation Pane.
2. Click on the right mouse button and choose the Rename command from the shortcut menu.
3. Type in the new name or edit the previous name, and press the ENTER key.

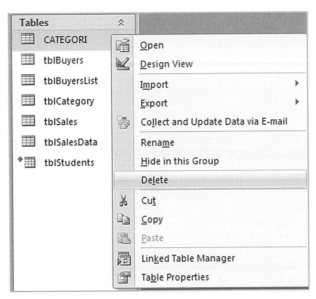

Figure 3.47 Deleting a table

TRY IT YOURSELF 3.4.5

A. Delete the table *CATEGORI* from the *G3_Ch3* database (see Figure 3.47).
B. Close the database, or continue on.

TRY IT YOURSELF 3.4.6

Using the *practice_Ch3* database:
A. Delete the table *tblSales*.
B. Rename the table *tblSalesData* as *tblSales*.
C. Close the database, or continue on.

Professional Tip: Copying and Hiding Objects

Here are some more tips from Jim Stiles:

You can copy an object without using the Edit menu's Copy and Paste commands. Simply select the object you want to copy and hold down the Ctrl key while you drag that object to the end of the object list and then release it. Access will create a duplicate and name it "Copy of filename." For example, if you want to copy a report named MyReport, you'd select it, hold down the Ctrl key, and drag MyReport to the end of the report list. Access would then display a new report named "Copy of MyReport" in your report list.

It's easy to hide a table so the average user doesn't know it exists. Right-click the table in the Navigation pane, then choose Properties from the submenu. In the resulting Properties dialog box, click the Hidden option at the bottom of the box. Next, click Apply and then click OK. When you're ready to work with the table, right-click on the Navigation pane and choose Navigation options. Click on the Show Hidden Objects check box. Finally, click OK to return to the Navigation Pane, which will now display your hidden table.

You can use the same process to hide and show any database object.

3.5 Setting and Removing Simple Relationships

Access is a relational database program in which data is organized into tables that are joined (related) to each other. This allows for data in one table to be accessible to another table, without redundancy and extra storage requirements. (A further discussion of relational databases is given in Chapters 1 and 7.)

The joins between tables are established by having the various tables share a common field. Typically, a primary key in one table is linked to the same field (which is not a primary key) in another table. A field that is not a primary key in another table is called a foreign key. Fields used in a join should be identical in design, that is, the same data type and size, and they should contain the same set of values. They don't need to have the same name nor do they have to be primary keys. It's easier to remember which fields are the common fields, however, if the same field names are used. When joining two tables where one table has an AutoNumber primary key, the foreign key should be set up as a long integer data type.

For example, in the *G3_Ch3* database, the field *CategoryID* in *tblCategory* is an autonumber primary key. The field *Category* in *tblSales* is a foreign key with a long integer type, The name of the category is looked up in *tblCategory* and displayed in *tblSales*. This way the category names are consistent and don't need to be retyped when a new record is entered in *tblSales*.

You must be able to create relationships to create queries, forms, and reports that use multiple tables. Remember that it is most efficient to design relational tables (see Chapters 1 and 7) so joining files is easily accomplished. Once two tables have been joined, data from the second table can be viewed as a subdatasheet in the first table.

There are four types of table relationships available in Access. They are outlined in Table 3.7.

Q: What data type should be used for an AutoNumber foreign key?

A: Use a long integer data type for the foreign key.

Table 3.7   Types of Relationships

Type of Relationship	Description
One-to-One Relationship	Records in first table linked to exactly one record in another table.
One-to-Many Relationship[a]	One record in first table linked to several (many) records in another table.
Many-to-One Relationship	Many records in first table linked to one record in another table.
Many-to-Many Relationship	Many records in first table linked to many records in another table.

[a]One-to-many and many-to-one relationships are essentially the same type of relationship seen from different viewpoints.

The one-to-many relationship is the most common join. In a one-to-many join, the first table has one record with a particular data value in the common field, while the second table has many records with that value. An example of a one-to-many relationship can be shown by considering the *tblCategory* and *tblSales* samples shown in Figure 3.48. The *tblCategory* table has only one record per category, but the *tblSales* table could contain many records for a single category as shown in Figure 3.49.

A many-to-many relationship would exist if an item could fit into more than one sales category. Then many items could be joined to one category and many categories to one sales item.

A one-to-one relationship exists when there is only one record in both tables with the same value in the common field. If two tables have a one-to-one relationship, they could theoretically be combined into one table. The data may be separated into two tables because there are so many fields that the table is difficult to work with, or because the data may be split into two groups that have different functions or security levels.

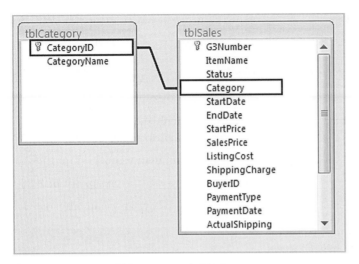

Figure 3.48 Joining *tblCategory* and *tblSales*

tblCategory	
CategoryID	CategoryName
1	Clothing
2	Books
3	Kitchen wares
4	Misc. Collectables

tblSales	
CategoryID	ItemName
1	Vintage Florida Map Scarf 50s Pink Silk
1	Antique Silver Ornate Glove Button Hook
1	Vintage 60's Satin Beaded Clutch Purse

Figure 3.49 A one-to-many relationship between *tblCategory* and *tblSales*

How to Create a Relationship in a Database

1. Select the Database Tools tab on the ribbon, and click on the Relationships button in the Show/Hide group (see Figure 3.50).

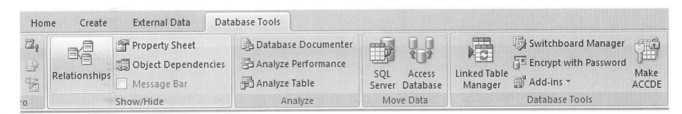

Figure 3.50 Relationships button on the ribbon

2. The Relationships window opens showing each table in the database (see Figure 3.51). If all tables are not displayed, click on the Show Table button on the ribbon, and select the tables to display.

3. Click on the linking field in the first table shown in the Relationships window. Drag that field to the matching field in the next table. This will probably be the primary key of the first table being dragged onto the foreign key in the second table.

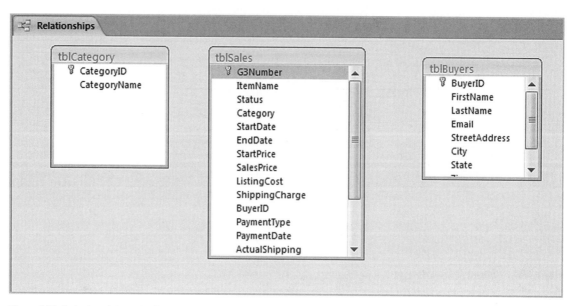

Figure 3.51 Relationships window

4. The Edit Relationships dialog box appears (see Figure 3.52) asking for confirmation of this procedure. Notice the relationship type at the bottom of this dialog box indicating the type of relationship created.

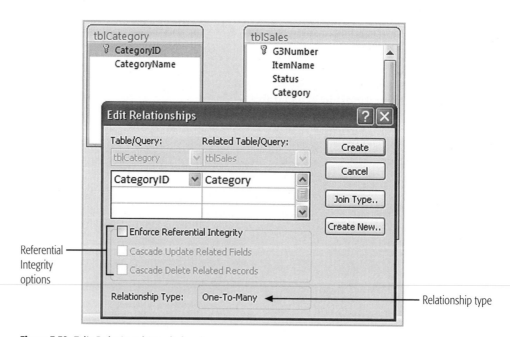

Figure 3.52 Edit Relationships dialog box

5. Click on the Create button (see Figure 3.52). Notice the dark line drawn between the linked tables (see Figure 3.53).

6. Repeat this procedure until all tables are linked.

7. Save the changes to the database.

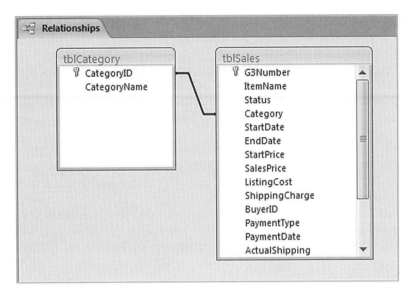

Figure 3.53 Tables linked in the Relationship window

How to Delete Relationships

1. Click on the Relationships button on the Database Tools tab of the ribbon.

   The Relationships window will display the links between the tables.

2. Click on the heavy line (link) that you wish to delete.

3. Press the [DELETE] key on the keyboard

   OR

   Right-click on the line and select Delete from the Shortcut menu.

   A dialog box will appear asking for confirmation of this operation.

4. Choose Yes. The relationship will be broken.

To print the relationships in a database, click on the Relationship Report button on the ribbon (see Figure 3.54). An Access report is created showing the relationships, and can be printed by clicking the Print button on the toolbar. Close the Relationships window by closing its tab, or by clicking on the Close button on the right end of the ribbon.

TRY IT YOURSELF 3.5.1

A. Open the Relationships window in the *G3_Ch3* database (see Figure 3.51).

B. Create a one-to-many relationship between *tblCategory* and *tblSales* (see Figures 3.52 and 3.53).

C. Create a one-to-many relationship between *tblSales* and *tblBuyers*.

D. Close the database, or continue on.

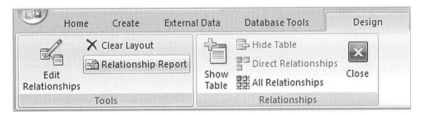

Figure 3.54 Relationship Report button

Introducing Referential Integrity

Once you begin joining tables, you should be aware of a database concept called referential integrity. Referential integrity is a system of rules that checks the validity of table joins and makes sure you don't accidentally delete or change related data. You can set referential integrity when two tables are in the same database and are joined with a primary key/foreign key common field. If tables are linked into a database, referential integrity must be set in the source database. There are several rules to ensure referential integrity.

When referential integrity is set, you must only enter values in the foreign key that already exist in the primary key of the first table. For example, when *tblSales* and *tblCategory* are joined, you can't add on item to *tblSales* unless the category of that item is already in *tblCategory*. Using a lookup field in *tblSales* ensures that valid categories are chosen from a list.

When referential integrity is set, you are not allowed to delete a record from a primary table if matching records exist in a related table. Using the same table join example as above, this means you can't delete a category from *tblCategory* until you first delete the items in that category in *tblSales*.

When referential integrity is set, you can't change a value in the primary key field in the first table if that record has related records (ones with the same value) in the second table. For example, you can't change the data value from 3 to 4 in the *CategoryID* field in *tblCategory*, if there are items in *tblSales* assigned to category 3 (Kitchen wares).

If you want to enforce referential integrity on a table join, select the Enforce Referential Integrity check box in the Edit Relationships dialog box as shown in Figure 3.52. You can open the Edit Relationships dialog box by double-clicking on the join line between the two tables in the Relationships window.

Once you have enforced referential integrity, you can select to have Access automatically repair any anomalies caused by deleting or changing a primary key value as described above. The options to Cascade Update Related Fields and Cascade Delete Related Records can be selected in the Relationships dialog box as shown in Figure 3.52. Cascade Update Related Fields will automatically change any foreign key values if the corresponding primary key value is changed, and Cascade Delete Related Records will automatically delete any records with a foreign key equal to the value of a deleted primary key record. These commands should be used with caution, and will be discussed in more depth in Chapter 7.

Once you set referential integrity on a table join, the appearance of the join changes in the Relationships window. Figure 3.55 Shows the 1–∞ symbols between *tblCategory* and *tblSales*. This indicates that there is a one-to-many join between the tables.

Q: What happens when you enforce referential integrity on a table join?

A: Access ensures that any changes or deletions to the primary key in the first table are reflected in the foreign key of the second table.

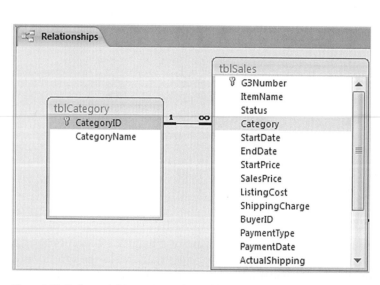

Figure 3.55 Referential Integrity enforced between *tblCategory* and *tblSales*

Using Subdatasheets

A subdatasheet is a feature of Access that allows you to view related records in a one-to-many join from the first table's Datasheet view. In other words, when you have the "one" table open in the Datasheet view, a subdatasheet displays all the matching records in the "many" table. For example, if *tblCategory* is open in Datasheet view, the related items in *tblSales* can be viewed in a subdatasheet.

If a table has a relationship set with another table, you can view the subdatasheet by clicking the expand indicator icon (+) next to a specific record (see Figure 3.56). You can hide the subdatasheet by clicking the collapse indicator icon (–) next to a specific record (see Figure 3.56).

If two tables haven't been joined, but meet the requirements to create a one-to-many join, then a subdatasheet can be created. Just open the Relationships window and join the two tables. When a join is deleted, the subdatasheet view is no longer available.

TRY IT YOURSELF 3.5.2

Using the *G3_Ch3* database:

A. Be sure a join has been established between *tblCategory* and *tblSales* (see Try It Yourself 3.51).

B. Open the *tblCategory* table in Datasheet view.

C. View the subdatasheet for a record by clicking the expand indicator icon next to the record (see Figure 3.56).

D. Hide the subdatasheet and close the *tblCategory* table.

Figure 3.56 *tblCategory* showing a subdatasheet from *tblSales*

Fast Track   A quick guide to procedures learned in this chapter

Adding Records to a Table

1. Position the cursor using one of the following ways:

   Click the mouse on the first field of a new record at the bottom of the table

   OR

   Use the navigation buttons at the bottom of the screen to position the cursor to the last record, then press the [ENTER] or [TAB] key to move to a new record

   OR

   Press the New Record button in the Records group of the ribbon Home tab.

2. Enter the new data in the appropriate fields.

3. Press the [TAB] key to move to the next field or move the mouse pointer to the next field.

4. Continue to enter as many new records as necessary. New records are automatically saved when the next new record is created or when the table is closed.

Editing Records

1. Position the data entry point by doing one of the following:

   Move the cursor to the field you want to edit either with keyboard movements ([TAB] or arrow keys) or by using the mouse to position the pointer in the field you want to edit.

2. Type in the new data value, if the field has no value entered in it. If the field already contains data, select the entire value and press the [DELETE] key to delete it—then type in the new data.

Moving and Copying Data

1. Select the data you want to move or copy. Remember that not all fields can be edited.

2. Click the Cut or Copy button in the Clipboard group on the ribbon Home tab

   OR

   Click the right mouse button to display the shortcut menu and choose Cut or Copy.

3. Position the cursor on the new record location.

4. Paste the data in the new location by using the Paste button on the ribbon.

Displaying the Office Clipboard

1. Click on the arrow in the lower right corner of the Clipboard group on the ribbon Home tab.

Deleting Records

1. Select the record or records you want to delete.

2. Press the [DELETE] key on the keyboard

   OR

   Click the Delete button in the Records group of the ribbon Home tab

   OR

   Click the right mouse button to bring up the shortcut menu. Choose the Delete Record command.

3. The Delete dialog box will appear, asking for confirmation of the delete operation. The Yes option permanently removes the records from your database file. You cannot undo such an operation. The No option will cancel the delete operation.

   Click the Yes button to delete the selected records.

Finding Data

1. Position the cursor in the field where you want to find the data.

2. Activate the Find command by doing one of the following:

   Click on the Find button in the Find group of the ribbon Home tab

   OR

Press the CTRL key and F key together to activate the Find command. The Find dialog box appears.

3. Fill in the Find What text box with the value you want to search for. Enter the entire value as it appears in the field or use the available wildcard characters.

4. Select the appropriate choice from the Match drop-down list. Unless the data value you're finding is the entire field, choose "Any Part of Field."

5. Select how to conduct the search from the drop-down list in the Search option. You can choose to search all the records, or only the records above or below the current record.

6. Choose from other Find options.

7. Click the Find Next button to proceed through the datasheet and locate the requested values. The Find dialog box will stay on the screen to allow for further searching.

8. Click the Close button to close the dialog box when the process is complete.

Using Quick Search

1. Type in the value you want to search for in the Search box on the status bar.

Replacing Data

1. Click on the Replace button in the Find group of the ribbon Home tab.

2. Enter the Find What data.

3. Enter the Replace With data.

4. Make selections from various options and check boxes.

5. Click the Find Next button or use the ENTER key to activate the find and replace. The first matching data will be highlighted.

6. Select Replace to replace that data and then press the Find Next button. This option will give you the opportunity to confirm each replacement.

   OR

   Choose the Replace All button to replace all occurrences of matching data globally without individual user confirmation.

Using the Spelling Function

1. Open the table in Datasheet view, and position the cursor in the first field of the first record

   OR

   Select the table name in the Navigation Pane.

2. Click the Spelling button in the Records group of the ribbon Home tab.

   The Spelling dialog box opens with the first instance of a word not in the dictionary indicated. Suggestions for replacing the word are presented along with buttons to ignore the word, change all occurrences, or to add it to the custom dictionary.

3. Click on the word or button of your choice.

4. Continue checking the spelling of all words in the table. Access will tell you when it has completed the process.

Importing Data from Another Access Database

1. Open the database file into which the data will be imported, or create a new one.

2. Click on the External tab of the ribbon, and then click on the Access button in the Import group. The Get External Data dialog box opens.

3. Specify the data source by clicking on the Browse button and finding the correct folder in the File Open dialog box.

4. Verify that the Files of Type box says "Microsoft Office Access." Select the name of the database, and make sure the name appears in the File Name box.

5. Click on the Open button. The File Open dialog box closes.

6. Click on the OK button in the Get External Data dialog box. The Import Objects dialog box opens.

7. Select the table to import or use the Select All button to choose all objects in a specific category.

8. Use the Options button to further define the importing procedure if necessary. The table can be imported with its design or just the data can be imported.

9. Click the OK button to import, and then click Close to finish the process. The imported object will be displayed in the object list.

Importing Data from Excel

1. Open the database into which you want to import the spreadsheet.

2. Select the External tab on the ribbon, and click on the Excel button in the Import group.

3. Select the name and location of the spreadsheet by clicking on the Browse button and choosing the folder and file name in the File Open dialog box. Click Open to return to the Get External Data dialog box.

4. Click on the OK button. The Import Spreadsheet wizard opens.

5. Choose the worksheet name, and then click on the Next button.

6. The second page of the wizard opens. If the spreadsheet has column headings that can be used for field names, select the check box for First Row Contains Column Headings. If not, leave it unchecked.

7. Click the Next button. The upper area of the window changes. If you want to change the name or data type of a column, change the selections in the Field Options area.

8. Click the Next button. The next screen appears for selecting the primary key. Click on the button to either let Access add a primary key, choose your own primary key, or not designate a primary key.

9. Click the Next button. The last screen appears. Specify the name of the table.

10. Click the Finish button and choose to either save or not save the steps.

Importing Data from a Text File

1. Open the database into which you want to import the text.

2. Select the External tab on the ribbon, and click on the Text File button in the Import group.

3. Select the name and location of the file by clicking on the Browse button, and choosing the folder and file name in the File Open dialog box. Click Open to return to the Get External Data dialog box.

4. Click on the OK button. The Import Text wizard opens.

5. Choose the format: Delimited or Fixed Width, and then click on the Next button.

6. The second page of the wizard opens. If the text file is delimited, select the delimiter. If it's fixed width, adjust the field widths.

7. If you are appending data to an existing table, skip to step 9

   OR

   Click the Next button. The data is shown in columns. If you want to change the name or data type of a column, change the selections in the Field Options area.

8. Click the Next button. The next screen appears for selecting the primary key. Click on the button to either let Access add a primary key, choose your own primary key, or not designate a primary key.

9. Click the Next button. The last screen appears. Specify the name of the table.

10. Click the Finish button and choose to either save or not save the steps.

Importing Data from Other File Types

1. Open the database into which you want to import the file.

2. Select the External tab on the ribbon, and click on the More button in the Import group.

3. Choose the file type from the list.

4. Select the name and location of the file by clicking on the Browse button, and choosing the folder and file name in the File Open dialog box. Click Open to return to the Get External Data dialog box.

5. Click on the OK button. Click the Finish button, and choose to either save or not save the steps.

   The new table will have the same name as the data source file.

Linking Tables

1. Open the database file into which you want to place the linked table.

2. Select the External tab on the ribbon, and click on the Access button in the Import group.

3. Select the source database file name and location containing the table to link, by clicking on the Browse button.

4. Select the option to "Link to the data source by creating a linked table." Click OK. The Link Tables dialog box opens.

5. Select the table you wish to link and click the OK button. The linked table from the external source will be displayed as a table in the destination database, with an arrow before the table name to show that it is an external linked object.

Refreshing Table Links

1. Open the database file containing the links.

2. Select the Database Tools tab on the ribbon and click on the Linked Table Manager button. The Linked Table Manager dialog box opens.

3. Click in the check box preceding each table name that needs to be refreshed, and click on the OK button. A window opens for you to select the location.

4. Select the location and database file name, then click the Open button. A message appears confirming that the links were refreshed.

5. Close the Linked Table Manager window.

Sorting on One Field

1. Open the table in the Datasheet view.

2. Click in the field to be sorted.

3. Click on the ascending or descending Sort button in the Sort & Filter group on the ribbon Home tab

OR

Right-click and select either Sort A–Z or Sort Z–A from the shortcut menu.

Sorting on Multiple Fields

1. Open the table in the Datasheet view. The primary sort field must appear to the left of the secondary sort field. If this is not the case, move the primary sort field to the left of the secondary sort field.

2. Select the fields for the multiple sort by clicking on the top row of the table—the row containing the names of the fields. Drag the mouse pointer across both the primary sort field and the secondary sort field names.

3. Click the Sort button (ascending or descending). Both levels of sorting are done simultaneously.

Moving a Field in Design View

1. Open the table in Design view.

2. Click the left mouse button in the gray row selector box to select the field you want to move.

3. Click the left mouse button and drag the field to the new location. A faint outline of a rectangle will move with the cursor arrow. Release the mouse button.

4. Save the table with the changes.

Moving a Field in Datasheet View

1. Open the table in Datasheet view.

2. Select the entire field by clicking the left mouse button on the field name. The entire column will be highlighted.

3. Click on the field name and drag the field (column) to the new location. A faint outline of a rectangle will follow the cursor arrow. A heavy black line will appear on the side of the column to indicate where the moved column will be inserted.

4. Release the mouse button to drop the field in the new location.

5. Save the table with the changes.

Filtering by Selection

1. Open the table in the Datasheet view.

2. Select the value to be matched. It can either be a whole field or any part of a field.

3. Select the Home tab on the ribbon. Click the Selection button in the Sort & Filter group

   OR

   Click the right mouse button and choose one of the filtering options from the lower portion of the shortcut menu.

Removing All Filters

1. In the Sort & Filter group on the ribbon, click on the Toggle Filter button

   OR

   In the status bar, click on the Filtered icon

   OR

   To permanently clear all filters, click on the Advanced button in the Sort & Filter group, and choose Clear All Filters from the menu.

Removing the Filter from One Field

1. Click on the field filter icon to the right of the field name to clear

   OR

   Right-click on any data in the field filter to clear.

2. Select the Clear Filter From Field command from the shortcut menu.

Filtering by Form

1. Open the table in Datasheet view.

2. Display an empty record by clicking on the Advanced button in the Sort & Filter group on the ribbon, and selecting Filter By Form.

   The Filter By Form window opens.

3. Click on the field to enter the filter criteria.

4. Specify the criteria:

   Select from the drop-down list

   OR

   Type in the criteria.

5. Click on the Toggle Filter button on the ribbon or select Apply Filter/Sort from the advanced menu.

Printing Filter Results

1. Click the Print button on the Quick Access toolbar after the filter has been applied and the results are displayed on the screen

   OR

   Select the Print command from the Office menu.

Adding a Field in Design View

1. Open the table in the Design view.

2. Click in the field below where the new field will be. The new field will be inserted above this field.

3. Click the right mouse button to display the shortcut menu, then select Insert Rows from the shortcut menu

OR

Select the Design tab on the ribbon, and click on the Insert Rows button in the Tools group.

4. Add the field name, data type, description (optional), and any field properties.

5. Save the table again to make sure the changes are saved. If you try to leave this screen without saving first, Access will prompt you to save the changes.

Adding a Field in Datasheet View

1. Open the table in Datasheet view.

2. Select the entire column to the right of the location where the new field will be inserted.

3. Select the Datasheet tab on the ribbon, and click on the Insert button in the Fields & Columns group

OR

Click the right mouse button to bring up the shortcut menu. Choose the Insert Column command.

Renaming Fields in Datasheet View

1. Select the entire field.

2. Select the Datasheet tab on the ribbon, and click on the Rename button

OR

Right-click on the field, and from the shortcut menu, choose the Rename Column command.

3. Type in the new field name.

Deleting a Field in Design View

1. Open the table in Design view.

2. Click in the field selector area to the left of the field you want to delete.

3. Select the Design tab on the ribbon, and click on the Delete Rows button in the Tools group

OR

Click the right mouse button to open the shortcut menu, then choose the Delete Rows command

OR

Press the ⌈DELETE⌋ key on the keyboard.

4. A dialog box will appear on the screen asking for confirmation of the delete operation. Choose the Yes button to confirm this operation or the No button to cancel the operation. The deletion can be reversed at this point by using the Undo Delete command from the Edit menu.

5. Save the file again to make the changes permanent.

Deleting a Field in Datasheet View

1. Open the table in Datasheet view.

2. Select the column to delete by clicking the field name at the top of the column.

3. Select the Datasheet tab on the ribbon, and click on the Delete button in the Fields & Columns group

   OR

   Use the right mouse button to display the shortcut menu, then choose the Delete Column command

   OR

   Press the ⌊DELETE⌋ key on the keyboard.

4. Confirm the deletion by clicking on the Yes button in the Confirmation dialog box. The new column will disappear from the table. The data associated with this column (field) will also be deleted.

5. Save these new changes to the design of the table.

Setting Captions

1. Open the table in Design view.

2. Click on the field to be assigned a caption.

3. Click on the Caption line in the Field Properties window.

4. Add text for the caption.

5. Save changes to the table.

Deleting a Table

1. In the Navigation Pane click on the name of table to delete.

2. Using the right mouse button, choose the Delete command from the shortcut menu

   OR

   Press the ⌊DELETE⌋ key on the keyboard.

3. Confirm the deletion.

Renaming a Table

1. Select the table you want to rename in the Navigation Pane.

2. Click on the right mouse button and choose the Rename command from the shortcut menu.

3. Type in the new name or edit the previous name, and press the ⌊ENTER⌋ key.

Creating a Relationship Between Two Tables

1. Select the Database Tools tab on the ribbon, and click on the Relationships button in the Show/Hide group.

2. The Relationships window opens showing each table in the database. If all tables are not displayed, click on the Show Table button in the Relationships group on the ribbon, and select the tables to display.

3. Click on the linking field in the first table shown in the Relationships window. Drag that field to the matching field in the next table. This will probably be the primary key all of the first table being dragged onto the foreign key in the second table.

4. The Edit Relationships dialog box appears asking for confirmation of this procedure. Notice the relationship type at the bottom of this dialog box indicating the type of relationship created.

5. Click on the Create button. Notice the dark line drawn between the linked tables.

6. Save the changes to the database.

Deleting Relationships

1. Click on the Relationships button on the Database Tools tab of the ribbon.

   The Relationships window will display the links between the tables.

2. Click on the heavy line (link) that you wish to delete.

3. Press the DELETE key on the keyboard

   OR

   Right-click on the line and select Delete from the shortcut menu.

   A dialog box will appear asking for confirmation of this operation.

4. Choose Yes. The relationship will be broken.

Review Questions

1. Where in a table are new records added?

2. What makes the replace command so powerful?

3. Can a deleted record be restored to a table?

4. Which buttons on the ribbon are used for copying and moving data? Which ribbon tab and which group are they in?

5. What command can you use to restore previous data if you make an editing mistake?

6. Why must a primary key be unique?

7. Can data from one Access database be imported into another Access database?

8. What's the difference between importing and linking a table?

9. Should an ascending or descending sort be used on a Price field of a table to show records with the highest priced item first?

10. Are sorts performed in the Datasheet or Design view?

11. Which records or fields are shown in a filter result?

12. Can you apply both a sort and a filter at the same time?

13. Name three things that can be changed to restructure a table's design.

14. Does adding a caption change the name of a field?

15. Which type of relationship between tables is most common?

16. Can two tables in a database have the same name?

17. Does the common field used to join multiple tables have to have the same name in each table?

18. What happens when you click on the Relationships button on the ribbon?

19. Can a deleted table be restored to a database?

20. What is rich text and how can it be stored in a memo field?

21. What's the easiest way to enter a date value into a field?

22. What does the Refresh button do?

23. What is a delimited text file?

24. Which Microsoft Office application is the easiest to import data from?

Exercises

Exercise 1—Review and Guided Practice

ACTIVITY

Use the *SDAL_Ch3* database.

Exercise 1A: Getting Data into the Tables

1. Type the following data into *tblCategory*:

CategoryID	CategoryName
CN	Country
DS	Disco
DW	DooWop
EL	Easy Listening
JZ	Jazz
RK	Rock

2. Type the following data into *tblRecordLabels*:

LabelNumber	LabelName
1	Columbia
2	Decca
3	Island
4	A & M
5	Interscope

3. To get *tblArtists* data:

   a. Import the table *tblBands* from the *Practice_Ch3* database.
   b. Delete the table *tblArtists*.
   c. Rename *tblBands* as *tblArtists*.

4. Import the data from the file *Media.txt* into *tblMedia*. The data is delimited by commas.

5. Import the data from the Excel spreadsheet *MusicAlbums.xls* into *tblRecordings*.

   a. Change the data type of the field *Label* in *tblRecordings* to a lookup field that gets its data from *tblRecordLabels*.

6. Import the data from the HTML document called *Inventory.html* into *tblInventory*.

   a. Add the following note to the *Notes* field in *tblInventory*, for the album "A Date With Elvis": This CD was once owned by Lisa Marie Presley. Format the text "Lisa Marie Presley" as bold and italic.

Exercise 1B: Creating Relationships

1. Display all six tables in the Relationships window.

2. Notice that the tables *tblRecordings* and *tblRecordLabels* are already joined. Why do you think this is? (Refer to Exercise 1A, step 5.)

3. Make the following joins:

   a. Join *tblInventory* and *tblRecordings* on the *MusicID* field.

   b. Join *tblInventory* and *tblMedia* on the *MediaType* field.

   c. Join *tblRecordings* and *tblCategory* on the *CategoryID* field.

   d. Join *tblRecordings* and *tblArtists* on the *ArtistID* field.

4. Change the data type of the field *Category* in *tblRecordings* to a lookup field that gets its data from *tblCategory*. Start the Lookup wizard and see what happens. You'll have to go back into the Relationship window and remove the join between these two tables first.

Exercise 1C: Creating Information

1. Open *tblInventory* in Datasheet view.

2. Add a total row, and average the prices of the items. What is the average price?

3. Sort into groups by media type, and alphabetize by title within those groupings. What's the first item in the list?

4. Filter the list down to show only those items with a quantity on hand of five or more. How many items are in the list now? What's the average price now?

5. What's the average price of an LP (long playing vinyl)?

6. How many LPs are in the store? (Sum the field *Quantity*.)

7. Open *tblRecordings* in Datasheet view.

8. How many disco albums are on file?

9. Each record in *tblRecordings* has a subdatasheet showing data from *tblInventory*. Open the subdatasheet for the "Best of the Monkees" album. Add a total row to the subdatasheet that displays the average price and the sum of the field *Quantity*. How many copies of this album are there in the store? What's their average price?

10. How many copies of "At Folsom Prison" are there in the store? What's their average price? How many CDs of "At Folsom Prison" are there in the store?

ACTIVITY

Exercise 2—Practicing New Procedures

Exercise 2A: Creating a Database

1. Create a new database called *Cruises_Ch3*.

2. Import the table *tblCruises* from the *Practice_Ch3* database. This is an empty table.

3. Import the data from the Excel spreadsheet *Cruise List.xls* into *tblCruises*.

Exercise 2B: Adding, Deleting, and Updating Records

1. Change the *Destination* field of record #2 to "Acapulco".

2. Change the departure dates on records #3 and #10 to June 1st.

3. Add the following record to the table:

   The Marvel Cruise Lines ship Mermaid will leave on June 15th from San Diego to Costa Rica for 14 days. The regular price is $4500 with eight seats left, and first class is $6600 with six seats left. Airfare is included.

4. Delete record #7.

5. Marvel Cruise Lines has changed its name to Calypso Cruises. Change the name in all records using one command.

Exercise 2C: Filtering and Sorting

1. Sort the records in date order from latest to the earliest departure date, and set a filter to show only seven-day cruises. Print the records. Remove the filter.

2. Sort the records in order by first class available seats, showing the cruise with the most available first. Set a filter that shows the cruises leaving from Miami that have at least 10 first class fares left. Print the records. Remove the filter.

3. Display only the cruises that include airfare.

Exercise 3—In-Class Group Practice

ACTIVITY AND
REFLECTION

Part 1

Divide into four groups as determined by your instructor. Each group will do one of the problems below. Use the *Cruise* database from Exercise 2. If you did not complete Exercise 2, create a new database called *Cruises*, and import the table *tblCruises* from the *Practice_Ch3* database. This is an empty table. Import the data from the Excel spreadsheet *Cruise List.xls* into *tblCruises*.

Group 1—Importing Data

1. Add the data from the text file *Vacations.txt* to *tblCruises*. The data in the text file is delimited by commas. Append the records to *tblCruises* at the same time as you import them. What happens?

2. Delete the erroneous records and try again. Import the data into a new table called *tblVacations*, let Access add a primary key, and then use the Clipboard to copy the records to *tblCruises*. Did this work?

3. Import the table *tblTours* from the database *Practice_Ch3*. Now, copy the records from *tblTours* to *tblCruises*. Did this work?

4. Print the records in *tblCruises*.

Group 2—Changing Table Structure

1. Would it be possible to calculate the end date of each cruise with the existing data? (Don't try to calculate it; you don't know how yet.)

What field property of *Length* needs to be changed in order to perform a calculation?

2. Make the change determined above. What happens when you go back to the Datasheet view? (Save the table, but do NOT proceed past the error message.) Why do you think the error occurred? Change the Data type back to text, or exit Design view without saving the table.

3. Go to Datasheet view and replace all occurrences of the word "days" with a blank.

4. Now change the Data type back to numeric. Did it work this time?

Group 3—Retrieving Information

1. Add a Total row to *tblCruises*. Use the Total row to determine:

a. What is the earliest departure date for a cruise?

b. What is the average first class fare? Average regular fare?

    c. What's the total number of first class seats available on all cruises? What's the total number of regular seats available?

    d. How many cruises include airfare?

2. If you wanted to travel on the ship Bahia, which cruise has the most available total seats? Use a filter to help find the answer.

3. Which cruise has the most expensive first class fare? Sort the records to help find the answer.

4. What's the average regular fare for a seven-day cruise to Puerto Rico?

Group 4—Setting a Relationship and Splitting a Table

1. Create a new table called *tblCruiseCompany*. Create an autonumber primary key. Add the following records:

    a. Adventure Cruises, 123 SeaShell Lane, Bay City, FL, 12222

    b. Calypso Cruises, 4908 South Harbor Drive, Shell City, CA, 92222

    c. Coracel Cruises, 87 Yacht Club Road, Miami, FL, 13333

    d. Getaway Cruises, 34127 West Spinnaker Street, San Diego, CA, 93333

2. Make a copy of *tblCruises* and call it *tblCruises2*. Create a lookup field in *tblCruises* that looks up the cruise company name in *tblCruiseCompany*. Why did the data in the *Company Name* field disappear? Use *tblCruises2* (the copy of the table) to add the company data back into *tblCruises*.

3. Import *tblPassengers* into the database from the *Practice_Ch3* database.

4. Open *tblPassengers* in Design view and make the *Cruise ID* a lookup field into *tblCruises*. Display the ship name in *tblPassengers* in the lookup field. Why was none of the data lost this time when creating the lookup field?

5. Open *tblCruiseCompany* and display the subdatasheet for *tblCruises*. You can also open a subdatasheet in *tblCruises* to see a passenger list.

6. Check the Relationships window and make sure the three tables *tblCruises*, *tblCruiseCompany*, and *tblPassengers* are all joined. Join them, if they aren't, and save the relationship window on closing.

Part 2

Form new teams composed of one person from each group in Part 1, so that each new team has one member from old group 1, 2, 3, and 4. Each team member is now a specialist in one or more aspects of using a table. Let the experts in the group show the others members how to do the following tasks:

1. Create a new database called *Swimwear* and import the tables *tblSwimwear* and *tblVendors* from the database *Practice_Ch3*.

2. Import the data from *Swimwear.xls*, an Excel spreadsheet, and append it to *tblSwimwear*.

3. Change the name of the field *Style* to *Bikini*, and make it a Yes/No field. Make a copy of *tblSwimwear* first, just in case it doesn't work the first time. Be sure all the data is retained in the field.

4. Make the field *Company* in *tblSwimwear* a lookup field that looks up *VendorID* in *tblVendors*. Again, retain all the data.

5. Change the field *Last Order Date* to a Date data type. Preserve all the data.

6. Change the field *Quantity* in *tblSwimwear* to a numeric field. Preserve all the data.

7. Add a Total row and calculate the following:

    a. The average cost of a suit.

    b. The total number of suits on hand.

    c. The date of the most recent order.

8. How many red suits are in the stock? Does it matter if red is in all capital letters or not?

9. What is the average cost of a small black bikini?

10. What's the most expensive blue suit in stock?

Exercise 4—Critical Thinking: Updating and Organizing Tables

ACTIVITY

Create a new database called *Birds* and import *tblBirds* in from the *Practice_Ch3* database. This is the log of a bird watcher.

1. Add a total row to *tblBirds*.

2. Set a filter that shows only those birds seen in Brown's Canyon. Show the total number of birds seen. Print and label the filtered records. Remove the filter.

3. Set a filter that shows all sightings of hawks (all kinds). Print and label the filtered records. Remove the filter.

4. Set a filter to determine where great blue herons have been seen. Print and label the filtered records.

5. Set a filter to determine where western tanagers have been seen. Print and label the filtered records.

6. Replace all occurrences of "Spruce Creek" with "Little Spruce Creek."

7. Add the following records:

    4 grosbeaks spotted at Crystal River on 7/17/09

    18 mallards seen at Talamas Reservoir on 7/20/09

8. Set a filter that shows all sightings of eagles (all kinds) at Talamas Reservoir. Print and label the filtered records. Remove the filter.

9. Delete the record for spotting the nighthawk at Talamas Reservoir.

10. Set a filter that shows all sightings of all eagles and hawks made before May 1, 2009. Print and label the filtered records. Remove the filter.

11. Sort the records in ascending date order. Print and label the sorted records.

12. Which bird was seen in the largest quantity? (Hint: Use Sort.) Print and label the sorted records.

13. Which location seems to be the worst place for bird watching? Print and label the sorted records.

14. Which birds have been seen least? Print and label the sorted records.

15. Import *tblBirdwatchers* from the *Practice_Ch3* database.

16. Assign any person in *tblBirdwatchers* to each record in *tblBirds* by creating a lookup field in *tblBirds*.

17. Sort the records in *tblBirds* in order by *Location* and *Date Seen*.

18. Print and label the sorted records.

ACTIVITY AND
REFLECTION

Exercise 5—Discussion Questions

1. Can you import data from another database, and append the records to an existing table? Can you only import to a new table? What is another way to append records to an existing table?

2. You are responsible for a hypothetical *tblSales* table containing all sales transactions for your company. You only want to keep the records from the past year in the table, so you want to move old records to an archive table once a month.

   a. Can you copy just the structure of the *tblSales* table to create the empty archive table? If so, how?

   b. List the steps needed to perform the monthly archiving procedure.

3. You are responsible for the personnel database for your company. The tables in this database contain employee information: personal data, such as name and address; job-related data, such as position name and pay rate; and benefit data, such as sick leave accrued, vacation taken, and health insurance coverage.

   a. What are your recommendations for making backups of the database? How much is backed up and how often?

   b. What do you suggest should be done with records of employees who leave the company?

4. What can you generalize about changing the data type of a text field to numeric? How does it depend on whether or not the values in the field include letters of the alphabet?

5. What's the easiest way to make the following updates to a table?

   a. Add 20 records from the same city and state.

   b. Change a text field into a lookup field that looks up data in an autonumber ID in another table?

6. Is it acceptable to change the data type of a primary key? Why or why not? How about changing the name of a primary key?

CASE STUDY A: MRS. SUGARBAKER'S COOKIES

Entering the Data

1. Enter the data into the tables. Some of the data is stored in existing files. Other data should be manually entered.

2. The existing data is stored in the following files in the *Case Study A* folder:

   - Order data is stored in an Excel file called *Orders.xls*.
   - Product data is stored in a Word file called *Valued Customer.doc*.
   - Payment data is stored in a dBase 5 file called *Payments.dbf*.

Need More Help?

   - You will have to type in the *tblCustomer* data. Refer to Figure 1.48 for the customer data.
   - Product data can be appended to the table by copying it from *Valued Customer.doc* and appending it to the table.

- *tblOrders* and *tblOrder Items* are imported from the Excel file, but the data will have to be split into two tables after importing.

- Import the data from the *Payments.dbf* file into its own table.

Controlling Data Entry

In order to keep the data in your tables consistent and accurate, it may be necessary to add validation controls. To determine whether or not controls are needed, you should examine each table for fields that contain critical data. Two good examples that often need validation controls are primary keys and common fields. Primary keys must contain unique data in every record and common fields must have the same data entered in all tables that will be joined.

Sometimes it is not critical but rather merely helpful to add controlling properties to fields. In the case of a table containing addresses, state data can be forced into the format of two uppercase letters. If most records contain a specific value in a field, that data can already be entered as a default. These controls make data entry easier and faster.

1. Review the table structure and field data in all the tables you have already created for Mrs. Sugarbaker.

2. Check the primary keys in all tables to make sure they are required and indexed.

3. Set field length for all fields to an appropriate length.

4. Make dollar amounts display as currency.

5. Create captions for any fields whose names are unclear.

6. Set input masks on any primary keys that are not completely numeric. Force data to be entered in uppercase or lowercase for consistency.

7. Set default values where appropriate.

8. Create lookup fields wherever possible.

Need More Help?

- *tblOrder Items* has a multiple-field primary key. Click on the first field and shift click on the second field before clicking on the Primary Key button. Also, set the properties of these fields to be required but not indexed.

- Captions might be used for name and city data.

- Consider setting a default value for the field *Freight Charges*.

- Lookup fields can be created for the following: *tblOrders*—Customer name, *tblOrderItems*—order number and product name, *tblPayments*—Customer name

Defining Relationships

Relational databases usually have many tables because data grouped into a single table is often separated into two or more tables after the normalization process is complete. These tables need to be joined to display and print the information the users require. There are three steps needed to define a relationship between two tables:

1. Identify the common field between the two tables.

2. Check that the common field has the same data type in both tables.

3. Join the tables on the common field.

It is helpful to think about the one-to-many relationship as the table joins are created. Which table has a different value in the common field for each record? This is the "one" table. Which table has the same value occurring multiple times in the common field? This is the "many" table.

If you create lookup fields, relationships between tables are created automatically.

Review the tables in the Sugarbaker database to determine the common fields and their place in the one-to-many relationship scheme. Check the Relationships window to see what joins have already been created by using lookup fields. Drag a table name from the Navigation Pane to the Relationships window, if the table doesn't already appear there. Rather than create a join in the Relationships window, consider making a lookup field. Lookup fields can only be created on un-joined tables.

CASE STUDY B: SANDY FEET RENTAL COMPANY

The Sandy Feet Rental Company (SFRC) is about ready to start using the new database system. They have data scattered in different files and formats but want to enter that data into the new database. Even though there are common amenities available for all properties at the resort, SFRC wants that data incorporated into the database so that it can be used in various reports and forms.

Because Access is a relational database, SFRC wants to be sure that data from all tables is easily accessible. That means making sure the tables are properly related on common fields.

Entering Data

1. The *tblRentalTransactions* does not have any data in it. The data is now in the *RentalTransaction.txt* file. Import the data from the text file into the *tblRentalTransactions* table.

2. Import the data from the *Clients.xlsx* into the *tblClients* table.

3. Import the data from the *Owners.accdb* into the *tblOwners* table.

4. Check the tables to be sure that

   a. All the data was imported from the source files.

   b. The fields are of the proper data type.

   c. There is a key field in each table.

5. Create a table to hold the amenities data.

   a. Enter the data from Chapter 1 identifying each amenity as a separate field.

   b. Which data type would be appropriate for these fields?

   c. Identify the key field for this table.

Creating the Table Relationships

1. Create the relationships between the tables.

   a. Look for one-to-many relationships using the key field from one table and the foreign key field in the other table.

   b. All tables should join to at least one other table.

CASE STUDY C: PENGUINS SKI CLUB

Importing Data and Checking Tables

1. You should have five or six tables in the *Penguins* database created in Chapter 2. Import the following data into these tables.

   a. *Attendance.xls*, another spreadsheet, has the data about event attendance.

   b. *Attendance.xls*, another spreadsheet, has the data about event attendance.

    c. *Events.txt* is a delimited text file that contains the event calendar.

    d. The HTML file *EquipmentRental.html* has all the equipment rental records.

    e. Payment data is in another database—*Payments.accdb*.

2. Check to see that all the primary keys are designated and working properly. Make sure that all lookup fields are operational.

3. Open the Relationships window. *tblMembers* should be joined to all tables except *tblEvents*.

Retrieving Information

1. Add a Total row to *tblMembers*. Using statistics from this row, answer the following questions:

    a. How many beginners are in the club?

    b. What's the average age of the beginners?

    c. How many beginners are renting equipment?

    d. In what city do all the advanced skiers live?

    e. What's the average age of the advanced skiers?

2. Add a Total row to *tblAttendance*. Count how many members are attending each event.

3. Use *tblEquipmentRental* to determine how many people rented equipment on 11/14/08.

4. Use *tblEquipmentRental* to determine what the latest rental date was, and who rented on that date.

5. Use *tblPayments* to find out which members have made multiple payments.

6. How much money will be collected from member fees this year?

Chapter

Queries

Objectives

After completing this chapter you will be able to

Understand what a query is:
- Define a query.
- Identify query types.
- Define criteria.
- Understand what a dynaset is.

Define query input:
- Add tables to the Query Design.
- Enter fields from one or multiple tables into the Design grid.
- Move, insert, and delete fields.

Define query criteria:
- Enter single and multiple criteria in the Design grid.
- Perform operations such as sorting, using show/hide fields, and entering common operators.

Perform simple queries:
- Create a new query.
- Distinguish between the Datasheet and Design views.
- Save the query.
- Exit Query Design.

Perform total queries:
- Define a group for subtotaling.
- Display the total row.
- Add totaling options.

Perform queries on multiple tables:
- Link two or more tables.
- Add fields from multiple tables.

Dictionary

Action query	Performs some action on data in a table.
Criteria	Limiting descriptors or conditions placed on fields that define the records to be included in the query.
Concatenate	Joining two text strings (fields) together to make a new field.
Crosstab query	Displays summary data in spreadsheet format.
Datasheet view	The window that displays the results of the query (the dynaset).
Design grid	The lower pane of the query design window which displays the fields, criteria and other elements of the design.
Dynaset	The set of records produced by the query.
Operator	Mathematical, relational, logical, and string commands used to extend or limit the criteria.

Query	Questions asked of a table (or tables) to obtain specific information. A query limits information to records that match specific criteria.
Query Design view	The view that allows the user to create the query.
Select query	Selects information from one or more tables based on criteria typed into the Query Design window.
SQL	Structured Query Language, a standard language used by many database software packages.
Table pane	The upper pane of the Query Design window that displays the data source(s) for the query (tables and/or queries).
Top(N)	Used in Query Design to limit the records displayed to a specified number or percentage.
Totals row	An additional row added to the Design grid for performing summarizing functions on defined groups of data.

4.1 Defining a Query

A database file can hold vast amounts of data stored in tables. As seen in the previous chapter, data can be edited, sorted, and filtered, but the resulting data is limited in usefulness as it is not stored. Queries are questions asked of a table, multiple tables, or other queries to obtain specific information that can be saved as a database object. A query extracts only certain records as defined by the criteria or conditions set by the user. When the query is run, the output is defined as the dynaset.

Queries are used as the data source for reports, forms, other tables, and queries. Queries can also perform calculations, summarize data, combine data from multiple sources, add, edit or delete records, and perform other database maintenance functions. Queries can be very simple or extremely complex using one table or several related tables.

Queries provide the answers to questions you have about the data in your database. For example, you might want to know which customers have not ordered from your company in the past year. The tables containing the customer data and order data from the past year are the data sources for this query. These two tables must be properly joined. The criterion is "no orders placed in the last year"; however, this criterion must be expressed using the fields in the tables which hold this data. The query produces a list of customers that can be printed or displayed on the screen, saved or used to produce letters, labels, or other output products.

How carefully a query is designed and run will affect the quality and validity of the information produced. If the query is incorrectly designed, the result will display inaccurate or incomplete information.

Types of Queries

There are several different types of queries which perform different actions on the tables. The Select query retrieves specific information from table data based on specified criteria. An Action query performs an action on a table such as deleting groups of records or creating a table from a group of records. An SQL query performs specialized processing on data and is written in SQL (Structured Query Language). The Specialized queries are designed for special purposes such as summarizing data in a spreadsheet format (Crosstab).

4.2 Creating a Simple Select Query

The input to a query is data from tables or other queries. This data is turned into information by applying criteria that mask out unwanted data and produce a dynaset. The dynaset is the result of the query and can be displayed or printed. The entire query can be saved so that the dynaset can be re-created at any time.

Let's start by creating a query from a single table in a database file that is already open. We will use Query Design rather than Query Wizard.

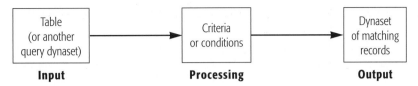

Figure 4.1 The query process

TRY IT YOURSELF 4.2.1

A. Open the *G3_Ch4.accdb* database file.

B. Create a query with the Query Design command.

C. Add the *tblBuyers* table (see Figures 4.2–4.4).

This activity continues in Try It Yourself 4.2.2.

How to Create a Query

1. Click the Create tab.

2. In the Other group, click the Query Design command (see Figure 4.2).

3. The Show Table dialog box appears (see Figure 4.3).

4. Choose the table(s) to be included in the query.

5. Click the Add button to add the tables to the Query Design. Click the Close button.

Sometimes you may find that you've added a table to the query twice. If this happens, click anywhere in the Table box in the upper area of the screen, the Table pane area (see Figure 4.4), and press the [DELETE] key. The table is easily removed. To add a table after closing the Show Table dialog box, right-click in the Table/Query entry area and select Show Table from the menu or click Show Table in the Query Setup group. The Show Table dialog box will reappear.

Q: How can I delete duplicate source tables in a query?

A: Click anywhere in the table box in the upper screen area, and press the [DELETE] key.

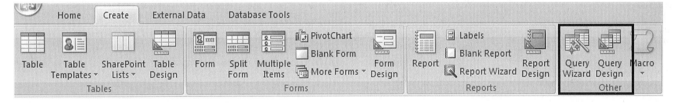

Figure 4.2 Creating a new query with Query Design

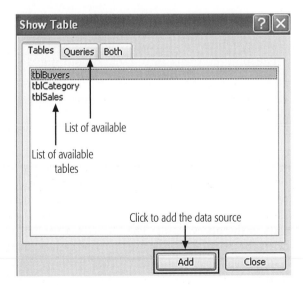

Figure 4.3 Show Table dialog box

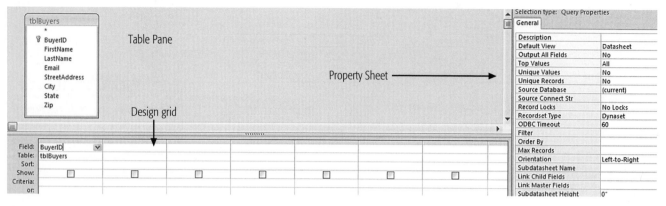

Figure 4.4 Query Design view

Examining the Query Design Window

After the data source for the query has been specified (either a table, multiple tables, or other queries), a Query Design window appears (see Figure 4.4).

There are two views for working with queries—the Design view and the Datasheet view. The Design view allows the user to carefully create the query, by specifying the records and fields to be included. The Datasheet view displays the dynaset, or set of records requested from the query criteria.

The Query Design window is divided into two sections—the Table pane and the Query Design grid (see Figure 4.4). The Table pane contains the names of the tables or queries and all their fields which will be used as input for the query. The Design grid is a display of columns and rows used to contain the fields and criteria of the query. Each column in the Design grid displays a single selected field and criteria for that field (if they exist). The field names appear across the top row.

The query document tab above the Table pane displays the name of the query. The default names queries as *Query1* and succeeding numbers until the query is saved with the name you select.

A dividing bar separates the two sections of the screen. This bar can be used to resize each section.

How to Resize the Design Window

1. Click the left mouse button on the dividing bar between the two sections and hold the mouse button down. The pointer turns into a dark pointing double arrow.

2. Drag the bar either up or down to reduce or enlarge the upper and lower panes.

The Query Design Ribbon

The Query Tools Design ribbon displays groups and commands used in designing and running queries. The Results group shows commands that change the query view and run the query. The Query Type group shows commands for creating different types of queries. The Query Setup group provides tools to edit the query design add additional data sources and limit the number of records in the query result. The Show/Hide group provides commands to add the Total row to the query design (summary functions), display the Table Names in the design grid, change query properties and create a Parameter query (see Figure 4.5).

Figure 4.5 Query Tools Design ribbon

Adding Fields to the Design Grid

Keep the end result in mind wnen selecting the fields for the Design grid. These fields will be included in the dynaset, and can be used to build criteria that will limit or define its scope. Queries are based on criteria, or conditions that are applied to the data held in particular fields of the table. It is important to choose the fields from the table that will produce the desired information. If the query fields are chosen incompletely or inaccurately, the resulting dynaset will be incomplete or inaccurate.

If you are unsure which fields to include, begin by including them all. You can remove them later or suppress their display in the dynaset.

Fields can be added to the Query Design in four ways. The method you choose is not as important as adding the correct fields. See Figure 4.6 for illustrations of each method.

How to Add a Field

Double-click on the desired field in the Table pane. This field will be entered into the field box of the first column in the Design grid

OR

Click on the desired field in the Table pane. Drag and drop the field icon to the Field box in a column

OR

Click in the empty field box. Click on the arrow at the right side of the Field box. Choose the desired Field from the drop-down list (see Figure 4.6)

Q: How do I add a field to a query?

A: Either
1. Double-click on a field name.
2. Click a field name and drag to a field box.
3. Choose a field from the drop-down list.
4. Type the field name in the field box.
Remember that "*" is not a field name; clicking it will add all fields.

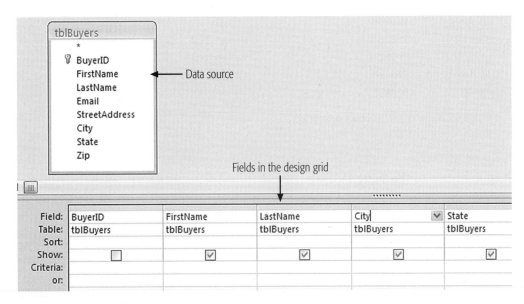

Figure 4.6 Adding fields to the Design grid

OR

Click in the empty Field box in the Design grid. Type in the field name when you see the cursor. You must be exact in typing the field name.

Q: If I use the * All Fields symbol, can I add any criteria to those fields?

A: No. To add criteria to a field, that field must be individually added to the Design grid.

How to Add All Fields from a Table

The asterisk (*) at the top of the table field list or the drop-down list is the "all fields" symbol (see Figure 4.6).

1. Add all the fields from the table to your query by treating the asterisk like any other field name and using one of the methods for adding fields described above

   OR

   Double click on the title bar of the table field list (see Figure 4.6). All fields are selected.

2. Drag selected fields to the leftmost empty column in the Design grid.

When a field name has been entered in the Design grid, all the data from this field will be displayed in the dynaset when the query is run, unless selecting criteria are placed on this field. This means that without criteria, the values contained in all the records will be included in the dynaset.

Q: How do I run a query?

A: Click on the Run button—it looks like an exclamation point (!).

3. Before moving on to determining criteria, decide which other fields should be included in the Query Design to fulfill the purpose of this query. Add these fields in the next columns by any of the methods previously described.

How to Run a Query

1. Click on the Run command in the Results group (see Figure 4.5)

   OR

   Click on the View command and choose Datasheet view (see Figure 4.5).

2. The results of the query (the dynaset) will be displayed in Datasheet view (see Figure 4.7).

FirstName	LastName	City	State
Jadyn	Walker	Toledo	OH
Penny	Stocks	Aspen	CO
Angie	Brown	Indianapolis	IN
Nina	Warren	Carmel	CA
Linda	Ashton	Jacksonville	NC

Figure 4.7 Results (dynaset) of a query

TRY IT YOURSELF 4.2.2

Create a new query using the *tblBuyers* table:

A. Add the fields *BuyersID, FirstName, LastName, City,* and *State.*

B. Run the query. You should see only the data from the fields which you entered into the Design grid (see Figure 4.7).

C. Sort the field *State.*

D. Filter records from CA (see Figure 4.9).

E. Save the query as *qryBuyers.*

How to Return to the Design View

1. Click the View command and choose Design view.

Saving a Query

Once the query has been designed and the correct results obtained, the query can be saved. Access considers a query as another database object such as a table, form, or report. Saved queries will be listed in the Navigation pane when All Access Objects are displayed. Saved queries can be used as the data source for form or report objects.

How to Save the Query (Initial Save)

1. To initially save the query, right click on the query document tab and choose Save from the menu.

2. Name the query with the *qry* prefix.

How to Save a Query with a New Name

1. Click the Office button (see Figure 4.8).

2. Point to Save As.

3. Click on the Save Object As command.

4. Enter the name for the new object.

5. Choose the object type.

6. Click the OK button.

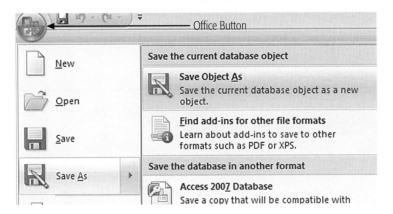

Figure 4.8 Saving the query

Working in Datasheet View

When a query is run, it appears in the Datasheet view which is very similar to the Datasheet View of a table. The same ribbon appears at the top of the screen when a query is shown in this view. Commands from all the groups are available for use on dynaset records.

Query results can be easily sorted or filtered for additional analysis. Formatting can be applied to the displayed records. Commands such as Find and Replace are also available in this view.

Note: The sort and filtered results are not saved with the query design if they are applied in Datasheet view. Therefore, if you want those functions saved with the query, include them within the query design.

How to Sort a Field in the Query Results

1. Click into the field to sort.

2. Click the Sort button on the ribbon, either ascending or descending order

　OR

　Click on the drop-down list to the right of the field name. Choose the sort function.

How to Filter a Query Result in Datasheet View

1. Click into the field cell that contains the data for the filter.

2. Choose the type of filter from the Selection command in the Sort & Filter Group (see Figure 4.9). Click in the check boxes that contain the data to filter

    OR

    Click on the drop-down list to the right of the field name. Click in the check boxes that contain the data to filter. Click OK.

How to Remove the Filter

1. Click the drop-down list to the right of the field name. Choose the Clear Filter command

    OR

    Click the Toggle Filter command in the Sort & Filter group on the ribbon.

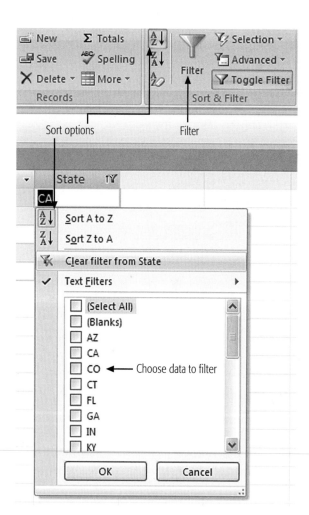

Figure 4.9 Filtering query results

Editing Fields in the Design Grid

The order in which the fields are entered will determine the order the data is displayed in the dynaset. If the fields in the Query Design are not in the order you want, you can move, delete, or insert new fields.

How to Move a Field

1. Select the field to move by clicking on the field selector above the field name. The entire field column will be selected.

2. Click and drag the field column on the field selector and move to the new location (see Figure 4.10).

3. Release the mouse button to drop the field in its new location.

Field:	FirstName	LastName	City	State	BuyerID
Table:	tblBuyers	tblBuyers	tblBuyers	tblBuyers	tblBuyers
Sort:					
Show:	☑	☑	☑	☑	☐
Criteria:					
or:					

Figure 4.10 BuyerID field moved in the Design grid

How to Delete a Field

1. Select the field to be deleted (see Figure 4.11).

2. Press the DELETE key

   OR

   Click the Delete Columns command from the Query Setup group

   OR

   Click the right mouse button to display the shortcut menu. Choose the Cut command.

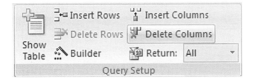

Figure 4.11 Deleting a field from the Design grid

How to Insert a Field

1. Select the field from the table field list in the Table pane.

2. Drag the field to the appropriate position in the Design grid.

3. Drop the field in place by releasing the mouse.

Entering Criteria

The criteria for the query are one of the most significant parts of query design. Field selection determines which fields to include in the dynaset and the criteria chosen on those fields determine which records will be included. Only fields entered into the Design grid can have criteria limitations placed on them.

TRY IT YOURSELF 4.2.3

Using the *qryBuyers* query:

A. Move the *BuyersID* field to the far left in the Design grid (see Figure 4.10).

B. Run the query. You should see the field in its new location.

C. Return to Design view.

D. Save the query.

TRY IT YOURSELF 4.2.4

Using the *qryBuyers* query:

A. Delete the field *FirstName* (see Figure 4.11).

B. Run the query. Verify that the field is deleted.

C. Return to the Design view.

D. Save the query.

TRY IT YOURSELF 4.2.5

Using the *qryBuyers* query:

A. Insert the field *FirstName* back into the first column of the Design grid.

B. Insert the field *Email* between the fields *BuyersID* and *State*.

C. Run the query to verify that the fields are inserted.

D. Return to the Design view.

E. Save the query.

Q: What are criteria?

A: Criteria are the rules used to decide which data is displayed in a query.

The records matching the designated criteria will be displayed in the dynaset. Criteria entry can be as simple as matching one word or character in a field or as complicated as a calculated expression that use predesigned functions. For example, *Status* = "Not Sold" is a simple criterion that includes only those records with a value of "Not Sold" in the *Status* field. A more complex criterion is *Status* = "Sold" and *ShippingDate* = >3/15/2008. The result of this query would display only those records for items sold and shipped after 3/15/08.

To set accurate criteria on a field, the type of data contained in the field must be determined. Is the field text, numeric, or another type of field? Is the text entered in all capitals or in proper case? A close examination of the table will help in entering accurate criteria. Remember only text criteria can be placed in a text field and only a numeric field can have numeric criteria entered. The criterion is entered in the Criteria row of the Design grid for the fields desired. Make sure each is in the correct field column (see Figure 4.12).

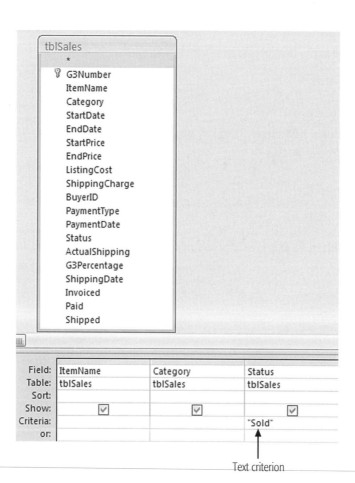

Figure 4.12 Entering criteria in the Design grid

TRY IT YOURSELF 4.2.6

Using the *tblSales* from the *G3_Ch4.accdb*, create the following query:

A. Enter the fields *ItemName, Category,* and *Status* into the Design grid.

B. Enter the Sold criterion for the *Status* field (see Figure 4.12).

C. Run the query. Only records that have items sold will be displayed (see Figure 4.13).

D. Save the query as *qryItemsSold*.

How to Enter Text Criteria

1. Click on the Criteria cell in the appropriate field column.

2. Enter the text to match in this field. When you move the cursor away from the field, quotation marks will appear around the text criteria.

3. If you need to edit the criterion later, be sure you keep the quotes on both the left and right ends. All records matching this criterion will be included in the dynaset.

ItemName	Category	Status
Vintage silver tone powder compact	Misc. Collectables	Sold
Vintage Bakelite Hair Comb Art Deco/Late Vict	Clothing	Sold
Vintage Hair Clippers Oster Model 105 Nice	Misc. Collectables	Sold
Vintage West German Cuckoo Clock	Misc. Collectables	Sold
Vintage Florida Map Scarf 50s Pink Silk	Clothing	Sold

Matches the text criterion

Figure 4.13 Dynaset of query design with text criteria

How to Enter T/F or Y/N Criteria

1. Click on the Criteria cell in the appropriate field column.
2. Enter the appropriate True/False or Yes/No criteria to match. It is very helpful to know how the data is displayed in this field.

TRY IT YOURSELF 4.2.7

Using the *qryItemsSold*:
A. Add the field *Shipped* to the Design grid.
B. Specify the criterion Yes in the *Shipped* field (see Figure 4.12).
C. Run the query (see Figure 4.14).
D. Save the query.

ItemName	Category	Status	Shipped
Vintage silver tone powder compact	Misc. Collectables	Sold	☑
Vintage Bakelite Hair Comb Art Deco/Late Vict	Clothing	Sold	☑
Vintage Hair Clippers Oster Model 105 Nice	Misc. Collectables	Sold	☑
Vintage West German Cuckoo Clock	Misc. Collectables	Sold	☑
Vintage Florida Map Scarf 50s Pink Silk	Clothing	Sold	☑

Yes/No Criterion

Figure 4.14 Dynaset of query design with Yes/No criteria

How to Enter Numeric or Currency Criteria

1. Click on the Criteria cell in the appropriate field column.
2. Enter the number to match in this field. Numeric criteria will appear as entered in the Criteria cell.

TRY IT YOURSELF 4.2.8

Using the *qryItemsSold*:
A. Delete the field *Shipped*.
B. Add the field *ShippingCharge* to the Design grid.
C. Specify the criterion 3 in the *ShippingCharge* field (see Figure 4.15).
D. Run the query. Only those records matching both criteria are displayed.
E. Save the query as *qryShippingCharge3*.

Field:	ItemName	Category	Status	ShippingCharge
Table:	tblSales	tblSales	tblSales	tblSales
Sort:				
Show:	☑	☑	☑	☑
Criteria:			"Sold"	3
or:				

Figure 4.15 Dynaset of query design with numeric or currency criteria

TRY IT YOURSELF 4.2.9

Using the *G3_Ch4.accdb* file, create a new query.

A. Add the *tblBuyers* to the query design.

B. Add all the fields to the Design grid.

C. Specify the criterion CA in the *State* field.

D. Run the query. There should be four records in the dynaset.

E. Return to the query design.

F. Specify the criterion Not CA in the *State* field (see Figure 4.16).

G. Run the query again. No records with CA in the *State* field should be displayed (see Figure 4.17).

H. Save the query as *qryBuyersNotCA*.

How to Enter Date Criteria

1. Click on the Criteria cell in the appropriate field column.

2. Enter the date in an accepted format, such as MM/DD/YY or Month-Day-Year. Access will add # symbols around the date. For example, if you enter 3/17/2008 or March-17-2008, Access will display #3/17/2008#.

The Not Operator

The Not operator in the Criteria cell will exclude all records matching the criteria from the dynaset.

How to Use the Not Operator

1. Click on the Criteria cell in the appropriate field column.

2. Enter the word "Not" and then enter the criteria.

Field:	BuyerID	FirstName	LastName	Email	StreetAddress	City	State	Zip
Table:	tblBuyers	tblBuyers	tblBuyers	tblBuyers	tblBuyers	tblBuyers	tblBuyers	tblBuyers
Sort:								
Show:	☑	☑	☑	☑	☑	☑	☑	☑
Criteria:							Not CA	

Figure 4.16 Query design using the Not operator

3. All records matching the criteria will be excluded in the dynaset.

BuyerID	FirstName	LastName	Email	StreetAddress	City	State	Zip
Babyneeds$	Jadyn	Walker	babyneeds@msn.com	P.O. Box 711	Toledo	OH	43614
bigDigree	Penny	Stocks	bigdig@bellsouth.net	8810 Richardson Rd	Aspen	CO	81611
blueangles	Angie	Brown	bluangie@msn.com	406 Palm Drive	Indianapolis	IN	46231
cachecloo	Linda	Ashton	cachecloo@yahoo.com	1502 West Commerce	Jacksonville	NC	28546
catchScatchcan	Eleanor	Trump	Trumpy@aol.com	3067 Hazleton St.	Milford	CT	06460
CoCoCocina	Pat	McDonald	Cocococina@aol.com	P O Box 273	Centralia	WA	98531

Figure 4.17 Dynaset using Not

TRY IT YOURSELF 4.2.10

A. Using the *qryBuyersNotCA* query, display the dynaset.

B. Print the dynaset from this query (see Figure 4.18).

C. Close the query.

Printing Query Results

The result of the query, or the dynaset, is displayed in a Datasheet view. These results can be printed to hard copy if needed.

How to Print a Dynaset

1. Click the Office button.

2. Move the mouse over the Print command.

3. Choose the print option from the Print menu (see Figure 4.18).

- The Print command will allow you to set the print settings.

- The Quick Print will send the query results to the printer using the settings that are currently available for the printer.

- The Print Preview will display the query results on the screen and allow you to make changes to the document before printing. A new Print Preview ribbon is displayed with the Print, Page Layout, Zoom, Data, and Close Preview galleries.

Q: How can I get all the fields on a page?

A: Use the Print Preview option to change margins or page orientation to accommodate your data.

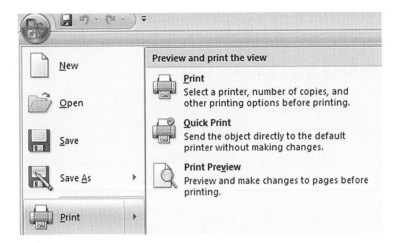

Figure 4.18 Printing a dynaset

Closing the Query Window

Several database objects (queries, forms etc.) can be opened at one time. All open objects are listed in the tabbed documents interface.

How to Close a Query

1. On the tab of the query to close, click the right mouse button.

2. From the shortcut menu, choose the Close or Close All command (see Figure 4.19). Close will close the active query. Close All will close all open database objects

   OR

   Click the Close box to the far right of the tabbed document ribbon to close the active database object.

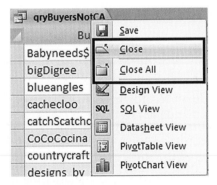

Figure 4.19 Closing the query

Q: What if I don't see any records when I run a query?

A: There may be no records that match the criteria. Check your criteria carefully, and visually check the data in the table for matches.

4.3   Working with Criteria

Entering a single criterion in a single field is a very simple query. There are other tools available in the Design window to define even more sophisticated queries. Entering criteria in more than one field, adding various common operators, adding totaling capabilities, sorting the fields in the dynaset, and showing or not showing a field are some of the other criteria tools that can be used.

Using Multiple Criteria and Common Operators

In select queries, it is sometimes necessary to specify more than one criterion. When criteria are entered for more than one field, they are usually joined by an AND. This will further limit the results of the query because all criteria must be matched for a record to be displayed. Using an AND operator makes the dynaset smaller. When multiple criteria are entered for a single field, they are joined by an OR operator, which expands the dynaset. It is also possible to create an OR condition based on multiple fields. Recall the use of AND/OR in Chapter 3 when we discussed filters.

When specifying multiple criteria in a query, it is essential to understand the common operators that are available. Table 4.1 summarizes these operators:

Table 4.1 List of Common Operators

Mathematical	Relational	Logical	String	Other
Addition (+)	Equal (=)	And	Like	Between . . . And
Subtraction (−)	Not Equal (<>)	Or	Concatenate (&)	In
Multiplication (*)	Greater Than (>)	Not		Is Null
Division (/)	Less Than (<)			

- Mathematical operators include the multiplication (*), division (/), addition (+), and subtraction (−) arithmetic operations, which are applied to numeric data.

  For example, *BillingPrice = ListingCost + ActualShipping* displays the result of this calculation. The field *BillingPrice* will display the result of adding the field *ListingCost* to the field *ActualShipping*.

- Relational operators include equal to (=), greater than (>), less than (<), not equal to (<>), and combinations thereof.

  For example, *EndPrice* > 15 displays all items costing more than $15.

- Logical operators include AND, OR, and NOT, which can be applied to any field type.

  For example, *Status* = Sold AND *Paid* = Yes will show all records of items that have been sold and paid. Both the criteria must be met for records to be displayed.

  A design using the NOT operator will exclude all records with that criterion. For example, *State* = Not CO will show all records that do not have CO in the *State* field.

- String operators are Like and & (Concatenate), which can be applied to text fields.

  For example, criterion Like *desk* in the *ItemName* field will show all items that have the word desk in that field. The asterisk (*) is placed before and after the word by Access.

- Miscellaneous operators are Between...And, In, and Is Null.

  For example, Between #3/1/2008# And #3/31/2008# in the *ShippingDate* field will show all records that have the shipping date between those two dates. The NOT operator can also be combined with the Between...And operator to exclude all dates within the specified range. Not Between #3/1/2008# And #3/31/2008# will display records that are not within those dates.

Using the AND/OR Operators

The AND/OR logical operators are used to join multiple criteria. When using the AND operator in a complex criteria query, both fields must match the criteria specified for a record to be included in the dynaset. When using the OR operator, the field must match one of the criteria specified. Remember, AND is used to join criteria on multiple fields and narrows down the dynaset. OR is used to specify multiple possible values for either a single field or multiple fields and expands the dynaset.

If no operators are specified, Access assumes an equal (=) sign before the criterion so that all matches must equal the criterion.

How to Use AND/OR Operators

AND

1. Enter the criteria in the desired first field column in a Criteria cell.

2. Enter the criteria in the desired second field column in a parallel Criteria cell. Both criteria should be on the same parallel line in the Criteria row (see Figure 4.20).

TRY IT YOURSELF 4.3.1

Using the *tblSales* from the *G3_Ch4.accmdb* file, create the following query:

A. Include the fields *ItemName, Category, Status,* and *Shipped*.

B. Set the criterion of "Sold" in the *Status* field.

C. Run the query. Notice that some items have been sold but not shipped yet.

D. Return to the Design view of the query.

E. Add another criteria in the *Shipped* field to display those records of sold but not shipped items. This is a Yes/No field so enter No in the criteria cell (see Figure 4.20).

F. Run the query again. Only those records of sold but not shipped items are displayed (see Figure 4.21).

G. Save the query as *qrySold_NotShipped*.

Field:	ItemName	Category	Status	Shipped
Table:	tblSales	tblSales	tblSales	tblSales
Sort:				
Show:	☑	☑	☑	☑
Criteria:			"Sold"	No

Figure 4.20 Query design using AND operator.

The dynaset records must match both criteria.

ItemName	Category	Status	Shipped
VEG O MATIC ...1961	Kitchen wares	Sold	☐
ALFRED MEAKIN SERVING PIECES...LOT OF 3	Kitchen wares	Sold	☐
Vintage Umbrella Navy Blue Stripes Excellent	Clothing	Sold	☐
Antique Baby Bonnet Lace Lawn Ribbon Gorgeous	Clothing	Sold	☐
Antique Infant Nightgown Lawn Lace Pretty	Clothing	Sold	☐
Vintage, 1963 Popeil Veg O Matic	Kitchen wares	Sold	☐

Figure 4.21 Dynaset using AND operator

OR

1. Enter the criteria in the desired first field column in the Criteria cell.

2. Enter the criteria in the desired second field column in the OR cell. Note that the OR criteria are below the original criteria (see Figure 4.22).

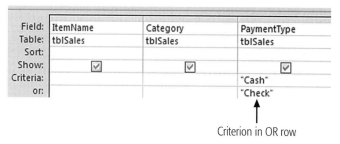

Field:	ItemName	Category	PaymentType
Table:	tblSales	tblSales	tblSales
Sort:			
Show:	☑	☑	☑
Criteria:			"Cash"
or:			"Check"

↑
Criterion in OR row

Figure 4.22 Query design using OR operator

The dynaset records can match either of the criteria (see Figure 4.23).

ItemName	Category	PaymentType
VINTAGE CERAMIC LIGHT FIXTURE	Misc. Collectables	Check
Antique Silver Ornate Glove Button Hook	Clothing	Check
Antique Sterling Silver Desk Eraser Tool	Misc. Collectables	Check
Vintage Indianapolis 500 ticket stub 1965	Misc. Collectables	Check
Shabby Chic Kitchen Vintage Egg Beater Red	Kitchen wares	Check
Antique Silver Money Clip Engraved Leaf W	Misc. Collectables	Cash
Antique Silver Money Clip Engraved Initial F	Misc. Collectables	Cash
LOT VINTAGE LIFE MAGAZINES JULY 1964	Books	Check

Figure 4.23 Dynaset using OR operator

TRY IT YOURSELF 4.3.2

Using the *tblSales* from the *G3_Ch4.accmdb* file, create the following query:

A. Include the fields *ItemName, Category,* and *PaymentType.*

B. Set the criterion on the field for Check or Cash (see Figure 4.22).

C. Run the query (see Figure 4.23).

D. Return to the query design.

E. Add the *ShippingDate* field to the Design grid.

F. Enter the criterion to show all records that were shipped after 4/3/2008. Be sure to specify the complete criteria on both rows (see Figure 4.24).

G. Run the query (see Figure 4.25).

H. Save the query *as qryCheck_Cash040308.*

Each row is considered a separate criterion, so be sure it contains the condition you want. For example if you want to show all records that were paid with cash or check and shipped after 4/3/2008, the Design grid should contain the criterion >4/30/2008 for the *ShippingDate* field on both Criteria rows (see Figure 4.24). The dynaset of this design will show records that match both sets of criteria (see Figure 4.25).

Field:	ItemName	Category	PaymentType	ShippingDate
Table:	tblSales	tblSales	tblSales	tblSales
Sort:				
Show:	☑	☑	☑	☑
Criteria:			"Cash"	>#4/20/2008#
or:			"Check"	>#4/20/2008#

Figure 4.24 Query design using multiple OR criteria

ItemName	Category	PaymentType	ShippingDat
VINTAGE CERAMIC LIGHT FIXTURE	Misc. Collectables	Check	6/4/2008
Antique Sterling Silver Desk Eraser Tool	Misc. Collectables	Check	5/15/2008
Vintage Indianapolis 500 ticket stub 1965	Misc. Collectables	Check	5/17/2008
LOT VINTAGE LIFE MAGAZINES JULY 1964	Books	Check	6/17/2008

Figure 4.25 Dynaset using multiple OR criteria

Using Arithmetic Operators

The most common usage of arithmetic operators is to create a new column containing a formula based on other fields in the query. For example, to calculate the difference between the original *StartPrice* and the *EndPrice,* create a column for a new field that will display the result of subtracting the *StartPrice* from the *EndPrice.*

To add a calculated column, click on the field row in the first empty column to the right of existing columns in the query and type the formula. The new column will be named according to the text that appears in front of the colon (:) in that cell. In Figure 4.26, the new field will be called *Difference.* If a new name is not included in the expression, Access will assign a new field name such as *Expr1.*

You can also use arithmetic operators to create a value for comparison in a criterion. For example, if you are tracking a stock portfolio, you can find all stocks that have had a 10% price increase over the last month by using the criterion *This Month = Last Month * 1.10.*

If you need to see a bigger view of the field cell, use the Zoom Command.

How to Open the Zoom Window for the Field Cell

1. In the field cell with the expression, click the right mouse button. A short-cut menu appears.

2. Click the Zoom command. The field cell is displayed in a larger view.

3. Click OK to close the Zoom window.

Each field in the Design grid has its own set of properties. These properties can be changed so that the field is displayed in a different format, i.e. currency. The format that is available for each field is based on the data type that was set when the fields were created in the table. Or in the case of a calculated field, the format can be set when the field is created in the query.

How to Change the Format of a Calculated Field

1. Click into the field cell in the Design grid.

2. Click the format line in the Property sheet for the field. If the Property Sheet is not displayed, click Property Sheet in the Show/Hide group (see Figure 4.26).

3. Choose the format for the field to be displayed in the dynaset.

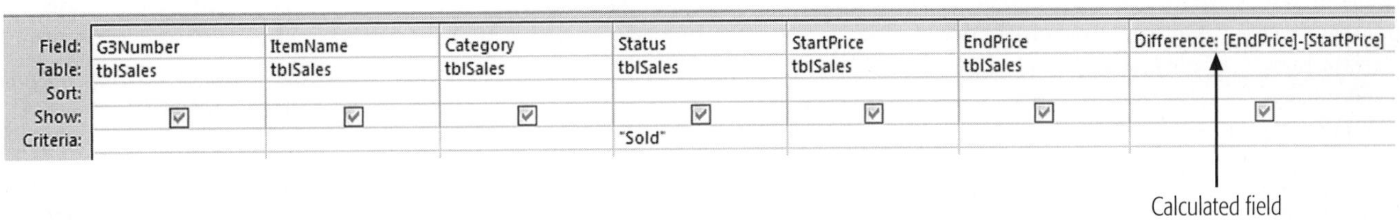

Field:	G3Number	ItemName	Category	Status	StartPrice	EndPrice	Difference: [EndPrice]-[StartPrice]
Table:	tblSales	tblSales	tblSales	tblSales	tblSales	tblSales	
Sort:							
Show:	☑	☑	☑	☑	☑	☑	☑
Criteria:				"Sold"			

Calculated field

Figure 4.26 Query design showing a calculated field

How to Create a Calculated Field

1. Click in an empty field cell in the Design grid.

2. Type the name of the new field to be created followed by a colon (:) (see Figure 4.26).

TRY IT YOURSELF 4.3.3

Create a new query using the *tblSales.*

A. Enter the following fields in the Design grid: *G3Number, ItemName, Category, Status, StartPrice,* and *EndPrice.*
B. Enter criterion on the *Status* field to display only Sold items.
C. Create a calculated field that will show the difference between the *StartPrice* and the *EndPrice* (see Figure 4.26).
D. Run the query.
E. Return to the Design view.
F. Enter criterion on the *Difference* field to display records that have a difference greater than $10.00 (see Figure 4.27).
G. Run the query (see Figure 4.28).
H. Save the query as *qry_Difference_>10.*

3. Enter the expression for the calculation. Field names must be enclosed in square brackets.
4. Enter any arithmetic operators needed.

Using Relational Operators

Relational operators can be used with number, currency, date, and counter field types and in some instances text fields. Greater than (>), less than (<), equal to (=), and not equal to (<>) can be used to compare the field data to another number, date, counter, or a text string. These comparison operators can also be combined to produce greater than or equal to (>=) or less than or equal to (<=) results.

How to Use Relational Operators on Numeric Data

1. Enter a comparison operator in the Criteria cell of the desired field column.
2. Enter the number you want to compare (see Figure 4.27).
3. The query result will match all criteria.

Field:	G3Number	ItemName	Category	Status	StartPrice	EndPrice	Difference: [EndPrice]-[StartPrice]
Table:	tblSales	tblSales	tblSales	tblSales	tblSales	tblSales	
Sort:							
Show:	☑	☑	☑	☑	☑	☑	☑
Criteria:				"Sold"			>10

Relational operator

Figure 4.27 Query design showing relational criteria

G3Number	ItemName	Category	Status	StartP	EndPr	Difference
2166598815	Vintage West German Cuckoo Clock	Misc. Collectables	Sold	$14.99	$51.09	$36.10
2170063175	VINTAGE,GERMAN PENDULUM CLOCK ORNATE	Misc. Collectables	Sold	$12.00	$75.00	$63.00
2304591635	Lot Vintage Birthday Candles 1950s Tugboats	Misc. Collectables	Sold	$2.99	$17.00	$14.01
2509255117	Antique Silver Ornate Glove Button Hook	Clothing	Sold	$7.99	$22.49	$14.50
2521794321	Antique Sterling Silver Desk Set Tool	Misc. Collectables	Sold	$7.99	$36.00	$28.01
2654038567	ALFRED MEAKIN SERVING PIECES...LOT OF 3	Kitchen wares	Sold	$8.75	$19.00	$10.25
2700496587	Vintage Colorado Ski Lift Tickets - 1960s	Misc. Collectables	Sold	$3.99	$22.50	$18.51
2836698359	Vintage Handheld Fan	Clothing	Sold	$1.99	$12.00	$10.01
2848166699	Vintage Umbrella Navy Blue Stripes Excellent	Clothing	Sold	$9.99	$26.00	$16.01
3407671211	Antique Silver Money Clip Engraved Leaf W	Misc. Collectables	Sold	$7.99	$19.45	$11.46
3505984948	Kitchen Digest Vintage Book Homemaking Dakota	Books	Sold	$7.99	$18.00	$10.01
3526669868	LOT VINTAGE LIFE MAGAZINES JULY 1964	Books	Sold	$4.75	$25.00	$20.25

Figure 4.28 Dynaset displaying records from relational criteria

Using Other Operators

There are a number of other operators that can be used to create criteria. Table 4.2 shows a complete list of them. Some of the most useful operators are Like, Between...And, and In. Like finds any record containing a specific word or phrase anywhere in a field;

Table 4.2   Acceptable Wildcards Used with the Like Operator

Wildcard	Use
*	Replaces any number of characters. Can be used before, after, or within a character string.
?	Replaces a single character within a character string.
#	Replaces any single digit within a numeric string.
[list]	Locates records for all instances of the field that begin with the characters specified within the list.
[!list]	Locates records for all instances of the field that do not begin with the characters specified within the list.

Between...And finds any record containing a value in a specified range of numbers; and In provides an easy way to specify multiple OR criteria.

The Like operator is useful for finding similar items or part of a field, such as all the people living on a certain street or all companies that list sporting goods in a product catalog. Use the asterisk (*) or other wildcard characters in combination with the Like operator to tell Access to locate the specified word anywhere within the words in the field. It is not necessary to type in the operator "Like" when using the wildcards. Access adds that operator into the Criteria when the query is run. Use the asterisk (*) or other wildcard characters to locate the specified word anywhere within the data in a particular field. For example, criteria entered as S* in the *City* field will display all records of cities that start with the letter S. The wildcard asterisk (*) is entered after the character which replaces all characters following the S. Criteria entered in the *City* field as *S will display records that end in the letter S, no matter what characters come before the S. The criteria *S* will display records with the letter anywhere within the data of the *City* field. It's easy to make an error when using this operator, so check your criteria carefully.

How to Use the Like Operator in Query Design

1. Enter criteria desired in the Design grid.

2. In the Criteria cell of the corresponding field, use any of the wildcards followed by the character string. The Like operator will be inserted by Access in the query design (see Figure 4.29).

3. The resulting dynaset displays all instances of the field matching the character string, depending on the design.

TRY IT YOURSELF 4.3.4

Create a new query using the *tblBuyers* table.

A. Enter the following fields in the Design grid: *BuyerID, FirstName, LastName, City,* and *State*.

B. Enter criteria to display all records that have a City starting with the letter S (see Figure 4.29).

C. Run the query (see Figure 4.30).

D. Save the query as *qryS_Cities*.

E. Return to the query design and experiment with other combinations of the asterisk wildcard (*).

Field:	BuyerID	FirstName	LastName	City	State
Table:	tblBuyers	tblBuyers	tblBuyers	tblBuyers	tblBuyers
Sort:					
Show:	☑	☑	☑	☑	☑
Criteria:				S*	

Figure 4.29 Using the * wildcard

BuyerID	FirstName	LastName	City	State
even-the-kitchen-sink	Vivian	Sedgewick	San Antonio	TX
FabulousKitchens	Nola	Johnson	Seattle	WA
JadeMaid	Denise	Arboles	Salem	OR
kitchenguru	Al	Bakirky	San Jose	CA
WachaGotcookin	Betty	Crockett	Salt Lake City	UT

Figure 4.30 Dynaset from wildcard criteria

The Between . . . And operator is useful for finding items that fall within a range of values. Between is inclusive; it retrieves records that match the values on either end of the range as well as those that occur between. For example, End Price Between 9 and 12 retrieves all items priced at or between $9 and $12. The same criteria could be expressed as Price >= 9 AND Price <= 12.

How to Use the Between . . . And Operator in Query Design

1. Enter criteria desired in the Design grid.

2. In the Criteria cell of the corresponding field, use the Between . . . And syntax for the criteria. Include a range of values for the result to fall within (see Figure 4.31).

Field:	ItemName	Category	EndPrice
Table:	tblSales	tblSales	tblSales
Sort:			
Show:	☑	☑	☑
Criteria:			Between 9 And 12

Figure 4.31 Using the Between . . . And operator

3. The resulting dynaset will display the records that fall within the range of values (see Figure 4.32).

ItemName	Category	EndPr
Vintage Bakelite Hair Comb Art Deco/Late Vict	Clothing	$10.19
VEG O MATIC …1961	Kitchen wares	$10.00
3 Vintage Colorado Ski Tickets 60s Winter Pk	Misc. Collectables	$10.50
Vintage Indianapolis 500 ticket stub 1965	Misc. Collectables	$10.37
Vintage Handheld Fan	Clothing	$12.00
Shabby Chic Kitchen Vintage Egg Beater Red	Kitchen wares	$11.00

Figure 4.32 Dynaset from the Between . . . And query design

The In operator is useful for identifying multiple values in a field. For example, State in ("CO", "CA") finds all records that have Colorado or California in the *State* field. This same criteria can be written as State = "CO" OR "CA". Using the In operator is most useful when more than two criteria values are used.

How to Use the In Operator in Query Design

1. Enter criteria desired in the grid.

2. In the Criteria cell of the corresponding field, use the In operator and then include a list of values separated by commas (see Figure 4.33).

3. The results of this query design would include all those values within the list.

Field:	BuyerID	FirstName	LastName	City	State
Table:	tblBuyers	tblBuyers	tblBuyers	tblBuyers	tblBuyers
Sort:					
Show:	☑	☑	☑	☑	☑
Criteria:					In ("CA","CO")

Figure 4.33 Query design showing the In operator

TRY IT YOURSELF 4.3.5

Using the *tblSales* table, create a new query.

A. Enter the following fields into the Design grid: *ItemName, Category,* and *EndPrice.*

B. Display all records that have an *EndPrice* between $9 and $12 (see Figure 4.31).

C. Run the query (see Figure 4.32).

D. Save the query as *qryEndPrice9-12.*

TRY IT YOURSELF 4.3.6

Using the *tblBuyers* table, create a new query.

A. Enter the following fields into the Design grid; *BuyerID, FirstName, LastName, City,* and *State.*

B. Display all records that have *State* data as either in CO or CA (see Figure 4.33).

C. Run the query (see Figure 4.34).

D. Save the query as *qryBuyersCO_or_CA.*

BuyerID	FirstName	LastName	City	State
bigDigree	Penny	Stocks	Aspen	CO
boomerbaby	Nina	Warren	Carmel	CA
dsdpurple	Denise	Martinez	Denver	CO
kitchenguru	Al	Bakirky	San Jose	CA
Over50	Anne	Jablonski	Oakland	CA
sukiyaki	Gus	Jones	Bakersfield	CA

Figure 4.34 Results of Try It Yourself 4.3.6

Using String Operators

There are a couple of other useful string operators, Concatenate (&) and Is Null. Concatenate means to join two text strings, so the & operator allows you to compare data to two joined text strings. For example, the criteria: PhoneNumber = AreaCode & Phone, finds all records where the *PhoneNumber* field equals the combination of *AreaCode* and *Phone*. If *AreaCode* = "(303)" and *Number* = "123-4567," then *Phone Number* is *AreaCode & Phone*, or "(303)123-4567."

Is Null matches a string that has no data in it. Text fields in a new record are null until data is entered into them, so using Is Null finds records where no values have been entered into a field. For example, in Figure 4.35, the Is Null operator is entered into the Criteria cell for the field *EndPrice*. This design will retrieve records where this is no end price entered into that field. That field is empty (null). Simply type the words "Is Null" into the criteria grid in the appropriate field column (see Figure 4.35).

Field:	G3Number	ItemName	EndPrice
Table:	tblSales	tblSales	tblSales
Sort:			
Show:	☑	☑	☑
Criteria:			Is Null

Figure 4.35 Using the Is Null operator

4.4 Creating Total Queries

A Total query is a type of query that performs summary calculations or aggregate functions on groups of data. All Total queries must include at least two fields—one field that's used to group the data, and another to provide values for calculating the summary information.

Total queries can be run on any data that is organized into categories or groups. In other words, the data source must have at least one field that has a finite number of possible values. For example, the *tblSales* can be grouped by the field *Category*, which identifies the group or type of item up for bid. There are only a few categories (a finite number) to classify the items. The field *ItemName* is not a good choice for grouping because every record will probably have a different value for that field. This would result in every record becoming its own group.

Total queries can calculate subtotals, averages, and other summary data on any numeric, date, or logical (Y/N) field in the data source. Some of the results can be difficult to interpret, however, such as the sum of values in a date field, which is given as a numeric value. A few of the calculations will work in any field. See Table 4.3 for a complete list.

The grouping and calculation options are entered on the Total row of the Design grid. Figure 4.37 shows the design to sum the *EndPrice* of all items for each *Category*. When the Total row is added to a query, the query then becomes a Total query.

How to Display the Total Row

1. On the Design tab, in the Show/Hide group, click Totals (see Figure 4.36). The Total row is displayed under the Table row in the Design grid.

There are a variety of grouping options available from the drop-down list in each of the cells in the Total row (see Figure 4.37). This row has a default value of Group By in each column although there are twelve (12) options available. We will work with only a few of these options: Group By, Sum, Avg, Min, Max, and Count.

Figure 4.36 Displaying the Total row

Field:	Category		EndPrice
Table:	tblSales		tblSales
Total:	Group By		Sum
Sort:			
Show:	☑		☑
Criteria:			

Total Row ⟶ (points to Total: row)

Figure 4.37 Grouping options

Using the Group by Option

The Group By option allows the user to specify a field as a grouping field. The data will be organized and displayed into groups based on the values in that field. For example you can group together all records that share a specific item category so that all books are grouped together, all kitchenware are grouped together and so forth. Subtotals can be calculated for each group for any numeric field. In Figure 4.37 a sum is calculated on the field *EndPrice* so that there is a price subtotal for all item groups. Notice that the grouping option for the field *Category* is Group By while the *EndPrice* has the grouping option of Sum.

This Group By option is useful when the data in a field is restricted to a set of discrete values—values that are specific and distinct. These values form natural groups when there are relatively few different values that can occur. An example would be a *Blood Type* field, where the set of possible values is small and distinct. There are only four different values—A, B, AB, or O.

The Group By option should be specified for only one field, unless subgroupings are needed. Be careful that only those columns that are part of the grouping scheme contain the value Group By in the Group row. Group By is the default value.

How to Calculate Subtotals

1. Identify the field that contains the different categories for grouping and the field that contains the numeric data to be totaled. Set up a query containing only those two fields.

2. Enter the Total row into the Design grid.

3. Choose Sum from the Total drop-down list for the field that contains the numeric data to be totaled (see Figure 4.37).

4. Run the query (see Figure 4.38).

TRY IT YOURSELF 4.4.1

Using the *tblSales* table, create a new query.

A. Add the fields *Category* and *EndPrice*.

B. Display the Total row.

C. On the Total row, Group By *Category* and Sum the *EndPrice* field (see Figure 4.37).

D. Run the query (see Figure 4.38).

E. Save the query as *qryCategory_Totals*.

Category	SumOfEndPrice
Clothing	$113.50
Books	$44.99
Kitchen wares	$75.99
Misc. Collectables	$405.20

Figure 4.38 Dynaset showing Category groups and EndPrice sums

Aggregate (Totaling) Options

There are twelve different options in the Total drop-down list. Seven of these options are used on numeric data only, two options are to display specific records and three are for other uses (see Table 4.3).

Table 4.3 Aggregate Options

Option	Description	Field Data Types
Count	Counts number of non-null values in a field. Produces a number count of records in each dynaset category.	All
Sum	Adds the values in a field. Calculates a total of field values for each dynaset category.	Number, Currency, Date/Time
Avg	Averages the values in a field. Calculates a numeric average for each dynaset category.	Number, Currency, Date/Time
Max	Finds the maximum value in a field in each dynaset category.	Number, Currency, Date/Time
Min	Finds the minimum value in a field in each dynaset category.	Number, Currency, Date/Time
StDev	Finds the standard deviation of values in a field in each dynaset category.	Number, Currency
Var	Finds the variance of values in a field.	Number, Currency
First	Finds the field in the first record of the group.	All
Last	Finds the field in the last record of the group.	All
Group By	Creates groups based on the values in fields of a record.	All
Exp	Creates a calculated field with an aggregate function.	Number, Currency, Date/Time
Where	Identifies criteria for a field not used in a grouping.	All

TRY IT YOURSELF 4.4.2

Open the *qryCategory_Totals* in Design view.
A. Edit the query and change the *EndPrice* totaling option to Avg.
B. Run the query (see Figure 4.39).

Category	AvgOfEndPrice
Clothing	$14.19
Books	$7.50
Kitchen wares	$6.33
Misc. Collectables	$16.88

Figure 4.39 Results of the Avg option

TRY IT YOURSELF 4.4.3

Using the *qryCategory_Totals*
A. Edit the query and change the *EndPrice* totaling option to Count.
B. Run the query (see Figure 4.40).
C. Ask yourself this question: What is actually being counted in this query design?
D. Close the query. Do not save the query.

Category	CountOfEndPric
Clothing	8
Books	6
Kitchen wares	12
Misc. Collectables	24

Figure 4.40 Results of the Count query design

Q: What did I do wrong if every record is displayed in a Total query?

A: Probably, more than one field has "Group By" on the Total row.

Total Query Mistakes

There are some mistakes that are easily made when first learning to use Total queries. The most common is using multiple "Group By" fields. Each time you add a field to a Total query, it defaults to "Group By" on the Total row. When this happens, Access groups by any change in value in any of these fields. The dynaset is grouped incorrectly (quite often there is no grouping at all) and a total is displayed for every record in the dynaset. Only one field should have "Group By" on the Total row.

Another mistake is using the Count option on a field that is blank in some records. Count only looks at records that have data in the specified field, so the counts are incorrect. For example, if the field *Artist* is sometimes left blank in a table, but the field *MusicNumber* is always filled in, then *MusicNumber* should be used as the field to count records. Generally, the primary key field is the best field to count in a table, as it is required to be filled in.

How to Remove the Total Row from the Grid

1. On the Design tab, in the Show/Hide group click Totals (see Figure 4.36).

Professional Tip: Displaying a Related Field

It's easy to get a summary value on one field in a Total query, but it's hard to get another field from the same record. Let's look at an example using the *Practice_Ch4.accdb* database. Let's say you want to see a list of customers and the last item they ordered. You would make a Total query using the table *tblOrders*, group by *Customer*, use the Max function on the field *Date_Sold*, and the Last function the field *PartNo*. But that doesn't work! The *PartNo* displayed is not the value found in the record for the last sale made to a customer. Instead, Access gets the *PartNo* for the last record as if the records were sorted in primary key order. Try it yourself and see: Open the *qryDevTip-GroupByWrongData* in the *Practice4* database.

Two queries need to be created to get the value you want. First create a Total query to retrieve the maximum value for the field *Date_Sold* for each customer. Look at the query *qryDevTipGroupByCorrectQ1* in *Practice4* as an example. Then, make another query that joins the first query to the table *tblOrders*. The tables should be joined on both the field *Customer* and the field *Date_Sold*. This query is a Select query, and displays the fields *Customer*, *Date_Sold*, and *PartNo* from the table *tblOrders*. Look at *QryDevTipGroupByCorrectQ2* to see the solution.

4.5 / Utilizing Other Query Features

Sorting a Query

One application of the Sort feature was discussed in a previous chapter with regard to sorting table data in the Datasheet view—using the Sort button. The same rules for sorting a table in the Datasheet view apply to sorting in a query. If sorting on multiple fields, the primary sort field must be to the left of the secondary sort field.

Sorting can also be applied to a field in a query. A Sort row is displayed in the Design grid (see Figure 4.41). When the cell is blank, the sorting function is not applicable. However, when the sort type—ascending or descending—is displayed in the cell, the data in the field will be sorted in the described order when the query is run.

TRY IT YOURSELF 4.5.1

Create a new query using the *tblBuyers* table:

A. Enter the fields *FirstName, LastName, City,* and *State* into the Design grid.

B. Sort in Ascending order on the *City* field.

C. Run the query.

D. Return to the Design view.

E. Move the *State* field to the left of the *City* field in the Design grid. Sort in Ascending order on both the *City* and *State* fields with the *State* field being the primary sort field (see Fig 4.41).

F. Run the query. Notice that the cities are now sorted alphabetically with each state (see Figure 4.42).

G. Save the query as *qrySortedCity*.

Field:	FirstName	LastName	State	City
Table:	tblBuyers	tblBuyers	tblBuyers	tblBuyers
Sort:			Ascending	Ascending ▾
Show:	☑	☑	☑	Ascending
Criteria:				Descending
or:				(not sorted)

Figure 4.41 Sorting in query design

When sorting on multiple fields, the primary sort field must be to the left of the secondary sort field in the Design grid.

FirstName ▾	LastName ▾	State ▾	City ▾
Andy	Gamboni	AZ	Flagstaff
Danny	Carbone	AZ	Tucson
Gus	Jones	CA	Bakersfield
Nina	Warren	CA	Carmel
Anne	Jablonski	CA	Oakland
Al	Bakirky	CA	San Jose

Figure 4.42 Multiple fields sorted

Using the Show Box

Only fields included in the Design grid are displayed in the dynaset and can have criteria applied to them. Even though a field is included in the Design grid and has criteria applied to it, the actual data results don't have to be displayed in the query run (see Figure 4.43).

Field:	FirstName	LastName	State	City
Table:	tblBuyers	tblBuyers	tblBuyers	tblBuyers
Sort:			Ascending	Ascending
Show:	☑	☑	☐	☑
Criteria:			"CA"	

Unchecked Showbox

Figure 4.43 The Show check box in the Design grid

The Show row controls whether or not a field will be displayed in the dynaset. Check the Show box in each field column when the data is to be displayed (see Figure 4.43). The

TRY IT YOURSELF 4.5.2

A. Open the *qrySortedCity* in Design view.

B. Enter CA as the criterion for the *State* field.

C. Run the query. Notice that only cities in the state of California are displayed.

D. Return to Design view.

E. Click into the Show box for the *State* field so that this field is not displayed in the dynaset (see Figure 4.43).

F. Run the query again. Notice that the redundant data of CA is not displayed (see Figure 4.44).

G. Close the query without saving it.

Q: How do I display only the top 25% highest priced items sold?

A: Enter the fields *EndPrice*, *ItemName*, and *Status*. Enter the criteria "sold" for the *Status* field. Sort in descending order on *EndPrice*. In the Return (Top values) drop-down list, choose 25%

default is to show all records from all fields in the query. When these boxes are not checked, the field and its criteria are still incorporated into the query, but no data in the field is displayed in the dynaset.

You might want to use a field in a calculation, a criterion, or a sort, but not actually display the field (see Figure 4.43).

FirstName	LastName	City
Gus	Jones	Bakersfield
Nina	Warren	Carmel
Anne	Jablonski	Oakland
Al	Bakirky	San Jose

Figure 4.44 Query results with State field not showing

Displaying Limited Records in the Dynaset

You can display only a particular number of records, or a percentage of the total number of records in a dynaset. For example, you might want to return the top 3 values or the top 10 percent of all values in a field. First, you must specify the field for which you want to display top values. Do this by selecting a sort order on that field, and by making sure that it is the leftmost field in the query design grid that has the Sort box selected. When you indicate an ascending sort, picking a range of values returns the records with the smallest values, while a descending sort returns the records containing the largest values.

Once the sort order has been established, you can select or type a range of top values in the Return drop-down list in Query Setup group (see Figure 4.45). You may select a value from the list, or type any valid number or any number between 1 and 100 followed by a percent symbol (%). For example, to see the top 10 values, type 10 in the box; to see the top ten percent of the values type 10% in the box. If you have designated an ascending sort on *StartPrice* in the *tblSales* table and have chosen to see the top five values, you'll see the five lowest priced items in the dynaset.

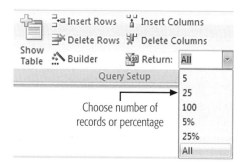

Figure 4.45 The Top Values list in the Query Setup Group

4.6 Creating Queries with Multiple Tables

Adding multiple related tables to the Table/Query area of the window can create even more complex queries. When working with multiple tables, a join must be created at either the table level or in query design. Once a relationship is established, you can use the data from those tables. Additional tables can be added initially from the Show Table dialog box, or later as needed.

How to Add Data Sources

1. Click the Show Table button on the Query Tools/Design ribbon (see Figure 4.46).

2. Choose the table or query from the Show Table Dialog box (see Figure 4.46).

3. Click the Add button to add the data source to the query design.

4. Click the Close button to close the Show Table dialog box.

TRY IT YOURSELF 4.6.1

A. Create a new query.

B. Add the *tblSales* table.

C. From the Query design screen, use the Show Table button to display other tables. Add the *tblBuyers* table to the query design (see Figure 4.46).

D. Notice that these two tables have been joined on the *BuyerID* field (see Figure 4.47).

E. This exercise continues in Try It Yourself 4.6.2.

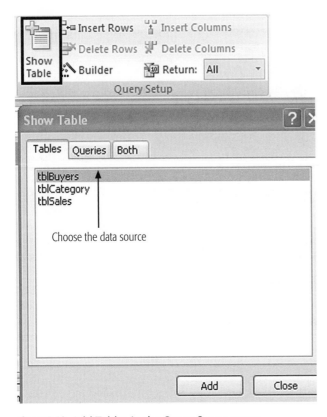

Figure 4.46 Add Tables in the Query Setup group

Joining tables on common fields in the query allows use of the fields from all tables in the Design grid. If relationships have been established between these tables, the related fields will have lines drawn between them. If no relationships have been established or no lines appear between the fields, temporary joins can be created at this time by following the steps below:

How to Join Tables in a Query

1. Select the field to join in the first table.

2. Drag this field to its related field in the second table. A relationship line will appear between the fields (see Figure 4.47).

3. Repeat as necessary to join all tables on related fields.

Tables are most often joined using the primary key and foreign key fields in two tables. For example, the primary key in the *tblBuyers* table is the field *BuyerID*. This same field in the *tblSales* is the foreign key. These two tables are joined using the field *BuyerID*.

Fields from multiple tables are added to the Design grid in the same fashion as adding fields from one table.

TRY IT YOURSELF 4.6.2

A. Add the fields *BuyerID,
FirstName,* and *LastName*
from the *tblBuyers.*

B. Add the fields *ItemName,
Status,* and *Paid* from the
tblSales.

C. Add the criterion "No" to the
Paid criteria row (see Figure
4.47).

D. Add the criterion "sold" to the
Status criteria row (see Figure
4.47).

E. Run the query. The results
should show all buyers who
have not paid for their items
(see Figure 4.48).

F. Save the query as
qryBuyers_NotPaid.

How to Add Fields from Other Tables

1. Double click on the desired field from the table in the Table/Query area (see Figure 4.47)

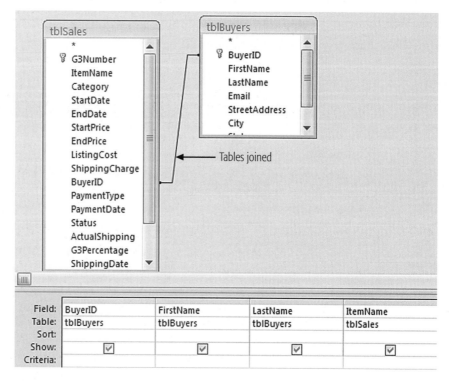

Figure 4.47 Adding fields from multiple tables

OR

Click on the desired field in the Table/Query area and drag the field icon to the Field box in the grid

OR

Click in the empty Field box. Click on the arrow on the right side of the Field box. Choose the desired field from the drop-down list. Notice that the table name appears first before the field name

OR

Click in the empty Field box. Type in the table name and field name separated by a period.

When the query is run, data from all joined tables is displayed (see Figure 4.48).

BuyerID	FirstName	LastName	ItemName	Status	Paid	EndPr
CoCoCocina	Pat	McDonald	Antique Infant Nightgown Lawn Lace Pretty	Sold	☐	$7.50
kitchenstuff2go	Eva	Olson	Vintage Umbrella Navy Blue Stripes Excellent	Sold	☐	$26.00
WachaGotcookin	Betty	Crockett	VEG O MATIC ...1961	Sold	☐	$10.00
WachaGotcookin	Betty	Crockett	ALFRED MEAKIN SERVING PIECES...LOT OF 3	Sold	☐	$19.00

Figure 4.48 Dynaset showing fields from multiple tables

Additional summarizing options can be added to query results in Datasheet view. The Totals row can be added to query results without adding it to the Design view. The Totals Row in Datasheet view does not offer as many options as those in Design view but the options do perform similar functions. For example, Sum in Datasheet view will add all the data in a numeric field. The Sum, Average, Count, Minimum, Maximum, Standard Deviation and Variance can be performed on number type data while a Count can be performed on other data types.

Figure 4.49 Displaying the Total Row in Data sheet view

TRY IT YOURSELF 4.6.3

A. Open the *qryBuyers_NotPaid* in design view.

B. Add the field *EndPrice* to the Design grid.

C. Run the query.

D. In the Datasheet view, add the Total row.

E. Sum the *EndPrice* field.

F. Save and close the query.

How to Add the Totals Row in Datasheet View

1. Run the query.

2. In Datasheet view, click the Totals command in the Records group. The Total row is added to the bottom of the datasheet.

3. Click in Total row cell for the field you wish to summarize.

4. Choose the summarizing function from the drop-down list.

5. If you wish to delete the Totals row, click the Totals command in the Records group.

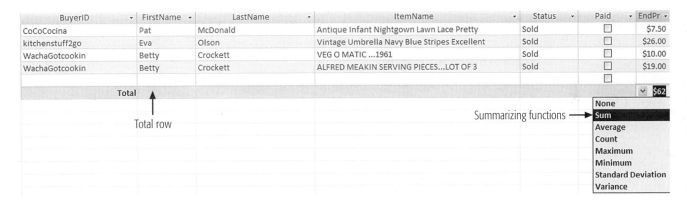

Figure 4.50 Adding Summarizing options to the Total row

Fast Track   Quick guide to procedures learned in this chapter

Creating a Query

1. Click the Create tab.

2. In the Other group, click the Query Design command.

3. The Show Table dialog box appears.

4. Choose the table(s) to be included in the query.

5. Click the Add button to add the tables to the Query Design. Click the Close button.

Resizing the Design Window

1. Click the left mouse button on the dividing bar between the two sections and hold the mouse button down. The pointer turns into a dark pointing double arrow.

2. Drag the bar either up or down to reduce or enlarge the upper and lower panes.

Adding a Field

1. Double-click on the desired field in the Table pane area. This field will then be entered into the field box of the first column in the Design grid

   OR

   Click on the desired field in the Table pane area. Drag and drop the field icon to the Field box in a column

   OR

   Click in the empty field box. Click on the arrow at the right side of the Field box. Choose the desired field from the drop-down list

   OR

   Click in the empty Field box in the Design grid. Type in the field name when you see the cursor. You must be exact in typing the field name.

Adding All Fields From a Table

1. Add the all fields symbol (asterisk*) using any of the methods to add a field.

Running a Query

1. Click on the Run command in the Results group

   OR

   Click on the View command and choose Datasheet view.

2. The results of the query will be displayed in Datasheet view.

Saving a Query (Initial Save)

1. To initially save the query, right click on the query document tab and choose Save from the menu.

2. Name the query with the *qry* prefix.

Saving a Query with a New Name

1. Click the Office button.

2. Point to Save As.

3. Click on the Save Object As command.

4. Enter the name for the new object.

5. Choose the object type.

6. Click the OK button.

Sorting a Query Result in Datasheet View

1. Click into the field to sort.
2. Click the Sort button either ascending or descending

   OR

   Click on the drop-down list to the right of the field name. Choose the sort function.

Filtering a Query Result in Datasheet View

1. Click into the field cell that contains the data for the filter.
2. Choose the type of filter from the Selection command in the Sort & Filter Group (see Figure 4.49)

   OR

   Click on the drop-down list to the right of the field name. Click in the check boxes that contain the data to filter. Click the Save button.

Removing a Filter

1. Click the drop-down list to the right of the field name. Choose the Clear Filter command

   OR

   Click the Toggle Filter command in the Sort & Filter group on the ribbon.

Returning to Design View

1. Click on the View command and choose Design view.

Moving a Field

1. Select the field to move by clicking on the field selector above the field name. The entire field column will be selected.
2. Click and drag the field column on the field selector and move to the new location.
3. Release the mouse button to drop the field in its new location.

Deleting a Field

1. Select the field to be deleted.
2. Press the Delete key

   OR

   Click the Delete Columns command from the Query Setup group

   OR

   Click the right mouse button to display the shortcut menu. Choose the Cut command.

Inserting a Field

1. Select the field from the table field list in the Table pane area.
2. Drag the field to the appropriate position in the Design grid.
3. Drop the field in place by releasing the mouse.

Entering Text Criteria

1. Click on the Criteria cell in the appropriate field column.

2. Enter the text to match in this field. When you move the cursor away from the field, quotation marks will appear around the text criteria.

3. If you need to edit the criterion later, be sure you keep the quotes on both the left and right ends. All records matching this criterion will be included in the dynaset.

Entering Numeric or Currency Criteria

1. Click on the Criteria cell in the appropriate field column.

2. Enter the number to match in this field. Numeric criteria will appear as entered in the Criteria cell.

Entering T/F or Y/N Criteria

1. Click on the Criteria cell in the appropriate field column.

2. Enter the appropriate True/False or Yes/No criteria to match. It is very helpful to know how the data is displayed in this field.

Entering Date Criteria

1. Click on the Criteria cell in the appropriate field column.

2. Enter the date in an accepted format, such as MM/DD/YY or Month-Day-Year.

Using the Not Operator

1. Click on the Criteria cell in the appropriate field column.

2. Enter the word "Not" and then enter the criteria.

3. All records matching the criteria will be excluded in the dynaset.

Printing a Dynaset

1. Click the Office Button.

2. Move the mouse over the Print command.

3. Choose the print option from the Print menu.

   - The Print command will allow you to set the print settings.

   - The Quick Print will send the query results to the printer using the settings that are currently available for the printer.

   - The Print Preview will display the query results on the screen and allow you to make changes to the document before printing. A new Print Preview ribbon is displayed with the Print, Page Layout, Zoom, Data, and Close Preview galleries.

Closing a Query

1. On the tab of the query to close, click the right mouse button.

2. From the shortcut menu, choose the Close or Close All command. Close will close the active query; Close All will close all open database objects

   OR

   Click the close box to the far right of the tabbed document ribbon to close the active database object.

Using AND/OR Operators

AND

1. Enter the criteria in the desired first field column in a Criteria cell.

2. Enter the criteria in the desired second field column in a parallel Criteria cell. Both criteria should be on the same parallel line in the criteria row.

   The dynaset records must match both criteria.

OR

1. Enter the criteria in the desired first field column in the Criteria cell.

2. Enter the criteria in the desired second field column in the OR cell. Note that the OR criteria are below the original criteria.

The dynaset records can match either of the criteria.

Using Relational Operators on Numeric Data

1. Enter a comparison operator in the Criteria cell of the desired field column.

2. Enter the number you want to compare.

Using the Like Operator

1. Enter criteria desired in the Design grid.

   In the Criteria cell of the corresponding field, use any of the wildcards followed by the character string. The Like operator will be inserted by Access in the query design.

2. The resulting dynaset displays all instances of the field matching the character string, depending on the design.

Using the Between...And Operator

1. Enter criteria desired in the Design grid.

2. In the Criteria cell of the corresponding field, use the Between...And syntax for the criteria. Include a range of values for the result to fall within.

3. The resulting dynaset will display the records that fall within the range of values.

Using the In Operator

1. Enter criteria desired in the Design grid.

2. In the Criteria cell of the corresponding field, use the In operator and then include a list of values separated by commas.

3. The results of this query design would include all those values within the list.

Creating a Calculated Field

1. Click in an empty field cell in the Design grid.

2. Type the name of the new field to be created followed by a colon :.

3. Enter the expression for the calculation. Field names must be enclosed in square brackets.

4. Enter any arithmetic operators needed.

Displaying the Total Row

1. On the Design tab, in the Show/Hide group, click Totals. The Total row is displayed under the Table row in the Design grid.

Calculating Subtotals

1. Identify the field that contains the different categories for grouping and the field that contains the numeric data to be totaled. Set up a query containing only those two fields.
2. Enter the Total row into the Design grid.
3. Choose Sum from the Total drop-down list (click where it says Group By) for the field that contains the numeric data to be totaled.
4. Run the query.

Removing the Total Row from the Grid

1. On the Design tab, in the Show/Hide group, click Totals.

Adding Data Sources

1. Click the Show Table button on the Query Tools/Design.
2. Choose the table or query from the Show Table Dialog box.
3. Click the Add button to add the data source to the query design.
4. Click the Close button to close the Show Table dialog box.

Adding the Total Row in Datasheet View

1. Run the query.
2. In Datasheet view, click the Totals command in the Records group. The Total row is added to the bottom of the datasheet.
3. Click in Total row cell for the field you wish to summarize.
4. Choose the summarizing function from the drop-down list.
5. If you wish to delete the Total row, click the Totals command in the Records group.

Joining Tables in a Query

1. Select the field to join in the first table.
2. Drag this field to its related field in the second table. A relationship line will appear between the fields.
3. Repeat as necessary to join all tables on related fields.

Adding Fields From Other Tables

1. Double-click on the desired field from the table in the Table pane area

   OR

   Click on the desired field in the Table pane area and drag the field icon to the Field box in the grid

OR

Click in the empty Field box. Click on the arrow on the right side of the Field box. Choose the desired field from the drop-down list

OR

Click in the empty Field box. Type in the table name and field name separated by a period.

Review Questions

1. Define a query.
2. What types of input can be used as a data source for queries?
3. What is a dynaset?
4. What are criteria and how are they used?
5. What are the two sections of the query design window?
6. Describe two methods for adding fields to the Design grid.
7. What is the "all field" symbol? What is its purpose?
8. In what order are the fields of a query displayed in Datasheet view?
9. What are criteria?
10. Can fields that are not entered into the Design grid have criteria placed on them?
11. What is the default operator if no other operators are entered in the Criteria cell?
12. Where are OR criteria entered for a field in the Design grid?
13. What function does the Not option in a Criteria cell perform on the dynaset?
14. What are the relational operators?
15. What results can be expected when using the Like, In, and Between... And operators?
16. What is a Total query?
17. Describe the method for displaying the Total row in the Design grid.
18. What is the significance of the Group By option?
19. Identify other options found in the Total row drop-down list.
20. What function does the Count option perform on the dynaset?
21. (T/F) The Sort row is always displayed in the Design grid.
22. (T/F) You cannot sort a query on multiple fields.
23. (T/F) You can hide a field that is used in query criterion.
24. (T/F) You can display a limited amount of the records in a dynaset with the Top Values list.
25. How can additional data sources be added to a query?
26. If two tables have been joined on common fields, what will appear between the tables in the query design view?
27. What is the advantage of having related tables in a query?

Exercises

Exercise 1—Practicing New Procedures

Using the *SirDanceALot_Ch4.accdb* file create queries to answer the following questions:

Exercise 1A: Creating Simple Queries

Using the *tblRecordings*, create the following queries.

1. Which recordings are in the Rock (RK) category? Show the *MusicID*, *Title*, *Artist*, *Category*, and *Label* fields. Save the query as *qry1A1_Rock*.

2. Which recordings are in the Rock (RK) from the Decca (2) label? Show the *MusicID*, *Title*, *Artist*, *Category*, and *Label* fields. Save the query as *qry1A2_Rock_Decca*.

3. Which recordings have the word hits anywhere in the title? Save the query as *qryEx1A3_Hits*.

Exercise 1B: Creating Queries with Complex Criteria

Using the *tblRecordings* and the *tblArtists*, create the following queries:

1. Which recordings are from the artist the BeeGees? Display *LastNameorBandName*, *Title*, and *Category*. Save the query as *qry1B1_BeeGees*.

2. Re-edit the *qryEx1B1_BeeGees*. Add the table *tblInventory* to the Table pane. How many BeeGees recordings are in stock and what type are they? Rename the query as *qry1B2_BeeGeesInventory*.

3. Which recordings have more than 5 in stock? Display *LastNameorBandName*, *Title*, *Category*, *Type*, and *QuantityonHand*. Save the query as *qry1B3_Inventory>5*.

Exercise 1C: Creating Queries with Calculations and Operators

Using any of the tables from *SirDanceALot_Ch4.accd*, create the following queries:

1. What records are there from the Decca (2) label other than Rock? Show the *Title*, *Artist*, *CategoryName*, and *LabelName* fields for all records that are not Rock. (Hint: Use the Not operator.) Save the query as *qry1C1_Decca_NotRock*.

2. Which Country recordings are less than $10? Show the *FirstnameOrBandName*, *LastName*, *Title*, *Type*, *Price*, and *CategoryName*. Save the query as *qry1C2_Country<10*.

3. Sir Dance A Lot is having a sale on all Easy Listening recordings. Create a calculated field that will show the sale price as 10% of the actual price. (Hint: The calculation for figuring the sale price would be the Price field minus the Price field times .10. Use the Zoom command to enlarge the field cell if you need to.) The query should display the fields *Artist*, *Title*, *Price*, and *Sale Price*. Format the *Sale Price* field to display as currency. Save the query as *qry1C3_EasyListeningSale*.

Exercise 1D: Using the Totals Row

Using any of the tables from *SirDanceALot_Ch4.accd*, create the following queries:

1. How many recordings in inventory for each category? (Hint: Sum the field *Quantity OnHand*.) Save the query as *qry1D1_CategoryInventory*.

2. How many recordings by type are there in stock? Save the query as *qry1D2_InventorybyType*.

3. What is the most expensive recording in stock? Show the Title and price. (Hint: Which Total function would you use to show the most expensive?) (Hint #2: Change the Top Values amount to 1 to display only the first record.) Save the query as *qry1D3_MostExpensive*.

EXERCISE 2—In-Class Group Practice

ACTIVITY AND REFLECTION

Divide into five groups as determined by your instructor. Each group represents the employees in one department of a corporation, and will do one of the following problems. Work with the tables in the *Practice_Ch4.accdb* database file.

Group 1–Personnel Department

You are responsible for the table called *tblEmployee*. Open it and browse the data and check the structure. Make sure each group member is familiar with it.

Group members will take turns being the database operator and the information seeker. Other group members may accompany either person and assist.

The operator's duty is to stay with the department table and find the information that is requested by another department.

The seeker's duty is to find the information requested in the list below, from the appropriate department. The departments are the other groups in class.

Select two people to be the first database operator and the first information seeker. After one item in the list has been found, rotate the duties of each to new group members. Go through the items in the list in the given order.

Data that your department needs:

a. What happened to the "Hypothetical ink" that we ordered from the warehouse? We ordered 25 cases last month. Why haven't we received them?

b. How much money was spent on employee travel? We need a list of all charges to the travel account.

c. What was the total commission that Mike Wanly received on orders this year? Commission is 10% of sales.

d. How many jobs is Rita Damply working on? Print a list of them.

The other departments are

- Sales (*tblOrders* table)
- Warehouse (*tblInventory* table)
- Accounting (*tblLedger* table)
- Manufacturing (*tblJobs* table)

Group 2–Sales Department

You are responsible for the table called *tblOrders*. Open it and browse the data and check the structure. Make sure each group member is familiar with it.

Group members will take turns being the database operator and the information seeker. Other group members may accompany either person and assist.

The operator's duty is to stay with the department table and find the information that is requested by another department.

The seeker's duty is to find the information requested in the list below from the appropriate department. The departments are the other groups in class.

Select two people to be the first database operator and the first information seeker. After one item in the list has been found, rotate the duties of each to new group members. Go through the items in the list in the given order.

Data that your department needs:

a. When is Herman DePloy due for his next salary review, given that salary reviews come once a year on the anniversary of your hire date?

b. One of our customers needs 45 units of "Passive formica." Do we have enough in stock in the warehouse?

c. What was the total amount in invoices to Western, Inc. over the last two months? What was the total amount of payments made? Does the company have a balance due? Print a list of all invoices and payments.

d. When will job #1585 be finished? How many hours have been charged to this job so far? Print a list of all work done on the job.

The other departments are

- Personnel (*tblEmployee* table)
- Warehouse (*tblInventory* table)
- Accounting (*tblLedger* table)
- Manufacturing (*tblJobs* table)

Group 3–Warehouse Department

You are responsible for the table called *tblInventory*. Open it and browse the data and check the structure. Make sure each group member is familiar with it.

Group members will take turns being the database operator and the information seeker. Other group members may accompany either person and assist.

The operator's duty is to stay with the department table and find the information that is requested by another department.

The seeker's duty is to find the information requested in the list below from the appropriate department. The departments are the other groups in class.

Select two people to be the first database operator and the first information seeker. After one item in the list has been found, rotate the duties of each to new group members. Go through the items in the list in the given order.

Data that your department needs:

a. How many orders for item C5777 have we received this year? Print a list of them. What is C5777?

b. How many times has "Tennessee scout" been used on jobs?

c. How much more will it cost per month if we give everyone in our department a 5% raise? Print a list of our employees, their current salary per month, and their new monthly salary.

d. How much money was spent on boxes? Print a list of all ledger entries for boxes.

The other departments are

- Sales (*tblOrders* table)
- Personnel (*tblOrders* table)
- Accounting (*tblLedger* table)
- Manufacturing (*tblJobs* table)

Group 4–Accounting Department

You are responsible for the table called *tblLedger*. Open it and browse the data and check the structure. Make sure each group member is familiar with it.

Group members will take turns being the database operator and the information seeker. Other group members may accompany either person and assist.

The operator's duty is to stay with the department table and find the information that is requested by another department.

The seeker's duty is to find the information requested in the list below from the appropriate department. The departments are the other groups in class.

Select two people to be the first database operator and the first information seeker. After one item in the list has been found, rotate the duties of each to new group members. Go through the items in the list in the given order.

Data that your department needs:

a. How many sales were made in September 2006? Print a list of these sales in ascending date order.

b. What has been the total cost to manufacture job #1422 so far?

c. You are working on the financial statements and find that you are missing the dollar value of all the items in stock that are in category NIZ. Get a list of these items and their total value.

d. We need a list of everyone who has less than a week's (40 hours) worth of vacation time left.

The other departments are

- Sales (*tblOrders* table)

- Warehouse (*tblInventory* table)

- Personnel (*tblEmployee* table)

- Manufacturing (*tblJobs* table)

Group 5–Manufacturing Department

You are responsible for the table called *tblJobs*. Open it and browse the data and check the structure. Make sure each group member is familiar with it.

Group members will take turns being the database operator and the information seeker. Other group members may accompany either person and assist.

The operator's duty is to stay with the department table and find the information that is requested by another department.

The seeker's duty is to find the information requested in the list below from the appropriate department. The departments are the other groups in class.

Select two people to be the first database operator and the first information seeker. After one item in the list has been found, rotate the duties of each to new group members. Go through the items in the list in the given order.

Data that your department needs:

a. How many times has the Helvetica machine been serviced so far? Print a list of all ledger charges we paid for this machine.

b. We need to call Susan Fellowman at home. What is her phone number?

c. The "Tepid trout" that we use to make rockets is not good enough. How much more, per unit, would it cost to use "Fancy stigmata" instead? Print the inventory records for each item.

d. We need a list of everything that "Superior Ironworks" has ordered from us this year.

The other departments are

- Sales (*tblOrders* table)
- Warehouse (*tblInventory* table)
- Personnel (*tblEmployee* table)
- Accounting (*tblLedger* table)

ACTIVITY

EXERCISE 3—Challenge: Queries on Multiple Tables

Use the database file *Practice_Ch4.accdb*.

Exercise 3A: New Query

Create a new query using the tables *tblOrders* and *tblInventory*. What field appears in both tables? Join the tables on this field.

1. Select the fields *Customer, Date_Sold, Quantity, Amount,* and *Descript.*
2. Add a new field *Quantity * Amount* and name the new field *Total Price.*
3. Sort by *Customer* and *Date_Sold.*
4. Use the criterion: *Date_Sold* after August 1, 2008.
5. Run the query. Save the query as *qry3A_Order Items.*

Exercise 3B: New Query

Create a query to summarize total sales amounts by customer. Re-edit the *qry3A_Order Items.*

1. Add a total row.
2. Remove all the fields except *Customer* and *Total Price.*
3. *Total Price* should be summed.
4. Run the query. Save the query as *qry3B_Customer Amounts.*

Exercise 3C: New Query

Create a new query using the tables *tblEmployee* and *tblOrders.* What field appears in both tables? Join the tables on this field.

1. Add the fields *Last Name, First Name.*
2. Create a new field, *Monthly Salary,* which divides the *Ann_Salary* by 12. Format the new field to currency.
3. Add a field to display the count of orders for each salesperson.
4. View the dynaset. You will notice that all the employees do not display, but only those that appear in the *tblOrders* table. Double-click on the join line between the tables. Change it to "Include ALL records from 'tblEmployee' and only those records from the 'tblOrders' where the join fields are equal."
5. Run the query and view the dynaset again. Save the query as *qry3C_Paychecks.*

Exercise 3D: Edit Query

Edit the query *qry3C_Paychecks.*

1. Add a column that is 10 percent of the *Amount* from the *tblOrders* table.
2. Add a Total row and sum the new column. Format the field to currency.

3. Save the query as *qry3D_Commissions*.

4. Run the query.

Exercise 3E: Edit Query

Open the *qry3D_Commissions* query.

1. Add the field *Department*, and remove the fields *First Name*, *Last Name*, and the field used to count orders.

2. Group by *Department* and sum the columns *Monthly Salary* and *Commission*.

3. Run the query.

4. Save the query as *qry3E_Dept Payroll*.

EXERCISE 4—More Practice: Using All Types of Queries

ACTIVITY AND REFLECTION

Exercise 4A: New Query

Create a query from the *tblEmployee* table in the *Practice_Ch4.accdb*. This query displays first and last name of the employee, the amount of vacation hours, and the number of vacation hours used.

1. Add a column that calculates the balance of vacation hours left.

2. Show only those records where 40 or more hours of vacation time remains.

3. Sort by *Last Name*.

4. Save the query as *qry4A_Vacation Remaining*.

Exercise 4B: New Query

Create a query from the *tblInventory* table.

1. Display the fields *Descript, Category, OnHand,* and *OnOrder*.

2. Add a column that adds the *OnHand* quantity to the *OnOrder* quantity.

3. Show only those records where the amount *OnOrder* is 1 or more, and category = "CKE" or "YWA."

4. Sort in *Category* order.

5. Save as *qry4B_Supply Orders*.

Exercise 4C: New Query

Create a query from the *tblLedger* table.

1. Have it display the total amounts posted for each account (not each individual amount, but a subtotal for each account description and account number).

2. Display the *Descript* and *AccountNo* fields and the sum of amounts.

3. Sort in *Descript* order.

4. Save as *qry4C_Account Summary*.

Exercise 4D: New Query

Create a new query using the tables *tblEmployee* and *tblJobs*.

1. Select the fields *Last Name, First Name* from *tblEmployee,* and *Hours* and *Cost* from *tblJobs*.

2. Sort by *Last Name*.

3. Display a subtotal of hours and costs for each employee.

4. Save as *qry4D_Employee Job Charges*.

REFLECTION

Exercise 5—Discussion Questions

1. Open the *tblLedger* table in the *Practice_Ch4.accdb* database in Datasheet view. Do you see a correlation between the fields *Account_no* and *Descript*? On paper (not on the computer), split the table into two tables that eliminate redundancy. What field is in both tables?

2. Under what circumstances might you use a filter rather than a query on a table to view a group of records?

3. Can you use the wildcard character * (asterisk) in the criteria of a query? Try it and find out.

4. How does changing the selection in the Return: Top Values drop-down list box affect the records displayed in a query? Try it and find out.

5. Can you sort on a field that isn't displayed in a query? Do you have to display the common field in a query consisting of two joined tables? Can you think of any rules where you must display a specific field in a query?

6. How can you make a calculated column (such as total job cost = *Cost* + *Price* in #5 of Exercise #4) display as currency?

CASE STUDY A: MRS. SUGARBAKER'S COOKIES

Now that the database is set up, Mrs. S wants to begin using it to retrieve data for customer questions, product information, and orders.

Design the query to answer the following questions. Add the appropriate tables and print out the dynaset (results) for each query. Save the queries with an appropriate name.

1. Which products have chocolate items in them? Name the query *qryCh4_1_ChocolateItems*.

2. How many customers are from each state? (Hint: Use the Count function.) Name the query *qryCh4_2_CustomerCount*.

3. Which products have either a cherry or strawberry cookie variety? (Hint: Use the Or criteria.) Name the query *qryCh4_3_Strawberry_Cherry*.

4. Which product is the biggest seller? (Hint: Use the Sum function and Sort descending order.) Name the query *qryCh4_4_BiggestSeller*.

5. Which cookie assortment is providing the most income? (Hint: Create a calculated field using the *Quantity* and *UnitPrice* fields.) Name the query *qryCh4_5_MostIncome*.

6. Which products are under $25? Name the query *qryCh4_6_Under25*.

7. Mrs. S wants to target her Colorado customers with a special offer. Retrieve all address data from customers only from Colorado. Name the query *qryCh4_7_COCustomers*.

8. Ms. Desdemona Savoy placed an order and would like to know when it was shipped. Retrieve this information for Ms. Savoy. Put in appropriate tables and field data in the query design. Name the query *qryCh4_8_SavoyOrder*.

9. Which customer has placed the most orders? (Hint: Identify who the customer is and count all his/her orders. Use Totaling functions.) Name the query *qryCh4_9_CountOrders*.

10. Mrs. S wants to be able to tell customers grand totals that would include all the costs for the items they've purchased plus the freight charge. Create a query that would give this information. (Hint: Create a calculate field and use the Sum function.) Name the query *qryCh4_10_TotalPrice*.

CASE STUDY B: SANDY FEET RENTAL COMPANY

Now that the database is set up, the Sandy Feet Rental Company will begin using it to retrieve data for customer questions, owner's queries, and other reports.

Design queries to answer the following questions.

1. Which owners are from Colorado? Show owner's name and all address data. Save the query as *qry1_Colorado_Owners*.

2. Which properties accept pets and have high speed Internet access? Save the query as *qry2_Pets_HighSpeed*.

3. Which properties are 2 bedroom condos? Save the query as *qry3_All_2BR*.

4. Modify the *qry3_All_2BR* to show only 2 bedroom condos that are ocean front. Save the query as *qry4_OF_2BR*.

5. Which clients have rented a condo and are bringing a pet? (Hint: Enter >0 for the criteria in the *Number of Pets* field). Save the query as *qry5_Renting_with_Pets*.

6. How many clients are there from each state? (Hint: Use Group By and Count from the Totals command.) Save the query as *qry6_Count_by_State*.

7. Which condos rent for $550 or less for the second week of July? Save the query as *qry7_July_550*.

8. Modify the *qry7_July_550* to show the property address and only those that accept pets. Save the query as *qry8_July_Pets*.

9. Which properties are rented during the month of May? Include the *Property Address,* the dates rented, *Deposit Amount,* and *Rental Number.* Save the query as *qry9_May_Rentals*.

10. What is the total of housekeeping fees for Property Number P1? Save the query as *qry10_Housekeeping_P1*.

CASE STUDY C: PENGUINS SKI CLUB

Using the *Penguins* database, create a series of queries, as described below.

1. Create the following three queries using *tblMembers*.

   a. *qryMembersBeginners* shows the names and ages of all the beginners in the group. Don't display the ability level, and sort by last name.

   b. *qryMembers7&8* shows the names, ages, ability levels, and equipment rental status of all 7 and 8 eight year olds. Sort in order by last name.

   c. *qryMembersIntermediate* shows the names and ages of all the intermediate skiers in the group, who are either 10 or 11 years old. Don't display the ability level, and sort by last name.

2. Create a query on *tblMembers* and *tblEquipmentRental* that shows the names of members who have rented equipment, the rental package number, rental date, and return date. Sort in order by last name. Save the query as *qryRentals*.

3. Create a query called *qryMemberDirectory* that shows member's names, phone numbers, parent's names, and parent's phone number. Sort in order by member's last name.

4. Create a total query called *qryMemberAbility* that groups members by ability level, and displays how many members are at that ability level, and what their average age is.

5. Create a total query called *qryMemberAttendance* that lists each member's name, and counts how many events each member has attended. Sort in order by member's last name.

6. Create a total query called *qryEventAttendance1*. List each event date, name, and location, and count the number of members that attended each event.

    a. Make a copy of *qryEventAttendance1* and call it *qryEventAttendance2*. Change the join type between *tblEvents* and *tblMembers* so that all records from *tblEvents* are included. Look at the difference in the data displayed. Save the query.

7. Create a total query called *qryAmountsPaid*. Total the payments made by each member.

    a. Create another query called *qryAmountsDue*. Use data from *tblMembers* (and *tblParents*, if you have this table in your database), and *qryAmountsPaid*. Show the member's names, amounts due, and total of payments made. Sort in order by member's last name.

Chapter 5

Forms

Objectives

After completing this chapter you will be able to

Understand forms:
- Define a form and identify uses for forms.
- Identify tools available to create forms.

Create a form:
- Choose the appropriate format and layout.
- Enter data sources into a form.
- Create a form based on table/query data using the following tools: Form tool, Split Form tool, Multiple Items tool, Form Wizard, and Datasheet.

Modify a form:
- Change to different form views.
- Identify the functions available in different form views.
- Use the Form Layout tools to edit a form.

Use a form:
- View, enter, and edit data through a form.
- Save and print forms.

Dictionary

Bound form	A form that is tied to a data source, such as a table or query.
Columnar	A form layout that displays all field names in a single column down the left side of the form. One record is displayed at a time.
Datasheet form	A type of form that displays all records in Datasheet view.
Design view	The view that allows manual creation or editing of a form. It comes with its own set of form design tools.
Field label	The label on a form that identifies a field data area. It can be any text you choose.
Form	A database object that displays table or query data, and is used instead of the Datasheet view. A form allows you to view, enter, and edit data.
Form tool	A tool that creates a form from a selected data source that displays one record at a time.
Form view	A view of the form which displays the data from the data source and allows for data entry and editing.
Form Wizard	A tool that asks the user for input to create the form.

Layout Tools ribbon	The ribbon which contains Layout tools for editing the form.
Layout view	A view of the form which allows for certain editing changes to the structure of the form as well as data entry and editing.
Main form	The form used to display data from the main or "one" table in a one-to-many relationship. Data is displayed in a columnar layout.
Main/subform	A type of form that combines two or more tables/queries into a single form with the tables having different layouts.
Multiple Items form	A type of form that displays multiple records in a columns and rows format.
One-to-many relationship	Two tables that are joined on a common field where a specific value for the common field appears only once in the main table, but can appear multiple times in the subtable.
Properties	The characteristics of a group of objects.
Property sheet	The list of properties for an object.
Split View form	A type of form that combines all fields from a datasource in two distinct views: Layout view and Datasheet view.
Subform	The form used to display data from the sub or "many" table in a one-to-many relationship. Data is displayed in a tabular layout.
Tabular	A form layout that has several fields and records displayed on the screen in a "table-like" design.
Unbound form	A form that is not tied to a data source.

5.1 Defining a Form

The data in tables and queries has been displayed and updated in one view, the Datasheet view. This view shows several records on the screen in a spreadsheet fashion with columns (table fields) and rows (table records). This view is acceptable to some for data entry. However, in other cases this screen might be too cluttered to use. An Access form is another way of displaying data in a table or query on the screen. Forms are used for data entry, viewing, and editing.

Forms have advantages over the Datasheet view, as they can be customized to suit the user's purpose. Objects and controls can be placed on the form in a more "user friendly" way. Objects such as instructions, lists of possible data values, and control buttons that activate procedures can be added to a form for ease of use. Only necessary data for a user need be displayed on a form, thus providing some measure of confidentiality.

Forms that are tied to a data source (a table or query) are called bound forms. Forms that are not tied to any data are called unbound forms. These unbound forms can be used to display user selections such as menus, or to display messages and information.

Access has several ways to create forms using the Forms group on the Create ribbon. Some of these tools require little user input and make use of a predesigned format, while others require that the user design the form. The forms created from these tools have different layouts that are conducive to data entry, editing, or viewing data. All forms can be modified through the Form Design view regardless of how they are originally created.

Table 5.1 shows different Forms tools, a description of the form that is created, and the layout of the form.

Notice the difference in the layouts of the forms in Figure 5.1. These forms all use the same data source but produce forms with different formats.

Q: When I edit the data in a form, is the data changed in the underlying table?

A: Yes. Records can be added and deleted this way, too.

Table 5.1　Forms Tools

Forms Tools	Form Layout	Description
Form	Columnar	All fields are arranged in one column on the left side of the screen. One record is displayed at a time.
Split view	Datasheet view and Layout view	All fields from the data source are displayed in two views: Datasheet view and Layout view.
Multiple Items	Similar to a Datasheet view with records (rows) and fields (columns)	All fields from the data source are displayed in a modified Datasheet view.
Pivot Chart	Chart	A graphical view of table or query data. The chart can be added to a form.
Blank Form	Various	An empty form is created in Layout view. Fields from tables/queries can be added.
Form Wizard (More Forms List)	Various	A guide to creating a form. Forms with subforms can be created through this tool.
Datasheet (More Forms List)	Datasheet	All fields are displayed in Datasheet view.
Modal Dialog (More Forms List)	Various	A custom form to display a dialog box for user input.
Pivot Table	Tabular	A tabular form which summarizes data.
Form Design	Various	An empty form is created in Design view. Fields from tables/queries can be added.

Figure 5.1　Samples of forms created with Forms tool

5.2 Creating a Form Using the Form Tool

The Form tool is a very easy way to create a form. This method uses all the fields from the data source in a columnar layout form, with one record displayed per page. The user need only choose the data source. (Note: If the table is part of a relationship with another table, the Form tool will create a form with a subform design, with the relationship table being the subform. If the table is part of a relationship with more than one table, then the subform will not be included into the form. Forms/subforms will be discussed later in this chapter.)

Q: What is the fastest way to create a form from a table?

A: Select the table and then click the Form tool. A form using all the fields from the table will be created.

How to Create a Form

1. Click on the table or query that will be the data source for the form. (Note: Do not open the table or query, simply select it.)

2. Click the Create tab. The Create ribbon will be displayed.

3. In the Forms group, click Form (see Figure 5.2).

4. The new form opens in Layout view. The data from the data source is displayed as well as the form controls. Changes can be made to the form design in Layout view.

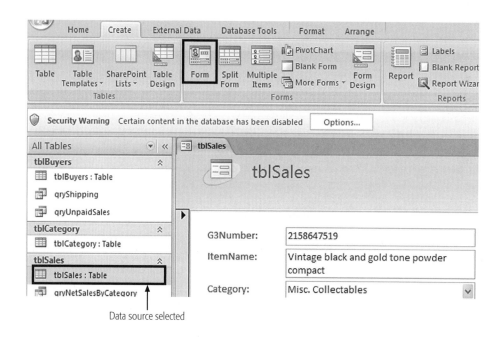

Figure 5.2 Creating a form with the Form tool

TRY IT YOURSELF 5.2.1

Using the *G3_Ch5.accdb* file, create the following form.

A. Click on the *tblSales* table to select it.

B. Using the Form tool, create a form from the *tblSales* table.

C. Save the form as *frmSales*.

How to Save a Form

1. Click the Office button.

2. Choose the Save As command.

3. Click Save Object As.

4. Enter the form name, beginning with the *frm* prefix.

5. Click OK

   OR

   Right-click on the form tab with the default name.

6. Choose the Save command from the shortcut menu and enter the name of the form in the Form Name text box (see Figure 5.3).

7. Click OK.

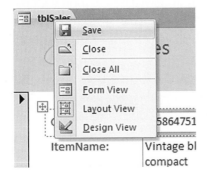

Figure 5.3 Save short-cut menu

How to Print the Form

1. Click the Office button.

2. Choose Print.

3. Click on the Print command.

4. Select the printer.

5. Select the page number or choose to print selected forms in the Print Range dialog box (see Figure 5.4).

6. Click OK.

Q: My form printout was multiple pages. What did I do wrong?

A: You forgot to select only one page or record in the Print Range dialog box.

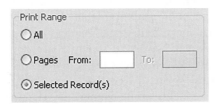

Figure 5.4 Print range dialog box

5.3 Working with Form Views

Depending on the method chosen for creating a form, it will open in one of three views. Each view displays a different screen and ribbon. The Form view displays the data within the form in their respective fields. No design changes to the form can be made in this view, but records can be added and edited here. The Design view does not display the data in the form but displays all the controls on the design side of the form. This view allows you to make changes to the structure of the form. The Layout view combines both Design view and Form view functionality: Records can be added or edited and some design changes can be made. Although formatting changes can be made to individual controls (fields, labels, and other objects on the form), other changes (such as resizing) require the change to be made to the entire group of controls on the form.

Introducing the Layout View

A form created with the Form tool opens in the Layout view. The Form Layout tools appear on the ribbon. Property Sheets for the form and its controls appear to the right of the screen. As you select different controls on the form, the Property Sheet changes (see Figure 5.5). The Property Sheet contains the characteristics of the control or Access object (such as a form). We will look at Property Sheets later in this chapter.

The properties that are set for a field in table design are applied to the field on a form. If a field data type is set for Currency, then the field is displayed on the form with the dollar sign and two decimal places. Other formatting can be applied to the controls on a form, such as font changes, colors, and autoformats. Controls can be moved and rearranged.

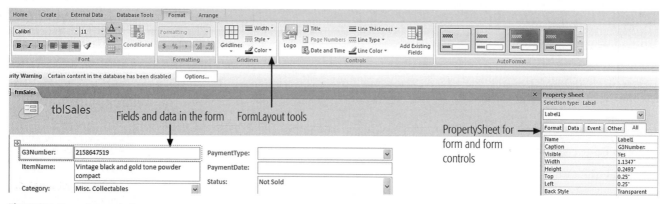

Figure 5.5 Form Layout view

Examining the Form Layout Tools Ribbon

The Form Layout Tools ribbon contains all the commands available to make some formatting changes to the form (see Figure 5.6). The Font group contains commands to make changes to any control such as bold, italics, font and background colors, alignment, font, and font size. The Formatting group contains commands to format a control with currency, percentage, and decimal place. The Gridlines group has commands to display the gridlines of the form and change the width, color, and style of gridlines on a form. The Controls group provides commands to make changes to different types of controls. For example, the Title command selects the title of the form so that any other formatting changes can be applied. Formatting for a date/time field can be changed by clicking on the Date/Time command. Changes to any control with lines can be made by clicking on the control and then selecting line width, color, and style. The Add Existing Fields command will display the list of available fields that can be added to the form. The AutoFormat group will make global changes to the look of a form based on predefined colors and styles. As with other actions in Access, these formatting changes can be reversed with the Undo command (see Figure 5.6).

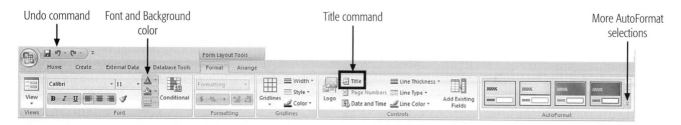

Figure 5.6 Form Layout Tools ribbon

How to Change the Format of the Form

1. In the AutoFormat group, click the More drop down arrow to display the format choices (see Figure 5.6).

2. Click on the format choice.

3. The form is displayed with the new color choices.

How to Format the Title

1. Click the Title command in the Controls group (see Figure 5.6).

2. Retype the text for the Title.

3. Add any formatting from the Font group.

How to Resize Controls

1. Click on the control to resize. (Note: In Layout View, all the controls of similar type, such as label, will be resized.)

2. Move the mouse to the border lines until a double-headed arrow appears. Click and drag to the desired size.

How to Delete a Control

1. Click on the control to delete. (Note: Some controls have multiple parts such as a label and a text box. Be sure to delete all the parts necessary.)

2. Push the Delete key.

How to Move a Control

1. Click on the control.

2. Move the mouse until a four-sided arrow appears. Click and drag the control to the new location.

Changing Individual Controls

Changes to individual controls are as simple as clicking on the control to change and then clicking or selecting the formatting change command. Changes to the font, font size, font color, line width, style, and color can all be achieved this way.

How to Change the Font

1. Click on the control for the font change.

2. Using the Font drop-down arrow, in the Font group, select a new font.

How to Change the Font Size

1. Click on the control for the font change.

2. Using the Font Size drop-down arrow, in the Font group, select a new size number.

Form View

The Form view shows the layout of the form and all data associated with the form. Fields are clearly identified with their names. If the form is based on an existing table or query, the data is shown. This view of a form is good for entering data into a table. Depending on the type of layout, one record at a time or several will be displayed on the screen. Notice that the ribbon now is the Home tab with the Views, Clipboard, Records, Sort &

TRY IT YOURSELF 5.3.1

Using the *frmSales* form, make the following changes:

A. Change the format of the form to the Civic AutoFormat (see Figure 5.6).

B. Edit the title of the form to "Sales Form." Change the font to Lucinda Sans and font size to 20.

C. Click on the control that holds the *G3Number* data. Add bold formatting to this control. Change the background color to Purple 2 (see Figure 5.6).

D. Click on the control that is the label for the *G3Number* field. Add bold formatting to this control.

E. Resize the controls of the form to make them smaller, but not so small as to cut off any data.

F. Save the changes to this form (see Figure 5.7).

Filter, and Find groups (see Figure 5.7). The Views group has one command to change the view of the form to Layout, Form, or Design view. The Clipboard group has commands to cut, copy, and paste record data. The Records group contains commands to check spelling, add new records, delete, and save records. The Sort & Filter group has commands to perform sorting and filtering actions on records—much like sorting and filtering in Datasheet view. The Find group contains commands to find and replace data in records, locate specific records, and select one or more records.

Figure 5.7 Form view ribbon

How to Change Views of a Form

1. Click the View command in the Views group on the Forms Layout ribbon (see Figure 5.8).
2. Choose Form View from the drop-down list

   OR

   Right-click on the name tab of the form.
3. Choose the view from the shortcut menu.

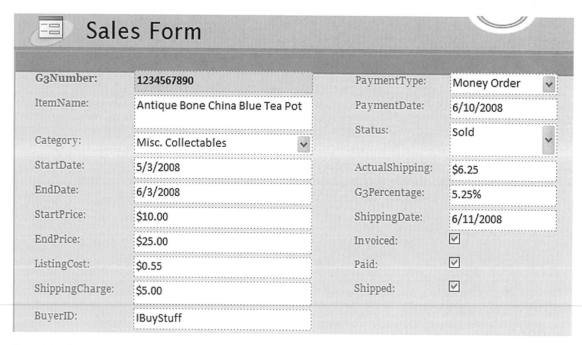

Figure 5.8 Changes made to form

Navigating Through the Form

In order to move between fields, make sure the form displayed on the screen is the active form by clicking into that form. Use the mouse to click on the desired field, and TAB or ENTER to move through the form. To move between records, use the navigation buttons at the bottom of the screen. Use the Search button on the navigation bar to search for character strings within a field (see Figure 5.9).

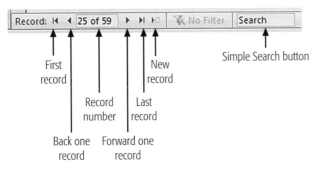

First record

Record number

Back one record

Forward one record

Last record

New record

Simple Search button

Figure 5.9 Record navigation buttons

TRY IT YOURSELF 5.3.2

Using the *frmSales* form:

A. Search for the character string "Vintage" in the *ItemName* field (see Figure 5.10).

B. Continue through all the records that have that character string.

C. Delete the string from the Search text box when the search is completed.

How to Use the Search Button in a Form

1. Click into the field to search.
2. Click into the Search text box (see Figure 5.10).

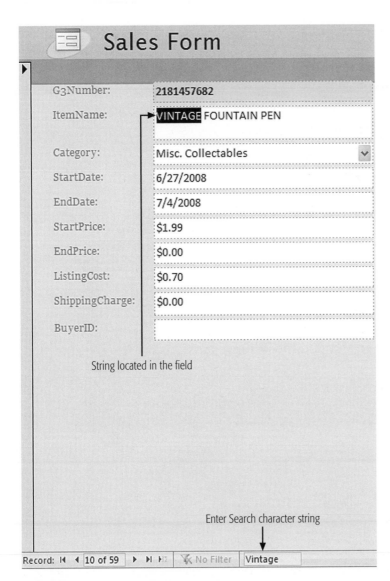

String located in the field

Enter Search character string

Figure 5.10 Using a Search character string

3. Type the character string to search.

4. Use $\boxed{\text{ENTER}}$ to progress through the forms with the search.

5. Click into another field in the form to end the search.

6. Delete the character string in the Search text box.

Using the Form to Enter Data

The most common use of a form is entering data. Make sure all the fields in the table data source are entered into the form. Otherwise not all field data will be entered into the table. Fields are formatted according to the data type set when the fields were entered at the time the table was created. Therefore, if a field data type is Currency, the dollar sign and two decimal points are automatically entered as data is typed into that field.

The Form view of a form allows you to enter new records, edit existing data, delete records, sort, filter, and spell check records. The Form view has its own ribbon with data editing commands (see Figure 5.11). To apply a filter, use the commands in the Sort/Filter

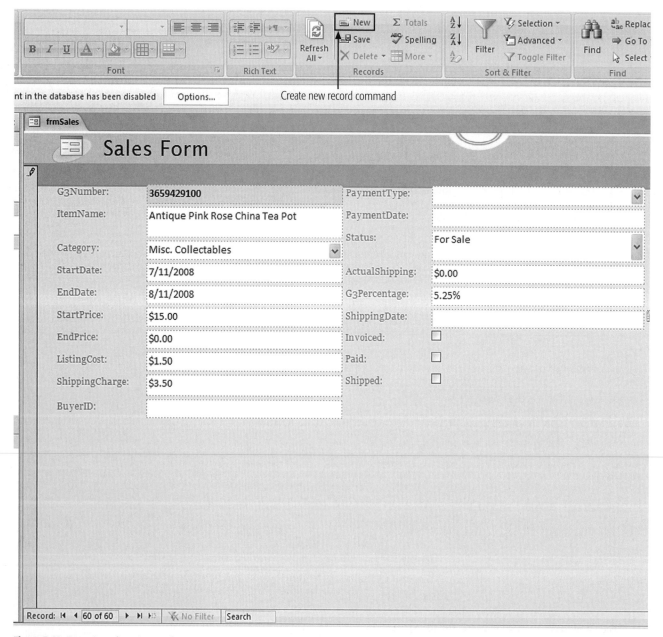

Figure 5.11 Entering data into a form

group for Filter by Selection or Advanced Filtering commands. To sort data in a form, click inside the field to sort. Then click either the Sort Ascending or Sort Descending command.

How to Add Data to a Table with a Form

1. In Form view, click the New (blank) record button on the navigation bar at the bottom of the form

   OR

   Click the New command in the Records group on the ribbon.

2. Add data to the form (see Figure 5.11).

3. Use the Tab key or the mouse to move between fields.

4. Data is saved when the form is closed or when another new record is added

   OR

   Click the Save command in the Records group.

How to Close the Form

1. Right-click on the form name tab.

2. Choose the Close command from the shortcut menu (see Figure 5.12).

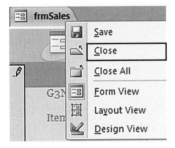

Figure 5.12 Closing the form

How to Open a Form

1. In the Navigation pane, double-click on the form name to open.

2. Change the view to Form view, if necessary, for data entry.

5.4 / Creating Other Types of Forms

Split Form

The Split Form command creates a form from a selected table or query with two distinctive views of the data. The Datasheet view is located at the bottom of the form while the same data is displayed in Layout view in the top half of the form. Both views are synchronized so that when fields are selected in the Datasheet view, that same record and field is displayed in Layout view. When records are selected and fields are

TRY IT YOURSELF 5.3.3

Using the *frmSales* form:

1. Add a new record (see Figure 5.11).

2. Enter the following data.

G3Number	3659429100
ItemName	Antique Pink Rose China Tea Pot
Category	Misc. Collectables
StartDate	7/11/2008
EndDate	8/11/2008
StartPrice	15.00
EndPrice	
Listing Cost	1.50
ShippingCharge	3.50
BuyerID	
PaymentType	
PaymentDate	
Status	For Sale
ActualShipping	
G3Percentage	0.0525
ShippingDate	
Invoiced	FALSE
Paid	FALSE
Shipped	FALSE

3. Save the record.

4. Close the form (see Figure 5.12).

TRY IT YOURSELF 5.4.1

Using the *tblBuyers* from the *G3_Ch5.accdb* file:

A. Create a Split Form (see Figure 5.13).

B. Add a new record with the following data. You can use either view of the form to add the new record.

Category	Data
BuyerID	ILuvT
FirstName	Earl
LastName	Gray
Email	ILuvT@open.net
StreetAddress	7878 Peach Street
City	Green River
State	MI
Zip	48345

C. Edit the record for GypsyKitchens (*BuyerID*). The address should be 2001 Vista Lane.

D. Save the form as *frmBuyers*. Close the form.

displayed in Layout view, that same record is displayed in Datasheet view. Records can be added, deleted or edited in either section of this type of form (see Figure 5.13). One advantage to this view would be the ability to see more of the records through the Datasheet view while having the ease of data entry and editing through the form Layout view.

How to Create a Split Form

1. Click the Create tab.

2. Click the data source (either table or query).

3. Click the Split Form command. The form is displayed in Layout view (see Figure 5.13).

How to Add a Record

1. Click the New command in the Records group

   OR

   Click the New (blank) record button on the form navigation bar.

2. Add data to the new record form in either view of the Split Form.

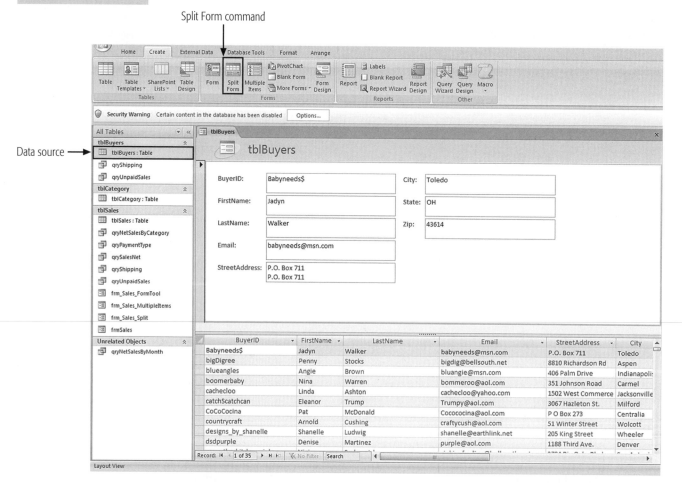

Figure 5.13 Creating a Split Form

Professional Tip: Creating an Autoformat Style

When a wizard is used to create a form, one of the options is to select a format or style. If you would like to give a new look to your forms, you can create your own style to apply to new forms.

First, you must create a form with the new style. Some ideas for changes are:

- Change control properties for text and background colors.
- Change the form's background picture to your own bitmap graphic.
- Change the background color of a section. (You can't have a background while displaying a graphic on the form's background.)

Save the form and move to either Layout or Design view. Click the directional arrows in the AutoFormat group to display the AutoFormat choices. Choose the AutoFormat Wizard and click the Customize button. Select the option to create a new format based on the open form and click the OK button. Type in a new name for the style and click OK. Close the AutoFormat Wizard after creating your new style.

Now you can apply your own style whenever you create a new form!

You can also remove styles by returning to the AutoFormat Wizard and choosing the Customize button. Choose the option to delete the selected format from the Customize Options list.

Multiple Items and Datasheet Forms

The Multiple Items form displays the records of a data source in a column and row format showing several records at a time. This form opens up in Layout view so that the table/query data is displayed and changes can be made to the design of the form (see Figure 5.14). The Datasheet form is very similar to the Datasheet view of a table with multiple records being displayed in the column and row format.

Figure 5.14 Creating a Multiple Items Form

How to Create a Datasheet Form

1. Click the Create tab.

2. Click the data source (either table or query).

3. Click the More Forms drop-down list. Choose Datasheet (see Figure 5.14).

4. The form is displayed in Datasheet view.

How to Create a Multiple Items Form

1. Click the Create tab.

2. Click the data source (either table or query).

3. Click the Multiple Items command. The form is displayed in Layout view (see Figure 5.14).

Introducing Property Sheets

Each group of objects in Access—tables, forms, queries etc.—has similar characteristics called properties. Properties, which can be found on the Property Sheet of the object, control the appearance and behavior of the objects to which they belong. Each field in a table has properties such as data type, size, and format. These are set when the table is created. Each control on a form or report has properties such as size, color, and font, as well as many other properties.

The properties for a control or Access object are listed on its Property Sheet. This Property Sheet might display when a form is created through one of the Forms commands, such as Multiple Items. The Property Sheet is only visible in the Layout and Design Views. If the Property Sheet is not displayed, it can be made visible by changing the view to either Layout or Design view and clicking the Database Tools tab. Then click on the Property Sheet command in the Show/Hide group. Close the Property Sheet by clicking on the Close X button in the top right corner of the sheet.

The Property Sheet has tabs that organize properties into groups. Each tab shows one property per line with the name of the property on the left and the actual setting on the right. The Property Sheets for different controls vary in types of properties listed. For example, the properties of a Form will be different than those of a form title or field holding data. Figure 5.15 shows some of the properties of the form itself. Notice the different tabs at the top of the property list to show only those properties. The All tab displays all properties for the selected object. Figure 5.16 shows the properties of the form title control. Remember this control was created when the form was created. Notice the Caption property. This shows the caption that is displayed in the title control. The title can be changed by editing that control in Layout view or by changing the Caption property to reflect the correct wording of the form title.

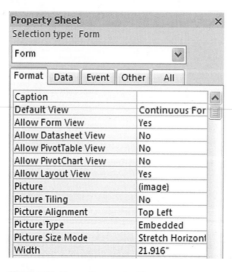

Figure 5.15 Form Property Sheet

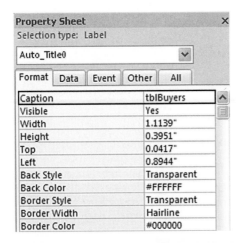

Figure 5.16 Title Property Sheet

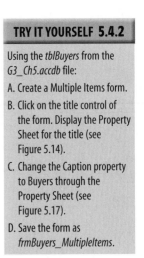

TRY IT YOURSELF 5.4.2

Using the *tblBuyers* from the *G3_Ch5.accdb* file:

A. Create a Multiple Items form.

B. Click on the title control of the form. Display the Property Sheet for the title (see Figure 5.14).

C. Change the Caption property to Buyers through the Property Sheet (see Figure 5.17).

D. Save the form as *frmBuyers_MultipleItems*.

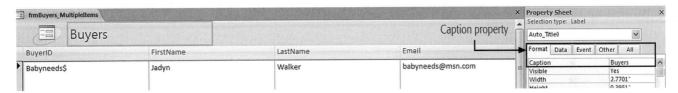

Figure 5.17 Title Caption changed

5.5 Using the Form Wizard

The Form Wizard is another way to create an Access form with more guidance from Access and more input from the user. Unlike the previous methods of creating a form where Access used all the fields from the data source, the Form Wizard allows for field selection as well as other formatting choices.

How to Use the Form Wizard

1. From the Create tab, click the More Forms drop-down list.

2. Click the Form Wizard command (see Figure 5.18).

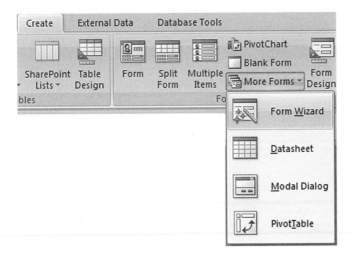

Figure 5.18 Starting the Form Wizard

3. On the first screen of the Wizard, choose the data source from the Table/Queries drop-down list (see Figure 5.19).

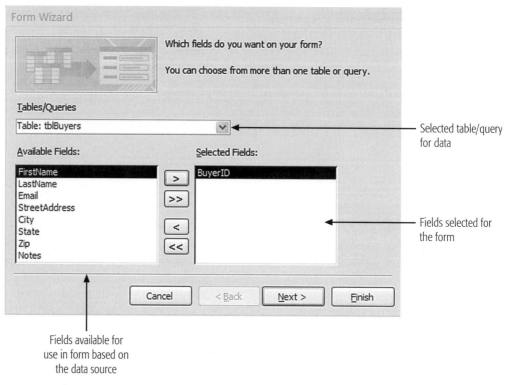

Figure 5.19 Selecting fields for the form

4. From the Available Fields box, click on a field to add to the form. Use the directional arrow (>) to move the highlighted field to the Selected Fields box (see Figure 5.19). The order in which you choose fields and move them to the Selected Fields window is the order they will appear on the form. See Table 5.2 for an explanation of other directional arrows.

Table 5.2 Directional Buttons for Field Selection

Buttom	Movement
>	Moves one highlighted field from Available Fields to Selected Fields window.
>>	Moves all fields from Available Fields to Selected Fields window in that order.
<	Moves one highlighted field from Selected Fields to Available Fields window.
<<	Moves all fields from Selected Fields to Available Fields window.

5. Select the desired fields in order. Click the Next button when finished.

6. Select the layout for the form. A sample layout appears on the left side of the screen (see Figure 5.20), Click the Next button to continue.

7. Select the style for the form. A sample style appears on the left side of the screen (see Figure 5.21). Click the Next button to continue.

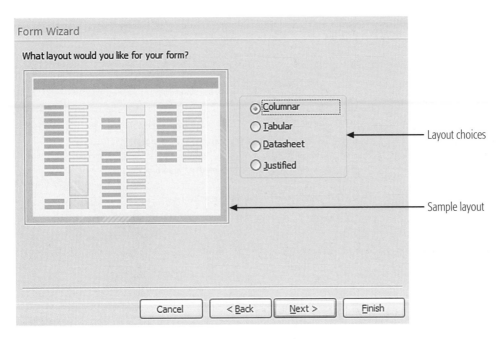

Figure 5.20 Form layouts

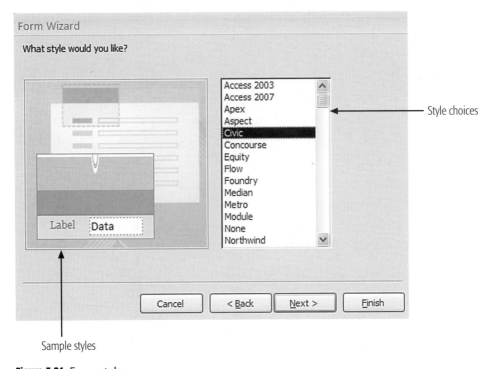

Figure 5.21 Form styles

8. Enter the title for the form. The default title is based on the name of the table/query used as the data source. Edit or delete the default to enter a new title (see Figure 5.22).

9. Choose the view in which to open the completed form (see Figure 5.22). *Open the form…* will open the form in Form view to enter data. *Modify the form's design…* will open the form in Design view to make changes to the structure of the form.

10. Click the Finish button. See Figure 5.23 for the finished form.

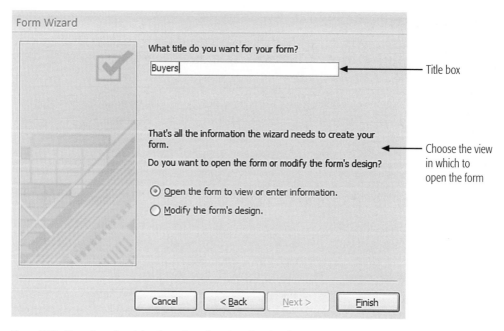

Figure 5.22 Entering the title choosing the view for the form

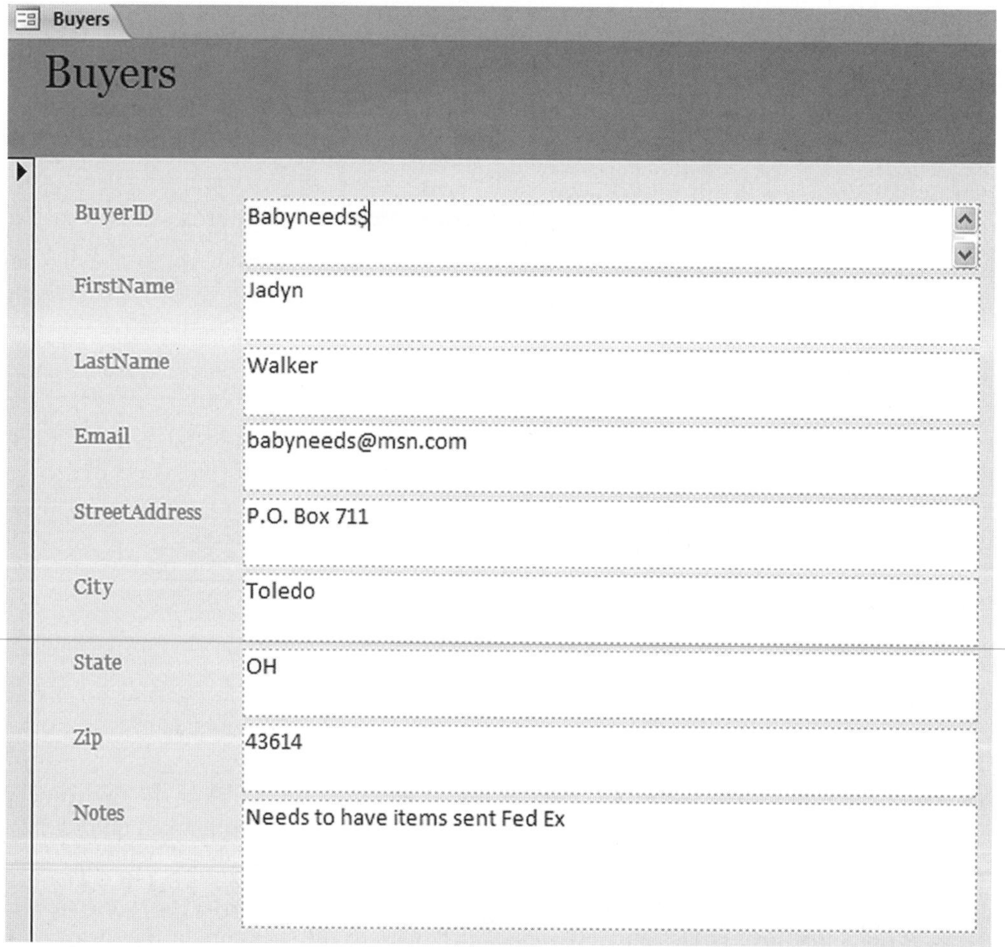

Figure 5.23 Completed form

Renaming an Access Form

Because Access picks up the name of the form from the title given in the last screen of the Form Wizard, you'll need to rename the form using proper naming conventions for database objects: Forms use the *frm* prefix.

How to Rename a Form

1. Close the form if it is opened.

2. Right-click on the form in the Navigation pane. Select the Rename command from the shortcut menu.

3. Edit the name of the Access object to include the prefix *frm* (see Figure 5.24).

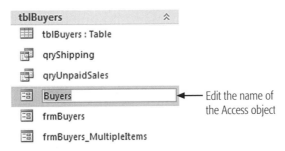
→ Edit the name of the Access object

Figure 5.24 Renaming the form

TRY IT YOURSELF 5.5.1

Using the *tblBuyers* table from the *G3_Ch5.accdb* file:

A. Create a form using the Form Wizard (see Figure 5.18).

B. Load all the fields into the form (see Figure 5.19).

C. Select the Columnar layout (see Figure 5.20).

D. Choose the Civic style (see Figure 5.21).

E. Enter the title as *Buyers* in the form (see Figure 5.22).

F. Open the form in Form view (see Figure 5.23).

G. Close the form.

H. Rename the form with the *frm* prefix to *frmBuyers_Wizard* (see Figure 5.24).

Using Multiple Tables in Forms

Multiple tables can be used as the data source for all types of forms, including those created by the Form Wizard, as long as the tables are joined in a relationship. There are two ways to show data from multiple tables in a form. You can create a query first to combine all preferred fields from several tables or you can add fields from other tables during the form building process. The tables used should already be joined through either the Relationship command (see Chapter 3) or through a temporary join in a query.

Making a Form with a Subform

A form/subform can be created to embed one form within another form, when a one-to-many relationship between the two tables exists. The main form displays data from the main or "one" table in a columnar format. The data, one record from the main table, is usually displayed at the top of the form. The subform displays multiple records from the "many" table in the one-to-many relationship. These records are displayed in a tabular or datasheet type layout. An example of a form/subform is shown in Figure 5.25. Two queries can be used instead of two tables but there must be two data sources to create the form/subform.

The main form is linked to the subform by a common field. The subform only displays the data that is related to the record displayed in the main form. Records in both tables must have the same value in the common field. The main form shows the data from the "one" side of the relationship with each record being unique to the table. The subform shows data from the "many" side of the relationship displaying all records related to the main form.

In the sample form illustrated in Figure 5.25, the record from the *tblBuyers* table is displayed in the main or upper area of the form with the matching records from the *tblSales* table displayed in the subform. The advantage to this type of form is that it allows the user to edit or add data to more than one table through a single form. It also allows all the related data to be viewed together on one screen.

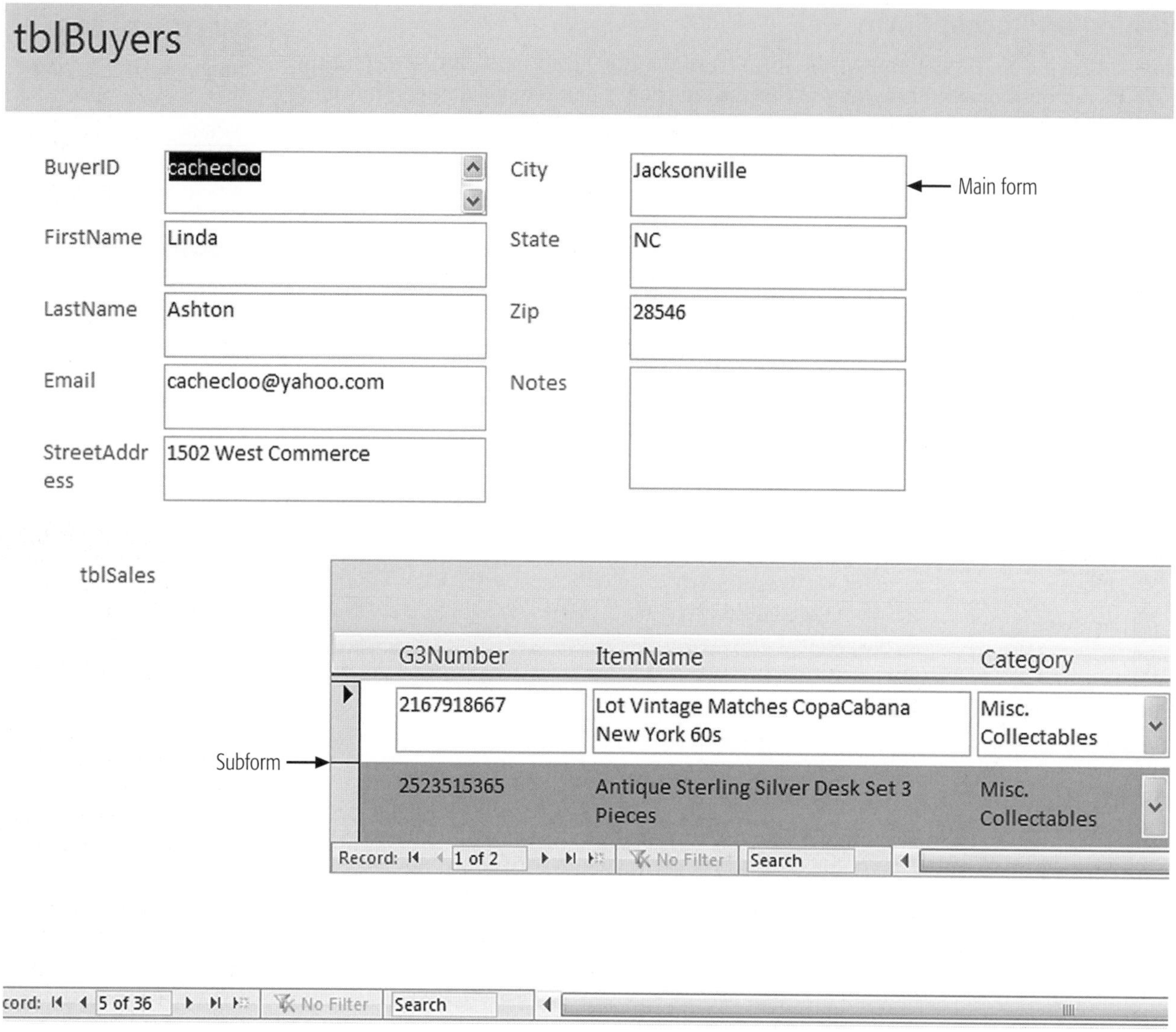

tblBuyers

BuyerID	cachecloo	City	Jacksonville	← Main form
FirstName	Linda	State	NC
LastName	Ashton	Zip	28546
Email	cachecloo@yahoo.com	Notes	
StreetAddress	1502 West Commerce		

tblSales

G3Number	ItemName	Category
2167918667	Lot Vintage Matches CopaCabana New York 60s	Misc. Collectables
2523515365	Antique Sterling Silver Desk Set 3 Pieces	Misc. Collectables

Subform →

Record: I ◀ 1 of 2 ▶ ▶I ▶* ⫶ No Filter Search

cord: I ◀ 5 of 36 ▶ ▶I ▶* ⫶ No Filter Search

Figure 5.25 A form/subform example

Before creating a form with a subform, make sure the data sources are related either through relationships or queries. Also be sure that the common field is a primary key field in the table on the "one" side of the relationship or the main table. If no primary key exists in the main table, the subform will not be created.

How to Create a Form/Subform with the Form Wizard

1. From the Create tab, click the More Forms drop-down list.
2. Click the Form Wizard command.
3. Choose the data source for the main form (the "one" table) from the Table/Queries drop-down list.
4. Select the desired fields from the Available Fields list for the main form.
5. Choose the data source for the subform (the "many" table) from the Table/Queries drop-down list.

6. Select the desired fields from the Available Fields list for the subform. Click the Next button when finished.

7. A screen appears showing the data view (see Figure 5.26). Click the Form with subform(s) option button. View the data by the main table. Click the Next button.

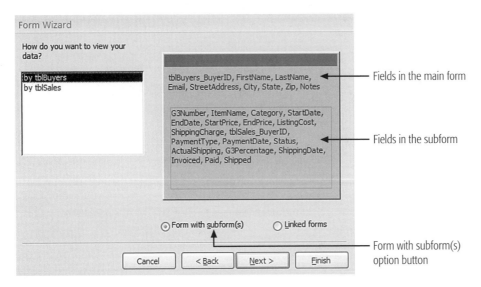

Figure 5.26 Choosing the Data view in a form/subform

8. Select the layout for the subform. Click the Next button to continue.

9. Select the style for the form. Click the Next button to continue.

10. Enter the title for the form and subform.

11. Choose the view in which to open the completed form.

12. Click the Finish button. See Figure 5.27 for the finished form.

The Form/Subform

The form/subform displays on the screen in one form although it is actually two separate forms. Each form has its own set of record navigation buttons at the bottom (see Figure 5.27). The two forms are synchronized by their common field (for this example, the *BuyerID* is the common field). When the main form record changes, the related records in the subform also change. The navigation buttons at the bottom of the subform will only change the records that are associated with the main form record.

Editing the Form/Subform in Layout View

As with any form, it is important to test the form by entering new records and editing current records. If the form will not accommodate data being entered or changed, it does not serve the purpose of making the data entry process easier.

While both forms can be edited from one screen when the form/subform is opened in Layout View, the subform will accept only minor changes. Simply click on the control in either the main form or subform to edit and make the change through the Form Layout Tools ribbon. Changes to the form will be displayed with the data included. Keep

TRY IT YOURSELF 5.5.2

Using the *tblBuyers* and the *tblSales* tables from the *G3_Ch5.accdb* file:

A. Create a form/subform using the Form Wizard.

B. Choose all the fields from the *tblBuyers* table as the data for the main form.

C. Choose all the fields from the *tblSales* table as the data for the subform.

D. View the data by *tblBuyers*.

E. Choose the Tabular layout.

F. Select the Access 2007 style.

G. Enter the names for the forms as *frmBuyers_Main* and *frmSales_Subform*.

H. See Figure 5.27 for the completed form.

TRY IT YOURSELF 5.5.3

Using the form *frmBuyers_Main*:

A. Create a new record.

B. Enter your name and information for the data in the *tblBuyers* table.

C. Enter information into the *tblSales* subform to purchase an item.

D. Close the form.

E. Open the *tblSales* table and the *tblBuyers* table. Check to see if the new records have been added.

frmBuyers_Main

BuyerID	Babyneeds$	City	Toledo
FirstName	Jadyn	State	OH
LastName	Walker	Zip	43614
Email	babyneeds@msn.com	Notes	Needs to have items sent Fed Ex
StreetAddress	P.O. Box 711		

← Main form

frmSales_Subform

	G3Number	ItemName	Category
	3213560172	Lot Vintage Painted Bottles Shal	Misc. Collectables
*			

Subform →

Record: ◄ ◄ 2 of 2 ► ►► ▼ No Filter | Search | ◄ ▬▬▬ |

Subform record navigation

Main form record navigation

Record: ◄ ◄ 1 of 36 ► ►► ▼ No Filter | Search |

Figure 5.27 Navigating a form/subform

TRY IT YOURSELF 5.5.4

Using the form *frmBuyers_Main*:
A. Open the form in Layout view.
B. Change the title to Buyers' Main Form.
C. Change the background of the field names (label controls) to a light green.
D. Change the font size for the field names (label controls) to 14.
E. Undo the font change.
F. Format the field name controls to a different font and change the size to 12.
G. Save the changes to the form.

the forms as simple as possible. Arrange objects in an eye-pleasing manner so that data is easy to read and understand. This will make data viewing, editing, and entry much easier.

If you make a change that is undesirable or unwanted, use the Undo command to erase that change and return to the previous format. Simply click the Undo command (see Figure 5.28).

Undo

Home   Create

Figure 5.28 Undo button

Creating a Form

1. Click on the table or query that will be the data source for the form. (Note: Do not open the table or query, simply select it.)
2. Click the Create tab so that the Create ribbon is displayed.
3. In the Forms group, click Form.
4. The new form opens in Layout view. The data from the data source is displayed as well as the form controls. Changes can be made to the form design in Layout view.

Saving the Form

1. Click the Office Button.
2. Choose the Save As command.
3. Click Save Object As.
4. Enter the form name, beginning with the *frm* prefix.
5. Click OK

   OR

   Right-click on the form tab with the default name.
6. Choose the Save command from the shortcut menu and enter the name of the form in the Form Name text box.
7. Click OK.

Printing the Form

1. Click the Office Button.
2. Choose Print.
3. Click on the Print command.
4. Select the printer.
5. Select the page number or choose to print selected forms in the Print Range dialog box.
6. Click OK.

Changing Views of a Form

1. Click the View command in the Views group on the Forms Layout ribbon.
2. Choose Form View from the drop-down list

   OR

   Right-click on the name tab of the form.
3. Choose the view from the shortcut menu.

Changing the Format of the Form

1. Change to Layout view.
2. In the AutoFormat group, click the More down arrow to display the format choices.
3. Click on the format choice.
4. The form is displayed with the new color choices.

Formatting the Title

1. Click the Title command in the Controls group.
2. Retype the text for the Title.
3. Add any formatting from the Font group.

Resizing Controls

1. Click on the control to resize. (Note: In Layout view, all the controls of similar type, such as label, will be resized.)
2. Move the mouse to the border lines until a double-headed arrow appears. Click and drag to the desired size.

Deleting a Control

1. Click on the control to delete. (Note: Some controls have multiple parts, such as a label and a text box. Be sure to delete all the parts necessary.)
2. Push the [DELETE] key.

Moving a Control

1. Click on the control
2. Move the mouse until a four-sided arrow appears. Click and drag the control to the new location.

Changing the Font

1. Click on the control for the font change.
2. Using the Font drop-down arrow in the Font group, select a new font.

Changing the Font Size

1. Click on the control for font changes.
2. Using the Font Size drop-down arrow, in the Font group, select a new size number.

Using the Search Button in a Form

1. Click into the field to search.
2. Click into the Search text box.
3. Type the character string to search.
4. Use the [ENTER] key to progress through the forms with the search.

5. Click into another field in the form to end the search.

6. Delete the character string in the Search text box.

Creating a Split Form

1. Click the Create tab.

2. Click the data source (either table or query).

3. Click the Split Form command. The form is displayed in Layout view.

Adding a Record

1. Click the New command in the Records group

   OR

   Click the New (blank) record button on the form navigation bar.

2. Add data to the new record form in either view of the Split Form.

Creating a Datasheet Form

1. Click the Create tab.

2. Click the data source (either table or query).

3. Click the More Forms drop down list. Choose Datasheet.

4. The form is displayed in Datasheet view.

Creating a Multiple Items Form

1. Click the Create tab.

2. Click the data source (either table or query).

3. Click the Multiple Items command. The form is displayed in Layout view.

Using the Form Wizard

1. From the Create tab, click the More Forms drop-down list.

2. Click the Form Wizard command.

3. On the first screen of the Wizard, choose the data source from the Table/Queries drop-down list.

4. From the Available Fields box, click on a field to add to the form. Use the directional arrow (>) to move the highlighted field to the Selected Fields box. The order in which the fields are chosen and moved to the Selected Fields window is the order they will appear on the form.

5. Select the desired fields in order. Click the Next button when finished.

6. Select the layout for the form. A sample layout appears on the left side of the screen. Click the Next button to continue.

7. Select the style for the form. A sample style appears on the left side of the screen. Click the Next button to continue.

8. Enter the title for the form. The default title is based on the name of the table/query used as the data source. Edit or delete the default to enter a new title.

9. Choose the view in which to open the completed form.

   ● *Open the form…* will open the form in Form view to enter data.

   ● *Modify the form's design…* will open the form in Design view to make changes to the structure of the form.

10. Click the Finish button.

Renaming a Form

1. Close the form if it is opened.

2. Right-click on the form in the Navigation pane. Select the Rename command from the shortcut menu.

3. Edit the name of the Access object to include the prefix.

Creating a Form/Subform with the Form Wizard

1. From the Create tab, click the More Forms drop-down list.

2. Click the Form Wizard command.

3. Choose the data source for the main form (the "one" table) from the Table/Queries drop-down list.

4. Select the desired fields from the Available Fields list for the main form.

5. Choose the data source for the subform (the "many" table) from the Table/Queries drop-down list.

6. Select the desired fields from the Available Fields list for the subform. Click the Next button when finished.

7. A screen appears showing the Data view (see Figure 5.26). Click the Form with subform(s) option button. View the data by the main table. Click the Next button.

8. Select the layout for the subform. Click the Next button to continue.

9. Select the style for the form. Click the Next button to continue.

10. Enter the title for the form and subform.

11. Choose the view in which to open the completed form.

Note: Remember that the tables must be linked on a common field for this type of form to be created.

12. Click the Finish button.

Review Questions

1. Are forms used for data input, output, or both?

2. Name three Forms tools available for creating forms.

3. What is the difference between a bound form and an unbound form?

4. What is the purpose of an unbound form?

5. What is the fastest way to create a form?

6. What changes to the form can be made in Layout view?

7. What is displayed in the Form view?

8. (T/F) Data displayed in a form can only be edited in Datasheet view.

9. (T/F) New records are created in Form view.

10. What keys assist in navigating through fields on a form?

11. What is the quickest way to move through form records?

12. How do you create a new record?

13. Describe the location of the Form Wizard command.

14. Which button loads all fields at one time from a table/query into a form?

15. Identify three layout choices available through the Form Wizard.

16. What is the difference between *opening the form to view or enter information* and *modifying the form's design?*

17. The Split Form displays data in two different views. What are they?

18. (T/F) The Multiple Items form displays one record at a time.

19. What is a Property Sheet?

20. What is the conventional naming prefix for a form?

21. (T/F) Only one table or query at a time can be used as the data source for a form.

22. When creating a form/subform, what type of relationship must be established between the tables?

23. (T/F) The main form is linked to the subform by the common field in the relationship.

24. (T/F) The subform displays the data from the "one" table in the relationship.

25. (T/F) Editing changes can be made only to the subform.

Exercises

Exercise 1—Creating Forms

ACTIVITY

Use the *SirDanceALot_Ch5.accdb* file to create the following forms.

Exercise 1A: Creating a Multiple Items Form

1. Create a form using the Multiple Items tool from the *tblArtists* table.

2. Change title of the form to "Artists."

3. Change the AutoFormat to Opulent (a purple background).

4. Save the form *as frmArtists.*

5. Change to Form View and enter the following records using the form:

   Electric Light Orchestra

   Beach Boys

   Blood, Sweat & Tears

   Three Dog Night

Exercise 1B: Creating a Split Form

1. Create a form using the Split Form tool from the *tblRecordLabels* table.

2. Change the title of the form to "Record Labels."

3. Save the form as *frmRecordLabels.*

4. Enter the following records using the form.

5. Change to Form view and enter the following records using the form. Enter data in either section of the form.

Dunhill

CBS

United Artists

Motown

Exercise 1C: Creating a Form with the Form Tool

1. Create a form using the Form tool from the *tblRecordings*. What other table appears as a subform in this form?

2. Change the title of the form to "Recordings and Inventory."

3. Change the AutoFormat to Trek.

4. Change all the field labels to Bold formatting.

5. Resize the controls in the main form to be shorter but to display all the data.

6. Save the form *as frmRecordings*.

7. Change to Form view and enter the following records using the form. Use the drop-down lists in the fields that have them to choose the data for that field. For the fields that have Autonumber fields, let Access automatically number the records.

Artist	Title	Category	Label	Type	Quantity on Hand	Price
Robinson	Anthology	Rock	Motown	Long Playing Vinyl	5	15.95
Electric Light Orchestra	Out of the Blue	Rock	United Artists	Compact Disk	3	18.95
Earth Wind and Fire	The Best of Earth Wind and Fire	Rock	CBS	Cassette	2	12.95
Blood, Sweat & Tears	Blood, Sweat & Tears	Rock	Columbia	Compact Disk	2	18.95
Three Dog Night	Suitable for Framing	Rock	Dunhill	Eight Track	4	9.95

8. Close the form. Open the *tblRecordings* table and verify that the data entered through the form is in the table.

Exercise 2—In-Class Group Practice

ACTIVITY AND REFLECTION

Divide into groups of two or three people, as determined by your instructor. Each group should work with the tables in the *Practice_Ch5.accdb* database file. Complete Part 1 as follows, with each group doing the steps that follow.

Part 1

1. Create a form to display the data in the table *tblInventory*.

   a. Include all fields.

   b. Use Columnar layout.

2. Go into the Design view and make any changes that make the form look better or make it easier to use.

3. Save the form as *frmInventory*.

4. Go back to the Table Design view for *tblInventory* and make these changes:

   a. *Partno* is the primary key.

   b. The *Category* field can only have the values "AIN," "CKE," or "NIZ."

5. Open the form and add the following record:

A1234, Arbitrary cob, 19 on hand, none on order, none on back order, $12.75, category "MBU."

6. Discuss how you can use the tools you have learned about so far to create a well-designed and effective data entry form for a table.

7. What changes can you add to the *frmInventory* form to make it better? Make those changes agreed upon by the group.

8. Resave the form and copy the database to a diskette.

Part 2

1. Exchange you diskette with another group, or duplicate the disk and exchange the duplicate.

2. Use the other group's database to add the following records. Note any problems you have, any data validation that is done, and any suggestions you have for changing the form.

   a. M9238, Mixed blessing, 47 on hand, 26 on order, none on back order, $8.59, category "CKE."

   b. M4749, Multiple catcall, 0 on hand, 133 on order, none on back order, $12.99, category "NIZ."

   c. J9876, Julep declaration, 146 on hand, none on order, none on back order, $34.00, category "MEW."

   d. J1234, Jaded harp, 72 on hand, 5 on order, none on back order $129.43, category "NIZ."

3. Exchange disks again so that each group now has the form it originally created. Discuss with the group the form's good features and suggest solutions for problems you found.

4. Make the suggested corrections to the form and test with your own data.

5. Write a list of at least three things that your group changed on the original form. Explain how and why these things were changed.

Exercise 3: Challenge: Modifying a Form

ACTIVITY AND REFLECTION

Exercise 3A: Editing a Form/Subform

1. Using the *tblBooks* and *tblCardholders* from the *Practice_Ch5.accdb* file

2. Create a form/subform with the *tblCardholders* as the main form and the *tblBooks* as the subform.

3. Change the format using the AutoFormat command.

4. Change the title of the form to "Cardholders and Books."

5. Italicize the title text.

6. Resize the main form controls to make them shorter but still wide enough to display the data.

7. Resize the subform control to make it shorter but still wide enough to display the data.

8. Move the subform control so that it is parallel to the controls on the main form.

9. Change the line thickness around the subform to 3 pt.

10. Change the color of the line around the subform to a dark blue.

11. Save the form as *frmCardholders*.

12. Change to Form view and add a new record with the following data:

DUNLA01 Hazel Dunlap 2776 W. Glendale Denver CO 80555 (303)555-7777.

Exercise 3B: Editing a Split Form

1. Using the *tblCustomers* table from the *Practice_Ch5.accdb* file, create a new form using the Split form tool.

2. Modify the text control for the Account Number data to Bold and red Font Color.

3. Change the title of the form to Customer Information.

4. Save the form as *frmCustomers*.

5. Switch to Form view. Add the following new record to the table using either section of the form. Notice in which section of the form the formatting changes were made.

Account Number 1026, Heavenly Trucks, 339 Tamasoa Lane, Cleo, CO 80129, (720) 410-1995.

Exercise 3C: Editing a Form

1. Using the *tblEmployee* table from the *Practice_Ch5.accdb* file, create a form using the Form Wizard.

- Load all fields.
- Use a Columnar layout.
- Select the Verve style.
- Name the form *frmEmployee*.

2. Open the form in Layout view and make the following changes:

- Change the title to Employee Information Form.
- Edit the field names (labels) to make the following changes. Use the Property Sheet for each control or edit the label by double-clicking into the label.

Old Label	New Label
EMPLOYEE_ID	EMPLOYEE ID
LASTNAME	LAST NAME
FIRSTNAME	FIRST NAME
VAC_ALLOW	TOTAL VACATION HOURS
SICK_ALLOW	TOTAL SICK HOURS
VAC_TAKEN	VACATION HOURS TAKEN
SICK_TAKEN	SICK HOURS TAKEN

- Resize the controls to make them show all the data and label text.

3. Using the Property sheet for each of the following controls, make the changes indicated:

- Format the text box (the control that holds the data for the field) for the field ANN_SALARY as currency. Right-click on this control and choose the Properties command. Use Data tab to locate the Currency property.
- Give the VAC_ALLOW field a default value of 80.
- Give the SICK_ALLOW field a default value of 120.

4. Save the form again. Change to Form view.

5. Enter a new record for yourself as a new employee. You are working in Department 3. Enter data for your record as you wish.

6. Save and close the form.

Exercise 4—Discussion Questions

1. Discuss the situations where using a query versus a table would be a better choice as the data source when creating a form.

2. Make a list of different form creation tools and the types of forms they create. Identify the uses, pros, and cons of each type of form.

3. What other features would you like to be able to add to a form? Think about design elements as well as what might be helpful to a user during data entry. Open one of the forms you have created in Design view. Examine the tools available and compare these to Layout view. Identify any elements or procedures that can be done in Design View and not in Layout View.

4. What are two different ways to change the field labels shown on a form?

CASE STUDY A: MRS. SUGARBAKER'S COOKIES

1. Create a form to enter new products using the *tblProducts* table. Use the Form Wizard tool to enter all fields. Choose the Columnar format and the Median style. Save the form as *frmProducts*. Make the following changes to the design of the form in Layout view:

   a. Change the title of the form to "Products Form".

   b. Change the style to the Flow style (blue).

   c. Change the labels for the fields (field names) to the Calibri font, font size 12.

   d. Resize the text boxes (data fields) to make them smaller and to allow for more space between the data and the names of the fields.

   e. Resize the Box Cover field to make the image of the cover smaller. Resave the form.

2. Using *frmProducts*, enter the information for a new product line:

   a. Peanut Butter Munchies; Crunchy peanut butter cookies that melt in your mouth. A favorite treat! $24.95. (There is no box cover graphic.)

3. Create a form using *tblCustomers* for customer data entry. Save the form as *frmCustomers*. Make the following changes to the design of the form in Layout view:

   a. Change the title of the form to "Customer Data."

   b. Change any other formats that you wish.

   c. Resave the form.

4. Using the form *frmCustomers*, enter your customer data into the form.

5. Create a form/subform using *tblOrderItems* and *tblOrders*. Save the form as *frmCustomer_Orders*. Make the following changes in Layout view:

   a. Change the title of the form to "Customer Orders."

   b. Change the title of the subform to "Order your cookies here!"

   c. Shorten the text boxes for the form data so as not to take up so much space on the form but still display all the data.

   d. Resave the form.

6. Using *frmCustomer_Orders*, enter the following order record:

   Order ID:7

   Customer ID: 011

   Order Date: 7/17/08

   Freight Charge: $7.79

   Product ID: Brownie Mini Bites, 2; Citrus Cooler Gift Box, 1; Peanut Butter Munchies 1.

CASE STUDY B: SANDY FEET RENTAL COMPANY

Sandy Feet Rental Company is very pleased with the way the database is working but some employees are having difficulty entering data in the Datasheet view. They have asked you to create a series of forms for easier and more accurate data entry. Make changes to the layout of the form to identify the form (through the Title) and to make it easier for data entry (such as resizing and moving controls).

Design the forms to match the following requirements.

1. A data entry form that combines *tblClients* and *tblRental Transactions*. Save the form as *frm1_Clients_Rentals*.

2. A data entry form that combines *tblOwners* and *tblProperties*. Save the form as *frm2_Owners_Properties*.

   a. Enter the following new records using the form.

New owner information	Property Information
Owner Number: 13	Property Number: P13
Property Number: P13	Property Address: 509S
Retriever, Jack	Condo Type: ShoresOF2BR
56 Battlefield Lane, Manassas VA 24567	Accepts Pets: Yes
(202)555-9009	High Speed Internet: Yes
iackretriever@woof.com	Amenities Code: 1

3. A form that shows all property information and all amenities. Save the form as *frm3_Properties_Amenities*.

4. A form that shows all property information plus rental rates. Save the form as *frm4_Properties_Rates*.

5. A split form for housekeeping information. Save the form as *frm5_Housekeeping*.

CASE STUDY C: PENGUINS SKI CLUB

Using the *Penguins.accdb* database, create a series of forms, as described below.

1. Create a form for entering and editing the records in *tblMembers*. Call it *frmMembers*. It should display only one record at a time. The title at the top of the form should be *Penguins Ski Club Members*.

2. Make a new form based on *qryRentals* and call it *frmRentals*. Show multiple records in rows, and change the title to "Equipment Rentals."

3. Use the Form Wizard to create a form on multiple tables: *tblEvents*, *tblAttendance*, and *tblMembers*. The form should show the event name, location, and date at the top of the form. The first name, last name, phone number, and age of each member attending should be shown in a list. Use any style you like. Name the form *frmEvents* with subform *frmAttendanceSubform*. Change the title to "Penguins Ski Club Events."

4. Use the Form Wizard to make another form on tables *tblEvents*, *tblAttendance*, and *tblMembers*. This time, show the name and phone number of the member at the top of the form, and show the list of events that the member attended below. Display the event name, location, and date in the list. Use a different style than in #3. Name the forms *frmMemberAttendance* and *frmEventsSubform*.

Chapter 6

Reports

After completing this chapter you will be able to

Understand reports:
- Define a report and know when to use one.
- Recognize different kinds of reports.
- Understand the different report views and their functions.

Create a report:
- Begin the report creation process using various Access report tools.
- Create a report using the Report tool.
- Create a report using the Labels tool.
- Create a report using the Report Wizard.

- Choose one or more data source(s) for the report.
- Group and sort report data to produce meaningful summary reports.
- Choose the appropriate format and layout.

Modify a report:
- Use the Layout view tools to edit a report.
- Preview and print a report.

Use reports with other applications:
- Export to Word, Text, and other file types.
- Mail Merge with Word.

Columnar report	A layout format for a report that presents data vertically in a column.
Exporting	Sending an Access report out to another application.
Grouping	A way to organize data in a report by placing all records that have the same value in a specific field together.
Labels tool	A reports tool to create various types of labels.
Mail merge	A feature in Word that allows for combining data from an Access table or query with a Word file to produce a customized document for each record in the table/query.
Report	An Access object that summarizes data from tables or queries into a concise, readable format.
Report tool	A reports tool to automate the process of generating an Access report from a table/query with little user input.
Report Wizard	A reports tool to guide the user through the process of creating an Access report from a table/query or multiple data sources.

Sort   An alphabetical or numeric organization of records based on any field in a report.
Tabular report   A layout format for a report that presents data in rows and columns, showing several records at a time.
Word   The word processing application of Microsoft Office.

6.1 / Defining a Report

There are two ways to produce output in Access—forms and reports. Forms are used for onscreen data display, but can also be input objects when used for adding and editing records. Reports are used only for output, but are more versatile than forms.

Reports summarize data from tables or queries into a concise, readable format that can be customized for any purpose. They can be printed on a printer or saved to a file—either in a variety of formats. They can also be previewed onscreen before printing. Access classifies a report as one of the objects that is saved with the database file.

It's easy to use multiple tables in a report; just be sure a relationship exists between the tables before starting to create the report. You can duplicate the structure of the form/subform type of data display in a report by using joined tables and proper data grouping.

Planning a Report

You should carefully plan a report before beginning the actual creation process on the computer. Let's look at some questions you can ask when planning a new report. In Table 6.1, we'll answer the questions using an example report—*rptStudent Transcript* from the *College Records* database.

Table 6.1   Planning a report

Planning Questions	Answers—Student Transcript Example
1. What is the purpose of the report?	To provide a list of courses and grades for one student.
2. What type of report is best—a standard report, a label report, or a chart?	A standard report.
3. How will the report look?	This report has the same structure as a form/subform. It's a combination of a columnar report on top and a tabular list of classes below. It will be printed with portrait orientation, in a grid format, and some lines and boxes could be used.
• Columnar or tabular style?	
• Portrait or landscape page orientation?	
• Grid or indented format?	
• Should special fonts, colors, lines, boxes, or other design features be used?	
4. What is the data source for this report—a table or a query?	The data source is a query that combines data from the *tblStudent* table and the *tblCourses Taken by Student* table. The tables are already joined, but the query has not been created yet.
• Must special queries be created first?	
• Are tables properly linked for a multitable report?	
5. Which fields are needed?	*tblStudent* table: *Name, Address, City, State, Zip, Student ID Number*
	tblCourses Taken by Student tabel: *Course Number, Grade, Date taken.*
6. Should data be sorted in a particular sequence?	Chronologically by the dates classes were taken—from oldest to most recent.
7. Are groupings, totals, or subtotals necessary?	Data is grouped by *Student ID Number*.
8. How should the report be created—by Design view, Report Wizard, or AutoReport?	Start by using the Report Wizard, then modify in the Design view.

Figure 6.1 shows a sample copy of the report. The *rptStudent Transcript* shows data from two tables—*tblStudent* and *tblCourses Taken by Student*. One record from the *tblStudent* table is shown at the top, with multiple records from the *tblCourses Taken by Student* table below. The relationship between the two tables is one-to-many, and the arrangement of the data as shown in the figure is similar to a form/subform.

Student Transcript

Name: Dupp, Stan
Address: 3672 N. Oak
          Glenisle, CO 89171
Student #: 16283

Semester	Course	Grade
Fall 97	CIS 140	A
Spring 97	CIS 120	B
Spring 97	ENG 201	A
Fall 97	MAT 150	B

Figure 6.1 Sample *rptStudent Transcript* report

Grouping Data in a Report

Grouping records in reports provides additional information to the reader of the report. When records are grouped together, summary information such as totals and counts can be calculated for each subgroup. All records that have the same value in a specified field are assembled to form a group. For example, a *tblEmployee* table grouped by *Department* would mean that all records where *Department* is "Human Resources" form a group, "Sales" records form another group, and so on.

Any field in a table can group records, but it makes most sense to use a field that has a relatively small set of values. For example, employees may be grouped by department because there are usually only a few different departments in a company. It wouldn't make sense to group the records by *Hire Date*, though, because it's possible that there could be as many different hire dates as there are employees. The groups would be meaningless. Figure 6.2 shows *tblEmployee* records grouped by the *Department* field, which provides more meaningful information than grouping by *Hire Date*.

Employee ID	Department	Last Name	First Name	Hire Date	YTD Pay
005	Human Resources	Green	Vivian	2-28-94	19796.39
002	Human Resources	Spawn	Melva	6-22-93	22059.82
004	Human Resources	Suspect	Velma	10-24-93	24908.64
003	Sales	Fluke	Harvey	1-3-96	21909.67
001	Sales	O' Reilly	Alvin	2-16-95	19950.57

Figure 6.2 *tblEmployee* records grouped by the *Department* field

If the table contains multiple levels of organization, then it's possible to create a report with subgroups within groups. For example, a large company might have a payroll report with subtotals grouped by branch and department as shown in Figure 6.3. Subtotals can be printed for each subgroup.

Employee ID	Branch	Department	Last Name	First Name	YTD Pay
002	Chicago	Human Resources	Spawn	Melva	22059.82
003	Chicago	Sales	Fluke	Harvey	21909.67
001	Chicago	Sales	O' Reilly	Alvin	19950.57
005	Denver	Human Resources	Green	Vivian	19796.39
004	Denver	Human Resources	Suspect	Velma	24908.64

Figure 6.3 *tblEmployee* records grouped by the *Branch* and *Department* fields

Access allows you to set different levels of grouping that can affect the size of the groups. The default setting groups data by everything in the field. Basing the group on the first few letters in the field can form larger groups. For example, instead of basing groups on the whole *Zip Code* field in a mailing list, larger regional groups could be defined by using only the first two digits in the field.

6.2 Creating a Report

There are several tools that can be used to create a report depending on the type of report needed. Some of the tools require more user input than others. The Labels tool creates a specialized report in the form of labels. See Table 6.2 for a comparison of the report tools.

Table 6.2 Comparing report tools

Report Creation Tool	Description
Report Tool	Creates a report from the selected data source with no user input. Opens in Layout view.
Labels Tool	Creates a label report from the selected data source with some user input. Opens in Print Preview.
Report Wizard	Creates a report from one or more data sources with user input. Opens in Print Preview or Design view.
Blank Report	Creates a blank report for the user to design. Opens in Design view.
Design view	Creates a report from one or more data sources that opens in Design view.

Using the Report Tool

The Report tool is one of the easiest ways to create a report from a single table or query. This tool requires no user input except to choose the data source and all the fields from that data source are entered into the report. Changes can be made to the report through the Layout view tools. Grouping levels and Sort functions can also be added to the report through the Layout View.

How to Use the Report Tool

1. Select the data source from the Navigation pane.

2. Click the Report tool command on the Create ribbon, the Reports group (see Figure 6.4).

3. The report opens in Layout View with the Report Layout Tools ribbon (see Figure 6.5).

TRY IT YOURSELF 6.2.1

Using the *tblBuyers* from the *G3_Chapter6.accdb* file:

A. Create a report using the Report tool.

B. Save the report as *rptBuyers_Report*.

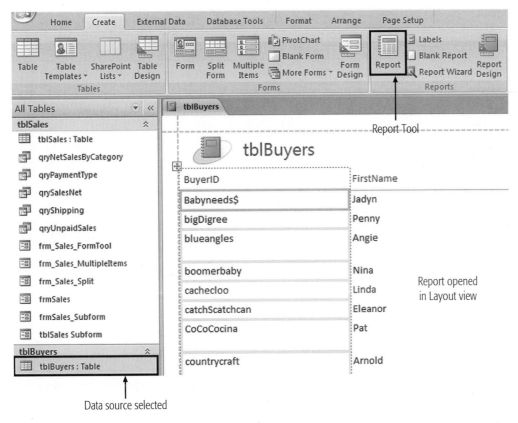

Figure 6.4 Creating a report with the Report Tool

Figure 6.5 Report Layout Tools ribbon

6.3 Working with a Report

Reports can be edited and customized, previewed, printed, or written to another file. You can open a report in four different views: Report view, Print Preview, Layout view and Design view. Within each of these windows, the report can either be modified or viewed with data before printing or saving. See Table 6.3 for a summary of the view options.

Table 6.3 Summary of view options

Report Views	Description
Report view	Shows the data in the report and allows for filtering and sorting of the data.
Print Preview	Shows different ways to view the report, including multiple pages, zoom, page orientation, exporting to other applications and printing.
Layout view	Shows the data in the report and allows for some formatting changes to the design of the report.
Design view	Allows for changes and editing to the design and structure of the report. Does not show the data in the report controls.

Editing the Report in Layout View

Like the Layout view with forms, the Report Layout view shows the data of the report and the controls that make up the report. Controls can be labels to identify the fields of the report or the title, text boxes to hold field data, images, lines, or other items on the report. The Layout view offers some editing tools for making changes to the report (see Figure 6.5). Not all the editing functions are available in Layout view. In addition to modifying the format of the report, sorts, filters, and grouping levels can be applied to modify the manner in which the data is presented or provide summary data.

How to Change the Report Style

1. Click the style of report in the AutoFormat group.

How to Delete a Control on a Report

1. Click the control (label, text box, image) to delete.
2. Click the right mouse button and choose the Delete command

   OR

   Push the DELETE key to delete the selected control.

How to Change the Font Style and Font Size

1. Click the control in which to make the font change.
2. Select the new font style from the Font drop-down list in the Font group.
3. Select the new font size from the Font Size drop-down list.

How to Change the Font Color

1. Click on the control in which to make the font change.
2. Click on the Font Color drop-down list and choose a new color.

How to Edit the Title

1. Click the Title command in the Controls group.
2. Edit the report title.

How to Add Page Numbers

1. Click the Page Numbers command in the Controls group (see Figure 6.6).
2. Set the parameters for the page number display.
3. Click OK.

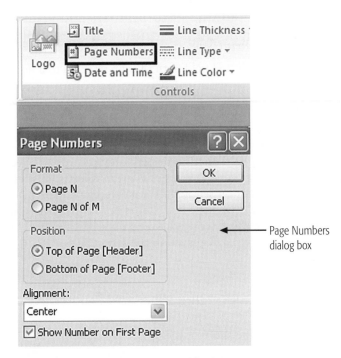

Page Numbers
dialog box

Figure 6.6 Editing report page numbering

How to Add the Date and Time Control

1. Click the Date and Time command in the Controls group.
2. Set the parameters for the date and time display (see Figure 6.7).
3. Click OK.

Figure 6.7 Editing Date and Time controls

Q: When I clicked the Date and Time control, Access adds another date and time control to my report? How do I fix that?

A: Delete the extra date/time controls that you don't want on your report.

TRY IT YOURSELF 6.3.1

Using the *rptBuyers_Report* make the following formatting changes:

A. Change the title to Buyers Report.

B. Delete the graphic control of a report in the title area.

C. Delete the time control.

D. Delete the date control.

E. Add a date control that shows the date in mm/dd/yy format.

F. Change the format of the report to the Trek Autoformat style.

G. Resize all the field controls on the report to make them smaller and closer together.

H. Resave the report.

How to Change the Size of Field Controls

1. Click on the field to resize. Note: All the controls associated with this field will be resized.

2. Move the mouse on the border of the selected field until the cursor turns to a double-headed arrow.

3. Click and drag the border to an appropriate size.

Using Filters, Groups and Sorts

In Layout view, the data of the report can be filtered to display only records of selected criteria. This is similar to applying filters in table Datasheet view, in queries and forms. There are several options for applying a filter on selected data including "equals," "does not equal," "contains," "does not contain," "begins with," "does not begin with," "ends with," and "does not end with." Choose the filtering option which best applies. Only those records matching the filter criteria will be displayed in the report.

How to Apply a Filter

1. Right-click on the data item to filter. For example, choose data that has more than one instance in the report, such as a state or city.

2. Select the Text Filters command from the shortcut menu (see Figure 6.8).

3. All records matching the filter criteria are displayed.

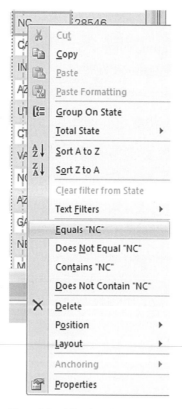

Figure 6.8   Filtering in Layout View

How to Remove a Filter

1. Right-click on the filtered field.

2. Select the Clear Filter command (see Figure 6.9).

3. All records in the report are now displayed.

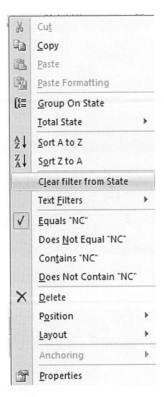

Figure 6.9 Removing the Filter

Sorting options can be applied to the data in any field in the report. Data can be sorted in Ascending or Descending order. This is similar to sorting the table in Datasheet view, in queries and forms. The Grouping and Sort command must be chosen to select sort fields.

How to Sort Data in a Report

1. Click the Grouping and Sort command in the Grouping & Totals group, the Format tab on the Report Layout Tools ribbon (see Figure 6.10).
2. The Group, Sort, and Total window opens. Select the Add a Sort command.
3. Select the field for sorting. The field is added to the Group, Sort, and Total window.
4. Choose the sort order, Ascending or Descending (see Figure 6.11), by clicking on the drop-down list next to the sort field.
5. The records in the report are sorted on the selected field.

How to Remove a Sort Option

1. Click the Delete button on the Sort Field ribbon (see Figure 6.11).

Grouping options arrange similar records together in a group based on a particular field. For example, all records that have the CO data in the *State* field will be organized together in the report. This is not only for visual clarity but summary functions can also be applied to the groups, For example, a subtotal or a count of records for the group can be put into the report. Only numeric field data can be summed but all data types can be counted.

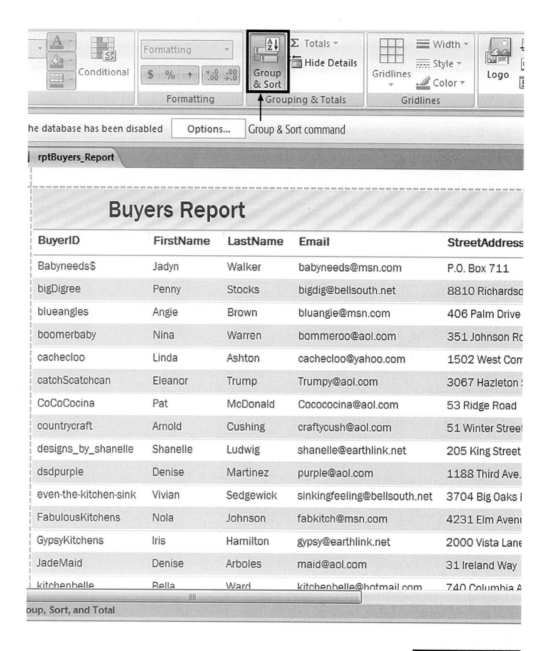

Figure 6.10 Adding a Sort field

Figure 6.11 Choosing the Sort option

How to Add a Grouping Level in a Report

1. Click the Grouping and Sort command in the Grouping & Totals group, the Format tab on the Report Layout Tools ribbon (see Figure 6.10).

2. The Group, Sort, and Total window opens. Click Add a Group (see Figure 6.10).

3. Select the field for grouping. The field is added to the Group, Sort, and Total window (see Figure 6.12).

4. The records in the Group field can also be ordered either Ascending or Descending by clicking on the drop-down list next to the group field.

5. Report records are now organized according to the grouping field which has been entered as the first field in the report (see Figure 6.13).

Figure 6.12　Selecting a Group field

State	BuyerID	FirstName	LastName	Email	StreetAddress	City
AZ						
	mamboitiliano	Andy	Gamboni	mambomambo@comcast.net	729 Elk Creek Road	Flagstaff
	princessqueen	Danny	Carbone	opq@msn.com	1495 Connaught Drive	Tucson

Buyers Report　　4/20/2007

Records grouped

Figure 6.13　Records grouped by State field

Other fields can be sorted within each group by adding a sorting level as described above. Groups can be deleted by the same method as removing a Sort Option (see Figure 6.11).

How to Count Records in a Group

1. Select a field other than the field used as the Group level field.

2. Click the Totals command drop-down list in the Grouping & Totals group (see Figure 6.14).

3. The count for the records of each group will be displayed after the last record of the group (see Figure 6.15).

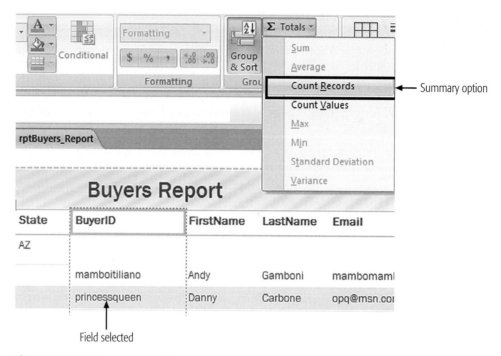

Figure 6.14 Adding summary data to a group

TRY IT YOURSELF 6.3.2

Using the *rptBuyers_Report* make the following changes:

A. Sort on the *State* field (see Figure 6.10).

B. Remove the Sort field (see Figure 6.11).

C. Add a Group on the *State* field (see Figure 6.12).

D. Add a Sort field to the Group on the *City* field (see Figure 6.10).

E. Create a Counted field for each of the groups (see Figure 6.13).

F. Save the report.

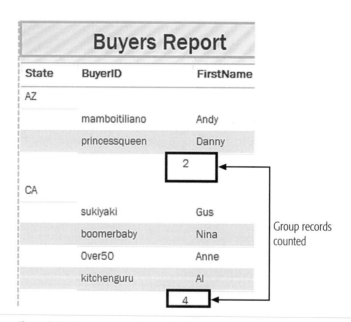

Figure 6.15 Group records counted

How to Delete the Count Control

1. Click on the control.

2. Right-click to display the shortcut menu. Choose the Delete command

   OR

   Push the DELETE key on the keyboard.

Previewing the Report

The Print Preview shows how the report will be printed. Changes to the page orientation, paper size and margins can be made through this view. The report can be viewed with one page at a time on the screen or with multiple pages on the screen. The Zoom command will increase the size of the report to see detail or decrease the size to view the layout of the report on the page. The report can be printed from this view. The report can also be exported to a Word file or into other file formats.

How to Select Print Preview

1. Click the View command on the Report Layout Tools ribbon.

2. Choose Print Preview (see Figure 6.16).

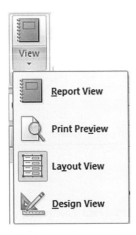

Figure 6.16 Print Preview

The Print Preview ribbon has several groups. The Print group contains the Print command to send the report to the Printer. The Page Layout group has the Page Orientation commands (Portrait, Landscape), Size, Margins, Print the data, and Page Setup. The Zoom group contains the Zoom command and commands for changing the number of pages displayed on the screen. The Data group has commands to send the Access report to other applications in different file formats. The Close Preview closes this window. See Figure 6.17 for the Print Preview ribbon.

Figure 6.17 Print Preview ribbon

How to Change the Page Orientation

1. Click on either the Portrait or Landscape command.

Q: What is actually being saved when I save a report?

A: When saving the report, only the report design is saved—not the data. If the data source is a query, it's run each time the report is run so the data is current. The same is true for forms.

TRY IT YOURSELF 6.3.3

Using the *rptBuyers_Report*:

A. Change to Print Preview (see Figure 6.16).

B. Change the Page Orientation to Landscape (see Figure 6.17).

C. Change the margins to Narrow.

D. Save the report.

E. Export the report to Word.

Note: Use the More command to export to another Access database, XML, HTML, or Snapshot viewer. Use the Text command to export the report as a .txt file format.

How to Change the Margins

1. Click on Margins.

2. Choose the margins desired from the selections.

3. If more customized margins are needed, click Page Setup. Enter the margins desired.

How to Save the Report

1. Click the Save icon.

   OR

   From the Office button, choose Save.

How to Print the Report

1. Click the Print command on the Print Preview ribbon.

   OR

   From the Office button, choose Print.

Exporting Reports to Other Applications

Reports can also be exported to Word and other file formats for use in different applications. The process is the same no matter the final format.

How to Export the Report to Word

1. In the Print Preview window, click the Word command in the Data group.

2. Choose the destination folder in which to save the report. Use the Browse button to navigate the appropriate folder. The report will be saved with an .rtf (Rich Text Format) file format.

3. Click OK.

6.4 / Creating a Report with the Labels Tool

Access can produce a number of different sizes and layouts of labels to meet a variety of needs, including mailing labels. Labels can be produced using the Labels tool which asks for user input to create customized labels.

How to Create Labels with the Label Tool

1. Select the data source for the labels, either a table or query.

2. From the Create tab, click Labels in the Reports group.

3. Select the labels size (see Figure 6.18). Click Next.

4. Select the font, font color, font size, and other formatting features. Remember not to choose a font size that is too large for the size of the label (see Figure 6.19). Click Next.

5. Select the fields for the labels from the list on the left side of the window. Use the arrow button to move the field to the Prototype label window or double-click on each

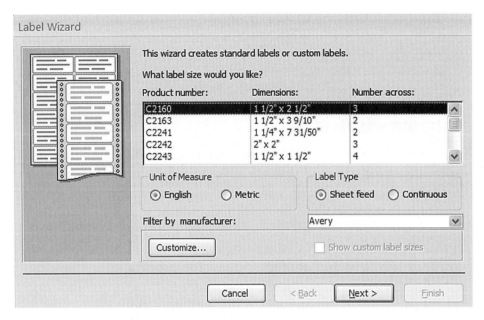

Figure 6.18 Choosing the size of the labels

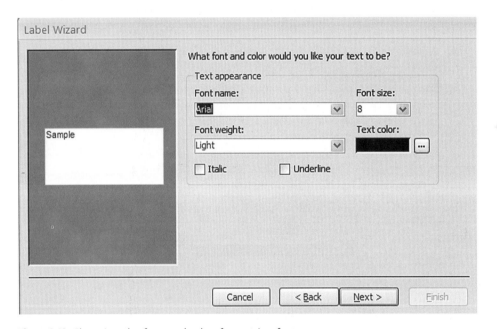

Figure 6.19 Choosing the font and other formatting features

field. The Prototype label window displays a preview of the label format (see Figure 6.20). Click Next.

- Put a space or comma where needed, such as a space between the first name and last name. Use the ENTER key to move to the next line in the label.

- Fields can be removed from the Prototype window by selecting the field and using the DELETE key on the keyboard.

6. Select the field on which to sort the labels (see Figure 6.21). Click Next.

TRY IT YOURSELF 6.4.1

Using the *tblBuyers* from the *G3_Ch6.accdb* file:

A. Create a set of mailing labels.

B. Use the C2160 Avery label size (see Figure 6.18).

C. Keep the default settings for the fonts (see Figure 6.19).

D. Choose all the fields needed for mailing labels and format appropriately. Put a space between *FirstName* and *LastName* fields and spaces and commas as needed between *City, State,* and *Zip* (see Figure 6.20).

E. Sort by State (see Figure 6.21).

F. Save the labels as *Labels tblBuyers* (see Figure 6.22).

G. Open in Print Preview (see Figure 6.23).

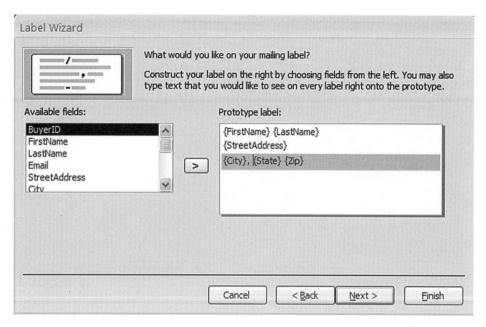

Figure 6.20 Selecting the fields for the labels

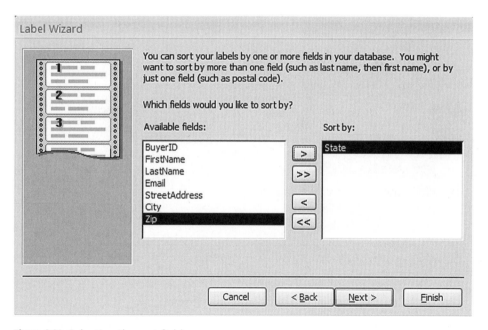

Figure 6.21 Selecting the sort field

7. Type in the name for the labels and choose how to view them. Labels can be opened in the Print Preview or Design view (see Figure 6.22). Click Finish.

8. The labels will be displayed (see Figure 6.23). They can now be printed or modified.

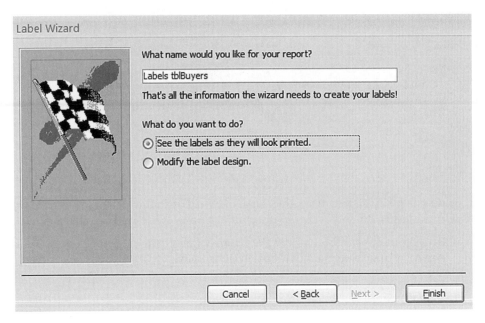

Figure 6.22 Naming the label report and finishing

```
Andy Gamboni
729 Elk Creek Road
Flagstaff, AZ 86004
```

```
Danny Carbone
1495 Connaught Drive
Tucson, AZ 85715
```

```
Gus Jones
515 East 79th Street
Bakersfield, CA 93304
```

```
Anne Jablonski
4052 Highland Drive
Oakland, CA 94602
```

Figure 6.23 Labels opened in Print Preview

6.5 Creating a Report with the Report Wizard

The Report Wizard is useful for creating most types of reports. It is a flexible tool that allows you to control much of the design during the report-building process. The Report Wizard, like other Wizards, asks several questions and creates the report based on the input. The Report Wizard accepts data from either a table or query or from multiple tables and queries provided they are properly joined. The finished report can be edited through Layout or Design View.

How to Use the Report Wizard

1. From the Create tab, the Reports group, click Report Wizard (see Figure 6.24).
2. Select the table or query for the data source from the drop-down list.

Figure 6.24 Starting the Report Wizard

TRY IT YOURSELF 6.5.1

Using the *G3_Ch6.accdb* file:

1. Create a report using the Report Wizard (see Figure 6.24).

2. Choose the *tblSales* and the *tblCategory* as the data sources for this report. Enter all fields (see Figure 6.25).

3. View by *tblCategory* (see Figure 6.27).

4. Choose the *StartDate* field as the Grouping Field. Enter Month as the Grouping Interval (see Figure 6.28).

5. Choose the *ItemName* as the field to sort (see Figure 6.29). Do not add any Summary Options.

6. Choose the Stepped layout and the Northwind style (see Figures 6.31 and 6.32).

7. Name the report *rptCategory* and open in Print Preview (see Figure 6.33).

8. The report should look similar to Figure 6.34.

3. Select the fields desired from the Available Fields window. Move these fields to the Selected Fields window with the directional arrows (see Figure 6.25). Click Next.

- If using multiple tables as the data source, select the next table from the drop-down list and select the fields as described above.

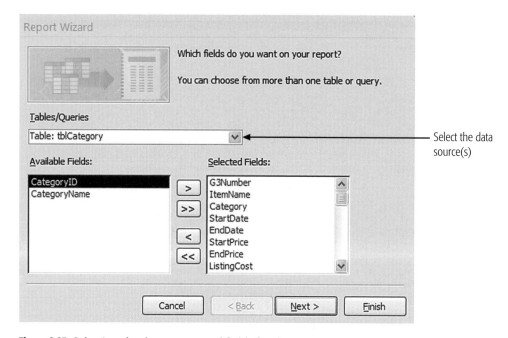

Figure 6.25 Selecting the data source and fields for the report

Q: Can I use more than two tables or queries in a report?

A: Yes, just be sure they are linked on common fields. To add another data source, select it from the Tables/Queries drop-down list, then add the fields (see Figure 6.25).

4. Select the data source on which to base the data view by clicking on it in the window on the left side of the screen. A sample view will appear in the right window (see Figure 6.26). (Note: This choice is available only in reports with multiple data sources.) Click Next.

5. Select any fields on which data should be grouped (see Figure 6.27). Choosing a Grouping Field creates headers in the report with the group name and footers that contact subtotals or other summary data for each group. Click Next.

- Click the Grouping Options button to set specific options for the groups. For example, in a Date field, the interval could be set to group by Month, Year, and Quarter, etc. Different data types suggest different options (see Figure 6.28).

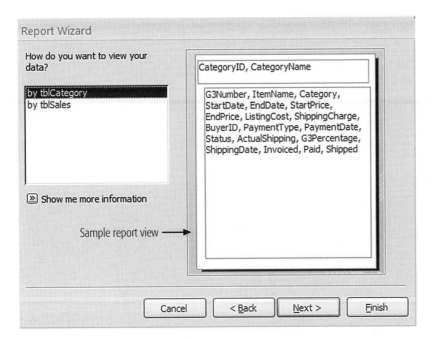

Figure 6.26 Viewing the data in the report

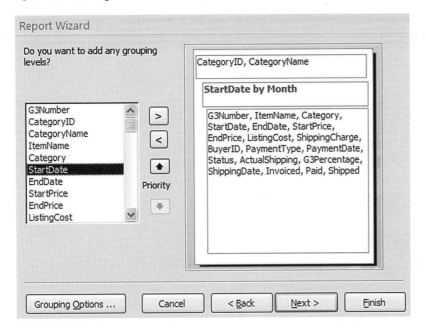

Figure 6.27 Setting the grouping level

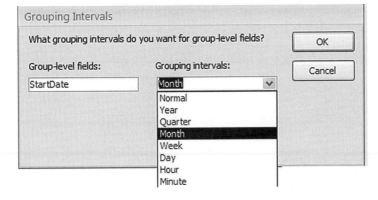

Figure 6.28 Grouping options

Q: I don't see the screen where I can choose the report view. What did I do wrong?

A: This screen is only available with multiple data sources. If you choose only one table or query for the data source, then this screen won't appear.

Q: What if I need to make a change within the Wizard? Can I go back?

A: Yes, there is a Back button on every Wizard screen. You can also edit the report in Layout and Design View.

6. Choose any fields on which to sort within the groups (see Figure 6.29). If no groups are chosen, the Sort Order will determine the record sequence of the overall report.

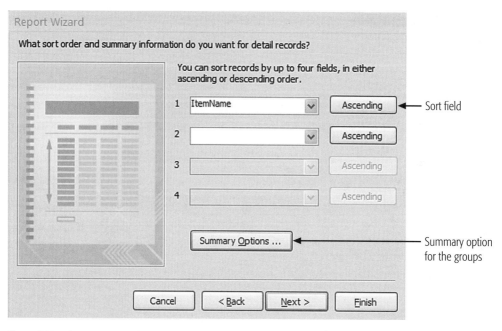

Figure 6.29 Choosing Sort fields

7. Choose any summary option for the groups (see Figure 6.30) by clicking into the desired check box. Click OK when finished setting the Summary Options.

- The summary options (Sum, Avg, Min, and Max) are available for numeric data. These values will print at the end of each group and at the end of the report.

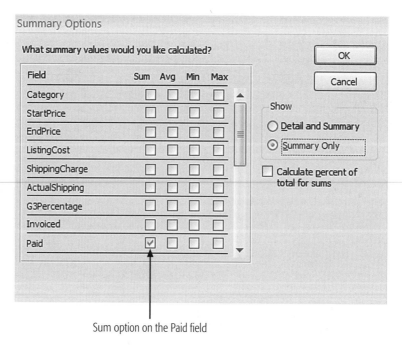

Sum option on the Paid field

Figure 6.30 Choosing Summary Options

- Select to display either detail or summary or just summary data.
- Click the check box to display the percent of total of sums. This displays group subtotals as percentages of the grand total (see Figure 6.30).

8. Choose the layout of the report and the page orientation (either Portrait or Landscape). Click Next (see Figure 6.31).

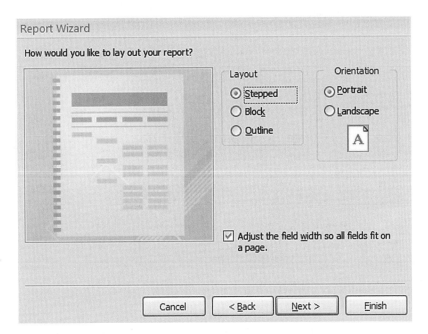

Figure 6.31 Choosing the report layout and page orientation

9. Choose the report style (see Figure 6.32). Click Next.

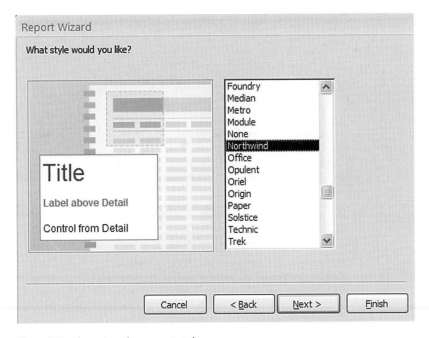

Figure 6.32 Choosing the report style

10. Enter the report title. This will be the name of the report object. Choose the view in which to open the report (see Figure 6.33). Click Finish.

TRY IT YOURSELF 6.5.2

Using the *rptCategory* make the following edits to the report.

1. Change the page orientation to Landscape (through the Print Preview).

2. In Layout view, delete the *CategoryID* field.

3. Make the *Category* field shorter to allow for more room across the page of the report.

4. Widen the fields *StartDate* and *EndDate* to show all the data in the column.

5. Widen or shrink the remaining fields so that they display the data in the columns.

6. Change the title of the report to Category Sales Report.

7. Resave the report.

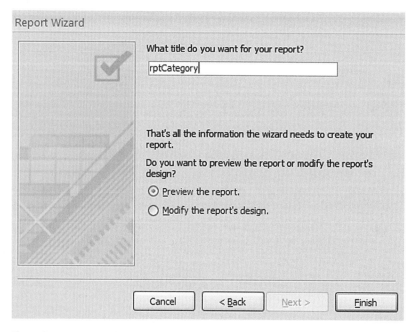

Figure 6.33 Entering the report title and finishing the report

11. The report will be generated and opened in the view selected. The report can be saved, printed or edited (see Figure 6.34).

Editing the Report

The report generated from the Report Wizard can be edited through Layout view or Design view. Limited editing tools are available through Layout view.

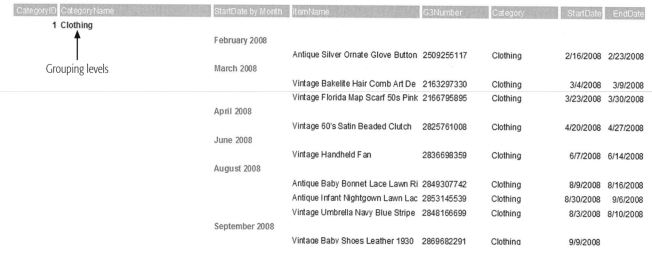

Figure 6.34 Completed report

6.6 Creating a Mail Merge Report with Word

Word is the word processing component of the Microsoft Office 2007 software package. A word processing application is useful when working with text documents in various ways, such as creating and editing reports, forms, tables, newsletter, and other types of documents. When integrating Access and Word, data from Access tables, queries or reports will most likely be moved into Word to facilitate formatting or using the data as text. You have already seen how easy it is to export an Access report to a Word document earlier in this chapter (section 6.3).

Using Access Data to Mail Merge into Word

The most useful and commonly used integrated application is Word's Mail Merge feature. Mail Merge combines a form letter with a table of names and addresses to create a customized or targeted mailing. The Mail Merge Wizard in Access is a simple and effective method for inserting Access data into an existing Word document or a new Word document. Word is used to create and edit the main document while Access supplies the data to insert into that document. The basis for the merge data can be a table or a query.

Note: Mail Merge does not have to be used specifically with a form letter. Any Word document can accept Access data fields in tables or queries.

How to Mail Merge Access Data into Word

1. Select the table or query for the data source.

2. Click the External Data tab to display the ribbon. In the Export group, click the More drop-down list (see Figure 6.35).

3. Choose Merge It with Microsoft Office Word.

4. Select the Merge option, either create a new document or use an existing (see Figure 6.36). Click OK.

   - Navigate to the location of the Word file or Word will open to a new document depending on the option chosen.

   - You will now be working in Word. The Mail Merge Wizard opens with a Mailings ribbon.

5. A task pane to the right of the document opens to assist with the Mail Merge (see Figure 6.37). Click the link at the bottom of the task pane: *Next: Write your letter.*

6. Begin inserting the merge fields, starting with the Address Block. Position the cursor at the location to insert this data (delete any prompts first). Click the *Address block* link on the Mail Merge pane to choose a style for the address data (see Figure 6.38). Click OK.

   - If there are different fields in the data source that Word does not recognize or other problems with the fields, click the *Match Fields* button. Then match the fields in the data source with Word's merge fields.

7. Move to the next merge field, the salutation. Click the *Greeting Line* link in the Mail Merge pane.

   - Select the format for the salutation, including the name and punctuation. Click OK (see Figure 6.39).

8. Add any additional fields that have been included in the data source. Note: When using Access data, all fields to be used in the Merge document must be included in the table or query data source.

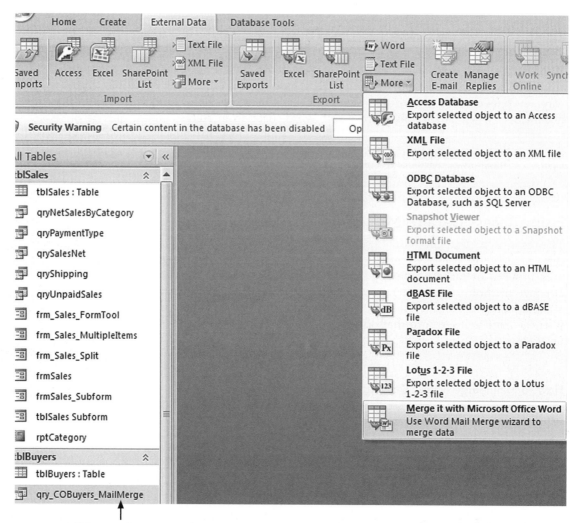

Data source for merge

Figure 6.35 Starting Mail Merge

TRY IT YOURSELF 6.6.1

Using the *tblBuyers* table

A. Create a Mail Merge between *tblBuyers* and the file *G3_MergeLetter.docx* (see Figures 6.36 and 6.37).

B. Select the appropriate fields for the Address block (see Figure 6.38).

C. Format the Greeting line as follows: "Dear [First Name]:" (see Figure 6.39).

D. Remove the prompt in the closing and add your name as the G3 Auctioneer. Preview the letters (see Figure 6.40).

E. Complete the Merge. Save the file as *G3_BuyersLetter.docx*. Close Word.

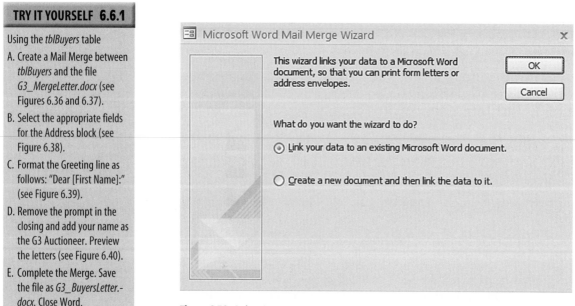

Figure 6.36 Selecting Merge options

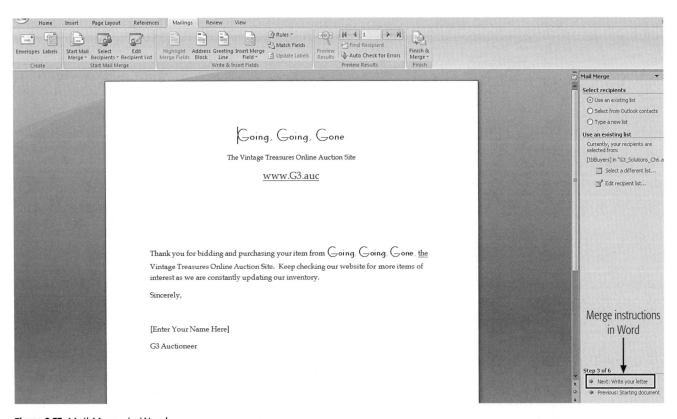

Figure 6.37 Mail Merge in Word

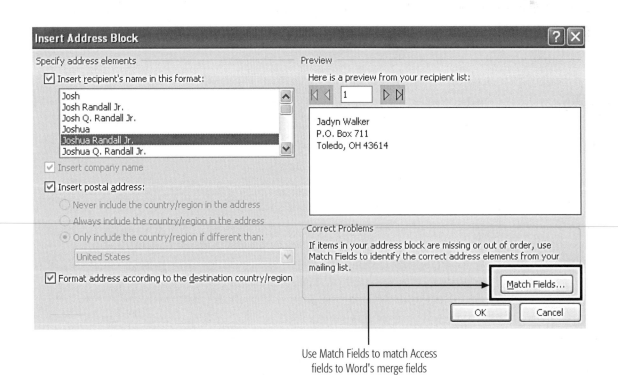

Use Match Fields to match Access
fields to Word's merge fields

Figure 6.38 Inserting Address block

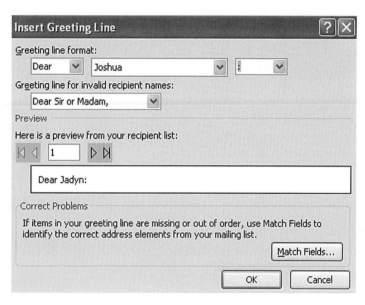

Figure 6.39 Selecting the Greeting line format

Q: Can I use the same address I used for mailing labels in a Mail Merge?

A: Yes, that's a good use of the table or query that was used for the labels.

9. Click the *Next: Preview you letters* link at the bottom of the Mail Merge pane. A preview of the merged letters will be displayed (see Figure 6.40).

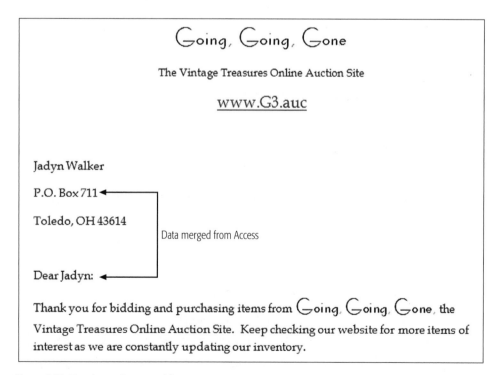

Figure 6.40 Preview of merged letters

10. Click the *Next: Complete the merge* link. Once the merge is completed, the letters can be edited, printed, or saved through Word (see Figure 6.41).

Figure 6.41 Completing the merge

Using the Report Tool

1. Select the data source from the Navigation pane.
2. Click the Reports tool command on the Create ribbon, the Reports group.
3. The report opens in Layout view with the Report Layout Tools ribbon.

Changing the Report Style

1. Click the style of report in the AutoFormat group.

Deleting a Control on a Report

1. Click the control (label, text box, image) to delete.
2. Click the right mouse button and choose the Delete command

   OR

   Push the ⌈DELETE⌉ key to delete the selected control.

Changing the Font Style and Font Size

1. Click the control in which to make the font change.
2. Select the new font style from the Font drop-down list in the Font group.
3. Select the new font size from the Font Size drop-down list in the Font group.

Changing the Font Color

1. Click on the control in which to make the font change.
2. Click on the Font Color drop-down list and choose a new color.

Editing the Title

1. Click the Title command in the Controls group.

2. Edit the report title.

Adding PageNumbers

1. Click the Page Numbers command in the Controls group.

2. Set the parameters for the page number display.

3. Click OK.

Adding the Date and Time Control

1. Click the Date and Time command in the Controls group.

2. Set the parameters for the date and time display.

3. Click OK.

Changing the Size of Field Controls

1. Click on the field to resize.

2. Move the mouse on the border of the selected field until the cursor turns to a double-headed arrow.

3. Click and drag the border to an appropriate size.

Applying a Filter

1. Right-click on the data item to filter.

2. Select the filter option from the shortcut menu, Text Filters command.

3. All records matching the filter criteria are displayed.

Removing a Filter

1. Right-click on the filtered field.

2. Select the Clear Filter command.

3. All records in the report are now displayed.

Sorting Data in a Report

1. Click the Grouping and Sort command in the Grouping & Totals group, the Format tab on the Report Layout Tools ribbon.

2. The Group, Sort, and Total window opens. Select the Add a Sort command.

3. Select the field for sorting. The field is added to the Group, Sort, and Total window.

4. Choose the sort order, Ascending or Descending, by clicking on the drop-down list next to the sort field.

5. The records in the report are sorted on the selected field.

Removing a Sort Option

1. Click the Delete button on the sort field ribbon.

Adding a Grouping Level in a Report

1. Click the Grouping and Sort command in the Grouping & Totals group, the Format tab on the Report Layout Tools ribbon.
2. The Group, Sort, and Total window opens. Click Add a Group.
3. Select the field for grouping. The field is added to the Group, Sort, and Total window.
4. The records in the Group field can also be ordered either Ascending or Descending by clicking on the drop-down list next to the group field.
5. Report records are now organized according to the grouping field which has been entered as the first field in the report.

Counting Records in a Group

1. Select a field other than the field used as the Group level field.
2. Click the Totals command drop-down list in the Grouping & Totals group.
3. The count for the records of each group will be displayed after the last record of the group.

Deleting the Count Control

1. Click on the control.
2. Right-click to display the shortcut menu. Choose the Delete command.

   OR

   Push the Delete key on the keyboard.

Selecting Print Preview

1. Click the View command on the Report Layout Tools ribbon.
2. Choose Print Preview.

Changing the Page Orientation

1. Click on either the Portrait or Landscape command.

Changing the Margins

1. Click on Margins.
2. Choose the margins desired from the selections.
3. If more customized margins are needed, click Page Setup. Enter the margins desired.

Saving the Report

1. Click the Save icon

   OR

   From the Office button, choose the Save command.

Printing the Report

1. Click the Print command on the Print Preview ribbon

   OR

   From the Office button, choose Print.

Exporting the Report to Word

1. In the Print Preview window, click the Word command in the Data group.

2. Choose the destination folder in which to save the report. Use the Browse button to navigate the appropriate folder. The report will be saved with an .rtf (Rich Text Format) file format.

3. Click OK.

Creating Labels with the Label Tool

1. Select the data source for the labels, either a table or query.

2. From the Create tab, click Labels in the Reports group.

3. Select the labels size. Click Next.

4. Select the font, font color, font size, and other formatting features. Remember not to choose a font size that is too large for the size of the label. Click Next.

5. Select the fields for the labels from the list on the left side of the window. Use the arrow button to move the field to the Prototype label window or double-click on each field. The Prototype Label window displays a preview of the label format. Click Next.

   a. Put a space or comma where needed, such as a space between the first name and last name. Use the ENTER key to move to the next line in the label.

   b. Fields can be removed from the Prototype window by selecting the field and using the DELETE key on the keyboard.

6. Select the field on which to sort the labels. Click Next.

7. Type in the name for the labels and choose view them. Labels can be opened in the Print Preview or Design view (see Figure 6.22). Click Finish.

8. The labels will be displayed. They can now be printed or modified.

Using the Report Wizard

1. From the Create tab, the Reports group, click Report Wizard.

2. Select the table or query for the data source from the drop-down list.

3. Select the fields desired from the Available Fields window. Move these fields to the Selected Fields window with the directional arrows. Click Next.

   ■ If using multiple tables as the data source, select the next table from the drop-down list and select the fields as described above.

4. Select the data source on which to base the data view by clicking on it in the window on the left side of the screen. A sample view will appear in the right window. Click Next.

5. Select any fields on which data should be grouped. Choosing a Grouping field creates headers in the report with the group name and footers that contact subtotals or other summary data for each group. Click Next.

   ▪ Click the Grouping Options button to set specific options for the groups.

6. Choose any fields on which to sort within the groups. If no groups are chosen, the Sort Order will determine the record sequence of the overall report.

7. Choose any summary option for the groups by clicking into the desired check box. Click OK when finished setting the Summary Options.

8. Choose the layout of the report and the page orientation (either Portrait or Landscape). Click Next.

9. Choose the report style. Click Next.

10. Enter the report title. This will be the name of the report object. Choose the view in which to open the report. Click Finish.

11. The report will be generated and opened in the view selected. The report can be saved, printed, or edited.

Mail Merging Access Data into Word

1. Select the table or query for the data source.

2. Click the External Data tab to display the ribbon. In the Export group, click the More drop-down list.

3. Choose Merge It with Microsoft Office Word.

4. Select the Merge option, either create a new document or use an existing. Click OK.

   ▪ Navigate to the location of the Word file or Word will open to a new document depending on the option chosen.

5. A task pane to the right of the document opens to assist with the Mail Merge. Click the link at the bottom of the task pane: *Next: Write Your letter.*

6. Begin inserting the Merge fields, starting with the Address Block. Position the cursor at the location to insert this data (delete any prompts first). Click the *Address block* link on the Mail Merge pane to choose a style for the address data. Click OK.

   ▪ If there are different fields in the data source that Word does not recognize or other problems with the fields, click the *Match Fields* button. Then match the fields in the data source with Word's Merge fields.

7. Move to the next Merge field, the salutation. Click the *Greeting Line* link in the Mail Merge pane.

   ▪ Select the format for the salutation, including the name and punctuation. Click OK.

8. Add any additional fields that have been included in the data source.

9. Click the *Next: Preview your letters* link at the bottom of the Mail Merge pane. A preview of the merged letters will be displayed.

10. Click the *Next: Complete the merge* link. Once the Merge is completed, the letters can be edited, printed, or saved through Word.

Note: When using Access data, all fields to be used in the Merge document must be included in the table or query data source.

Review Questions

1. Name two database objects that can be used as data sources for a report.

2. You can create a multitable report as long as the tables are _____ before-hand. (Fill in the blank).

3. Data groups are best formed on fields that have few/many values. (Choose one.)

4. Name two report creation tools.

5. (Y/N)   Is report data displayed in the Layout view?

6. What does Sorting do to records in a report?

7. What is the purpose of setting Grouping fields?

8. Name two summary (Totals) options that can be applied to groups.

9. Which View lets you change the page orientation of the report before printing?

10. Does the Labels tool automatically insert spaces between fields on a label?

11. (Y/N) Is it possible to print labels with colored text on them?

12. (Y/N) Are only mailing labels created through the Labels tool?

13. Identify three summary options available through the Report Wizard.

14. When a grouping level is identified in a report, what does this do to the look of the report?

15. Name two file formats to which an Access report can be saved.

16. What is the purpose of a Mail Merge?

17. What Access data can be used in a Mail Merge?

18. Name the application that accepts the Access data for a Mail Merge.

Exercises

ACTIVITY

Exercise 1—Practicing New Procedures

Exercise 1A: Using the Report Tool

Using the *SDAL_Ch6.accdb* database file

1. Create a report from the *tblRecordings*.

2. Make the following changes to the report design:

   a. Delete the Date control.

   b. Delete the Time control.

   c. Delete the report icon in the title.

   d. Change the title to "Recordings Report by Your Name."

   e. Resize the fields in the report to have the report print on two pages.

3. Save the report as *rptRecordings*.

Exercise 1B: Using the Label Tool

1. Create a query using the *tblArtists*, *tblRecordLabels*, and *tblRecordings*.

   a. Add the *FirstName* and *LastNameOrBandName* from the *tblArtists* table; *Title*, *Category* fields from the *tblRecordings* table; and *LabelName* from the *tblRecord Labels* table.

   b. Save the query as *qryArtists_Recordings_Labels*.

2. Using the *qryArtists_Recordings_Labels*, create labels using the following settings.

   a. Product Number C2242 size 2″×2″.

   b. Font Arial, font size 10, Bold weight, color dark blue.

   c. Enter the *FirstName* and *LastNameOrBandName* fields on the first line of the label separated by a space. The remaining fields are on separate lines.

   d. Sort on *LabelName*.

   e. Save the report as *lblArtists_Recordings_Labels*.

Exercise 1C: Using the Report Wizard

1. Create a report using the tables *tblInventory, tblRecordings, tblArtists,* and *tblRecord-Labels*.

2. Enter all the fields from *tblInventory*, the field *Title* from *tblRecordings*, *LastName-OrBandName* from *tblArtists*, and *LabelName* from *tblRecordLabels*.

3. View by *LabelName*.

4. Group on *LastNameOrBandName*.

5. No sorting level.

6. Choose the Stepped layout and the Origin style.

7. Name the report *rptRecordings_Information*.

8. Change to Layout View and make the following changes:

   a. Change the style to Access 2007.

   b. Delete the *Notes* field.

   c. Delete the *InventoryID* field.

   d. Delete the *tblInventory_MusicID* field.

   e. Change the label on the *LastNameOrBandName* field to Artist.

   f. Change the label on the QuantityonHand field to Quantity.

   g. Resize the fields to show as much data as possible on the report.

9. Resave the report.

Exercise 2—In-Class Group Practice: Comparing Report Tools

ACTIVITY AND REFLECTION

Divide into groups as determined by your instructor. Work with the tables in the *Practice_Ch6.accdb* database file.

Group 1: Using the Report Tool

1. Create a report using the *tblCruises* table using the Report Tool showing Cruise information.

2. In Layout View, make the following changes:

   a. Change the title.

   b. Change font, font size, and color.

   c. Add grouping levels and sorts.

  d. Resizing and moving fields.

  e. Delete unnecessary fields.

  f. Add totals (or summary) data.

Answer the following questions:

1. How easy was it to create a report? Report any problems creating the report.

2. How easy was it to modify the report? Report any problems making modifications. Report any changes that could not be made to the report.

3. Critique the look of the report. Is it easy to understand? Does it display all the data and information needed to make a useful report?

4. What is the purpose of the Report Tool? When would this be useful in creating a report? In which instance would this not be the tool to use to create an Access report?

Group 2: Using the Labels tool

1. Create a report using the *tblPassengers* table showing passenger information.

2. In Layout View, make the following changes:

  a. Change the title.

  b. Change font, font size, and color.

  c. Add grouping levels and sorts.

  d. Resizing and moving fields.

  e. Delete unnecessary fields.

  f. Add totals (or summary) data.

Answer the following questions:

1. How easy was it to create a report? Report any problems creating the report.

2. How easy was it to modify the report? Report any problems making modifications. Report any changes that could not be made to the report.

3. Critique the look of the report. Is it easy to understand? Does it display all the data and information needed to be useful?

4. What is the purpose of the Labels Tool? When would this be a useful tool to use when creating a report? In which instance would this not be the tool to use to create an Access report?

Group 3: Using the Report Wizard

1. Create a report using the *tblCruises* and *tblPassengers* tables. Show Passenger and Cruise data.

2. In Layout View, make the following changes:

  a. Change the title.

  b. Change font, font size, and color.

  c. Add grouping levels and sorts.

d. Resizing and moving fields.

e. Delete unnecessary fields.

f. Add totals (or summary) data.

Answer the following questions:

1. How easy was it to create a report? Report any problems creating the report.

2. How easy was it to modify the report? Report any problems making modifications. Report any changes that could not be made to the report.

3. Critique the look of the report. Is it easy to understand? Does it display all the data and information needed to make a useful report?

4. What is the purpose of the Report Wizard? When would this be a useful tool to use when creating a report? In which instance would this not be the tool to use to create an Access report?

Conclusion

Be prepared to report back to the class on your findings about each report tool.

Exercise 3—Practice: Grouping, Multiple Tables and Mail Merge

Use the *Practice_Ch6.accdb* file.

ACTIVITY AND REFLECTION

Exercise 3A: Creating an Inventory Report

1. Using the *tblInventory*, create an Inventory report.

2. The data should be grouped on *Category*, printed in *PartNo* order.

3. Include a sum for the *OnHand* field for each group.

4. Choose the layout and the style.

5. Name and save the report as *rptInventory*.

6. Make the following changes to the report design in Layout view:

    a. Change the title to Inventory Report by Your Name.

    b. Add bold formatting to each of the controls in the group summary section.

    c. Add a light background color to the controls in the group summary section.

    d. Change the font size for the Grand Total controls to 12.

7. Resave the report.

Exercise 3B: Creating a Reorder Report

1. Using the tables *tblInventory* and *tblVendors*, create a Reorder report.

2. List the items in the inventory that need reordering from the vendor, that would be items with less than five on hand. (Hint: Make sure the tables are joined properly and create a query.)

3. The report should look similar to Figure 6.42.

4. Make changes to the title, the location of the *Zip* field, and the font size for the fields *PartNo*, *Description*, and *Price*.

5. Save the report as *rptReorderReport*.

Reorder Report

Company name	Banzai Productions
Address	3203 West Word Lane
City	DeRockey
State	CO

Zip   85349

PartNo	Description	Price
B7769	Blue gopher	$126.72
C0741	Cocoa ice	$234.73
C4867	Combination leer	$99.42
L0007	Lateral avalanche	$59.51
M2687	Midnight tank	$195.38
P2745	Punster oval	$40.71
R6734	Retro coffee	$3.64

Figure 6.42 Reorder report

Exercise 3C: Creating Mailing Labels and Customized Mail Merge

1. Using the table *tblPassenger*, create a set of mailing labels. Save the label report as *lblPassenger_MailingLabels*.

2. Using the same data, create a Mail Merge letter advertising special prices for current cruisers. Include the address data for the Address block. Include name data for the Greeting line.

3. The text of the letter should read:

Because you have been a regular Crusin' Customer, we are offering special pricing for our fall cruises. Book now and save!

September 10–20: Ten sun-filled days on the *Sun Goddess* to Cozumel. Special price: $2,200, which includes airfare to Miami.

September 1–21: Twenty-one days of exquisite scenery to nature's wonderland—Alaska. Cruise the *Chinook,* the luxury liner in the fleet. Special price: $3,000, which includes airfare.

September 7–10: A three-day getaway to Cabo. Let the *Mermaid* sail you away for a refreshing three-day adventure. Special price: $1600, including airfare.

Call now for reservations.

Your Travel Agent

4. Save the merged letters as *CruisingLetter.docx*.

Exercise 4—Discussion Questions

REFLECTION

1. What are some good applications of Columnar style reports? Think of specific examples—what situations are best handled by grouping data this way? What data tables might lend themselves to this format?

2. Can you print labels to serve the same function as Columnar style reports? When might that be appropriate? When isn't it appropriate?

3. What are some criteria to be considered when choosing between a Columnar or Tabular style report?

4. Compare and contrast forms and reports in the following areas:

   a. How easy are they to create?

   b. How many different formats, layouts, and styles are available?

   c. How do you use them to input and output data?

   d. How do they look in Layout view and what modifications can be made in this view?

CASE STUDY A: MRS. SUGARBAKER'S COOKIES

Mrs. Sugarbaker needs a lot of different reports for her business. Some of the reports require using a query or multiple joined tables as a data source. She wants the reports to have a professional look.

1. Create a customer report that shows all the customers grouped by states. Complete any edits you feel are necessary to give the report a professional look. Name the report *rptCustomerReport*.

2. Create a set of mailing labels for Colorado customers only. Save the report as *lblColorado-Customers*.

3. Create a Mail Merge letter for Colorado customers only. This letter should advertise a special sale of 20% off the total (excluding shipping and tax) for Colorado customers when they order three or more boxes of delicious Mrs. Sugarbaker's Cookies. Use data for both the Address block and the Greeting line from Access. Save and name the letter as *ColoradoCustomers.docx*.

4. Create a report that shows a sum of all orders for each product item. Include the ProductName, Description, and Price of the product. Create a query first to assemble this information. Name the report *rptProduct_Order_Report*. Format the report to change the Title and produce an attractive report.

5. Create a report that shows customer ID information (*CustomerID, FirstName,* and *LastName*) and order information (*ProductName, Quantity,* and *UnitPrice*). Sum the *Quantity*. Modify the report to add the title Customer Orders Summary and to produce an attractive report. Save the report as *rptCustomer_Orders*.

   - Revise the report to have the title display Property Rates Report.

   - Change the grouping level to Condo Type and Property Address.

   - Resize the controls to make sure all the data is displayed.

   - Resave the report.

Property Rates Report

Condo Type	Property Address	1/01-3/31	4/01-5/31	6/01-8/31	9/01-10/31	11/01-12/31	Accepts Pets	High Speed Internet
Outrigger2BR								
	3170							
		$325.00	$350.00	$400.00	$350.00	$325.00	☐	☑
	4090							
		$325.00	$350.00	$400.00	$350.00	$325.00	☑	☐

Figure 6.43 Property Sales Report

CASE STUDY B: SANDY FEET RENTAL COMPANY

Now Sandy Feet must generate both reports for owners and internal rental reports. SFRC also wants to mail special offers to its loyal customers. Create reports for the following situations. you may need to create queries first to use as the data source before making the reports. Make changes in Layout view to ensure that the report is clear and easy to read.

1. Create a rental report for each property that has been rented. Include the *property address*, *date arrived*, *date departed*, *amount of deposit*, *method of payment*, and any *pet deposit*. Save the report as *rpt1Rental_Properties*.

   - Revise the report to have the title display Rental Report.
   - Sort on the *date arrived* field.
   - Sum the *pet deposit* field.
   - Resave the report.

2. Create a set of mail labels for all owners. Save the report as *lblOwners_Labels*.

3. Create a Mail Merge with the *tblOwners* to a new Word document. The letter to Owners will give information about upcoming pool maintenance. Use data from the *tblOwners* in the Address block and Greeting line. Save the letter as *OwnersLetter.docx*. The body of the letter is as follows:

   > As discussed at the last Home Owners Association meeting, we will be resurfacing the outdoor pool deck and conducting pool maintenance. The outdoor pool will be out of service during the week of May 1–May 7. Please note that the indoor pool will be available for owner and renter use during this time.
   >
   > Sincerely,
   >
   > The Management

4. Create a report showing all housekeeping charges that have been paid. (*Hint:* Create a query first. Use the Is Not Null criterion in the *Date Paid* field.) Save the report as *rpt4_Housekeeping Report*.

   - Sort on the Date Paid field and group by *Property Number*.
   - Revise the report to have the title display *Housekeeping Charges*.
   - Sum the *Fees*. Using the Properties sheet, change the format of the sum to Currency. (*Hint:* Right-click on the sum for the group and choose the Properties command. In the Format property line, choose Currency from the drop-down list.)
   - Resave the report.

5. Create a report showing the property information (*Address, Pets,* and *Internet*) and rental rates. Group by *Property Address*. Save the report as *rpt5_PropertyRates*.

   - Revise the report to have the title display *Property Rates Report*.
   - Change the grouping level to *Condo Type* and *Property Address*.
   - Resize the controls to make sure that all the data are displayed.
   - Resave the report.

CASE STUDY C: PENGUINS SKI CLUB

Using the *Penguins* database, create a series of reports, as described below.

1. Create a report that prints a directory of members and their parents. The directory should include each member's name, address, and phone number, as well as the parents' names and phone number(s). Print in order by the member's last name. The report should print in landscape mode. Use the Flow style, and name the report *rptMemberDirectory*.

2. Make a report that prints mailing labels to members and name it *rptLabels*. The labels should print in alphabetical order by last name. Use the template for Avery USA 5160 labels.

3. Create a report showing members' names, phone numbers, ages, ability levels, and whether or not they rented equipment. Group by ability level and sort in order by last name. Select the Urban style. Name the report *rptAbilityLevels*.

4. Create a report that lists the names, ages, ability levels, and phone numbers of all members attending each event. Group by event, and show the name, location, and date of each event. Sort members by ability level, and secondarily by age. Use the Aspect style. Name the report *rptEventAttendance*.

Chapter 7

Database Design and Maintenance

Objectives

After completing this chapter, you will be able to

Understand database principles and terms:
- Entities, entity classes, attributes, tuples, and relations.
- Normalization.
- Referential integrity.
- Data dependency.
- Data anomalies.
- Data integrity.

Design a database:
- Create an entity-relationship (E-R) diagram.
- Normalize tables developed from an E-R diagram.
- Define table relationships and foreign keys.

Tune up a database:
- Add and modify lookup fields for easy data display.
- Add attachment fields for storing media, Microsoft office documents, and other types of files.
- Create multiple-field primary keys.
- Create indexes on tables for faster searching and sorting.

Maintain a database:
- Compact and repair a database.
- Split a database into a front end and a back end.
- Print documentation.
- Analyze database performance.
- Enforce referential integrity.

Understand and maintain proper table relationships:
- Create and delete table joins.
- Set field properties to help enforce referential integrity.
- Know how changing a key field affects table joins.
- Understand the difference between inner and outer joins.
- Maintain correct joins between tables, including enforcing referential integrity.
- Produce a Find Duplicate Records query using the Query Wizard.
- Produce a Find Unmatched Records query using the Query Wizard.

Dictionary

Anomaly	An instance of incorrect or inconsistent data.
Attribute	A field in a table. This term is also used to mean a characteristic of an entity class in an E-R diagram.
Bridge table	A table created to simplify a many-to-many relationship between tables.

Composite, complex, or compound key	A multiple-field primary key.
Data integrity	The accuracy of data in a database.
Deletion anomaly	An anomaly that happens when data is deleted from a relation.
Domain integrity	When values in any given field are within an accepted range.
Entity	One specific member of an entity class.
Entity class	A group of like items (or entities).
Entity integrity	When a database has no duplicate records in any table.
First Normal Form	A standard for a table that requires that all the fields describe the entity represented by the table, the candidate for primary key be defined, and all fields contain the simplest possible values.
Foreign key	Field(s) containing the same values as those in the primary key of another table.
Functional dependency	When the value of one attribute determines the value of another attribute.
Index	A field property that, when set, speeds up searches on that field.
Inner join	Join type containing only the records from both tables having at least one corresponding record in the other table.
Insertion anomaly	An anomaly that happens when data is added to a relation.
Left outer join	A one-to-many join type containing all the records in the "one" table, and only those records in the "many" table containing a data value in the foreign key that matches one in the primary key of the "one" table.
Lookup field	A special type of field that displays a value from another table.
Lookup table	A table that holds data about groups or categories of information, and is used by other tables for looking up data values.
Master table	A fairly static (mostly unchanging) table that holds data about people and things.
MDE file	A read-only database (except for data) that is much smaller than a regular database.
Multiple-field primary key	A primary key made up of more than one field.
Non-key attribute	An attribute that is not a primary key, nor part of a key.
Normal form	A representation of a table that meets a set of rules intended to eliminate data redundancy and errors.
Normalization	The process of making a table match a relational database design standard called a normal form.
Overnormalization	The process of normalizing data to the point where work becomes difficult.
Partial dependency	When a non-key attribute is determined by only one of the attributes in the key.
Referential integrity	A set of rules that ensures that data in joined tables remains accurate.
Relation	A table in a relational database.
Right outer join	A one-to-many join type containing all the records in the "many" table, and only those records in the "one" table containing a data value in the foreign key that matches one in the primary key of the "many" table.
Second Normal Form	A standard for a table that requires it to be in First Normal Form and have no partial dependencies.
Third Normal Form	A standard for a table that requires it to be in Second Normal Form and have no transitive dependencies.
Transaction/event table	A table that contains data about transactions or about events that occur to the data in tables.
Transitive dependency	When a non-key attribute determines the value of another attribute.
Tuple	A record in a table.
Update anomaly	An anomaly that happens when data is changed in a relation.
User-defined integrity	When the data in a database complies with specific business and user rules.

7.1 / Designing a Relational Database

Databases really have two main functions—to update data and retrieve data. Updating data provides a means to keep data current by adding, editing, and deleting records. Retrieving data provides information the user needs by producing accurate queries, forms, and reports. Proper database design is critical to ensure that data is updated correctly and can be retrieved quickly and easily.

Relational database rules govern how tables are designed, created, and joined. These rules make relational databases very powerful by eliminating data redundancy, reducing errors, and preventing data loss while providing the flexibility needed to supply user information. In order to understand relational database rules, basic concepts and terminology need to be revisited.

Relational Database Terminology

Relational database theory is based on the principles of relational algebra, the branch of mathematics that deals with set theory. The language of relational algebra is used to define the database design and table design processes as precisely as possible. This language can be difficult to understand without a thorough understanding of relational algebra. In order to understand the terminology, it's helpful to review the basics.

A table is often represented by a grid or matrix—the way a table appears when examined in the Datasheet view. A table is also referred to as a relation. A record in a table is a row in the grid, and is also known as a tuple. A field is a column in the grid, and is also called an attribute. This information can be summarized as follows:

Database Object	Graphical Representation	Relational Term
Table	Grid or matrix	Relation
Record	Row	Tuple
Field	Column	Attribute

Relations, or tables, have several characteristics:

- No two tuples, or records, can be exactly the same. One or more of the attributes in any two tuples must be different, so a primary key can be designated for the relation.

- The order in which tuples appear has no significance, so any two tuples can be interchanged without affecting the relation. The same is true for attributes: They can appear in any order in a relation without affecting the data.

- Each attribute in a relation must have a unique name and must describe a characteristic of the relation.

- An attribute can contain only one value in any given tuple. When you look at the intersection of a row and column, you see only one value.

- The possible set of values for an attribute, known as the domain of an attribute, must be the same in each tuple. In other words, an attribute can't be numeric in one tuple and text in another tuple.

Entity-Relationship Diagrams

The first step in designing a relational database is to analyze the data, organize it into groups, and determine the relationships between groups of data. An entity-relationship (E-R) diagram is a tool that helps you analyze and organize the data you need to capture.

Q: Aren't all databases different?

A: The data differs, but the functions of almost every database are the same to update and retrieve data.

Q: What's an entity relationship diagram?

A: An entity relationship diagram helps you analyze and organize data so you can begin developing tables.

An E-R diagram arranges data into entity classes—the first draft of the database tables. It also helps you determine primary keys, table joins, and additional tables in the database.

By creating an E-R diagram, you are developing entity classes, determining attributes, and defining relationships between entity classes. An entity class is a group of like items, and an entity is one specific member of the group. For example, an entity class might be all the courses taught at your college, and the class you are taking now is an entity in that class. Relating these terms to table design, think of an entity class as the first draft of a table and an entity as a prototype record in a table. An attribute is a characteristic of an entire entity class. So, the attributes of an entity class will most likely become the fields in the associated table. Attributes provide information about an entity, uniquely identify an entity, or describe a relationship between entities. For example, some attributes of an entity class representing college courses could be course number, section number, course name, and course level (graduate/undergraduate). Course number and section number uniquely identify a course; course name provides information about a course; and course level describes a relationship among the courses in the entity class.

The relationship between two entity classes defines how they interact, or how one entity class acts upon another. The relationship also determines how many entities in each class will interact. Is their relationship one-to-one, or one-to-many? Or can many entities in one class interact with many entities in another class? For example, consider the following entity classes: courses, course sections (individual classes), instructors, and college employees. The entity classes instructors and course sections interact with each other when instructors teach sections. Given the assumption that a course section is taught by only one instructor, instructors and course sections have a one-to-many relationship because one instructor can teach many sections. The entity classes instructors and college employees have a one-to-one relationship because each instructor is an employee. There is one entity in each class for every instructor. The entity classes courses and instructors have a many-to-many relationship. One instructor is able to teach many classes, and one class can be taught by multiple instructors. These relationships between entity classes will be developed into table joins or may grow into additional tables.

You can create an E-R diagram on paper or with a software tool on the computer. There are some products designed specifically for creating E-R diagrams—you can search the Web and find several tools. It's probably easiest to begin by sketching it on paper, then develop a more formal presentation over time, and keep it with the database documentation.

All E-R diagrams should represent entity classes, attributes, and relationships. However there are many ways to draw E-R diagrams using several different sets of symbols. The information represented, not the symbols used, is the main focus of an E-R diagram. You can begin by just drawing circles and lines on a piece of paper, and writing in the necessary information. One example of a more formal E-R diagram is shown in Figure 7.1.

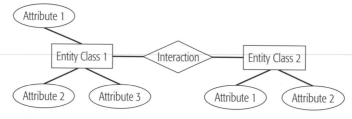

Figure 7.1 The layout of an entity-relationship diagram

The symbols used in this E-R diagram are described as follows:

- A rectangle is used to represent an entity class.

- An oval is used to represent an attribute.

- A diamond is used to represent a relationship.

- The 1s and ∞s (infinity symbols) represent the one (1) and many (∞) sides of a one-to-many relationship. 1s on both sides of a diamond represent a one-to-one relationship, and ∞s on both sides indicate a many-to-many relationship.

E-R diagrams can be used to expand the *G3* (Going, Going, Gone online auctions) example database to handle a problem that has occurred. When the same person buys multiple items, a lot of the data in *tblSales* is repeated. Figure 7.2 shows two sales to the same person. The data in the shaded area is repeated in both records.

G3Number	ItemName	BuyerID	Actual Shipping	Shipping Date	Shipped
2158347238	Vintage Tablecloth Fruit Cherries 1940s Excellent Condition	Linen*Lady	$2.00	5/1/2008	Yes
2152735340	6 Vintage Red Yellow Striped Napkins Linen Never Used	Linen*Lady	$2.00	5/1/2008	Yes

Figure 7.2 Multiple sales to the same buyer

It seems clear that another table is needed for shipment data, and the shaded fields need to be moved to that table. Here's an E-R diagram showing the possible splitting of *tblSales* into two tables—*tblSales* and *tblShipments*. Figure 7.3 shows only a few of the attributes or fields in *tblSales*.

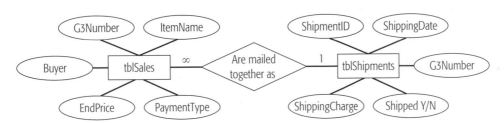

Figure 7.3 E-R diagram showing the relationship between *tblSales* and *tblShipments*

The field *G3Number* is needed to join the two tables together, but when there are multiple items in the same shipment, the same problem of repeating data occurs again. Perhaps a better design would be to put the field *ShipmentID* in *tblSales*. That way all items would be assigned a shipment number, shipment data is only recorded once, and the two tables can still be joined. The join will be one-to-many from *tblShipments* into *tblSales*. The adjusted E-R diagram is shown in Figure 7.4.

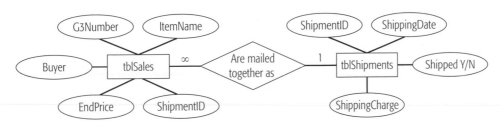

Figure 7.4 E-R diagram showing a better relationship between *tblSales* and *tblShipments*

TRY IT YOURSELF   7.1.1

A. Read the description of the E-R diagram in the college example.

B. Draw the rectangles for the entity classes in the E-R diagram on paper.

C. Add the attribute ovals.

D. Place an asterisk next to the primary key attribute for each entity class.

E. Fill in each relationship diamond, and mark the sides of the relationship with the appropriate 1 and ∞ symbols.

F. Compare your diagram with the solution shown in Appendix B.

Let's step through another example together. The text will describe the E-R diagram for this database; you can create the E-R diagram by doing the steps in the Try It Yourself 7.1.1. You may find it easier to write the attributes of the entity class inside the rectangle below the class name.

We are going to develop the faculty/department/degree side of the college database example begun in Chapter 1. We need to keep data about faculty, the courses they develop, the degrees for which they are advisors, and their class schedules. We also want to know which courses are required for each degree, how much credit is given for each course, and when and where a course can be taken.

Let's assume that our entity classes are: faculty, courses, degrees, and class schedules. A list of the attributes of each entity class are:

Faculty—Name, address, department, phone, email address

Courses—Course number, description, credit hours, textbook

Degrees—Degree name, department, description, advisor, required courses

Class Schedules—Course number, section number, location, instructor, day(s), time(s)

Primary keys are needed for faculty, degrees, and class schedules. Course number is the primary key for the Courses entity class because it's unique for each class, and degree name is the primary key for Degrees for the same reason. Name could be the primary key for the Faculty entity class; however, it's possible that two faculty members could have the same name. A different primary key, such as Social Security Number, should be selected when the table is created. The Class Schedules entity class needs both the course number and section number to uniquely identify an entity, thus the primary key will be a combination of the two.

Q: Can you give me a hint to help in defining a relationship?

A: Think concretely. How and when do two entities interact? What verb describes an action taken by one or both entities?

Try to think of a word that describes how each pair of entity classes interacts. Faculty **teach** courses; faculty **advise about** degrees; and faculty **teach** class section in the schedule. Degrees **require** courses; degrees don't have a relationship with the class schedule. Courses are **offered as** class sections in the schedule.

Now, break down each relationship into one-to-one, one-to-many, or many-to-many. There are several many-to-many relationships in this example. To determine relationship types, ask questions such as "How many courses can a faculty member teach?" and "How many faculty members can teach a course?" Be sure to reverse each question. When you're finished, you can compare your diagram with the solution shown in Appendix A.

TRY IT YOURSELF   7.1.2

A. Create the tables for the college database example, using the format shown at the right. Write the information on paper, don't create the tables in Access.

B. Compare your tables with the solution shown in Appendix A.

Designing Tables

Designing tables from E-R diagrams is straightforward. Assign the entity class name as the table name, list the attributes as fields enclosed in parentheses after the table name, and underline the primary key field. A table is represented as follows:

Tablename(Primary Key Field, Field2, Field3, . . . , Fieldn)

Figure 7.5 Syntax for representing a table

Using the *G3* database example, the table *tblShipments*, with *ShipmentID* as the primary key, would be represented in the following way:

tblShipments(ShipmentID, ShippingDate, Shipped, ShippingCharge)

Figure 7.6 The *tblShipments* table

ShipmentID was added to the field list as the primary key because no primary key naturally occurred in the table. It often happens that primary keys need to be created, and AutoNumber fields are designed for this purpose.

Be sure to also examine the relationships between tables shown in the E-R diagram, so the appropriate foreign keys can be included in field lists. In the *G3* database example, the field *ShipmentID* was added to *tblSales* to join it to *tblShipment*. There is a one-to-many relationship between the tables—one shipment can include many sales. The new *tblSales* is shown in Figure 7.7.

---

tblSales(G3Number, ItemName, Category, Buyer, StartDate, EndDate, StartPrice, EndPrice, ListingCost, ShippingAmountPaid, PaymentType, PaymentAmount, Status, G3Percentage, Invoiced, Paid, ShipmentID)

Figure 7.7 The new table, *tblSales*

Table Types

There are three basic groupings for database tables—master tables, lookup tables, and bridge or transaction/event tables. These types describe the type of data stored in these tables, how the tables are used, and their update frequency.

A master table holds data about people and things such as customers, faculty members, or college courses. Master tables are static—the data in them usually doesn't change often.

A lookup table holds data about groups or categories of information, and other tables use them to look up data values. Lookup tables are often dynamic, with values being added at times. In the *G3* database, *tblCategory* is a lookup table. It's better to make category a lookup table rather than type in a list of values for a category field because the categories can change at any time—whenever new items are sold.

Transaction/event tables are generally dynamic: Their data is frequently changed. Transaction/event tables can contain data about transactions that occur to the data in tables such as a customer placing an order or paying an invoice. Transaction/event tables can also hold data about an event such as a faculty member being scheduled to teach a course, or an item being shipped.

Bridge tables are created when a many-to-many relationship exists between two tables, and are often used to store transaction or event data. Bridge tables are sometimes called junction tables. If you don't create bridge tables during this first design step, they will be created in the next step as you normalize the tables. Many-to-many joins are difficult to manage in a relational database, so bridge tables are created to connect the two (usually master) tables. The *G3* database doesn't have a many-to-many join, but the College database does. Consider the tables *tblCourses* and *tblDegrees*. One course can be required in multiple degree programs, and one degree program requires the completion of multiple courses. A bridge table should be created to handle this join, it can be called *tblCoursesDegrees* as it joins *tblCourses* and *tblDegrees*. The new table contains only the primary key fields from the other two tables. Figure 7.8 shows how the tables *tblCourses*, *tblDegrees*, and *tblCoursesDegrees* might look. Notice that the primary key for *tblCoursesDegrees* is made up of both fields, because either field by itself is not unique.

---

tblCourses(CourseID, CourseTitle, Description, CreditHours, Textbook)
tblDegrees(DegreeID, DegreeName, DepartmentName, DegreeDescription, FacultyAdvisor)
tblCoursesDegrees(CourseID, DegreeID)

Figure 7.8 *tblCourses, tblDegrees* and *tblCoursesDegrees*

Q: Why use lookup tables? Isn't it easier to put all the data values in a list.

A: Use a list of values when values don't change. If a list changes, keep the values in a separate table.

Q: How can I tell if a table needs a multiple-field primary key?

A: If no single field is unique, but a combination of fields defines a unique instance, you need a multiple-field primary key.

7.2 Normalizing Tables

The next step in creating a database is to normalize the tables created from the E-R diagram. Table normalization is the process of making a table match a relational database design standard called a normal form. There are five normal forms, each form representing an ideal table that meets a set of rules intended to eliminate data redundancy and errors. Normalizing tables ensures that:

- Tables will not need restructuring later.
- More tables can be added without restructuring existing tables.
- Data updates produce consistent and accurate data.
- Table joins can be made to represent any entity or event in the database.
- Queries, forms, and reports produce correct information.
- All database functions can be done without complexity.

Each successive normal form molds the table into a more efficient and error-free structure. All normal forms assume that the requirements for previous normal forms have been met, so if a table is in third normal form, it must also be in first and second normal form by definition. You apply a normal form by changing the structure of a table until it meets the requirements of that form. New tables are often created during the process.

Usually, database developers ensure that their tables meet only the first three normal forms. Tables normalized to this point are generally considered normalized enough for most purposes. It is possible to overnormalize your data, or normalize it to the point where it becomes difficult for you to work with. We will discuss the first three normal forms in detail, and briefly look at two others. First, however, we need to understand the concepts of data dependency and data anomalies.

Q: Why is it important to understand functional dependency?

A: Because it defines the relationship between a primary key and all the other fields in a table.

Data Dependency

We know that an attribute (or combination of attributes) that uniquely identifies a tuple is a primary key. If an attribute is not a primary key, it's called a non-key attribute. If a non-key attribute is a primary key in another relation, it's called a foreign key.

When an attribute determines the value of another attribute, a dependency exists. If attribute 2 is dependent on attribute 1 and you change the value of attribute 1, the value of attribute 2 changes also. Consider the relation, *Courses*, where *CourseNumber* is the primary key (see Figure 7.9).

CourseNumber	CourseTitle	CreditHours	Textbook	Author
CIS 140	Introduction to Databases	3	*Access Guidebook*	Trigg
CIS 150	Introduction to Spreadsheets	2	*Excel Guidebook*	Dobson
CIS 160	Introduction to Visual Basic	3	*Visual Basic Guidebook*	Trigg

Figure 7.9 *CourseTitle* and *Textbook* are dependent on *CourseNumber*

The attribute *CourseTitle* is dependent on the attribute *CourseNumber*. If the course number changes, then the title of the course changes also. The attribute *Textbook* is also dependent on *CourseNumber*. When one attribute determines another attribute, a functional dependency exists between the two. All non-key attributes in a relation should be functionally dependent on the primary key attribute. So, in the *Courses* relation shown above, all the attributes should be functionally dependent on the *CourseNumber*.

What about the attribute *Author*? It isn't functionally dependent on the *CourseNumber*. Two tuples contain the value "Trigg" for the attribute *Author*, but have different values for *CourseNumber*. When the *CourseNumber* is changed, the *Author* doesn't always change. *Author* is dependent on the attribute *Textbook*, a non-key attribute. This is called a transitive dependency—when a non-key attribute determines the value of another attribute. Transitive dependencies are eliminated during normalization.

There is a third type of dependency, partial dependency, that occurs only in relations that have a multiple-field or composite primary key. When a non-key attribute depends on only one of the attributes in the key, a partial dependency exists. The relation below demonstrates an example of partial dependency. This relation is called *ClassSchedule* and has a multiple-field primary key consisting of *CourseNumber* and *SectionNumber*. This relation is shown in Figure 7.10.

CourseNumber	SectionNumber	CourseTitle	Location	Instructor
CIS 140	L01	Introduction to Databases	A202	Sweeney
CIS 140	L02	Introduction to Databases	A355	Bates
CIS 160	L01	Introduction to Visual Basic	A310	Almazen

Figure 7.10 *CourseTitle* is partially dependent on the primary key

The attribute *CourseTitle* is only partially dependent on the primary key. *CourseTitle* is functionally dependent on *CourseNumber*, but it is independent of *SectionNumber*. If the *SectionNumber* changes, the *CourseTitle* does not always change. Partial dependencies are removed during normalization.

Data Anomalies

Normalization not only eliminates transitive and partial dependencies, but also eliminates the occurrence of data anomalies. Anomalies are instances of incorrect or inconsistent data caused by redundant data (the same data stored in more than one relation), transitive dependencies, or partial dependencies. There are three types of data anomalies: insertion anomalies, deletion anomalies, and update anomalies. The example shown in Figure 7.11 will be used to illustrate the various types of data anomalies.

StudentID	Course Number	Credit Hours
100	CIS 140	3
200	CIS 140	3
300	CIS 160	3

Figure 7.11 Poorly designed relation that will create anomalies

Insertion anomalies occur when data is added to a database. If data is inserted into only one relation, but should be inserted into more than one relation, an insertion anomaly arises. If data can't be added because the value for the primary key is unknown, this is also an insertion anomaly. In Figure 7.11, if a new course needs to be added, an insertion anomaly occurs if nobody has enrolled in the new course. The new course can't be added without a value for *Student ID*.

Deletion anomalies happen when data is deleted from one relation, but remains in another relation. They also occur when data can't be deleted without removing other important data. In the relation shown in Figure 7.11, if the student with a *Student ID* of "300" drops out, a deletion anomaly will occur. If the tuple for *Student ID* = "300" is removed, it will also remove the data for the course "CIS 160."

Update anomalies come about while changing the value of an attribute. If the value should be changed elsewhere, and isn't, the data will be inconsistent and create an update anomaly. Using the example shown in Figure 7.11, an update anomaly will happen if the course "CIS 140" changes to 4 credit hours. If the tuple for *Student ID* = "100" is changed to 4 credit hours, but the tuple for *Student ID* = "200" isn't changed, the data is inconsistent. An update anomaly will have occurred.

First Normal Form or 1NF

A table is in First Normal Form when all attributes describe the entity represented by the relation, the candidate for the primary key is defined, and all attributes contain the simplest possible values.

This means for a table to be in 1NF:

- You should only include fields that describe the people, events, or objects in the table.

- You should identify a possible primary key.

- Fields should be broken down into the smallest meaningful pieces.

- There should be no repeating groups of data where the same data values appear in multiple records.

- Fields should not contain multiple values for any data items.

A *G3* database expansion will be the first example to consider. The client is starting to buy goods for resale in G3 auctions and would like to track purchases. She is especially interested in knowing how much an item cost so that the cost can be subtracted from the sales price and the amount of profit can be calculated.

The first entity to consider is purchases. Purchases will have a name, cost amount, date purchased, place purchased, and the same categories as *tblSales*. Purchases and sales will have to be joined so that cost information is available. An E-R diagram showing these two entities/tables is shown in Figure 7.12 (not all fields are shown for *tblSales*).

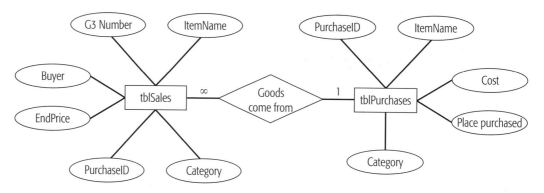

Figure 7.12 E-R diagram for *G3* database expansion

Putting the primary key from *tblPurchases, PurchaseID,* into *tblSales* joins the two tables. You can't reverse it, putting *SalesID* into *tblPurchases,* because one purchase may be split up into more than one sale and that would put multiple values into the *SalesID* field. There's a one-to-many relationship from *tblPurchases* into *tblSales*. Not every record in *tblPurchases* will have a value in the *SalesID* field, because at any given time, some items will not yet have been put up for sale. Neither will every record in *tblSales* have a corresponding record in *tblPurchases*—found items are not in *tblPurchases*.

Referring to Figure 7.12, it is obvious that the *Category* field isn't needed in both tables, unless the client wants to track the categories of purchases before they become sales. There has been no mention of it, so it's better to remove the field from *tblPurchases* to avoid data anomalies.

Sometimes, creating the tables and putting sample data into them will reveal if additional steps are needed to normalize the data. Figure 7.13 shows some sample records for *tblPurchases*. Look at the field *PlacePurchased*. It has the same data values in multiple records and similar values with slightly different text. In order to comply with first normal form, a separate table for purchase locations needs to be created.

PurchaseID	ItemName	Cost	PlacePurchased
1	1950s Tablecloth with Cowboy Motif	$2.00	Garage Sale
2	4 Antique Tablecloths with Lace	$6.00	Auction
3	2 Candlewick Bedspreads from the 1940s	$8.50	Thrift Store
4	Box of Assorted Dinner Napkins Linen	$5.00	Estate Auction
5	Box of Kitchen Towels Embroidered 1940s	$3.50	Auction
6	Embroidered Pillow Case	$1.00	Thrift Store

Figure 7.13 *tblPurchases* with sample data

Upon closer examination, another problem might be in store. Some of the item names, notably those in records 2–5, indicate that there are multiple items. If all the items aren't sold together as one, but are broken apart and sold separately, then the cost field needs to be divided amongst all the items sold. Another table could be created for separate items in a lot, but it might just be easier to have two cost fields—*TotalCost* and *UnitCost*. When there's only one item in a record, the fields *TotalCost* and *UnitCost* will have the same value. Figure 7.14 shows these tables in the *G3* database in first normal form, based on these changes.

---

tblSales(<u>G3Number</u>, ItemName, Category, Buyer, StartDate, EndDate, StartPrice, EndPrice, ListingCost, ShippingAmountPaid, PaymentType, PaymentAmount, Status, G3Percentage, Invoiced, Paid, ShipmentID, PurchaseID)
tblPurchases(<u>PurchaseID</u>, ItemName, TotalCost, UnitCost, PlaceID)
tblPurchasePlaces(<u>PlaceID</u>, PlaceName)

Figure 7.14 *tblSales* and additional *G3* tables in first normal form

Next, consider the set of tables developed for the college database in Try It Yourself 7.1.1 and put them into 1NF. The first draft of these tables is shown in Figure 7.15, with the candidates for primary keys underlined.

FACULTY(<u>SSN</u>, Name, Address, Dept. Code, Dept. Name, Phone, Email Address, Course Name Taught 1, Course Number 1, Course Name Taught 2, Course Number 2, etc.)

COURSES(<u>Course#</u>, Course Title, Description, Credit Hours, Book, Taught by Faculty 1, Taught by Faculty 2, etc., Required by Degree 1, Required by Degree 2, etc.)

DEGREES(<u>DegreeID</u>, Degree Name, Dept. Code, Dept. Name, Degree Description, Advisor1, Advisor2)

CLASS SCHEDULES(<u>Course#</u>, <u>Section#</u>, Course Title, Location, Instructor SSN, Day1, Day2, Day3, Time1, Time2, Time3)

Figure 7.15 First draft of tables for college database

There are several changes that need to be made to these tables to get them into 1NF. Some fields can be broken down into smaller units of data, repeating groups can be eliminated, fields with multiple values can be moved to new tables, and better primary keys can be found for some tables. Refer to Figure 7.15 as you go through this example.

First, we'll identify the fields that contain too much data. The *Faculty* table has two: *Name* and *Address*. Break *Name* down into two fields—*FirstName* and *LastName*—so that faculty can be sorted in alphabetical order by last name. Also, break *Address* into four fields—*Address, City, State,* and *Zipcode*. This allows labels to be printed for faculty, and allows data to be sorted on any of those fields.

Next, look for repeating groups of data, or data that appears in more than one table. There's only one: *Degrees Advised* in the *Faculty* table, and *Faculty Advisors* in the

Q: How do I know when a field is broken down into the smallest possible unit?

A: When the field can easily be sorted and searched, it's small enough. For example, if you group data by area code, it's much easier to store the area code separately from the phone number.

Degrees table. Both of these fields tell us who the advisors are for each degree program. Let's eliminate *Degrees Advised* in the *Faculty* table.

Now, look for fields with multiple values—there are several.

- The *Faculty* table has *Courses Developed* repeated because a faculty member usually develops more than one course. A bridge table, *Courses Developed*, can be added to hold this information. It should contain at least the field *Course#* and the primary key field from the *Faculty* table.

- The *Courses* table repeats the field *Degrees Required By* because a course can be required in multiple degree programs. Another bridge table, *Courses In Degrees*, should be created to hold the field *Course#* and the primary key field from the *Degrees* table.

- The *Degrees* table has the field *Faculty Advisors* repeated. Again, a bridge table should be created for this data. Make a new table, *Degree Advisors*, containing the primary key fields from the *Faculty* and *Degrees* tables.

- The *Class Schedules* table repeats the fields *Days Scheduled* and *Times Scheduled* because many classes are offered more than once a week, and are not always held at the same time each day. Once more, a bridge table can be made to hold the data. Let's call it *Class Schedule Times*, and move the days and times here.

Lastly, take a look at the candidates for primary keys in each table.

- The *Faculty* table uses *Name*—not a good choice if two faculty members have the same name. Change it to Social Security Number, or SSN, as each faculty has a unique SSN.

- The *Courses* table uses *Course#*, which meets the requirements for a primary key.

- The *Degrees* table uses *Degree Name*, which certainly meets the requirements, but is long and easy to misspell in repetitive use. Errors in the values of a primary key will prevent tables from joining correctly, so a simpler primary key is recommended. Because no other candidate naturally occurs, an AutoNumber field called *Degree ID* can be created.

- The *Class Schedules* table has a multiple-field primary key because neither *Course#* nor *Section#* alone is unique, but when they are combined they create a distinct identifier for each record. This primary key can stand as it is.

Figure 7.16 shows the changes made to the college database after the tables are put into 1NF.

FACULTY(SSN, FirstName, LastName, Address, City, State, Zipcode, Dept. Code, Dept. Name, Phone, Email Address)
COURSES(Course#, Description, Credit Hours, Book)
DEGREES(DegreeID, Degree Name, Dept. Code, Dept. Name, Degree Description)
CLASS SCHEDULES(Course#, Section#, Course Title, Location, Instructor SSN)
FACULTY COURSES(Faculty SSN, Course#, Course Title)
COURSES IN DEGREES(DegreeID, Course#, Degree Name)
CLASS SCHEDULE TIMES(Course#, Section#, Course Title, Day, Time)
DEGREE ADVISORS(Faculty SSN, DegreeID)

Figure 7.16 College database tables in 1NF

Second Normal Form or 2NF

A table is in Second Normal Form when it is in First Normal Form and it includes no partial dependencies. If a primary key is a single field, the table is automatically in Second Normal Form.

A few changes need to be made to the tables in the college database (see Figure 7.16) to get them into 2NF. The *Course Title* field needs to be removed from the *Class Schedules*, *Faculty Courses*, and *Class Schedule Times* tables. In each instance, *Course Title* depends only on part of the multiple-field key—the field *Course#*. In the tables *Class Schedules* and *Class Schedule Times*, *Course Title* is not determined by the field *Section#*. In the *Faculty Courses* table, *Faculty SSN* does not determine *Course Title*, it's determined by *Course#* and should be removed from this table. Also, the *Degree Name* field needs to be removed from the *Courses in Degrees* table because it depends on only the *DegreeID* part of the primary key. The result of these changes is shown in Figure 7.17.

FACULTY(SSN, FirstName, LastName, Address, City, State, Zipcode, Dept. Code, Dept. Name, Phone, Email Address)

COURSES(Course#, Description, Credit Hours, Book)

DEGREES(DegreeID, Degree Name, Dept. Code, Dept. Name, Degree Description)

CLASS SCHEDULES(Course#, Section#, Location, Instructor SSN)

FACULTY COURSES(Faculty SSN, Course#)

COURSES IN DEGREES(DegreeID, Course#)

CLASS SCHEDULE TIMES(Course#, Section#, Day, Time)

DEGREE ADVISORS(Faculty SSN, DegreeID)

Figure 7.17 College database tables in 2NF

Third Normal Form or 3NF

A table is in Third Normal Form when it is in Second Normal Form and contains no transitive dependencies. 3NF eliminates repetitive data and calculated data, and sometimes creates lookup tables in the database.

To put the college database into 3NF, we need to create another table. In the *Faculty* table, the fields *Department Office* and *Department Secretary* are dependent on the *Department Name* field, which is a non-key attribute. A new table, *Departments*, should be created to hold the fields *Department Name*, *Department Office*, and *Department Secretary*.

The *Departments* table needs a primary key. *Department Name* is not a good choice for a primary key for the same reason *Degree Name* didn't work in the *Degrees* table. Colleges often use abbreviations for their departments, such as "CIS" for "Computer Information Systems," so let's introduce a *Department Code* field that contains abbreviations already in use.

Figure 7.18 shows the college database tables after departmental data has been moved to another table, and the field *Department Code* has been added to the tables *Faculty* and *Degrees*.

FACULTY(SSN, FirstName, LastName, Address, City, State, Zipcode, Dept. Code, Phone, Email Address)

COURSES(Course#, Description, Credit Hours, Book)

DEGREES(DegreeID, Degree Name, Dept. Code, Degree Description)

CLASS SCHEDULES(Course#, Section#, Location, Instructor SSN)

FACULTY COURSES(Faculty SSN, Course#)

COURSES IN DEGREES(DegreeID, Course#)

CLASS SCHEDULE TIMES(Course#, Section#, Day, Time)

DEGREE ADVISORS(Faculty SSN, DegreeID)

DEPARTMENTS(Dept. Code, Dept. name)

Figure 7.18 College database tables in 3NF

Q: How much is enough
normalization?

A: Through either 3NF or 4NF.
You'll learn to recognize a
normalized table once you
have a little experience.

Advanced Normal Forms

Once all tables in a database are in 3NF, most people consider the data normalized, though one can continue on to 4NF and 5NF. Let's take a quick look at both.

A table is in 4NF when it has at most one independent multivalued dependency (MVD). A multivalued dependency exists when a field can contain multiple values for one given value in the primary key (or part of the primary key, if it's a multiple-field primary key). For example, the table *Degree Advisors* shown in Figure 7.18 has one MVD. One faculty member can advise students about multiple degrees, so the field *DegreeID* can contain multiple values for one given value in the field *Faculty SSN*. This means that there could be more than one record with the same value for *Faculty SSN*.

The tables shown in Figure 7.18 are already in 4NF; let's create a table that's not in 4NF using the same data. The *FacultyDegreesAndCourses* table, shown in Figure 7.19, contains the courses developed by and the degrees advised by a faculty member. Both of the fields *Course#* and *DegreeID* have a multivalued dependency on the primary key *Faculty SSN*. One faculty member can advise students about multiple degrees and can develop multiple courses. There is no relationship, however, between the fields *Course#* and *DegreeID*. It's easy to see this problem when examining the data because many records have blank values.

FACULTY DEGREES AND COURSES

Faculty SSN	Course#	DegreeID
123-45-6789	CIS100	BUSINESS
123-45-6789	CIS150	CIS
123-45-6789	CIS200	
123-45-6789	CIS210	
456-78-9012	CIS100	CIS
456-78-9012	CIS120	
456-78-9012	CIS150	

Figure 7.19 The table *FacultyDegreesAndCourses* with sample data

A table is in 5NF when it can no longer be split into two more tables because further splitting would make tables that can't be re-joined. Taking normalization too far can create one-to-one relationships in the database and force you to create many queries that re-join tables. When you make it difficult to obtain data for forms and reports, you may have overnormalized the database. Sometimes people deliberately break a normalization rule because enforcing it requires more steps to produce information from the database. One example of this might be storing a total in a table, when the individual amounts that make up the total are also stored there.

Professional Tip: Normalization

This tip comes from Daniel Roth, an Information Architect at a large insurance company. He has many years of data processing experience as an application programmer, technical support specialist, DBA, and for the last several years as a data analyst. The full article can be found online at http://www.inconcept.com/JCM/December2000/roth.html.

I believe the goal of every logical model should be to normalize to 3rd Normal Form. Much to the horror of many lifetime data analysts, many of whom have no practical experience, I also believe there are exceptions. Logical models should graphically represent the business in a way that is useful and understandable. The success of a model can be determined by the clarity in which it represents the business.

I recently worked on a model that would be used to store data about business recovery. The table in question contained the business activities that are essential and need to be quickly replaced if the building blows up or burns down. Two of the attributes needed were the employee ID of the disaster recovery plan owner (the person responsible for the activities plan upkeep) and the employee ID of the plan approver (typically, but not always, the plan owner's manager). When looking at this data from a logical stand-point, the two employee IDs are a repeating group and therefore should be normalized to a separate table as shown below.

Business Activity (Activity ID, Activity Description, Recovery Time, Recovery Priority)

Business Activity Employee (Employee Role ID, Activity ID, Employee ID)

The other choice, not as logically pure, would be to denormalize the IDs to the business activity table as shown below.

Business Activity (Activity ID, Activity Description, Recovery Time, Recovery Priority, Activity Owner Employee ID, Activity Approver Employee ID)

When reviewing this I asked myself the following questions:

1. Would the separate entity be shareable?

    No, the business activity employee table would only have value in the context of its relationship to the business activity table. No other entity would relate directly to the business activity employee table. The table only has value because it further describes the business activity (Who is the approver of the business activity? Who is the owner of the business activity?).

2. Does creating a separate entity make the model easier to understand?

    No; you must know the values of the type code to understand the model. In some cases Employee ID would represent the approver and in other cases it would represent the owner. When the two employee IDs are stored and properly named on the main table, they are clearly identifiable. The separate entity makes the model more difficult to understand.

3. Does creating a separate entity make the model more flexible?

    Yes; if a new role is created for an employee it could be added to the model without altering the structure. You would simply have to add another type code. But it would still require changes to the application to edit, verify, display, and update the new role. The likelihood of new roles should play a factor in the decision. Existing business rules, which must be built into the application, must be evaluated to ensure they are still valid. In this case the flexibility is at the expense of usability.

Based upon the above answers I fail to see a practical benefit of creating a separate entity.

7.3 Using Advanced Field Properties

The next step in the database development process is to create the tables. When you're making customized tables, it's best to create your own tables in Design view. Choose the field names carefully—omitting spaces in names will eliminate the need to enclose field names in parentheses later. Specify the data type, appropriate field properties, and primary key. Refer to Chapter 2 if you need to review these topics. This section describes some tools that can help fine tune your tables—adding attachment fields for media, editing lookup fields, assigning a multiple-field primary key, and setting the index property.

Lookup Fields

Lookup fields are fields that display a value from another table. Sometimes a code or ID number doesn't convey much information to a user, and it's better to display a name or description. The table containing the lookup field should have a one-to-many join with the other table. The lookup field contains a foreign key, and displays a name or description found in the table for which this field is a primary key. A foreign key is a field containing the same values as those in the primary key of another table.

In the *G3* database expansion example shown in Figure 7.14, *PlaceID* is the primary key for the table *tblPurchasePlaces*, but is used as a foreign key in *tblPurchases*. A foreign key is usually a lookup field that displays data from the first table. In this example, *PlaceID* is actually stored in *tblPurchases*, but the field *PlaceName* from *tblPurchasePlaces* is actually displayed. Refer back to Chapter 3 for further information about creating lookup fields.

A lookup field is based on a query that is tied to the other table. You can edit the query behind the lookup field the same way you edit all queries in Access. You can control the data that's displayed in the lookup field—which additional fields are shown, and how the data is filtered and sorted.

How to Edit a Lookup Field Query

1. Open the table in Design view, and select the lookup field.

2. Click on the Lookup tab in the field properties area and click on the Row Source property row (see Figure 7.20).

3. Click on the Build button (...) on the right end of the Row Source property row (see Figure 7.20). The query grid opens.

TRY IT YOURSELF 7.3.1

A. Using the *G3* database, create a new table, *tblPurchasePlaces* following the specifications shown in Figure 7.14.

B. Add records to *tblPurchaseG3_Ch7 Places* for Garage Sale, Auction, and Thrift Store.

C. Close *tblPurchasePlaces*.

D. Make the field *PlacePurchased* in *tblPurchases* a lookup field into *tblPurchasePlaces*.

E. Close the table, or continue on.

Field Name	Data Type	Descri
EndPrice	Currency	
ListingCost	Currency	
ShippingAmountPaid	Currency	
BuyerID	Text	
PaymentType	Text	
PaymentDate	Date/Time	
Status	Text	
G3Percentage	Number	
Invoiced	Yes/No	
Paid	Yes/No	
ShipmentID	Number	
PurchaseID	Number	

Field Properties

Display Control	Combo Box
Row Source Type	Table/Query
Row Source	SELECT [tblPurchases].[PurchaseID], [tblPurchases].[ItemName] FROM tblPurchases;
Bound Column	1
Column Count	2
Column Heads	No
Column Widths	0";2.0521"
List Rows	16
List Width	2.0521"

Figure 7.20 The Row Source property for the lookup field

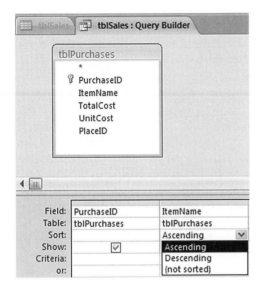

Figure 7.21 Sorting a field in the lookup query

Q: When I try to make a look-up field, I get an error message saying the data type can't be changed because of existing relationships. What should I do?

A: Open the Relationships window and remove the join between the two tables needed to create the lookup field. Close the window and save the relationships, then create the lookup field. The relationship, will be remade after the lookup field is generated.

4. Edit the query grid, adding a field to the query (see Figure 7.21), or make another edit. Make changes to other lookup properties if necessary, as explained below.

5. Close and save the query.

When you add a field to a drop-down list, you must also change the lookup properties so the new field can be displayed. Specifically, the properties Column Count, Column Widths, and List Width should be changed.

Other properties of the lookup field can be set to control the format of the list of values. When the table is opened in Design view, these properties can be edited by selecting the Lookup tab (see Figure 7.20). The properties and their descriptions are as follows:

- Bound Column—the value stored in the table, which is usually not the value shown in the list. Generally, it's the primary key from the lookup table.

- Column Count—the number of columns or fields in the underlying query.

- Column Heads—when set to "yes," the field names are shown as headings over the columns.

- Column Widths—the width (in inches) of each column. When the first column width is zero, the data in the first field is not displayed.

- List Rows—the number of rows displayed in the list.

TRY IT YOURSELF 7.3.2

A. Open *tblSales* in Design view.

B. Edit the query behind the lookup field *PurchaseID*.

C. Sort the query in alphabetical order by *ItemName* (see Figure 7.21). Save the query and the table.

D. View the *PurchaseID* field in Datasheet view. It should look like Figure 7.22.

E. Close the table, or continue on.

ShipmentID ▾	PurchaseID ▾
23	Box of Assorted Dinner Napkins Liner
23	1950s Tablecloth with Cowboy Motif
41	1950s Tablecloth with Cowboy Motif
7	2 Candlewick Bedspreads from the 1ç
22	4 Antique Tablecloths with Lace
	Box of Assorted Dinner Napkins Line
4	Box of Kitchen Towels Embroidered
34	Embroidered Pillow Case

Figure 7.22 Lookup field with a new sort order

- List Width—the width of the list (in inches).

- Limit To List—when set to "yes," no new values can be added by typing them into the list. When set to "no," values may be added.

Multivalued Fields

Access 2007 has a new field data type—the multivalued field. The multivalued field is a special lookup field that lets you store more than one data value in a field. It lets you create a one-to-many relationship without making a separate table. In reality, Access is creating the second table, you just can't see it. It's far better to avoid this data type as multivalued fields are incompatible with SQL servers, other databases, and even older versions of Access. Create your own tables and joins to facilitate proper database design, and to avoid possible problems.

If you must create a multivalued field, use the Lookup Wizard to create a lookup field. On the very last screen of the Lookup Wizard, select the check box to Allow Multiple Values.

Attachment Fields

The attachment data type is also new to Access 2007. If a field is an attachment field, you can store pictures, sounds, Office documents, and other files in the field. These other files are actually stored inside the database. Storing too many or too large a file as an attachment could slow the database down.

How to Create an Attachment Field

1. In Design view, add a new field to a table.

2. Type in a name and select the Attachment data type (see Figure 7.23).

3. Save the table.

TRY IT YOURSELF 7.3.3

A. Open *tblSales* in Design view.

B. Add a new attachment field called *ItemPhoto* as shown in Figure 7.23.

C. Change the caption of *ItemPhoto* to "Item Photo" as shown in Figure 7.24.

D. Save the table and change to Datasheet view.

E. Close the table, or continue on.

Field Name	Data Type
BuyerID	Text
PaymentType	Text
PaymentDate	Date/Time
Status	Text
G3Percentage	Number
Invoiced	Yes/No
Paid	Yes/No
ShipmentID	Number
ItemPhoto	Attachment
	Text
	Memo
	Number
	Date/Time
	Currency
	AutoNumber
	Yes/No
	OLE Object
	Hyperlink
	Attachment
	Lookup Wizard...

General | Lookup

Caption	
Required	No

Figure 7.23 Creating an attachment field

Be sure to type a value into the Caption property for the attachment field. If there's no caption set, then a paper clip graphic appears as the column name in Datasheet view. Figure 7.24 shows the attachment field without a caption at the top and with a caption on the bottom.

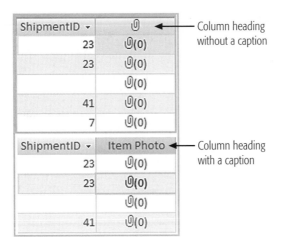

Figure 7.24 Attachment field with and without a caption

When an attachment field contains no data, a paper clip icon with a zero in parentheses is displayed in Datasheet view. Once data is added, the number 1 appears in parentheses after the paper clip.

How to Add Data to an Attachment Field

1. In Datasheet view, double-click on the attachment field

   OR

   In Datasheet view, right-click on the attachment field, and select Manage Attachments from the shortcut menu.

   The Attachments window opens (see Figure 7.25).

2. Click on the Add button. The Choose File dialog box opens.

3. Locate the file name of the attachment and double-click on it, or click once on the name and click on the Select button. The Attachments window displays the file name (see Figure 7.26).

4. Click the OK button to close the window. The number 1 appears in parentheses after the paperclip in the field.

TRY IT YOURSELF 7.3.4

A. Open *tblSales* in Datasheet view.
B. Add file *tablecloth.jpg* to any record in the *ItemPhoto* field. Refer to Figures 7.25 and 7.26.
C. View the attachment.
D. Save the table.
E. Close the table, or continue on.

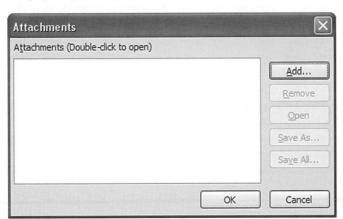

Figure 7.25 Adding data to an attachment field

How to View Data in an Attachment Field

1. In Datasheet view, double-click on the attachment field

   OR

   In Datasheet view, right-click on the attachment field, and select Manage Attachments from the shortcut menu.

   The Attachments window opens showing the attachment name (see Figure 7.26).

2. Double-click on the file name, or click once and click on the Open button (see Figure 7.26).

   The attachment opens.

3. Close the attachment when finished. Click the OK button to close the Attachments window.

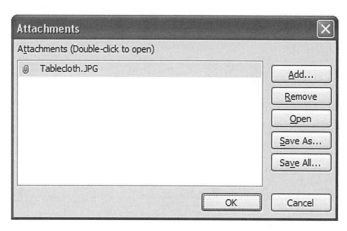

Figure 7.26 File added to an attachment field

Q: How many fields can be combined into a primary key?

A: All of the fields in a table can be part of the primary key if they meet the requirements.

Multiple-Field Primary Keys

When two or more fields are combined to create a primary key it's called a multiple-field primary key. Multiple-field primary keys can also be called compound, composite, or complex primary keys. If a table has a multiple-field primary key, then the unique combination of key fields defines a record because none of the key fields alone defines it.

The *G3* database doesn't have any tables with a multiple-field primary key, but it's easy to create a situation that calls for one. Suppose that the client finds that she has several identical items to sell. Going, Going, Gone has an auction type called a dutch auction where several items can be sold in the same auction. Several buyers can each buy an item in the auction. In this case, there will be a many-to-many join between *tblBuyers* and *tblSales*. One buyer can buy multiple items and one auction can have multiple buyers.

The best way to represent this situation in the database is to create a third table, a bridge table, which contains records that join *tblBuyers* and *tblSales*. The only data in the new table are the primary key fields in the other two tables. Figure 7.27 shows the hypothetical table, *tblSalesBuyers*.

tblSalesBuyers(SalesID, BuyerID)

Figure 7.27 Bridge table *tblSalesBuyers* with a multiple-field primary key

The primary key in *tblSalesBuyers* is composed of the only two fields in the table, *SalesID* and *BuyerID*. Neither of these fields alone is unique, and each can occur multiple times. Only the combination of one *SalesID* and one *BuyerID* together will be unique. A buyer can only buy a specific item one time. This table can be sorted by either field in the primary key to produce a list grouped by sales or by buyers.

How to Create a Multiple-Field Primary Key

1. Open the table in Design view.

2. If the fields aren't next to each other, move them together.

3. Select all fields to be included (see Figure 7.28).

4. Click on the Primary Key button on the ribbon (see Figure 7.28). A key symbol appears to the left of each selected field.

   If you create a multiple-field primary key on a table containing data, you may have problems unless you change the Indexed property to "Yes (No Duplicates)" as described on the next page.

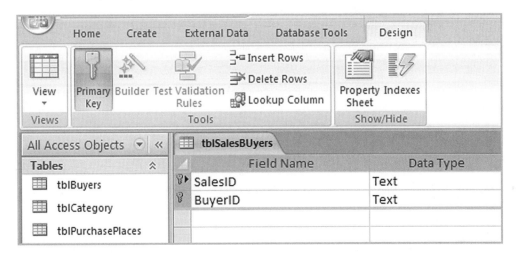

Figure 7.28 Creating a multiple-field primary key

Indexes

Setting the Indexed field property to Yes will speed up record searches and sorts by creating an index on the field. If you build a query criterion based on a range of values in a field, it will run faster if the field is indexed. If you sort a table on an indexed field, it will sort more quickly than without an index. It's also faster to retrieve data from indexed tables when searching within a Visual Basic procedure.

An index on a table works like an index in a book. The table index is stored in sorted order, so when you look for a value it's easy to find in the sorted list. You can then retrieve the entire record matching that value, the same way you would turn to the indicated page in a book index to find specific information.

How to Create an Index

1. Open the table in Design view.

2. Select the field to be an index.

3. Click on the Indexed property line and select either "Yes (Duplicates OK)" or "Yes (No Duplicates)."

TRY IT YOURSELF 7.3.5

A. Using the *G3_Ch7* database, create a new table called *tblSales Buyers*.

B. Add two fields—*SalesID* and *BuyerID*. They should both be lookup fields.

C. Make both fields the primary key for the table (see Figure 7.28).

D. Save the table, and close it.

TRY IT YOURSELF 7.3.6

A. Open the table *tblSales* in Design view.

B. Create an index on the field *ItemName*, and allow duplicates.

C. Save the table.

D. Create an index on *Category* and don't allow duplicates.

E. Save the table. Click OK to clear the error message (see Figure 7.29).

F. Allow duplicates and save again.

G. Close the table, or continue on.

You should set the Indexed property to "Yes (No Duplicates)" for a primary key made up of one field. This ensures that each record contains a different value for the field. If you have a multiple-field primary key, you should set the Indexed property to "Yes (Duplicates OK)" for both fields. The individual fields of a multiple-field primary key can have duplicate values, but the combination of the fields cannot. If the Indexed property is set to "Yes (No Duplicates)" for either field, an error message may displayed as shown in Figure 7.29. The error occurs if multiple records have the same value in the field. When the error message is displayed, click on the OK button to close the message. A second error message may be displayed. If so, click on the OK button to close this message also. Change the Indexed property to "Yes (Duplicates OK)" to prevent the error from happening again when the table is saved.

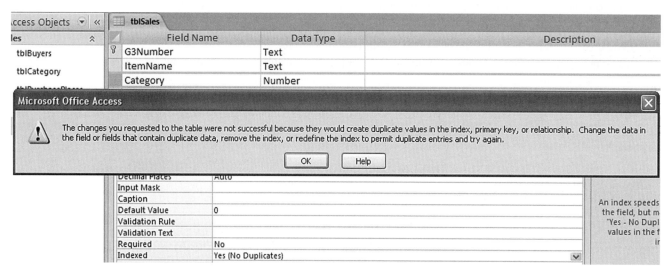

Figure 7.29 Error encountered when setting the Indexed property to "Yes (No Duplicates)"

When you have a table open in Design view, the view, Indexes command on the menu displays all the indexes on the table.

7.4 Maintaining Referential Integrity

The next step in database development is creating relationships, or joins, between the database tables. The key concept governing table relationships is that of referential integrity—the idea of preserving data accuracy by using proper relationships. Data accuracy is called data integrity, and can be broken down into four different types.

- User-defined Integrity—the data complies with specific business and user rules.

- Entity Integrity—no duplicate records exist in any table.

- Domain Integrity—the values in any given field are within an accepted range.

- Referential Integrity—all foreign keys have values that correspond to records in the referenced table (the table in which the value is the primary key).

Enforcing Data Integrity

The most important part of database design is establishing and preserving data integrity. Normalizing tables, setting field properties, creating relationships, and using lookup tables all contribute to data integrity. In some cases, writing macros or programs may be the only way to implement the necessary rules.

User-defined integrity means that data meets the requirements determined by the database users. For example, a student grade records system may require that when an incomplete grade is replaced with a letter grade, a corresponding record be added to the table containing the transaction date, the reason, and the name of the faculty member changing the grade. Other examples include financial ledger applications that need a debit to be recorded for every credit (and vice versa), inventory applications where counts are reduced when shipments are made, and payroll applications that update year-to-date figures after processing the current period. Many user-defined integrity rules must be implemented with macros and programs. User-defined integrity ensures that a database performs the job for which it was intended.

Entity integrity ensures that every record in a table is unique. Normalization is the best tool for establishing entity integrity, as normalization produces a primary key and eliminates transitive and partial dependencies. Even in normalized tables, however, it's possible for two records in a table to be the same except for the value in the primary key. For example, a salesperson may inadvertently add a customer who's already in the table. In this case, providing a list of existing customers can eliminate the problem. The easiest way to do this is by creating a Combo box on a form that contains an alphabetized list of customers (see Chapter 9 for details on Combo boxes). Entity integrity removes the possibility of data occurring in multiple records, thereby eliminating insertion, deletion, and update anomalies.

Domain integrity restricts the range of values that are valid for any field. The domain of a field is the set of all possible values that can occur in the field. For example, the domain of a field named *State* is the group of fifty, two-letter abbreviations used by the post office. Domains can be large—all positive numbers—or very small—true or false. The domain of a field can be defined by specifying a data type; by setting field properties such as format, input mask, and validation rule; by creating a lookup field; or by writing a macro or program. Domain integrity makes certain that query criteria can be written so the resulting dynaset includes all possible matches. It also ensures that searches perform properly, expressions evaluate correctly, and operations execute appropriately.

Joining Tables

Before discussing referential integrity, we need a better understanding of table joins. There are three types of table joins: one-to-one, one-to-many, and many-to-many. Many-to-many joins should be eliminated if possible, and replaced with a bridge table having a one-to-many join with each original table. One-to-one joins are rare; however, there are some instances where splitting a table into two tables can be helpful. You might consider splitting a table with a large number of fields that won't easily display on the screen, or a table containing some data that is sensitive or private in nature. The two tables would have the same primary key and a one-to-one join.

Keep in mind that most joins create a one-to-many relationship between two tables. The "one" table contains only a single occurrence of a specific value in the common field, and that field must be the primary key in this table. The "many" table can contain multiple occurrences of a specific value in the common field. This field is not the primary key in the "many" table, but it's a foreign key and should be a required field.

Table joins are the key to a relational database. They can be made at either the database level or the query level.

1. You can create a permanent join between the tables at the database level. This means that the join is activated any time you use the two tables. Use the Relationship button on the ribbon to set this join. Also, when a lookup field is created, a permanent join is established between the two tables involved.

2. You can create a temporary join in the Query Design window if the tables are not already joined. This is not a permanent relationship, however; it's only valid during the current query. If you select tables for a query that have a primary key/foreign key relationship, the tables will appear already joined in the Query Design window.

How to Join Tables in the Query Design View

1. Create a new query.

2. Add the appropriate data sources (tables or queries).

3. Select the field in the "one" table, drag it to the same field in the "many" table, and drop it there. A join line will appear between the two tables on those fields, symbolically showing the connection between the two tables.

Removing Joins

It's easy to remove a join if it is incorrect or if two tables are joined that shouldn't be.

How to Delete a Join

1. In the Relationships window, or in a query, click on the join line to be deleted.

2. Press the DELETE key.

3. The join line should be eliminated from the screen. If you delete the join from inside the Query Design window, the join will be deleted for the current query. If the join is removed in the Relationships window, it is permanently deleted.

Types of Joins

Different types of joins can be established between tables. These different types of joins produce different results in queries. The two join types are described in Table 7.1.

Table 7.1 Types of Joins

Type of Join	Description
Inner Joins or Equi-Joins	Default join type in Access. Selects only the records from both tables that have at least one corresponding record in the other table.
Outer Joins	Selects all records in one table, and only the corresponding records in the other table. Can be further described as left or right outer joins.

Using the *G3* database, consider *tblCategory* and *tblSales*, as shown in Figure 7.30. These two tables are joined on the field *CategoryID*.

Figure 7.30 *tblCategory* and *tblSales*

An inner join selects only the records from both tables that have at least one corresponding record in the other table. Notice in Figure 7.30 that *tblCategory* has a "Clothing" category, but *tblSales* has no items in this category. Also, the last record in *tblSales* has not been assigned a category. Neither of these records are included in an inner join. The records included in an inner join are shown in Figure 7.31 below.

CategoryID	CategoryName	ItemName
1	Books	Kitchen Digest Vintage Homemaking Book
2	Linens	Vintage Tablecloth Fruit Cherries 1940s
2	Linens	6 Vintage Red Yellow Striped Linen Napkins
3	Kitchen Tools	Vintage 1963 Popeil Veg O Matic

Figure 7.31 Inner join between *tblCategory* and *tblSales*

An outer join selects all records in one table, and only the corresponding records in the other table. There are two types of outer joins: a left outer join and a right outer join. The outer join dynasets for the above example are shown in Figures 7.32 and 7.33.

In the left outer join shown in Figure 7.32, all the records in the "one" table are included (in this case *tblCategory*) and only corresponding records from the "many" table. The item "Vintage Black and Gold Tone Powder Compact" is missing because it is in the "many" table and has no corresponding record in *tblCategory*.

CategoryID	CategoryName	ItemName
1	Books	Kitchen Digest Vintage Homemaking Book
2	Linens	Vintage Tablecloth Fruit Cherries 1940s
2	Linens	6 Vintage Red Yellow Striped Linen Napkins
3	Kitchen Tools	Vintage 1963 Popeil Veg O Matic
4	Clothing	

Figure 7.32 Left outer join between *tblCategory* and *tblSales*

CategoryID	CategoryName	ItemName
1	Books	Kitchen Digest Vintage Homemaking Book
2	Linens	Vintage Tablecloth Fruit Cherries 1940s
2	Linens	6 Vintage Red Yellow Striped Linen Napkins
3	Kitchen Tools	Vintage 1963 Popeil Veg O Matic
		Vintage Black and Gold Tone Powder Compact

Figure 7.33 Right outer join between *tblCategory* and *tblSales*

In the right outer join shown in Figure 7.33, all the records in the "many" table are included (in this case *tblSales*) and only corresponding records from the other table. The Clothing category record is missing because it has no corresponding record in *tblSales*.

Changing Join Types in a Query

When tables are joined the default type is the inner join. Generally, this type of join is sufficient for most types of queries. However, the join type can be changed to produce other query results.

Q: When I double-click on the join line, the Query Properties box opens, not the Join Properties box. What am I doing wrong?

A: You're double-clicking on the background of the query window. Be sure to point at the join line before clicking.

How to Change the Join Properties in the Relationships Window

1. Double-click on the join line that connects the tables. The Edit Relationships dialog box appears.

2. Click on the Join Type button (see Figure 7.34). The Join Properties dialog box will appear, showing several options.

3. Click the bullet next to the join property (see Figure 7.34).

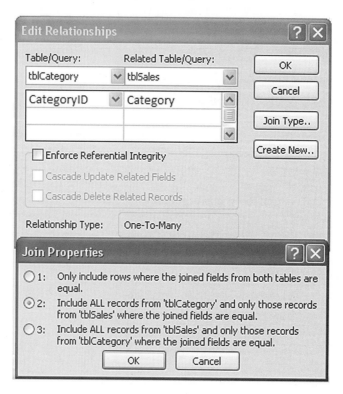

Figure 7.34 Edit Relationships and Join Properties dialog boxes

- The first choice is the default and will produce the inner join. Only the records from both tables that have at least one corresponding record in the other table will be included.

- The second choice will produce the left outer join. All records from the "one" table will be included and only matching records from the "many" table will be included.

- The third choice will produce the right outer join. All records from the "many" table will be included and only matching records from the "one" table will be included.

4. Click the OK button.

Notice that the join type is graphically displayed as a line with an arrow pointing to either the "one" or "many" table, depending on the type of outer join selected (see Figure 7.35). The default or inner join is displayed as a line with no arrow heads.

Enforcing Referential Integrity

Referential integrity is a set of rules that Access uses to maintain consistent data in joined tables. Referential integrity exists when every foreign key is related to the primary key in another table. When tables are properly joined and maintained, the resulting related data used in queries, forms, and reports has greater accuracy. If we assume that tables have a one-to-many relationship, the following rules will be used to enforce referential integrity:

- When a record is added to the "many" table, the value for the foreign key must correspond to a valid value in the primary key in the "one" table.

- If the foreign key is updated in the "many" table, the new value must correspond to a valid value in the primary key in the "one" table.

- A record in the "one" table cannot be deleted if related records exist in the "many" table.

- The primary key in the "one" table cannot be changed if related records exist in the "many" table.

Referential integrity can be enforced in Access by five different means:

- Setting field properties
- Selecting specific join settings
- Creating special queries
- Normalizing tables
- Creating lookup fields

To ensure referential integrity, you can set rules on field properties when a table is created, or modify them later. You should set the field properties of primary keys so that they are unique and required fields (see Chapter 2). You should also change the properties of the foreign key in the "many" table of the join so that it is a required field. If this rule were enforced in the example shown in Figure 7.33, the record for the vintage compact would not be in the *tblSales* table because it has no corresponding value in *tblCategory*.

You can also enforce referential integrity by activating join maintenance settings to keep the join maintained properly. These settings are activated by turning on the referential integrity rules in the Relationships dialog box. (See How to Enable Referential Integrity Maintenance Rules below.) These rules keep you from making changes to your tables that would invalidate the relationships you have established. When these rules are activated, Access checks each time a key field is changed, and displays a message if this change violates the referential integrity of the table. Note that referential integrity cannot be enforced on a join in a query.

When referential integrity rules are set, and the data in a primary key is changed, then changes are made automatically to tables containing the foreign key. You can choose automatic table maintenance by selecting the Cascade Update and/or Cascade Delete functions in the Relationships dialog box. Both refer to actions that are taken when a primary key field is changed or deleted. The resulting actions, update and delete, are performed on the "many" table. A Cascade Update changes the values in the foreign key in the "many" table to reflect the change made to the primary key data. A Cascade Delete deletes the records in the "many" table that share the same value in the foreign key as the deleted primary key data.

Use caution with Cascading Updates and Cascading Deletes. Cascading Updates should be avoided because primary key values should not be changed without strong justification, such as when an erroneous value is found. Cascading Deletes can cause the unintentional deletion of large amounts of data. For example, consider a database that contains a table for items sold and another table for items in inventory. If Cascade Delete is set and an item is deleted from the inventory table because it's discontinued, all the related records in the items sold table will be deleted also. There would be no remaining sales data about that item, and sales reports would be inaccurate. It's a good idea to avoid both Cascading Updates and Cascading Deletes while learning to use Access. Enforcing referential integrity without choosing either Cascading Updates or Cascading Deletes will

Q: What if I don't see the Edit Relationships dialog box as shown in Figure 7.35?

A: You are trying to enforce referential integrity from inside a query, and it can't be done. Close the query and join the tables in the Relationships window on the database level.

cause a warning message to appear when actions are taken that violate referential integrity. No data will be changed automatically.

Lookup fields can also help enforce referential integrity. When using a foreign key in a table, make it a lookup field that gets its values from the table containing the primary key. For example, the field *Category* in *tblSales* is a lookup field whose values come from *tblCategory*. When a record is added to the table *tblSales*, the values for the field *Category* are restricted to valid values for the primary key, *CategoryID*, in the table *tblCategory*.

Setting referential integrity rules ensures that data is maintained correctly on joined tables. When referential integrity has not been imposed on a database, you can use queries to help clean up your data before setting referential integrity rules. You can use the Find Unmatched Query Wizard and the Find Duplicates Query Wizard to locate records that violate referential integrity. After using these wizards, you can create a Delete or Update query to alter all related records in both tables. You should then set referential integrity on all joins. Erroneous data problems are difficult to detect and have to be corrected manually.

TRY IT YOURSELF 7.4.2

A. Open the Relationships window in the *G3_Ch7* database.

B. Enforce referential integrity on the join between *tblCategory* and *tblSales*, and select both Cascade Update and Cascade Delete (see Figures 7.35 and 7.36).

C. Open *tblCategory* and delete the record for Books (*CategoryID* =2).

D. Open *tblSales* and verify that all the books have been deleted from the table.

E. Close the table, or continue on.

How to Enable Referential Integrity Maintenance Rules

1. With a database open, click the Relationships button on the ribbon. The Relationships window opens.

2. Double-click on the join line of the relationship to be edited.

3. The Edit Relationships dialog box will appear so that you can further define the related fields and tables (see Figure 7.35).

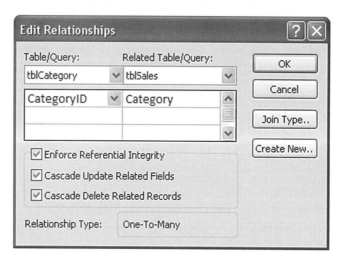

Figure 7.35 Edit Relationships dialog box with referential integrity enforced

4. Check the Enforce Referential Integrity check box.

5. Check the Cascade Delete Related Records check box. (Optional)

6. Check the Cascade Update Related Fields check box. (Optional)

7. Click the OK button. When referential integrity is set, the symbols 1 and ∞ are displayed on the join line between the tables (see Figure 7.36).

Once you have selected the Cascade Delete Join setting, you can set up a Delete query as in the previous section. A Delete query on tables with this join setting will delete all related records in multiple tables. Be cautious!

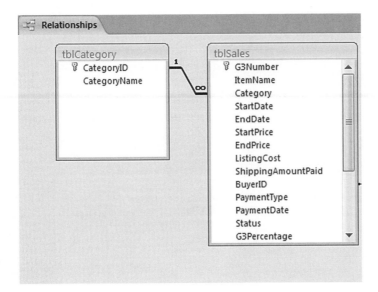

Figure 7.36 Relationships window showing a one-to-many join with referential integrity enforced

Using Wizards to Maintain Referential Integrity

Besides setting join characteristics, you can use the Query wizard to assist in maintaining referential integrity. You may want to run these wizard checks before performing a Delete query to remove duplicates or unmatched records in joined tables. Table 7.2 describes the two types of queries.

Table 7.2 Query Wizard selections

Type of Query Wizard	Description
Find Duplicate Records Wizard	Shows any records in a table that have duplicate values in a field or part of a field.
Find Unmatched Records Wizard	Shows records in one table that have no matching record in a related table.

Find Duplicate Records Wizard

The Find Duplicate Records query helps you locate records in a table with duplicate data values in a specified field. This type of query would be useful if the primary key is being created or changed in a table. This query can be used to see if the new key field has a unique value in each record.

How to Use the Find Duplicate Records Wizard

1. Click on the Query Wizard button in the Other group of the ribbon Create tab (see Figure 7.37).

2. Select the Find Duplicates Query Wizard from the list in the New Query dialog box (see Figure 7.37).

3. Click the OK button. The Table Selection dialog box appears (see Figure 7.38).

4. Choose the table (or query) containing the records to be checked. You can specify what's displayed in the View list—tables, queries, or both—by selecting one of the View buttons (see Figure 7.38).

TRY IT YOURSELF 7.4.3

A. Use the Wizard to find any duplicate values in *tblCloths* in the field *ItemName*. Refer to Figures 7.37–7.41 to check your screen during the process.

B. View the resulting records. There should be five of them.

C. Close the query and continue on.

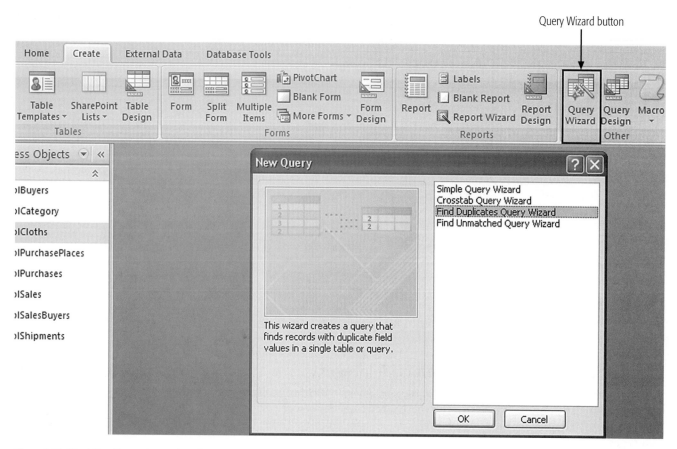

Figure 7.37 Find Duplicate Records selection in the New Query dialog box

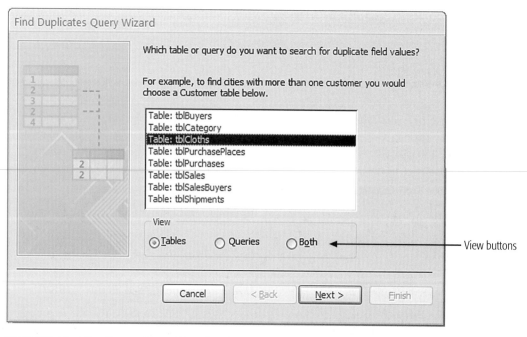

Figure 7.38 Find Duplicates Query Wizard–Table Selection dialog box

5. Click the Next button. The next screen appears (see Figure 7.39).

Directional arrows to move fields

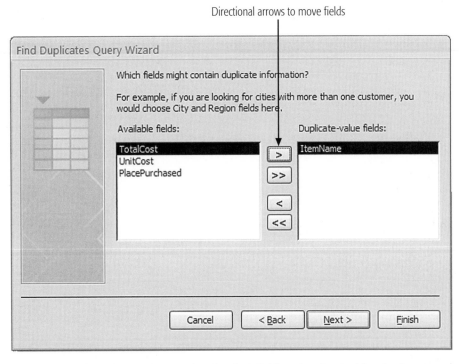

Figure 7.39 Find Duplicates Query Wizard–select fields to be checked for duplicates

6. Select the fields(s) that you want searched for duplicate records.
7. Move the field(s) to the Duplicate-value fields window with the right directional arrow key.
8. Click the Next button. The next screen appears (see Figure 7.40).

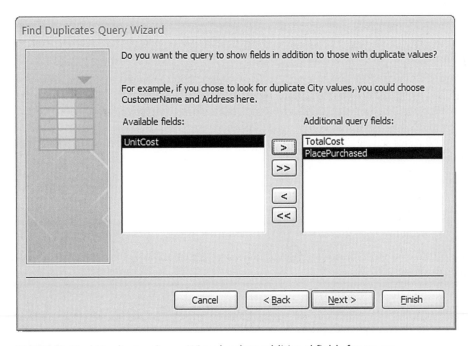

Figure 7.40 Find Duplicates Query Wizard–select additional fields for query

9. Select any additional fields to be included in this query.

10. Click the Next button. The final screen appears (see Figure 7.41).

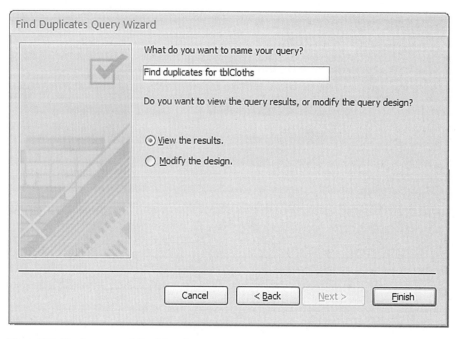

Figure 7.41 Final screen of Find Duplicates Query Wizard

11. Add the title for the query, and choose the action to be taken next—view the results or modify the design.

12. Click the Finish button to complete the process.

Find Unmatched Records Wizard

The find Unmatched Records Query wizard will create a query to locate records in a "many" table that have no associated records in the related "one" table. This query will display records based on the linking field. It's important to remove these records or to add the data that's missing in the common field, otherwise these orphaned records won't show up in any queries where an inner join is used (the default). You will have to make the necessary changes manually.

TRY IT YOURSELF 7.4.4

A. Use the Wizard to find any records in *tblCloths* that are unmatched in *tblPurchasePlaces*. Refer to Figures 7.42–7.46 to check your screen during the process.

B. View the resulting records. There should be three of them.

C. Close the query and continue on.

How to Use the Find Unmatched Records Wizard

1. Click on the Query Wizard button in the Other group of the ribbon Create tab.

2. Select the Find Unmatched Query Wizard on the New Query dialog box (see Figure 7.42).

3. Click the OK button.

4. Select the table containing the records to be checked (usually the "many" table). Figure 7.43 shows an example.

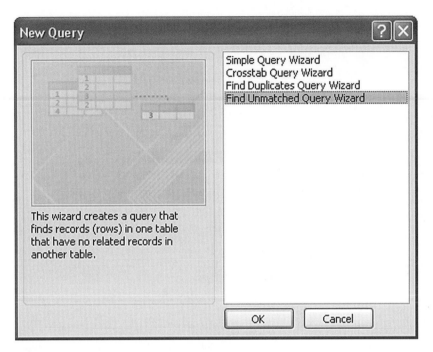

Figure 7.42 Find Unmatched Query Wizard in the New Query dialog box

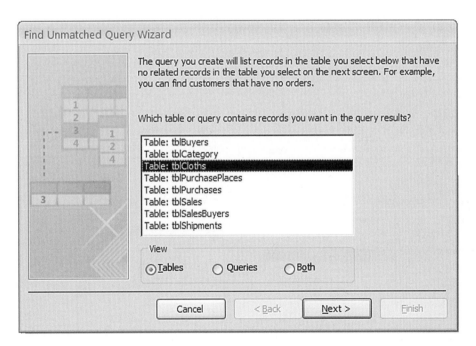

Figure 7.43 Find Unmatched Query Wizard–Table Selection dialog box for first table

5. Click the Next button to move to the next screen.

6. Select the data source containing the related records (usually the "one" table) so that the previous table can be checked against it (see Figure 7.44).

7. Click the Next button to move to the next screen.

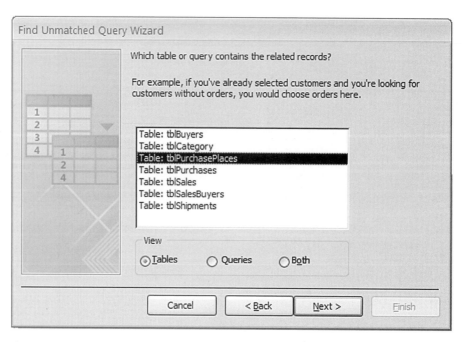

Figure 7.44 Find Unmatched Query Wizard–Table Selection dialog box for second table

8. Select the related fields in the joined tables, and click on the button showing a double-headed arrow (see Figure 7.45). If the tables were joined correctly, Access will select those fields on the basis of that established relationship.

9. Click the Next button to move to the next screen.

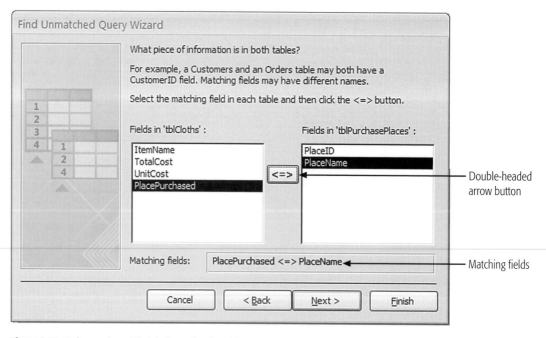

Figure 7.45 Select related fields from both tables

10. Select the fields to be displayed in the query results by clicking on the arrow buttons to move the desired fields between windows (see Figure 7.46).

11. Click the Next button to move to the next screen.

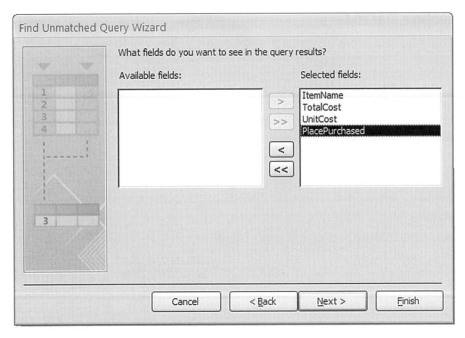

Figure 7.46 Select additional fields for the query

12. Type in a title for the query and choose the view to open the query.

13. Click the Finish button to complete the process.

Remember that the query doesn't correct the problem, it just shows it to you. You will probably want to delete these records, or update the data in the blank fields. Either way, you'll need to build a criterion to test whether the field is blank or not. A blank field is represented in criteria by the words "Is Null." For example, to select only records with nothing in the *PlacePurchased* field, you would type "Is Null" in the Criteria row of the *PlacePurchased* field.

How to Begin Enforcing Referential Integrity on an Existing Database

If you have a database in which you have not been enforcing referential integrity, it's a good idea to begin doing so. Follow the steps below to start enforcing referential integrity.

1. List all joins between tables.

2. Run Find Unmatched and Find Duplicates queries on all joined tables.

3. Run Delete queries on those tables to remove the duplicates and unmatched records found in step 2.

4. Be sure every table has a primary key that doesn't allow duplicates, and that in every table the common field is required. Change field properties as required.

5. Change the join settings to enforce referential integrity on all joins.

7.5 Maintaining Databases

Maintaining a database is more than maintaining data and table joins. Queries, forms, and reports need to be edited and added from time to time, and table structures may need to be changed. There are also some procedures that can be carried out on the entire database to increase performance, provide additional information, and enhance ease of use.

Q: What happens to my Access 2002–2003 database when it's converted to:. Access 2007?

A: The file extension is changed in Access 2007, so the original database name is unchanged.

TRY IT YOURSELF 7.5.1

A. Open the database *Practice_Ch7.mdb*.

B. Convert the database to Access 2007 keeping the same name.

C. Close the database.

Converting Databases

Whenever a new version of Access is released by Microsoft, old databases need to be converted to the latest version so they can utilize the new commands and features of the software. Databases created by Access 2003, the previous version of Access, can either be converted to Access 2007 or they can be used in Access 2007 without converting. When you convert a database to Access 2007, the old version is still kept. Older databases can use the new features of Access 2007 without conversion, but those features won't be available if the same database is opened in the older version again.

How to Convert an Access 2002–2003 Database to Access 2007

1. Open the database to be converted. The words "(Access 2002–2003 file format)" are shown in the title bar of the Database window.

2. Click on the Office button and select Convert (see Figure 7.47). The Save As dialog box appears.

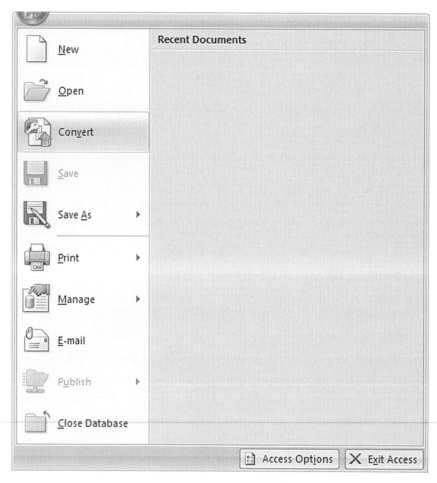

Figure 7.47 Convert command on the Office menu

3. Select the folder in which to store the new database, and type a new name for the database into the File name box (see Figure 7.48). You can use the same filename if you want, as the file extension will change from .mdb to .accdb. Click the Save button.

4. The database is converted and saved. The new database in Access 2007 format is open.

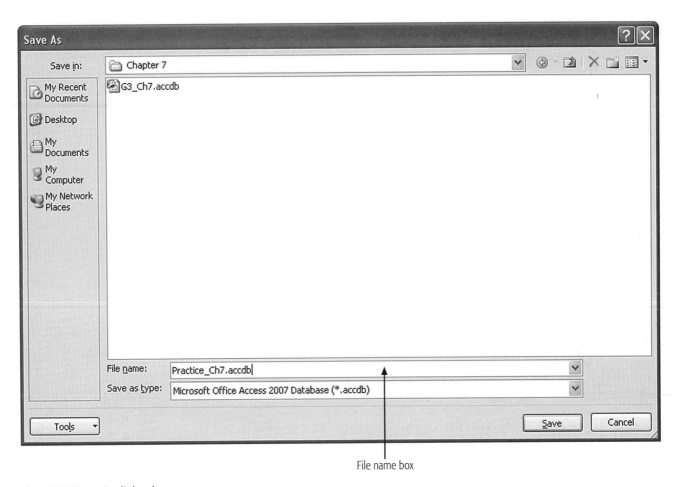

File name box

Figure 7.48 Save As dialog box

You can also convert an Access 2007 database back to an earlier version. You might convert a database backwards if a user doesn't have the latest version of the software.

How to Convert an Access 2007 Database to an Earlier Version

1. Open the database you want to convert.

2. Click on the Office button and select Save As. A secondary menu opens as shown in Figure 7.49.

3. Select the format—either Access 2002–2003 or Access 2000 (see Figure 7.49).

4. Select the folder and type in the name of the new database, then Click the Save button.

Compacting, Repairing and Backing Up Databases

Compacting and repairing a database are done with a single command. If you delete data or objects in an Access database, the database file can become fragmented and use excess disk space. Compacting the database rearranges how the file is stored on your disk so that it takes up less space. If you need to copy a database to a CD or send it as an email attachment, you should first compact the database to make it as small as possible. Access usually repairs any damage to a database when it is opened. However, a database may sometimes behave erratically and have to be repaired manually.

Figure 7.49 Save As command on the Office menu

TRY IT YOURSELF 7.5.2

A. Open the Explorer window, make sure the view shows all details, and check the size of the *G3_Ch7* database.

B. Open the *G3_Ch7* database in Access and compact it.

C. Check the file size again as in step A, and note that the size has changed.

D. Continue on.

How to Compact and Repair a Database

1. Open the database.

2. Click on the Office button, select Manage, and click on Compact and Repair Database (see Figure 7.50). No changes to the database can be seen within Access—the file size must be checked to see the difference.

Access can compact all databases automatically when they are closed. It's probably a good idea to select this option, especially when working with databases that will be copied to CDs or uploaded online. The Compact on Close command is found in the Current Database group of the Access Options window.

A database should be backed up on a regular basis. How frequently a backup is done depends on how often the data is updated and how critical the system is. Access will create a backup for you—click on the Office button and select Manage. The Backup command appears on the sub-menu as shown in Figure 7.50. Access will create a default database name by adding today's date to the end of the database name, and will save the file in the current folder. If these choices are not what you want, you can type your own database name and select a different folder.

Q: Why split a database?

A: It's the most efficient way to structure a database that is shared by several people over a network.

Splitting Databases

Many developers like to split a database. When a database is split, the two resulting databases are called the front-end and back-end databases. The front-end database contains all the database objects, while the back-end database contains all the data. The data tables are linked into the front-end database, and can easily be refreshed whenever necessary. Chapter 3, Section 3 contains more information about working with linked tables.

Figure 7.50 Compact and Repair Database command

Databases stored on networks are split so that the data resides on the file server, and each user has a copy of the object database stored on their local computer. Databases are also split because it's easier to update users to new versions of database objects, such as new forms, reports, and queries when only the object database needs to be replaced.

How to Split a Database into Two Databases

1. Open the database.

2. Select the Database Tools tab on the ribbon, and click on the Access Database button (see Figure 7.51). The Database Splitter wizard begins (see Figure 7.51).

3. Click on the Split Database button as shown in Figure 7.51. The Create Back-end Database window opens (see Figure 7.52).

4. Change the suggested name for the back-end database if necessary. Access will use the old database name and add the characters _be to the end of the name (see Figure 7.52).

5. Click on the Split button as shown in Figure 7.52. The split will take a few seconds, then a message box will appear telling you the database was successfully split.

6. Click the OK button in the message box. The Database window of the front-end database appears. This database has the same name as your original database, and the tables should be linked to the back-end database.

7. Open a file management tool, such as Explorer, to verify that there are now two databases.

TRY IT YOURSELF 7.5.3

A. Open the *G3_Ch7* database.

B. Split into two databases. Use Figures 7.51 and 7.52 as guidelines.

C. Verify that the objects work with the tables linked to the back-end database.

D. Open the *G3_Ch7_be* database and note that it contains only the tables.

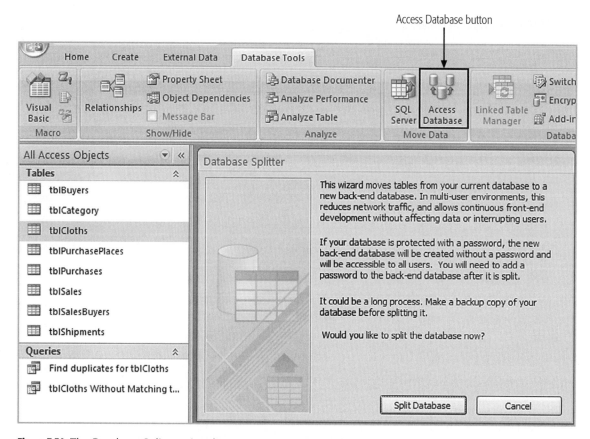

Figure 7.51 The Database Splitter wizard screen

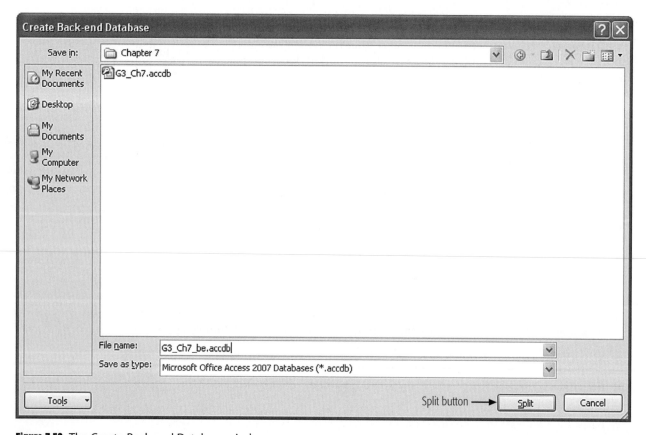

Figure 7.52 The Create Back-end Database window

Printing Documentation

It's good to keep a set of documents describing the database for your own reference, and to help others who may need to make changes to the database. You can print documentation about any database object, and can control the level of detail about much of the information printed. Table documentation can include any or all of the following: table properties, relationships, field names, field data types, field sizes, field properties, and indexes. The details available for other object types are just as detailed. To see what details are available, click on the Options button in every tab of the Documenter window (see Figure 7.53).

How to Print Documentation

1. Open the database.

2. Select the Database Tools tab on the ribbon, and click on the Database Documenter button (see Figure 7.53). The Documenter window opens (see Figure 7.53).

TRY IT YOURSELF 7.5.4

A. Using the *G3_Ch7* database.

B. Print documentation for the *tblSales* table. Select the options as shown in Figure 7.54.

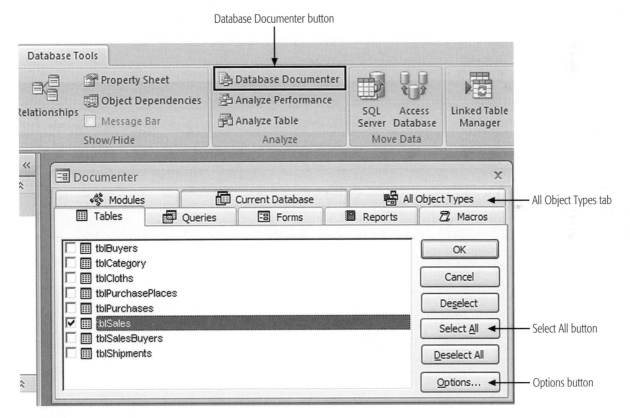

Figure 7.53 The Documenter window

3. Select the objects you want to print documentation for by clicking the check box in front of the object. You can also select all objects using the Select All button. Click on the different tabs to see different groups of objects. Click the All Object Types tab to view a list of all database objects at once. Refer to Figure 7.53 for guidance.

4. The Print Table Definition window appears when you click the Options button (see Figure 7.54). Choose any Options for the documentation and click the OK button to close the Options window.

5. Click the OK button in the Documenter dialog box. The documentation appears in the report preview window.

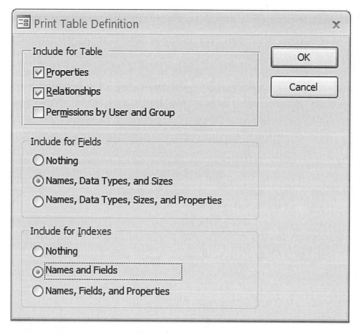

Figure 7.54 The Print Table Definition window

Professional Tip: Documentation

Most database developers agree that good database documentation should include, at least, the following items:

1. Data dictionary—a list of table names, field names, field data types, appropriate field properties (length of text fields, validation rules, etc.), indexes, and primary keys. A short verbal description of each table and field can also be included.

2. Object dependency charts—charts showing the tables and queries used as data sources for queries, forms, and reports.

3. Code printouts—printed Visual Basic programs and macros.

4. Table relationship diagrams or database schema—a diagram showing all tables, primary keys, foreign keys, and join types.

5. User guide—instructions for using the database.

Access doesn't produce this level of documentation, though the Documenter can be used to develop the data dictionary. An online search can help you locate several software tools you can use to produce additional documentation. These tools cannot produce user guides, however, which must be written by the developer.

Analyzing Performance

The Performance Analyzer can optimize the database and potentially reduce the time it takes to perform database tasks. It categorizes the analysis results into three groups: Recommendation, Suggestion, and Idea. Recommendation and Suggestion optimizations can be made for you, but you will have to implement the Idea optimizations yourself. Access will not do any of the optimizations without your consent, and there is no guarantee that you will see a measurable difference in performance.

Some examples of the types of optimizations advised by Performance Analyzer might include:

- Join tables
- Create indexes
- Use fewer controls on forms
- Convert macros to Visual Basic
- Convert the whole database to an ACCDE file

An ACCDE file is an alternative database file type that is execute only. Converting your database to an ACCDE file will reduce the size of the database by removing all Visual Basic source code and the ability to edit any database object. Essentially an ACCDE file is a read-only database (except for data). To create an ACCDE file, select the Database Tools tab on the ribbon, and click on the Make ACCDE button in the Database Tools group.

How to Analyze Database Performance

1. Open the database.
2. Select the Database Tools tab on the ribbon, and click on the Analyze Performance button in the Analyze group (see Figure 7.55). The Performance Analyzer window appears (see Figure 7.55).

TRY IT YOURSELF 7.5.5

A. Using the *G3_Ch7* database, run the Performance Analyzer. Refer to Figures 7.55 and 7.56.
B. Observe the results and close the analysis window.
C. Continue on.

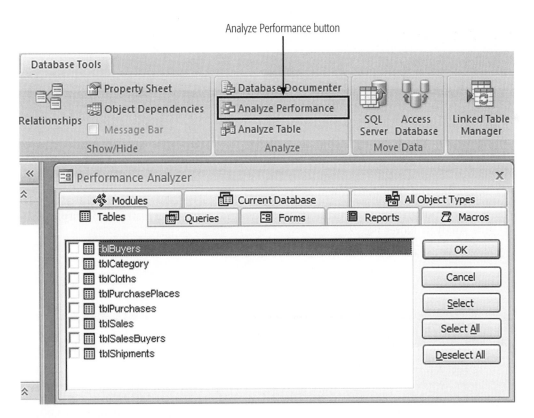

Figure 7.55 The Performance Analyzer window

3. Select the objects you want to analyze by clicking the check box in front of the object. You can also select all objects using the Select All button. Click on the different tabs to see different groups of objects. Click the All Object Types tab to view a list of all database objects at once. Refer to Figure 7.55 for guidance.

4. Click the OK button to start the analysis. After a few moments a list of ideas appears in the Performance Analyzer Results window, or a message box appears telling you it has no suggestions to improve the object(s). Refer to Figure 7.56 to see a sample list displayed in the Performance Analyzer window.

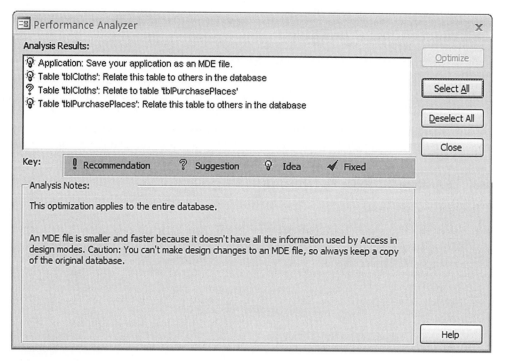

Figure 7.56 The Performance Analyzer Results window

5. To implement a Recommendation or Suggestion optimization, select it and click on the Optimize button. You can also implement all suggestions by clicking Select All before clicking the Optimize button. The Performance Analyzer will perform the optimizations and then mark them as fixed.

6. To carry out an idea optimization, click on it and follow the instructions displayed in the Analysis Notes box.

7. Click on the Close button when you're finished.

Professional Tip: Database Performance

The following tips help speed up the performance of a database:

- Choose appropriate data types for fields. Choosing the smallest data type or field size saves space in your database. Be sure foreign keys have the same data type and size as primary keys to improve join operations.

- Create indexes on all fields used in sorting, setting criteria in queries, and table joins. Queries run faster when fields on both sides of joins are indexed (often the primary and foreign keys).

- Compact the database. Compacting restructures the records in a table so they are stored all together in primary key order, which can speed up queries.

- Use only the fields needed in the dynaset when building a query. If other fields are needed to set criteria, uncheck the Show check box for those fields.

- If expressions are used in a form or report, place them in a control on the form or report. Access runs slower if the expression comes from an underlying query.

- Use Make Table queries to create tables from a query dynaset. Use the new tables rather than queries as the data source in forms, reports, or other queries.

- Close any forms that aren't in use.

- Use graphic objects in moderation. They take up a lot of space and can be slow to load in.

Object Dependencies

The Object Dependencies window shows the relationships between all tables, queries, forms, and reports. The data source (table or query) can be displayed for any of these objects, or the objects that use a specific data source can be shown. This information helps users avoid data errors, and is invaluable when the database is maintained or updated. Name Autocorrect tracking must be enabled (Tools, Option command) for object dependencies to be viewed.

How to View Object Dependencies

1. Open the database.

2. Select the Database Tools tab on the ribbon, and click on the Object Dependencies button (see Figure 7.57). A window appears warning that this could take a few minutes. Click the OK button.

3. Click the OK button to continue. The Object Dependencies window opens (see Figure 7.57).

4. Click on the plus sign to expand the view of the dependencies for an object.

TRY IT YOURSELF 7.5.6

Using the *G3_Ch7* database:
A. Display the object dependencies for all tables.
B. Expand the view of one or two objects. Your screen should resemble Figure 7.57.
C. Close the Object Dependencies window.

Grouping Objects

Access has the ability to keep a group of object shortcuts together in the Navigation Pane, so working with objects is fast and easy. A shortcut to any type of database object can be included in a group. Adding, renaming, and deleting these shortcuts does not affect the actual objects themselves. You can see the objects in a group by selecting Custom from the Navigate to Category group in the Navigation Pane (see Figure 7.58).

You may want to create object groups to keep together all objects used in a particular form or report. This group would contain the form or report, subforms or subreports, and the tables and queries that provide source data to the form or report. Other groups can be created around functions of the database. If the information in the database can be categorized, the involved objects can be grouped. For example, the college database contains data about faculty, classes, degrees, and departments. All of the objects involved in each function can be grouped, which makes it easier to work on each part of the database.

How to Create a Custom Group

1. Right-click on the Navigation Pane title bar and select Navigation Options from the shortcut menu (see Figure 7.59).

2. In the Navigation Options window, select the Custom grouping option from the left column (see Figure 7.60).

TRY IT YOURSELF 7.5.7

A. Using the *G3_Ch7* database, create a custom group named Buying. Refer to Figures 7.59 and 7.60.
B. Continue on.

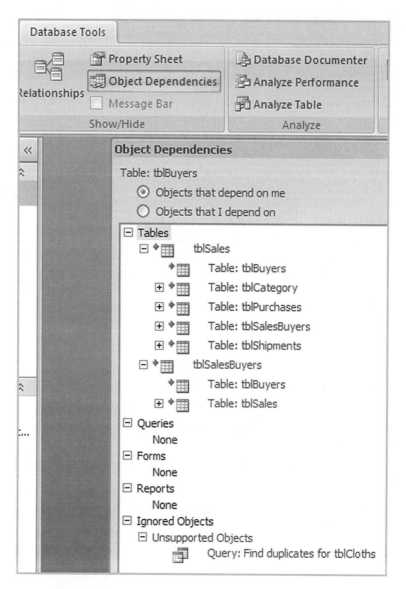

Figure 7.57 Object Dependencies window

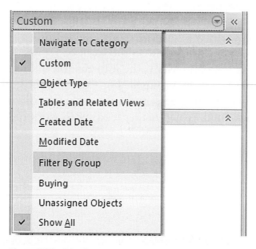

Figure 7.58 Displaying a custom group

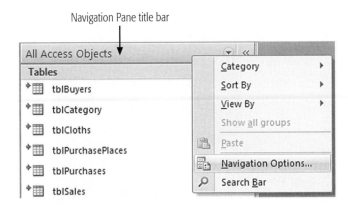

Navigation Pane title bar

Figure 7.59 Displaying Navigation Options

3. Click on the Add Group button, and type the new group name (see Figure 7.60).
4. Click the OK button.

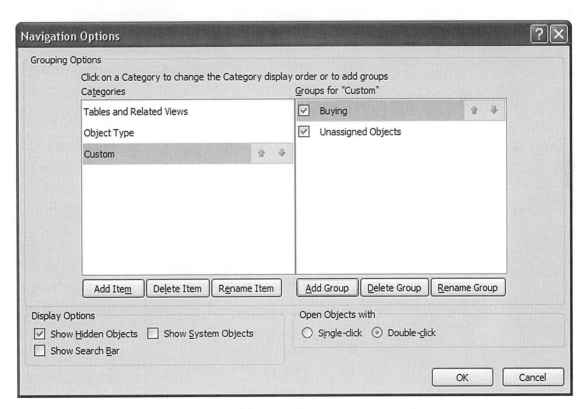

Figure 7.60 Creating a new group in the Navigation Options window

How to Add an Object to a Group

1. Be sure that Custom grouping is selected in the Navigation Pane.
2. Right-click on the object name and select Add to group... from the shortcut menu. Choose the group name from the submenu. Refer to Figure 7.61.

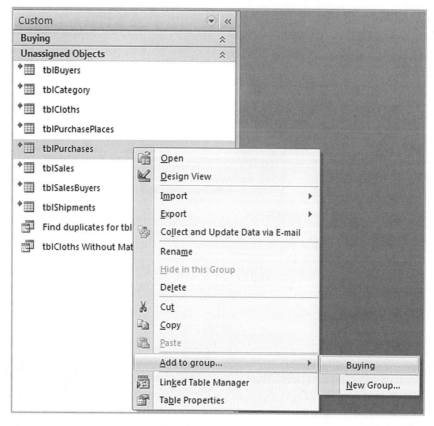

Figure 7.61 Adding an object to a group

TRY IT YOURSELF 7.5.8

A. Using the *G3_Ch7* database, add the following tables to the custom group named Buying: *tblCloths*, *tblPurchases*, and *tblPurchasePlaces*. Refer to Figures 7.61 and 7.62.

B. Close the *G3_Ch7* database.

3. The name of the object should appear under the group name as seen in Figure 7.62.

4. To remove an object from a group, select the object name, right-click, and choose Remove from the shortcut menu (see Figure 7.62).

Figure 7.62 Removing an object from a group

Editing a Lookup Field Query

1. Open the table in Design view and select the lookup field.

2. Click on the Lookup tab in the field properties area and click on the Row Source property row.

3. Click on the Build button (…) on the right end of the Row Source property row. The query grid opens.

4. Edit the query grid, adding an ascending sort order to the non-key field, or make another edit.

5. Close and save the query.

Creating a Multiple-Field Primary Key

1. Open the table in Design view.

2. If the fields aren't next to each other, move them together.

3. Select all fields to be included.

4. Click on the Primary Key button on the ribbon. A key symbol appears to the left of each selected field.

Creating an Index

1. Open the table in Design view.

2. Select the field to be an index.

3. Click on the Indexed property line and select either "Yes (Duplicates OK)" or "Yes (No duplicates)."

Joining Tables in the Query Design View

1. Create a new query.

2. Add the appropriate data sources (tables or queries).

3. Select the field in the "one" table, drag it to the same field in the "many" table, and drop it there. A join line will appear between the two tables on those fields, symbolically showing the connection between the two tables.

Deleting a Join

1. In the Relationships window, or in a query, click on the join line to be deleted.

2. Press the DELETE key.

3. The join line should be eliminated from the screen. If you delete the join from inside the Query Design window, the join will be deleted for the current query. If this relationship was created at the database level, it is permanent until deleted at the database level.

Changing the Join Properties in Query Design View

1. Double-click on the join line that connects the tables. The Edit Relationships dialog box appears.

2. Click on the Join Type button. A Join Properties dialog box will appear showing several options.

3. Click the bullet next to the Join property.

4. Click the OK button.

Enabling Referential Integrity Maintenance Rules

1. With an open database, click the Relationships button on the toolbar. The Relationships window opens.

2. Double-click on the join line of the relationship to be edited.

3. The Relationships dialog box will appear so that you can further define the related fields and tables.

4. Check the Enforce Referential Integrity check box.

5. Check the Cascade Delete Related Records check box. (Optional)

6. Check the Cascade Update Related Fields check box. (Optional)

7. Click the OK button. When referential integrity is set, the symbols 1 and ∞ are displayed on the join line.

Using the Find Duplicate Records Wizard

1. Click on the Query Wizard button in the Other group of the ribbon Create tab.

2. Select Find Duplicates Query Wizard from the list in the New Query dialog box.

3. Click the OK button. The Table Selection dialog box appears.

4. Choose the table (or query) containing the records to be checked.

5. Click the Next button. The next screen appears.

6. Select the field(s) that you want searched for duplicate records.

7. Move the field(s) to the Duplicate-value fields window with the right directional arrow keys.

8. Click the Next button. The next screen appears.

9. Select any additional fields to be included in this query.

10. Click the Next button. The next screen appears.

11. Add the title for the query, and choose the action to be taken next.

12. Click the Finish button to complete the process.

Using the Find Unmatched Records Wizard

1. Click on the Query Wizard button in the Other group of the ribbon Create tab.

2. Select the Find Unmatched Query Wizard on the New Query dialog box.

3. Click the OK button.

4. Select the table containing the records to be checked (usually the "many" table).

5. Click the Next button to move to the next screen.

6. Select the data source containing the related records (usually the "one" table) so that the previous table can be checked against it.

7. Click the Next button to move to the next screen.

8. Select the related fields in the joined tables.

9. Click the Next button to move to the next screen.

10. Select the fields to be displayed in the query results by clicking on the arrow buttons to move the desired fields between windows.

11. Click the Next button to move to the next screen.

12. Type in a title for the query and choose the view to open the query.

13. Click the Finish button to complete the process.

Beginning to Enforce Referential Integrity on an Existing Database

1. List all joins between tables.

2. Run Find Unmatched and Find Duplicates queries on all joined tables.

3. Run Delete queries on those tables to remove the duplicates and unmatched records found in step 2.

4. Be sure every table has a primary key that doesn't allow duplicates and that in every table the common field is required. Change field properties as required.

5. Change the join settings to enforce referential integrity on all joins.

Converting an Access 2002–2003 Database to Access 2007

1. Open the database to be converted. The words "(Access 2002–2003 file format)" are shown in the title bar of the Database window.

2. Click on the Office button and select Convert. The Save As dialog box appears.

3. Select the folder in which to store the new database, and type a new name for the database into the File name box. Click the Save button.

4. The database is converted and saved. The new version of the database is opened.

Converting an Access 2007 Database to an Earlier Version

1. Open the database you want to convert.

2. Click on the Office button and select Save As. A secondary menu appears.

3. Select the format or Access version.

4. Select the folder and type in the name of the file, then click the Save button.

Compacting and Repairing a Database

1. Open the database.

2. Click on the Office button, select Manage, and click on Compact and Repair Database.

Splitting a Database into Two Databases

1. Open the database.

2. Select the Database Tools tab on the ribbon, and click on the Access Database button. The Database Splitter wizard begins.

3. Click on the Split Database button. The Create Back-end Database window opens.

4. Change the suggested name for the back-end database if necessary. Access will use the old database name and add the characters _be to the end of the name.

5. Click on the Split button. The split will take a few seconds, then a message box will appear telling you the database was successfully split.

6. Click the OK button in the message box. The Database window of the front-end database appears. This database has the same name as your original database, and the tables should be linked to the back-end database.

7. Open a file management tool, such as Explorer or My Computer, to verify that there are now two databases.

Printing Documentation

1. Open the database.

2. Select the Database Tools tab on the ribbon, and click on the Database Documenter button. The Documenter Window opens.

3. Select the objects you want to print documentation for by clicking the check box in front of the object. You can also select all objects using the Select All button. Click on the different tabs to see different groups of objects. Click the All Object Types tab to view a list of all database objects at once.

4. The Print Table Definition window appears when you click the Options button. Choose any Options for the documentation and click the OK button to close the Options window.

5. Click the OK button in the Documenter dialog box. The documentation appears in the report preview window.

Analyzing Database Performance

1. Open the database.

2. Select the Database Tools tab on the ribbon, and click on the Analyze Performance button in the Analyze group. The Performance Analyzes Window appears.

3. Select the objects you want to analyze by clicking the check box in front of the object. You can also select all objects using the Select All button. Click on the different tabs to see different groups of objects. Click the All Object Types tab to view a list of all database objects at once.

4. Click the OK button to start the analysis. After a few moments a list of ideas appears in the Performance Analyzer Results window, or a message box appears telling you it has no suggestions to improve the object (s).

5. To implement a Recommendation or Suggestion optimization, select it and click on the Optimize button. You can also implement all suggestions by clicking Select All before clicking the Optimize button. The Performance Analyzer will perform the optimizations and then mark them as fixed.

6. To carry out an Idea optimization, click on it and follow the instructions displayed in the Analysis Notes box.

7. Click on the Close button when you're finished.

Viewing Object Dependencies

1. Open the database.

2. Select the Database Tools tab on the ribbon, and click on the Object Dependencies button. A window appears warning that this could take a few minutes. Click the OK button.

3. Click the OK button to continue. The Object Dependencies window opens.

4. Click on the plus sign to expand the view of the dependencies for an object.

Creating a Custom Group

1. Right-click on the Navigation Pane title bar and select Navigation Options from the shortcut menu.

2. In the Navigation Options window, select the Custom grouping option from the left column.

3. Click on the Add Group button, and type the new group name.

4. Click the OK button.

Adding an Object to a Group

1. Be sure that Custom grouping is selected in the Navigation Pane.

2. Right-click on the object name and select Add to group... from the shortcut menu. Choose the group name from the submenu.

3. The name of the object should appear under the group name.

Removing an Object From a Group

1. Select the object name, right-click, and choose Remove from the shortcut menu.

2. The name of the object is removed from the group.

Review Questions

1. What are the two main functions of a database?

2. What is an entity-relationship diagram?

3. (T/F) Attributes of an entity class determine the fields in the corresponding table.

4. What is the function of a lookup table?

5. Bridge tables hold data from two tables having what type of relationship?

6. Which type of table is most dynamic?

7. What is normalization?

8. Which branch of mathematics forms the basis for relational database theory?

9. (T/F) If the field *SSN* determines the field *Name,* the field *SSN* is functionally dependent on *Name.*

10. (T/F) If a field in a table can be broken down into smaller fields, the table is not in 1NF.

11. (T/F) A partial dependency is when only some of the non-key fields are functionally dependent on the primary key.

12. (T/F) A table containing a calculated field is in 3NF.

13. (T/F) If a data anomaly occurs, it means that further normalization is needed.

14. (T/F) A lookup field in a table is the primary key in another table.

15. How do you change the sort order of a lookup field drop-down list?

16. (T/F) A multiple-field primary key can be made up of four different fields.

17. (T/F) You can create a multiple-field primary key on a table that already has data in it.

18. Why index a field?

19. What is the default join type?

20. When would you run a Find Duplicates query?

21. What is the purpose of a Find Unmatched Records query?

22. Describe the problem that can arise after turning on Cascade Delete.

23. (T/F) Databases created by previous versions of Access can be opened in Access 2007 without converting them to 2007.

24. What is the purpose of database compacting?

25. When a database is split, what does the front-end database contain?

26. What does it mean to optimize a database?

Exercises

ACTIVITY

Exercise 1—Review and Guided Practice

"Sir Dance-A-Lot" is a growing business. They've been adding data to the database, and may have made some mistakes that need to be corrected. In addition, the database will needs to be expanded to handle a new product. One of the business partners is creating custom CD mixes for parties, and will start selling them in the store soon. Each CD will have a title and price, and will contain several songs taken from different existing recordings. The store needs a catalog of custom CDs, including CD title, a list of songs on the CD, and which recording each song comes from. In addition, the store will need written permission to use each song, and so will require contact information for each record label on file

A. Draw an E-R diagram for the planned expansion to handle the custom CDs. Include the new tables required, as well as the existing tables that will be joined to the new tables. You don't need to list the attributes in the existing tables unless they are new attributes. Remember that one custom CD contains many songs, and one song can appear on many custom CDs.

B. Create a set of tables on paper, based on the E-R diagram. The tables should be normalized to 3NF. Identify the primary key in each table. Create a bridge table to handle the many-to-many join between custom CDs and songs. Include any new fields in existing tables, but don't list all existing fields.

C. Open the *SDAL_Ch7* database. Add a new field to *tblRecordings*. Call it *AlbumCover*, make it an attachment data type, and add a caption. There are two album covers in the *Chapter7* folder—*champs.jpg* and *darin.jpg*. Add these files to the appropriate records in *tblRecordings*. Edit *frmRecordings* and add the new field *AlbumCover* to the form. Save the form.

D. Using the *SDAL_Ch7* database, open *tblInventory* in Design view. Edit the query behind the lookup field *MusicID*. Add the field *Artist* to the query. Be sure the Column Count property is now three. Click on the *MusicID* field in Datasheet view, and notice that the artist's number, not name, is displayed. Edit the query for *MusicID* again. Remove the field *Artist* that you added above. Add *tblArtists* to the query and display the field *LastNameOrBandName*. Now, return to Datasheet view and look at the drop-down list for *MusicID*. The artist's name should now be visible.

E. Run the Query wizard and find the records in *tblArtists* that have no matching records in *tblRecordings*.

F. Run the Query wizard and find the records in *tblRecordings* that have duplicates.

G. Analyze the performance of the *SDAL_Ch7* database. To improve performance, Access recommends indexes be created on what table and fields? Why do you think the Performance Analyzer recommends this? Go ahead and create one or more of these indexes.

H. Compact and close the database.

Exercise 2—Practicing New Procedures

Exercise 2A: Normalizing Tables

A public relations company wants a database developed to track its clients' projects, special events, and attendees at these events. Each client can have multiple projects, and each project can have multiple events. For example, the Redfield Corporation might have the projects "Health Fair" and "New Office Opening." The "New Office Opening" project could have the events "Press Release," "Office Tour," and "Black Tie Dinner." The public relations company maintains a file of contacts—people who receive mailings or are invited to attend scheduled events. These people have areas of interest, such as Business, Arts, Sports, etc., and they are affiliated with organizations of one of the following types: Print Media, TV Media, Radio Media, Other Media, Non-Media Corporation, or Non-Media Non Profit. The public relations company gets information about the projects and events, invites the potential attendees, and maintains a list of who will be attending each event. So far, the following tables have been established:

> tblClients(Organization Name, Address, Phone, Email, Contact Person)
> tblProjects(Name, Description, Start Date)
> tblEvents(Name, Description, Date, Time, Location)
> tblContact Organizations(Organization Name, Address, Phone, Email, Organization Type)
> tblContact People(Name, Address, Phone, Email, Job Title, Interest Area 1, Interest Area 2, Interest Area 3)

1. Add a primary key to each table.
2. Add fields to tables to connect related entities (foreign keys). For example, *tblProjects* needs a field that will connect it to *tblClients*.
3. Create a bridge table called *tblAttendees* to hold the contact people invited to each event.
4. Create any needed lookup tables.
5. Normalize the tables through 3rd Normal Form.

Exercise 2B: Enforcing Referential Integrity

Open the *MusicMedia_Ch7* database.

1. Cascade Update
   a. Enforce referential integrity on the join between the tables *tblProducts* and *tblMedia Type*. Check the box to Cascade Update Related Fields on the join. Save the relationship layout when you close the window.
   b. Open the table *tblProducts* and note the values for *Media Type ID* for records one and three.
   c. Open the table *tblMedia Type* and change the value in the field *Media Type ID* for a CD to 1, and a Book to 3 (the opposite of existing ID values). You'll have to change the ID for a CD to a value greater than 4 first, then change Book 3, and then change CD to 1. If you don't you'll get an error message indicating duplicate values in the primary key.
   d. Open the table *tblProducts* and note the values for *Media Type ID* for records one and three. They should be changed.

2. Cascade Delete

   a. Enforce referential integrity on the join between the tables *tblProducts* and *tblMedia Type*. Check the box to Cascade Delete Related Fields on the join. Save the relationship layout when you close the window.

   b. Open the table *tblProducts* and sort on the field *Media Type ID* in descending order. Note the values for *Media Type ID* for the first two records.

   c. Open the table *tblMedia Type* and delete the record for Cassette.

   d. Open the table *tblProducts* and sort on the field *Media Type ID* in descending order. Note that the old records with a *Media Type* of 4 are deleted.

3. Create and run a Find Unmatched query on the tables *tblProduct Level* and *tblProducts* to find those products without a *ProductLevel ID*. Save the query and call it *qryUnmatchedLevels*.

Exercise 2C: Changing Field Properties

Continue to use the *Musicmedia_Ch7* database.

1. Using the table *tblProducts*, change the fields *ProductLevel ID* and *MediaType ID* to lookup fields. They should look up values in the *tblProduct Level* and *tblMedia Type* tables, respectively.

2. Using the table *tblProducts*, change the underlying query in the lookup field *InstrumentID* so that instruments are displayed in alphabetical order by name.

Exercise 2D: Restructuring Tables

Use the database *Musicmedia_Ch7*.

1. Examine the table *tblArtists*. Normalize the table, creating any new tables you think are necessary to complete the normalization.

2. Define a primary key for any new tables created in step 1.

3. Join the new table created in step 1 to the table *tblArtists* and enforce referential integrity between the two tables.

Exercise 2E: Using an Index

Use the database *Musicmedia_Ch7*.

1. Open the report *rptProducts* in Preview mode, noting how long it takes to open, more or less.

2. Go to Design view and notice the grouping on the field *MediaType ID*.

3. Close the report.

4. Open the table *tblProducts* and create an index on the field *MediaType ID* (duplicates OK).

5. Close the table.

6. Open the report *rptProducts* in Preview mode again, and compare the length of time it takes to open with the last time, before indexing. Is there any significant difference? Do you think there would be a larger difference with more data in the table?

Exercise 2F: Creating an Object Group

Use the database *Musicmedia_Ch7*.

1. Create an object group named *MusicProducts*. Place shortcuts to the following objects in the group: *tblArtists*, *tblProducts*, *tblInstruments*, *tblMediaType*, *tblProduct Level*, and *tblProducts*.

Exercise 2G: Documenting Tables

Uuse the database *Musicmedia_Ch7*.

1. Print the documentation on *tblProducts*—show properties and relationships; include names, data types and sizes for fields; and names, fields, and properties of indexes.

Exercise 2H: Identifying Table Types

Use the database *Musicmedia_Ch7*.

1. Using the tables in the group *MusicProducts*, identify master, lookup, and bridge tables.

Exercise 2I: Compacting a Database

1. Note the size of the *Musicmedia_Ch7* database by looking at it in the Explorer or My Computer window. Compact it, and compare the new size with the old.

Exercise 2J: Splitting a Database

1. Make a copy of the *Musicmedia_Ch7* database and name it *Musicmedia_Ch7B*. Split the *Musicmedia_Ch7B* database into a front end and a back end.

Exercise 3—In-Class Group Practice

ACTIVITY AND REFLECTION

Split into groups of two or three as specified by your instructor. Each group will do the following set of tasks in the time frame noted by your instructor.

1. Think of one database example that contains at least one many-to-many join and at least five tables. You can get suggestions from your instructor—they are in the solutions document for Chapter 7.

2. Draw an E-R diagram on paper of the example.

3. Select one member of the group to write a short, but adequate description of the database without listing the exact tables. One of the other teams will have to create their own E-R diagram, so be sure there is enough information for them to do it.

4. Exchange your database description papers with those from one of the other groups.

5. Create an E-R diagram from the other group's description.

6. Get together with the other group and compare the two E-R diagrams for the database. Discuss any differences and see if you can come to a consensus on one E-R diagram.

Exercise 4—Critical Thinking: Exploring Join Types and Referential Integrity

ACTIVITY AND REFLECTION

Using the *Personnel_Ch7* database, do the following:

1. Examine the *tblEmployee* and *tblDepartment* tables. What is their common field? In which table is this field the primary key? Which table is the "one" table in the one-to-many relationship? Join the two tables.

2. What field property changes should be made on these two tables to ensure referential integrity? Make necessary changes.

3. Create four queries to find duplicate records and unmatched records in the *tblEmployee* and *tblDepartment* tables. Print the dynaset from each query, and label them.

4. What should you do about these duplicate and/or unmatched records? Be specific about queries that you could run to correct the problems. Assign the unmatched employees to the unmatched department.

5. Make the field *Department* in *tblEmployee* a lookup field.

6. Print both tables.

ACTIVITY AND REFLECTION

Exercise 5—Challenge: Designing Databases

Create an E-R diagram and a normalized table list for the following database descriptions. Be sure to clearly mark joins and join types (one-to-one, one-to-many, and many-to-many).

1. Design a database for managing a public recreational facility. The database needs to track memberships and special classes, generate billings, and record payments. There are three different types and prices for memberships. Two types of memberships are for individuals, and one type is a family membership for which you need to track family members. There are a number of special classes offered in various rooms at the recreation center. You need to track the class, location, day and time, price, staff member who is teaching it, and participants (members). The database needs to generate a monthly billing that includes both membership fees and any special classes taken, and record payments made by members.

2. Design a database to manage a messenger service. The service employs messengers who deliver packages in an urban area. The messengers are paid an hourly rate plus a fixed dollar amount for every package delivered. Customers are billed by the weight of the package and the distance traveled by the messenger. The service offers three special flat rates to customers who send many packages per month. There is a special rate for ten to twenty packages, twenty to thirty packages, and thirty or more packages per month. The database should track the number of packages delivered per day by each messenger, and the number and weight of packages delivered for customers. The data will feed into the payroll system and will generate monthly invoices to send to customers.

3. Design a database for tracking service data about aircraft for a small airport. There are several models of aircraft, and each model has a specific manufacturer, size (number of seats), and description. Records of maintenance need to be kept—which mechanic made what repair to which aircraft. Mechanics are trained and certified for each model of aircraft separately, but not all mechanics are certified for all aircraft. The hourly rate paid to mechanics varies according to the number of models a mechanic is certified to work on.

REFLECTION

Exercise 6—Discussion Questions

1. Why is referential integrity important?

2. What happens to a database if the value in a key field is changed in a "one" table in a one-to-many join, but the same field in the "many" table is not changed?

3. What happens to a database if a "many" table is allowed to have a record with an empty or incorrect value in the common field?

4. If you haven't enforced referential integrity in a database, what process should you follow to begin doing so?

5. What do you know about relational algebra? How about set theory and Venn diagrams? List five ways in which relational algebra and relational databases are alike. Use the Internet to find more information.

6. Create a set of step-by-step rules to use when creating a bridge table. Step 1 might be: Identify the primary key and foreign key fields in the two tables making up the many-to-many relationship.

7. Are there any benefits to creating your own AutoNumber primary key instead of using a primary key consisting of three fields in a table? Or vice versa?

8. What should be included in a good set of documentation?

CASE STUDY A: MRS. SUGARBAKER'S COOKIES

The business is growing and more data needs to be tracked. Mrs. Sugarbaker would like to add inventory information, reorganize the product line, and track production costs.

Part 1: Adding Inventory Information

The inventory consists of all the ingredients used to make the cookies, and sufficient data needs to be stored so ingredients can be easily reordered when supplies run low. This means that data pertaining to the source or supplier of the ingredient and data regarding the ingredient's quantity on hand should be stored in the database.

1. Create the *tblInventory* table containing the data found in the Excel spreadsheet *Ingredients.xls*. See Chapter 3 if you need more information about importing an Excel spreadsheet.

2. Split *tblInventory* into two tables—*tblInventory* and *tblSuppliers*.

3. Normalize the tables and designate primary keys. Be sure to add a foreign key where needed to enable a join.

4. Join the two tables together.

5. Change the field *SupplierId* in *tblInventory* to look up the supplier's name in *tblSupplier*.

Need More Help?

Look for repeating data, and move it to another table. Use AutoNumber primary keys, if no other keys naturally occur.

Part 2: Adding and Editing Fields

1. Add a field called *BoxCover* to *tblProducts*, and make it an attachment data type.

2. Add the following files to the *BoxCover* field for each record in *tblProducts*: BonBon.bmp, Brownie.bmp, Capuccino.bmp, ChocIndulgence.bmp, Citrus.bmp, FruitJewels.bmp, Holiday.bmp, OldWorld.bmp, and PeanutButter.bmp.

3. Either use the form *frmProducts* previously created, or make a new form for *tblProducts* and call it *frmProducts*. Be sure the new field *BoxCover* is displayed on the form.

4. Open *tblOrders* in Design view and edit the lookup query for the *CustomerID* field. Add both the *LastName* and *FirstName* fields to the query. Edit the properties Column Count, Column Widths, and List Width so that all data is displayed properly.

Part 3: Joins

Create a query called *qryJoins* using *tblProducts* and *tblOrderItems*. Display the fields *ProductName*, *OrderID,* and *Quantity*.

a. Use the default inner join for the two tables. How many records display?

b. Use an outer join for the two tables, showing all records in *tblProducts*. How many records display?

c. Use an outer join for the two tables, showing all records in *tblOrderItems*. How many records display?

What does that tell you about the two tables? What would you expect to see if you created an Unmatched Records query? Create the query and call it *qryProductsNotOrdered*.

CASE STUDY B: SANDY FEET RENTAL COMPANY

Now that the SFRC database is working, it's a good idea to perform some database maintenance and revision. Be sure to make a backup of the database file before attempting any of the tasks that make major changes.

1. Create a lookup field in the *tblHousekeeping* table to connect the *tblHousekeeping* table to the *tblProperties* table on the *PropertyNumber* field. Access should lookup the data for the *PropertyNumber* field from the *tblProperties* table. (Note: Since this table is joined to another table, the relationship might have to be deleted temporarily to make this change.)

2. Several owners have asked to add pictures of their condo or the resort. Create an attachment field to the *tblProperties* table. Add one image to the records from the folder *Images_CSB_Ch7* found in your student data files. Add any image to a record in this table. (Note: There will be some properties that have not sent in any images.)

   a. Create a form for the *tblProperties* to display the photos. Name the form *frmProperty_Photos*.

3. SFRC wants to add another table to the database to keep track of maintenance issues. Import the data from the *tblMaintenance.xlsx*.

   a. The key field is the *Invoice* field.

   b. Change the *Property Number* field to a look-up field joining the *tblProperty* table. Display both the *Property Number* and the *Property Address* fields in the look-up list.

   c. Change the Issue field to a look-up field and enter the data choices as follows:

   Carpet Cleaning

   Plumbing

   Smoke Detectors

   Locks and Keys

   Electrical

   Appliance Repair

   Minor Repair

   Flooring

   d. Add the new table to the Relationships window and join it to the *tblProperties* table.

4. Create an Unmatched Records query to show which properties have not had any maintenance issues. Name the query *qry_UnmatchedProperties_Maintenance*.

5. Create an Unmatched Records query to show which properties have not had any rentals. Name the query *qry_UnmatchedProperties_Rentals*.

6. Import the data from the *MoreClients.xlsx* spreadsheet and append the records to the *tblClients* table. Note: There should be 25 records after this import.

7. Create a Find Duplicates query using the *tblClients* table. Name the query as *qry_Find_Duplicates_tblClients*.

8. Run the Performance Analyzer on all tables in this database. Copy all the results of this report to a Word document. What actions did you take based on these recommendations?

9. Run the Database Documenter report. Export this report to Word. What information is presented in this report? In which situations would this information be useful?

10. What is the file size for this database? (Note: To determine file size, close the database file. Navigate to the file through Windows Explorer. Right-click on the file and choose Properties.)

  a. Return to Access and open this database file. Compact the file.

  b. Determine the file size after compacting.

  c. What is the size difference? Write this information in a Word document.

CASE STUDY C: PENGUINS SKI CLUB

E-R Diagrams, Table Design, and Normalization

The Penguins Ski Club is adding private coaching for members. Members can have 1, 2, or 3 hour coaching sessions with one of the coaches, but members are charged an extra fee for each coaching session. The Excel spreadsheet *CoachingSessions.xls* contains the first two weeks of coaching data. Print a copy of *CoachingSessions.xls* and examine the data.

1. Draw an E-R diagram that shows the new tables that will be created to manage the coaching sessions. If existing tables will be joined to the new tables, include them, but it's not necessary to list all the attributes or fields in each existing table.

2. Using the E-R diagram, list the new tables and all their attributes or fields. Underline primary key fields.

3. Normalize these tables through 3NF. Be sure there are no repeating groups of data or many-to-many joins between tables. If these tables are different from those produced in step 2, list them and their fields. Again, underline primary key fields.

Creating Tables and Fields

4. Import the spreadsheet *CoachingSessions.xls* into the database. Create the tables shown in step 3. Check that the data types for fields are appropriate. Create a primary key for all tables.

5. Be sure that any foreign keys such as *CoachID* and *MemberID* are lookup fields.

Examining Data

6. Create a query that will list all members who have not had a coaching session. Show the name, age, and ability levels of the members. Call the query *qryMembersWithoutCoachingSessions*.

7. Create a query that will list all members who have not attended an event. Show the name, age, and ability levels of the members. Call the query *qryMembersWithoutEventAttendance*.

Maintaining the Database

8. Make an object group called Coaching and add *tblCoaches*, *tblCoachingSessions*, and *qryMembersWithoutCoachingSessions*.

9. Analyze the performance of the database. Note two suggestions that are made for improving the database, and make those changes if they seem reasonable.

10. Check the size of the database. Compact the database, and check the size again. Note any change.

Chapter 8

Advanced Queries and SQL

Objectives

After completing this chapter, you will be able to

Create and run complex queries:
- Make a simple and multifield Parameter query.
- Produce a Crosstab query using the Query Wizard, or in Design view.

Create and run action queries:
- Build Update queries.
- Build Make-Table queries.
- Build Append queries.
- Build Delete queries.

Use operators and functions in expressions:
- Utilize the Expression Builder to create expressions.
- Create calculated fields using numeric, text, and date fields.

- Create calculated fields using functions.
- Use expressions as query criteria.
- Zoom in on expressions and edit them manually.
- Create expressions that refer to fields and controls in other objects.

Create and execute SQL statements:
- Write a SELECT statement that includes criteria and sort options
- Write a SELECT statement that uses the GROUP BY clause and aggregate functions.
- Create a Union query.
- Use multiple tables in SQL statements.

Dictionary

Action query	A type of query that performs an operation on a table, such as deleting specified records.
Aggregate function	A function that returns a summary value for a group of data, such as sum or avg.
Append query	A query that adds records from one table to another.
Archiving	Moving outdated or unused data to another table for storage.
Argument	A data value passed to a function.
Calculated field	A new query field that uses one or more fields in a calculation.
Concatenating fields	Combining two text fields to make a new field.
Crosstab query	A type of query that displays summarized data in row and column format.
Data Definition query	A query that creates a table or changes the structure of a table.

Data Manipulation query	A query that retrieves, organizes, or updates data.
Delete query	A query that deletes records from a table.
Expression	A set of symbols used to define a calculation or other operation.
Expression Builder	A tool used to create expressions and object identifiers.
Function	A mini program within Access that performs a special operation, such as rounding a number.
Join	A relationship between tables based on a common field or fields.
Literal value	A data value that is constant—it doesn't change. For example, "12" or "Smith" are literal values.
Make-Table query	An action query that creates a new table with selected records from another table.
Object identifier	The complete name and location of an Access object.
Operator	A symbol representing the action to be performed in an expression.
Parameter query	A type of query that allows the user to specify the criteria each time the query is run.
Prompt	A message to the user displayed on the screen.
Property sheet	A dialog box that allows you to change the properties or attributes of an object.
Query Wizard	A feature of Access that helps the user create several different types of queries.
Select query	A type of query that selects records based on certain criteria. This is the default query type.
SQL (Structured Query Language)	A universal language for expressing queries.
Union query	A query that displays data from multiple tables, even if the tables have no common fields.
Unique Values	A query property that selects only records with unique values in the fields included in the query.
Unique Records	A query property that returns only unique records in the dynaset.
Update query	An action query that makes global changes to table data.
Zoom	A feature in query design that enlarges the screen display of a cell.

8.1 Building Parameter Queries

Queries are a very powerful feature of Access that can perform many advanced procedures. In Chapter 4, we examined Select queries. These basic queries select records, called a dynaset, based on criteria specified in the query design. This chapter will explore how several other very powerful types of queries can be developed in Access. All these queries create a dynaset, all can be saved, and all dynasets can be printed, except for those created by an Action query.

What Is a Parameter Query?

Parameter queries are interactive queries. Interactive means that the query requires input from you, the user. When you run a Parameter query, you are prompted to enter the criteria using the keyboard. Parameter queries are flexible—they allow users to change the query criteria. Instead of changing the criteria in the query design, it's entered interactively each time the query is run.

When a Parameter query is run, it displays a prompt on the screen asking you to enter data. This prompt, or message, helps you enter the appropriate data. You specify the prompt when you create the query, so you must be sure that it clearly states what data needs to be entered.

A Parameter query is really a query with a piece of information missing. Access interprets the prompt you type on the Criteria row as an unidentified data item, and displays a message box asking for more information because of this reference to unknown data. When you type a field name incorrectly in a query, Access displays the same message box asking for more clarification. Therefore, some erroneous queries will behave like Parameter queries.

How to Create a Parameter Query

1. Create a new query in Design view.

2. Select the tables for the data source and click the Add button. Close this window when you have finished selecting tables.

3. Enter all fields desired in the query grid.

4. In the Criteria line for the field designated as the parameter field, type a prompt message (see Figure 8.1).

How to Run the Parameter Query

1. Click the Run button on the ribbon, located in the Results group of the Design tab (see Figure 8.1)

   OR

   Click the Datasheet View button on the ribbon in the Results group.

   The Parameter dialog box will appear, prompting you to enter a value (see Figure 8.2).

TRY IT YOURSELF 8.1.1

A. Open the *G3_Ch8* database.

B. Create a query using *tblSales*. Add the fields *Category*, *ItemName*, *EndPrice*, and *Status*.

C. Add the criteria "[Type Category 1, 3, or 4]" in the *Category* field (see Figure 8.1).

D. Run the query. Your screen should display a prompt similar to Figure 8.2.

E. Type "3" into the prompt text box. You should see 23 records in the dynaset.

F. Run the query again for category 1 (nine records).

G. Save the query as *qrySalesCategories*.

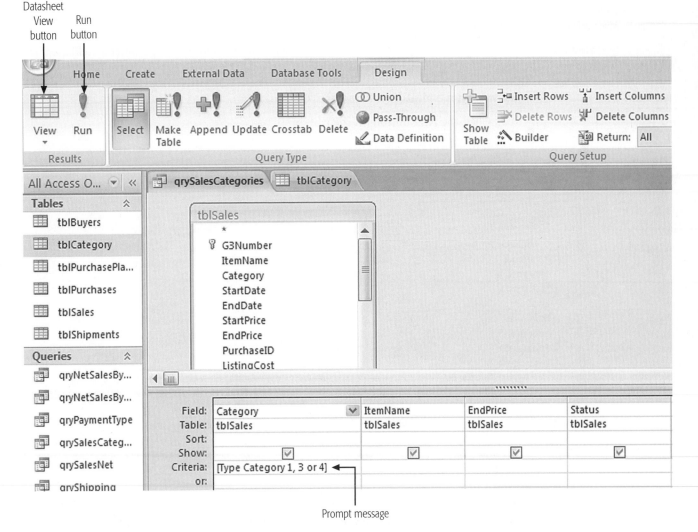

Figure 8.1 Query grid showing prompt for Parameter query

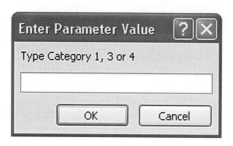

Figure 8.2 Parameter dialog box

2. Enter the criteria you want to match.

3. Click the OK button. The dynaset appears based on the criteria you entered.

   If the value entered is a valid criterion, the matching records will be displayed; the results can then be printed and the query saved. This type of query can be run repeatedly with different values entered each time.

How to Create a Multifield Parameter Query

1. Create or edit a query in Design view.

2. Select the tables for the data source and click the Add button. Close this window when you have finished selecting tables.

3. Enter all fields desired in the query grid.

4. In the Criteria line for each of the fields designated as the parameter fields, enter a prompt message in square brackets (see Figure 8.3).

How to Run a Multifield Parameter Query

1. Click the Run button on the ribbon

   OR

   Click the Datasheet button on the ribbon.

Q: Sometimes a message box is displayed when I'm not working with a Parameter query. What's going on?

A: You mistyped a field name or made a reference to a field not available to the query.

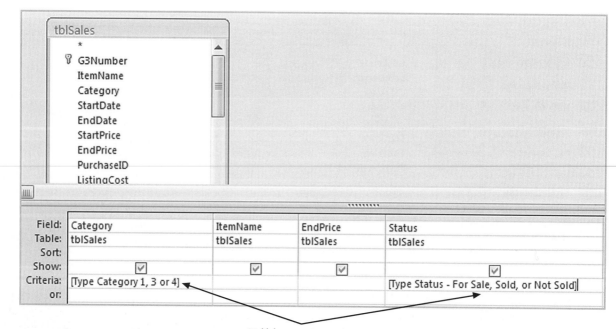

Multiple prompt messages

Figure 8.3 Multifield Parameter query

A Parameter dialog box will appear for each parameter field, prompting you to enter a value. These dialog boxes will appear in the same order as the criteria appear on the query grid, from left to right.

2. Enter the values you want to match.

3. Click the OK button. If the values entered are valid criteria, the matching records will be displayed.

The data in a record must match all the criteria or the record won't be displayed.

TRY IT YOURSELF 8.1.2

Using the query *qrySalesCategories* created in Try It Yourself 8.1.1:

A. Go to the Design view.

B. Add another parameter criterion on the *Status* field (see Figure 8.3).

C. Run the query to find all clothing for sale. You should see one record.

D. Save the query.

8.2 / Creating Action Queries

An Action query performs some type of action or operation on table records based on the query criteria. For example, you could use an Action query to delete all items in inventory that are no longer available. Action queries are useful if global updates need to be made, such as changing the records for all employees in the Marketing department to reflect the new department name, Sales Facilitation.

Four different types of Action queries can be created, as seen in Table 8.1.

Q: Can I undo an Action query?

A: No, your data is permanently changed. Back up original files before running Action queries!

Table 8.1 Types of Action Queries

Type of Action Query	Operation
Delete	Deletes specific records from the table.
Append	Adds records from one table to another table.
Update	Globally changes record data in a table to a new value.
Make-Table	Makes a new table from specific records in another table.

As you can see by the actions performed, these queries make permanent changes to table data and cannot be reversed. Therefore it is crucial that you understand the action about to be performed on the data and take appropriate steps to back up the original data before performing the actions.

It would be wise for you to first create a Select query to determine the records that will be affected before actually performing an Action query. This allows you to visually check which records will be affected.

Update Queries

An Update query allows you to globally change data in a field without editing each individual record. With one Update query, all records matching certain criteria will have data changed to new values. You can use an expression to calculate a new value for the field to be updated. An expression is an operation performed on data such as a numerical calculation. Expressions are covered in detail later in this chapter.

How to Create an Update Query

1. Create a new query using the Design view. Add table(s) and field(s).

2. Click the Update button in the Query Type group on the ribbon Design tab.

   An Update To: row is added to the grid.

3. Type the new data value in the correct field column of the Update To: row (see Figure 8.4). This is the new value that will be written to all matching records.

4. Add the criteria to select the records for updating (see Figure 8.4).

TRY IT YOURSELF 8.2.1

A. Create a new query using *tblSales*.

B. Change the *ListingCost* to $2.00 for all items with a *StartPrice* of more than $10.00. Refer to Figure 8.4.

C. Save the query and name it *qryChangeListingCosts*.

D. Open the *tblSales* table to verify that the change was made.

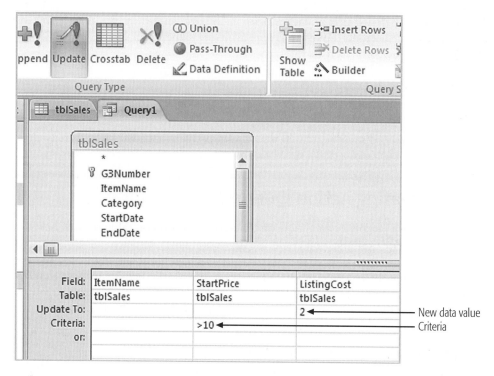

Figure 8.4 Update Query

5. Click the Run button.

A dialog box is displayed with a message warning that records will be updated (see Figure 8.5).

6. Click the Yes button to complete the update process.

Clicking the No button will cancel the entire process before any records are updated.

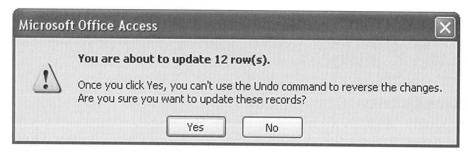

Figure 8.5 Update Query dialog box

Make-Table Queries

The Make-Table Query will create a new table based on query criteria applied to records in a table. Only those records that match the criteria are copied to the new table. The records are not removed from the original table; they are copied into the new table. The fields selected in the query will be the fields for the new table.

Make-Table queries are useful for archiving data. If a table contains a large amount of data or some data that is outdated, part of the table's data can be archived or moved to another table. Once the archive table has been made, the archived data can be deleted from the main table. Archived tables should be placed in another database and stored elsewhere, leaving only the current data in the active database. The archives are available if old data needs to be checked.

How to Create a Make-Table Query

1. Create a new query in the Design view.

2. Click the Make-Table button in the Query Type group on the ribbon (see Figure 8.6).

   A Make-Table dialog box appears (see Figure 8.6).

3. Type the new table name.

4. Select the location for the new table—either in the current database file or another database file.

5. Click the OK button.

TRY IT YOURSELF 8.2.2

A. Create a Make-Table query using *tblPurchases* and *tblPurchasePlaces*. Create a new table called *tblGarageSale-Purchases* that contains only items bought at a garage sale (see Figure 8.6).

B. Save the query and call it *qryMakeGarageSaleTable*.

C. Run the query (see Figure 8.7). Three records should be added to the new table.

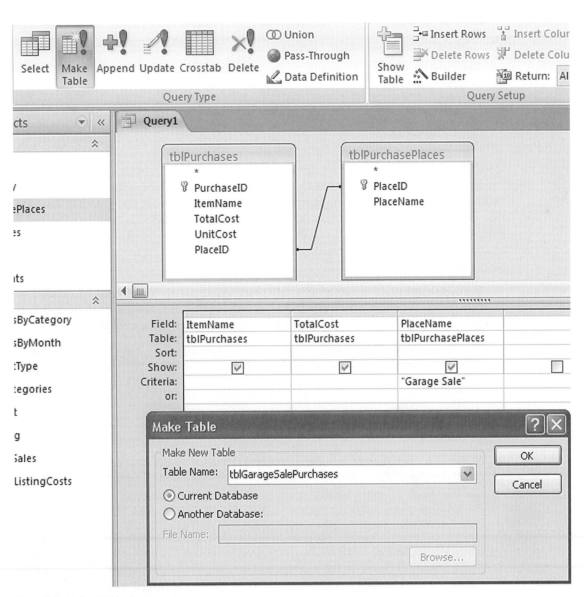

Figure 8.6 Make-Table Query

6. Select all fields you want in the new table and enter the criteria.

7. Click the Datasheet View button on the toolbar to preview the result of the query before actually running it, then return to the Design view.

8. Click the Run button on the ribbon.

   A dialog box appears, indicating how many records will be copied to the new table (see Figure 8.7).

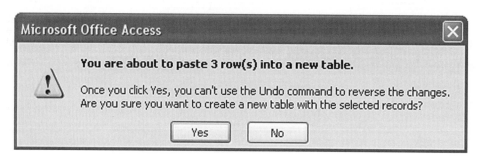

Figure 8.7 Dialog box to allow the Make-Table query to run

9. Click the Yes button to complete the process. Clicking the No button cancels the process entirely.

   Open the new table to verify that it has the records and fields you selected. The old table does not change at all.

Append Queries

An Append query will add records from one table to another table. The table that is open and in use for the query will supply the records. We'll call this the source table. The table that will receive the records must already exist either in the same database file or in another Access database. We'll call this the destination table.

Notes about Appending Records

- Records can be added to an open table but you won't see them until you reread the table after appending. Refresh the table and display the new records by using the SHIFT + F9 keys, or the Refresh button on the Quick Access toolbar.

- The append process may not be the most efficient process if you are copying all the fields and records in a table. It's probably faster to use the Copy and Paste buttons to copy the entire table.

- Another option for copying all records to another table is the Import command. This process will take both records and structure to a new table without having to previously create it.

- Make sure that the records being appended have unique values in the destination table's key field. Records will not append if there are duplicate values or no values in the key field. In other words, if the source table has multiple records containing "CO" in the *State* field and *State* is the primary key of the destination table, only the first "CO" record will be appended.

- Enter all the desired fields in the query grid individually and do not use the asterisk (*) to select all fields. If the asterisk is used, individual fields from the same table cannot be used to define criteria, as they will have to be added to the grid again. An error message will indicate that there are duplicate fields trying to be appended.

- Do not include an AutoNumber field in records to be appended. You can modify the table design to add that field after appending the records.

- An Append query will only work with one table at a time.

How to Create an Append Query

1. Create a new query in the Design view. Use the table containing the data you want to append to the new table. Add the fields and criteria for the records to be appended (see Figure 8.8).

2. Run the query to view the result, then return to the Design view.

3. Convert the Select query to an Append query by clicking the Append button in the Query Type group on the ribbon (see Figure 8.8).

   An Append dialog box appears (see Figure 8.8).

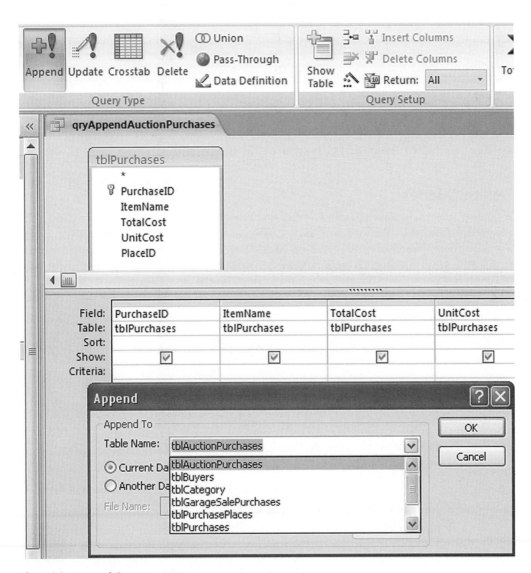

Figure 8.8 Append Query

TRY IT YOURSELF 8.2.3

A. Open the table *tblAuctionPurchases* in Datasheet view. It should have no records. Close it.

B. Create an Append query using the table *tblPurchases* as the source, and append the records to the table *tblAuctionPurchases*.

C. Include all the fields from *tblPurchases*, but append only those records with a value of 2 in field *PlaceID*.

D. Save the query and name it *qryAppendAuctionPurchases*.

E. Run the query.

F. Open the table *tblAuction-Purchases* and verify that it contains the seven new records.

4. Type the name for the destination table, or select it from the drop-down list.

5. Choose the location of the table in either the current database file or in another file.

6. Click the OK button.

7. Run the query by clicking the Run button to run the query.

A dialog box appears, showing the number of rows about to be appended (see Figure 8.9).

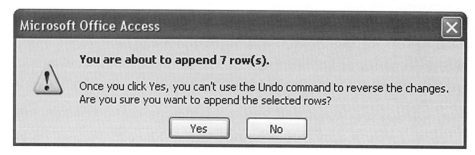

Figure 8.9 Dialog box showing the number of rows to be appended

8. Click the Yes button to complete the process, and records will be appended to the table. If you click the No button to cancel the process, no records will be appended.

The append process cannot be reversed by using the Undo command. If you did not make a backup copy of the destination table beforehand, you will have to perform a Delete query (see the next section) to remove the new records.

Delete Queries

A Delete query eliminates records from a table permanently. This action cannot be reversed, so always make a backup copy of the data before proceeding. When you create a Delete query, you need only include fields that are part of the criteria. There is no way to delete only certain fields from a record; the entire record is deleted. Consequently, field selection has no impact (beyond criteria selection) on the final result.

How to Create a Delete Query

TRY IT YOURSELF 8.2.4

A. Create a Delete query based on the table *tblAuctionPurchases* created previously. The query should delete all items with a *TotalCost* greater than $5. Refer to Figure 8.10.

B. Save the query and name it *qryDeleteOverFive*.

C. Run the query. Four records should be deleted (see Figure 8.11).

D. Open the table *tblAuction-Purchases* and verify that it contains three records (see Figure 8.12).

1. Create a new query, enter the criteria, and verify the records to be deleted by clicking the Datasheet View button. Return to the Design view.

2. Convert the query to a Delete query by clicking on the Delete button in the Query Type group on the ribbon (see Figure 8.10).

A Delete row is added to the grid (see Figure 8.10).

3. Run the query by clicking on the Run button on the ribbon.

A Delete dialog box appears, indicating that records will be deleted (see Figure 8.11).

4. Click the Yes button to complete the process. The selected records will be deleted. If you click the No button to cancel the process, no records will be deleted.

You can turn off the warnings that are displayed when Action queries are run. You might want to do this if you have an Action query that is routinely run, as it will eliminate a step for users. Don't suppress the warning messages, however, until you are sure the query runs correctly.

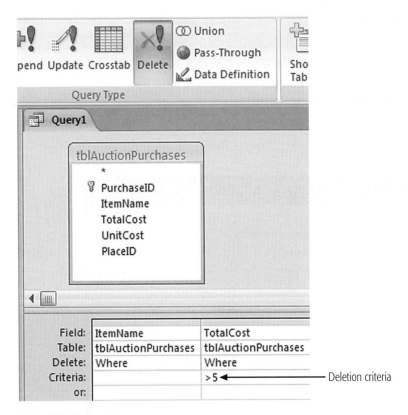

Figure 8.10 Delete Query

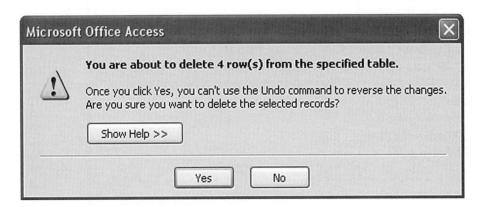

Figure 8.11 Dialog box showing the number of rows to be deleted

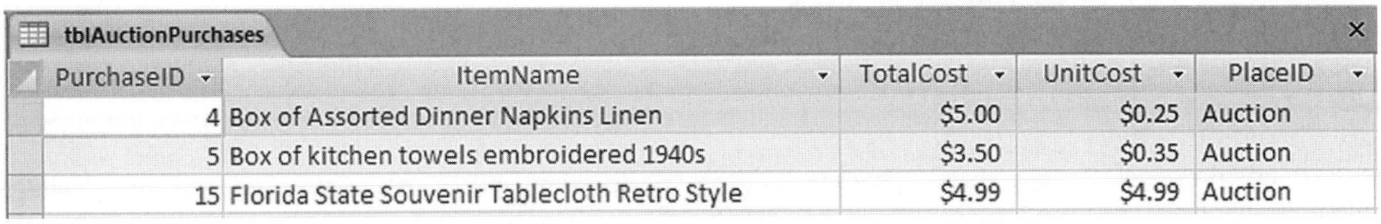

PurchaseID	ItemName	TotalCost	UnitCost	PlaceID
4	Box of Assorted Dinner Napkins Linen	$5.00	$0.25	Auction
5	Box of kitchen towels embroidered 1940s	$3.50	$0.35	Auction
15	Florida State Souvenir Tablecloth Retro Style	$4.99	$4.99	Auction

Figure 8.12 Result of Try It Yourself 8.2.4 showing the three remaining records

How to Suppress Warning Messages for Action Queries

1. Click on the Office button and click on the Access Options button. The Access Options dialog box appears as shown in Figure 8.13.

2. Click on the Advanced group in the left pane (see Figure 8.13).

3. Uncheck the Action queries check box (see Figure 8.13).

4. Click the OK button to close the access Options dialog box.

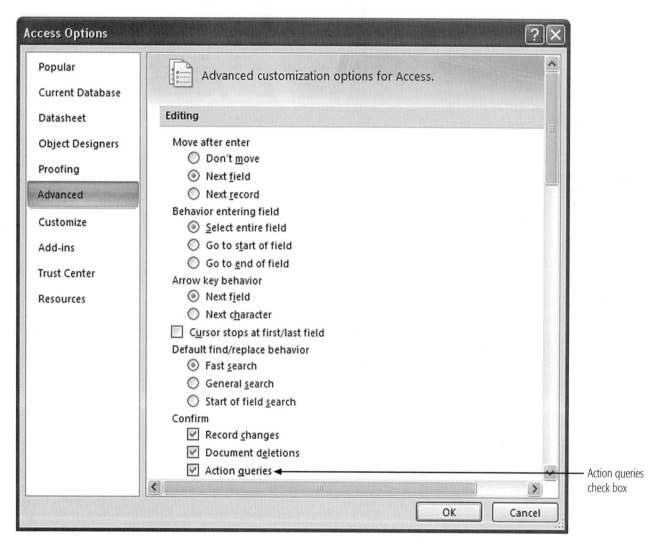

Figure 8.13 Suppressing Action Query warnings

Professional Tip: Using "Is Null" in Criteria

This tip comes from Allen Browne, a Microsoft MVP (Most Valuable Professional) who lives in Perth, Australia. Allen has a background in dBase/Foxbase, and switched to MS Access when version 1.0 was first released in 1992. He provides tuition and assistance for Access users, and is the author of Essential Access 95 (SAMS, 1995, now out of print). His Web site, Allen Browne's tips for Microsoft Access can be found online at http://allenbrowne.com/tips.html.

You wish to create two different tables—one for your WA friends and another for those in other states. You create two queries: one where the Criteria line under State reads WA, and a second query where the Criteria line reads Not "WA." You could think this would take care of all cases. It doesn't!

The problem is the way Access and other true relational databases handle Nulls. If the entry under State has been left completely blank, the record will not show up in either of the above queries. You must specifically ask Access to check for Nulls, by using a Criteria such as Is Null Or Not "WA." Whenever you enter criteria for a query, think about the possibilities of Nulls.

In some cases, you will want to prevent Nulls occurring. In Access 2 or later, open the table in Design view, click on the field, and in the properties at the bottom of the screen, set Required to "Yes."

8.3 Summarizing Data with Crosstab Queries

A Crosstab query displays summarized data in a spreadsheetlike format (in rows and columns). You can display sums, averages, counts, and other statistical information about the data in a table. The records are grouped two ways by values in two different fields, and then statistics are calculated where the two groups meet or cross—hence the name Crosstab query, a query that produces a cross-tabulated result. For example, you can group student records by major and gender so that students' average ages can be calculated. Figure 8.14 shows how this Crosstab query looks.

You can create a Crosstab query by two different methods—using the Crosstab Query Wizard or creating the query "from scratch" in the Query Design view. Both methods take a little bit of planning and thought to ensure accurate results.

There are three parts to a Crosstab query: Row Headings, Column Headings, and Values (see Figure 8.14). A Crosstab query must have an entry for each of these. The Column Headings and Row Headings are descriptive labels that identify how the Values are grouped, and Values are summarized numeric data. In Figure 8.14, the Row Heading field is *Major,* the Column Heading field is *Gender,* and the Value field is *Age.* Several Row Headings can be used in a Crosstab, but only one Value and one Column Heading are used. Also, criteria cannot be entered in Value fields. You can create a Crosstab query on multiple tables if they can be joined.

Column heading (gender)

Row heading (major)

Values (average age)

	Male	Female
Business	32	35
English	26	25
Math	21	21
Psychology	29	42

Figure 8.14 Parts of a Crosstab query

There's an example of a Crosstab query in the database *MusicMedia_Ch8.* The query is called *qryProductsCrosstab.* The query counts the items in the table *tblProducts* organized by media type and instrument type. The query dynaset is shown in Figure 8.15.

The field *MediaTypeID* is used as the Row Heading. Figure 8.15 shows the media types listed in the column furthest left. The field *Name* from the table *tblInstruments* is used as the Column Heading. Both *MediaTypeID* and *InstrumentID* are lookup fields, qryProductsCrosstab

Media Type	Banjo	Drums	Guitar	Piano	Tuba
Book	2	4	3	3	3
Video	3	3	3	3	3
CD	4	3	4	3	5
Cassette		1		1	

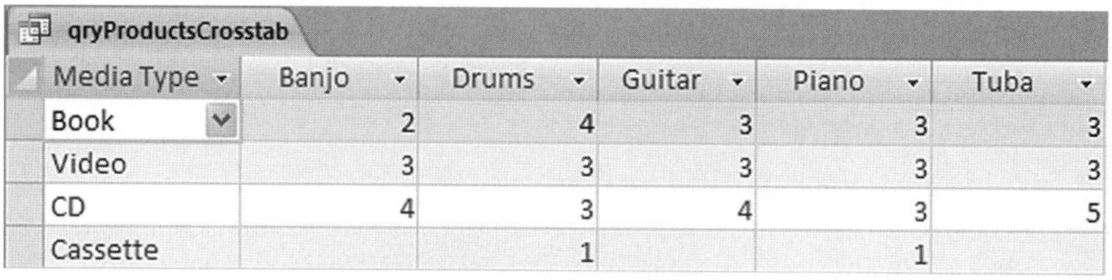

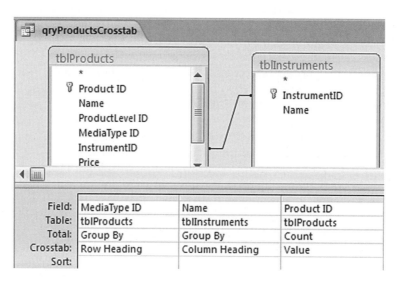

Figure 8.15 Dynaset for query *qryProductsCrosstab*

but the query will not display the instrument name when *InstrumentID* is used. Figure 8.15 shows the instrument names listed along the top row. The field *ProductID* is counted to provide the values in the query dynaset. This field was chosen because it's the primary key in the table *tblProducts,* so an accurate count is guaranteed, as there must be value in the primary key of every record. The Design view of the query *qryProductsCrosstab* is shown in Figure 8.16.

Figure 8.16 Design view for query *qryProductsCrosstab*

A number of different values can be calculated in a Crosstab query: count, sum, average, min (smallest value), max (largest value), standard deviation, variance, first (value in first record), last (value in last record), or any expression (see the next section). Only one of these may be selected as the value in a query—multiple values can't be calculated.

One of the easiest mistakes to make is in the selection of Row and Column Headings. Row and Column headings should be fields representing groups or categories of data. If a field is used that has many different values, a row will be displayed for each value, and totals become meaningless. Let's change the query *qryProductsCrosstab* as an example. Figure 8.17 shows the Design view and the dynaset when the Row Heading is changed to *Name*. One row is shown for each record in *tblProducts,* so all counts are one. No totals or other statistics can be properly calculated.

Creating a Crosstab Query with the Crosstab Query Wizard

The Query wizard helps you create a Crosstab query by asking specific questions about the fields to be used. If fields from more than one table are necessary to create the Crosstab,

Field:	Name	Name	Product ID
Table:	tblProducts	tblInstruments	tblProducts
Total:	Group By	Group By	Count
Crosstab:	Row Heading	Column Heading	Value
Sort:			

Name	Banjo	Drums	Guitar	Piano	Tuba
Advanced Piano				1	
Advanced Tuba					1
Always Banjo	1				
Banjo Chords		1			
Beginning Piano				1	
Beginning Tuba					1
Bluegrass Banjo 1	1				
Bluegrass Banjo 2	1				
Bluegrass Banjo 3	1				

Figure 8.17 Design View and dynaset for query *qryProductsCrosstab* with *Name* as the Row Heading

create a new query with these fields first and then use that query as the data source. The Crosstab wizard will allow for only one data source (table or query). The Crosstab wizard will also not allow any criteria to be entered in the Crosstab grid. If criteria are necessary, go back to the query in Design view and edit the query after you create it.

How to Use the Crosstab Query Wizard

1. Click on the Query Wizard button in the Other group of the ribbon Create tab. The New Query dialog box appears (see Figure 8.18).

2. Select Crosstab Query Wizard, and click on the OK button. The Table Selection screen appears (see Figure 8.19).

TRY IT YOURSELF 8.3.1

A. Using the *G3_Ch8* database, create a Crosstab query with the wizard. Use *tblSales* and make *Category* the Row Heading and *PaymentType* the Column Heading. Calculate the sum of the field *EndPrice*. See Figures 8.18–8.23.

B. Save the query as *qrySalesCrosstab*, and view the results (see Figure 8.23).

C. Close the query.

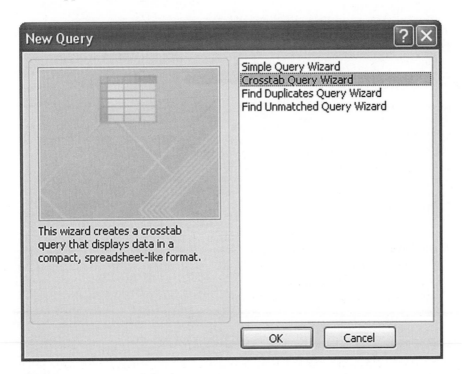

Figure 8.18 New Query dialog box

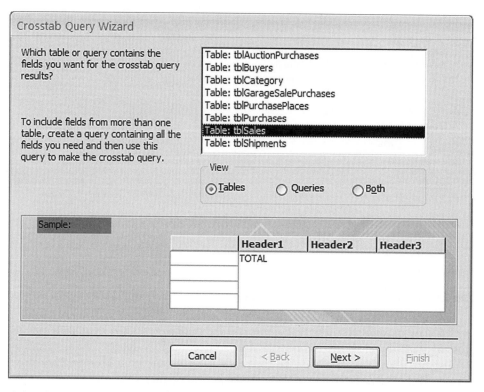

Figure 8.19 Table Selection screen of the Crosstab Query Wizard

3. Select the data source for the Crosstab query. Remember that you can use only one table/query for the data source in the wizard.

4. Click the Next button. The Row Heading Selection screen appears (see Figure 8.20).

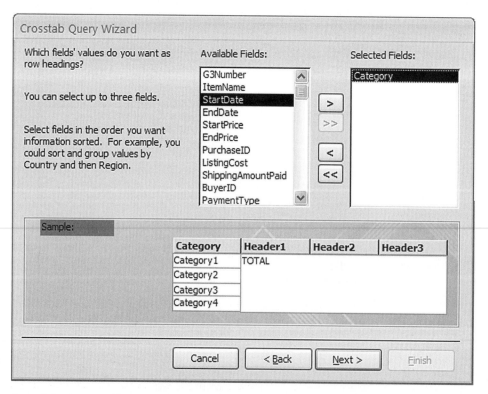

Figure 8.20 Row Heading Selection screen of the Crosstab Query Wizard

5. Select the field for the Row Headings. Use the right directional arrow buttons to move the field to the Selected Fields window.

6. Click the Next button. The Column Heading Selection screen appears (see Figure 8.21).

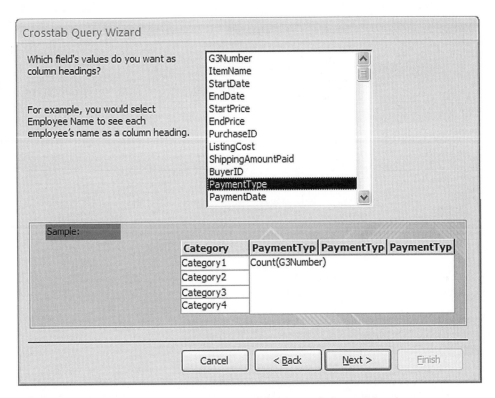

Figure 8.21 Column Heading Selection screen of the Crosstab Query Wizard

7. Select the Column Heading field.

8. Click on the Next button. The Value Selection screen appears (see Figure 8.22).

9. Select the field containing the Value to be tabulated.

10. Select the calculation to be performed on this field to produce the Value.

11. Click the Next button. The final screen appears.

12. Enter the title for the Crosstab query and select the view to open the query.

13. Click the Finish button to complete the process.

The Crosstab Query wizard also adds a total of each row to the query. Figure 8.23 shows both the dynaset and Design view of the query. The total appears in the dynaset as the first column to the right of the Row Headings, and in the Design view at the far right.

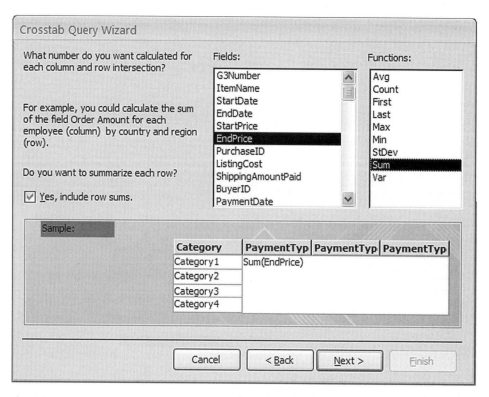

Figure 8.22 Value Selection screen in the Crosstab Query Wizard

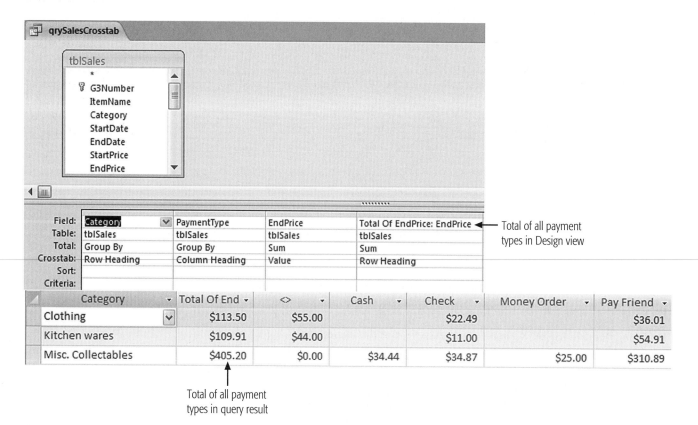

Figure 8.23 Dynaset and Design view of the Crosstab query created by the wizard

Notice that the dynaset of *qrySalesCrosstab* shown in Figure 8.23 has a column heading "<>." This symbol represents data that has no value in the Column Heading field. In this example, it contains the sum of the *EndPrice* for records with no data in the field *PaymentType*. These records are for items that are unsold, or are still for sale. See the Professional Tip at the end of this section for information about eliminating these records.

Creating a Crosstab Query in Design View

Creating a Crosstab query in Design view gives you more flexibility than the wizard. Both multiple data sources and criteria can be employed when the wizard isn't used. You can also sort the Row Heading and Column Heading fields. The most important thing to remember is to specify one or more Row Headings, only one Column Heading, and only one Value field.

How to Create a Crosstab Query in Design View

1. Create a new query in the Design view.

2. Select the table(s) for the data source.

3. Click the Crosstab button in the Query Type group of the ribbon.

   Notice that the grid now has a Total row and a Crosstab row (see Figure 8.24).

4. Add the field for the Row Heading to the grid.

5. Select Row Heading from the drop-down list in the Crosstab row, and keep the Group By selection entered in the Total row (see Figure 8.24).

6. Add the field for the Column Heading to the grid.

TRY IT YOURSELF 8.3.2

A. Create a Crosstab query in Design view using *tblSales*. Make *Category* the Row Heading, *Status* the Column Heading, and count the field *G3Number*. Refer to Figures 8.24 and 8.25.

B. Run the query and save it as *qrySalesCrosstab2*.

C. Close the query.

Q: What if my Crosstab query doesn't display any data?

A: Check to be sure that you have clicked the Crosstab query button and have designated fields for the column heading, row heading, and value.

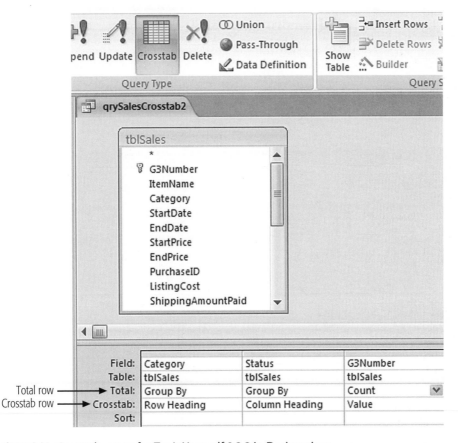

Figure 8.24 Crosstab query for Try It Yourself 8.3.2 in Design view

7. Select Column Heading from the drop-down list in the Crosstab row, and keep the Group By selection entered in the Total row (see Figure 8.24).

8. Add the field for the Value to the grid.

9. Select Value from the drop-down list in the Crosstab row.

10. Select the calculation for the value (sum, count, and so forth) in the Total row (see Figure 8.24).

11. Specify criteria or a sort order either on the heading field or another field you add to the query.

12. Run the query from the Run button on the ribbon.

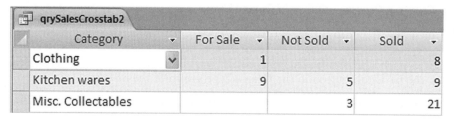

Figure 8.25   Crosstab query dynaset for Try It Yourself 8.3.2

Professional Tip: Eliminating Null Values

Sometimes blank or unlabeled rows will appear in the dynaset of a Crosstab query, or values will be listed with a "<>" heading. This is the result of having no data values in either the Row Heading or Column Heading field in some of the records in the data source. The query *qrySalesCrosstab*

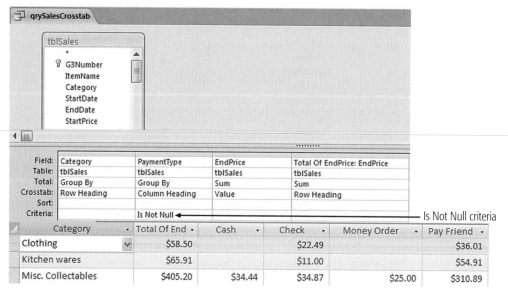

Figure 8.26   Eliminating Null values

created in Try It Yourself 8.3.1 and shown in Figure 8.23 includes data with no values in the field *PaymentType*. Access refers to these blanks as null values.

To eliminate null values from a Crosstab query, the criterion "Is Not Null" can be added to the query. Access will then ignore null values. In this case, the *PaymentType* field has null values, so the criterion "Is Not Null" is placed in that field. Figure 8.26 shows *qrySalesCrosstab* with this criterion and the resulting dynaset.

8.4 Using Expressions in Queries

An expression is a set of symbols used to define a calculation or other operation. There are many forms of expressions that can be used in a variety of ways within Access. Expressions can be used to define new fields for queries, reports, forms, and filters; to define criteria in a query; to change records using an Update query; or within macros and modules. They can be very simple or extremely complex.

A calculated field is a new field that you can add to a query. Performing a calculation on an existing field or fields creates this new field. You can create calculated fields using numeric, date, currency, and text data. You can also incorporate an Access function, a preprogrammed operator, into a calculation. Calculated fields are created by carrying out a specific expression. In the previous section, Crosstab queries automatically calculate expressions such as count and sum of the values in a field.

There are several parts to an expression. All are listed below, but are not necessarily included in all expressions. See Figure 8.27 for an example of an expression used to create a new field.

Q: What's an expression?

A: An expression is a formula or mathematical computation.

- Operators indicate the type of action to be performed.

- Object names identify the objects used in the expression (fields, tables, forms, reports, or controls). Always enclose field names in square brackets ([ ]) when you use them in an expression.

- Functions transform values into new values by running Access miniprograms.

- Literal values are actual values supplied by you—numbers, dates, or character strings.

- Constants represent values that do not change (Yes, No, Is Null, True, False).

The Is Null criterion in a query will find records without data in the specified field.

Creating an Expression

You can manually type an expression, or use the Expression Builder, a tool that helps create a valid expression. Expressions are made up of two or more data values or fields connected by an operator, or a function representing a data value. Expressions can be entered in the field name portion of the Query Design grid to create a calculated field, or in the Criteria row to create a calculated criterion. Figure 8.27 shows an expression used to define a new field in a query.

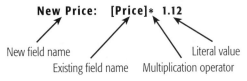

Figure 8.27 Expression to define a new field

Operators

An operator is a symbol or word that lets you perform a specific action on two data values or fields. Operators are used in Access expressions to define an operation. There are several different types of operators that can be used; some of them are the same symbols used in other software applications. They are shown below in Table 8.2.

Table 8.2 Types of Operations

Operations	Description	Operators
Mathematical	Perform mathematical operations on number or number type fields.	Multiply (*), Divide (/), Add (+), Subtract (−), Exponent (^), Integer Divide (\)
Relational	Compare two values or expressions in an equation.	Equal (=), Not Equal (<>), Less Than (<), Less Than or Equal To (<=), Greater Than (>), Greater Than or Equal To (>=)
String	Perform operations only on text fields.	Concatenation (&), Similar to (Like)
Logical	Set conditions in an expression.	And (And), Inclusive (Or), Equivalence (Eqv), Implication (Imp), Exclusive (Xor), Not (Not)
Other	Perform other operations.	Range (Between…And), Compare to a List (In), Null Object (Is Null)

These operators have a precedence order that Access follows in evaluating the expression and performing the operations. In Table 8.3, operators are listed in the order of precedence, with the operation listed first being executed first. If two operations have the same level of precedence, the leftmost operation is carried out first, followed by the next operation to the right, and so forth. Parentheses can be used to group sections of the expression and override the order of precedence.

Table 8.3 Order of Precedence for Operators

Operators	Precedence Order	Operators	Precedence Order
Mathematical	1. Exponentiation 2. Negation 3. Multiplication/Division 4. Integer Division 5. Addition/Subtraction 6. String Concatenation 7. Like	Relational	1. Equal 2. Not equal 3. Less than 4. Greater than 5. Less than or equal to 6. Greater than or equal to
Logical	1. Not 2. And 3. Or 4. Xor 5. Eqv		

For example, let's examine how the following expression would be evaluated:

6 + 4 * 3 − 5 * 2

The multiplication operations are carried out first, from left to right. So, 4 * 3 = 12, and 5 * 2 = 10. Substituting these values into the expression gives us:

6 + 12 − 10

Now, the addition and subtraction are carried out from left to right, giving a result of 8. If the addition should be carried out first, use parentheses as follows:

(6 + 4) * 3 − 5 * 2

In this case, 6 + 4 = 10, making the expression:

10 * 3 − 5 * 2

Next, the multiplication operations are executed, giving us:

30 − 10

The result is now 20.

You can also use text data in expressions. The string operators manipulate text, just as mathematical operators manipulate numbers. A new text field can be made by connecting (concatenating) two other text fields using an ampersand (&). For example, a new field combining City and State would be created by evaluating the following expression:

CityState: [City] & ", " & [State]

The comma inside quotes inserts a comma between the two text fields. If *City* = "Denver" and *State* = "CO", then *CityState* = "Denver, CO".

You can also select a records containing a specific word or phrase by using the Like string operator. For example, to select all records with the words "Fire Department" in the field Organization Name, you would use the following criterion in the Organization Name column:

Like *Fire Department*

The asterisks (*) before and after the text tell Access that the text can appear anywhere in the field—at the beginning, in the middle, or at the end of the name.

How to Create a Calculated Field with the Expression Builder

1. Create a new query in the Design view.

2. Click on a blank field name in the Field row, where the expression will be entered.

3. Click the right mouse button and select Build from the shortcut menu (see Figure 8.28)

TRY IT YOURSELF 8.4.1

A. Open the query *qryG3Amount* in the Design view.

B. Use the Expression Builder to add a new Column called *G3Amount* that multiplies *EndPrice* by *G3Percentage*. Refer to Figure 8.29.

C. Save the query, and view the results. It should look like Figure 8.30.

D. Close the query.

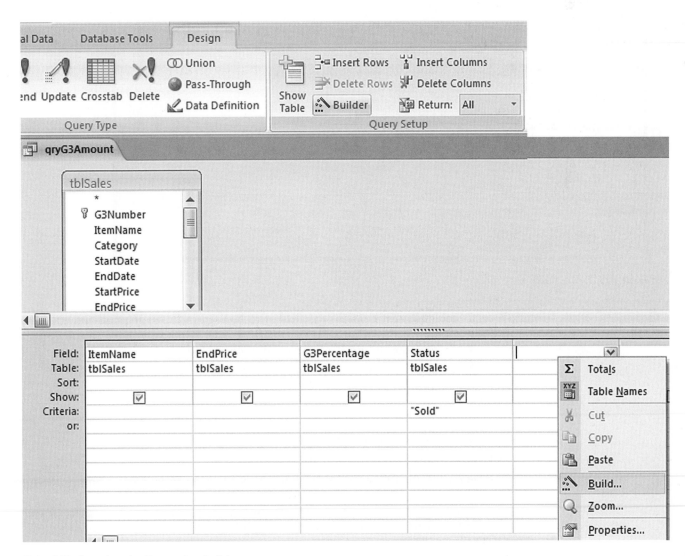

Figure 8.28 Opening the Expression Builder

Q: Why do some calculated fields display a row of #s in a query?

A: The column is too narrow to display the data. Just widen the column and the data will display.

OR

Click the Builder button on the Design tab of the ribbon, in the Query Setup group (see Figure 8.28).

The Expression Builder dialog box opens (see Figure 8.29).

4. Type in the expression in the Expression Builder window

OR

Build the expression by clicking buttons and selecting from drop-down lists.

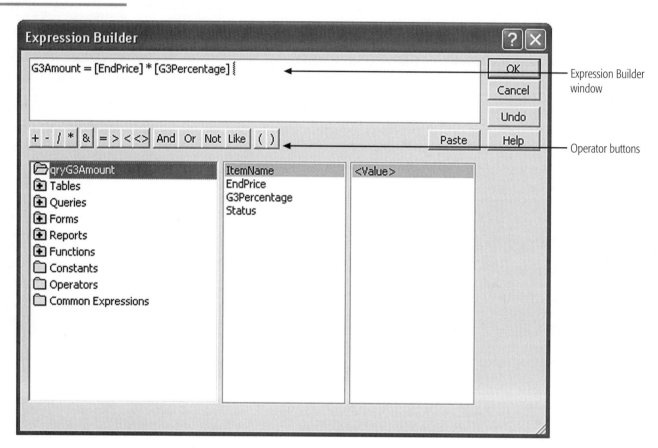

Figure 8.29 Expression Builder dialog box

Select the table that contains the field(s) to be used in the expression and click the Paste button to enter it into the Expression Builder window. Double-clicking on an item will also enter it into the Expression Builder window.

Numbers will always have to be typed in.

Additional operations can be added to create a more complex expression.

5. Click the OK button to close the Expression Builder dialog box and return to the Query Design screen. The expression will be entered into the field cell.

6. Complete and run the query to see the results of the expression.

Even though the Expression Builder is intended to aid you in creating an expression, sometimes it can actually get in the way. It's easy to accidentally enter items into the Expression Builder window by double-clicking. You can always delete or backspace unwanted items. If you remember to type in field names surrounded by square brackets, it's easier to manually create or edit an expression.

qryG3Amount				
ItemName ▾	EndPrice ▾	G3Percentage ▾	Status ▾	G3Amount ▾
6 Vintage Red Yellow Striped Napkins Linen Never Used	$14.07	5.25%	Sold	0.738674976937473
Vintage Tablecloth Fruit Cherries 1940s Excellent Condition	$19.85	5.25%	Sold	1.04212496746331
Vintage silver tone powder compact	$5.53	5.25%	Sold	0.290324990935624
Vintage Bakelite Hair Comb Art Deco/Late Vict	$10.19	5.25%	Sold	0.534974983297288
Vintage Hair Clippers Oster Model 105 Nice	$8.00	5.25%	Sold	0.419999986886978
Vintage West German Cuckoo Clock	$51.09	5.25%	Sold	2.68222491625696
Vintage Florida Map Scarf 50s Pink Silk	$8.83	5.25%	Sold	0.463574985526502
Lot Vintage Matches CopaCabana New York 60s	$6.05	5.25%	Sold	0.317624990083277

Figure 8.30 Results of Try It Yourself 8.4.1

How to Manually Create and Edit a Calculated Field

1. Create or edit a query in the Design view. Add the appropriate table(s) and fields for the query.

2. Click on an empty field cell to create an expression

    OR

    Click on an existing expression to edit.

3. Click the right mouse button and choose the Zoom command. This will allow for easier typing in the cell (see Figure 8.31)

    OR

    Press the ⎡SHIFT⎤ and ⎡F2⎤ keys to zoom.

Q: Why are there sometimes square brackets around object names?

A: Square brackets must enclose an object name if it contains a space. Brackets around object names are optional if the name contains no spaces however, Access often adds them anyway.

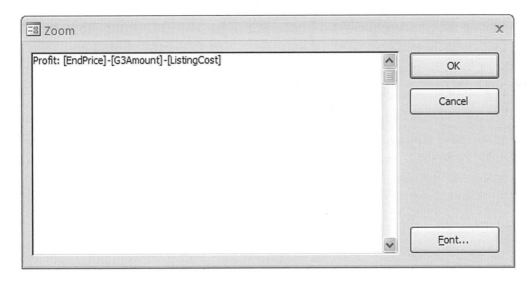

Figure 8.31 Zoom screen

4. Type the new field name followed by a colon. For example,

    Profit:

TRY IT YOURSELF 8.4.2

A. Open the query *qryG3Amount* in Design view.

B. Add a new field, called *Profit*, calculated by subtracting *G3Amount* and *ListingCost* from *EndPrice*. Refer to Figure 8.31.

C. View the query dynaset, then save and close the query.

5. Next type the first value to be used in the calculation. If this value is a field name containing one or more spaces, enclose it in square brackets. For example,

   Profit: [EndPrice]

6. Type in the arithmetic operator to be used in the calculation. For example,

   Profit: [EndPrice] —

7. Type in the second field or literal value used in the calculation. For example,

   Profit: [EndPrice] — [G3Amount]

8. Repeat steps 6 and 7 until the expression is complete, then click the OK button to move from the Zoom screen back to the grid.

9. Click the Run button on the ribbon to see the results of the calculated field.

Functions

Access provides many built-in functions that can be used in calculations on fields in queries, forms, and reports. A function is a prewritten miniprogram that produces a result representing a data value. Functions often require data values as input, which are processed by the function into another value. These data values are called arguments.

There are financial, mathematical, text, date, and various other functions available. Appendix C contains a complete list of Access functions. For example, you can display today's date by using the function Date(). You must use parentheses with a function, and if you want the function to use an argument, it must be inside the parentheses. For example, Weekday(*Birthdate*) would return the day of the week corresponding to the date value in the *Birthdate* field. Other useful functions include Month(*SalesDate*) which gives the month of the field *SalesDate*, and Ucase(*State*), which converts the field *State* to uppercase. Appendix B contains a list of all functions.

TRY IT YOURSELF 8.4.3

A. Open the query *qryG3Amount* in Design view.

B. Add a new field called *SalesMonth* that displays the month in field *EndDate*. Refer to Figure 8.32.

C. View the query dynaset, then save and close the query.

How to Display Available Functions in the Expression Builder

1. Open the Expression Builder.
2. Click on the Functions folder on the left side of the screen (see Figure 8.32).
3. Click on the Built-In Functions subfolder (see Figure 8.32).
4. A list of all available functions will appear in the next two windows.
5. Click on the function you wish to use in the expression and then click the Paste button.
6. When the expression is complete, click the OK button to move back to the Query Design screen.

Some of the most frequently used functions are those used for values in Crosstab queries: count, sum, average, min, and max. All of these functions can be used in expressions. For example, to create a query field to count the number of records in the table *tblSales*, you can count the primary key field as follows:

   SalesCount: Count([G3Number])

Or, to find the average price of all purchases:

   AveragePurchase: Avg([TotalCost])

These functions are called aggregate functions because they return only one value for all the records in the table. When using an aggregate function in a query, don't try to add other fields unless they also return a single value. The query should be treated like a Crosstab query.

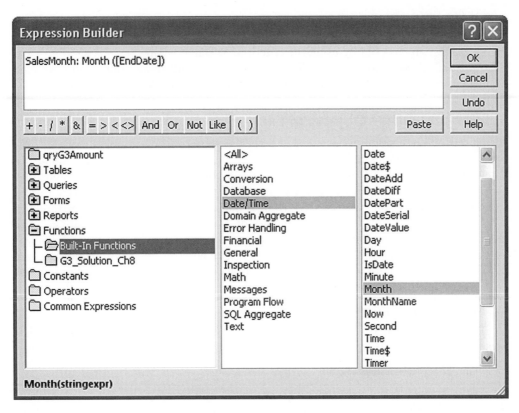

Figure 8.32 Expression Builder window showing functions

Now, let's take a look at a few examples of string functions, those used with text to create new text strings or transform existing ones. As previously noted, Ucase and Lcase are string functions that convert the case of letters in a string. Other string functions Left, Right, and Mid can be used to create new strings of text from existing text data. The Left function extracts characters from the left end of a string; the Right function takes characters from the right end of a string; and the Mid function takes characters from the middle of a string. The Left function has two data values: the text string and the number of characters to extract. The syntax of the Left function is:

Left(string, number of characters)

For example, Left("Spring Break",6) returns the string "Spring." The Right function is used the same way—Right("Spring Break",5) returns the string "Break." The Mid function has the syntax:

Mid(string, start position, number of characters)

For example, Mid("Spring",3,4) returns the string "ring" (four characters beginning in the third position). Remember that each space in a string counts as a character position—in the string "Spring Break," there is a space in position seven. You can use any string function with any field having a data type of text. For example, if *PhoneNumber* is a text field, Left(PhoneNumber,3) returns the three leftmost characters in a phone number, most usually the area code.

Date functions are also widely used. Sometimes you need to use only a portion of a date in a calculation, such as only the month or only the year. The Month() function returns the month in the form of an integer, while the Year() function returns the four-digit year. For example, Month(#9-May-2001#) returns 5 (May is the 5th month), and Year(#05/09/01#) returns 2001. The number symbols (#) are used to mark the beginning and end of a date. The function Date() and the function Now() both return today's date and are useful in criteria. For example, you might want to specify only those items that are more than 30 days old by using the criterion: < Date() − 30.

Appendix B contains a list of all Access functions with descriptions and examples. You can also find out more about a specific function by using Access help.

Referencing Other Objects in Expressions

An expression can include any data found in the database by using an object identifier. The object identifier contains the name of the object and the field or control containing the data. A calculation in one query can use a field in another query, a field in a table, or a control on a form. For example, a date entered by a user on a form could be used to control the data displayed in a query. Only records that match the month would be shown.

Object identifiers are the complete names of Access objects. All objects are grouped into collections such as tables, forms, queries, and so forth. Objects are grouped this way in the Navigation Pane. Every object identifier begins with the collection name, followed by the object name, and then the field or control name. Names of collections and objects are separated by exclamation points. In general, the format for an object identifier is:

> **[Collection name]![Object Name]![Field or Control Name]**

For example, there's a form in the *G3_Ch8* database called *frmSalesMonth* with a combo box named *cboMonth*. To refer to this combo box, use the following object identifier:

> **[Forms]![frmSalesMonth]![cboMonth]**

Try It Yourself 8.4.4 uses this object identifier in a query parameter to control the records displayed in the query.

8.5   Viewing Property Sheets

All Access objects have properties that describe and define the object. Chapter 2 introduced field properties, characteristics of fields that can be set in a table's Design view. Forms and reports have properties, as do all the controls found on a form or report. Queries and the fields used in them also have properties. All properties can be changed by opening their property sheet to customize the behavior or appearance of an object.

Query Property Sheets

A property sheet is a dialog box that allows you to view or edit the properties or characteristics of an object. Property sheets can be opened in the Design view of any object by clicking on the Property Sheet button or selecting the Properties command from the shortcut menu (see Figure 8.33).

Queries have properties that affect the overall query, such as the location of the data source and which records should be included in the dynaset. The properties of a field used in a query are a subset of the field properties defined in the source table, such as format and caption.

How to Set Properties for a Query and Its Fields

1. Open a query in Design view.

2. Select the query or a field. The entire query can be selected by clicking anywhere outside the design grid and the field lists. The easiest way is to click on the background in the upper part of the query screen.

3. Open the property sheet by:

   Right-clicking and selecting the Properties command from the menu (see Figure 8.33)

TRY IT YOURSELF 8.4.4

A. Open the query *qryG3Amount* in Design view.

B. Add the following criteria to the calculated field *SalesMonth*:

   [Forms]![frmSalesMonth]! [cboMonth]

C. Save and close the query.

D. Open the form *frmSalesMonth*, and select a month.

E. Run the query *qryG3Amount*. It should display only those items sold in the selected month.

F. Close both the form and the query.

Q: What if I don't understand a property?

A: Click on the property row in the property sheet, and press F1 for help.

TRY IT YOURSELF 8.5.1

A. Open the query *qryG3Amount* in Design view.

B. Change the Format property of field *G3Amount* to Currency. Refer to Figures 8.33 and 8.34.

C. Save the query.

D. Open *frmSalesMonth* and select month 5.

E. Run the query and note the format of *G3Amount*.

F. Close the query and the form.

OR

Clicking on the Properties Sheet button in the Show/Hide group of the ribbon Design tab (see Figure 8.33).

The property sheet opens on the right side of the screen.

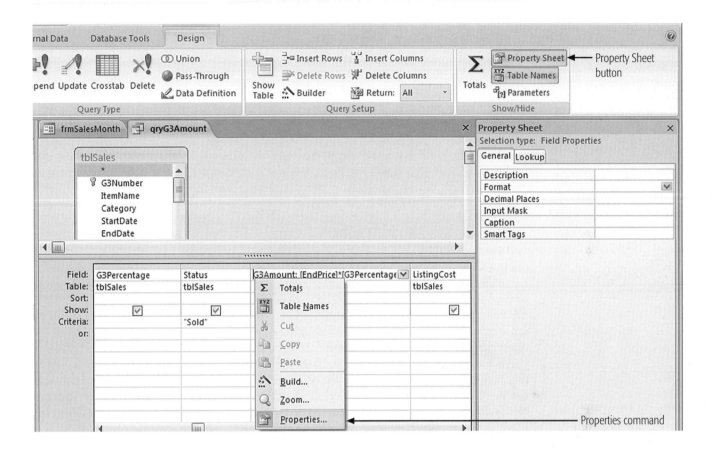

4. In the property sheet, click on the row next to the property you want to set and change the value (see Figure 8.34). You can change values by selecting from a drop-down list (see Figure 8.34), by typing, or by using the Expression Builder.

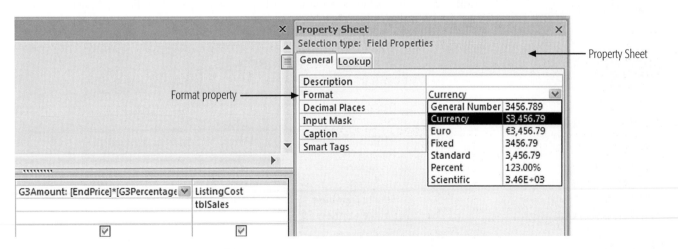

Figure 8.34 Property Sheet for *G3Amount* field

You may find that data values produced by multiplication and division often have too many decimal places in their display. When this happens, data doesn't match the format of other numbers displayed in the dynaset and can be difficult to read. Use the field properties to change the format and the number of decimal places of the data to remedy this problem.

The property sheet can be moved around the screen by dragging the title bar. It can be closed by clicking on the X or Close button in the upper right corner of the property sheet.

Displaying Unique Values and Records

There are two properties that make a query display only unique data values, the Unique Records property and the Unique Values property. Either of these properties can be set to "Yes" or "No," but only one of these properties can be set to "Yes" at a time. If the Unique Values property is set to "Yes," Access automatically sets the Unique Records property to "No" and vice versa. One important detail to remember is that if either property is set, you can't update the data in the query Datasheet view.

When the Unique Records property is set, the query will return only unique records in the dynaset. A record will not be included if it contains the same data in every field as another record. All of the fields in the data source are compared, not just those fields included in the query. The Unique Records property is only available when more than one table is used in the query, so the data must be unique in all the fields from all the tables or queries used in one joined record.

The Unique Records property is often used to display data from the "one" table in a one-to-many join, with criteria being applied to the "many" table. Because the same record from the "one" table may match many records, multiple occurrences of the same data could appear in the dynaset. The trick is to not include any fields from the "many" table that may have different data values in records that are otherwise the same. If a field must be included because it's included in the query criteria, uncheck its Show box in the query grid, and duplicates will not be included in the dynaset.

For example, using the *G3* database, the table *tblPurchasePlaces* shows all possible places to buy. If you want to see a list of all the actual places items have been bought, you can run a query showing all the records in *tblPurchasePlaces* plus matching records from *tblPurchases*. To see only the unique records, uncheck the Show box for all fields except *PlaceName* from *tblPurchases* and set the Unique Records property to Yes.

TRY IT YOURSELF 8.5.2

A. Using the *G3_Ch8* database, open the query *qryPurchase-Places*. There are 15 records.

B. Go to the Design view and set the Unique Records property to "Yes" (see Figure 8.35).

C. View the dynaset again. You should still see 15 records because all the values in the *ItemName* field are different.

D. Go to the Design view and uncheck the Show box for the *ItemName* field.

E. View the dynaset again. You should now see only three unique records.

F. Save and close the query.

How to Display Unique Records in a Query

1. Open the query in Design view.

2. Display the property sheet for the query.

3. Change the value of the Unique Records property to Yes (see Figure 8.35).

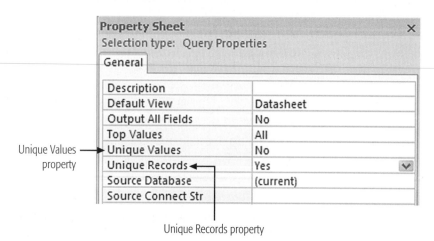

Figure 8.35 Setting the Unique Records property

When the Unique Values property is set, the query will select only records with unique values in the fields included in the query. If multiple fields are used in the query, the combination of values in all fields must be different for a given record to be included when the query is run. This property can't be set for just one field, unless the query contains only one field.

How to Display Unique Values in a Query

1. Open the query in Design view.
2. Display the query property sheet.
3. Change the value of the Unique Values property to Yes.

Professional Tip: Eliminating Ambiguous Joins

When three or more joined tables are used as a data source in a query, it's possible to get more than one dynaset, depending on how the tables are joined. When joins can be interpreted in more than one way, Access generates an error message saying the query cannot be executed because of ambiguous outer joins. Using only inner joins in queries will eliminate this error; however, inner joins don't always produce the dynaset you want.

Here's an example that you can follow along with by using the query *qryTalentInstruments* found in the *MusicMedia_Ch8* database. The purpose of this query is to list all talent used in the production of the music media, and the instrument(s) they play. The names of the talent come from the table *tblTalent*, the products they created are found in the table *tblTalentProducts*, and the instruments are listed in the table *tblProducts*. All talent should be included in the list, even if they have no matching products and instruments.

Open the query *qryTalentInstruments* in Design view and you'll see that *tblTalent* has an outer join to *tblTalentProducts*. This should include all records from *tblTalent*, and only those records from *tblTalentProducts* that match a record in *tblTalent*. Table *tblTalentProducts* has an inner join to *tblProducts*, which will include only records that have a match in both tables. This should produce the list you want. However, an error occurs when you try to run the query because these joins can be interpreted in two ways:

1. The tables *tblTalent* and *tblTalentProducts* are outer joined first, giving a list of all people in *tblTalent* (with or without a matching product). Then, this dynaset is inner joined to *tblProducts*, giving a list of instruments for matching records only. Only the people in *tblTalent* that have created a product are listed.
2. The tables *tblTalentProducts* and *tblProducts* are inner joined first, giving a list of all products, instruments, and the talent they feature. Then, *tblTalent* is outer joined to this dynaset, giving a list of all talent, even if they have no matching products and instruments.

Two queries for each of the above scenarios have been constructed to show these results. For scenario 1, look at the queries *qryTalentProductJoin1A* and *qryTalentProductJoin1B*. For scenario 2, look at the queries *qryTalentProductJoin2A* and *qryTalentProductJoin2B*.

The original query, *qryTalentInstruments*, needs to have the joins changed so that the ambiguity is removed and the data can be obtained from one query. Changing both joins to inner joins doesn't produce the right list. You must set up the joins as follows:

- Tables *tblTalent* and *tblTalentProducts* are outer joined, with all records from *tblTalent* included.
- Tables *tblTalentProducts* and *tblProducts* are outer joined, with all records from *tblTalentProducts* included.

Change the joins and run the query. Now, all that remains is to eliminate duplicate records. Enable the Unique Values property on the query and the result should produce the list you want.

Q: What if I set the Unique Values property to Yes and still see multiple duplicate records?

A: You probably included too many fields. Restrict the query to display only the field or fields that contain duplicate values.

TRY IT YOURSELF 8.5.3

A. Create a new query using *tblPurchases* and include all fields. The dynaset should include 15 records.
B. Go to the Design view and set the Unique Values property to "Yes," and remove the field *PurchaseID* from the query.
C. View the dynaset. You should see only 13 records. The duplicates have been removed.
D. Save and close the query.

8.6 Defining SQL

SQL stands for Structured Query Language; it is pronounced "sequel" or by saying each letter separately. SQL is used to manage data in a database. SQL can be used to create data objects, such as tables, and also to retrieve data from existing data objects. SQL is part of most database products, not just Access, and is the most commonly used query language. Although there's a standard set of SQL commands, not all database products use the entire set. However, most SQL queries are portable from one database product to another.

Using SQL, it's possible to construct queries that can be run with data stored on a remote server. Multiple users, using client computers, can access the data simultaneously. When a database can respond to SQL queries originating from client computers, it's called an SQL server database. The back end of a database, the database containing all objects except tables, controls the application from your computer. The front end of the database, the tables, are stored on the SQL server.

Introducing SQL

SQL is a language for query building. SQL statements are instructions for retrieving data, creating tables, or modifying tables. SQL is not a true programming language because SQL statements specify the task to be done, but not how to do it. For example, most programming languages have constructs for looping (repeating a set of instructions) and branching (switching to another set of instructions), but SQL does not.

Every query created in Access has an underlying SQL statement. You can see the SQL statement by opening a query in Design view, and switching to the SQL view. You can create or edit a query using the SQL view, then save it the same way all queries are saved. If the SQL statement is changed in a query, the corresponding changes are automatically made to the query in Design view. Most of the time, it's easiest to create queries in the Design view, but a few SQL commands cannot be created in the Design view grid, making it necessary to enter the SQL statement directly.

TRY IT YOURSELF 8.6.1

A. Open the query *qryPurchases*, then go to Design view.

B. Go to the SQL view (see Figure 8.36).

C. Examine the SQL statement. It should resemble Figure 8.37.

D. Insert the field *UnitCost* into the list (see Figure 8.37). Be sure to put a comma in front of the item.

E. Run the query.

F. Close and save the query.

How to View and Edit an SQL Statement

1. Open the query in Design view.

2. Click on the View button at the left end of the ribbon Home or Design tab, and select the SQL View command (see Figure 8.36)

   OR

   Right-click on the query name on the tab (see Figure 8.36), and select SQL View from the Shortcut menu.

3. The SQL window appears as shown in Figure 8.37. Once the SQL statement is visible, it can be edited and saved.

Text can be added and edited in the SQL window in the same way as any other text-processing software. Items can be cut, copied, and pasted using the toolbar buttons. However, items can't be moved by selecting and dragging them.

When you save and close a query while in SQL view, it will re-open in SQL view next time you open it in Design view. To return to the Design view, click on the Design View command on the View button menu.

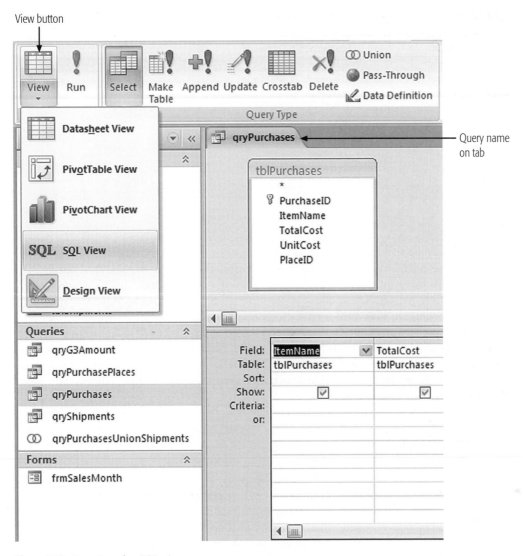

Figure 8.36 Opening the SQL view

Field added in Try It Yourself 8.6.1

Figure 8.37 The SQL window

Comparing Query Types

SQL commands can create all Access query types. Table 8.4 shows the Access query types and their equivalent SQL commands. Using the TRANSFORM command to create a Crosstab query is legal in Access, but it's not part of the standard set of SQL commands. All other queries are standard.

Table 8.4 Access Query Types and Their Equivalent SQL Statements

Access Query Type	Equivalent SQL Command
Select queries	SELECT
Total queries	SELECT with a GROUP BY clause
Append queries	INSERT INTO
Update queries	UPDATE
Delete queries	DELETE
Make-Table queries	SELECT INTO
Crosstab queries	TRANSFORM
Parameter queries	PARAMETER

Data manipulation queries use the Data Manipulation Language, or DML, part of SQL. DML commands retrieve, update, and organize the data in tables, and can be created in Design view. All of the commands shown in Table 8.4 are DML commands.

There are three additional query types—Union queries, Pass-Through queries, and Data Definition queries. These query types must all be created using SQL. Union queries allow data from multiple tables to be combined, even if the tables have no fields in common. Pass-Through queries allow queries to be run on a server rather than on a local machine. Running queries locally is the default. Data Definition queries use the Data Definition Language, or DDL, part of SQL. DDL commands create new tables and change the structure of tables. Table structure changes include adding, editing, and deleting fields and field properties.

Examining SQL Syntax

The easiest way to compare an SQL statement with its Access counterpart is to switch between the Design view and SQL view of the query. Examining different types of queries in both views can provide insight into how SQL statements are constructed.

An SQL statement always starts with a command, followed by a list of parameters. The parameters provide additional information needed to carry out the command. Parameters are composed of variables—user-defined information—and keywords—special words that designate how the variable is to be used with the SQL command. For example, the following SQL statement retrieves data from five fields in *tblSales*.

SELECT ItemName, StartDate, EndDate, StartPrice, EndPrice

FROM tblSales;

In this example, SELECT is the SQL command and everything else is a parameter. The word FROM is a keyword specifying that the table or query name that follows is the data source. The table name *tblSales* is a variable identifying the table to be used, and the five field names between the words SELECT and FROM are variables that identify the fields to be included. Notice that the keywords and commands are typed in uppercase letters, and variables are typed in lowercase with initial capitals. This helps you easily identify the parts of an SQL statement.

Punctuation is used in several places in a statement. Field names are separated by commas, as are all items in lists of variables. Field names begin with the name of the table or query, which is separated from the rest of the field name by a period. For example, *tblSales.ItemName* indicates the field *ItemName* from the table *tblSales*. SQL statements always end with a semicolon (;), although Access will execute statements without it (other software may not).

An SQL statement can continue over multiple lines without any special end-of-line or continuation characters. This allows you to break the statements into lines that are easy to read.

Square brackets must be used to enclose any object names that contain spaces. For example, the field *Dept ID* must be written as [Dept ID] in an SQL statement. Square brackets must also enclose any object names containing characters that SQL considers illegal, such as the forward slash (/).

Parentheses are often used to group items in an SQL statement. Use them in the same manner as in expressions—to force precedence in operations or to enclose arguments in functions. SQL will often add parentheses to criteria, as in the following example.

SELECT tblSales.ItemName, tblSales.EndPrice, tblSales.G3Percentage, tblSales.Status

FROM tblSales

WHERE (((tblSales.Status)="Sold"));

In this example, parentheses enclose the criteria following the WHERE keyword. SQL added an extra set of parentheses to the command; the query will run with or without the extra parentheses.

When describing the syntax of SQL statements, certain conventions will be used. They are described in Table 8.5 below.

Table 8.5 SQL Syntax Elements

Element	Convention
COMMANDS	Uppercase letters
KEYWORDS	Uppercase letters
variables	Lowercase letters
[]	Optional item
, ...	List can contain as many items as needed
|	Use only one of the items in the list, read as "or"

Consider the following example.

CREATE [UNIQUE] INDEX indexname ON tablename (fieldname [ASC | DESC], ...)

[WITH PRIMARY | DISALLOW NULL | IGNORE | NULL];

In this statement, CREATE INDEX is the command and UNIQUE is an optional keyword. The words indexname, tablename, and fieldname are variables. Actual object names are substituted in their places in a statement. Field names are required, and must be enclosed in parentheses. A field name may be followed by either the word ASC or DESC (optional), and there can be as many field names listed as needed. The WITH clause is optional, but if it's used, it must be followed by either PRIMARY, DISALLOW NULL, IGNORE, or NULL. So an actual CREATE INDEX statement might look like this:

CREATE INDEX StateIndex ON (tblBuyers (State)) WITH DISALLOW NULL;

This statement creates an index named *StateIndex* on the table *tblBuyers*, using the field *State*. For the index to be created, null values are not allowed in either of these fields.

8.7 Retrieving Data with the Select Statement

The SELECT statement is the most frequently used SQL command. It selects field values, or columns of data, from one or more tables. The SELECT command can sort, group, use multiple tables, and apply criteria to restrict records.

When Access creates an SQL statement from an existing query, it always adds the name of the table in front of the field name and separates them with a dot. The SQL statement does not require this format if only one table is used, so in that case the table name and dot can be omitted from the field name.

TRY IT YOURSELF 8.7.1

A. Using the *Practice8* database, create a new query *qrySalesSQL* by typing an SQL statement.

B. Include the fields *Category*, *EndPrice*, and *ItemName*.

C. View the dynaset.

D. Save and close the query.

Selecting Data From One Table

The simplest form of the SELECT command has the following syntax.

SELECT fieldname [, ...] FROM tablename;

The field names must be valid fields in the table, and are separated by commas if more than one field is listed. For example, the following statement retrieves the fields *ItemName*, *Category*, and *EndPrice* from *tblSales*.

SELECT ItemName, Category, EndPrice FROM tblSales;

To retrieve all fields from a table, use the symbol * as follows:

SELECT * FROM tblSales;

The WHERE keyword allows criteria to be added to restrict the number of records retrieved, and is the equivalent of adding criteria to the query grid. The syntax of a SELECT statement containing WHERE criteria is as follows:

SELECT fieldname [, ...] FROM tablename
WHERE expression;

Any valid expression can follow the WHERE keyword, as long as it contains a field name, a relational operator, and a value. For example, the expression **EndPrice > 20** contains a field name (EndPrice), an operator (>), and a value (20). The relational operators used by SQL are the same as those used by other Access expressions, and are shown below in Table 8.6.

Table 8.6   Relational Operators

Operator	Meaning
=	Equal
<>	Not Equal
<	Less Than
>	Greater Than
<=	Less Than or Equal To
>=	Greater Than or Equal To
LIKE	Match a text string using a combination of values and wildcards
BETWEEN... AND	Match values that fall within a range of values

Let's take a look at some examples of SELECT statements that include criteria. The following statement retrieves only those records where the field *Category* equals 1 (1 is the *CategoryID* for clothing).

SELECT ItemName, Category, EndPrice FROM tblSales
WHERE Category = 1;

TRY IT YOURSELF 8.7.2

A. Open the query *qrySalesSQL* in SQL view and add a criterion to select only clothing.

B. View the dynaset and save the query as *qrySalesSQL-2*.

C. Change the query to retrieve all items with an end price of more than $20.

D. View the dynaset and save the query as *qrySalesSQL-3*.

To find records in which the field *EndPrice* is greater than $20.00, use the following statement:

SELECT ItemName, Category, EndPrice FROM tblSales
WHERE EndPrice > 20;

Date values should be delimited with the symbol # as shown below.

SELECT ItemName, EndPrice FROM tblSales
WHERE EndDate > #5/1/08#;

Text values should be enclosed with either single or double quotes as in the following example.

SELECT ItemName, Category FROM tblSales
WHERE Status = "Not Sold";

The LIKE operator is used to match text strings using a combination of values and wildcards. LIKE retrieves records where the value in a field contains the text specified in the LIKE parameter. The wildcard * matches anything. When it follows a string, the string must occur at the beginning of the field. When it precedes a string, the string must occur at the end of the field. When it encloses the string, the string may occur anywhere in the field. For example, **ItemName LIKE 'vintage*'**, retrieves all records where the field *ItemName* starts with the word 'vintage', **ItemName LIKE '*vintage'**, retrieves all records where the field *ItemName* ends with the word 'vintage'; and **ItemName LIKE '*vintage*'**, retrieves all records where the field *ItemName* contains the word 'vintage'. The following statement retrieves all items with names containing the word 'vintage':

SELECT ItemName FROM tblSales

WHERE ItemName LIKE '*vintage*'

The BETWEEN operator is used to match values that fall within a range of values. The syntax of BETWEEN is:

Fieldname BETWEEN value1 AND value2;

If the value in the named field is greater than or equal to value1, and less than or equal to value2, the record is retrieved. The following statement retrieves all records where the field *EndPrice* is greater than or equal to 9.99, and less than or equal to 15.

SELECT ItemName, EndPrice FROM tblSales

WHERE EndPrice BETWEEN 9.99 AND 15;

Expressions in WHERE criteria can be joined using the operators AND and OR. When two expressions are joined by AND, both expressions must be true for the record to be included. When two expressions are joined by OR, either expression can be true for the record to be included. The following statement retrieves records where the item name contains the word 'vintage' and where the field *EndPrice* is greater than or equal to 9.99 and less than or equal to 15.

SELECT ItemName, EndPrice FROM tblSales

WHERE ItemName LIKE '*vintage*' AND EndPrice BETWEEN 9.99 AND 15;

The dynaset resulting from this query contains seven records, and is shown in Figure 8.38.

ItemName	EndPr
6 Vintage Red Yellow Striped Napkins Linen Never Used	$14.07
Vintage Bakelite Hair Comb Art Deco/Late Vict	$10.19
3 Vintage Colorado Ski Tickets 60s Winter Pk	$10.50
Vintage Indianapolis 500 ticket stub 1965	$10.37
Vintage Handheld Fan	$12.00
Shabby Chic Kitchen Vintage Egg Beater Red	$11.00
Vintage, 1963 Popeil Veg O Matic	$15.00

Figure 8.38 Result for Try It Yourself 8.7.3

TRY IT YOURSELF 8.7.3

A. Use *tblSales* to create a new query called *qrySalesVintage*. Include the fields *ItemName* and *EndPrice*.

B. Add a WHERE criterion to select records where the item name contains the word 'vintage' and where the field *EndPrice* is greater than or equal to 9.99 and less than or equal to 15.

C. View the dynaset. It should resemble Figure 8.38.

D. Save and close the query.

When multiple ANDs and ORs are used in criteria, parentheses may be needed to specify the order of evaluation. ANDs are executed before ORs, so use parentheses if an OR should be evaluated first. For example, let's say we need a list of all items in Category 1 or 3 that are for sale. The criteria we type in first are:

WHERE Category = 1 OR Category = 3 AND Status = "For Sale"

TRY IT YOURSELF 8.7.4

A. Create a new query named *qrySalesAndOr* using *tblSales*. Include the fields *ItemName*, *Category*, and *Status*.

B. Add a WHERE criterion to select a list of all items in Category 1 and 3 that are for sale, but omit the parentheses as shown in the first example at right.

C. View the dynaset. It should resemble in Figure 8.39.

D. Add the parentheses to the WHERE criterion as shown in the second example at right.

E. View the dynaset. It should resemble in Figure 8.40.

F. Save and close the query.

Because ANDs are evaluated first, all records where **Category = 3 AND Status = "For Sale"** are selected. Then the OR is evaluated, which adds all records where **Category = 1** regardless of status. Parentheses need to be added to the expression as follows:

WHERE (Category = 1 OR Category = 3) AND Status = "For Sale"

Now, the OR is evaluated first, giving all items in Category 1 or 3, then the AND is evaluated, giving only items for sale in those groups. Figure 8.39 shows the dynaset from queries using the two WHERE clauses above.

ItemName	Category	Status
Beautiful Antique Lace Tablecloth	Kitchen wares	For Sale
6 Vintage Red Yellow Striped Napkins Linen Never Use	Kitchen wares	Sold
Vintage Tablecloth Fruit Cherries 1940s Excellent Cond	Kitchen wares	Sold
Salt&Pepper shakers glass&silverplated tray	Kitchen wares	Not Sold
VEG O MATIC ...1961	Kitchen wares	Sold
WOODEN HAMBURGER PRESS...RETRO 60's	Kitchen wares	For Sale
WOODEN RECIPE FILE BOX...RETRO 60's	Kitchen wares	For Sale
Silver plated tea and coffee pot set	Kitchen wares	For Sale
William Rogers silver plate water pitcher	Kitchen wares	For Sale
Japanese Lusterware Salt and Pepper Set	Kitchen wares	Sold
ENGLISH VILLAGE SERVING BOWL..JAPAN	Kitchen wares	Not Sold
PAIR OF PITCHERS FOR OIL & VINEGAR..JAPAN	Kitchen wares	Not Sold
ALFRED MEAKIN SERVING PIECES...LOT OF 3	Kitchen wares	Sold
FIRE-KING CREAM AND SUGAR	Kitchen wares	For Sale
FRANKOMA Bean Pot/Casserole	Kitchen wares	For Sale
Vintage Baby Shoes Leather 1930 Good Cond	Clothing	For Sale
Shabby Chic Kitchen Vintage Egg Beater Red	Kitchen wares	Sold
VINTAGE SILVER PLATE CREAM AND SUGAR SET	Kitchen wares	Not Sold
Lot 2 Canisters 40s Ransburg Black Floral VG	Kitchen wares	Sold
ANTIQUE KITCHEN FOOD GRATER	Kitchen wares	Sold
Vintage..Daher Ware serving tray	Kitchen wares	Not Sold
Vintage, 1963 Popeil Veg O Matic	Kitchen wares	Sold
VINTAGE WOODEN BREAD BOX...C@@L!!	Kitchen wares	For Sale
Vintage Foley Flour Sifter..Three Screen	Kitchen wares	For Sale

Figure 8.39 Dynaset from Query Without Parentheses

ItemName	Category	Status
Beautiful Antique Lace Tablecloth	Kitchen wares	For Sale
WOODEN HAMBURGER PRESS...RETRO 60's	Kitchen wares	For Sale
WOODEN RECIPE FILE BOX...RETRO 60's	Kitchen wares	For Sale
Silver plated tea and coffee pot set	Kitchen wares	For Sale
William Rogers silver plate water pitcher	Kitchen wares	For Sale
FIRE-KING CREAM AND SUGAR	Kitchen wares	For Sale
FRANKOMA Bean Pot/Casserole	Kitchen wares	For Sale
Vintage Baby Shoes Leather 1930 Good Cond	Clothing	For Sale
VINTAGE WOODEN BREAD BOX...C@@L!!	Kitchen wares	For Sale
Vintage Foley Flour Sifter..Three Screen	Kitchen wares	For Sale

Figure 8.40 Dynaset from Query with Parentheses

The WHERE clause isn't the only way of restricting the records retrieved. A keyword can be added immediately following the word SELECT to eliminate duplicates or include only the top values. These keywords are ALL, DISTINCT, DISTINCT ROW, and TOP. The syntax of this clause is:

SELECT ALL | DISTINCT | DISTINCT ROW |

TOP number | TOP percent PERCENT

fieldname [, ...] FROM tablename;

The ALL keyword returns all records, and is the default value. DISTINCT and DISTINCT ROW eliminate duplicate records in the same way as setting the properties Unique Records and Unique Values. DISTINCT is the equivalent of the property Unique Records, and DISTINCT ROW is the equivalent of the property Unique Values. The keyword DISTINCT ROW, like property Unique Values, is used only with joined tables. TOP can only be used when the records are sorted, and will return the top number or percentage of records as specified. It has the same effect as selecting a value from the Top Values box in query Design view.

The following statement retrieves a list of item names from *tblPurchases* with each name appearing only once in the list.

SELECT DISTINCT ItemName FROM tblPurchases;

The resulting dynaset of this query is shown in Figure 8.41.

ItemName
1950s Tablecloth with Cowboy Motif
2 Candlewick Bedspreads from the 1940s
4 Antique Tablecloths with lace
Antique Souvenir Tablecloth Hawaii Unused
Box of Assorted Dinner Napkins Linen
Box of kitchen towels embroidered 1940s
Embroidered Pillow Case
Florida State Souvenir Tablecloth Retro Style
Souvenir California State Map Tablecloth
Vintage Germany Souvenir Tablecloth
Vintage Souvenir Tablecloth Alaska

Figure 8.41 Result for Try It Yourself 8.7.5

> **TRY IT YOURSELF 8.7.5**
>
> A. Create a new query called *qryDistinctPurchases*. Use *tblPurchases* and add only the field *ItemName*.
> B. View the dynaset.
> C. Go to the SQL view and add the DISTINCT keyword as shown in the example in the text at right.
> D. View the dynaset. It should resemble Figure 8.41.
> E. Save and close the query.

Sorting records is done by adding the ORDER BY keywords. The syntax of a SELECT statement containing ORDER BY criteria is as follows:

SELECT fieldname [, ...] FROM tablename

ORDER BY fieldname [, ...] [DESC];

The field name following the keywords ORDER BY determines the sort order, and more than one field may be listed. The optional keyword DESC sorts in descending order.

For example, the following statement sorts the list of items in ascending alphabetical order.

SELECT DISTINCT ItemName FROM tblPurchases ORDER BY ItemName;

To sort the records in descending order, add the DESC keyword at the end of the ORDER BY clause, as shown below.

SELECT DISTINCT ItemName FROM tblPurchases

ORDER BY ItemName DESC;

To sort the records on multiple fields, list the fields separated by commas. The records will be sorted by the first field, then records that have the same value in that field are sorted by the values in the next field listed, and so forth. The following example sorts albums by place purchased and item name.

SELECT PlaceID, ItemName FROM tblPurchases

ORDER BY PlaceID, ItemName;

To select top values from a sorted dynaset, use both the TOP and ORDER BY keywords. For example, to select the top 8 records from the list of purchases, use the following statement:

SELECT TOP 8 PlaceID, ItemName FROM tblPurchases

ORDER BY PlaceID, ItemName;

The resulting dynaset for the above query is shown in Figure 8.42.

TRY IT YOURSELF 8.7.6

A. Create a new query called *qryTopPurchasesSorted*. Use *tblPurchases* and add the fields *PlaceId* and *ItemName*.

B. Add an ORDER BY clause that will perform an ascending sort by *Place* and *Name* as shown in the example in the text at right.

C. Select only the top 8 records.

D. View the dynaset. It should resemble Figure 8.42.

E. Save and close the query.

PlaceID	ItemName
Garage Sale	1950s Tablecloth with Cowboy Motif
Garage Sale	Florida State Souvenir Tablecloth Retro Style
Garage Sale	Vintage Germany Souvenir Tablecloth
Auction	4 Antique Tablecloths with lace
Auction	Antique Souvenir Tablecloth Hawaii Unused
Auction	Box of Assorted Dinner Napkins Linen
Auction	Box of kitchen towels embroidered 1940s
Auction	Florida State Souvenir Tablecloth Retro Style

Figure 8.42 Result for Try It Yourself 8.7.6

A percentage of records is retrieved by adding the keyword PERCENT after the value. For example, to select the top 10% of the records from the purchases table use this statement:

SELECT TOP 10 PERCENT PlaceID, ItemName

FROM tblPurchases ORDER BY PlaceID, ItemName;

Of course, SQL statements can contain both the WHERE and ORDER BY keywords. The example below will display the fields *PlaceID*, *ItemName*, and *TotalCost* in *tblPurchases*. It will select only records for items bought at garage sales, and records will be sorted on *ItemName* and *TotalCost*.

SELECT PlaceID, ItemName, TotalCost FROM tblPurchases

WHERE PlaceID = 1

ORDER BY ItemName, TotalCost;

Using Joined Tables

Data can be retrieved from multiple tables using the JOIN keyword. Adding JOIN to a statement is the equivalent of adding tables in the query Design view, and specifying their join types. The syntax for a JOIN in a SELECT statement is:

SELECT fieldname [, ...] FROM table 1

INNER JOIN | LEFT OUTER JOIN | RIGHT OUTER JOIN table2 ON table1.keyfield=table2.foreignkeyfield;

SQL requires that you specify the join type—inner, left outer, or right outer. Access will accept LEFT JOIN and RIGHT JOIN, allowing the omission of the word OUTER. In an SQL statement, left and right refer to the position of a table relative to the JOIN keyword. The table in which the common field is the primary key, table1, is always listed on the left side. In a one-to-many join, table1 is the "one" table and table2 is the "many" table. A LEFT OUTER JOIN would join all records from table1 to all matching records in table2; a RIGHT OUTER JOIN would join all records from table2 to all matching records in table1; and an INNER JOIN would include only those records that have a matching value in both tables.

All field names are listed before the FROM keyword, regardless of the source table. When using multiple tables, field names must be preceded by the source table name and a dot. For example, the field *ItemName* in *tblPurchases* must be expressed as *tblPurchases.ItemName*.

Here are some examples using the tables *tblPurchases* and *tblSales*. In this case, *tblPurchases* is table1 and *tblSales* is table2 because every item in *tblPurchases* can have multiple records in *tblSales*.

To see a list of all item names, costs, and sales prices use the following statement:

SELECT tblPurchases.ItemName, tblPurchases.TotalCost, tblSales.ItemName, tblSales.EndPrice FROM tblPurchases

LEFT JOIN tblSales on tblPurchases.PurchaseID = tblSales.PurchaseID;

This example produces a list of item names, costs, and sales prices from every purchase in *tblPurchases*. There are 15 records in the dynaset, as shown in Figure 8.43. No data is shown in field *tblSales.ItemName* if the item hasn't been put up for sale yet.

> **TRY IT YOURSELF 8.7.7**
>
> A. Create a new query called *qryPurchasesLeft* based on *tblPurchases* and *tblSales*. Include the *ItemName* field from both tables, the *TotalCost* from *tblPurchases* and *EndPrice* from *tblSales*.
> B. Specify a left join where all records from *tblPurchases* are included.
> C. View the dynaset and save the query. It should look like Figure 8.43.
> D. Change the query to an inner join where only the records with values in both tables are included.
> E. View the dynaset and save the query as *qryPurchasesInner*. It should look like Figure 8.44.

tblPurchases.ItemName	TotalCost	tblSales.ItemName	EndPrice
1950s Tablecloth with Cowboy Motif	$2.00	Vintage Tablecloth Fruit Cherries 1940s Excellent Cond	$19.85
4 Antique Tablecloths with lace	$6.00	Beautiful Antique Lace Tablecloth	$0.00
2 Candlewick Bedspreads from the 1940s	$8.50		
Box of Assorted Dinner Napkins Linen	$5.00	6 Vintage Red Yellow Striped Napkins Linen Never Use	$14.07
Box of kitchen towels embroidered 1940s	$3.50		
Embroidered Pillow Case	$1.00		
Vintage Souvenir Tablecloth Alaska	$9.99		
Florida State Souvenir Tablecloth Retro Style	$6.99		
Antique Souvenir Tablecloth Hawaii Unused	$14.99		
Souvenir California State Map Tablecloth	$9.99		
Vintage Souvenir Tablecloth Alaska	$3.99		
Vintage Germany Souvenir Tablecloth	$8.99		
Florida State Souvenir Tablecloth Retro Style	$4.99		
2 Candlewick Bedspreads from the 1940s	$8.50		
Embroidered Pillow Case	$1.00		

Figure 8.43 Result for Try It Yourself 8.7.7 query *qryPurchasesLeft*

An inner join eliminates those records with no data in *tblSales.ItemName*. The SQL for an inner join is:

SELECT tblPurchases.ItemName, tblPurchases.TotalCost, tblSales.ItemName,tblSales.EndPrice

FROM tblPurchases INNER JOIN tblSales ON tblPurchases.PurchaseID = tblSales.PurchaseID;

This example retrieves only three records as shown in Figure 8.44.

qryPurchasesInner				
tblPurchases.ItemName	TotalCost ▾	tblSales.ItemName	EndPrice ▾	
1950s Tablecloth with Cowboy Motif	$2.00	Vintage Tablecloth Fruit Cherries 1940s Excellent Cond	$19.85	
4 Antique Tablecloths with lace	$6.00	Beautiful Antique Lace Tablecloth	$0.00	
Box of Assorted Dinner Napkins Linen	$5.00	6 Vintage Red Yellow Striped Napkins Linen Never Use	$14.07	

Figure 8.44 Result for Try It Yourself 8.7.7, query *qryPurchasesInner*

Grouping Data

Using the GROUP BY keywords in a SELECT statement is the equivalent of creating a Total query. GROUP BY arranges data into groups depending on the values in one or more fields. Aggregate functions, such as SUM and AVG, can be evaluated for each resulting group of data. In addition, a criterion can be applied to the retrieved records by adding the HAVING keyword. The syntax of the SELECT statement with a GROUP BY clause is:

SELECT fieldname [, ...], *FUNCTION*(fieldname) [, ...] FROM table GROUP BY fieldname[, ...];

The word FUNCTION is not actually used; it represents any function that can be used in a Total query, and should be replaced by one of these function names. The most frequently used functions are sum, avg, count, max, and min. For example, use the following statement to find the average selling price of each category of items:

SELECT Category, Avg(EndPrice) FROM tblSales

GROUP By Category;

This statement finds the highest priced item in each category:

SELECT Category, Max(EndPrice) FROM tblSales GROUP BY Category;

A caption can be added to any field by including the AS keyword and caption text. The caption displays as the column heading in the dynaset. The following statement is the same as the previous example, except the column containing the maximum price is labeled "Highest Price."

SELECT Category, Max(EndPrice) AS HighestPrice

FROM tblSales GROUP BY Category;

When this query is run, three records are retrieved, as shown in Figure 8.45.

qrySalesMaxPrice	
Category ▾	HighestPrice ▾
Clothing	$26.00
Kitchen wares	$19.85
Misc. Collectables	$75.00

Figure 8.45 Result for Try It Yourself 8.7.8

TRY IT YOURSELF 8.7.8

A. Use *tblSales* to create a new query called *qrySalesMaxPrice*. The query should find the item that sold for the highest price in each category.

B. Add the caption "Highest Price" to the column containing the maximum price.

C. View the dynaset. It should resemble Figure 8.45.

D. Save the query.

The HAVING keyword is used with GROUP BY so criteria can be applied to select specific records, because a WHERE clause will not work with grouped data. The syntax for a statement using the HAVING keyword is:

SELECT fieldname [, ...], *FUNCTION*(fieldname) [, ...] FROM table GROUP BY fieldname

HAVING condition;

The condition following the keyword HAVING has the same format as a WHERE condition and can include any field, relational operator, or aggregate function. The condition can contain multiple expressions joined by the AND and OR operators. The following example counts the number of items in each category having four or more items.

> **SELECT tblSales.Category, Count(tblSales.G3Number) AS CountOfItems FROM tblSales**
>
> **GROUP BY tblSales.Category**
>
> **HAVING Count(tblSales.G3Number) > 20;**

The statement above returns two records, as shown in Figure 8.46.

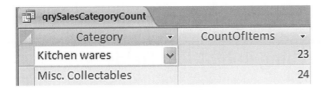

Category	CountOfItems
Kitchen wares	23
Misc. Collectables	24

Figure 8.46 Result for Try It Yourself 8.7.9

The COUNT function can also be used without using GROUP BY. COUNT creates a new column in the query containing a count of records, or a count of values in a specified field. It can be used with either a field name or a wildcard character. The syntax of COUNT is:

> **SELECT COUNT (*) | COUNT(fieldname)**
>
> **AS columnname FROM tablename;**

When COUNT is used with the symbol *, it counts the number of records in the dynaset. The following example counts the number of records in *tblSales* and labels the column "Total Sales."

> **SELECT COUNT(*) AS [Total Sales]**
>
> **FROM [tblSales];**

When COUNT is used to count a field, it returns the number of records without a null value in that field. In the following example, the field "Sold Purchases" displays the number of records with data entered in the *PurchasesID* field.

> **SELECT Count (PurchaseID)**
>
> **AS [Sold Purchases]**
>
> **FROM tblSales;**

Union Queries

Union queries are queries that allow data from two or more tables to be joined and displayed, even though the tables have no fields in common. A union query will display similar data from each table in the same output fields, and it will combine text and number data types if the values in the fields are comparable.

To create a union query, you must use SQL. In the SQL statement, select the fields from each table and join them using the keyword UNION. The easiest way is to first make a query for each table and save it. Each query should contain the fields to be included from the source table. Each query can then be copied and pasted to the union query, which will combine all the queries into one set of output.

For example, the client for the *G3* database would like to see approximately how much money she has spent on acquiring items for sale and how much has been spent on shipping. Since the tables *tablPurchases* and *tblShipping* have no common fields, the only way to collect this data is by using a union query. The following SQL statement creates this union query.

TRY IT YOURSELF 8.7.9

A. Create a new query called *qrySalesCategoryCount* based on *tblSales*. Include the *Category* field and count the number of items in each category. Show only those categories that have more than 20 items sold.

B. Add the caption CountOfItems to the column containing the count.

C. View the dynaset and save the query. It should look like Figure 8.46.

TRY IT YOURSELF 8.7.10

A. Create a new query called *qrySalesCount* using *tblSales*. Count the number of sales and add the caption "Total Sales" to the column containing the count.

B. View the dynaset. It should show a count of 56 sales.

C. Change the query to count the values in the field *PurchaseID*, and have a caption "Sold Purchases" on the column containing the count.

D. View the dynaset. It should show a count of 3 purchases.

E. Save the query as *qrySoldPurchases*.

TRY IT YOURSELF 8.7.11

A. Open the query called *qryPurchasesUnionShipments* and view the dynaset.

B. Change to the SQL view to see the statement behind the union query.

SELECT tblPurchases.ItemName, tblPurchases.TotalCost FROM tblPurchases;

UNION SELECT tblShipments.ShipmentID, tblShipments.ShippingCharge FROM tblShipments

WHERE (((tblShipments.ShippingCharge) Is Not Null));

The query shows the data for *ItemName* and *ShippingID* in the same field, and the data for *TotalCost* and *ShippingCharge* in the same field.

Professional Tip: Matching in Multiple Fields

This tip comes from Jim Stiles, who was introduced in a Chapter 3 tip. Jim hosts a Microsoft Access Tutorial at his Web site "Uncle Jim's Web Designs" located at http://www.jdstiles.com/mso2k/access/.

To search for a criterion in more than one field in a query, use the following SQL:

SELECT Tablename.* FROM TableName

WHERE ((([Field1] & [Field2] & [Field3])

Like "*abc*");

The above example will return any records that contain "abc" in the fields (*Field1*, *Field2*, *Field3*).

Fast Track   A quick guide to procedures learned in this chapter

Creating a Parameter Query

1. Create a new query in Design view.
2. Select the tables for the data source and click the Add button. Close this window when you have finished selecting tables.
3. Enter all fields desired in the query grid.
4. In the Criteria line for the field designated as the parameter field, type a prompt message.

Running the Parameter Query

1. Click the Run button on the ribbon, in the Results group of the Design tab
   OR
   Click the Datasheet view button on the ribbon in the Results group.
   The Parameter dialog box will appear prompting you to enter a value.
2. Enter the criteria you want to match.
3. Click the OK button. The dynaset appears based on the criteria you entered.

Creating a Multifield Parameter Query

1. Create or edit a query in Design view.

2. Select the tables for the data source and click the Add button. Close this window when you have finished selecting tables.

3. Enter all fields desired in the query grid.

4. In the Criteria line for each of the fields designated as the parameter fields, enter a prompt message in square brackets.

Running a Multifield Parameter Query

1. Click the Run button on the ribbon

   OR

   Click the Datasheet button on the ribbon.

   A Parameter dialog box will appear for each parameter field prompting you to enter a value. These dialog boxes will appear in the same order as the criteria appear on the query grid, from left to right.

2. Enter the values you want to match.

3. Click the OK button. If the values entered are valid criteria, the matching records will be displayed.

Creating an Update Query

1. Create a new query using the Design view. Add table(s) and field(s).

2. Click the Update button in the Query Type group on the ribbon Design tab.

   An Update To: row is added to the grid.

3. Type the new data value in the correct field column of the Update To: row. This is the new value that will be written to all matching records.

4. Add the criteria to select the records for updating.

5. Click the Run button.

   A dialog box is displayed with a message warning that records will be updated.

6. Click the Yes button to complete the update process.

   Clicking the No button will cancel the entire process before any records are updated.

Creating a Make-Table Query

1. Create a new query in the Design view.

2. Click the Make-Table button in Query Type group on the ribbon.

   A Make-Table dialog box appears.

3. Type the new table name.

4. Select the location for the new table—either in the current database file or another database file.

5. Click the OK button.

6. Select all fields you want in the new table and enter the criteria.

7. Click the Datasheet view button on the toolbar to preview the result of the query before actually running it, then return to the Design view.

8. Click the Run button on the ribbon.

   A dialog box appears indicating how many records will be copied to the new table.

9. Click the Yes button to complete the process.

   Clicking the No button cancels the process entirely.

Creating an Append Query

1. Create a new query in the Design view using the table containing the data you want to append to the new table. Add the fields and criteria for the records to be appended.

2. Run the query to view the result, then return to the Design view.

3. Convert the Select query to an Append query by clicking the Append button in the Query Type group on the ribbon.

   An Append dialog box appears.

4. Type the name for the destination table, or select it from the drop-down list.

5. Choose the location of the table in either the current database file in another file.

6. Click the OK button.

7. Run the query by clicking the Run button on the ribbon.

   A dialog box appears showing the number of rows about to be appended.

8. Click the Yes button to complete the process, and records will be appended to the table. If you click the No button to cancel the process, no records will be appended.

Creating a Delete Query

1. Create a new query, enter the criteria, and verify the records to be deleted by clicking the Datasheet view button. Return to the Design view.

2. Convert the query to a Delete query by clicking on the Delete button in the Query Type group on the ribbon.

   A Delete row is added to the grid.

3. Run the query by clicking the Run button on the ribbon.

   A Delete dialog box appears, indicating that records will be deleted.

4. Click the Yes button to complete the process. The selected records will be deleted. If you click the No button to cancel the process, no records will be deleted.

Suppressing Warning Messages for Action Queries

1. Click on the Office button and click on the Access Options button. The Access Options dialog box appears.

2. Click on the Advanced group in the left pane.

3. Uncheck the Action queries check box.

4. Click the OK button to close the Access Options dialog box.

Creating a Crosstab Query in Design View

1. Create a new query in the Design view.

2. Select the table(s) for the data source.

3. Click the Crosstab button in the Query Type group on the ribbon.

4. Add the field for the Row Heading to the grid.

5. Select Row Heading from the drop-down list in the Crosstab row, and keep the Group By selection entered in the Total row.

6. Add the field for the Column Heading to the grid.

7. Select Column Heading from the drop-down list in the Crosstab row, and keep the Group By selection entered in the Total row.

8. Add the field for the Value to the grid.

9. Select Value from the drop-down list in the Crosstab row.

10. Select the Calculation for the value (sum, count, and so forth) in the Total row.

11. Specify a criterion or sort order either on the heading field or another field you add to the query.

12. Run the query from the Run button on the ribbon.

Using the Crosstab Query Wizard

1. Click on the Query Wizard button in the Other group of the ribbon Create tab. The New Query dialog box appears.

2. Select Crosstab Query Wizard, and click on the OK button. The Table Selection screen appears.

3. Select the data source for the Crosstab query. Remember that you can use only one table/query for the data source in the wizard.

4. Click the Next button. The Row Heading Selection screen appears.

5. Select the field for the Row Headings. Use the right directional arrows to move the field to the Selected Fields window.

6. Click the Next button. The Column Heading Selection screen appears.

7. Select the Column Heading field.

8. Click on the Next button. The Value Selection screen appears.

9. Select the field containing the Value to be tabulated.

10. Select the Calculation to be performed on this field to produce the Value.

11. Click the Next button. The final screen appears.

12. Enter the title for the Crosstab query and select the view to open the query.

13. Click the Finish button to complete the process.

Creating a Calculated Field With the Expression Builder

1. Create a new query in the Design view.

2. Click on a blank field name in the Field row, where the expression will be entered.

3. Click the right mouse button and select Build from the shortcut menu

   OR

   Click the Builder button on the Design tab of the ribbon Query Setup group. The Expression Builder dialog box opens.

4. Type in the expression in the Expression Builder window

   OR

   Build the expression by clicking buttons and selecting from drop-down lists.

Select the table that contains the field(s) to be used in the expression and click the Paste button to enter it into the Expression Builder window.

Double-clicking on an item will also enter it into the Expression Builder window.

Numbers will always have to be typed in.

Additional operations can be added to create a more complex expression.

5. Click the OK button to close the Expression Builder dialog box and return to the Query Design screen. The expression will be entered into the field cell.

6. Complete and run the query to see the results of the expression.

Manually Creating and Editing a Calculated Field

1. Create or edit a new query in the Deisgn view. Add the appropriate table(s) and fields for the query.

2. Click on an empty field cell to create an expression

   OR

   Click on an existing expression to edit.

3. Click the right mouse button and choose the Zoom command

   OR

   Press the [SHIFT] and [F2] keys to zoom.

4. Type the new field name followed by a colon.

5. Next type the first value to be used in the calculation. If this value is a field name, enclose it in square brackets.

6. Type in the arithmetic operator to be used in the calculation.

7. Type in the second field used in the calculation.

8. Repeat steps 6 and 7 until the expression is complete, then click the OK button to move from the Zoom screen back to the grid.

9. Click the Run button on the ribbon to see the results of the calculated field.

Displaying Available Functions in the Expression Builder

1. Open the Expression Builder.

2. Click on the Functions folder on the left side of the screen.

3. Click on the Built-In Functions subfolder.

4. A list of all available functions will appear in the next two windows.

5. Click on the function you wish to use in the expression and then click the Paste button.

6. When the expression is complete, click the OK button to move back to the Query Design screen.

Setting Properties for a Query and its Fields

1. Open a query in Design view.

2. Select the query or a field. The entire query can be selected by clicking anywhere outside the design grid and the field lists. The easiest way is to click on the background in the upper part of the Query screen.

3. Open the property sheet by:

Right-clicking and selecting the Properties command from the menu

OR

Clicking on the Properties Sheet button in the Show/Hide group of the ribbon Design tab.

The property sheet opens on the right side of the screen.

4. In the property sheet, click on the row next to the property you want to set and change the value. You can change values by selecting from a drop-down list, by typing, or by using the Expression Builder.

Displaying Unique Records in a Query

1. Open the query in Design view.

2. Display the property sheet for the query.

3. Change the value of the Unique Records property to Yes.

Displaying Unique Values in a Query

1. Open the query in Design view.

2. Display the query property sheet.

3. Change the value of the Unique Values property to Yes.

Viewing and Editing the SQL Statement in a Query

1. Open the query.

2. Click on the View button at the left end of the ribbon Home or Design tab and select the SQL View command

OR

Right-click on the query name on the tab and select SQL View from the Shortcut menu.

3. The SQL window appears. Once the SQL statement is visible, it can be edited and saved.

SQL Statements:

RETRIEVING RECORDS

    SELECT fieldname [, ...] FROM tablename

    WHERE expression;

    SELECT ALL | DISTINCT | DISTINCT ROW |

    TOP number | TOP percent PERCENT

    fieldname [, ...] FROM tablename;

RETRIEVING SORTED RECORDS

    SELECT fieldname [, ...] FROM tablename

    ORDER BY fieldname [, ...] [DESC];

RETRIEVING RECORDS FROM MULTIPLE TABLES

SELECT fieldname [, ...] FROM table1

INNER JOIN | LEFT OUTER JOIN | RIGHT OUTER JOIN table2 ON table1.keyfield =
table2.foreignkeyfield;

RETRIEVING AGGREGATE DATA (TOTAL QUERY)

SELECT fieldname [, ...] FUNCTION(fieldname) [, ...] FROM table GROUP BY fieldname
[HAVING condition];

RETRIEVING FIELD AND RECORD COUNTS

SELECT COUNT (*) | COUNT(fieldname)

AS columnname FROM tablename;

Review Questions

1. What is a Parameter query?

2. How might this type of query be used?

3. In a multifield Parameter query, must the records match all parameters entered to be included in the dynaset?

4. Write the identifier for a control named *txtLastName* found on a form named *frmCustomer*.

5. What is an Action query?

6. Why is it important to back up original data before running an Action query?

7. Why would you use a Delete query?

8. What action does an Append query perform?

9. Why is it a good idea to make a Select query before an Action query?

10. Which records will be changed in an Update query?

11. Can you reverse the append process using the Undo command?

12. What is the purpose of a Crosstab query?

13. What are the three parts of a Crosstab query?

14. (T/F) Any field can be used for a Row Heading.

15. (T/F) Crosstab queries created by the wizard automatically have totals added.

16. What is a function?

17. What is an expression?

18. How can you access the Expression Builder screen in Query Design?

19. What is an operator?

20. What is the order of precedence?

21. What is a calculated field?

22. How can you combine two text fields?

23. What is a property sheet?

24. How do you open the property sheet of a query?

25. What is the difference between the Unique Records and Unique Values properties?

26. What does SQL stand for?

27. (T/F) Access creates an SQL statement for every query.

28. (T/F) All SQL statements start with the word SELECT.

29. Which statement is the most frequently used SQL command?

30. When can the table name and dot be omitted in identifying a field?

31. Which keyword allows criteria to be added to restrict the number of records retrieved?

32. To retrieve all addresses on Elm Street, what value should be used after the operator LIKE?

33. Are ANDs or ORs evaluated first?

34. (T/F) Using the TOTAL BY keywords in a SELECT statement is the equivalent of creating a Total query.

Exercises

Exercise 1—Review and Guided Practice

ACTIVITY

Use the *SDAL_Ch8* database.

Exercise 1A: Finding Recordings by Specific Artists or Music Categories

1. Using *tblRecordings*, create a Parameter query that displays all items in any category entered by a user. The query must accept the category name, not the *CategoryID*, and include the fields *Artist*, *Title*, and *Category*. Name the query *qryCategoryParameter*.

2. Using *tblRecordings*, *tblInventory*, and *tblArtists*, create a Parameter query that displays all items in the inventory by any artist entered by a user. The query must accept the artist's name, not the *ArtistID* number. Include the fields *Title*, *Type*, *QuantityOnHand*, and *Price*. Don't display the field *Artist*. Save the query as *qryArtistsParameter*.

Exercise 1B: Using Action Queries to Control Inventory

1. Construct a Make-Table query that creates a table called *tblRockCountryReorders*. The query should include the fields *LabelName*, *Artist*, *Title*, *Type*, *QuantityOnHand*, and *Price*. The table should list all rock or country albums with less than two copies on hand, sorted in order by record label name and artist's name. The new table should display the artist's name, not the *ArtistID* number. Name the query *qryRockCountryReorders*. Run the query.

2. Make a copy of *tblInventory* and name it *tblInventoryBeforeUpdate*. Create an Update query called *qryUpdatePrices* that raises the prices of items in *tblInventory*. If the current price of the item is less than $10, raise the price by 10%. Run the query and compare the data in the two tables, *tblInventory* and *tblInventoryBeforeUpdate*. The easiest way to compare is to open both tables and sort each by *Price*.

Exercise 1C: Analyzing Sales

1. Create a Crosstab query named *qryInventoryCount* that analyzes data from *tblInventory* and *tblRecordings*. The query should show the sum of the quantities on hand, broken down by category of recording and type of media. The category name, not the *CategoryID*, should be displayed. Also, the media description, not the *Type* field, should be displayed. List the categories as row headings, and media descriptions as column headings.

2. Copy the Crosstab query *qryInventoryCount* and name it *qryInventoryPriceAverage*. Edit the query so that the value calculated is now the average price. Save your work.

3. Create a query using *tblInventory* and name it *qryInventoryValue*. Show all fields except *InventoryID*. Add a new column to the query with a calculated field *InventoryValue*, equal to *QuantityOnHand* multiplied by *Price*. Add a total row to the dynaset in Datasheet view that displays the total of the field *QuantityOnHand* and the new field *InventoryValue*.

ACTIVITY

Exercise 2—Practicing New Procedures

Open the *Personnel_Ch8* database.

Exercise 2A: Using Expressions in Queries

Use the *tblEmployee* table to create a query that displays an employee's name, salary, and how long they have been employed.

1. Create a calculated field to show the number of years of employment. You will need to use the Date() function, which provides today's date, in the calculation. The period of time between two dates is measured in days. Call the new field *YearsEmployed*, and format it to only one decimal place.

2. Sort by *Department* and *LastName*, and don't display *LastName*.

3. Create another new column that displays *FirstName* and *LastName* together. Call the new field *FullName*. Use the ampersand operator (&) to join the fields *FirstName* and *LastName* together, and leave a space between them.

4. Print the dynaset.

5. Save the query as *qryEmployeeInfo*.

Exercise 1B: Using Action Queries

1. Create a Make-Table query on the *tblEmployee* table that selects only those records for people hired after December 31, 1999. Include all fields and name the new table *tblNewEmployee*. Call the query *qryNewEmployee*.

2. Create an Update query on the *tblNewEmployee* table that changes the Sales department code, SAL, to MKT for Marketing. Name the query *qryEmployeeMKT*.

3. Make a Delete query on the *tblNewEmployee* table that removes all records where the phone number prefix is 931. Save the query as *qryEmployee931*.

4. Make an Append query table that adds the employees working in the CIS department from the *tblMoreEmployees* table to the *tblNewEmployee* table. Save the query as *qryEmployeeAppend*.

Exercise 2C: Using Crosstab Queries

1. Create a Crosstab query on *tblEmployee* that shows the number of employees enrolled in each health plan, organized by department. Use the department name, not the abbreviated code, as the column heading. Name the query *qryCrosstabHealthDept*.

2. Create a Crosstab query on *tblEmployee*, *tblDepartments*, and *tblHealthPlan*. Show the total amount spent by the employees in each department on each health plan. Health plan name should be the row heading. Name the query *qryCrosstabHealthAmounts*.

Exercise 2D: Using Parameter Queries

1. Create a query on the *tblEmployee* table that shows the names, departments, and monthly salaries of employees. Set up the query so that the employee last name is a parameter, and write an appropriate prompt. Save the query as *qryEmployeeByName*.

2. Use *tblEmployee* table and create a query that shows how many vacation hours remain for each employee. Save and name the query *qryEmployeeVacation*.

   a. Show only these remaining hours, the employee name, and the department code. The *RemainingVacationHours* field can be calculated from the existing fields by subtracting the hours used from the accrued hours.

   b. Sort the *RemainingVacationHours* field in descending order.

   c. Set the query up so that the department code is a parameter, and write an appropriate prompt.

Exercise 2E: Displaying Unique Records and Values

1. Create a query using the tables *tblDepartments* and *tblEmployee*. The query should show a list of departments that have hired employees after July 1, 2003. A department name should appear only once in the dynaset. Save the query as *qryDepartmentsUnique*.

Exercise 2F: Debugging SQL Statements

Each of the following SQL statements contains an error. Rewrite each statement so as to correct the error.

1. SELECT FirstName, LastName from tblMailList WHERE State = CA;

2. SELECT LastName, OrderDate from tblMailList INNER JOIN tblOrders on MailingID = CustomerID;

3. SELECT Avg(ItemPrice) from tblItems;

Exercise 3—In-Class Group Practice: Data Hunt

ACTIVITY AND REFLECTION

Work in small groups as determined by your instructor. Use the *Students_Ch8* database. Each team will complete the following steps, retrieving data using queries to find the necessary information to go to the next step. The first team to finish with the correct answer wins.

1. Append the records from *tblStudentsToo* to *tblStudents*. Create a query on *tblStudents* showing only those people born after January 1, 1980, and sort in ascending order by *LastName*. Write down the last name of the student who's last in this list.

2. Create a query that shows all the students enrolled in all classes. Sort in ascending order by class name and grade. Find the class taught by the instructor with the same last name as the student found in step 1. What is the record number of the student who got the only A grade in this class?

3. Create a query that shows all students' names, addresses, and birth dates. View only those students who have the number found in step 2 as part of their address. Sort in ascending order by birth date. Who is the oldest student in the list?

4. Create a query that shows all the classes in which the student from step 3 has enrolled. In which class did this student get an A?

5. Create a Crosstab query that counts the number of students receiving each letter grade in the class found in step 4. How many students received a B in this class?

Exercise 4—Crosstabs Challenge: Expressions, Joins, and Functions

Exercise 4A: Using Joins and Expressions

Use the *MusicMedia_Ch8* database.

1. Create a Crosstab query called *qryLevelMediaTotals*. Show the total number of products on hand for each product level and media type. Use media type as the column heading and display the *Description* field for media, not the ID number. Eliminate any records from the count that have a null value for the product level.

2. Create a Crosstab query called *qryTalentInstrumentCounts*. Show the number of products developed for each instrument by each person in *tblTalent*. Use the instrument name, not the ID number, as the column heading. Use a new column showing the person's full name as the row heading—full name is *FirstName* and *LastName* separated by a space.

3. Edit the query joins so that all the people in *tblTalent* are included in the query, even if they haven't developed a product. You'll have to edit all the table joins in the query. Save this query as *qryTalentInstrumentCounts2*.

Exercise 4B: Using Functions

Use the *Personnel_Ch8* database.

1. Create a Crosstab query using *tblEmployee* and name it *qryEmployeeSalaryAverages*. Use the following specifications:

   a. The row heading should show the year a person was hired. Use the function Year, which extracts the year from a date field, on the field *Hire_Date*. Add the caption "Hire Year" to the column.

   b. The column heading should be the field *Department*. Display the *Description* field for the department, not the code.

   c. The value should be the annual salary amount. Format it as currency.

   d. Include only data that has a value in the *Department* field (Is Not Null).

   e. Save the query and print the dynaset. It should resemble the data shown in Figure 8.47.

Hire Year	Accounting	Computer Information	Human Resources	Manufacturing	Marketing	Sales	Warehouse
1995							$36,500.00
1997		$34,500.00				$37,600.00	
1998		$38,000.00				$40,000.00	
1999				$41,000.00		$31,500.00	$41,500.00
2000	$32,400.00						$38,000.00
2001		$41,000.00			$40,000.00		
2002		$36,250.00				$29,500.00	$36,850.00
2003	$27,500.00				$28,500.00		
2004			$31,000.00				$40,100.00
2006				$46,500.00		$36,500.00	
2007			$31,300.00	$32,000.00			

Figure 8.47 Dynaset for Exercise 4B, #1

2. Create a Total query that's grouped by the health care plan name and shows the total monthly cost for each plan for everyone in the company. Add a Total row in Datasheet

view, so the total dollars spent on all health plans is shown at the bottom of the screen. Save the query as *qryMonthlyHealthCareCosts*.

   a. Open the form *frmDepartmentSelect* in Design view and display the property sheet. Note the name of the combo box on the form.

   b. Edit *qryMonthlyHealthCareCosts* and add the field *DepartmentID* from *tblEmployee* to the query. On the Total row for this field select "Where" so the field can be used with a criterion. Be sure the Show box is unchecked.

   c. On the Criteria row for *DepartmentID*, add the identifier for the combo box on *frmDepartmentSelect*. Use the expression builder to help create the identifier.

   d. Save the query.

   e. Open form *frmDepartmentSelect*, and choose a department from the combo box. Leave the form open and run the query *qryMonthlyHealthCareCost*. The department entered in the combo box on the form makes *qryMonthlyHealthCareCost* behave like a parameter query. It should only display information for the department selected on the form.

Exercise 5—Discussion Questions

ACTIVITY AND REFLECTION

1. Discuss at least three ways to use a Parameter query. Think in terms of using a control on a form as a parameter, or getting data from a macro or a Visual Basic procedure to use as a parameter.

2. Use Appendix B to look up what the following functions are and how they work:

- InStr
- Weekday
- IsNull

Create an example of how each function could be used in a query criterion.

3. The process of data archiving is used to remove old data from a table and place it into another table. What kind of query would be used to create a new empty table to contain archived records? Assuming that data is archived based on the value in the *DateCreated* field, discuss how queries could be used to move data from one table to another. (Data is to be moved if the *DateCreated* field is prior to January 1 of the current year.)

CASE STUDY A: MRS. SUGARBAKER'S COOKIES

Mrs. Sugarbaker needs more information about cookie sales and the supplies inventory. The company also needs a way to archive sales data. Creat the following queries to provide this information. Get the database *CSA_Ch8* from your instructor, and use it to create all queries.

1. Create a Crosstab query named *qryRegionalPreferences* that shows cookie sales by product and the state where a customer resides. The query should show the total number of boxes of each product sold.

2. Create a query called *qryReOrders* based on *tblInventory* and *tblSuppliers*. The query should have the following specifications:

   a. Include the fields *Description, Unit, Price*, and *Quantity* from *tblSuppliers*.

   b. Include the fields *Name, Address, City, State*, and *Zip* from *tblSuppliers*.

   c. Create a new column named *Order Quantity* that shows the quantity to be ordered. The quantity to be ordered should bring the quantity in inventory up to 10 units of each inventory item.

    d. Create a new column named *TotalPrice* that calculates the price of the item ordered.

    e. Include only those items that have a quantity on hand of four or less.

    f. Sort the records in alphabetical order by the supplier's name.

3. Archiving data is moving older data to a separate storage table. These older records are used less frequently than current ones. By archiving, the tables containing current data are kept smaller so queries can be run much faster. The process of archiving consists of two steps: copying older data to another table, and removing older data from the current table.

    a. Create an Append query that appends data from *tblOrders* to *tblOrders-Nov08*. Name the query *qryArchiveOrdersAppend*. The query should allow the user to enter the month to be archived as a parameter. The month is expressed as a digit 1–12. The query will have a new calculated field called *OrderMonth* that uses the function Month with the *OrderDate* field to display the month of the order. The parameter criterion should be placed in this new field, so that *OrderMonth* equals the month entered by the user.

    b. Run the query *qryArchiveOrdersAppend* for the month of November (11), and verify the data was added to *tblOrders-Nov08*.

    c. Create a Delete query that deletes those records from *tblOrders* that were copied to *tblOrders-Nov08* in step A. Again, use a parameter to allow the user to enter the month of sales to be deleted. Name the query *qryArchiveOrdersDelete*.

    d. Make a copy of *tblOrders*, and then run *qryArchiveOrdersDelete*. Verify that the data was removed from *tblOrders*.

Need More Help?

1. The query *qryRegionalPreferences* should include the tables *tblCustomers, tblOrderItems,* and *tblProducts.* Include only three fields: the product name, the state where the customer lives, and the sum of the quantity ordered.

2. In the query *qryReOrders*, the column *OrderQuantity* can be calculated by subtracting the field *Quantity* from 10. The column *TotalPrice* should multiply *Price* by the *OrderQuantity*.

CASE STUDY B: SANDY FEET RENTAL COMPANY

Sandy Feet Rental Company needs some changes made to its database that will require you to design advanced queries. You'll be making permanent changes to the data tables so be sure to back up the database before starting these queries.

Design the appropriate queries to accomplish the tasks as described below:

1. SFRC wants to make a rental fee change. The rates for the time frame of 1/1–3/31 will be increased by $25 and the time frame of 11/1–12/31 will be decreased by $25. Run the query. Save the query as *qry_Ch8Ex1_RateChange*. Close the query and open the table to verify that the rates have been changed.

2. SFRC wants to see a count of the clients per state and the type of condo they rent. Create a Crosstab query to show this information. (Hint: This will take fields from three different tables.) Save the query as *qry_Ch8Ex2_Crosstab*.

3. The housekeeping company is charging a 7% tax rate on each cleaning service. Calculate the tax amount and the total with tax for each of the properties. Save the query as *qry_Ch8Ex3_HousekeepingTax*.

4. Which property has had the most maintenance charges? Show the property number and address and the total amount of maintenance charges. Save the query as *qry_Ch8Ex4_-MaintenanceCharges*.

5. There are duplicate records for five of the clients (Client Numbers 21–25). Create a Delete query that deletes these records. Save the query as *qry_Ch8Ex5_DeleteRecords.*

CASE STUDY C: PENGUINS SKI CLUB

The Penguins Ski Club needs various queries written. They need some analysis of the new coaching program, a way to determine what fees are still unpaid by members, some information about members organized by their ages, and a mailing list for their new newsletter.

Use the database *CSC_Ch8* for the case study. It's available from your instructor; it's not in the student data set.

Property Sheets

1. Create a query that shows a list of coaches and the members they have worked with. Each coach/member combination should appear only once. Show only the coach's name and the member's first and last name. Sort by coach's name, then by member's last name. Save the query as *qryMemberCoaches.*

Expressions

2. Create a query to show the name of each member, the name of the member's parent, and the amount of any outstanding balance. The outstanding balance is the member fees + coaching fees − payments. Sort by members' last names. Save the query as *qryMemberAmountsDue.*

Need More Help?

Create a Total query that shows the sum of coaching fees for each member. Use this query as one of the data sources for *qryMemberAmountsDue.* Create a second Total query that shows the sum of payments made by each member. Use this query as another of the data sources for *qryMemberAmountsDue.*

Crosstab Queries

3. Write a Crosstab query that counts members by age and ability level. Save the query as *qryAgeAbilityXTab.*

4. Write a Crosstab query that shows the number of members who attended each event type by ability level. Use *Ability Level* as the row heading. Save the query as *qryEventAbilityXTab.*

5. Create a Total query that shows the number of members who received coaching, grouped by ability level. Save the query as *qryCoachingAbilityCount.*

6. Combine the queries *qryEventAbilityXTab* and *qryCoachingAbilityCount* so that counts are made by ability level of members who attended each type of event plus members who received coaching. Add a caption to the count field from *qryCoachingAbilityCount* that says "Coaching". Save the query as *qryAbilityAllCounts.* The final dynaset should look like Figure 8.48.

AbilityLevel	Coaching	Lesson	Recreation
Advanced	2	2	3
Beginner	11	11	25
Intermediate	9	6	12

Figure 8.48 Dynaset for Case Study C, #6

Union Queries

7. Create a Union query with both coaches' and parents' names and addresses. This will be used to generate mailing labels to mail out the new newsletter to both parents and coaches. Save the query as *qryUnionAddresses.*

Need More Help?

Create a query showing parents' name and address data, and combine the first and last name fields into one field—*FullName.* Create a second query showing the coaches' name and address data. Open both queries in SQL view, and copy both queries' SQL to the clipboard. Create a new Union query and paste both in, then edit the SQL to make it a Union query.

Chapter 9

Custom Forms

Objectives

After completing this chapter you will be able to

Design custom forms from single and multiple data sources:
- Understand the functions of form sections.
- Add various types of controls, including Labels, Text boxes, Combo boxes, List boxes, Option buttons, Toggle buttons, Check boxes, images, and bound and unbound objects.

Modify forms and controls:
- Move, resize, and align controls.
- Create Header and Footer sections.
- Add visual enhancements such as lines, rectangles, colors, and special effects.
- Add conditional formatting to controls.

Set properties:
- Understand the use of Property Sheets for forms and controls.
- Modify controls and forms through the Property Sheet.

Print the form:
- Preview the form.
- Use page breaks in printing the form.

Create complex forms:
- Create a tabbed form.
- Create an expression in a Text box control.
- Add a subform to a form.
- Create a Pivot Table form.
- Create a Pivot Chart form.
- Save the form as a report.

Dictionary

AutoFormat	A form design command that automatically formats a form.
Bound control	An object in a form or report that is tied directly to a field in the data source.
Check box	A control representing a Yes/No field that appears as a box with a check mark inside.
Combo box	A control that enables the user to select data from a drop-down list displayed on the form.
Command button	An interactive control that performs an action when checked.
Conditional formatting	Formatting placed on a control based on a condition.
Control	An object in a form or report.
Hyperlink control	A control that contains a URL, email address, or internal link to another document.
Image control	A control to add a picture or saved graphic file.
Label	A control that holds descriptive text data.

List box	A control that displays a list of data values and allows the user to select from the list.
Logo	An image used as a logo usually placed in the header section of a form or report.
OLE	Object Linking and Embedding.
Option button	A control representing a Yes/No field that appears as a circle with a dot inside.
Page break	A control that creates an additional page to a form or report.
Pivot Chart	A type of form that displays summary data in a graphical format that can be switched (pivoted) for different views.
Pivot Table	A type of form that summarizes data in groups that can be switched (pivoted) for different views.
Property	An attribute of a control in a form or report.
Property sheet	A list of attributes of a control in a form or report.
Smart Tags	Links to actions that can be performed in other programs. Can be attached to a table or query or to controls in a form, report, or data access page.
Tabbed form	A control that displays multiple pages (tabs) on a form.
Tab order	The order in which the cursor tabs between the fields in a form.
Text control	A box where field data or an expression is displayed.
Toggle button	A control representing a Yes/No field that appears as a raised or sunken box.
Unbound control	An object in a form or report that is not directly tied to a field in the data source.

Chapter 5 introduced basic forms created using wizards and Forms commands. There are times, however, when these basic forms are not sufficient and a custom-designed form is needed.

In this chapter, you will be creating a form "from scratch" in the Design view. By learning how to work with various controls, labels, and properties, you will be able to create a more complex custom form.

9.1 Planning, Designing, and Starting a Form

It's important for you to plan the form design before actually sitting down at the computer. A clear idea of the purpose of the form is necessary to ensure the form's accuracy. Before starting the form, it sometimes helps to draw a sketch of the form on a piece of paper, while looking at the table(s) that will be used in the form in Design view. (Design view will show you all the fields and their properties.)

Prepare the data sources for the form. If multiple data sources are to be used, be sure that all tables are properly linked. If a query will be the data source for the form, be sure the query is created and produces the correct dynaset.

Ask some questions about the usage of the form. Who will be the ultimate user or users? What is their level of comfort with Access? Consider the reason for the form's existence—what data needs to appear and why? Think of the function of the form—will it be used for data entry or just for data display?

The form should have an eye-appealing design and should be easy to use. When you are laying out the objects on the form, think of the preferred order for viewing or entering data. Consider symmetry and spacing of objects, clustering of similar objects, and other design issues. View the form with sample data loaded. If the form will be used for entering data, try entering and editing some sample data. If multiple forms are used in the same database, make them consistent in layout, color scheme, and operations.

Not all Access forms have a data source. An unbound form, one that is not attached to a table or query, can be created in Design view by not selecting any data sources. You can place labels, graphics, and other controls on unbound forms. Unbound forms are used to provide information or to allow users to make selections. They can be splash screens—forms that appear briefly when an application is opened and display the application name, developer's name, date, and other general information. Unbound forms may also be menus, such as a Switchboard form (see Chapter 12), or they may allow a user to specify other input such as the criteria for a custom query.

Q: What's the fastest way to create a custom form?

A: Use one of the form commands to create a basic form, then edit it.

An Access form, whether created by a wizard or custom designed, has the same objects and attributes. The easiest way to create a form is to use one of the Forms commands from Chapter 5 and edit the result to your liking. A form is made up of various controls and properties. How these controls and properties are set and used will determine the complexity of the form.

Controls

Controls are a large class of objects used in Access forms and reports. They can be labels, text boxes, lines, rectangles, expressions, pictures, or graphs. The controls used in reports and forms are the same.

Controls can be either unbound or bound to a field in a table or query. Unbound controls do not have a field associated with them. They can be text labels or other objects, such as graphics. Unbound controls don't vary, and are usually decorative or explanatory objects. Bound controls are directly related to fields in the data source, and the data displayed in them changes as the record pointer moves to a different record. When data is entered in the text box that represents the field, the record in the table is updated.

Table 9.1 describes the types of controls that can be incorporated in an Access form.

Table 9.1 Types of Controls

Control	Description
Bound Controls	
Bound object frame	Frame that holds an OLE object that is a field in a table.
Check box	Yes/No control shown as a square on the form; can display field data.
Combo box	Displays as a pop-up list of values from which to choose data.
List box	A box displaying a list of values from which to choose data.
Option button	Yes/No control shown as a circle on the form; can display field data.
Option group	A frame control that holds several option buttons/toggle buttons relating to field data.
Text box	Displays field data as it appears in the active record.
Unbound controls	
Attachment	Used to attach other files to the form. This can also be a bound control if there is an attachment field in the data source.
Command button	Push button used to run a command, macro, or module.
Image	Unbound graphic.
Label	Displays text as typed.
Line	Drawn line used for enhancement purposes.
Logo	Image used as a logo.
Page break	Creates additional pages on a form.
Rectangle	Drawn rectangle used for enhancement purposes.
Subform	Form inserted into another form that shows data from both forms.
Toggle button	Typically used as part of an option group to select/deselect an option.
Unbound object frame	Frame that holds an OLE object that is not associated with a field in a table.

How to Start a Custom Form

1. Click the Create tab.

2. Click the Form Design command in the Forms group (see Figure 9.1).

Figure 9.1 Creating a new form in Design view

3. A blank form opens up ready for controls to be added (see Figure 9.2).

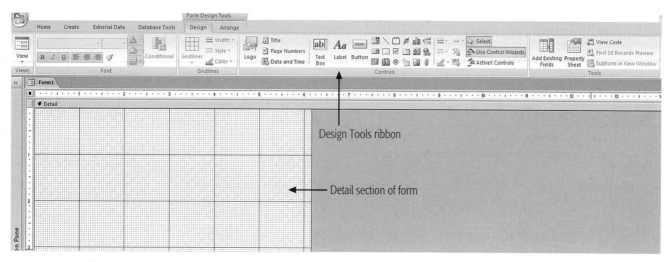

Design Tools ribbon

Detail section of form

Figure 9.2 Blank form in Design view

Working in Design View

When using the Form Design tool, the new form opens up in Design view. In a previous chapter, we worked in Layout view, which displayed the fields of the form and the data in the form. Design view displays the structure of the form and not the data. More changes can be made to the design and structure of the form in Design view than in Layout view. The form is empty and there is no data in it until a data source is chosen and fields are added. The form area displays a grid and top and side rulers to help with form design.

The Form Design Tools ribbon (see Figure 9.3) shows several groups and many commands. Some of these groups and commands are available in the Layout view, while others are specific to the Design view.

Controls group to add bound and
unbound controls to a form

Figure 9.3 Form Design Tools ribbon

A new group, Controls, contains commands for adding various controls to the form design. The Controls group is divided into three sections. The first section of this group gives controls for the header section of the form. The second section has commands to add different bound or unbound controls to the form. The third section of this group provides commands to format controls including adding special effects, line width, and type. There are also commands to select all the controls at one time to make global changes, to select control defaults, and to use the Control Wizards.

The Tools group on this ribbon has commands to add fields to the form and display property sheets for the form and its controls. Other commands in this group open Visual Basic code attached to the form, preview the first ten records of the form, and open a subform in a new window. The Gridlines group has controls to add gridlines to a tabular or stacked layout and then modify the gridlines.

Sections of a Form

There are three main sections to a form—the Header section, the Detail section, and the Footer section. When the form opens in the Design view, only the Detail section is displayed with no field data. The Header section appears at the top of the form and can be used to hold controls for titles, logos, pictures, and other data that appear only once on each form. The Detail section holds data from a data source. A Subform can also be added to the Detail section to display data from another form (the data in both forms must be joined). The Form Footer section appears at the bottom of the form. It is used for summary data, totals, or other general information such as a date or page number. The Header and Footer sections are most likely to contain unbound controls such as text, graphics, and other objects. The Page Header and Footer do not appear on the form unless it is printed and then they appear on each page.

Q: How do I turn on the Page Header/Footer sections?

A: Right-click in the Detail section of the form and choose that command from the shortcut menu.

How to Display the Form Header/Footer Sections

1. In the Detail section of the form, right-click.
2. From the shortcut menu, choose the Form Header/Footer command (see Figure 9.4).
3. Choose the Page Header/Footer command to display the Page Header/Footer section.

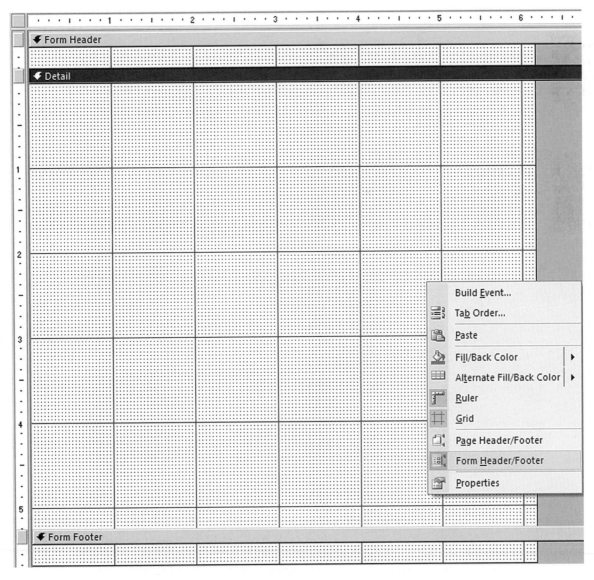

Figure 9.4 Displaying the Header/Footer sections

TRY IT YOURSELF 9.1.1

Use the *G3_Ch9.accdb* database file.

A. Create a new form in Design view (see Figure 9.4).

B. From the *tblSales* table, add all the fields to the Detail section of the form (see Figure 9.5).

C. Save the form as *frmSales* (see Figure 9.6).

Displaying the Data Sources For a Form

When you create a form with the Form Design tool, no data source is available in the form. You must choose the data for the form from the list of tables or queries, and then enter the fields into the form by dragging and dropping them. Fields from multiple sources can be added, provided the tables are properly joined in the Relationships window.

How to Choose Data for a Form

1. On the Form Design Tools ribbon, click the Add Existing Fields command.

2. A list of tables and queries will appear. Click the + in front of the table/query to display the fields from that source (see Figure 9.5).

Click the + to display the fields in the table

Figure 9.5 Adding data to a form

3. Drag and drop the desired fields into the Detail section of the form (see Figure 9.6).

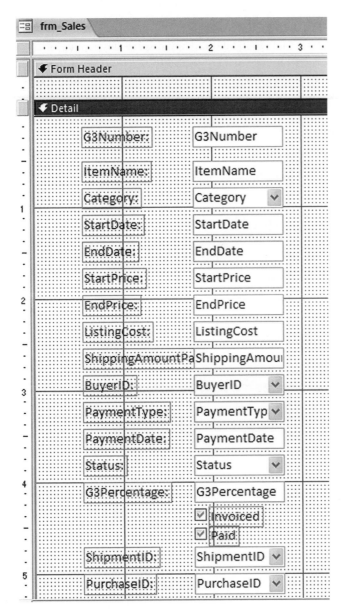

Figure 9.6 Fields added to the Detail section

9.2 / Working with Unbound Controls

Unbound controls include decorative objects such as lines and rectangles, and informational objects such as titles and labels. These controls can be formatted for visual effect or emphasis. These types of controls are not bound to any data source. They are static and do not vary as different records are displayed on the form.

Since forms are used for data entry, it is important to organize the form in a clear manner. Directions for use, visual effects to highlight certain sections of the form and a descriptive title are good design elements of a form. Commands to create these elements can be found on the Design Tools ribbon, in the Controls group.

Title and Label Controls

Label controls are used for titles or labels for data. They display descriptive or informational text. Titles are usually entered in the Form Header and will appear at the top of the form when displayed or printed. There are two different controls for each of these elements, but they are very similar.

TRY IT YOURSELF 9.2.1

Using the *frmSales* form:

A. Add a Title control.

B. Modify the Title to display *Sales Form*.

C. Enlarge the Header section.

D. Move the Title control to the center of the Header section.

E. Change the font and font size of the title.

F. Resize the Title control.

G. Resave the form.

How to Add a Title to a Form

1. Click the Title control (see Figure 9.7).

2. The title will appear in the Form Header section (see Figure 9.7).

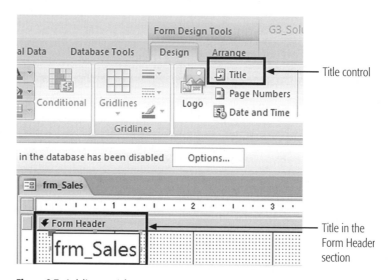

Figure 9.7 Adding a title

How to Modify the Title

1. Click into the Title control. Select text to delete.

2. Type new text. The size of the Title control will expand as text is added (see Figure 9.8).

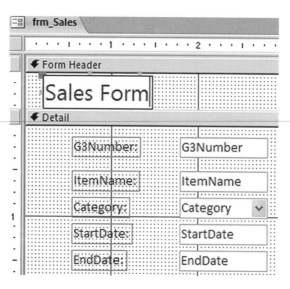

Figure 9.8 Form title modified

Enhancing the Title

The default text and size of the title may not be satisfactory for the look of your form. Perhaps the text should be a larger size or a different font style. Perhaps you want to move the title to a different location in the Form Header section. If you make changes to the Title control, the Form Header section or the control itself might need to be resized. All sections of the form can be resized to either enlarge or shrink the size by dragging the boundary lines between sections.

Using Color

Color and special effects add visual interest to the form and also provide an opportunity for creativity. You can change colors on the background for sections of the form, label controls, and several other control types. Text colors can be changed in any control with text, and line controls can also have color added to them. If the form is to be used for screen display data entry, be sure to use colors that are easy to read and do not distract from the form. Use contrasting colors for text so that it stands out clearly against the background.

Special Effects

Special effects can be placed on form controls to create visual interest and draw attention. You can apply effects to any control that has a box or circle around it. Special effects can be added through the Property Sheet for the control or through the Form Design Tools ribbon, the Controls section.

A description of each type of special effect is given in Table 9.2.

Table 9.2 Types of Special Effects

Special Effect	Description
Flat	Flat on the form background with no special effects.
Raised	Raises the box above the form background.
Sunken	Lowers the box below the form background.
Shadowed	Provides a dark shadowed effect around the box.
Etched	Shows a sunken effect without a sunken inside.
Chiseled	Adds a chiseled line underneath a control.

How to Change the Font Style and Size

1. Click the control to select it. Handles will appear around the control.

2. Using the Font drop-down list, select the new font style.

3. Using the Font Size drop-down list, select the new font size.

How to Change the Font Color

1. Click the label.

2. Click the Font Color command in the Font group.

3. Choose the color.

How to Change the Label Background Color

1. Click the label.

2. Click the Fill/Back Color command in the Font group.

3. Choose the color.

How to Add Color to a Form Section

1. Click the title bar for the section (Header, Detail, Footer).
2. Click the Fill/Back Color command in the Font group.
3. Choose the color.

How to Resize Form Sections

1. Move the mouse pointer to the boundary line between sections. The pointer will change to a double-headed arrow.
2. When that double-headed arrow is displayed, click and drag to resize the section (see Figure 9.9).

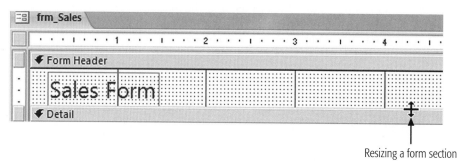

Resizing a form section

Figure 9.9 Resizing a form section

How to Move a Control

1. Click on the control to select it. Handles will appear around the control.
2. Click and drag the control using the Move handle (the large handle in the upper left corner) to its new location. Notice the pointer changes to a four-sided arrow.

How to Resize a Control

1. Click on the control to select it. Handles will appear around the control.
2. Move the pointer to the Resizing handles. The pointer will change shapes to display a double-headed arrow.
3. Drag the Resizing handles to the appropriate size (see Figure 9.10).

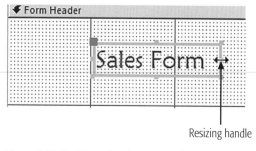

Resizing handle

Figure 9.10 Resizing the title control

Q: How can I change the font and format of a label?

A: Formatting and alignment features can be applied to the Label text when the control is selected. The bold, underline, and italic formats can be applied as well as font change and font size.

How to Add Special Effects

1. Click on the control to select it.
2. Click the drop-down list next to the Special Effects command in the Controls group.
3. Choose the desired effect.

Adding Other Controls to the Form

Other unbound controls such as line, rectangles, and OLE (object linking and embedding) objects can be included on a form for added visual interest. You can add lines to divide objects into groups or separate sections of the form. Rectangles can be used to draw borders around certain fields on the form. These objects can be modified to enhance their appearance by changing characteristics such as the width, style, and color of the line or border. Note that an OLE object could also be a bound control if it is a field in a table.

New controls are added to the form by clicking the desired button in the Controls group and then clicking into the form for object placement. Format the object by clicking on it to select it. Handles will appear around the object showing that it is selected. Select the formatting features to apply to the control. Several objects can be selected at one time so that formatting can be applied to all at one time. The Format Painter command will capture the formatting from a selected control and apply those features to another control or several controls at one time.

How to Add a Line to the Form

1. Click the Line command in the Controls group (see Figure 9.11).
2. Click the location in the form to place the line (see Figure 9.11).

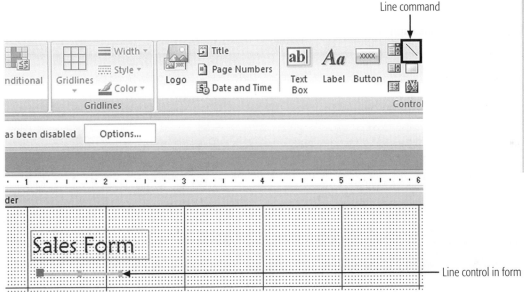

Figure 9.11 Adding a Line control

How to Format the Line Control

1. Click the Line control to select it. Handles should appear around the line (see Figure 9.12).
2. Use the drop-down list by the Line thickness, Line style, and Line color commands to choose the formatting features (see Figure 9.12).

How to Add a Rectangle to the Form

1. Click the Rectangle command in the Controls group (see Figure 9.13).
2. Draw the rectangle in the form from its top left corner by clicking and dragging the mouse pointer. Drag down to the right to draw the size of the rectangle (see Figure 9.13).

TRY IT YOURSELF 9.2.2

Using the *frmSales* form in Design view:

A. Add a Line control under the form title (see Figure 9.11).

B. Format the Line control to 3-pt. thickness.

C. Change the color of the line to red (see Figure 9.12).

D. Add a Rectangle control around both the Title and the Line controls (see Figure 9.13).

E. Change the view to Form view to see the changes.

F. Save the form.

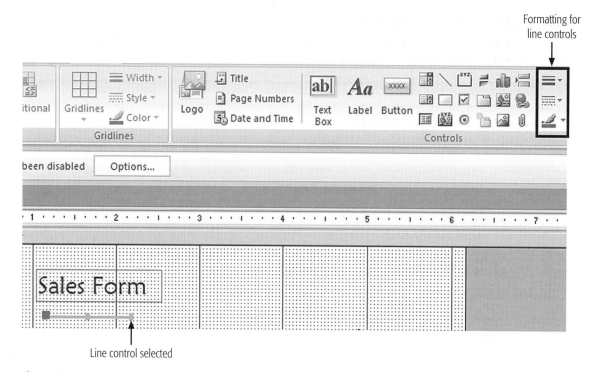

Figure 9.12 Formatting a Line control

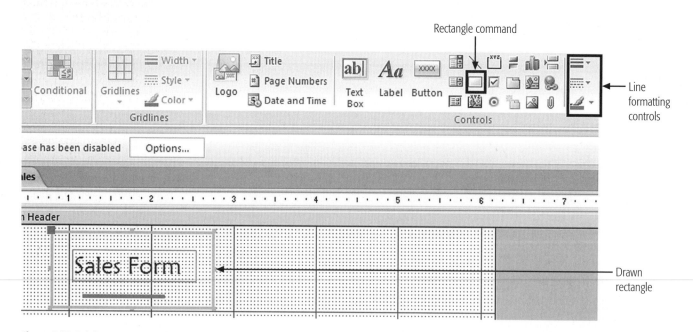

Figure 9.13 Adding a Rectangle control

How to Delete a Control

1. Click on the control to select it.

2. Push the DELETE key.

Images and Other Nontext Objects

Graphics and other nontext objects can be added to forms and reports. Access provides several controls to include these objects in a form:

- Image control, which adds any valid graphic file type including .bmp and .jpg file formats.
- Unbound Object Frame, which adds an object created by a compatible software application such as clip art. This object can be edited in the source application.
- Bound Object Frame, which adds an object that is stored as a field in a table.
- Chart control, which will create a chart out of table or query data.
- Attachment control, which adds data from other programs (such as PowerPoint) into the form.
- Logo control, which adds an image in the left corner of the Header section.

When using an Unbound Object Frame, an OLE object is inserted into the form. Linking and embedding are two ways foreign data objects can be contained. Embedded objects are copied into the form or report while linked objects have the link to the object stored. OLE objects can be graphics, sounds, or any file type that can be created within the Windows environment. Use the Image control (rather than the Unbound Object Frame control) for a saved graphic in order to reduce the size of the actual database file. Only the size of the image itself is added to the database, as opposed to the size of the OLE control and its associated file. (Note: Too many of these types of objects in a database can cause performance issues.)

How to Add a Logo

1. Click the Logo control (see Figure 9.14).
2. Navigate to the logo graphic file. Click on it to select it.
3. Click OK.
4. The Logo is placed in the left corner of the Header section. Move or resize as necessary (see Figure 9.14).

TRY IT YOURSELF 9.2.3

Using the *frmSales* form in Design view:

A. Add a logo to the form. Use the *G3_Logo.jpg* file provided in the dataset.

B. Resize and move the image to the left corner of the form (see Figure 9.14).

C. Add an Image control to the Detail section of the form.

D. Use the *Tea_cup.jpg* file provided in the dataset (see Figure 9.15).

E. Save the form.

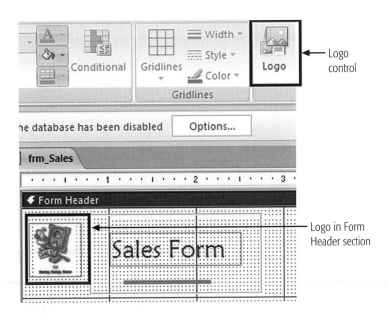

Figure 9.14 Adding a logo

How to Add an Image

1. Click the image control (see Figure 9.15).

2. Drag a frame to hold the image at an appropriate place in the form.

3. An Insert Picture dialog box appears. Locate the saved image file, select it and click OK. The image is inserted into the form (see Figure 9.15). Move or resize as necessary.

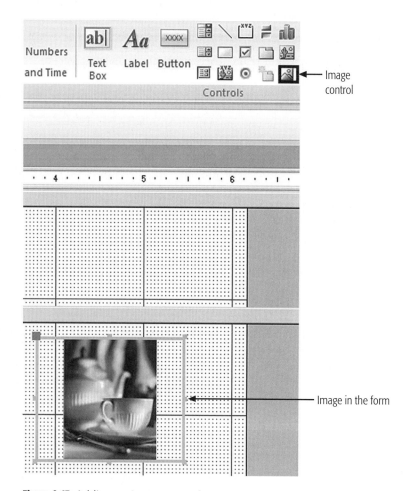

Figure 9.15 Adding an Image control

Setting Properties

Every control, each section, and even the form itself has a list of properties associated with it. Properties are the attributes associated with that particular object. These attributes further describe the appearance of the object and how that object behaves. An object's properties are displayed on the property sheet.

A control must be selected to display its property sheet. To select an entire section—Header, Detail, or Footer—click on the gray square to the left of the section boundary.

How to Display the Property Sheet

1. Click the Property Sheet command in the Tools group (see Figure 9.16).

2. Select a control or section of the form. The Property Sheet is displayed to the right of the form in Design view (see Figure 9.16).

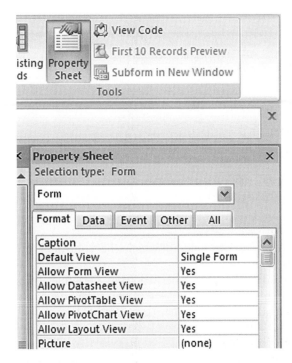

Figure 9.16 Displaying the Property Sheet

Looking at the Property Sheet

Every class of objects in Access has a different set of properties, but the format of their property sheets is similar. Different groups of properties can be displayed by clicking on the tabs located at the top of the Property dialog box. See Table 9.3 for types of properties.

Table 9.3 Types of Properties

Property	Description
Format	Describes how an object will appear on the form: font, size, color, caption, and so forth.
Data	Describes how the values will appear on the form, the data source to which it is bound, formats, and other table-related properties.
Event	Named events to which a response can be added. The response can be to run a macro or Visual Basic procedure.
Other	Additional attributes of the control.

Both bound and unbound controls have a Name property. The data entered in the Name property uniquely identifies the control. Unbound objects (those objects that are not associated with a field in the table) have an Access-generated name describing the type of control. Bound objects (those objects that have a table field associated with them) take the name of the related field.

There are some standard conventions used to name the controls on forms. These naming conventions help you identify the type of control, which is helpful when you are using it in a macro or Visual Basic program. Naming the controls on a form properly also helps you distinguish between the control and the underlying field in the data source. Control names usually have a three-letter prefix indicating the control type. Text box names begin with the letters "txt." For example, a text box that contains someone's last name might be called "txtLastName." Commonly used control prefixes are listed in Table 9.4.

Table 9.4   Common Control Name Prefixes

Control Type	Prefix
Text box	txt
Combo box	cbo
Command button	cmd
Label	lbl
Option button	opt
Option group	grp
Subform	sub

The Control Source property identifies the field to which the control is bound. Unbound fields have no Control Source property.

Other properties listed for a bound control are inherited from the table definition when the table is created. Changes made to these properties will only affect the control in the form and not change values in the table definition. They are listed below.

- Format
- Decimal Places
- Status Bar Text

- Input Mask
- Caption
- Default Value

- Validation Rule
- Validation Text
- Smart Tags

A useful form property of a control is the ControlTip Text property. A tip is a piece of text that appears when you rest the mouse pointer on the object and provides information about that object. The ControlTip Text property lets you assign a tip to a control. Type the message (up to 255 characters) in the property line.

How to Add a ControlTip Text

1. Display the Property Sheet for the control.

2. Click the All tab.

3. Scroll down to locate the ControlTip Text property.

4. Right-click into the property box to display the shortcut menu. Choose the Zoom command (see Figure 9.17).

5. Type the ControlTip Text into the Zoom screen. Click OK. The ControlTip will be displayed in Form view when the mouse pointer is rolled over the control.

You can also make changes to the border style, color, and width of a label through the Property Sheet. Two of the most powerful properties, though, are the Enabled and Locked properties. When a control is not enabled (Enabled = No), the control is dimmed when the form is displayed and users can not tab into that control. When a control is locked (Locked = Yes), users can tab to the control but are not allowed to enter data. For example, a primary key could be disabled or locked on a form so that users can only view the value in that field.

There are several properties that change the appearance, format, and location of controls. The Left and Top properties specify the location of a control in the number of inches from the left edge and the top of the section. The Width and Height properties define the dimensions of a control. The Scroll Bars property displays vertical scroll bars for text or memo fields that are too large to fit in a control.

For images it might be necessary to change the Property Sheet settings to have the entire image displayed. Some images are too large for a frame drawn on a form. There

TRY IT YOURSELF   9.2.4

Using the *frmSales* form in Design view:

A. Display the Property Sheet for the *Tea_cup.jpg* image control.

B. Add the ControlTip Text that says "A sample teapot from our collection" (see Figure 9.17).

C. View the ControlTip in Form view.

D. Save the form.

Q: How can I find out the purpose of a specific property?

A: Click on the line of the property sheet for that property, and press [F1].

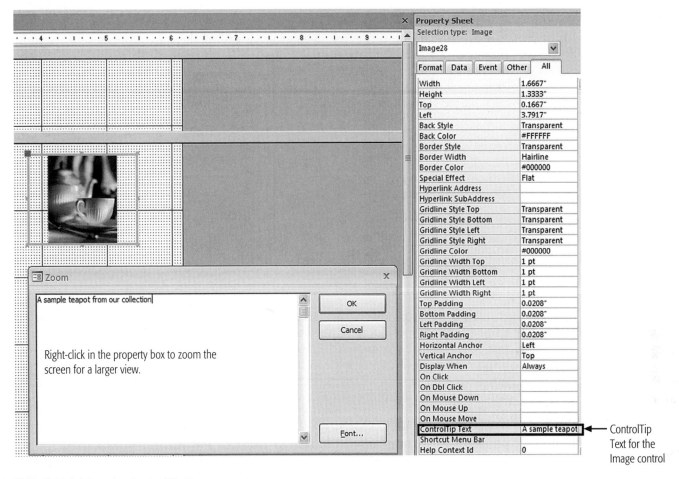

Figure 9.17 Adding the ControlTip Text property

are three different size modes for images. Each size mode displays the object differently (see Figure 9.18). Table 9.5 describes the way the image is displayed with each size mode.

Figure 9.18 Image Size mode property

Table 9.5　Size Modes

Size Mode	Result
Clip	Displays a picture in its original size.
Stretch	Image fits into the size of the control. Sometimes results in disproportionate images.
Zoom	Image fits into the size of the control with its proportions intact.

Form Properties

In addition to the properties for all controls on a form, there are properties for the entire form and each section of the form. To open the form Property Sheet, click in the Form Selection button (see Figure 9.19) in the upper left corner of the form. Make sure the Property Sheet command in the Tools group is selected. To open a section Property Sheet, click on the section bar between the sections of the form.

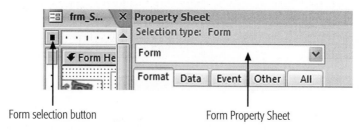

Figure 9.19 Form Property Sheet

There are many other from properties. The Record Source property contains the name of the table or query providing data to the form. The Caption property contains text displayed in the form's title bar. The Default View property governs whether the form displays one record or multiple records. When set to Single Form, the form shows only one record (columnar); when it's set to Continuous Form or Datasheet, the form shows multiple records. The properties Allow Edits, Allow Deletions, and Allow Additions manage the form's data entry capabilities. When these properties are set to Yes, records can be edited, deleted, and added, respectively. So to prevent unwanted data entry, set all these properties to No. The properties Record Selectors and Navigation Buttons determine whether or not these controls are displayed on a form. Record selectors and navigation buttons are the buttons that move from record to record, seen at the bottom of every form and in Datasheet view. It's often convenient to turn these off in the subform of a form/subform. The user must move through the records on the main form only, with the records in the subform updating automatically.

The section properties are the same for the Header, Detail, and Footer sections of the form. The most useful property for a section is the Back Color property. The color selection made here will color the background of the entire section. This is important because you cannot assign a background color to an entire form, only to a particular section. Several properties for the form sections can be changed either on the Property Sheet or through commands on the Design Tools ribbon. The Back Color property is one of those which can be changed either through the Property Sheet or the command button (see Figure 9.20).

All property sheets have an Event tab that displays the events that can happen to an object. For example, a form can open, a command button can be clicked, or data in a control can be changed. Each Event row in a property sheet can be assigned a macro or Visual Basic procedure that runs when the event occurs. We will examine events in detail in a later chapter.

Q: How can I change the background color of a form?

A: You can't. You must change the background color of each section separately.

Professional Tip: Creating Consistent Forms Quickly

Forms are the most visible part of a database so it is important to design them well. One key part of the design is to use a consistent format and layout on all forms in a database. For example, all labels and text boxes should have the same background color, font style, and size. Formatting each control to look alike can take a lot of time, unless the default properties are changed for each control type. Setting default values for a form will save time in the design phase.

To change the defaults, create the form. Create the object, such as a label. Display the Property Sheet for that object. Set the desired properties and then save the form. The next time this type of control is used, the properties will be set automatically.

If many forms are needed, consider making one master form that has all the default control properties set. Do not connect a data source to the form or add any controls (those that have been created can be deleted). Save the form and set it as a template. To set this form design (or report design) as a template, click the Office button. Click the Access Options command at the bottom of the screen. In the Forms/Reports section, type in the name of the form (or report) to use as a default template. The default is Normal for both forms and reports.

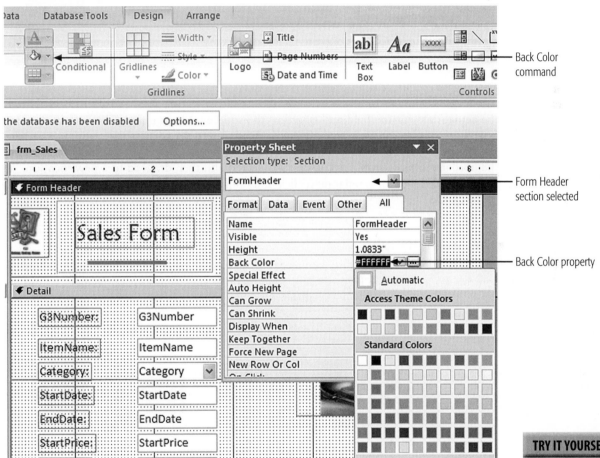

Figure 9.20 Changing the Back Color property

9.3 Working with Bound Controls

Fields are called bound controls because they are bound or tied directly to the data source. There are two controls that appear on the form for each field—the Label control and the Text Box control. The Label control is the descriptive text associated with the field and

TRY IT YOURSELF 9.2.5

Using the *frmSales* form in Design view:

A. Display the Property Sheet for the Form Header Section.

B. Change the Back Color property to a gray tone.

C. Save the form.

D. Change to Form view to see the changes (see Figure 9.21).

Figure 9.21 Form changed to new color

Q: Is there an easy way to apply the format of one control to several other controls?

A: Yes. Select the formatted control, double-click on the Format Painter button, and click on each control.

Q: How can I move only one part of a bound control?

A: Click and drag on the larger handle (rectangle) in the upper left corner of the control.

can be the field name or any other appropriate identification. The Text Box control holds the actual data for the field and is tied to the source table or query. The data in the Text Box changes with each new record that is displayed in the form.

Bound control pairs can be moved separately or together. They will move together if the border around one of the controls is selected and then dragged to a new location. To move one of the controls separately, click and drag on the large handle in the top left corner of the control.

The Arrange Ribbon

The Arrange ribbon contains commands to help with aligning, sizing, and positioning controls on a form (see Figure 9.22). Alignment, sizing, and position changes can affect the overall layout and usefulness of the form. These changes can be made to either bound or unbound controls.

Figure 9.22 Arrange ribbon

The AutoFormat command is also located on this ribbon so that global formatting can be applied and changed to the form. The Control Layout group contains commands that affect the layout of the control on the form:

- Tabular/Stacked, which creates a tabular or stacked form.
- Control Margins, which specifies the location of the information in the control.

- Control Padding, which sets the space between controls.
- Group/UnGroup, which groups/ungroups controls together so that they can be moved or formatted together.
- Snap to Grid, which adjusts the size so that the boundaries are on gridlines.
- Tab Order, which adjusts the order in which the pointer moves through the form.

One useful tool in form design is the drawing grid—a series of horizontal and vertical lines that construct a grid pattern on the background of the form. The grid actually appears as rows and columns of dots. The purpose of the grid is to help with object sizing and placement on the form. To turn the grid on/off, use the Grid command in the Show/Hide group on the Arrange ribbon. When the grid is turned on, the Snap To Grid command can be useful in object placement. This command aligns objects so that the upper left corner of the control is placed on an intersection point of a horizontal and vertical grid line. When the Snap To Grid command is turned off, controls can be placed or moved anywhere on the form. The default spacing between each gridline is 0.13 inch, but both the vertical and horizontal spacing between gridlines can be changed. The GridX and GridY properties on the Form Property Sheet control the spacing between the dots in both directions. The default is set to 24 both horizontally and vertically. As the number is increased, the grid dots move closer together.

Aligning Controls

In order to create a well-organized and appealing form, the controls should be properly aligned. There are several alignment choices (see Table 9.6) and each will line up the controls differently. These Alignment commands are found on the Arrange ribbon in the Control Alignment group. Alignment selections are usually applied to several controls at once and can be reversed with the Undo command.

Q: How can I move several controls at the same time?

A: Hold down the [SHIFT] key while selecting the controls, then drag one and all of them will move together.

Table 9.6 Types of Alignments

Alignment	Effect on Controls
Left	All selected controls will be aligned to the leftmost edge.
Right	All selected controls will be aligned to the rightmost edge.
Top	All selected controls will be aligned to the topmost edge.
Bottom	All selected controls will be aligned to the bottommost edge.
To Grid	All selected controls will be aligned to a grid marker.

How to Align Multiple Controls

1. Select the controls to be aligned. To select multiple controls, press the [SHIFT] key while clicking on the controls one at a time. Handles will appear around all the selected controls.
2. Click the desired Alignment command (see Figure 9.23).

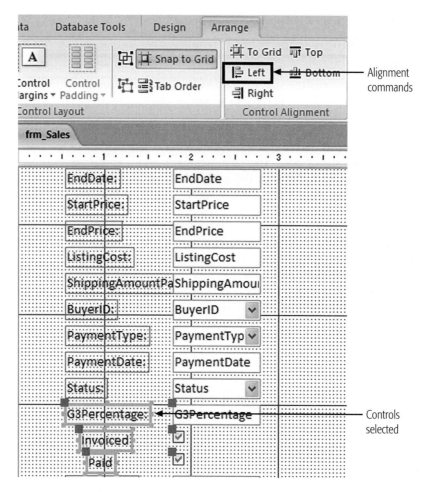

Figure 9.23 Aligning multiple controls

Resizing Controls

Any control can be resized individually by dragging on any of the seven small handles that appear when the control is selected. The Arrange ribbon has a group of commands to resize controls based on the size of other controls on the form. There are several commands from which to choose and each affects the controls differently. Table 9.7 describes the effect of each sizing command. The Anchoring command ties one control to another so that if there are changes made to that control, the same changes will be made to the other control.

Table 9.7 Sizing Controls

Size	Effect on Control
To Fit	Will size the control to fit the largest entry.
To Grid	Will size the control to a point on the grid.
To Tallest	Will size the control to the size of the tallest selected control.
To Shortest	Will size the control to the size of the shortest selected control.
To Widest	Will size the control to the size of the widest selected control.
To Narrowest	Will size the control to the size of the narrowest selected control.

How to Resize Multiple Controls

1. Select the controls to be resized. To select multiple controls, press the ⎡SHIFT⎤ key while clicking on the controls one at a time. Handles will appear around all the selected controls. (Note: Be sure to select the control that has the size characteristics to apply to the other controls.)

2. Click the desired Size command (see Figure 9.24).

Note: Use the Form view to check the progress of the design of the form.

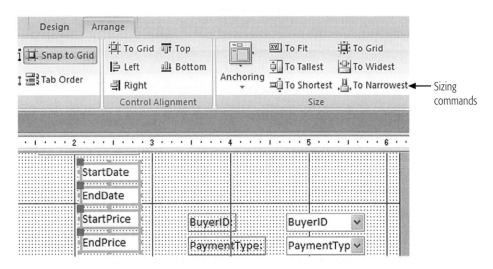

Sizing commands

Figure 9.24 Resizing multiple controls

Figure 9.25 Sales form after moving and resizing controls

TRY IT YOURSELF 9.3.1

Using the *frmSales* form:

A. Delete the *G3Percentage* control.

B. Move the *G3Number* control closer to the top of the Detail section.

C. Move the following controls under the *G3Number* control toward the left side of the form: *Item name, Category, StartDate, EndDate, StartPrice, EndPrice, ListingCost, ShippingAmountPaid, Status, Invoiced, ShipmentID,* and *PurchaseID.*

D. Move the following controls to the right side of the form: *BuyerID, PaymentType, PaymentDate,* and *Paid.*

E. Resize the following controls so that the entire Label and all the data is displayed in the Text Box: *ItemName, Category, ShippingAmountPaid,* and *PurchaseID.*

F. Resize the following controls to shorten the width of the Text Box holding the data: *StartDate, EndDate, StartPrice, EndPrice, ListingCost, ShipmentID,* and *PaymentDate.*

G. Align the *BuyerID, PaymentType, PaymentDate,* and *Paid* controls so that the Text Boxes are aligned to the right and their Lables are aligned to the left.

H. Align the remaining controls so that the Labels are aligned to the far left edge of the form and the Text Boxes are aligned right (see Figure 9.25).

I. Save the form.

Q: Is there an easier way to select all the controls on a form?

A: Yes, there is a Select All command on the Form Design Tools ribbon, the Controls group. That will select all the controls on the form.

Positioning Controls

The Position group on the Arrange ribbon provides commands to bring certain controls to the front or back of other controls. For example, if a shaded rectangle is drawn around a group of controls, the rectangle might obstruct the display of those controls. If the rectangle was positioned in the background, the controls would display in the front of the rectangle. The Send to Back command positions the shaded rectangle in the background. Several useful alignment commands found in this group are the Horizontal and Vertical spacing commands. These commands will align controls that are on the same row or arranged into a vertical column. Before using these commands, select a row or column of controls. Each of these commands has three choices:

- Make Equal, which puts equal spacing between controls.
- Increase, which increases the spacing between controls.
- Decrease, which decreases the spacing between controls.

The Show/Hide group contains commands to display or hide the Grid, Ruler, Page/Form Headers and Footers.

How to Send an Object to Back

1. Select the object.
2. Click on the Send to Back (or Send to Front) command (see Figure 9.26).
3. The selected object is now in the background (see Figure 9.27).

TRY IT YOURSELF 9.3.2

Using the *frmSales* form:

A. Draw a rectangle control around the *BuyerID*, *PaymentType*, *PaymentDate*, and *Paid* controls.

B. Add background (Fill/Back color control on the Form Design Tools ribbon) color to the rectangle.

C. Send the Rectangle control to the back (see Figure 9.26).

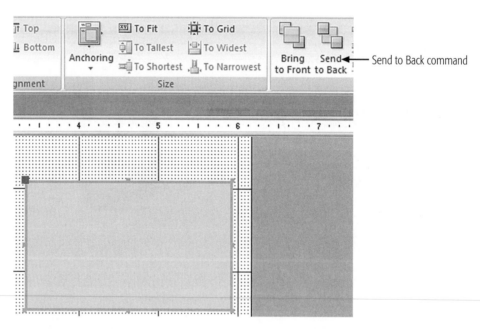

Figure 9.26 Rectangle in front of controls

Adding Special Controls

Check boxes, Option buttons, List boxes, and most of the other types of controls found in any Windows dialog box can be added to a form. These are bound controls used to view or enter field data. Command buttons are interactive controls that perform an action when clicked. Command buttons are connected to macros or Visual Basic modules, and will be discussed in a later chapter.

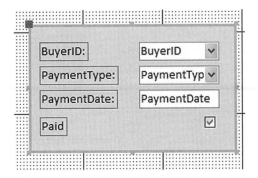

Figure 9.27 Rectangle in back of controls

Creating Check Boxes, Option Buttons, and Toggle Buttons

Option buttons, check boxes, and toggle buttons can be used to represent data from a Yes/No field. When the data value in the field is true (yes), the check box will appear with a check mark displayed in it, the option button will have a bullet displayed in it, and the toggle button will appear depressed. All of these controls can be clicked on or off with the mouse button.

When a Yes/No field type is chosen in table design, a check box is automatically displayed for that field when it is used in a form. That check box can be changed to show an option button or toggle button in Design view of the form.

How to Change an Existing Check Box into an Option Button/Toggle Button

1. In Design view of the form, right-click on the Check Box control. A shortcut menu will display.

2. Choose the Change To command (see Figure 9.28).

3. Select the new control type.

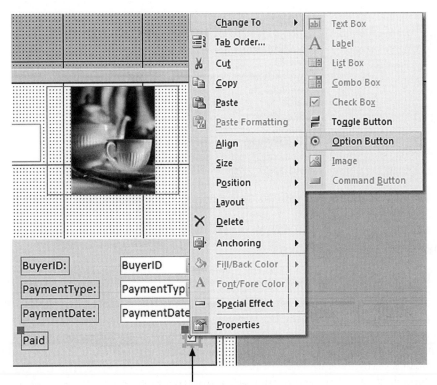

Check box control selected

Figure 9.28 Changing the Check Box control

An Option Button, Toggle Button, or Check Box control can be added to a form using the commands in the Controls group of the Form Design Tools ribbon. These controls must then be associated with a field in the data source through the control's Property Sheet. These boxes and buttons can be resized, moved, and have their properties changed like other controls. To see how the new button looks, change the view to Form view.

TRY IT YOURSELF 9.3.3

Using the *frmSales* form:
A. Change the Check Box control in the Paid field to an Option Button (see Figure 9.28).
B. Save the form.

How to Create a Check Box, Option Button, or Toggle Button

1. Click the desired control type in the Controls group, the Form Design Tools ribbon.

2. Click on the form in the location to place this control. The control plus its associated label is displayed on the form. Click the Option Button (Check Box or Toggle Button) control only.

3. In the Property Sheet for this control, select the Data tab. Pull down the arrow to display the drop-down list of available fields in the Control Source property line (see Figure 9.29). Choose the Yes/No field.

4. Click the associated Label control for the button/box. Change the Caption property of this control to a more descriptive label.

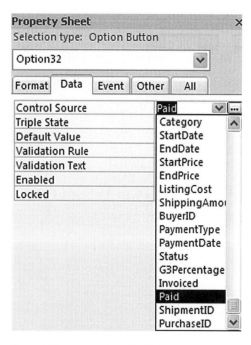

Figure 9.29 Associating the field with the Option Button

List Boxes and Combo Boxes

Lists Boxes and Combo Boxes are ideal for displaying a list of values so that the user can select the correct data from the list. Both types of controls are similar because they display lists of data. The Combo Box must be opened for the list to appear, but the List Box is always open on the form with the list showing.

List Boxes and Combo Boxes are good for fields that have a specific list of choices available as data values for the field. They restrict the user to selecting only from the displayed list of data values. Wizards for both types of boxes make them easy to create. The Use Control Wizards command must be selected (from the Controls group) in order to use the Wizards.

Both the List Box and the Combo Box Wizards offer choices as to where the data for the lists will be drawn and whether or not an action will result from making a selection from the box.

When creating a List Box or Combo Box, you can get the input for the field by

- Looking up the values in the box from another table or query. Data can be displayed from a joined table.

- Typing in the values for the lists.

- Finding a record and displaying it on a form after selecting it from the box.

These controls can be resized, moved, and formatted to match the style of the other controls on the form. Change to Form View to see how the List Box or Combo Box looks on the form. There are similar properties on the Property Sheets for the List and Combo boxes that can be useful for customization. The Column Count property (Format tab) specifies the number of columns that are displayed in the box. The Column Heads property determines whether or not the field names are displayed on the top row of the box. The Column Width property specifies the width of each column in inches. The measurements are separated by a semicolon (;) if there is more than one column. If the column width is set to 0", it will not be visible in the box.

How to Change a List Box to a Combo Box

1. In Design view, right-click on the List Box/Combo Box control to display the shortcut menu.

2. Choose the Change To command and choose the desired control type. Note: The List Box control displays an open list on the form so be sure there is enough room to display this control.

How to Create a List Box or Combo Box

1. Click the desired control type in the Controls group, the Form Design Tools ribbon.

2. Click on the form in the location to place this control. The control plus its associated label is displayed on the form. The Wizard opens.

3. Choose the method for entering the list data, either from a table/query or from typing in the list.

4. Choose the table/query for the data source. Click Next (see Figure 9.30).

Note: Combo Boxes might already be displayed as fields on the form. This is due to the data type that was chosen when the table was designed. If the data type chosen for the field was a Lookup field, a Combo Box will be displayed on the form.

Q: How is the key field hidden in a Combo box?

A: By setting the Combo box Column Width property to 0" for the first column.

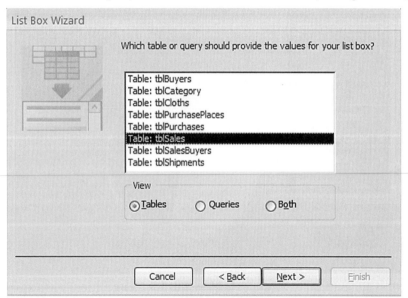

Figure 9.30 Choosing the data source for the list values

5. Select the field(s) for the list data (see Figure 9.31). Click Next.

6. Choose the sort order if desired. Click Next.

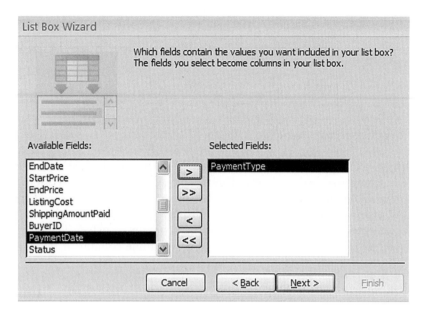

Figure 9.31 Field(s) to include in list

7. Adjust the width of the list. Click Next.

8. Choose the corresponding field to store the data (see Figure 9.32). Click Next.

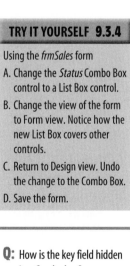

TRY IT YOURSELF 9.3.4

Using the *frmSales* form

A. Change the *Status* Combo Box control to a List Box control.

B. Change the view of the form to Form view. Notice how the new List Box covers other controls.

C. Return to Design view. Undo the change to the Combo Box.

D. Save the form.

Q: How is the key field hidden in a Combo box?

A: By setting the Combo box Column Width property to 0" for the first column.

Note: With form/subforms, any subtotals or aggregate data must be displayed in the subform footer. A control that calculates summary data for records displayed in the subform should not be placed in the Detail section of the main form.

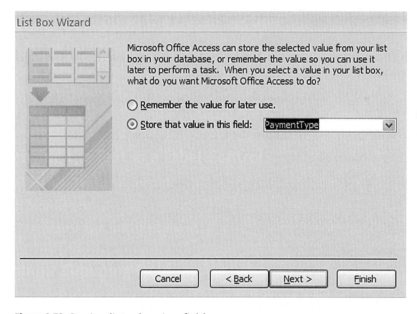

Figure 9.32 Storing list values in a field

9. Enter the name of the control. Click Finish.

10. Resize or move the control so it fits on the form.

Using an Expression in a Control

Text Box controls can be added to a form to hold data that is created through an expression using fields, functions, and data values. An expression in a control can calculate a number or dates, process a string of text or look up data in another table. Expressions in the Form Footer section can calculate subtotals, counts, and other summary information. Expressions can be entered into the Text Box control by hand or through the Expression Builder. The Expression Builder provides help in writing complex expressions. The Expression Builder can

be accessed through the Text Box Property Sheet in the Control Source property line. Click the ellipsis in that property line or right-click on the Text Box control and choose the Build Event command on the shortcut menu (see Figure 9.33).

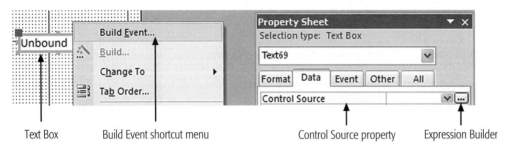

Figure 9.33 Creating a calculated control

Working with Text Box Controls

Text Box controls hold data from a table/query or an expression. When you add a field to a form, it is in the form of a Text Box control. There are two parts to a Text Box control—the Label holds the text describing the data in the actual Text Box, which holds the data itself. When creating a Text Box control, it is necessary to add a control source (found in the Property Sheet of the Text Box) or a source for the data. This can be a field in a table or query, a calculation using fields from a table or query, a calculation using fields and numeric values, or other expressions that are available in Access. Two of the most common expressions now have specific commands on the Form Design Tools ribbon for easy incorporation into a form. The Page Number and Time and Date commands in the Controls group are really expressions held in Text Boxes without the Label section. Their control sources are Access Common Expressions.

How to Add a Calculated Control

1. Click the Text Box command on the Form Design Tools ribbon, Controls group.
2. Add the Text Box control to the form.
3. Display the Property Sheet for the control.
4. In the text box or the Control Source property line (Data tab), enter the expression starting with an equals sign. Enclose field names used in the expression in square brackets (see Figure 9.34). Example: [FieldName].

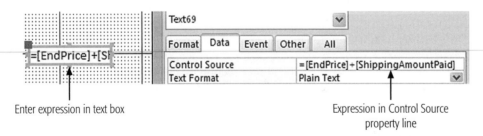

Figure 9.34 Entering the expression

5. Choose the appropriate format for the text box from the Format property line (Format tab).
6. Change the name of the control from the default to a more descriptive name. Ex: TotalCost.

Figure 9.35 Form with new control added Total Cost

7. Change the text in the Label control for the Text Box (see Figure 9.35).
8. Move, resize, and format as necessary.

Creating Subtotals

Aggregate data, usually a subtotal, often appears in a subform because subforms frequently list items in a group. The aggregate data, one piece of data that summarizes a value for an entire group, can be a sum, count, average, or other statistic. Aggregate data should be placed in a control on the Footer section of the subform.

If the Form Footer section is not displayed, click the Form Header/Footer command in the Show/Hide group on the Arrange tab.

Use the functions Sum, Count, and Avg to total, count, and average data. An expression is placed in a text box, which is the same type of control used to display a field. Use the same method for creating a calculated control Text Box, and then type the expression into the text box or the Control Source property line. The expression to total a numeric type field is =Sum([FieldName]). The expression to average a numeric data type field is =Avg([FieldName]). Be sure to start the expression with an equal sign (=) followed by the function and then the field upon which to perform this function. The field is enclosed in parentheses and Access will add the square brackets around the field name.

Q: How can I add a subtotal to a form?

A: Add a new text box to the footer, and type "=sum (*name of control*)" into the box.

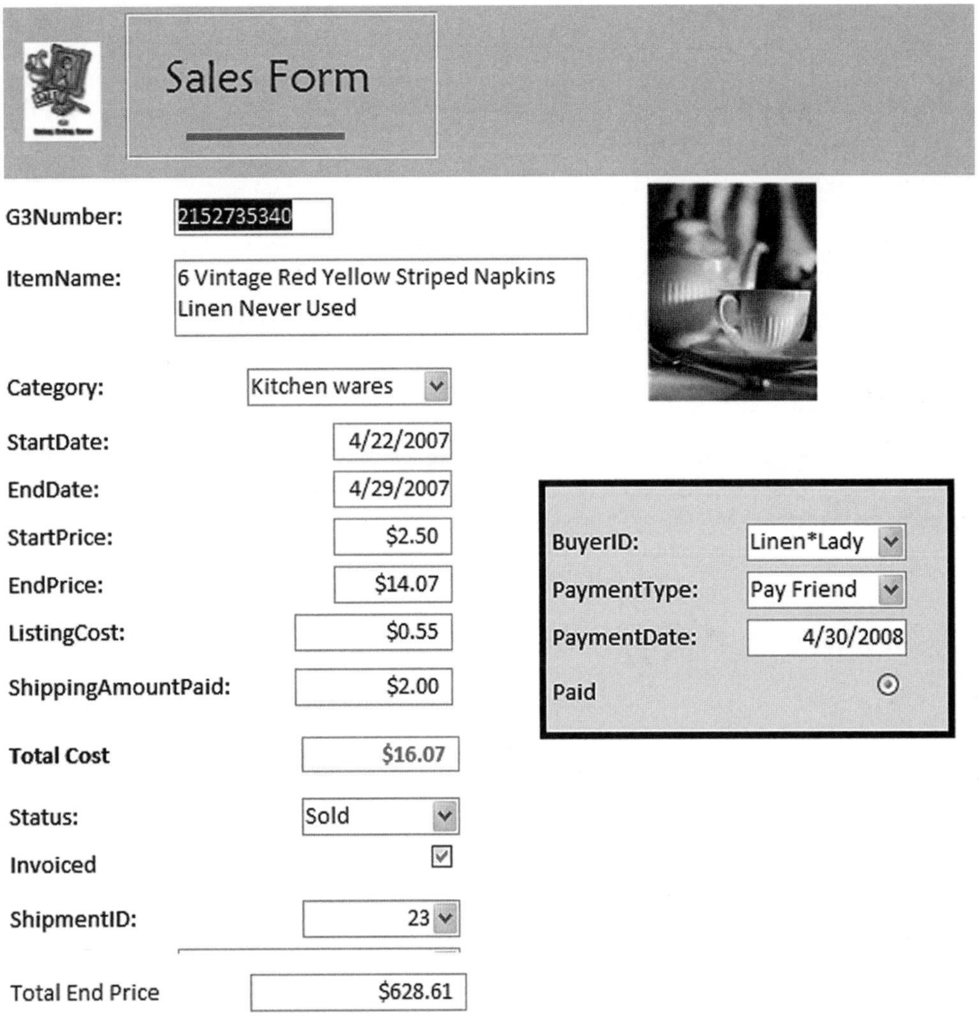

Figure 9.36 Form with subtotal in Footer section, Total End Price

TRY IT YOURSELF 9.3.5

Using the *frmSales* form:

A. Add a calculated control that sums the *EndPrice* and the *ShippingAmountPaid* fields.

- Create a Text Box control to hold this calculation. Enter the expression in the Text Box (see Figure 9.33).
- Using the Property Sheet for this control, change the name the control *TotalCost* (see Figure 9.34).
- Format to currency.
- Change the associated Label to display the caption Total Cost.
- Move the Text Box between the *ShippingAmountPaid* and *Status* controls. Resize and move as needed (see Figure 9.35).

B. Add a calculated control to show the sum of *EndPrice* in the Footer section of the form.

- Create a Text Box control to hold this calculation. Enter the expression in the Text Box.
- Use the =Sum ([FieldName]) format.
- Format to currency.
- Change the associated Label to display the caption Total End Price.
- Align the new control with the others on the form (see Figure 9.36).

C. Save the form.

Working with Subforms

Access can create a form with another form embedded in it, a subform which holds related data. When using the Form commands to create a form, Access will automatically make a form/subform when the table (data source) is properly joined to one other table. If the table is joined to more than one other table, the subform will not be automatically generated. Through the Form/Subform command on the Form Design Tools ribbon, Controls group, a subform can be added to an existing form if the data sources for each form are properly joined. The forms can be created separately and then combined through the Subform/Subreport command.

The subform can be generated using any of the forms tools or created in Design view. When designing a subform, keep in mind that this form will become part of another form. The subform should be very simple and only have the necessary data rather than a lot of embellishments. Because these commands create forms in predesigned formats, it is necessary to release the form from its format before making any changes. In Layout view, it was difficult to make changes, such as moving or resizing, individual controls. If a change was made to one, it affected all the controls on the form. In Design view, this autoformatting can be removed so that changes can be made separately to each control. Subforms can be quickly created and then easily edited.

How to Create the Subform

1. Click the data source (table).

2. Display the Create ribbon. Click the Form command. The form is created with the selected table as its data source.

3. Change to Design view.

4. Display the Arrange ribbon.

5. Select all the controls on the form (Press [SHIFT] + click the right mouse button).

6. Click the Remove command in the Control Layout group (see Figure 9.37).

7. All controls can be moved, resized, and formatted individually.

8. Save the form.

Once the subform is created, it can be added to an existing form. The two forms will be joined on the common field which joins their source data (tables). The Subform Wizard will provide prompts through this process.

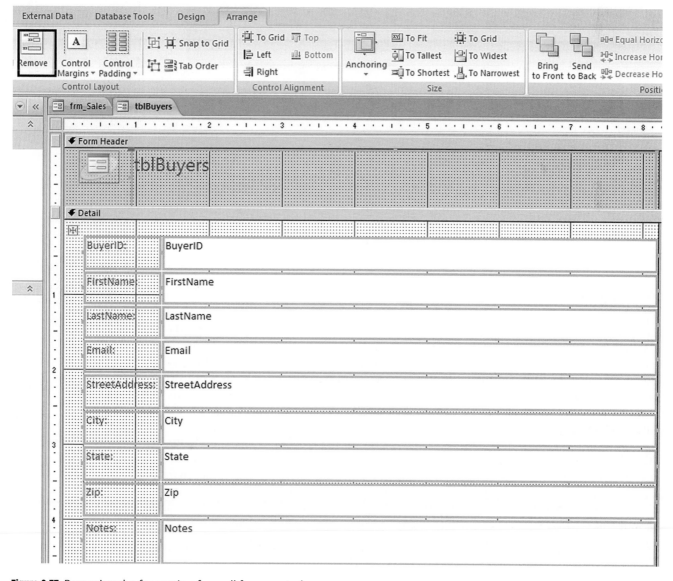

Figure 9.37 Removing the formatting from all form controls

How to Add a Subform to a Form

1. Open the "main" form in Design view. Resize the form sections (Detail) if necessary to hold the subform control.

2. Click the Subform/Subreport command on the Form Design Tools ribbon, the Controls group.

3. In the main form, click and drag to draw the subform control. The Subform Wizard will open (see Figure 9.38).

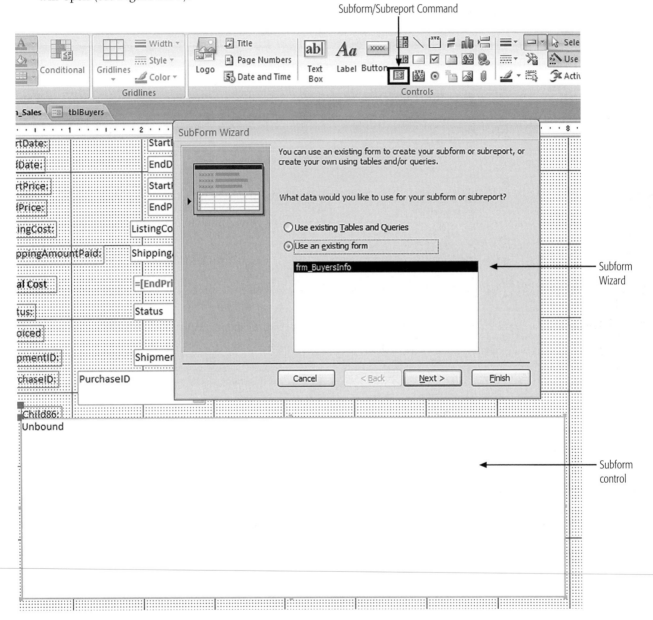

Figure 9.38 Subform Wizard

4. Choose the subform source. Click Next.

5. Choose the linking field. Click Next (see Figure 9.39).

6. Enter the name of the subform control and click Finish.

7. The subform can be moved and resized as needed. Figure 9.40 shows the form with subform.

8. Save the form.

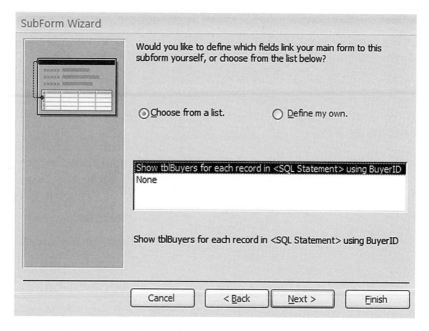

Figure 9.39 Choosing the linking field for the forms

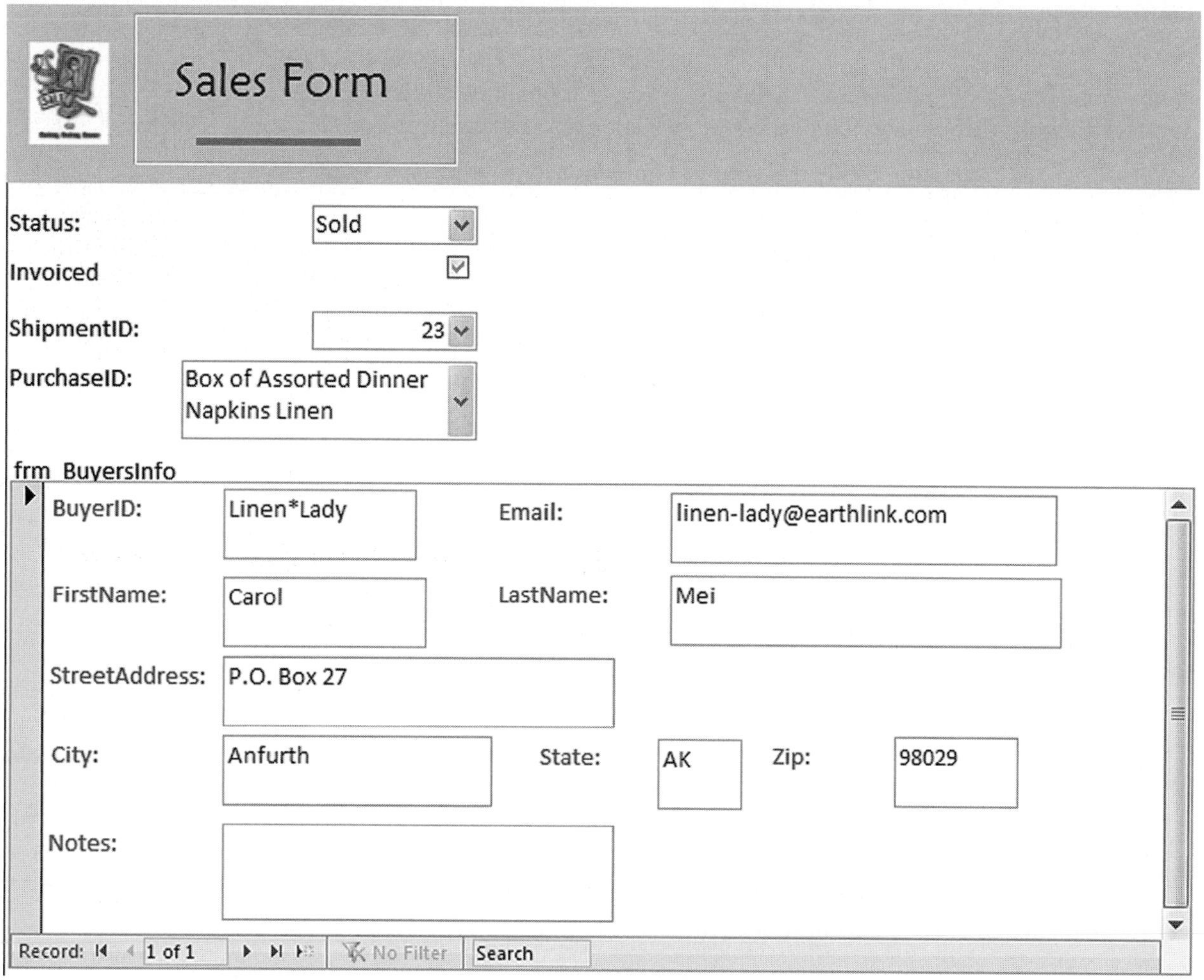

Figure 9.40 Form with subform displayed

Data entered into either section of the form is entered into the original data source. The subform should only display data that is directly related to the record of the main form. If this is not the case, review the table relationships to ensure that the data sources used for these forms are correctly linked.

Professional Tip: Using Form Properties

Here are some additional form properties that can be set. Open the form's property sheet to make these changes.

1. To use a form only for entering new data, set the Data Entry property to Yes. The form will always open with no data displayed, and existing records can't be accessed.

2. To add your own title to a form, type the title text into the Caption property line.

3. To stop the next record from displaying when the TAB key is pressed while in the last control of a form, change the Cycle property to Current Record. When the TAB key is pressed, the focus returns to the first control in the current record.

9.4 Customizing the Form: Working with Other Controls

There are several other commands that can be added to a form to further customize the functionality or look of the form. The Hyperlink, Tab Control, and the Page Break commands are available on the Form Design Tools ribbon, the Design tab in the Controls group. The Tab Order command is available on the Arrange tab, the Control Layout group. These commands add controls such as hyperlinks and page breaks. Conditional Formatting in the Font group allows for formatting to be placed on a text box or combo box control based on specific conditions. All these controls provide more opportunities to improve the use of the form for data entry or data display.

Tab Order

The Tab Order is the order the cursor moves when you tab (press the TAB key) to move from control to control. The order in which the controls are added to the form will determine the initial Tab Order. When controls are added or moved on the form design, it will affect the Tab Order. Always check Tab Order after changing the controls on a form.

Test the Tab Order by opening the new form and tabbing between controls. Generally, a form is filled out, from top to bottom and from left to right. The cursor should not jump randomly around the form. If several controls are related, as in an address group, you should tab through them in succession. If the Tab Order is not appropriate, it can be changed.

Always check the Tab Order after making changes to a form (adding or deleting controls) and make corrections if necessary.

How to Change the Tab Order

1. In Design view, click the Arrange tab.

2. Click the Tab Control command found in the Control Layout group.

3. Choose the section in which to recorder the controls.

4. In the Custom Order field list, drag and drop the fields in the proper order (see Figure 9.41).

TRY IT YOURSELF 9.3.6

Using the *G3_C9.accdb* database file:
A. Create a new form using the *tblBuyers* table. Use the Form command.
B. Open the form in Design view.
  a. Delete the Form Header section.
  b. Select all the remaining controls on the form.
  c. Click the Remove command in the Control Layout group (see Figure 9.37). The controls should move separately.
  d. Revise the form so that the controls are parallel to each other to minimize the length of the form (see Figure 9.40).
  e. Save the form as *frmBuyers_Information*.
C. Use the *frmBuyers_Information* as the subform in the *frmSales* form.
  a. Place the subform control in the Detail section of the *frmSales* form.
  b. Delete the Total End Price controls in the Form Footer section.
  c. Save the form (see Figure 9.40).

Q: What if I move a control on a form and mess up the Tab Order?

A: The AutoOrder button automatically reorganizes the controls by their position on the form. The order is left to right and top to bottom. The AutoOrder button may produce the result you want, so that no controls need to be moved manually.

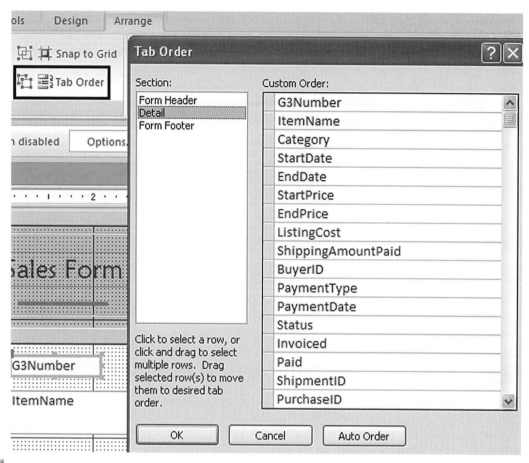

Figure 9.41 Tab Order dialog box

TRY IT YOURSELF 9.4.1

Using the *frmSales* form:

A. Rearrange the Tab Order for the controls so that they match the order of the fields on the form (see Figure 9.41).

B. The last controls should be the *BuyerID* and other controls that are to the right of the form.

C. Test the new Tab Order in Form view.

D. Save the form.

5. Continue this process until all fields are in the desired order.

6. Click OK to complete the process.

Fields can be manually reordered by dragging and dropping them in the proper sequence in the Custom Order field list. However, an easy way to reorder fields according to natural sequence is the AutoOrder button in the Tab Order dialog box. Access will reorder the Tab Order according to the placement of the fields on the form. If a custom order is desired, use the drag and drop method.

Creating Page Breaks and Printing the Form

Unless page breaks are added at the end of the form, the form will print in a continuous fashion with several forms on a single page. Inserting a page break is one way to have only one form printed per page.

Page breaks can also be used to create a multiple-page form for viewing. Having more than one page on your form will allow you to add more information than can fit on one screen. You can organize information better so that the form will appear less jumbled and thus be more useful to the data entry process. Be advised that when you place any controls on another page, they will print on their own separate page. Consequently, one record may require several pieces of paper to print.

The Page Break button in the Controls group makes inserting a page break easy. If you want to place controls on a second page, place the page break mark in the middle of the Detail section and move or copy those controls to the next page.

Q: Why doesn't the Form Header print on every page of the form?

A: The Form Header prints once on the first page at the top of the form. To have a header section print on every page of a form, put the information in a Page Header section.

How to Insert a Page Break

1. In Design view, click the Page Break control in the Controls group.
2. Click into the form at the location for the page break (see Figure 9.42)

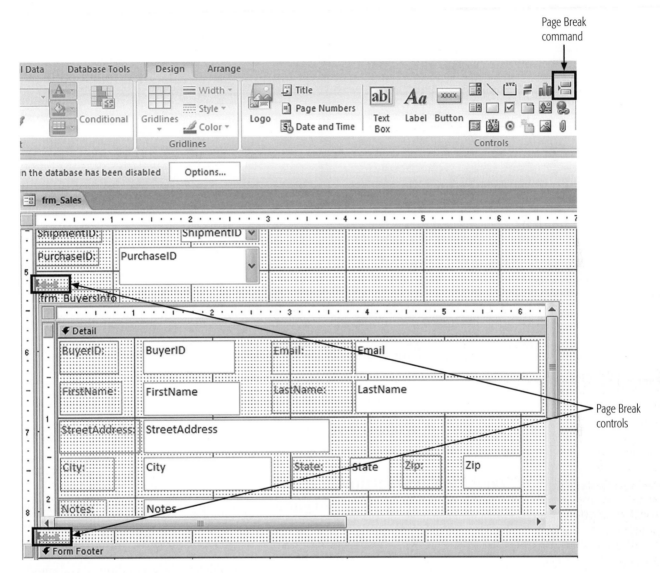

Figure 9.42 Creating a page break on a form

3. Move any controls necessary to the new page (below the page break). It might be necessary to enlarge the entire form area to 7.5 inches to accommodate the next page.
4. Check the form in Print Preview (Office Button, Print, Print Preview) (see Figure 9.43).

Hyperlinks and Button Commands

Adding Hyperlink controls and Buttons are ways to move from the form to the Internet or to move to various places within the form. The Hyperlink command will accept Internet URL, email addresses, and locations within the database.

TRY IT YOURSELF 9.4.2

Using the *frmSales* form:
A. Add a page break control before and after the subform. This will move the subform to a separate page (see Figure 9.42).
B. Preview the form in Print Preview view (see Figure 9.43).
C. Save the form.

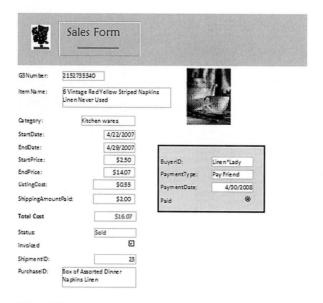

Figure 9.43 Form on two pages

TRY IT YOURSELF 9.4.3

Using the *frmSales* form:

A. Add a Hyperlink command to the Form Header section. Use the http://www.G3Auctions.com URL (see Figure 9.44).

B. Save the form.

How to Add a Hyperlink

1. Click the section of the form to place the Hyperlink control.

2. Click the Hyperlink command in the Controls group.

3. Select the type of Hyperlink to include.

   - Navigate to the location within the database.
   - Enter the URL.
   - Enter the email address.

4. Click OK (see Figure 9.44).

5. Save the form.

TRY IT YOURSELF 9.4.4

Using the *frmSales* form:

A. Apply conditional formatting to the Total Cost text box.

B. Set the condition so that if the value of Total Cost is greater than $20 a yellow background will appear (see Figure 9.45).

C. Test the form in Form view by scrolling through the records (see Figure 9.46).

D. Save the form.

Conditional Formatting

Conditional formatting can be used with text boxes and combo boxes. A format can be specified if the value in the text box complies with the condition. If a field holds data that is greater than $100, for example, that field can be highlighted with special background colors, bold formatting, or a different text color. Up to three formats can be applied matching different conditions. You can also delete these conditions as desired.

How to Add Conditional Formatting

1. Click the control on which to add the formatting.

2. Click the Conditional command in the Font group. The Conditional Formatting dialog box appears.

3. Enter the condition for the field.

4. Enter the formatting to be applied if the condition is met. Click OK (see Figure 9.45).

5. In Form view, scroll through the forms to verify that the conditional formatting works (see Figure 9.46).

6. Save the form.

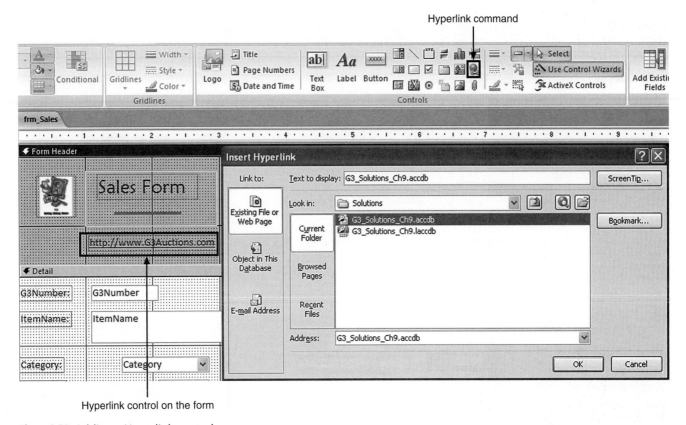

Hyperlink command

Hyperlink control on the form

Figure 9.44 Adding a Hyperlink control

Conditional Command

Conditions on the field

Formatting to be applied

Figure 9.45 Adding conditional formatting

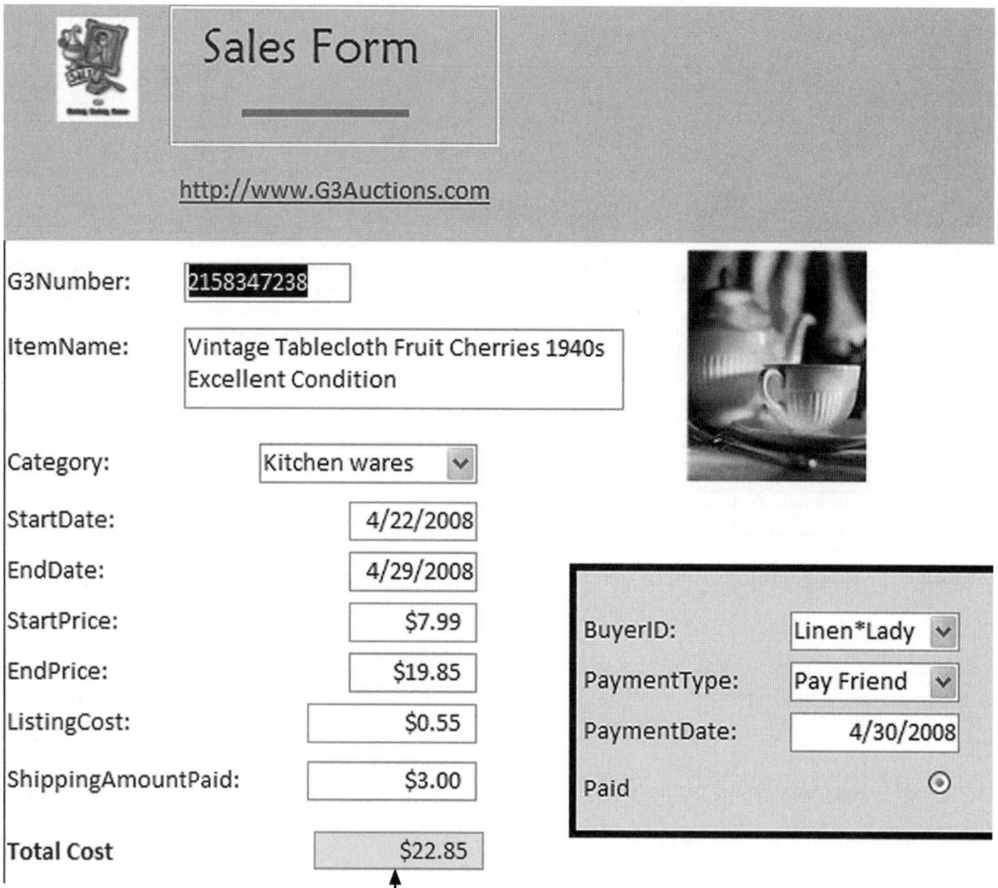

Formatting applied to the Total Cost text box if the amount is greater than $20

Figure 9.46 Form with conditional formatting

9.5 Creating Other Forms

- Tabbed Form
- Blank Form
- Pivot Chart
- Pivot Table

There are several other types of controls and commands that can be used to create specialized forms. The Tab control (Controls group) creates a tabbed form with tabs identifying the pages of the form. The Blank Form command creates a blank form that is not tied to a data source. A form created with the Blank Form command opens in Layout view. Fields can be added through the field list as in both Layout and Design views. The Pivot Table form is similar to a Crosstab query with numeric data summarized in groups. The Pivot Chart form displays the data in a graphical format.

Tabbed Form

A tabbed form enhances data entry by grouping related controls under one tab page and eliminating a cluttered look on a form. The Tab control can create any number of tabs or pages needed for the form. Any type of field or control can be entered on a tab page. The Tab control does not take up the entire area of the form and controls can be placed outside the boundaries of the Tab control for a further customized look. It is much easier to start with a new form rather than try and modify an existing form into a tabbed format. The Tab control itself can be resized and moved like any other form control. Fields placed on the tab pages can be formatted, aligned, and sized using the Design View Tools. The caption that is displayed on the tab can be changed by changing the Name property on the Property Sheet for each tabbed page.

How to Create a Tabbed Form

1. Select the table/query data source. Create a new form with the Form Design command.

2. Click the Tab Control command. Click and drag for the placement of the control on the form (see Figure 9.47).

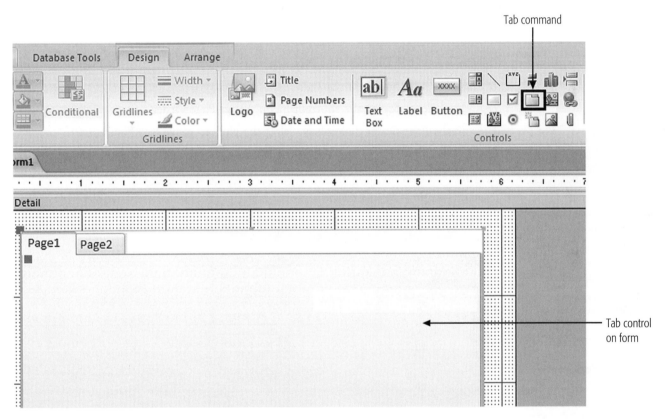

Figure 9.47 Creating a tabbed form

3. Display the Add Existing field list.

4. Drag the desired fields to the first tab page. Add any other controls. Use sizing and alignment commands.

5. Add additional pages to the tab control by right-clicking into the Tab control. From the shortcut menu, choose Insert Page.

6. To change the name of the tab page, click on the page. On the Property Sheet for that page, change the Name property line to reflect the desired name (see Figure 9.48).

7. Save the form. View the form through Form view.

TRY IT YOURSELF 9.5.1

Using the *G3_Ch9.accdb* database file:

A. Create a new form using the Form Design command.

B. Add a Tab control to the Detail section of the blank form (see Figure 9.47).

C. Display the Add Existing Fields list

D. From the *tblSales* table
- Add the following fields to Page 1 of the Tab control: *G3Number, ItemName, Category, StartDate,* and *EndDate.*
- Arrange and align the fields so that they are easily viewed.
- Rename Page 1 to "Item Information" (see Figure 9.48).

E. On Page 2
- Add the following fields: *G3Number, ItemName, StartingPrice, EndPrice, ListingCost,* and *ShippingAmountPaid.*
- Arrange and align the fields so they are easily viewed.
- Rename Page 2 to "Pricing Information".

F. Add another page to the Tab control.
- Add the following fields from *tblSales* and *tblBuyers*: *BuyerID, PaymentType, PaymentDate, Status, FirstName, LastName, Email, StreetAddress, City, State,* and *Zip.*
- Arrange and align the fields so they are easily viewed.
- Rename Page 3 to "Buyer Information".

G. Reorder the pages if necessary so that they are in this order: Item Information, Buyer Information, Pricing Information (see Figure 9.49).

H. Save the form as *frmSales_Buyers_Tabbed* (see Figure 9.50).

I. View the form in Form view.

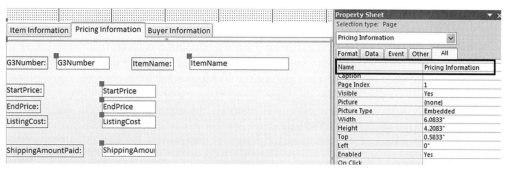

Figure 9.48 Changing the name for the tab pages

When working with multiple pages of a Tab control, it might be necessary to change the order of the pages. It does not matter the order the pages are created. They can be moved to any order using the Page Order dialog box.

How to Change the Page Order

1. Select the Tab control (any page).
2. Right-click to display the shortcut menu. Select Page Order.
3. From the Page Order dialog box, select the page to move (see Figure 9.49).
4. Click the Move Up or Move Down button as appropriate. Click OK when finished.

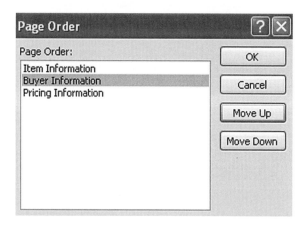

Figure 9.49 Changing the Page Order on a Tab control

Pivot Tables

A Pivot Table summarizes numeric data in groups. The rows and columns in a Pivot Table (and their related data) can be switched or pivoted for different views of the data. Data for the Pivot Table can be from a table or query. There are three elements for creating a Pivot Table—a field containing the Row Headings, a field containing the Column Headings, and a Data field that holds numeric data for performing calculations. The Row and Column headings are fields used for defining the data groups. Access has a Pivot Table command found on the Create ribbon, the Forms group, under the More Forms command.

Item Information	Buyer Information	Pricing Information

G3Number: 2152735340   Category: Kitchen wares ⌄

ItemName: 6 Vintage Red Yellow Striped Napkins
             Linen Never Used

StartDate: 4/22/2007

EndDate: 4/29/2007

Figure 9.50 Tabbed form

How to Create a Pivot Table

1. Click the Create tab to display the Create ribbon. Click the More Forms command. Choose the PivotTable command.

2. The form is opened in PivotTable view with its own ribbon (see Figure 9.51).

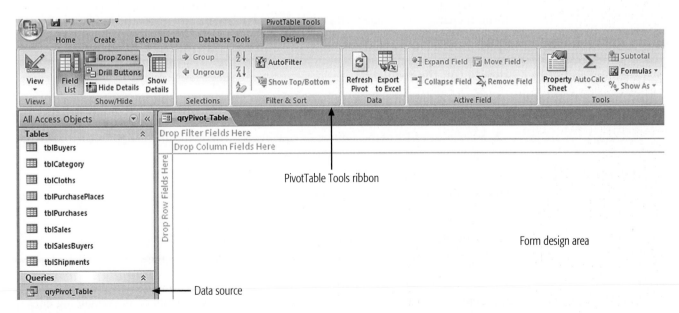

Figure 9.51 Creating a Pivot Table

3. Select the data source (table/query). Double-click on the Field List command.

4. Drag and drop the fields from the data source into the Row, Column, or Data section of the form (see Figure 9.52).

		CategoryName ▾			
		Clothing	Kitchen wares	Misc. Collectables	Grand Total
		+│−	+│−	+│−	+│−
State ▾		EndPrice ▾	EndPrice ▾	EndPrice ▾	No Totals
AK	+−		▸ $14.07		
			$19.85		
AZ	+−	$8.83		$19.45	
CA	+−			$51.09	
				$19.99	
				$17.00	
				$22.50	
CO	+−			$7.50	
				$14.99	
CT	+−	$10.19		$36.00	
FL	+−	$4.99			
GA	+−			$10.50	
IN	+−		$11.00	$25.00	
KY	+−	$21.50			
MA	+−			$10.37	

Figure 9.52 Adding data to a Pivot Table form

5. Click the + or − in front of each section to display or hide the details.

6. Save the form.

The purpose of the Pivot Table form is to view the data from various perspectives. Column and row headings can be switched so that the columns become rows and vice versa. The order of the items in the rows and columns can also be rearranged. A filter can be set to view only a certain percentage of the data and subtotals and items can be sorted in ascending or descending order. Calculated fields and totals can also be added to the form. If changes are made to the underlying data source, the Pivot Table form will automatically be updated to reflect the changes.

How to Edit the Pivot Table

1. To pivot the data, drag and drop the row or column field to the other location in the form.

2. Switch the order of the column or row items by dragging and dropping each item into a new location in the column or row.

How to Add Totals to the Pivot Table

1. Select a cell with numeric data from the detail section.

2. Click the AutoCalc command. Choose the Sum command.

3. The subtotal and totals will be displayed within the Grand Total area and at the bottom of each detail section (see Figure 9.53).

Filters can also be added to a Pivot Table. As with other filters, the remaining data is simply not displayed but can be recalled by removing the filter.

CategoryName ▾						
	Kitchen wares		Clothing		Misc. Collectables	Grand Total
	+ −		+ −		+ −	+ −
State ▾	EndPrice ▾		EndPrice ▾		EndPrice ▾	EndPrice ▾
AK	$14.07					$14.07
	$19.85					$19.85
	$33.92					$33.92
AZ			$8.83		$19.45	$8.83
						$19.45
			$8.83		$19.45	$28.28
CO					$7.50	$7.50
					$14.99	$14.99
					$22.49	$22.49

← Subtotals and Totals

Figure 9.53 Adding subtotals and totals

How to Filter Data

1. Click the drop-down list in the Row or Column Heading. A list of all the data in the field will be displayed (see Figure 9.54).

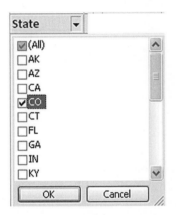

Figure 9.54 Filter list

2. Choose the data to display. Only the checked boxes will display in the Pivot Table. The default is All (see Figure 9.55).

3. To remove a filter, choose All from the drop-down list to display all data.

Drop Filter Fields Here			
	CategoryName ▾		
	Misc. Collectables	Grand Total	
	+ −	+ −	
State ▾	EndPrice ▾	EndPrice ▾	
CO	$7.50	$7.50	
	$14.99	$14.99	
	$22.49	$22.49	
Grand Total		$7.50	
		$14.99	
	$22.49	$22.49	

Figure 9.55 Pivot Table with filtered data

TRY IT YOURSELF 9.5.2

Using the *G3_Ch9.accdb* database file:

1. Create a query from the *tblSales, tblBuyers,* and *tblCategory.*

2. Choose the fields *EndPrice, State,* and *CategoryName.* Save the query as *qryPivot_Table.*

3. Create a Pivot Table form using the *qryPivot_Table* query as the data source (see Figure 9.51).

4. Enter the *CategoryName* as the Column Heading, the *State* as the Row Heading, and the *EndPrice* as the data (see Figure 9.52).

5. Add totals to the data (see Figure 9.53).

6. Filter on the *State* of CO (see Figure 9.54).

7. Remove the filter and display all the data.

8. Pivot the data so that the *CategoryName* is now the Row Heading and the *State* is the Column Heading.

9. Save the form as *frm_PivotTable.*

Pivot Charts

A Pivot Chart displays data in a graphical format. The data can be manipulated or pivoted similar to the Pivot Table form. The Chart can be filtered to display specific data and summary options. There is a Pivot Chart command on the Create ribbon, the Forms group.

How to Create a Pivot Chart

1. Click the Create tab to display the Create ribbon. Click the Pivot Chart command.
2. The form is opened in PivotChart view with its own ribbon.
3. Select the data source (table/query). Double-click on the Field List command.
4. Drag and drop the fields from the data source into the Filter, Category, and Detail sections on the form (see Figure 9.56). The detail area will display the data to be summarized.

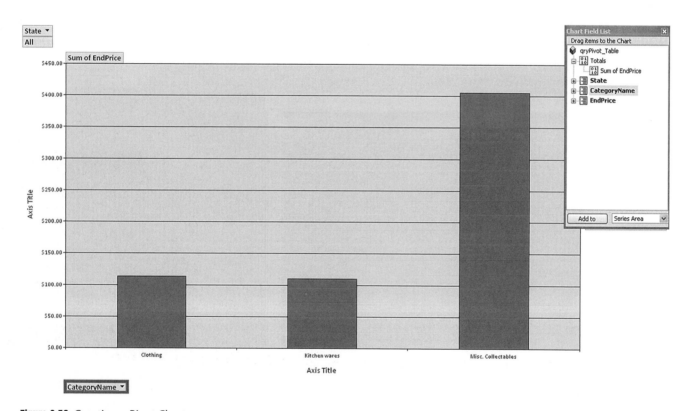

Figure 9.56 Creating a Pivot Chart

TRY IT YOURSELF 9.5.3

Using the *qryPivot_Table* query:

1. Create a Pivot Chart form.
2. Add the *State* field as the filter, the *EndPrice* as the detail data, and the *CategoryName* as the Category (see Figure 9.56).
3. Change the chart type to 3D column type (see Figure 9.57).
4. Save the form as *frm_PivotChart*.

How to Modify the Pivot Chart

1. To pivot the filter and category areas, drag and drop the fields into the new location on the form.
2. To filter the data displayed, use the drop-down list for the field. Choose the data to filter.
3. To change the calculation function in the detail section, click the title of the function and then click the AutoCalc command. Choose a new calculation.
4. To change the chart type, click into the middle of the chart. Click the Change Chart Type command. Choose a new chart type (see Figure 9.57).

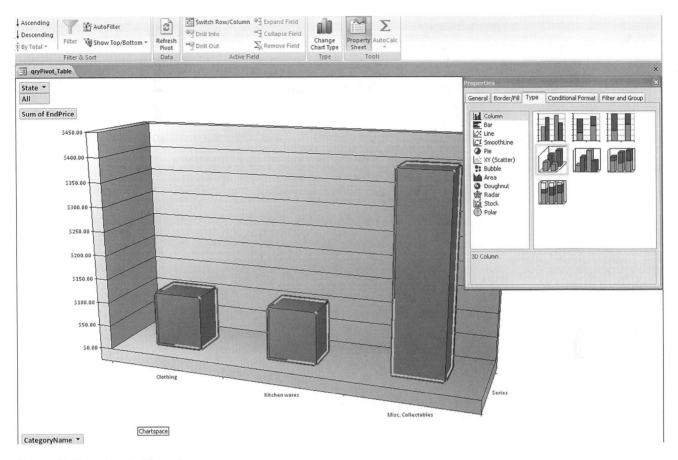

Figure 9.57 Changing the Chart Type

9.6 Saving a Form as a Report

It is possible to save a form as a report object within the same database. This might be useful if a form contains the data needed for a report so that you don't have to re-create the same information in a report format.

How to Save a Form as a Report

1. Select the form. It is not necessary to open it.

2. Click the Office Button, the Save As command.

3. Choose the Save Object As command.

4. Choose report from the As drop-down list (see Figure 9.58).

5. Type a name for the report. Click OK.

Figure 9.58 Saving a form as a report

Fast Track   **A quick guide to procedures learned in this chapter**

Starting a Custom Form

1. Click the Create tab.

2. Click the Form Design command in the Forms group.

3. A blank form opens up ready for controls to be added.

Displaying the Form Header/Footer Sections

1. In the Detail section of the form, right click.

2. From the shortcut menu, choose the Form Header/Footer command.

Choosing Data for a Form

1. On the Form Design Tools ribbon, click the Add Existing Fields command.

2. A list of tables and queries will appear. Click the + in front of the table/query to display the fields from that source.

3. Drag and drop the desired fields into the Detail section of the form.

Adding a Title to a Form

1. Click the Title control.

2. The title will appear in the Form Header section.

Modifying the Title

1. Click into the Title control. Select text to delete.

2. Type new text. The size of the Title control will expand as text is added.

Changing the Font Style and Size

1. Click the control to select it. Handles will appear around the control.

2. Using the Font drop-down list, select the new font style.

3. Using the Font Size drop-down list, select the new font size.

Changing the Font Color

1. Click the label.

2. Click the Font Color command in the Font group.

3. Choose the color.

Changing the Label Background Color

1. Click the label.

2. Click the Fill/Back Color command in the Font group.

3. Choose the color.

Adding Color to a Form Section

1. Click the title bar for the section (Header, Detail, Footer).
2. Click the Fill/Back Color command in the Font group.
3. Choose the color.

Resizing Form Sections

1. Move the mouse point to the boundary line between sections. The pointer will change to a double-headed arrow.
2. When that double-headed arrow is displayed, click and drag to resize the section.

Moving a Control

1. Click on the control to select it. Handles will appear around the control.
2. Click and drag the control using the move handle (the large handle in the upper left corner) to its new location. Notice the pointer changes to a four-sided arrow.

Resizing a Control

1. Click on the control to select it. Handles will appear around the control.
2. Move the pointer to the resizing handles. The pointer will change shapes to display a double-headed arrow.
3. Drag the resizing handles to the appropriate size.

Adding Special Effects

1. Click on the control to select it.
2. Click the drop-down list next to the Special Effects command in the Controls group.
3. Choose the desired effect.

Adding a Line to the Form

1. Click the Line command in the Controls group.
2. Click the location in the form to place the line.

Formatting the Line Control

1. Click the Line control to select it. Handles should appear around the line.
2. Use the drop-down list by the Line thickness, Line style, and Line color commands to choose the formatting features.

Adding a Rectangle to the Form

1. Click the Rectangle command in the Controls group.
2. Draw the rectangle in the form from its top left corner by clicking and dragging the mouse pointer. Drag down to the right to draw the size of the rectangle.

Deleting a Control

1. Click on the control to select it.
2. Push the DELETE key.

Adding a Logo

1. Click the Logo control.
2. Navigate to the logo graphic file. Click on it to select it.
3. Click OK.
4. The Logo is placed in the left corner of the Header section. Move or resize as necessary.

Adding an Image

1. Click the Image control.
2. Drag a frame to hold the image at an appropriate place in the form.
3. An Insert Picture dialog box appears. Locate the saved image file, select it, and click OK. The image is inserted into the form. Move or resize as necessary.

Displaying the Property Sheet

1. Click the Property Sheet command in the Tools group.
2. Select a control or section of the form. The Property Sheet is displayed to the right of the form in Design view.

Adding a ControlTip Text

1. Display the Property Sheet for the control.
2. Click the All tab.
3. Scroll down to locate the ControlTip Text property.
4. Right-click into the property box to display the shortcut menu. Choose the Zoom command.
5. Type the ControlTip Text into the Zoom screen. Click OK. The ControlTip will be displayed in Form view when the mouse pointer is rolled over the control.

Aligning Multiple Controls

1. Select the controls to be aligned. To select multiple controls, press the SHIFT key while clicking on the controls one at a time. Handles will appear around all the selected controls.
2. Click the desired Alignment command.

Resizing Multiple Controls

1. Select the controls to be resized. To select multiple controls, press the SHIFT key while clicking on the controls one at a time. Handles will appear around all the selected controls. Be sure to select the control that has the size characteristics to apply to the other controls.
2. Click the desired Size command.

Sending an Object to Back

1. Select the object.

2. Click on the Send to Back (or Send to Front) command.

3. The selected object is now in the background.

Changing an Existing Check Box into an Option Button/Toggle Button

1. In Design view of the form, right-click on the Check Box control. A shortcut menu will display.

2. Choose the Change To command.

3. Select the new control type.

Creating a Check Box, Option Button, or Toggle Button

1. Click the desired control type in the Controls group, the Form Design Tools ribbon.

2. Click on the form in the location to place this control. The control plus its associated label is displayed on the form. Click the Option Button (Check Box or Toggle Button) control only.

3. In the Property Sheet for this control, select the Data tab. Pull down the arrow to display the drop-down list of available fields in the Control Source property line. Choose the Yes/No field.

4. Click the associated Label control for the button/box. Change the Caption property of this control to a more descriptive label.

Changing a List Box to a Combo Box

1. In Design view, right-click on the List Box/Combo Box control to display the shortcut menu.

2. Choose the Change To command and choose the desired control type. (Note: The List Box control displays an open list on the form so be sure there is enough room to display this control.)

Creating a List Box or Combo Box

1. Click the desired control type in the Controls group, the Form Design Tools ribbon.

2. Click on the form in the location to place this control. The control plus its associated label is displayed on the form. The Wizard opens.

3. Choose the method for entering the list data, either from a table/query or from typing in the list.

4. Choose the table/query for the data source. Click Next.

5. Select the field(s) for the list data. Click Next.

6. Choose the sort order if desired. Click Next.

7. Adjust the width of the list. Click Next.

8. Choose the corresponding field to store the data. Click Next.

9. Enter the name of the control. Click Finish.

10. Resize or move the control so it fits on the form.

Adding a Calculated Control

1. Click the Text Box command on the Form Design Tools ribbon, Controls group.

2. Add the Text Box control to the form.

3. Display the Property Sheet for the control.

4. In the Text Box or the Control Source property line (Data tab), enter the expression starting with an equals sign. Enclose field names used in the expression in square brackets.

5. Choose the appropriate format for the Text Box from the Format property line (Format tab).

6. Change the name of the control from the default to a more descriptive name.

7. Change the text in the Label control for the Text Box.

8. Move, resize, and format as necessary.

Changing the Tab Order

1. In Design view, click the Arrange tab.

2. Click the Tab Control command found in the Control Layout group.

3. Choose the section in which to recorder the controls.

4. In the Custom Order field list, drag and drop the fields in the proper order.

5. Continue this process until all fields are in the desired order.

6. Click OK to complete the process.

Creating the Subform

1. Click the data source (table).

2. Display the Create ribbon. Click the Form command. The form is created with the selected table as its data source.

3. Change to Design view.

4. Display the Arrange ribbon.

5. Select all the controls on the form (Press SHIFT + click the right mouse button).

6. Click the Remove command in the Control Layout group.

7. All controls can be moved, resized, and formatted individually.

8. Save the form.

Adding a Subform to a Form

1. In Design view, resize the form sections (Detail) if necessary to hold the subform control.

2. Click the Subform/Subreport command on the Form Design Tools ribbon, the Controls group.

3. In the main form, click and drag to draw the subform control. The Subform Wizard will open.

4. Choose the subform source. Click Next.

5. Choose the linking field. Click Next.

6. Enter the name of the subform control and click Finish.

7. The subform can be moved and resized as needed. Save the form.

Inserting a Page Break

1. In Design view, click the Page Break control in the Controls group.

2. Click into the form at the location for the page break.

3. Move any controls necessary to the new page (below the page break). It might be necessary to enlarge the entire form area to 7.5 inches to accommodate the next page.

4. Check the form in Print Preview (Office Button, Print, Print Preview).

Adding a Hyperlink

1. Click the section of the form to place the Hyperlink control.

2. Click the Hyperlink command in the Controls group.

3. Select the type of Hyperlink to include.

   - Navigate to the location within the database.
   - Enter the URL.
   - Enter the email address.

4. Click OK.

5. Save the form.

Adding Conditional Formatting

1. Click the control on which to add the formatting.

2. Click the Conditional command in the Font group. The Conditional Formatting dialog box appears.

3. Enter the condition for the field.

4. Enter the formatting to be applied if the condition is met. Click OK.

5. In Form view, scroll through the forms to verify that the conditional formatting works.

Creating the Pivot Table

1. Click the Create tab to display the Create ribbon. Click the More Forms command. Choose the PivotTable command.

2. The form is opened in PivotTable view with its own ribbon.

3. Select the data source (table/query). Double-click on the Field List command.

4. Drag and drop the fields from the data source into the Row, Column, or Data section of the form.

5. Click the + or − in front of each section to display or hide the details.

6. Save the form.

Editing the Pivot Table

1. To pivot the data, drag and drop the row or column field to the other location in the form.

2. Switch the order of the column or row items by dragging and dropping each item into a new location in the column or row.

Adding Totals to the Pivot Table

1. Select a cell with numeric data from the detail section.

2. Click the AutoCalc command. Choose the Sum command.

3. The subtotal and totals will be displayed within the Grand Total area and at the bottom of each detail section.

Filtering Data

1. Click the drop-down list in the Row or Column Heading. A list of all the data in the field will be displayed.

2. Choose the data to display. Only the checked boxes will display in the Pivot Table. The default is All.

3. To remove a filter, choose All from the drop-down list to display all data.

Creating a Pivot Chart

1. Click the Create tab to display the Create ribbon. Click the Pivot Chart command.

2. The form is opened in PivotChart view with its own ribbon.

3. Select the data source (table/query). Double-click on the Field List command.

4. Drag and drop the fields from the data source into the Filter, Category, and Detail sections on the form. The detail area will display the data to be summarized.

Modifying the Pivot Chart

1. To pivot the filter and category areas, drag and drop the fields into the new location on the form.

2. To filter the data displayed, use the drop-down list for the field. Choose the data to filter.

3. To change the calculation function in the detail section, click the title of the function and then click the AutoCalc command. Choose a new calculation.

4. To change the chart type, click into the middle of the chart. Click the Change Chart Type command. Choose a new chart type.

Review Questions

1. What is a control?

2. What is the difference between an unbound and a bound control?

3. List and describe three types of unbound controls.

4. What is the purpose of an unbound form?

5. How do you add fields to the form in Design view?

6. Which section of a form holds the data fields?

7. If you wanted to add a logo to a form, in which section would you add it?

8. Which control will add a title to a form?

9. How do you resize a control?

10. (T/F) Once the Title control is added to a form, it cannot be modified.

11. What is the difference between a Label and a Title control?

12. Name two enhancements that can be made to either a Label or Title control.

13. What is the difference between an Image control and an Unbound Object Frame control?

14. (T/F) If the file is to be edited in its original program, use the Bound Object Frame control to insert it into a form.

15. What is a property sheet?

16. (T/F) Only the form sections have property sheets.

17. What is the naming convention for a Combo Box control?

18. What is the purpose of aligning controls on a form?

19. What is the method for selecting multiple controls?

20. What is the purpose of a List Box?

21. (T/F) The Combo Box always appears open on a form.

22. For which field data type would a Toggle button, Option button, or Check Box be used?

23. What effect does a page break have on printing the form?

24. What is the value of using a Combo Box on a form?

25. What field data type can be used in an expression for a calculated control?

26. Where would you place calculated control for a subtotal?

27. Give an example for using conditional formatting on a control.

28. How to you release a form from its AutoFormat?

29. (T/F) Data entered into a form/subform is therefore entered into the data source tables.

30. What is the Tab Order?

31. Why would you want to change or modify the Tab Order?

32. What does the AutoOrder feature do?

33. What is the purpose of a Tabbed form?

34. What are the three data elements needed for a Pivot Table form?

35. Why would you want to save the form as a report?

Exercises

Exercise 1—Practicing New Procedures

ACTIVITY

Use the *SDAL_Ch9.accdb* database file.

Exercise 1A: Creating a New Form

1. Use the Form Design command to create a new form with the *tblRecordings* as the data source.

2. Load all the fields into the form Detail section.

3. Display the Form Header section. Resize the Header section to include the title of the form (Recordings) and SDAL's logo (*SDAL_Logo.jpg*).

   - Change the font size of the title to 22. Resize the control if necessary.
   - Enlarge the Logo control to display SDAL's logo more clearly.
   - Change the background color of the Form Header to light pink.

4. Arrange the following fields on the left side of the form: *MusicID, Artist, Title,* and *Category.*

5. The field *AlbumCover* should be on the same line as *MusicID.*

6. The field *Label* should be parallel with *Category.*

7. Use the alignment commands to be sure the controls are aligned properly. Align the right edge of the *AlbumCover* and Label controls.

8. Resize the *Title* Text Box so it displays the entire title.

9. Add a horizontal line below the *Category* and *Label* controls.

   - Change the color to dark pink.
   - Change the line thickness to 4pt.

10. Change the background color of the Detail section to light pink.

11. Check and fix the Tab Order so that it matches the order the controls are located on the form.

12. Save the form as *frmRecordings.*

Exercise 1B: Creating a Subform

1. Create a form using the Form tool with the *tblInventory* as the data source.

2. Delete the Title and the Logo.

3. Do not display the Form Header.

4. Remove the AutoFormat on the controls so that the controls can be formatted individually.

5. Resize the controls to make them small enough to hold their data. Align them so that the Labels are on the left edge of the form and the Text Boxes are aligned left.

6. Save the form as *frmInventory.*

7. Add the *frmInventory* as a subform in the *frmRecordings* form.

8. Save the *frmRecordings.* View the form in Form view. Compare with Figure 9.59.

Exercise 1C: Creating a Tabbed Form

1. Create a tabbed form using the *tblRecordings* and *tblInventory* tables.

2. Load all the fields from the *tblRecordings* on Page 1 of the Tab control.

3. Align and arrange the fields for clear display. Resize to display all data in each field and label.

4. Load all fields from the *tblInventory* on Page 2 of the Tab control.

5. Add a line or rectangle control for visual interest on Page 1.

6. Add the *AlbumCover* and *Artist* fields to Page 2 (they are also on Page 1).

7. Rename the Page 1 "Recordings Information." Rename Page 2 to "Inventory Information."

8. Save the form as *frmRecordings_tabbed.*

Figure 9.59 Sample form for Exercise 1B, *frmRecordings*

Exercise 2—In-Class Group Practice

ACTIVITY AND REFLECTION

Divide into groups of two to four people, as determined by your instructor. Work with the tables in the *Practice_Ch9.accdb* database file. Each team will do the following set of tasks, divided into parts. Your instructor will tell you how long you have to complete each part.

Part 1

1. Work within your group to create a form for entering and displaying information from the *tblEmployee* table. Use the Form Design tool to create *frmEmployee* form and include all fields from the employee table except the *Department* field.

2. Arrange and format the form in any way you wish, as long as the following minimum conditions are met.

   a. There should be a centered title Header "Employees" that is in a font larger than the other form labels.

   b. Change at least the background color of the detail section.

   c. Add a Combo box for the *Department* field that looks up the *Department Name*.

   d. Calculate the balance of remaining vacation and sick hours.

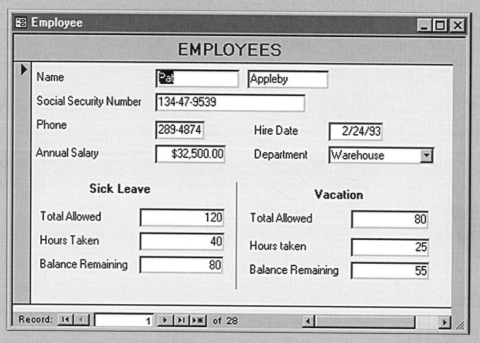

Figure 9.60 Sample form for Exercise 2

3. Check for correct tab order.

4. Save the form as *frmEmployee*.

Part 2

1. Exchange forms with another group.

2. Open the form and take turns using it to add each group member to the database as a new employee in the Computer Information Systems department. Note any problems you encountered and any changes you think should be made to the form.

3. Discuss these changes and summarize them on paper or in a file for the other group to read.

Part 3

1. Give the page or file containing your findings to the group that created the form.

2. Use the feedback you got on your own group's form to make improvements. It's OK to borrow ideas from the other group's form. Save your form.

Part 4

If possible, display the forms developed by all groups to the class and discuss the best features of each.

ACTIVITY AND REFLECTION

Exercise 3—Challenge: Creating an Order Form

Using the *Practice_Ch9.accdb* file, create a form to display orders, as shown in Figure 9.61. This will require creating queries to combine fields from five different tables.

Exercise 3A: Creating the Main Form

1. Display the table relationships in the database (click the Relationships button). Review the relationships for the tables:

   tblCustomers

   tblOrders

   tblEmployee

   tblInventory

   tblDepartments

   tblOrder Items

2. Create a query that joins the *tblCustomers*, *tblOrders*, and *tblEmployee* tables and name it *qryOrderQuery*. Be sure to include the common fields that join the tables. This query will contain the data for the main form (see Figure 9.61).

3. Create a form called *frmOrders* that displays data from the *qryOrderQuery*. It should display all the data shown in the main form, but it can be formatted and moved if you want (see Figure 9.61).

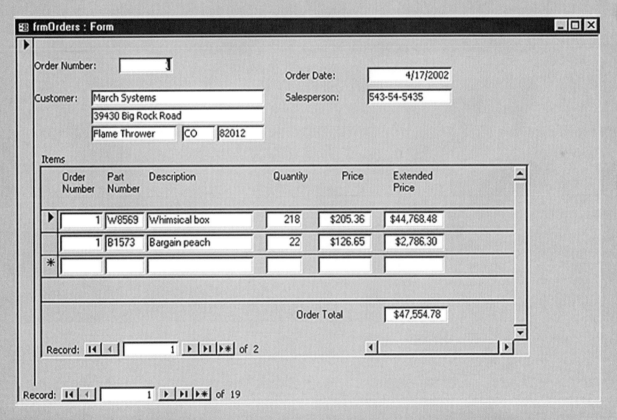

Figure 9.61 Sample form for Exercise 3

Exercise 3B: Creating the Subform

1. Create a query that joins the *tblOrder Items*, *tblOrders*, and *tblInventory* tables and name it *qryItemQuery*. Be sure to include the common fields that join the tables. Create a calculated field called *Extended Price* based on the expression *Quantity *Price*. This query will contain the data for the subform (see Figure 9.61).

2. Create a form called *frmItems* that displays data from the *qryItemQuery*. It should display all the data shown in the subform (including the total). The total shown is the sum of the query field *Extended Price*. Turn off the Record Selectors and Navigation Buttons. Save the form.

Exercise 3C: Combining the Forms

1. Open the *frmOrders* form in Design view and extend the form boundary downward (or if the Footer section is displayed, extend the Detail section). Using the SubForm/SubReport command draw a large rectangle on the lower part of the form. When the SubForm Wizard starts, choose to build the subform from the existing form *frmItems*.

2. View the form and adjust it so that all information is displayed clearly (see Figure 9.61).

3. Save the form.

ACTIVITY AND REFLECTION

Exercise 4—Discussion Questions

1. What are the pros and cons of using queries versus forms for:

   a. Creating expressions for new calculated values?

   b. Calculating totals or other summary statistics?

   c. Using data from multiple tables?

2. What differences might a form have if it is going to be used to enter and edit data, rather than being used for viewing data?

3. Do you think Access forms could be created to duplicate many paper forms?

   What form controls could be used to duplicate different features found on paper forms, such as check boxes or choices to be circled?

   What advantages might there be to using an Access form that looks like a paper form?

4. Think about the use of color, lines, rectangles, special effects, and graphics on a form. Write three principles that you could use to govern their usage.

5. List all the controls you can use on a form that make data entry and editing easier when using the mouse, rather than typing data in from the keyboard. What advantage is there to including these mouse-based controls?

CASE STUDY A: MRS. SUGARBAKER'S COOKIES

Mrs. Sugarbaker wants a form to show her customers' data, with a Combo box to select a customer name in the header of the form.

1. Create a query to combine data from the following tables: *tblOrderItems, tblOrders,* and *tblProducts.*

   a. Include all the fields from *tblOrderItems, tblOrders,* and *UnitPrice* from *tblProducts.*

2. Save the query as *qry_OrderForm.*

3. Create a form using all the fields from the *tblCustomers* table.

   a. Delete the *LastName* control.

   b. Move the *FirstName* and the *CustomerID* controls to the Form Header section.

    c. Arrange the fields so that address information is located together along the left edge of the Detail section.

    d. Add visual enhancements such as a rectangle or line control. Add color.

    e. Add a Combo Box control to the Form Header that shows a list of alphabetized customer *LastNames*. When a *LastName* is selected from the Combo Box, the form should display the record for the customer.

    f. Save the form as *frm_Customers*.

4. Create a form using the *qry_OrderForm* as the data source.

    a. Open the form in Design view.

    b. Remove all AutoFormats.

    c. Delete the icon in the Form Header.

    d. Change the Title of the form to "Order Information."

    e. Resize the controls to make them shorter but still display the data and labels.

    f. Move the *ProductID* field to be parallel to the *OrderID* field.

    g. Move the *UnitPrice, Quantity*, and *FreightCharge* fields to the right of the form.

    h. Add a calculated control which calculates the Total Price for the order. Hint: (UnitPrice *Quantity) + FreightCharge.

    i. Format this control as currency.

    j. Set Conditional Formatting on the Total Price control to change background color and Bold for Total Price greater than $50.

    k. Through the Property Sheet, turn off the Record Selector and Navigation Button properties.

    l. Save the form as *frm_OrderForm*.

5. Add the *frm_OrderForm* to the *frm_Customers* as a subform.

6. Test the form in Form view to be sure it displays the data correctly when the *LastName* is selected.

7. Save the *frmCustomers*.

Need More Help?

To display the customers in alphabetical order in the Combo Box:

1. Open the Combo Box Property Sheet, and open the Row Source query.

2. Sort the *LastName* field in ascending order.

3. Close and save the query.

4. To format a control *Price* as currency, open its property sheet and change the Format property.

5. To turn off the Record Selector and Navigation Buttons on the form, open the Form property sheet and change those properties.

6. To display the Field list in alphabetical order in the Combo box:

    a. Open the Combo box property sheet and open the Row Source query.

    b. Sort the field list in ascending order.

    c. Close and save the query.

CASE STUDY B: SANDY FEET RENTAL COMPANY

SFRC wants a form to hold client rental information. It should display all client information, rental rates, and additional fees. The form should show the total the client owes for the rental.

1. Create a Client Information form using the *tblClient* table. Include all the fields from the table.

   a. Delete the icon and the title in the Form Header section.

   b. Resize the Header section to make it larger.

   c. Delete the *LastName* control.

   d. Add the title, "Client Rental Information."

   e. Resize the fields to make them shorter but still display all the data.

   f. Move the *FirstName* and *ClientID* fields into the Form Header section.

   g. Add a Combo Box control on the using the *LastName* field to select a record. Place this control in the Form Header section.

   h. Arrange the contact information into a block on the left side of the form in the Detail section.

   i. Add a separator line under the Client information.

   j. Save the form as *frm_ClientInformation*.

2. Create a query using the *tblRentalTransactions*, *tblRentalRates*, and *tblProperties* tables.

   a. Add all the fields from the *tblRentalTransactions* table.

   b. Add all the fields from the *tblRentalRates* table.

   c. Add the field *PropertyAddress* and *CondoType* from the *tblProperties* table.

   d. Save the query as *qry_RentalInformation*.

3. Create a form using the *qry_RentalInformation* query.

   a. Delete the icon from the Form Header.

   b. Change the title of the form to "Rental Information."

   c. Resize all controls to make them shorter but still display the data.

   d. Remove the AutoFormat formatting from all controls.

   e. Group the controls to have all condo information together, the rental rates together, client information together, and payment information together.

   f. Add lines, rectangles, etc. for visual interest and to set sections of the form apart.

   g. Add a Combo Box control that will allow for choosing values from a list. Enter the values from $300–675 in $25 increments (300, 325, 350, etc.). Store the values in the *RentalFee* field.

   h. Save the form as *frm_RentalInformation*.

   i. Use the form to enter the Fee data into all the records.

4. Add the *frm_RentalInformation* as a subform to the *frm_ClientInformation*.

   a. Save the *frm_ClientInformation*.

   b. Be sure the *frm_ClientInformation* runs correctly.

CASE STUDY C: PENGUINS SKI CLUB

The Penguins Ski Club needs some new forms for viewing table and query data.

Use the database *CSC_Ch8* for the case study. The queries developed in the Chapter 8 case study will be used as data sources for some of the forms.

Tabbed Forms

1. Create the following forms based on three queries developed in Chapter 8.

Query Name	FormName
qryMemberCoaches	*frmMemberCoaches*
qryAgeAbilityXTab	*frmAgeAbilityXTab*
qryAbilityAllCounts	*frmAbilityAllCounts*

   Format the forms with the same colors and fonts—use the same styles if you create the forms with a wizard. Change the Record Selectors property to "No" and the Navigation Buttons property to "No" for each form.

2. Create a tabbed form named *frmTabbedInfo,* and put each of the forms created in step #1 onto a separate page of the tabbed form. Change the tab page names to be more descriptive. Add a title to the form *frmTabbedInfo* that says "Penguins Ski Club." Put the logo file *penguins.jpg* next to the title.

Forms and Sub Forms

1. Edit the query *qryMembersCoaches* created in Chapter 8. Add the fields *AbilityLevel* and *Age* to the query and save it.

2. Create a form based on *qryMembersCoaches* that displays members' first name, last name, age, and ability level in a tabular view. Name the form *frmMemberSub.*

3. Create another form from *tblCoaches* and call it *frmCoachesMembers.* It should show the name of one coach at a time.

4. Add a subform to *frmCoachesMembers* that displays the form *frmMemberSub.* The two forms are joined by *CoachID.* Save the form. It should display all the members who have taken a session with the coach whose name appears in the upper part of the form.

Combo Boxes

1. Create a new form based on *tblMembers.* Include all fields and arrange them in columnar format. Group the address fields together. Save and name the form *frmMembers.*

2. Add a Combo Box to the Form Header—be sure the wizard is turned on when you add the Combo Box so that the wizard runs. Choose the option to "Find a record on my form based on the value selected in my combo box." Include the fields *MemberID, LastName,* and *FirstName.* Hide the key column (*MemberID*). Once the field has been created, open the Property Sheet for the Combo Box and edit the query in the Row Source property. Sort the query in ascending order on *LastName* and save the query. View the form. When you choose a different member from the Combo Box, the form should display all the information for the selected member.

Chapter 10

Custom Reports

Objectives

After completing this chapter you will be able to

Plan and design custom reports.
Create and modify custom reports:
- Create a report using Report Design.
- Choose data source(s).
- Enter various types of controls, including Labels, Text boxes, drawn objects, bound controls, unbound controls, expressions, functions, and calculated fields.
- Move, resize, and align controls.
- Create Page, Header, and Footer sections
- Group and sort records.
- Create grand totals and group subtotals.

- Add visual enhancements such as colors, borders, and special effects.
- Create a separate title page using the Blank Report command.

Set properties:
- Modify properties for the report and its controls.

Create a report with a subreport.
Print reports:
- Add page breaks.
- Create a Snapshot.

Dictionary

AutoFormat	A report design command that automatically formats a report.
Bound control	An object in a form or report that is tied directly to a field in the data source.
Calculated control	A control based on an expression.
Control	An object on a report.
Forced page break	A page break placed in a specific location by the report designer.
Grouping	A method of organizing fields based on the data values in a descriptive field.
Image control	A control to add a picture or saved graphic file.
Label	An object in a report that holds descriptive text.
Property	An attribute of a control in a form or report.
Property sheet	A list of attributes of a control in a form or report.
Report	Printed result of table or query summaries.
Report sections	Parts of a report, such as the Report Header/Footer, Page Header/Footer, Detail, or Group Header/Footer.

Snapshot	An Access report converted to a .snp file format for e-distribution. All elements of the report are saved in this format.
Sorting	A method of organizing records based on ascending or descending order of values in a field or fields.
SubReport	A report that is inserted into another report.
Text Box	A box where field data or calculated data is displayed.
Unbound control	An object in a form or report that is not directly tied to a field in the data source.

10.1 Getting Started with a Custom Report

Access reports are the printed result of table or query summaries. Reports can display detailed data from records, data summaries, totals, and subtotals. A report can be detailed, which means it would show every record in the table. The report could summarize data showing counts, averages, or statistics about groups of records. The report can also display totals and subtotals for both detailed and summary data.

Reports can be printed with one or more records on each page depending on the purpose of the report. Reports with a vertical layout print all the data in one record in a block format, followed by a block containing the next record and so forth. Tabular layouts print records in rows, similar to the way data appears in table Datasheet view.

The Report Design tools are almost identical to those of the Form Design tools and the procedures for creating a custom report are very much the same as creating a custom form. Reports are designed to be printed, rather than displayed on the screen; therefore the design perspective differs from that used to design a custom form. Reports are often formal documents in that they can be widely distributed and are used to provide written records of data and transactions. Reports need to present table or query data in a well-organized, easy-to-read fashion.

Planning a Report

As with everything we have done with Access, a little planning of the report will go a long way to ensure its accuracy and neat appearance.

1. First, design the report on paper. Answer the following questions to help determine the design.

   - What is its purpose?

   - Who will see or use it?

   - What sections are necessary for the report?

   - How often must this report be generated?

2. Identify the data source. Answer the following questions to help determine the source.

   - What data is necessary to create this report?

   - Is the data source a table, multiple tables, a query, or a form?

   - Are these data sources already created (and joined)?

3. Organize the data. Answer the following questions to help determine how to organize.

   - Will the data be sorted?

   - Will the data be more meaningful if it is grouped? On which field(s)?

- Should the data be printed in detail or summarized?

- Are totals or subtotals needed?

4. Add other features that should be included in this report. Answer the following questions to help determine other features.

    - Are graphics needed?

    - What is the title of the report?

    - Should page numbers, date, and so forth be included?

    - Will boxes, lines, and so forth help emphasize or clarify information?

    - Should data groups be on separate pages?

5. Begin to create the report.

Starting a Custom Report

The Report Design command on the Create ribbon is the starting place to design a custom report. Other report commands can be used to create reports and then customized through the Report Design Tools.

How to Start a Custom Report

1. From the Create ribbon, click the Report Design command in the Reports group.

2. A blank report opens (see Figure 10.1).

The report opens a blank report in which data sources must be added much the same way as adding data to a form. Report Design Tools has three tabs (ribbons) which contain commands to design, format, and print the report. The Design ribbon has commands to add numerous

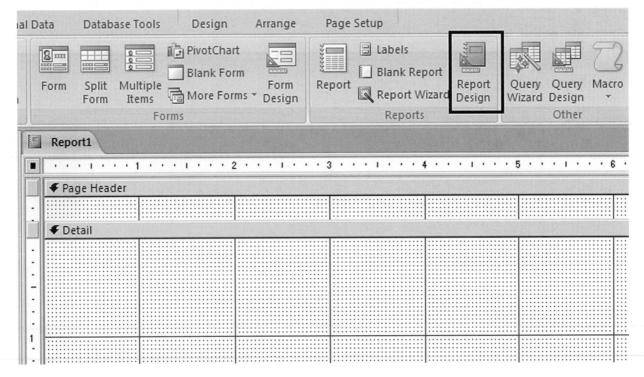

Figure 10.1 Starting a custom report

report controls, data, and formatting commands (see Figure 10.2). The View drop-down command gives access to different report views; the Report view, Print Preview, Layout view, and Design view. The Font group gives commands for formatting the text on the report: Font style, font size, color, bold, italics, and underline formatting, the Format Painter, Conditional Formatting, back/fill colors, and alignment choices. The Grouping and Totals group provides commands for creating data groups, adding totals, and other summary functions. The Gridlines group gives commands to add gridlines between controls in a tabular report for visual effect. There are also commands to change the size, color, and style of the lines. The Controls group provides numerous commands to add controls to the report. The Add Existing Fields and Property Sheet commands are found in the Tools group.

Figure 10.2 The Design ribbon

Report Design Screen

The Report Design view is the place to create and modify a report. The menu bar, Design toolbar, Formatting toolbar, Toolbox, and rulers will help you in this process.

Identifying Report Sections

The Design view screen is divided into several different sections. Not all sections may be visible on your screen, and not all of them must be used for every report. Each section has a different purpose in a report and may display its contents in a different manner. The report sections and their descriptions are listed in Table 10.1 and shown in Figure 10.3.

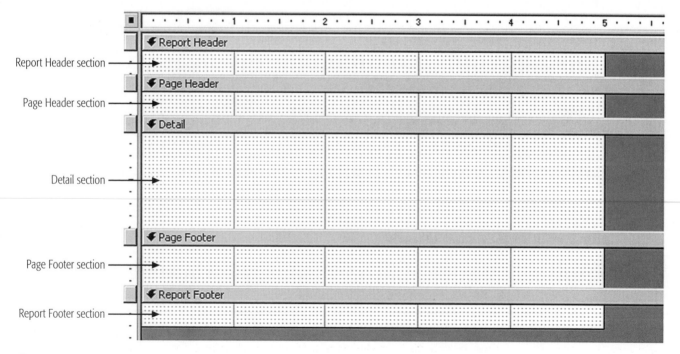

Figure 10.3 Typical report sections

Table 10.1 Sections of a Report

Report Section	Description
Report Header	Section that prints only at the beginning of the report.
Page Header	Section that prints at the beginning of each page of the report.
Group Header	Section that prints before the first record of each group.
Detail section	Section containing all records from the table/query data source.
Group Footer	Section that prints after the last record of each group.
Page Footer	Section that prints at the bottom of each page of the report.
Report Footer	Section that prints only at the end of the report.

Any type of control or object can be placed in any section of the report. The accuracy, neatness, and visual appeal of the report depend on the placement of these controls in the proper locations on the report.

Report Header Section

Anything placed in this section is printed only at the beginning of the report. Formatting features that draw attention to the text or controls are often used in the Report Header section. Usually, data is not placed in the Report Header section because it is only printed once and data changes from record to record. Text that identifies the name and purpose of the report, such as titles, can be placed in this section. If this section is not visible on the screen, click on the arrange tab and choose the Report Header/Footer command from the Show/Hide group.

Page Header Section

Anything placed in this section is printed at the top of every page. Identifying text such as the report name and data or column headings are appropriate for the Page Header section. In addition, formatting and special effects can be applied to controls in this section for visual interest.

Group Header Section

In a Group Header, a specific value is identified to make it clear that all the records following the header share that value and belong in a group. This section appears before the Detail section containing the group of records. It will be displayed only if the records are specifically grouped based on a certain value in a field.

Detail Section

This section contains the data records drawn from the table or query data source. All or only some of the fields from the table/query, as well as calculated fields, can be displayed in this section.

Group Footer Section

The Group Footer section summarizes records from the detail section for each group. Totals or other summary data for each group can be displayed here.

Page Footer Section

The Page Footer section contains text that is printed at the bottom of every page. Page numbers are typically placed in this section.

Report Footer Section

The Report Footer section is printed once at the end of the report. Grand totals, other report summaries, and text can be included in this section.

Resizing the Report Area and Sections

It is sometimes necessary to widen or lengthen the report size to accommodate all controls for the report. Keep in mind the size of the paper on which the report will be printed and stay within appropriate margins. You do not want your report size to be larger than the paper size. The ruler line across the top of the Design window shows you the inch markers across the width of the page. A typical printed page is 6½ inches wide and 9½ inches high, with an inch margin all round. You can change a report to print in landscape mode (paper is rotated 90 degrees) and make fonts smaller to increase the amount of information printed across a report row.

TRY IT YOURSELF 10.1.1

Using the *G3_Ch10.accdb* file:

A. Create a report using the Report Design tool (see Figure 10.1).

B. Expand the right border of the report.

C. Expand the Page Header section of the report (see Figure 10.4).

How to Adjust the Size of the Report

1. Move the cursor to the right edge of the report area (see Figure 10.4). The cursor will change to a double-headed arrow.

2. Click and drag the right border to the right to widen the report area.

3. Move the cursor to the bottom edge of the report area. The cursor will change to a double-headed arrow.

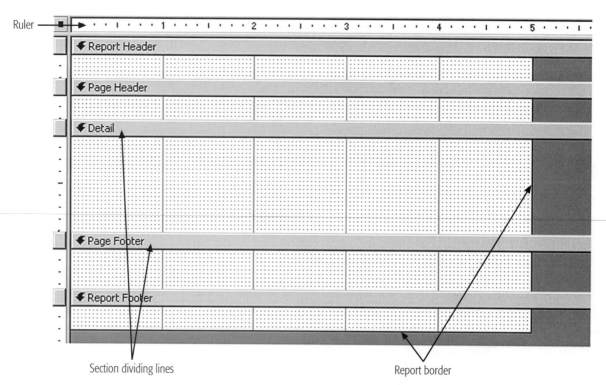

Figure 10.4 Report borders and sections

4. Click and drag the bottom border downward to lengthen the report area.

You can resize any report section using the same method as for resizing the report area. The sections can be enlarged or reduced to meet your needs.

How to Resize the Sections of the Report

1. Move the cursor to the dividing line between the sections (see Figure 10.4). The cursor will change to a double-headed arrow.

2. Click and drag the dividing line to enlarge or reduce the size of the section.

The Arrange Ribbon

The Arrange ribbon has controls to align, arrange, and size controls on the report. The AutoFormat command offers report formatting styles. The Report Header/Footer and Page Header/Footer sections can be added or removed from the report from this ribbon (see Figure 10.5).

Figure 10.5 The Arrange ribbon

How to Add the Report Header/Footer Sections

1. Click the Arrange tab.

2. Click the Report Header/Footer command in the Show/Hide group (see Figure 10.5).

Working with Field Controls

The fields in a report are connected to the table(s) data source and the printed field data will come directly from that source. Fields from multiple tables can be added to a report provided the tables are properly joined. Fields from multiple data sources can also be combined into a query and the query can then be used as the data source for the report when using other report creation tools. Any or all of the fields can be added to the Detail section of the report. When a field is added to the Detail section, the corresponding data in all the records from the data source will be displayed on the report.

Two controls are added to the report for each field: the Label control and the Text control. The Label control is a descriptive name associated with the field, and can be the field name or any other appropriate identification. The Text control holds the actual data for the field and is tied or bound to the source table.

How to Add Fields to the Report

1. Click the Design tab.

2. Click the Add Existing Fields command. A list of all the data sources available will be displayed (see Figure 10.6).

3. Click the Expand icon (+) to display the fields in the tables and queries.

4. Click and drag the fields into the report Detail section.

Q: Can I use a query as the data source when using the Report Design command?

A: When you choose the Add Existing Fields command, all tables in the database will be displayed. If the tables are properly joined, there is no need to create a query as you can choose any field from any related tables. If you need to create a query as a data source, create the report using the Report Wizard command.

TRY IT YOURSELF 10.1.2

A. Add fields from the following tables to the report:

   a. *tblSales*: G3Number, ItemNumber, PurchaseID, BuyerID, EndPrice, ShippingAmountPaid, PaymentType, and PaymentDate

   b. *tblShipments*: ShippingDate

   c. *tblBuyers*: FirstName, LastName, Email, Address, City, State, and Zip

B. Display the Page Header/Footer.

C. Add a Label control to the Page Header as the Title for the report. Enter the text "INVOICE" into the Label control.

D. Save the report as *rptInvoice*.

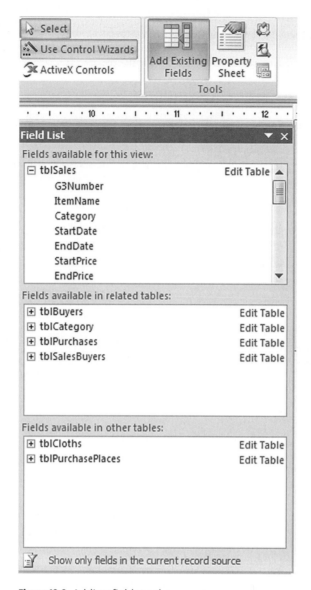

Figure 10.6 Adding fields to the report

10.2 Working with Bound Controls

Once fields have been entered into the Detail section of the report (see Figure 10.7), they can easily be moved, modified, and otherwise customized. Controls can be moved around the form for better organization and aligned to create a well-organized appearance. Any unnecessary labels can be deleted.

Q: What if I want to move several controls together?

A: Holding down the [SHIFT] key while you click on a control allows you to select multiple controls for a single operation.

How to Move Controls in the Detail Section

1. Click on the control to move. Handles should appear around the control.

2. Click and drag the control to the new location. This will move the control and its label together.

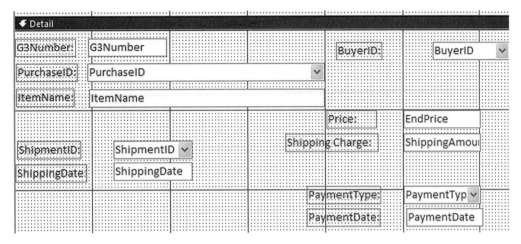

Figure 10.7 Moving and aligning controls

How to Delete Multiple Label Controls

1. Click on the first label to delete.
2. Hold down the SHIFT key and click the mouse to select the remaining Label controls.
3. Press the DELETE key to delete the labels.

How to Make Global Formatting Changes to Text

1. Click on the first control to select it.
2. Press SHIFT and click on the remaining controls to select them.
3. Click on the formatting feature. All selected controls will be formatted with the chosen feature.

How to Align Controls in the Detail Section

1. Click on the control that is aligned properly.
2. Press SHIFT + click on the remaining controls to be aligned.
3. Click the Arrange tab.
4. Choose one of the alignment commands for the type of alignment desired.

The types of alignments outlined in Table 10.2 are the same as the alignments discussed in Chapter 9. Each type of alignment will produce different results.

How to Change the Text in a Label Control

1. Click into the Label control.
2. Select the text.
3. Retype new text into the control.

Table 10.2 Effects of Alignments

Alignment	Effect on Control
Left	All selected controls will be aligned to the leftmost edge.
Right	All selected controls will be aligned to the rightmost edge.
Top	All selected controls will be aligned to the topmost edge.
Bottom	All selected controls will be aligned to the bottommost edge.
To Grid	All selected controls will be aligned to a grid marker.

TRY IT YOURSELF 10.2.1

A. Using the *rptInvoice* report, align the *G3Number*, *PurchaseID*, and *ItemName* labels to the left edge of the report at the top of the Detail section.

B. Resize the text boxes for these fields so all the data is displayed in the report.

C. Group the *EndPrice* and *ShippingAmountPaid* controls to the right side of the report.

  a. Change the *Shipping AmountPaid* label to "Shipping Charge."

  b. Change the *EndPrice* label to "Price."

D. Group the Payment controls together below the *EndPrice* and *ShippingAmountPaid* controls.

E. Group the Shipping information together on the left edge of the report.

F. Save the report. View the report in Report view.

TRY IT YOURSELF 10.2.2

A. Using the *rptInvoice* report, add a grouping level to the report (see Figure 10.8).

B. Group on the *BuyerID* field (see Figure 10.9).

C. Save the report.

Sorting and Grouping Records

One of the most powerful features of reports is the ability to sort and group records by specific fields and add summary data to those groups. Sorting organizes records on any specified field. The sorted records can be within a group or in the Detail section of the report. The sort can be in ascending or descending order on any data type.

Grouping organizes records into groups based on a common value in a field, the same way records are grouped in a query. All records with this common value will be printed together. When a group is created, a new report section appears—the Group Header section. Fields can now be added or moved into the Group Header section. These fields will print at the top of each group.

How to Add a Grouping Field

1. On the Design ribbon, click the Group & Sort command.

2. Click the Add a Group button at the bottom of the report (see Figure 10.8).

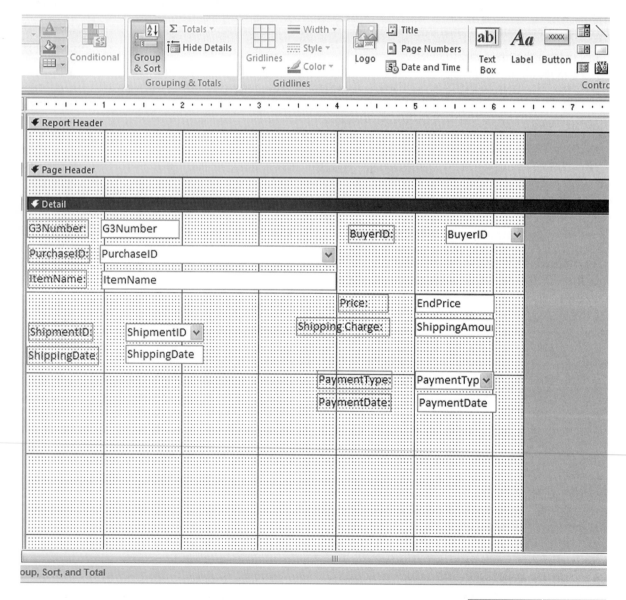

Figure 10.8 Adding a grouping level to the report

3. Choose the field by which to group the records.

4. The Group Header section is created (see Figure 10.9).

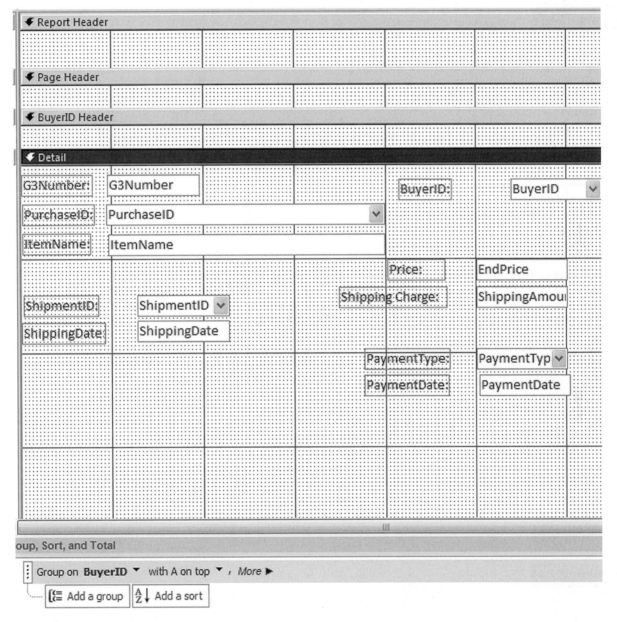

Figure 10.9 Group Header section

How to Add Field to the Group Header Section

1. From the Field list, click and drag the field to the Group Header section.

2. If the field is located in the Detail section, click and drag the field to the Group Header section.

3. Align, resize, and format with the Form commands.

TRY IT YOURSELF 10.2.3

A. Resize the Group Header section.

B. Move the *BuyerID* field controls to the Group Header section.

C. Add the following fields from the *tblBuyers* table:

   a. *FirstName, LastName, StreetAddress, City, State, Zip,* and *Email.*

D. Delete the *LastName* Label control.

E. Move the *LastName* text box next to the *FirstName* text box.

F. Move the address information below the name information.

G. Move the *BuyerID* and *Email* fields to the right side of the Group Header section.

H. Resize and align as needed. See Figure 10.10.

I. Save the report. View the report from Report view.

Q: I have changed my mind about a group that I created. How do I delete it?

A: Select the group level to delete and click the Delete (X) button in the Group on pane at the bottom of the report.

TRY IT YOURSELF 10.2.4

A. Using the *rptInvoice* report, enter the following settings for the *BuyerID* group:

   a. With A on top, by entire value, with no totals, with a header section, without a footer section, keep whole group together.

B. Sort on the State field (see Figure 10.12).

C. Save the report. View the report through Report view.

Figure 10.10 Group Header fields added

The Grouping Property Sheet

The Grouping level Property Sheet has several properties that can be set to customize the look of the group in the report. If there are multiple groups added into the report, each grouping level will have its own set of properties. Group properties can be accessed through the Property Sheet and additional settings are found in the Group, Sort, and Total pane window at the bottom of the report. Note that each field used as the Group level field has different settings available in the Group, Sort, and Total pane window (see Table 10.3).

How to Display Group Properties

1. In the Group, Sort, and Total Pane, click the More Options link (see Figure 10.11).
2. Click in the Group Header section.
3. Click the Property Sheet command on the Design ribbon (see Figure 10.11).

Table 10.3 Group settings in the Group, Sort, and Total pane

Group Setting	Options	Description
With A on Top	Select A on top or Z on top	Displays the Group field in ascending or descending order
Grouping Interval	Select the interval	Gives a valid interval for the group
With No Totals	Select the totaling option choice. Numeric data can have totals while text fields can be counted.	Provides a method to include totals in the group
With title	Type the text for the title	Enters a specialized title for the summary field
With Header Section	Turns Group Header section on/off	Creates/removes a Group Header section
Without Footer Section	Turns Group Footer section on/off	Creates/removes a Group Footer section
Keep Whole Group Together on One Page	• Keep group together • Do not keep group together • Keep header and first record together	Print options for keeping groups together

Sorting Levels

Sorting levels can be added on any field and within the group. If sorting is added in a group, the selected sort field in the group will be sorted.

How to Add a Sort Level

1. In the Group, Sort, and Total pane, click the Add a Sort button.
2. Choose the field to sort.
3. Select the sort settings (see Figure 10.12).

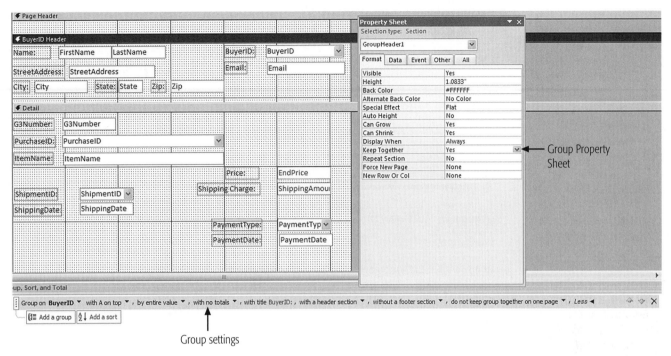

Figure 10.11 Group Header settings and properties

Figure 10.12 Sort settings

10.3 / Formatting the Report

Formatting commands located in the Report Design ribbon are the same as formatting commands for forms. Simply click the control to format and then click the formatting choice. For a review of the formatting commands, see Chapter 9. These formatting commands are also available through the controls Property Sheet.

A report can contain several sections and these sections print differently. A Report Header prints only one time at the beginning of the report, whereas data in the Page Header section prints on every page. Data in a Group Header will print each time the grouping field changes. Adding visual enhancements will draw attention to the report sections and data in the report. These objects also provide visual interest and a professional appearance to the report.

The AutoFormat command will automatically format a report from a list of predefined formats. This feature is useful for maintaining a sense of unity in the format of reports. The AutoFormat command is found on the Design ribbon.

10.4 / Using the Report

Since reports are usually printed, the location of page breaks is important to the appearance and continuity of the report. Forced page breaks and page breaks that are added manually through the Page Break command can be added to any section of the report.

Q: When I drew a rectangle around text, the text disappeared. How can I display the text?

A: Click on the Rectangle control. From the Arrange ribbon, click the Send to Back command. The rectangle is placed in back of the text.

TRY IT YOURSELF 10.3.1

A. Using the *rptInvoice* report, add a Label control in the Page Header section with the text "Customer Invoice."

   a. Increase the font size.

   b. Change the color of the text.

   c. Add a rectangle control around the text.

B. Add the *G3_Logo.jpg* image to the Page Header.

C. Add a Date and Time control to the Page Header section.

D. Add a line control in the Group section after all the controls. Note that it might be necessary to enlarge the group section.

   a. Increase the thickness of the line to 4pt.

E. Move the *Shipping* fields parallel to the item information.

F. Move the *Price* and *Shipping Charge* to the left side of the report under the Item information.

G. Move the *Payment information* parallel to the Price and *Shipping Charge* (see Figure 10.13).

H. Make all the Label controls Bold.

I. Add any Special Effects.

J. Add a calculated control that adds the *ShippingAmountPaid* and *EndPrice* fields. Locate that new field under the *ShippingAmountPaid* control. Name it *TotalDue*.

   a. Make the Label bold and change the color to red.

   b. Format the text box as bold.

   c. Align and size to match the *ShippingAmountPaid* and *EndPrice* controls.

K. Save the report.

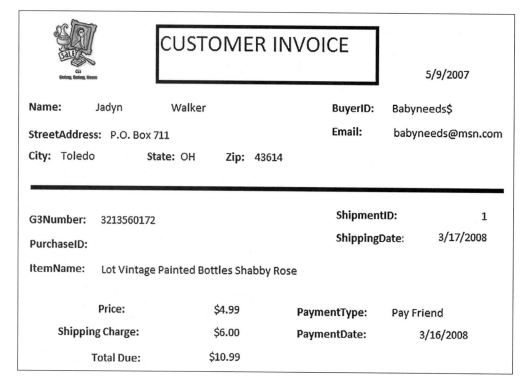

Figure 10.13 Formatting the report

With a report that has grouped data, page breaks can be based on group breaks forcing a new page to begin each time a new group is printed. Remember how each section of the report prints for correct placement of the forced page break. Check the Print Preview to see how the report will print per page.

The Force New Page is a section property that has four settings controlling how the page break occurs in relationship to the section. These settings are shown in Table 10.4.

Table 10.4 Page Break Settings

Setting	Description
None	Produces no forced page breaks
Before Section	Prints this section at the top of a new page.
After Section	Prints this section on the current page, then goes to the top of a new page to print the next section.
Before and After	Prints this section at the top of a new page, then goes to the top of another new page and prints the next section.

How to Create a Forced Page Break

1. Click into the section to place the forced page break.

2. Display the Property Sheet.

3. Click the All tab.

4. Select the Force New Page property line and click the drop-down arrow (see Figure 10.14).

5. Choose the setting.

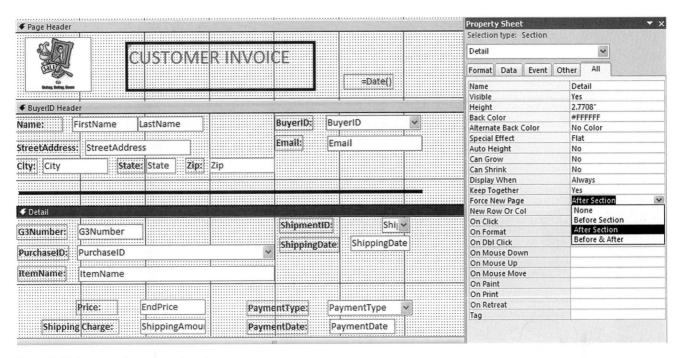

Figure 10.14 Setting a force page break

Printing the Report

The report can be saved during the creation, testing, and preview process. Once the report is saved, it can be printed as needed. Each time the report is printed, the current data in the source table(s) or query will be shown. It is a good idea to use Print Preview to be sure the report will print as expected. Check to be sure that all objects on the report are visible and that the report conforms to the margins of the paper size. Revise the margins and other printer settings from the Print Preview ribbon or the Page Setup tab.

How to Preview and Print the Report

1. Choose Print Preview from the drop-down list on the View command (see Figure 10.15).

TRY IT YOURSELF 10.4.1

A. Using the *rptInvoice* report, create a forced page break to have each group report print on a separate page with the Page Header printing at the top of the page (see Figure 10.14).

B. Check to see how the report prints through Print Preview.

C. Save the report.

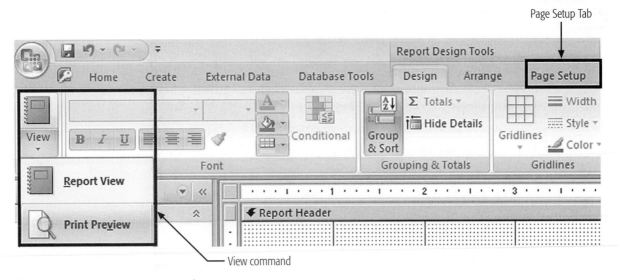

Figure 10.15 Print Preview command

2. Make changes to margins or page orientation as needed.

3. Click the Print command to send the report to the printer (see Figure 10.16).

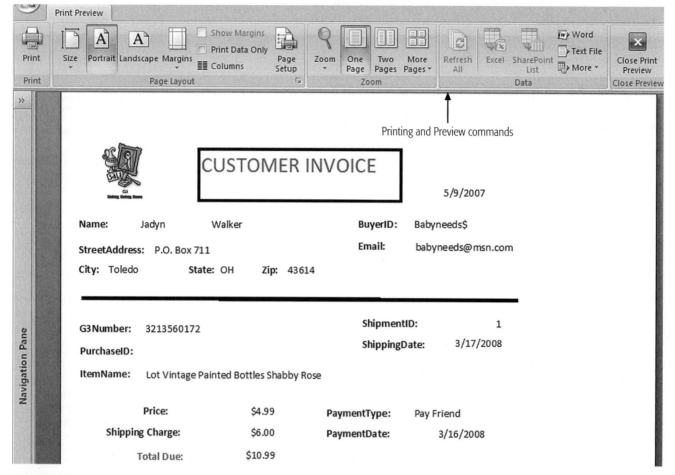

Figure 10.16 Report in Print Preview

TRY IT YOURSELF 10.4.2

A. Save the *rptInvoice* report as an .rtf file format.

Other Options for Sending the Report

There are other options for distributing the report. It is easy to send the report as an email attachment of various file formats. Access does the conversion for you. There are also plug-in downloads available to covert the report to a .pdf file format. The Snapshot file format (.snp) contains the entire report including any graphics, charts, and formatting. A Snapshot viewer is needed to open the .snp file. This add-in is installed when a Snapshot report is created or can be downloaded from the Microsoft Web site.

How to Send the Report through Email

1. Click the Office Button.

2. Click Email. The Send Object As dialog box opens (see Figure 10.17).

3. Choose the file format for the attachment.

4. A blank email message appears with the report attached. Complete the email information and send.

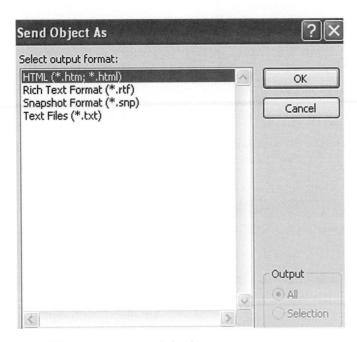

Figure 10.17 Send Object As dialog box

10.5 Working with Subtotals, Totals, and Subreports

The Grouping features in reports are also valuable to provide totals and subtotals for groups of records. Totals can be placed in any section of the form but these totals act differently in each section. If you need a subtotal for a group of records, place the calculated field in the Group Footer section, as these subtotals would print at the end of every group. If a grand total is needed for all records, place the calculated field in the Report Footer section, as this total would summarize data for the entire report. Remember that only numeric fields can be calculated. The Group, Sort, and Total pane makes it easy to place a total or subtotal field in the report.

To make the report more meaningful, field labels can be deleted and changed to clearly show the groups. Move fields into the proper group sections so that the subtotals calculate accurately.

How to Create Group Subtotals

1. Create the report with the desired groups (see Figure 10.18).

2. Click the More Options link to expand the Group Options.

3. Set Options such as Interval value, title, and other options (see Figure 10.19).

TRY IT YOURSELF 10.5.1

1. Using the *rpt_MonthlySales-Report* in the *G3_Ch10.accdb*, modify the report to include a group subtotal of the *EndPrice* field by *Category*.

2. Include a Grand Total on the *EndPrice* field.

3. Delete, move, align, and resize controls as necessary.

4. See Figure 10.21.

5. Save the report.

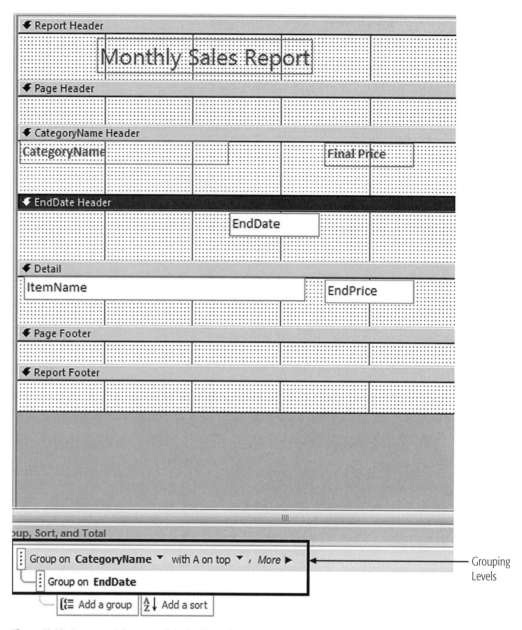

Figure 10.18 Report with group labels identified

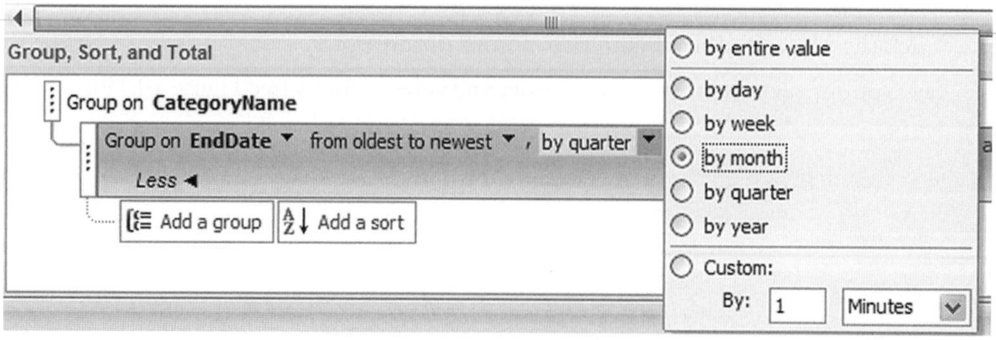

Figure 10.19 Set the interval

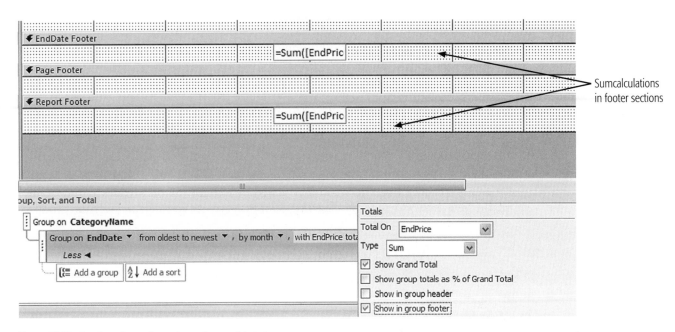

Figure 10.20 Setting the subtotals and grand total

4. Set the Totals. Access will enter the summary calculation in the appropriate footer section (see Figure 10.20).

5. Add any descriptive labels or elements to distinguish the groups.

6. Save the report (see Figure 10.21).

Figure 10.21 Report with subtotals and grand total

Running Sums

Another form of subtotals is the Running Sum. This is a sum expression placed in the Detail section. The Running Sum property of this control can be set to calculate running sums over a group or over the entire report. The subtotal resets itself to zero for each group if the property is set to sum over a group of records. The Running Sum is different than an expression placed in the Group footer section that sums a group. Such an expression displays the total of values in a field for that group. Think of a running sum as a subtotal that shows how each item in a group contributes to the total or how each group of items contributes to the total. Figure 10.22 shows a report with both a running sum and a group total. The Group Subtotal amount is calculated by a control in the Group Footer section. The Running Sum is calculated by a control in the Detail section containing the field *EndPrice* with the Running Sum property set to calculate over the group.

Monthly Sales Report

Clothing

		Running Sum
Vintage Bakelite Hair Comb Art Deco/Late Vict	$10.19	$10.19
Antique Silver Ornate Glove Button Hook	$22.49	$32.68
Vintage Florida Map Scarf 50s Pink Silk	$8.83	$41.51
Antique Infant Nightgown Lawn Lace Pretty	$7.50	$49.01
Antique Baby Bonnet Lace Lawn Ribbon Gorgeous	$21.50	$70.51
Vintage Umbrella Navy Blue Stripes Excellent	$26.00	$96.51
Vintage Handheld Fan	$12.00	$108.51
Vintage 60's Satin Beaded Clutch Purse	$4.99	$113.50
Group SubTotal		$113.50

Figure 10.22 Report showing running sum on each record

How to Set a Running Sum

1. Add a text box control in the Detail section or the Group Footer section.

2. Open the Property Sheet for the text box control. Select a field or type in an expression in the Control Source property line.

3. Select the appropriate value on the Running Sum property line (Over Group or Over All) (see Figure 10.23).

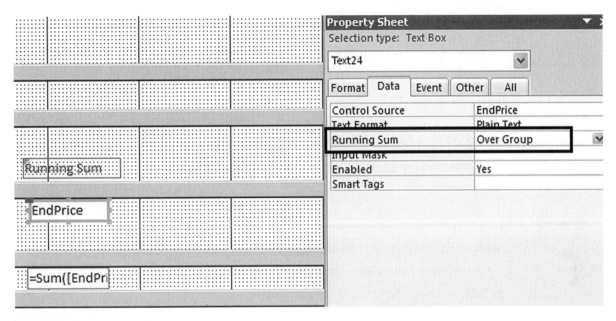

Figure 10.23 Running Sum property line

4. View the report with the running sums in Report view (see Figure 10.22).

The Running Sum property can also be used to number each detail line in a report. Add a control to the Detail section containing the expression "=1" (set the Control Source to =1). Set the Running Sum property to "Over Group" to number each item within the group, or "Over All" to number items continuously throughout the report (see Figure 10.24).

TRY IT YOURSELF 10.5.2

A. Using the *rpt_RunningSums* in the *G3_Ch10.accdb*, create a Running Sum on the *EndPrice* field to calculate Over a Group (see Figure 10.22).

B. Create a Running Sum to number each record in the group (see Figure 10.24).

C. Save the report.

Monthly Sales Report

Clothing

				Running Sum
1	Vintage Bakelite Hair Comb Art Deco/Late Vict	$10.19		$10.19
2	Antique Silver Ornate Glove Button Hook	$22.49		
3	Vintage Florida Map Scarf 50s Pink Silk	$8.83		$41.51

Figure 10.24 Running Sum used to number detail items

Reports with Subreports

Reports can also contain other reports as subreports to show related data. The procedure for creating this type of report is similar to that of creating a form with a subform, as discussed in previous chapters. It is crucial that the data sources (tables) be properly linked so that the correct data is incorporated into the report. Include the linking field in both reports.

Both report objects (the main report and the subreport) should be created and saved using any of the Report commands available. It is also important to determine where the subreport will be located on the main report. Locate it in the most appropriate section to display the data to its maximum value.

How to Create a Report/Subreport

1. Create both report objects, the main report and the subreport.
2. Open the main report in Design view.
3. Make any adjustments necessary to have sufficient room on the main report for the subreport. (Enlarge sections or move controls to accomplish this.)
4. Drag and drop the subreport object into the report location (see Figure 10.25).
5. Resize, move, and align as necessary.
6. Save and view the report in Report view (see Figure 10.26).

TRY IT YOURSELF 10.5.3

Using the *rpt_Buyers_Main-Report* in the *G3_Ch10.accdb* file:
1. Open the report in Design view.
2. Resize the Detail section.
3. Drag and drop the *rpt_Sales_ SubReport* into the Detail section (see Figure 10.25).
4. Move and resize the subreport control.
5. View the report in Report view (see Figure 10.26).
6. Save the report.

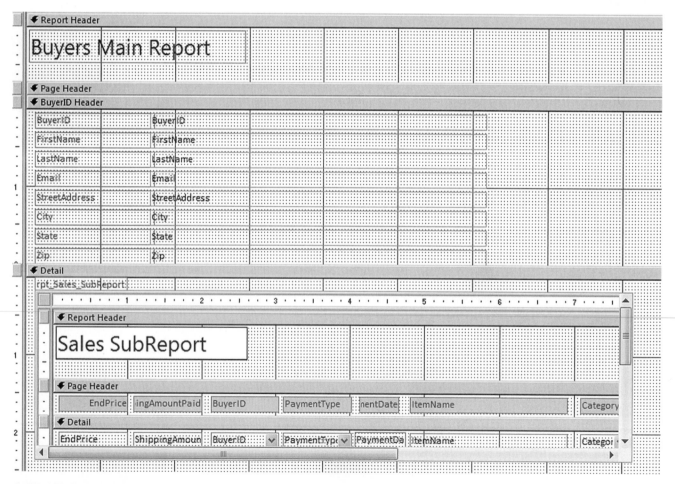

Figure 10.25 Report with subreport in Design view

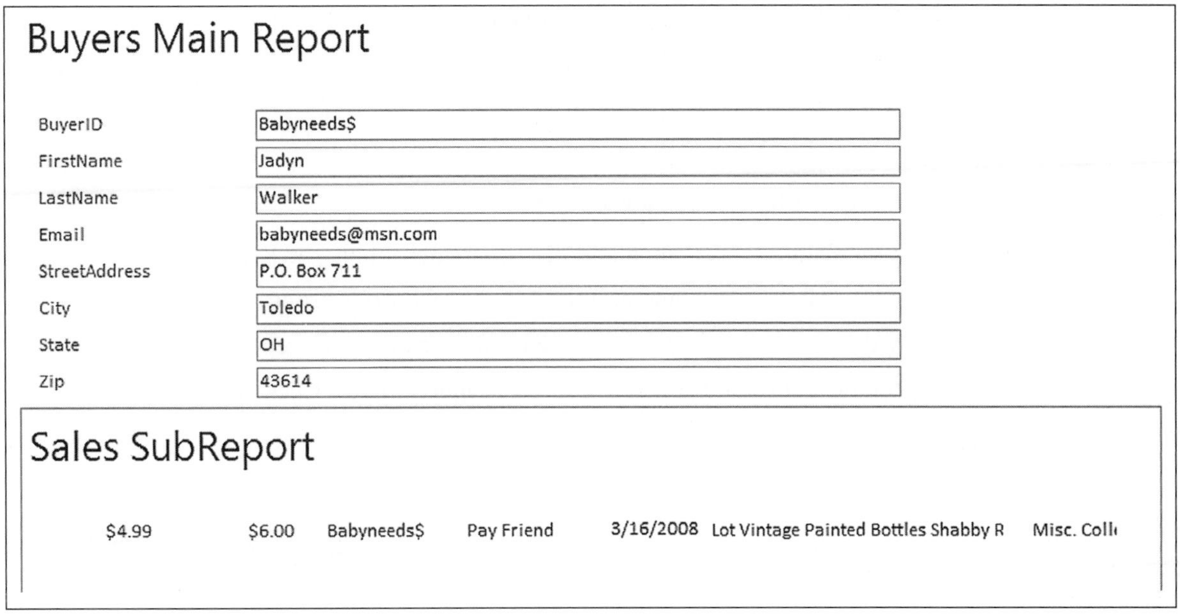

Buyers Main Report

BuyerID	Babyneeds$
FirstName	Jadyn
LastName	Walker
Email	babyneeds@msn.com
StreetAddress	P.O. Box 711
City	Toledo
State	OH
Zip	43614

Sales SubReport

| $4.99 | $6.00 | Babyneeds$ | Pay Friend | 3/16/2008 | Lot Vintage Painted Bottles Shabby R | Misc. Coll |

Figure 10.26 Report with subreport

10.6 Using the Blank Report

The Blank Report command creates a blank report without a data source. This blank report can be used to create title sheets or other specialty reports such as Charts. Change to Design view to have the full set of Design commands available. To create a title, simply add unbound Label controls to enter Title text. Use design elements to enhance the look of the title page. Another way to create a title page is to enlarge the Report Header section of the original report, enter title information, and end that section with a page break control to keep all the title data on one page.

Another use for the blank report would be to enter a Chart control to show Access data in a graphical format. Use table data or create a query with minimal fields for the chart. Charts can be embedded in a report or can be created in another application (such as Excel) and imported into the report using an Unbound Object frame (see Figure 10.27).

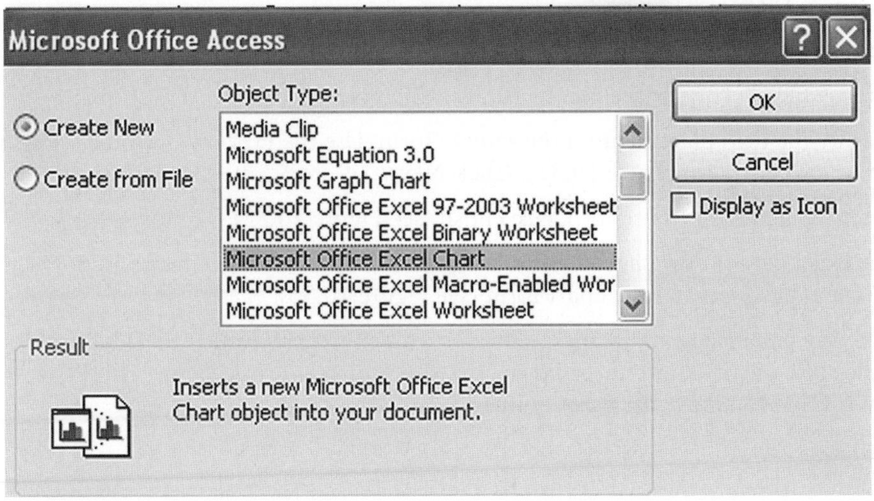

Figure 10.27 Unbound Object dialog box

The Insert Chart command is available in the Controls group to create a chart that can be embedded within a report or an individual chart not embedded within a report. The Chart Wizard opens as a guide to creating the chart. Have the data source ready before beginning to create a chart.

How to Create a Chart in a Blank Report

1. Click the Blank Report command on the Create ribbon, the Reports group.
2. Click the Insert Chart command found in the Controls group.
3. Draw the outline for the Chart in the Detail section of the report.
4. Choose the data source for the chart (see Figure 10.28). Click Next.

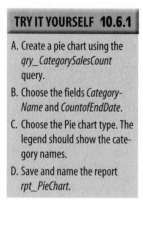

TRY IT YOURSELF 10.6.1

A. Create a pie chart using the *qry_CategorySalesCount* query.

B. Choose the fields *Category-Name* and *CountofEndDate*.

C. Choose the Pie chart type. The legend should show the category names.

D. Save and name the report *rpt_PieChart*.

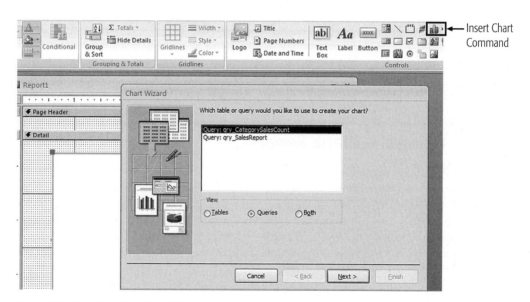

Figure 10.28 Starting the Chart Wizard

5. Choose the fields from the data source (see Figure 10.29). Click Next.
6. Choose the chart type (see Figure 10.30). Click Next.
7. Modify the field placement on the sample form. Use the Preview button to see a sample of the chart (see Figure 10.31). Click Next.
8. Enter the name for the chart. Click Finish (see Figure 10.32).
9. The exact data for the chart does not display in Design view. Switch to Report view to see the table/query data in chart form (see Figure 10.33).
10. Add any enhancements to the report. To edit the chart, return to Design view and right-click on the chart to bring up the shortcut menu (see Figure 10.34). Choose Chart Object and use the Edit command.

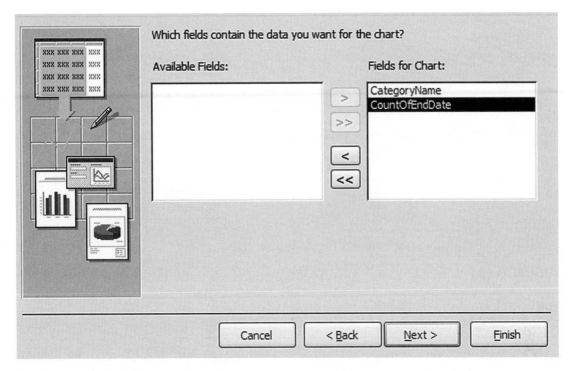

Figure 10.29 Choosing the fields for the chart

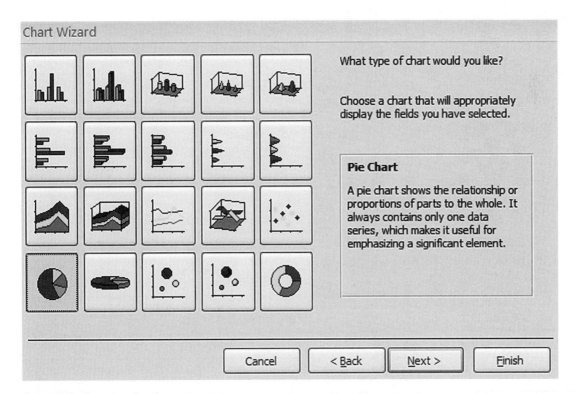

Figure 10.30 Choosing the chart type

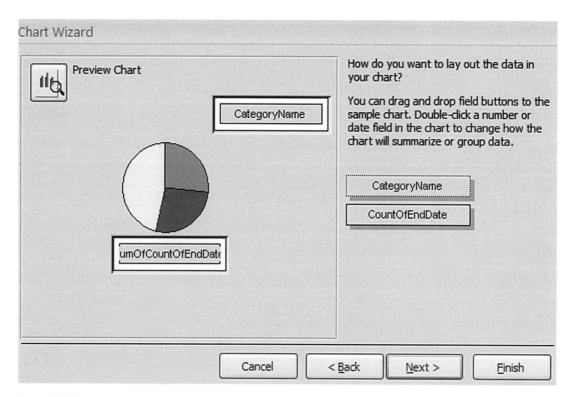

Figure 10.31 Previewing the chart

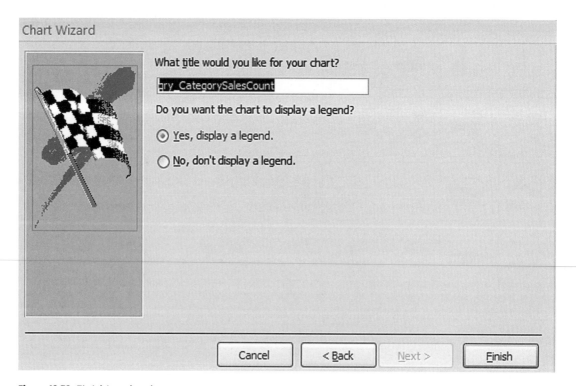

Figure 10.32 Finishing the chart

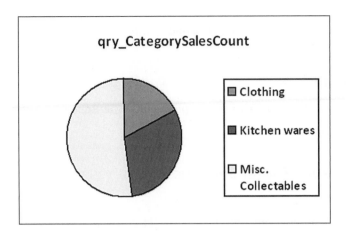

Figure 10.33 Viewing the chart

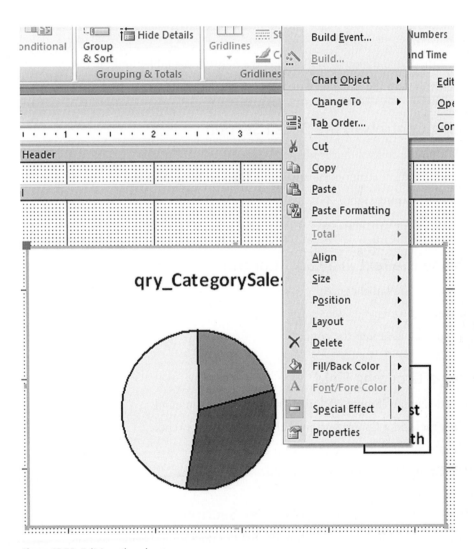

Figure 10.34 Editing the chart

Fast Track   A quick guide to procedures learned in this chapter

Starting a Custom Report

1. From the Create ribbon, click the Report Design command in the Reports group.
2. A blank report opens.

Adding the Report Header/Footer Sections

1. Click the Arrange tab.
2. Click the Report Header/Footer command in the Show/Hide group.

Adding Fields to the Report

1. Click the Design tab.
2. Click the Add Existing Fields command. A list of all the data sources available will be displayed.
3. Click the Expand icon (+) to display the fields in the tables and queries.
4. Click and drag the fields into the report Detail section.

Aligning Controls in the Detail Section

1. Click on the control that is aligned properly.
2. Press [SHIFT] + click on the remaining controls to be aligned.
3. Click the Arrange tab.
4. Choose one of the alignment commands for the type of alignment desired.

Changing the Text in a Label Control

1. Click into the Label control.
2. Select the text.
3. Retype new text into the control.

Adding a Grouping Field

1. On the Design ribbon, click the Group & Sort command.
2. Click the Add a Group button at the bottom of the report.
3. Choose the field by which to group the records.
4. The Group Header section is created.

Adding Field to the Group Header Section

1. From the Field list, click and drag the field to the Group Header section.
2. If the field is located in the Detail section, click and drag the field to the Group Header section.
3. Align, resize, and format with the form commands.

Displaying Group Properties

1. In the Group, Sort, and Total Pane, click the More Options link.
2. Click in the Group Header section.
3. Click the Property Sheet command on the Design ribbon.

Adding a Sort Level

1. In the Group, Sort, and Total pane, click the Add a Sort button.
2. Choose the field to sort.
3. Select the sort settings.

Creating A Forced Page Break

1. Click into the section to place the forced page break.
2. Display the Property Sheet.
3. Click the All tab.
4. Select the Force New Page property line and click the drop-down arrow.
5. Choose the setting.

Previewing and Printing the Report

1. Choose Print Preview from the drop-down list on the View command.
2. Make any changes to margins or page orientation.
3. Click the Print command to send the report to the printer.

Sending the Report Through Email

1. Click the Office Button.
2. Click Email. The Send Object as dialog box opens.
3. Choose the file format for the attachment.
4. A blank email message appears with the report attached. Complete the email information and send.

Creating Group Subtotals

1. Create the report with the desired groups.
2. Click the More Options link to expand the Group Options.
3. Set Options such as Interval value, title and other options.
4. Set the Totals. Access will enter the summary calculation in the appropriate footer section.
5. Add any descriptive labels or elements to distinguish the groups.
6. Save the report.

Setting a Running Sum

1. Add a Text Box control in the Detail section or the Group Footer section.
2. Open the Property Sheet for the Text Box control, Select a field or type in an expression in the Control Source property line.

3. Select the appropriate value on the Running Sum property line (Over Group or Over All).

4. View the report with the running sums in Report view.

Creating a Report/Subreport

1. Create the main report and the subreport.

2. Open the main report in Design view.

3. Make any adjustments necessary to have sufficient room on the main report for the subreport. (Enlarge sections or move controls to accomplish this.)

4. Drag and drop the subreport object into the report location.

5. Resize, move, and align as necessary.

6. Save and view the report in Report view.

Creating a Chart in a Blank Report

1. Click the Blank Report command on the Create ribbon, the Reports group.

2. Click the Insert Chart command found in the Controls group.

3. Draw the outline for the Chart in the Detail section of the report.

4. Choose the data source for the chart. Click Next.

5. Choose the fields from the data source. Click Next.

6. Choose the chart type. Click Next.

7. Modify the field placement on the sample form. Use the Preview button to see a sample of the chart. Click Next.

8. Enter the name for the chart. Click Finish.

9. The exact data for the chart does not display in Design view. Switch to Report view to see the table/query data in chart form.

10. Add any enhancements to the report. To edit the chart, return to Design view and right-click on the chart to bring up the shortcut menu. Choose Chart Object and use the Edit command.

Review Questions

1. What is the purpose of a report?

2. What other database objects are similar in look and design to reports?

3. What is the purpose of grouping data on a report?

4. Which section will print at the beginning of each page?

5. Which section contains the data for the report?

6. Why would it be necessary to resize the report area?

7. What important point is necessary for you to consider when resizing the report?

8. Which sections of the report can be resized?

9. What is the purpose of adding a drawn object to a report?

10. Why is it necessary to use the Send to Back command when drawing a rectangle around text?

11. Why would you use the AutoFormat command?

12. In which section of the report would you put a report title?

13. In which orders can records be sorted?

14. What is the purpose of grouping records in a report?

15. When setting the group field, what new section appears on the report?

16. How can the Group Footer section be displayed?

17. Which type of alignment lines the controls up by their left most edge?

18. How can you select more than one control at a time?

19. What is the purpose of a running sum?

20. Where should the control for the running sum be placed?

21. Where is the Force New Page property?

22. How will the report print if the page break is set as "After Section" on a group header?

23. What are two uses for a Blank Report?

24. Where is the control to create a chart?

Exercises

Exercise 1—Practicing New Procedures

ACTIVITY

Exercise 1A: Creating a Report Using Report Design

Using the *SDAL_Ch10.accdb*

1. Create a report using the following tables: *tlbInventory*, *tblArtists*, and *tblRecordings*.

   a. Use *Title*, *Category*, *Artist*, and *Label* from *tblRecordings*.

   b. Use *Price*, *Quantity*, and *Type* from *tblInventory*.

   c. Use *LastNameorBandName* and *FirstName* from *tblArtists*.

2. Load all the fields into the Detail section of the report.

3. Enter a title for the report "Inventory Report."

4. Group on *Artist*.

   a. Move the *LastNameorBandName* and *FirstName* to the Group Header section. Delete the *Artist* field.

   b. Delete the Labels but keep the Text Box controls. Format to a larger font size. Resize to show all data in the text boxes.

5. Group on *Title* within the *Artist* group.

   a. Move the *Title* field controls to the Group Header.

6. Arrange the fields as shown in Figure 10.35.

7. Add a horizontal line control in the *Artist* Header section. Change the color and line thickness.

8. Save the report as *rpt_Ex1A_InventoryReport*.

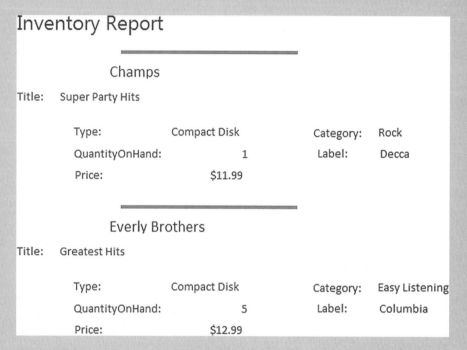

Figure 10.35 Inventory Report example 1A

Exercise 1B: Enhancing the Report

Using the *rpt_Ex1A_InventoryReport*

1. Open the report in Design view.

2. Add today's date to the Report Header section.

3. Add your name to the Report Header section.

4. Add page numbers to the Page Footer section.

5. Add the *SDAL_Logo.jpg* file as a Logo to the report. Refer to Figure 10.36.

6. Format the *Artist* Group to keep all records together.

7. Add Conditional Formatting to the *Quantity* field where the *Quantity* is 1. Change the background color of the field.

8. Save the report as *rpt_Ex1B_InventoryReport*.

Exercise 1C: Grouping and Subtotaling

Using the *rpt_Ex1B_InventoryReport*

1. Group on *Type*. Remove any other group levels.

   a. Move the *Type* field into the Group Header section.

   b. Delete the Label for the *Type* field.

Figure 10.36 Inventory Report example 1B

c. Format the text box so that the font is 16pt. Enlarge the text box so that it displays all the data for that field.

2. Move the *Title, LastNameorBandName,* and *FirstName* fields to the top left corner of the Detail section.

   a. Delete the labels from the *LastNameorBandName* and *FirstName* fields.

   b. Align the controls.

   c. Draw a rectangle control around these fields.

3. Arrange the *Category* and *Price* fields under the rectangle control. Align so they are in line with each other.

4. Move the *QuantityonHand* field parallel with the *Price* field.

5. Add a subtotal of the *Type* field in the Group Footer section. Add a label identifying the new control. (Hint: Use the Count function.)

6. Add a grand total of the *Type* in the Report Footer section. Add a label identifying the new control. (Hint: Use the Count function.)

7. Save the report as *rpt_Ex1C_InventoryReport* (see Figure 10.37).

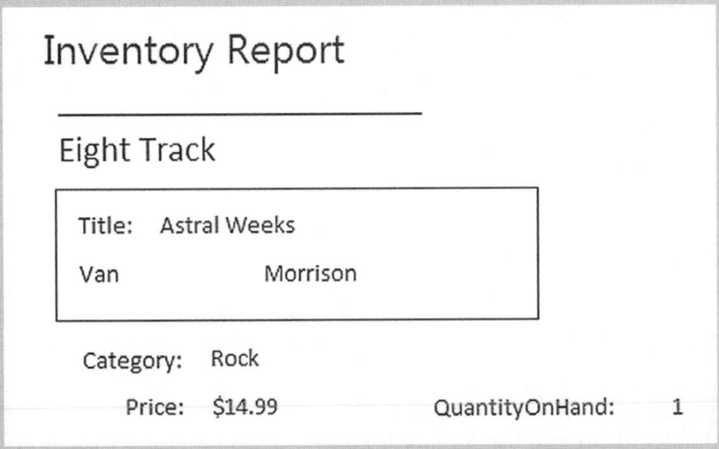

Figure 10.37 Inventory Report example 1C

ACTIVITY AND
REFLECTION

Exercise 2—In-Class Group Practice

Divide into groups as determined by your instructor. Work with the tables in *Practice_Ch10.accdb*. Each group will do the following set of tasks, divided into parts. Your instructor will tell you how long you have to complete each part, and what needs to be turned in at the end of the exercise.

Part 1

1. Create a query that could be used to print a customer statement. A statement is a summary of orders showing amounts, with a total amount due by the customer printed at the bottom of the page. Save the query to a floppy disk and name it *qryStatement Query*.

   You will need to include fields from the following tables:

   - *tblOrders*
   - *tblOrder Items*
   - *tblInventory*
   - *tblCustomers*

2. The statement must show the customer's name and address, the total amount of each order, and the grand total of these amounts—the total amount due from the customer.

Part 2

1. Exchange the file with another group. Use the *qryStatement Query* as the data source to create the *rptStatement* report. The report should include the following features:

   a. Group the report by customer and subgroup by order number.

   b. Print a new page for each customer.

   c. Print the customer's name and address and today's date at the top of the page.

   d. Print the total amount of each order, and the grand total of these amounts—the total amount due from the customer—below the orders.

2. Modify the query if necessary. If the query needs modification, make a note of each change made and why. Save the report as *rptStatement* and print the first page.

Part 3

1. Return the file to the original group along with the notes of any query modifications you made. Briefly discuss the notes you receive from the other group within your own group.

2. Tape the sample page of your report on the board or other area of the room as indicated by your instructor.

3. View all the reports and note which one you liked best and why.

ACTIVITY AND
REFLECTION

Exercise 3—Challenge: Creating a SubReport

Use *Practice_Ch10.accdb*.

Exercise 3A: Creating a Sales Commission Report

Create a report showing the total commission for each salesperson. Salespeople receive a 5% commission on every sale.

1. Combine the *tblEmployee*, *tblOrders*, *tblOrderItems*, and *tblInventory* tables into a query named *qrySalesCommissions*.

   a. Include the fields *SSN* from *tblEmployee*, *Order Number* from *tblOrders*, *Part Number* and *Quantity* from *tblOrderItems*, and *Price* from *tblInventory*.

   b. Create a new field called *Commission* that multiplies *Quantity* times *Price* times 5%.

2. Create a report from the query *qrySalesCommissions* using the Report Wizard.

   a. Include all fields.

   b. Group on the salesperson's *SSN* and subgroup by *Order Number*.

   c. Add a summary option that sums the commissions.

   d. Name the report *rptSalesCommissions*.

   e. Edit the report in any way that makes it easier to read.

   f. Save the report as *rpt_Ex3A_SalesCommissions*.

Exercise 3B: Creating a Salesperson Information Report

Create another report to display the names and phone numbers of salespeople.

1. Create a Columnar report using the *tblEmployee* table using the Report Wizard.

   a. Include the salesperson's *LastName*, *FirstName*, and *Phone*.

   b. Name the report *rpt_Ex3B_SalespersonInfo* and save it.

2. Edit the report.

   a. Remove the *FirstName* and *LastName* controls. Add a new control to show the person's full name as *LastName, FirstName* (example: Malderer, Kevin).

   b. Remove the report header.

   c. Save the report.

Exercise 3C: Adding a SubReport to the Sales Commission Report

Combine the *rpt_Ex3A_SalesCommission* report and the *rpt_Ex3B_SalespersonInfo* report.

1. Edit the *rptSalesCommissions* report and add the *rptSalespersonInfo* report as a subreport in the SSN Header section. Be sure all totals are displayed: a total of the commission on an order, a total of the commissions due each salesperson, and a grand total of all commissions at the end of the report.

2. Save this report as *rpt_Ex3C_SalesCommission*.

Exercise 4—Challenge: Creating a Chart Report

ACTIVITY

Using the *Practice_Ch10.accdb* database file

1. Create a query using the *tblEmployee* showing the vacation hours remaining for each Department. (Hint: Create an expression which calculates the difference between hours allowed and hours taken.)

2. Save the query as *qry_Ex4_DepartmentHoursSummary*.

3. Using the *qry_Ex4_DepartmentHoursSummary* create a report with an Access chart.

4. Enlarge the report and chart control to display the entire chart.

5. Save the report as *rpt_Ex4_HoursSummary_Chart*.

Exercise 5—Discussion Questions

1. Forms and reports are similar in many ways. Compare the following aspects of forms and reports:

   - Design view
   - Controls used
   - Property sheets
   - Purpose
   - Usage

CASE STUDY A: MRS. SUGARBAKER'S COOKIES

Now Mrs. Sugarbaker would like a customized report that can be used as a packing slip for each order.

1. Create a report that combines fields from multiple tables. Include the following data:
   - *Order ID*
   - Complete customer name
   - Customer address information
   - Order date and ship date
   - Quantity, product name, and unit price
   - Freight charges

2. Group each order by *CustomerID.*

3. Create calculated fields in the report for the total price per item and total of all items purchased. Add in the freight charge for an Order Total Due.

4. Create a report title using Mrs. S's logo.

5. Resize, align, or delete extra labels. Re-caption labels as needed.

6. Add other controls or enhancements for visual interest or data identification.

7. Force a new page so that each group prints on its own page.

8. Save the report as *rpt_PackingSlip* (see Figure 10.38).

CASE STUDY B: SANDY FEET RENTAL COMPANY

Report 1: Client Receipt

SFRC needs a customer receipt to send to their renters when they make a deposit and book a rental property.

1. Create a custom report that shows the following information:
   - Client information such as *CustomerID,* name, and address fields.
   - Rental information such as arrival and departure dates, rental number, condo type, condo address, method of payment, number of pets, and rental fee.
   - Payment information such as deposit and pet deposit.

2. Arrange the fields in groups so that all client address information is together and all payment information is together.

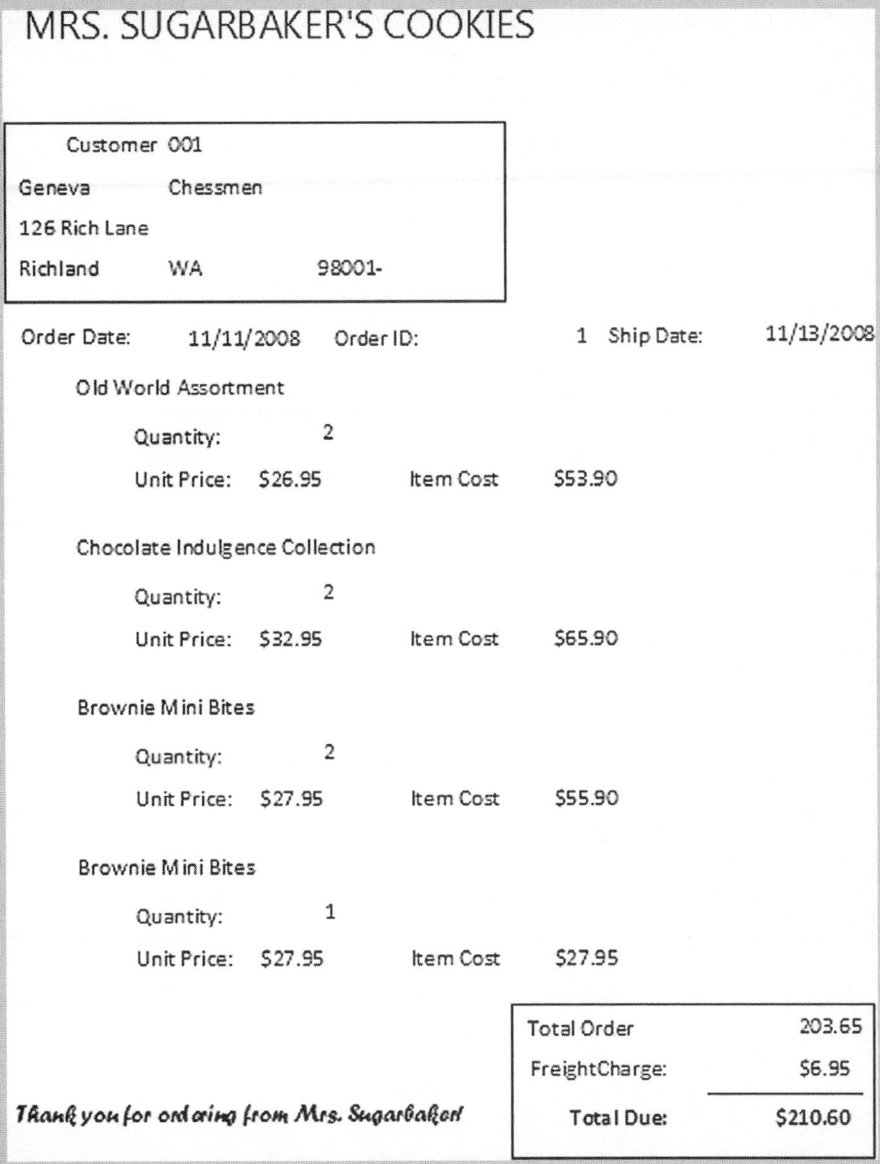

MRS. SUGARBAKER'S COOKIES

Customer 001

Geneva   Chessmen

126 Rich Lane

Richland   WA   98001-

Order Date: 11/11/2008   Order ID: 1   Ship Date: 11/13/2008

Old World Assortment

Quantity: 2

Unit Price: $26.95   Item Cost $53.90

Chocolate Indulgence Collection

Quantity: 2

Unit Price: $32.95   Item Cost $65.90

Brownie Mini Bites

Quantity: 2

Unit Price: $27.95   Item Cost $55.90

Brownie Mini Bites

Quantity: 1

Unit Price: $27.95   Item Cost $27.95

Total Order	203.65
FreightCharge:	$6.95
Total Due:	$210.60

Thank you for ordering from Mrs. Sugarbaker!

Figure 10.38 Packing slip for Mrs. Sugarbaker

3. Add the SFRC logo (SandyFeet.jpg) and a title on the report.
4. Calculate the total amount of deposit and show that on the report
5. Calculate the toal amount of fee, including the rental fee and pet charges. Remember that the pet charge is $150 per pet.
6. Calculate the Total Due per rental.
7. Add a note on the report reminding clients that the pet charge is $150 per pet.
8. Add a note on the report thanking clients for renting from Sandy Feet.
9. Group the report on *CustomerNumber* and *DateArrive* field so that there is one report per customer per rental.

10. Format the report attractively with additional visual interest elements. Align, resize, and remove controls as needed.

11. Ensure that one receipt prints for each rental.

12. Save the report as *rpt_RentalReceipt* (see Figure 10.39).

Figure 10.39   Rental receipt for Sandy Fleet Rental Company

Report 2: Owner's Report

SFRC wants to send their owner a payment report summarizing the rentals and any maintenance charges that have been debited from their account.

1. Create a report that shows the following:

   - All Owner information

   - Rental information for their property including the arrival date, the rental fee, and rental number.

   - Any maintenance charges including the vendor, date paid, and issue repaired.

2. Calculate SFRC's commission, which is 25% of the rental fees.

   - Deduct that amount from the rental fee. This is the owner's payment.

3. Deduct any maintenance charges. Show the actual payment back to the owner.

4. Use enhancements to draw attention to the data and to provide visual interest.

5. Make sure one owner's report prints on one page.

6. Save the report as *rpt_OwnersReport* (see Figure 10.40).

Figure 10.40 Owner's Report

CASE STUDY C: PENGUINS SKI CLUB

Using the *Penguins* database, create two reports, as described below.

1. Create a report that prints a calendar of Penguins' events. Print the event date, type, name, and location. Events should be printed in chronological order. The title of the report in the header should be "Penguins Ski Club Calendar" and the logo found in file penguins.jpg should also print in the header. Save the report as *rptCalendar.*

2. Create a statement to be sent to parents showing any outstanding amounts due. Each parent's statement should print on a separate page, with today's date, the parents name and address, and the member's name at the top. Below this, show the fee amount due, any unpaid coaching charges, and payments made. At the end, print the balance due. If the balance due is $100 or more, print it in red. Save the report as *rptStatement.*

Need More Help?

Use the query created in Chapter 8 called *qryMemberAmountsDue*, it contains all the amounts needed for the statement. Add the member's name, and the parents' names and addresses to the query. Rename or save this query as *qryStatement*, and use it as the data source for the report.

Chapter 11

Macros

Dictionary

Action	One step of a task performed by a macro.
Action pane	The upper part of the Macro Builder window used for entering actions, conditions, names, and comments.
Argument	Additional information needed by a macro. Arguments determine the object or objects involved in the action, the conditions placed on an object, text to be displayed, and other important specifics.
Argument pane	The lower part of the Macro Builder window used for entering arguments.
AutoExec macro	A special macro that automatically runs when a database is first opened.
AutoKeys macro	A special macro that is assigned to run when a specified key or combination of keys is pressed.

Command button	A button on a form or report that runs an associated macro or other event procedure.
Comment	The optional documentation of the macro action.
Condition	An expression, evaluated as either true or false, that is used to control the actions of a macro. If the expression is true, the action will be performed.
Control name	A field or other object name included in the Condition column of a macro.
Debug	To find and correct the bugs, or errors, in a macro or other program.
Event	A change occurring to an object within a database, such as a command button being clicked or a form being opened.
Event procedure	An object, such as a macro or module, that executes when triggered by an event.
Macro	A database object containing a series of steps or actions that are run to complete a specific task.
Macro Builder	A feature that assists you in creating a macro in the Form Design view.
Macro group	One macro containing several related macros.
Module	A database object containing a Visual Basic program that can be attached to a command button.
Null	The condition of having no data in a control or field.
Splash screen	An unbound form displaying information about a database—its name, developer, version, date, and so forth.

11.1 Introducing Events and Macros

A macro is a series of commands that tell Access to perform a specific task. Macros are really programs, but are set up in a simplified manner so you don't need to learn a programming language to use them. There are 53 different actions (commands) you can use in a macro, including an action that activates any menu command. A macro can contain up to 999 separate actions and may run menu commands, other macros, and Visual Basic procedures. All macros are listed in the Navigation Pane, unless they're embedded in another database object.

Macros are designed to help you automate any type of task that you routinely perform on your database. Macro actions run queries, open forms, print reports, open and close database objects, and so forth. Macros can be run with a button click, by pressing a key or combination of keys, or run in response to an event occurring within the database.

Macros can be attached to forms and reports. These macros are called embedded macros and can only be run or edited through the form or report they're embedded in. Macros that are independent of another database object are called standalone macros. These macro names appear in the Navigation Pane.

Events

A database event is the occurrence of a change to a database object. Some events are user controlled, such as clicking a command button, while other events are system controlled, such as writing a record to a table when a form is closed.

Most programming in the Windows environment is event driven, which means programs are run when an event happens. When writing an event-driven program, you need to analyze the circumstances under which it is run. You should decide which event will trigger the program, identify which object the event happens to, and attach the program to the object/event combination.

Macros are often run in response to events on forms, reports, form and report controls, command buttons, and toolbar buttons. If a macro is responding to a form, report, command button, or other control, it should be attached to the property sheet of that object. Macros that run in response to keystrokes and macros that automatically execute when the database opens are not attached to any specific objects.

Macro Structure

Macros can range from being very simple—some macros are only one action—to being extremely complex, with many actions and many additional features. You can add conditional actions to a macro that run only when a specified condition is true. You can assign names to a number of macros and group them together inside another macro. You can perform iterations or loops by opening another macro and telling it how many times to run.

No matter how complex the macro, it is made up of a series of actions. The actions perform a task one step at a time. Every task in a database is comprised of a series of steps. For example, if you want to find a record in a form and enter new data, you are really performing several steps. You are opening the form, specifying which record to find, entering the new data, and closing the form. Just as a database task can be broken down into smaller tasks, so can a macro task be broken down into smaller tasks or actions.

Each line of a macro contains an action, an optional comment, and any necessary arguments. Arguments supply any additional information needed by the action. Arguments determine the object or objects involved in the action, the conditions placed on an object, text to be displayed, and other important specifics. Some actions have no arguments, while others have one or more. In addition, a comment box is available for every action to be documented.

11.2 / Creating a Macro

There are no wizards available to help you create a macro; you must build a macro one action at a time using the Macro Builder. Complex macros may need to be outlined on paper before creating them in Access. Begin by listing the steps needed to complete the task, then each step will become an action in the macro.

The Macro Builder

The Macro Builder is a screen with a set of tools for creating and editing macros. Both standalone and embedded macros use the Macro Builder.

How to Display the Macro Builder

1. Click on the Create tab on the ribbon.

2. Click on the Macro button in the Other group, then select Macro from the dropdown menu (see Figure 11.1). The Macro Builder window opens.

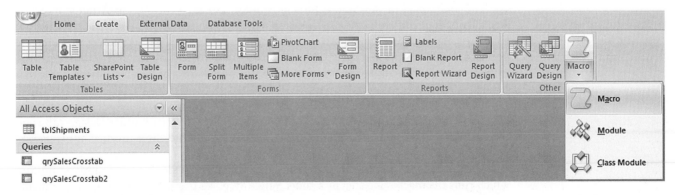

Figure 11.1 Opening the Macro Builder

Examining the Macro Builder Window

There are two parts to the Macro Builder window—the Action pane and the Action Arguments pane. The Action pane is located at the top part of the design screen and contains three columns—the Action column, the Arguments column, and the Comment column. The Action Arguments pane appears at the bottom when an action is selected (see Figure 11.2).

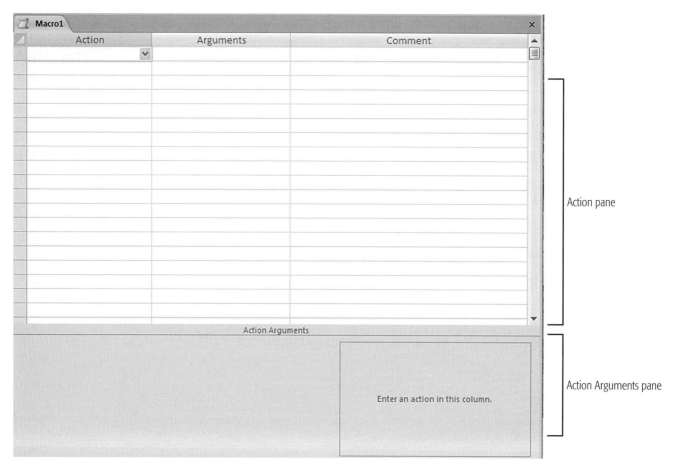

Figure 11.2 The Macro Builder window

A macro can have one or more actions or individual tasks written into it. The Action pane is a list of the actions in the macro, each row contains a separate action. The Comment column is optional and is used to document and describe each action. It is always a good idea to thoroughly document each macro action for yourself and other users.

The lower part of the Macro Builder window is called the Action Arguments pane. Arguments or specific objects used in each action are entered here. These arguments are summarized in the Arguments column in the upper, or Action, pane. These arguments are necessary to supply the macro action with additional information to carry out the required step. For example, macro arguments can be the name of a form to open, or the name of a control containing data for comparisons.

The Macro Builder window has a Design tab on the ribbon with several command buttons. These buttons are identified in Figure 11.3. The Macro Builder Design tab is on the far right end of the ribbon. The buttons are organized into three groups: Tools, Rows, and Show/Hide.

The Tools group has the Run command button and the Single Step command button, which runs the macro one step at a time. Single Step is a useful tool when trying to debug or track down an error in a macro.

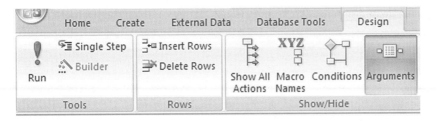

Figure 11.3 Macro Builder Design tab buttons

The Rows group allows rows to be inserted and deleted from the macro. Each row contains one macro action.

The Show/Hide group controls which columns are viewed in the Action pane and which actions are permitted. By default, the Action, Arguments, and Comments columns are displayed. You can also turn on a Macro Names column, for working with macro groups, and a Conditions column, for creating conditional actions. These will be discussed later in this chapter. The Show All Actions button turns the security filter on and off. If Show All Actions is selected, all actions are permitted, otherwise only those considered secure for the database are allowed.

TRY IT YOURSELF 11.2.1

A. Open the *G3_Ch11* database.

B. Open the Macro Builder and add the Open Table action to the first step or row in the Action pane (see Figure 11.4).

C. Notice that two arguments can be entered for this action.

D. Continue on.

Entering Actions and Arguments

When adding a new step to a macro, both the Action and Action Arguments panes of the window must be completed. Each step has an action, and most actions have different arguments that must be provided for the macro to run. There are only one or two actions that don't have any arguments. Most actions have at least one argument.

Before entering any actions for the macro, you should identify the task or tasks that you want the macro to perform. If you find it difficult to compose the macro at the computer, list each action on paper before starting. You should also know the name of the object on which you wish to perform each action and include the object name or names in the list.

How to Enter Actions

1. Position the pointer in the first empty cell in the Action column (see Figure 11.4).

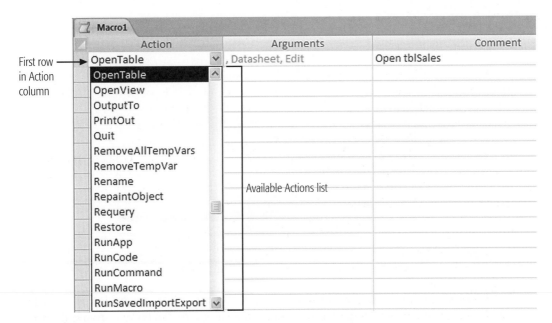

Figure 11.4 Adding an action to a macro step

2. Click on the drop-down list arrow and choose the action from the list (see Figure 11.4)

OR

Type in the action name.

3. Fill in any required arguments (see below).

4. Complete the Comment cell to document the macro action.

The arguments displayed in the Action Arguments pane will vary according to the macro action.

How to Enter Arguments

1. Click the mouse in the first Argument cell (see Figure 11.5).

2. Click on the drop-down arrow to display the list.

3. Select the correct argument.

4. Continue to fill in all necessary arguments listed in the Action Arguments pane.

TRY IT YOURSELF 11.2.2

A. Edit the macro begun in Try It Yourself 11.2.1.

B. Add the argument *tblSales* to the OpenTable action. Refer to Figure 11.5.

C. Choose Read Only as the Data Mode.

D. Continue on.

Figure 11.5 Adding an argument to a macro step

You can also add actions to a macro using the drag and drop method. You can select an object from the Navigation Pane and drag and drop it into an empty Action cell. Access will enter an Open action in the Action column and all the associated arguments in the

Action Arguments pane. This method is useful when a macro opens various database objects.

How to Drag and Drop Macro Actions

1. Open the Macro Builder window.

2. Bring the object you're going to use into view in the Navigation Pane.

3. Select the appropriate object in the Navigation Pane, drag it to the first open cell in the Action column, and drop it into this cell (see Figure 11.6). The cursor becomes a small icon during the process.

4. The appropriate action will be automatically entered into the Action cell.

5. Add necessary arguments, and complete all documentation in the Comment cell.

TRY IT YOURSELF 11.2.3

A. Add another OpenTable action to the macro created in Try It Yourself 11.2.2 using drag and drop as shown in Figure 11.6.

B. Save the macro with the name *mcrOpenTables* by clicking the Save button.

C. Close the Macro Builder window.

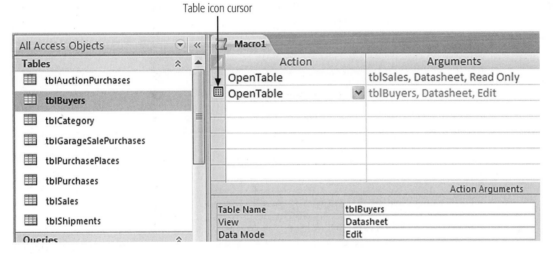

Figure 11.6 Using the drag-and-drop method to enter actions

Saving, Printing, and Testing a Macro

Once a macro is written, it is a good idea to test it out to see if it runs accurately. Before running a new macro, it's necessary to save it first. You should also save the macro each time you make any changes to its design. Each time you save the macro, the new changes are incorporated into the macro so it will run with these changes. Macros can be saved at any time by clicking on the Save button on the ribbon, but running the macro forces a save to occur.

A macro can be printed by clicking on the Office button, and choosing the Print command while the Macro Builder is open. The commands listed in the macro are printed, as well as the arguments, values, and properties if you specify to include them.

Macro are often run by attaching them to the event properties of objects by embedding them within objects. You can also run a macro from the Navigation Pane or from the Macro Builder window. This is a good way to test a standalone macro.

TRY IT YOURSELF 11.2.4

A. Run the macro *mcrOpenTables*. The two tables *tblSales* and *tblBuyers* should open in Datasheet view.

B. Try to edit data in *tblSales*. Because you designated the Read Only mode in the macro, you can't edit the data.

C. Close both tables and the macro, if it's open.

How to Run a Standalone Macro

1. Click the Run button on the ribbon (see Figure 11.3)

    OR

    Double-click on the macro name in the Navigation Pane.

A message box will prompt you to save the macro first if it has been changed or not saved previously. The Save As dialog box will appear, so the macro can be named.

2. The result of the macro steps are displayed on the screen.

11.3 / Enhancing Macros

It's probable that you'll want to edit a macro after you have originally designed it. You can delete, insert, and rearrange actions in the macro. You can also add, remove, or change arguments.

TRY IT YOURSELF 11.3.1

A. Edit the *mcrOpenTables* macro created in Section 11.2.

B. Add the OpenQuery action to the macro as shown in Figure 11.7.

C. Add the PrintOut and Close actions, appropriate arguments for Close, and comments as shown in Figure 11.8.

D. Save and run the macro. If a warning icon is displayed—a small yellow triangle to the left of an action—it indicates that the action won't be allowed to run unless the database is trusted. In Figure 11.8, the Printout command and the Close command have Warning icons.

How to Edit a Macro

1. From the Navigations pane, select the macro to edit.

2. Right-click on the macro name and select Design view from the shortcut menu. The Macro Builder window opens.

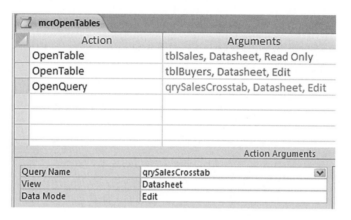

Figure 11.7 Adding more actions to a macro

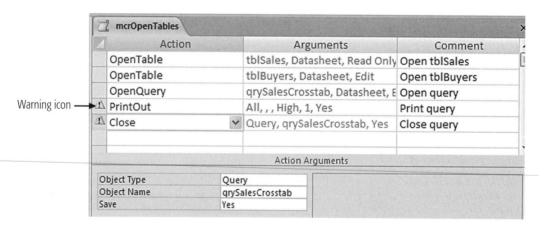

Figure 11.8 *mcrOpenTables* macro example

Adding and Changing Actions

Often times having just one action on a macro is not sufficient for your needs. You will want to include several actions in a macro that are related to a single task. Be sure to consider the order in which you write the actions, and the method you will use to close out this particular task. Actions such as beeps, hourglass displays, and warning messages may not be necessary but can also be included in the macro. These actions are already preprogrammed into Access and can be found on the pull-down list in the Action column.

How to Insert an Action

1. Click on the row where you want to insert an action (see Figure 11.9). The new action will be inserted above the selected row.

2. Display the shortcut menu with the right mouse button and select the Insert Rows command

   OR

   Click the Insert Rows button in the Rows group of the ribbon Design tab.

A blank row will be inserted. You can now add the new action to the inserted row.

TRY IT YOURSELF 11.3.2

A. Insert a row in the *mcrOpenTables* macro before the Printout action (see Figure 11.9).
B. Add the action Beep on the new row.
C. Save and close the macro.
D. Run the macro.

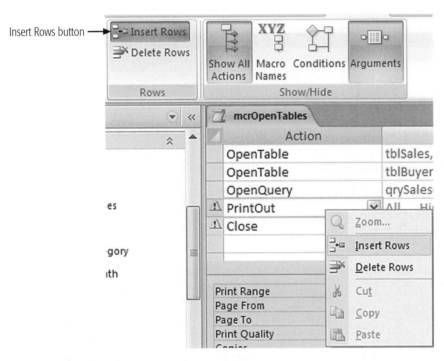

Figure 11.9 Inserting a row

How to Delete a Macro Action

1. Click on the row of the action you want to delete (see Figure 11.9).

2. Display the shortcut menu and choose the Delete Rows command

   OR

   Click the Delete Rows button in the Rows group of the ribbon Design tab

   OR

   Press the ⌈DELETE⌉ key on the keyboard. This will also delete the entire row that is selected.

If necessary, you can undo the Delete command to restore the deleted action.

TRY IT YOURSELF 11.3.3

A. Using the *mcrOpenTables* macro created previously, delete the action PrintOut and the action OpenTable for *tblBuyers* (see Figure 11.10).
B. Save the macro.
C. Continue with Try It Yourself 11.3.4.

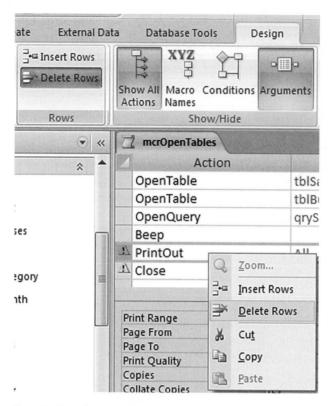

Figure 11.10 Deleting a row

TRY IT YOURSELF 11.3.4

A. Using the *mcrOpenTables*
macro, move the Beep action
to the bottom row.

B. Run and save the macro.

C. Close the macro window.

How to Move a Macro Action

1. Click in the shaded area just to the left of the action to be moved.

2. Drag the row to the new location. The cursor changes to a white arrow with an attached rectangle during the move (see Figure 11.11).

	Action	Arguments	Comment
	OpenTable	tblSales, Datasheet, Read Only	Open tblSales
	OpenQuery	qrySalesCrosstab, Datasheet, E	Open query
Selected row →	Beep		
	Close	Query, qrySalesCrosstab, Yes	Close query

Figure 11.11 Selecting a row to move

Q: What if I can't find a macro
action in the drop-down
list?

A: Click the Show All Actions
button in the Show/Hide
group on the ribbon.

3. Release the mouse button. The action will now be in its new location.

Be sure to save all changes to your macro.

Other Macro Actions

Let's take a look at some widely used macro actions. These actions are especially useful in automating forms, so they are often used in macros that run in response to form events. The Show All Actions button in the Show/Hide group of the ribbon Design tab controls which actions appear in the drop-down list. Be sure it is activated to see all available actions.

The MsgBox action displays a window containing a warning or informational message. The message can be up to 255 characters long, and can be an expression that includes data from fields and form controls. There are four arguments used with the MsgBox action: Message, Beep, Type, and Title; however, you need only specify a message, as the other arguments have default values. Type the text or expression of the message into the Message argument. The Beep argument can be set to Yes or No depending upon whether or not you'd like a beep to sound. The Type argument affects the icon displayed in the message box. If you specify Critical, you'll see a red circle with an X superimposed on it in the message box. A Warning? message displays a dialog balloon containing a question mark; a Warning! message displays a yellow triangle containing an exclamation point; and an Information message displays a dialog balloon containing the letter "i." Text typed into the Title argument will appear in the title bar of the message box.

The RunCommand action executes any Access command appropriate within the context to the macro. For example, you can't execute the command GoToNextRecord in an unbound form without a data source; the command only works with tables and bound forms. The Command argument has a drop-down list that allows you to pick a command.

The SetWarnings action controls whether or not system warnings are displayed. These messages include warnings when records are deleted and when action queries are run. The SetWarnings action has one argument, Warnings On, that can be set to Yes or No. When Warnings On is set to No, system messages are not displayed.

Let's write a sample macro that includes the actions MsgBox, RunCommand, and SetWarnings. Our macro should open a table, find a specific record, and delete it. We would like to display our own warning message, rather than use the Access standard warning message. This macro will contain the five commands shown in Figure 11.12. First, we open the *tblAuctionPurchases* table and locate the record with the primary key (*PurchaseID*) equal to 15. Next, we set the system warnings off. Then we display a message box with a Warning icon, a title bar that says "Record Deletion," and a message that says "One record will be deleted." The next step actually deletes the record. The only way to write a macro that deletes a record is to use the RunCommand action and select DeleteRecord as the command argument.

Q: If I turn system warnings off in a macro, will they automatically turn back on after the macro ends?

A: Yes.

Action	Arguments
OpenTable	tblAuctionPurchases, Datasheet, Edit
FindRecord	=15, Whole Field, No, All, No, Yes, Yes
SetWarnings	No
MsgBox	One record will be deleted, Yes, None,
RunCommand	DeleteRecord

Figure 11.12 *mcrDelete no space Purchase*

TRY IT YOURSELF 11.3.5

A. Using the *G3_Ch11* database, create the macro shown in Figure 11.12.
B. Save the macro as *mcrDeletePurchase* and close the Macro Design view.
C. Make a copy of *tblAuctionPurchases*.
D. Run the macro.
E. Verify that the correct record was deleted and close the table.

Let's look at another useful macro action. The SendKeys action sends a keystroke to Access as if you had pressed the key on the keyboard. You can use SendKeys to answer questions in dialog boxes, to simulate pressing the ENTER key to bypass warning screens, and so forth. SendKeys has two arguments—Keystrokes and Wait. The Keystrokes argument contains one or more keystrokes you'd like to generate. To specify a letter or number key, enclose it in quotes; to specify a special key, such as ENTER, place it in curly brackets {}. For example, to specify pressing the letter A followed by a TAB, type: "A" {TAB}. The Wait argument tells Access whether or not to wait until the

action caused by the keystroke is complete. Figure 11.13 shows a macro containing the SendKeys action. This macro opens a table, tabs to the next field, and sorts on that field in ascending order.

TRY IT YOURSELF 11.3.6

A. Create the macro shown in Figure 11.13.

B. Save the macro as *mcrSortSales* and close the Macro Builder.

C. Run the macro.

D. Verify that the table was sorted and close the table.

mcrSortSales	
Action	**Arguments**
OpenTable	tblSales, Datasheet, Edit
⚠ SendKeys	{TAB}, Yes
RunCommand	SortAscending

Figure 11.13 *mcrSortSales*

Table 11.1 is a list of all macro actions, and a short description of each. Actions marked with an asterisk can be used only in an Access project. For more information about any action, use the Help feature. The easiest way to get help on an action is to select the command in the macro Action column, then press F1.

Table 11.1 All Macro Actions

Action	Description
AddMenu	Creates a custom menu or shortcut menu.
ApplyFilter	Applies a filter (query) to a table, form, or report.
Beep	Sounds a beep.
CancelEvent	Cancels the event that triggered the macro.
Close	Closes a specified object, or the current window.
CloseDatabase	Closes the current database. No actions following this command will be run.
CopyDatabaseFile	Makes a copy of the database connected to your project. Use only with SQL Server.
CopyObject	Copies a specified object to another database, or to the same database with a new name.
DeleteObject	Deletes the specified object.
Echo	Hides (when turned off) the results of a macro while it's running.
FindNext	Finds the next record that meets the criteria specified in a previous FindRecord action, or previous use of the Edit, Find menu command.
FindRecord	Finds the next record that meets the criteria specified in the arguments.
GoToControl	Moves the focus to a specified field or control on a form, or in the Datasheet view of a table or query.
GoToPage	Moves the focus to a specified page on a form.
GoToRecord	Makes the specified record the current record in a table, query, or form.
Hourglass	Displays an hourglass while a macro is running.
LockNavigationPane	Locks the Navigation pane so database objects can't be deleted.
Maximize	Maximizes the current window.
Minimize	Minimizes the current window.
MoveSize	Moves or resizes the current window.
MsgBox	Displays a message box containing information.
NavigateTo	Controls the display of objects in the Navigation pane.
OpenDiagram	Opens a database diagram in a project.
OpenForm	Opens a form.
OpenFunction	Opens a user-defined function in a project.
OpenModule	Opens a Visual Basic module.
OpenQuery	Runs the specified query.
OpenReport	Opens the specified report.
OpenStoredProcedure	Opens and runs a stored procedure in a project.
OpenTable	Opens the specified table.
OpenView	Opens a view in a project.
OutputTo	Converts the data in a table, form, report, or data access page to a different format such as an Excel spreadsheet, an HTML file, or a text file.

(Continued)

Table 11.1 All Macro Actions (*Continued*)

Action	Description
PrintOut	Prints the currently active object, which can be a form, table, report, module, or data access page.
Quit	Exits Access.
RemoveAllTempVars	Removes any temporary variables from use.
RemoveTempVar	Removes any specified temporary variable from use.
Rename	Renames the specified object.
RepaintObject	Forces the completion of any pending screen updates to occur immediately.
Requery	Updates a control by rerunning the underlying query. Useful for updating the list of values in a Combo or List box, after an item has been added to the list.
Restore	Restores a maximized or minimized window to its previous size.
RunApp	Runs another application, such as Excel or Word.
RunCode	Runs a Visual Basic function in a module.
RunCommand	Runs any command from the menu, toolbar, or shortcut menu.
RunMacro	Runs another macro.
RunSQL	Runs the SQL statement in a query. This is the only way to run a data definition query within a macro.
Save	Saves the specified or active object.
SearchForRecord	Searches for a specific record.
SelectObject	Selects a specified object.
SendKeys	Sends a keystroke to Access as if the key had been pressed on the keyboard.
SendObject	Attaches a specified object to an email.
SetMenuItem	Changes the state of menu items (enabled or disabled, checked or unchecked) on the menu bar.
SetProperty	Sets a property for a control on a form or report.
SetTempVar	Creates a temporary variable and assigns it an initial value.
SetValue	Changes the value of a field, control, or property.
SetWarnings	Turns system messages on or off.
ShowAllRecords	Turns off any active filters, so all records are shown.
ShowToolbar	Displays or hides a toolbar.
StopAllMacros	Halts all running macros.
StopMacro	Halts only the macro containing this action.
TransferDatabase	Copies data from the current database to another database, or links tables from another database.
TransferSpreadsheet	Imports data from or exports data to a spreadsheet.
TransferSQLDatabase	Transfers databases stored using SQL Server.
TransferText	Imports data from or exports data to a text file.

11.4 Running and Debugging Macros

You can run a macro many ways within the database, including from within the Macro Builder window. You can also double-click on the name of the macro in the Navigation pane to run the macro. If a macro is embedded in another object, it can be run by clicking on a command button in that object, or it may be run automatically when a specified event occurs.

Debugging a Macro

Sometimes macros don't work exactly the way you planned, and although having your macro run perfectly the first time is the most desirable situation, it doesn't always happen that way. Access provides a way to debug macros with problems. Debugging is finding and correcting the errors in a macro or other program.

If you run an incorrect macro and find the problem difficult to pinpoint, you can single step through the entire macro, one action at a time. Single stepping allows you to

see each individual task and the associated actions and arguments, so you can locate and correct the problem. Often the problems are simple to correct, such as changing an incorrect object name in the argument. These types of errors are easily fixed by editing the macro.

If a macro action causes an error, Access will display another dialog box or a series of dialog boxes that describes the problem. The only exit from this dialog box is to click the Halt button to stop execution of the macro (see Table 11.2). You can then correct the problem. This error message will be displayed when running the macro all at once or when using the Single Step mode.

Table 11.2   Single Step Buttons

Button	Results
Step	Executes the macro one action at a time. If no error message appears as a result of this action, the next macro action will appear in a dialog box.
Halt	Stops running the macro at this point. Closes the Single Step dialog box.
Continue	Runs the remaining macro actions, but not in the Single Step mode.

TRY IT YOURSELF 11.4.2

A. Run the macro *mcrProblem Macro*.

B. You should see an error message indicating that you need to specify a new name or different database for the object being copied. Note the suggested solution. Click OK to clear the error message.

C. Click Stop All Macros in the Action Failed dialog box (see Figure 11.14). Close the *tblCategory* table.

D. Close the macro.

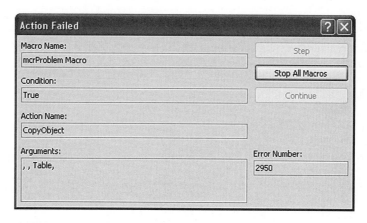

Figure 11.14 The Action Failed dialog box

How to Use the Single Step Mode for Debugging

1. Open the macro in the Design view.

2. Click the Single Step button on the ribbon, in the Tools group of the Design tab (see Figure 11.15).

Figure 11.15 The Single Step button

3. Run the macro. The Macro Single Step dialog box will appear on the screen. This dialog box shows the macro name, condition, action name, and arguments (see Figure 11.16)

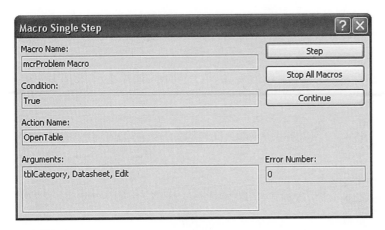

Figure 11.16 Macro Single Step dialog box

4. Click the Step button. The macro action described in the dialog box is executed, and another Macro Single Step dialog box appears on the screen describing the next step.

5. Continue to step through all the actions of the macro until you discover the error. When an error is encountered, an error message displays exactly as it does when Single Step is turned off. The same Action Failed dialog box is shown as is in Figure 11.14. Figure 11.17 shows the step displayed right before the error. This is the action that needs to be corrected.

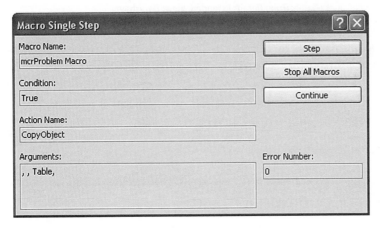

Figure 11.17 Erroneous action displayed in Single Step mode

6. Make any corrections necessary by opening the macro in Design view.

7. Resave the new macro instructions.

8. Run the new macro to see if the error is corrected; if necessary, debug the macro again.

TRY IT YOURSELF 11.4.3

A. Run the macro *mcrProblem Macro* in Single Step mode.

B. Step until you see the screen shown in Figure 11.17.

C. Check the arguments closely and note that no new table or database name is listed. This causes the error message encountered in Try It Yourself 11.4.2, Step B.

D. Halt the macro.

E. Correct the error in the macro by deleting the CobyObject action.

F. Save the macro.

G. Run the macro again.

Professional Tip: Displaying a "Please Wait" Message

This tip comes from Ray White, who runs a Web site called Mr. Access. The Web site is located at http://mr.access2000.itgo.com. Many of these Access 2000 tips still work in Access 2007.

Sometimes you may want to display a status message to inform users that they must wait for an action to be completed. For example, you may want to display the text "Please Wait" while

Microsoft Access is initializing a database, running a long query, and so on. To display a status message in Microsoft Access, do the following:

1. Create the following form, not based on any table or query:

   Form: PleaseWait

   Caption: TestForm

   ScrollBars: Neither

   Popup: Yes

   Modal: Yes

   RecordSelectors: No

   NavigationButtons: No

2. Create a label on the form with the following properties:

   Caption: Please Wait
   Font Size: 18

   The label caption is the message you want to display.

3. Create the following macro named Test 1:

Action	Arguments
OpenForm	Form Name: PLEASEWAIT, View: Form, Data Mode: Read Only, Window Mode: Normal
RepaintObject	Object Type: Form, Object Name: PLEASEWAIT
OpenQuery	Query Name: Order Details Extended, View: Datasheet
Close	Object Type: Form, Object Name: PLEASEWAIT, Save: No

NOTE : The above argument for OpenQuery is just an example of what you may want to run; this can be anything. The main macro actions in Test1 are OpenForm, RepaintObject, and Close.

4. Run the macro. Note that the PleaseWait form opens. As soon as the query completes processing, the form disappears and the query results appear.

11.5 Creating Conditional Macros

Adding decision-making capabilities such as conditional actions that are performed only when specific criteria are met can create more powerful macros. Criteria used to perform a conditional action are similar to those used to select a query dynaset.

A condition is an expression that can be evaluated as true or false. The macro action will be performed if the condition proves true. If the condition is false, the macro will ignore the action and execute the next action in the list.

You can add conditions to any macro action in an existing macro, or you can write a new macro that includes conditions. The Condition column must be visible in order to enter conditional expressions in the Design view.

How to Display the Condition Column

1. Open the Macro Builder.

2. Click the Conditions button in the Show/Hide group on the ribbon.

The Condition column is displayed to the left of the Action column. Figure 11.18 shows the Conditions button and the Condition column.

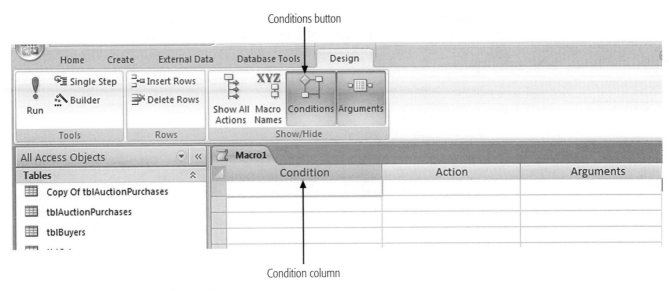

Figure 11.18 notes: Conditions button, Condition column

Figure 11.18 Displaying the Condition column

Writing the Conditional Expression

Conditional expressions are those that evaluate as true or false, such as

State = "CO"

Amount > 10

and so forth. The generic format, or syntax, for a condition involving a control is:

[Object Identifier] Operator Value

An object identifier refers to the name of a control. A control is the name of a text box or other control found on a report or form. An operator is a relational operator, such as =, >, <, and so forth. The value at the end of the expression is the data used to compare to the control. An example of a macro condition is shown in Figure 11.19.

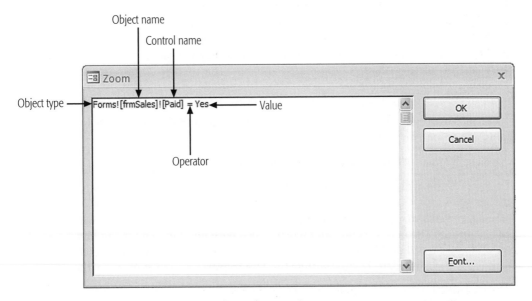

Figure 11.19 notes: Object name, Control name, Object type, Operator, Value — Forms![frmSales]![Paid] = Yes

Figure 11.19 Zoom window showing conditional expression

When specifying the control name, you cannot use a field stored in the source table or query unless the field is also included in the form or report. Be sure you know the name of the form or report you're referencing in the condition. The syntax of a control is as follows:

Forms!FormName!ControlName

OR

Reports!ReportName!ControlName

The complete identifier for a control has three parts—an object type name, the form or report name, and the control name. In these examples, FormName is the name of a valid form, ReportName is the name of a valid report, and ControlName is the name of a control on the form or report. The macro conditional expression always starts with either the word Forms! or the word Reports! If the FormName, Report-Name, or ControlName contains a space, enclose the name in square brackets. For example, a text box named *Grand Total* on the *frmOrder* form would be written as follows:

Forms!frmOrder![Grand Total]

The easiest way to create the identifier for a control is to use the Expression Builder. You can launch the Expression Builder by right-clicking in the Condition column and selecting Build from the menu. Refer to Chapter 8 for more information about using the Expression Builder and object identifiers.

Let's take a closer look at some conditional expressions. The example shown in Figure 11.19 will evaluate as true when the current record in the form has a Yes value in the Paid check box. When the condition is true, the macro action on the same row executes. If the rows below the condition contain an ellipsis (...) in the Condition column, these actions are executed also. If the condition is false, the macro skips to the next row without an ellipsis (see Figure 11.20).

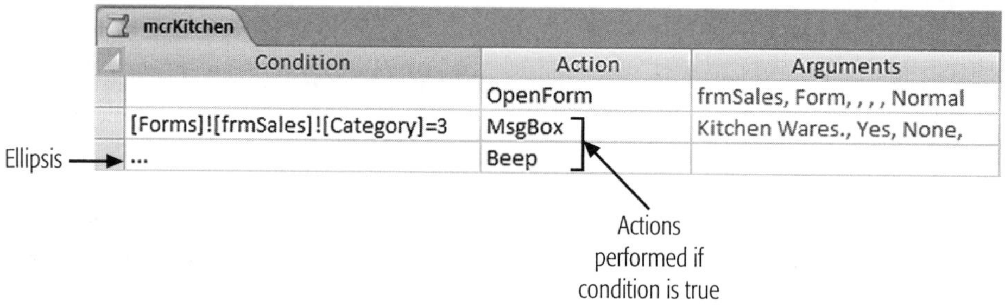

Figure 11.20 Conditional actions in a macro

Conditional expressions can contain all data types and can be two or more expressions joined with an "And" or an "Or." Examine the following condition:

[Forms]![frmSales]![PaymentDate] > Date() – 30

This expression will be true whenever the *PaymentDate* control on the *frmSales* form is greater than today's date minus 30 days. In other words, it will be true for every record where *PaymentDate* is within the last 30 days. Conditions joined with an "And" must all be true for the action to execute, and when joined with an "Or," either can be true for the action to be carried out. In the following example, the expression will be true for a record where the payment date occurs within the last month and the item is in the "Kitchen Wares" Category.

[Forms]![frmSales]![PaymentDate] > Date() – 30 And [Forms]![frmSales]!Category = 3

How to Write a Macro Condition

1. Edit or create a macro in Design view.

2. Display the Condition column.

3. Click in the Condition cell next to the action that depends on the condition (see Figure 11.20).

4. Click on the right mouse button. Select the Zoom command to enlarge the cell. (You can also zoom by pressing the SHIFT and F2 keys together.)

5. Enter the conditional expression.

6. Click the OK button to close the Zoom window.

7. Finish writing the macro.

8. Save the macro.

9. Run the macro.

TRY IT YOURSELF 11.5.1

A. Write a macro that displays the *frmSales* form.

B. Add a condition to the action MsgBox as shown in Figure 11.20.

C. Add the action Beep to the macro.

D. The condition and actions should resemble those shown in Figure 11.20.

E. Save as *mcrKitchen*, run, and close the macro.

To add more commands that are executed if the condition is true, list them below the row containing the condition. Put an ellipsis (...) in the Condition column and the action to its right in the Action column.

You can create an If-Then-Else construct by using an ellipsis and the Stop-Macro command. This construct allows you to perform one set of macro actions when a condition is true, and a different set of actions when a condition is false. An example of a macro with an If-Then-Else construct is shown in Figure 11.21. If *Status* is "Not Sold" then the Set-Value and MsgBox actions are executed. The StopMacro action ends the macro immediately, so the next commands aren't executed. The last two commands are executed only when the *Status* is "For Sale."

Condition	Action	Arguments
[Forms]![frmSales]![Status]="Not Sold"	SetValue	[tblSales]![G3Percentage], =0
...	MsgBox	Item not sold., Yes, None,
...	StopMacro	
[Forms]![frmSales]![Status]="For Sale"	MsgBox	Still for sale, Yes, None,

Figure 11.21 Macro with an If-Then-Else construct

Notice the SetValue action shown in Figure 11.21. This action assigns a value to an object or the property of an object. In Figure 11.21, the SetValue action sets the *G3Percentage* field in *tblSales* to zero.

11.6 Using Special Macros

There are three types of special macros that you can use to automate or simplify a database—an AutoExec macro, an AutoKeys macro, and a macro group. Each of these macros is created in Design view, and each can contain any valid macro actions. The differences lie in the usage of the macros.

Autoexec Macros

AutoExec macros are automatically executed when a database first opens. You can create an AutoExec macro to carry out any database initialization tasks, display a series of forms, or other appropriate actions. To create an AutoExec macro, just save it with the name AutoExec. In this case, don't use the prefix "mcr" because you must use the exact

Q: What if I want another form to display after the splash screen closes?

A: Add another action to open the second form at the end of the macro that closes the splash screen.

name AutoExec for it to work correctly. If you specify an AutoExec macro for a database, you can bypass it by holding down the SHIFT key while the database loads.

One common usage for an AutoExec macro is to display a splash screen (see Figure 11.24). A splash screen is an unbound form with the name, date, and other descriptive information about a database. Splash screens usually display for a few seconds when a database opens, then they are closed and replaced with a Switchboard or other main form. A splash screen is timed to display for just a few seconds by using the On Timer and Timer Interval properties of the form (see Figure 11.23). The On Timer property is set to the name of a macro or procedure to run after the expiration of the specified time interval, and this macro or procedure closes the form (see Figure 11.22). The Timer Interval property contains the length of time to wait before executing the On Timer macro. The time interval is expressed in milliseconds, so an interval of 5000 really represents 5 seconds. Be sure to open the property sheet for the entire form, not just one of the form sections. The easiest way is to right-click on the form title bar while in Design view, and choose Properties from the shortcut menu.

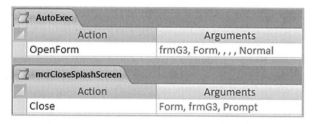

Figure 11.22 Macros for displaying and closing a splash screen

Figure 11.23 Splash screen timer properties for *frmG3*

TRY IT YOURSELF 11.6.1

A. Create an AutoExec macro that displays the form *frmG3* (see Figure 11.22).

B. Create another macro called *mcrCloseSplashScreen* that closes *frmG3* (see Figure 11.22).

C. Change the On Timer property of *frmG3* to run *mcrCloseSplashScreen*, and the Timer Interval property to 3000 (see Figure 11.23).

D. Close the *G3* database and reopen it to verify that the splash screen works (see Figure 11.24).

How to Create an AutoExec Macro to Display a Splash Screen

1. Create a splash screen form.

2. Create an AutoExec macro with an OpenForm action to open the splash screen (see Figure 11.22).

3. Create a macro with a Close action to close the splash screen form (see Figure 11.22).

4. Open the splash screen form in Design view and bring up the property sheet for the form (see Figure 11.23).

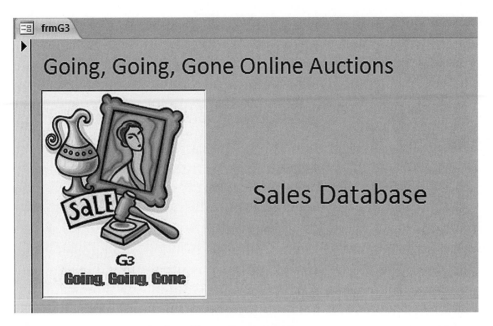

Figure 11.24 Splash screen displayed by an Autoexec macro

5. Assign the macro created in step 3 to the On Timer event.

6. Type the number in milliseconds for the screen to display on the Timer Interval property row.

7. Close the property sheet and form.

You can open the form to test the splash screen. It should display for the specified interval, then close. To see the AutoExec macro open the splash screen, you'll have to close the database and reopen it.

Macro Groups

Macro groups help keep your macros organized. You can group all the macros that are attached to a particular form's events, or group macros with similar functions, such as macros that open forms. A macro group is a single macro containing several related macros. Each macro in a group is assigned a different name. When you refer to a macro in a group, use the syntax: GroupName.MacroName. For example, if you have a macro group named *mcrEmployeeForm* and a macro in the group named *CloseForm*, you would refer to the macro as *mcrEmployeeForm.CloseForm*. Only the name of the container macro will show in the Macro group of the Database window. However, the individual macro names show on all event drop-down lists on property sheets (see Figure 11.26).

Q: Can I add conditional actions to macro groups?

A: Yes, each named macro can have conditional actions.

How to Create a Macro Group

1. Create or open a macro in Design view.

2. Click on the Macro Names button in the Show/Hide group on the ribbon (see Figure 11.25). The Macro Name column appears to the left of the Action column (see Figure 11.25).

3. Type the name of the macro into the first row of the macro in the Macro Name column.

4. Add actions, arguments, and comments for the macro.

TRY IT YOURSELF 11.6.2

A. Create a new macro called *mcrSalesForm*.

B. Turn on the Macro Name column and make two named macros, *OpeningMessage* and *ClosingMessage*. Each macro should display a message and beep. Use Figure 11.25 as a guide.

C. Save the macro.

D. Open the form *frmSales* in Design view.

E. Open the property sheet for the form and attach the macros to the On Open and On Close events as shown in Figure 11.26.

F. Save the form.

G. Test the macro group by opening and closing the form (see Figure 11.27.)

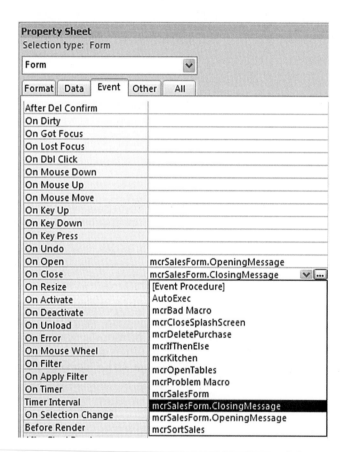

Macro Name	Action	Arguments
OpeningMessage	MsgBox	The sales form is opening, Yes, None,
	Beep	
ClosingMessage	MsgBox	The sales form is closing, Yes, None,
	Beep	

Figure 11.25 Macro group

Figure 11.26 Attaching group macros to form open and close events

5. Repeat steps 3 and 4 for each macro in the group.

6. Save and name the group.

In the example shown in Figure 11.25, the group of macros is named *mcrSalesForm* because all the macros are triggered by events on the form *frmSales*. There are two macros, *mcrSalesForm.OpeningMessage* and *mcrSalesForm.ClosingMessage*, each displaying a message and sounding a beep. Figure 11.26 shows the two macros in the group being attached to the On Open and On Close events of the *frmSales* form.

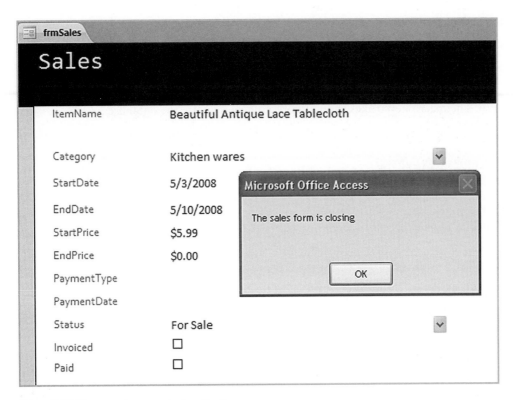

Figure 11.27 Message box on closing the form

AutoKeys Macros

AutoKeys macros let you assign macro actions to keystrokes, so when that key is pressed, the macro action is performed. You can use any key or keystroke combination, such as pressing the CTRL or SHIFT key in conjunction with other keys. If Access is already using a keystroke combination you assign, you will override and replace the Access default. You can only assign one macro action per keystroke combination. If you want several actions to run, save the actions as a separate macro and use the RunMacro action in the AutoKeys macro to execute the second macro.

AutoKeys keystrokes are represented in the same way as in the SendKeys macro action (see Section 11.3). The carat (^) symbol represents pressing the CTRL key, and the plus sign (+) symbolizes pressing the SHIFT key. Letters and numbers are typed as is, and special keys are enclosed in curly brackets {}. For example, ^c represents pressing CTRL and c simultaneously, while +{HOME} represents pressing the SHIFT and HOME keys simultaneously.

How to Create an AutoKeys Macro

1. Create a new macro.

2. Turn on the Macro Name column.

3. Type the key or key combination into the Macro Name column (see Figure 11.28).

| AutoKeys | | |
Macro Name	Action	Arguments
^C	OpenForm	frmSales, Form, , , , Normal
^Z	Close	Form, frmSales, Prompt

Figure 11.28 AutoKeys macro

TRY IT YOURSELF 11.6.3

A. Create an AutoKeys macro that opens the form *frmSales* when CTRL and c are pressed together, and closes the same form when CTRL and z are pressed together. Use Figure 11.28 as a guide.

B. Close and save the macro as *AutoKeys*.

C. Test the macro by pressing the key combinations.

4. On the same row, select an action and its appropriate arguments.

5. Repeat steps 3 and 4 for any other keystroke assignments you'd like to make.

6. Save the macro group with the name AutoKeys.

To test the macro, try pressing the key or key combination listed in the AutoKeys macro. The macro keystrokes should work anywhere inside the database.

Professional Tip: / **Assigning AutoKeys for Aligning Controls**

This tip comes from Allen Browne, who was introduced in a Chapter 8 tip. His Web site, MS Access Tips for Casual Users, can be found online at http://allenbrowne.com.

Getting controls to align correctly after dragging them around can be a chore! "Snap to grid" is useful, but often doesn't give the precise placement you want. Too often you find yourself roughly aligning the controls and then going to the *Format* menu to get *Align, Left* for text boxes and *Align, Right* for labels. Then you select the ones on the same row and go back to the menu for *Align, Top* or *Align, Bottom*. A keystroke such as Ctrl+L for align left or Ctrl+R for align right could speed things up. Here are the steps to get that result.

1. Create a new macro and save it with the name *AutoKeys*.
2. If you cannot see a column called "Macro Name," check Macro Names on the View menu.
3. In the first row of the Macro Name column, enter ^L.
4. In the Action column beside this, choose DoMenuItem. Then, in the bottom of the window, fill in which menu item you want, i.e., Form Design, Format, Align, Left.
5. In the second row, enter ^R under Macro Name, and DoMenuItem under Action. Again fill in the menu item details in the bottom of the window, i.e., Form Design, Format, Align, Right.
6. Enter another two rows using ^T for Align, Top, and ^B for Align, Bottom.
7. Save the macro and test it. Select two or three controls that are not aligned correctly, press Ctrl and L together, and watch them move into place.

11.7 / **Running Macros from Command Buttons**

An excellent way to use macros is to incorporate them into forms for data entry or viewing. A command button is added to the form and when the button is clicked a macro is run. The button is placed on the form, then a macro is attached to the button. Macros that are attached to forms and reports, are called embedded macros. You can also attach an existing macro to a command button, and still edit it from the Navigation pane.

An easy way to create a command button is by using the Command Button Wizard. This wizard assists you in attaching a macro to the button. You can use a macro already created and saved or you can make a selection from the action list, and Access will create a macro for you. If Access creates the macro automatically, it will not appear in the Navigation Pane.

How to Add a Command Button with an Embedded Macro

1. Open an existing form in Design view.

2. Be sure that the Control Wizard button is pressed, and click the Command Button button in the Controls group on the ribbon Design tab. Refer to Figure 11.29 for the location of these buttons.

TRY IT YOURSELF 11.7.1

A. Open the form *frmBuyers* in the *G3_Ch11* database in Design view.

B. Add a command button to the form footer. The button should display the next record when clicked. Refer to Figures 11.30 and 11.31.

C. Continue on.

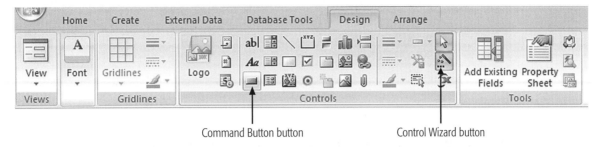

Command Button button   Control Wizard button

Figure 11.29 Controls group on the ribbon Design tab

3. Click on the form where you want the command button located, and the Command Button wizard begins (see Figure 11.30).

4. Select an item from the Categories list on the left, then select an Action from the list on the right. All will produce an embedded macro, except the Run Macro action in the Miscellaneous category. Click the Next button.

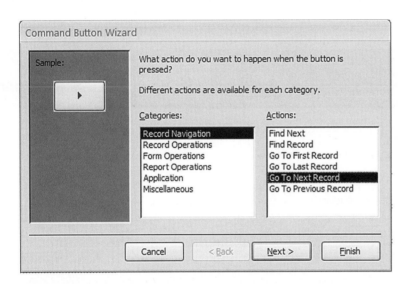

Figure 11.30 First screen in Command Button Wizard

5. Finish making selections to create the command button. For more detailed instructions refer back to Chapter 9.

Table 11.3 shows all the actions available with the Command Button wizard. Selecting any action except Run Macro will create an embedded macro.

The name of an embedded macro will not appear in the Navigation pane. It is attached to the object, the form or report in which it was created. It can only be viewed or edited by opening that object.

How to Add a Command Button to Run a Macro Using the Wizard

1. Open a form you previously saved, or create a new form. Display the form in Design view.

2. Click the Command Button button on the ribbon (see Figure 11.29). Be sure the Control Wizards button is pressed before clicking the command button.

3. Click on the form, or click and drag for a custom-sized frame for the command button. The Command Button wizard begins.

Figure 11.31 *frmBuyers* command button with embedded macro

Table 11.3   Command Button Wizard Actions

Category	Actions	Description/Usage
Record Navigation	Find Next Find Record Goto First Record Goto Last Record Goto Next Record Goto Previous Record	Use on forms to create your own navigation buttons. To replace the default buttons, turn off the record selectors and navigation buttons on the form's property sheet.
Record Operations	Add New Record Delete Record Duplicate Record Print Record Save Record Undo Record	Use on forms for data entry functions.
Form Operations	Apply Form Filter Close Form Edit Form Filter Open Form Open Page Print a Form Print Current Form Refresh Form Data	Use on forms to create filters and turn them on and off. This function creates an ad hoc query capability for users.

(Continued)

Table 11.3 Command Button Wizard Actions (*Continued*)

Category	Actions	Description/Usage
Report Operations	Mail Report Preview Report Print Report Send Report to File	Use on a form to control report functions. They can be used as a report function menu, or placed on a form to invoke a report containing the same data as a form.
Application	Quit Application Run Application Run MS Excel Run MS Word Run Notepad	Use on unbound forms as menu selections that open other softwre tools.
Miscellaneous	Auto Dialer Print Table Run Macro Run Query	Use on forms to perform these miscellaneous functions. Auto Dialer lets you connect to the Internet or another computer with your modem.

4. Choose the Miscellaneous category, and the Run Macro action (see Figure 11.32).

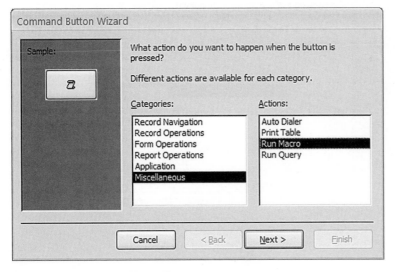

Figure 11.32 Command Button Wizard opening screen

5. Click the Next button to move to the next screen.

6. Choose the macro from the list of macro names (see Figure 11.33).

7. Click the Next button to move to the next screen.

8. Choose the Text option button to display text on the face of the command button, and retype the caption for the command button. Refer to Figure 11.34 to locate these items. (You can select the Picture option button and browse for a graphic file. This is covered later in this chapter.)

9. Click the Next button to move to the next screen.

10. Choose a name for the command button (see Figure 11.35). This name will be used to refer to the command button in other macros or modules.

11. Click the Finish button to complete the process.

Always test a new command button to see if it runs and executes the macro as expected.

TRY IT YOURSELF 11.7.2

A. Open the *frmBuyers* form in Design view.

B. Add a command button to the form footer that runs the macro *mcrSendEmail*. Refer to Figures 11.32 through 11.36 to assist with the process.

C. Save, run, and test the button.

D. Close everything when you're finished.

Figure 11.33 List of macro names

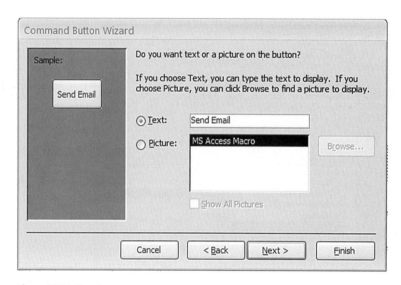

Figure 11.34 Caption screen

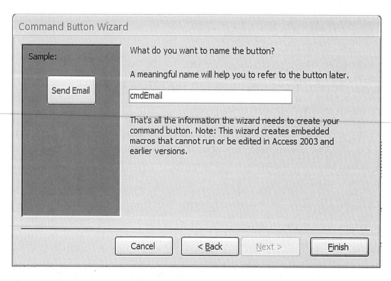

Figure 11.35 Final screen of Command Button Wizard

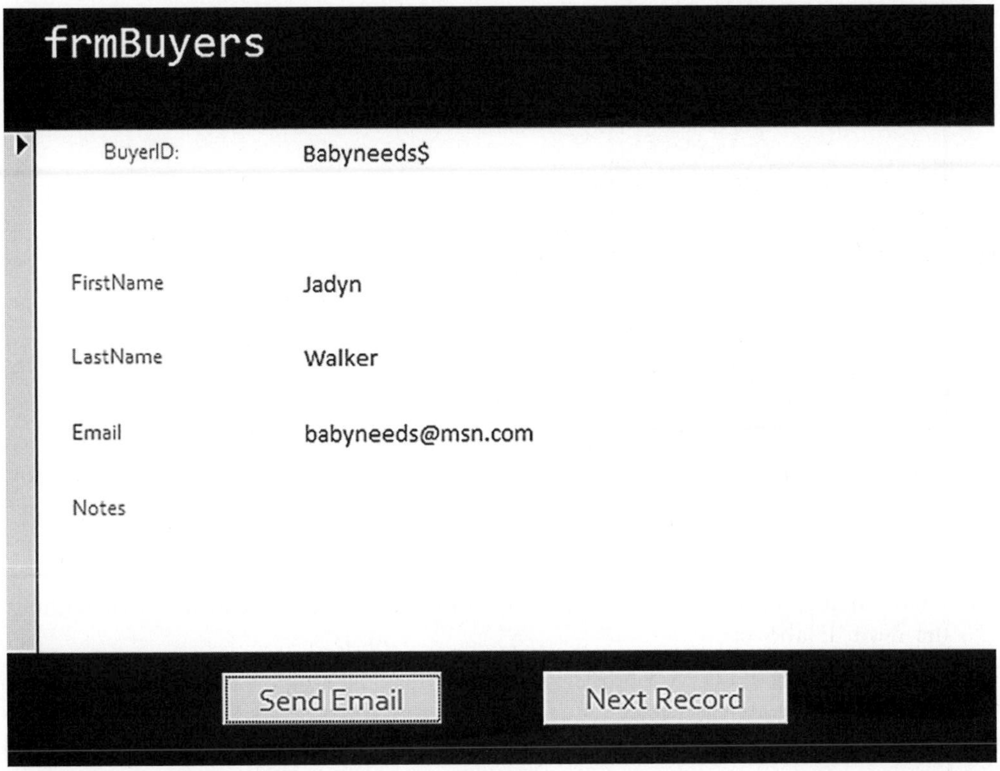

Figure 11.36 Command button on form

Working with Macro Builder and Event Properties

You can also manually add a command button to a form and attach a macro to the command button. The end result is the same as using the wizard—you have a command button with a macro attached to the On Click event of its property sheet. The command button is created without the wizard in this case. Once the command button is created, you can either use the Macro Builder to write and attach the macro or you can do the steps manually. To create a command button without the wizard, be sure the Control Wizards button (the Toolbox button with a wand icon) is **not** pressed in or toggled on.

How to Add a Command Button and Embedded Macro Without the Wizard

1. Open the form in Design view or create a new form.
2. Click the Command Button icon on the Toolbox.
3. Click on the form, or draw a frame for a custom-sized command button. Click the Cancel button to cancel the Command Button wizard, if it starts.
4. Click the right mouse button while pointing at the command button to display the shortcut menu. Select the Build Event command. The Choose Builder dialog box will appear (see Figure 11.37).
5. Select the Macro Builder command (see Figure 11.37).
6. Click the OK button. The Macro Builder window opens. Create and save the macro.

You can also add an existing macro to a command button through the property sheet of the command button.

Figure 11.37 Choose Builder dialog box

How to Attach an Existing Macro to a Command Button

1. Follow steps 1–3 of "How to Add a Command Button and Embedded Macro Without the Wizard" above.

2. Open the command button property sheet by right-clicking on the command button and selecting Properties.

3. Click on the Event tab.

4. Click on the On Click row and select the macro from the drop-down list of names (see Figure 11.38).

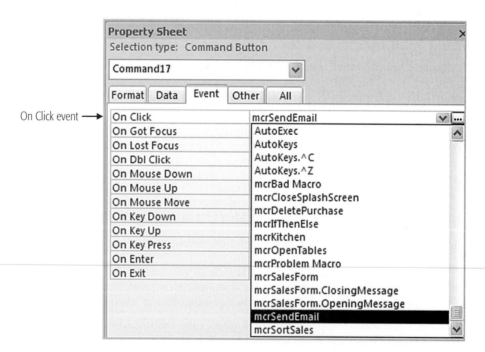

Figure 11.38 Attaching a macro to the On Click event of a command button

You can make a command button respond to a keystroke combination, the ALT key plus any letter, by changing its caption. The letter part of the keystroke combination will appear underlined on the caption. For example, a caption "Send" means that the command button can be invoked by pressing the ALT key and the S key together. To do this, add an ampersand (&) before the letter in the Caption row of the property sheet (see Figure 11.39).

Caption → Caption
property

Figure 11.39 A command button with an assigned keystroke combination

TRY IT YOURSELF 11.7.3

A. Edit the command button created in Try it Yourself 11.7.2 and make It respond to pressing the ALT and S keys as shown in Figure 11.39.

B. Test the keystrokes.

If you need to use the ampersand as part of the caption, as in "Save & Print," you can use two ampersands together (&&) in the Caption property: "Save && Print."

A command button can display either a caption or an icon. If both are assigned to the button, the picture displays, but not the caption. If the icon is deleted, the caption will be shown. You can choose an icon from the Access set, or assign any icon file (.ico) or a bitmap file (.bmp) to a command button. If the picture is too large for the button, it will be clipped and only a portion of the image will be displayed. The only way to display both a caption and a picture is to create your own image that includes the caption text.

How to Add an Icon to a Command Button Caption

1. Select the command button and use the right mouse button to display the shortcut menu.

2. Select the Properties command. The property sheet for the command button will be displayed (see Figure 11.40).

3. Click on the Format tab of the property sheet (see Figure 11.40).

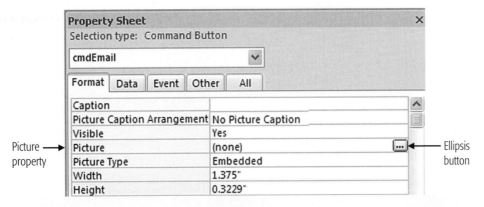

Picture → Picture
property

Ellipsis button

Figure 11.40 Button properties

4. Delete the text on the Caption property line.

5. Click the ellipsis button on the Picture property line (see Figure 11.40). You will have to click on the Picture property line to make the Ellipsis button appear, if it's not visible. The Picture Builder dialog box will be displayed (see Figure 11.41).

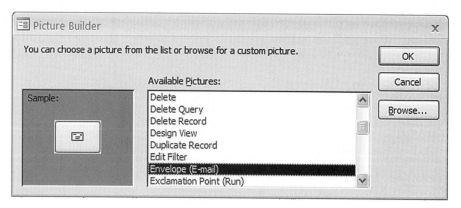

Figure 11.41 Picture Builder dialog box

TRY IT YOURSELF   11.7.4

A. Edit the command button on *frmBuyers* that sends email.

B. Display an envelope icon on the button face as shown in Figure 11.42. Figures 11.40 and 11.41 show the various screens in this process.

C. Save the form and test the button.

D. Continue on.

6. Scroll through the Available Pictures list box and make an appropriate selection.

7. Click the OK button. The chosen picture will be displayed on the face of the command button.

8. Close the property sheet for the command button.

A command button will not run the attached macro until you click on the button. This act of clicking on the button is an event that triggers the corresponding macro. Clicking on the Event tab of the property sheet for a command button displays all possible events that

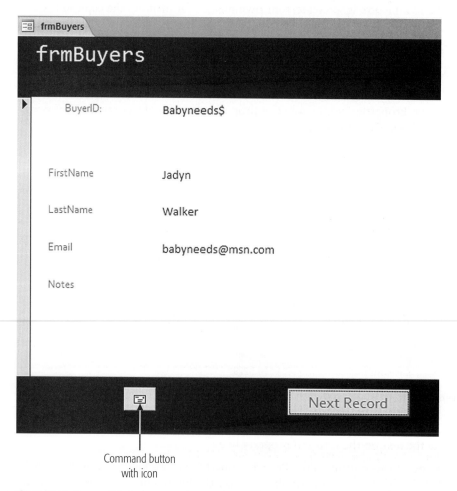

Command button
with icon

Figure 11.42 Form with an icon on the command button

can occur to the button. These events include left mouse click, right mouse click, double-click, keyboard key presses, and so forth. Any of these events can be linked to a macro.

The only way to edit an embedded macro is by opening the property sheet of the object containing the macro. In most cases, this object is a command button.

How to Edit an Embedded Macro

1. Open the property sheet of the command button or other object containing the macro.
2. Click on the Event tab. The On Click property line should contain the value [Embedded Macro].
3. Click in the ellipsis button on the On Click property line. The Macro Builder window opens as shown in Figure 11.43.
4. Edit the macro as needed and save.

TRY IT YOURSELF 11.7.5

A. Open *frmBuyers* in Design view.
B. Open the property sheet for the command button that displays the next record.
C. Edit the embedded macro. It should resemble Figure 11.43.
D. Close the Macro Builder window without making any changes, and close the form.

Condition	Action	Arguments
	OnError	Next,
	GoToRecord	, , Next,
[MacroError]<>0	MsgBox	=[MacroError].[Description], Yes, None,

Figure 11.43 Embedded macro in Macro Builder window

Fast Track   A quick guide to procedures learned in this chapter

Displaying the Macro Builder

1. Click on the Create tab of the ribbon.
2. Click on the Macro button in the Other group, then select Macro from the drop-down menu. The Macro Builder window opens.

Entering Actions

1. Position the pointer in the first empty cell in the Action column.
2. Click on the drop-down list arrow and choose the action from the list

   OR

   Type in the action name.
3. Fill in any required arguments.
4. Complete the Comment cell to document the macro action.

Entering Arguments

1. Click the mouse into the first Argument cell.
2. Click on the drop-down arrow to display the list.
3. Select the correct argument.
4. Continue to respond to all the arguments listed in the Action Arguments pane.

Dragging and Dropping Macro Actions

1. Open the Macro Builder window.

2. Bring the object you're going to use into view in the Navigation Pane.

3. Select the appropriate object, drag it to the first open cell in the Action column, and drop it into this cell. The cursor becomes a small icon representing the object during the process.

4. The appropriate action will be automatically entered into the Action cell.

5. Complete all necessary arguments and documentation in the Comment cell.

Running a Standalone Macro

1. Click the Run button on the ribbon

   OR

   Double-click on the macro name in the Navigation Pane.

   A message box will prompt you to save the macro first if it has been changed or not saved previously.

2. The result of the macro is displayed on the screen.

Editing a Macro

1. From the Navigation Pane, select the macro to edit.

2. Right-click on the macro name and select Design view from the Shortcut menu. The Macro Builder window opens.

Inserting an Action

1. Click on the row where you want to insert an action. The new action will be inserted above this row.

2. Display the shortcut menu, and select the Insert Rows command

   OR

   Click the Insert Rows button in the Rows group of the ribbon Design tab.

   A blank row will be inserted. You can now add the new action to the inserted row.

Deleting a Macro Action

1. Click on the row of the action you want to delete.

2. Display the shortcut menu and choose the Delete Rows command

   OR

   Click the Delete Rows button in the Rows group of the ribbon Design tab

   OR

   Press the [DELETE] key on the keyboard. This will also delete the entire row that is selected.

Moving a Macro Action

1. Click in the shaded area just to the left of the action row to be moved. The cursor changes to a white arrow with an attached rectangle during the move.

2. Drag the row to the new location.

3. Release the mouse button. The action will now be in its new location.

Using the Single Step Mode for Debugging

1. Open the macro in the Design view.

2. Click the Single Step button on the ribbon, in the Tools group of the Design tab.

3. Run the macro. The Macro Single Step dialog box will appear on the screen. This dialog box shows the macro name, condition, action name, and arguments.

4. Click the Step button. The macro action described in the dialog box is executed, and another Macro Single Step dialog box appears on the screen describing the next step.

5. Continue to step through all the actions of the macro until you discover the error. Be sure to check each entry shown in the dialog box for accuracy. Look closely at the arguments listed to make sure the action does what you intend.

6. Make any corrections necessary by opening the macro in Design view.

7. Resave the new macro instructions.

8. Run the new macro to see if the error is corrected; if necessary, debug the macro again.

Displaying the Condition Column

1. Open the Macro Builder.

2. Click the Conditions button in the Show/Hide group on the ribbon.

Writing a Macro Condition

1. Edit or create a macro in Design view.

2. Display the Condition column.

3. Click in the Condition cell next to the action that depends on the condition.

4. Click on the right mouse button. Select the Zoom command to enlarge the cell, or press SHIFT + F2.

5. Enter the conditional expression.

6. Click the OK button to close the Zoom window.

7. Finish writing the macro.

8. Save the macro.

9. Run the macro.

Creating an AutoExec Macro to Display a Splash Screen

1. Create a splash screen form.

2. Create an AutoExec macro with an OpenForm action to open the splash screen.

3. Create a macro with a Close action to close the splash screen form.

4. Open the splash screen form in Design view and bring up the property sheet for the form.

5. Assign the macro created in step 3 to the On Timer event.

6. Type the number in milliseconds for the screen to display on the Timer Interval property row.

7. Close the property sheet and form.

Creating a Macro Group

1. Create or open a macro in Design view.

2. Click on the Macro Names button in the Show/Hide group on the ribbon. The Macro Name column appears to the left of the Action column.

3. Type the name of the macro into the first row of the macro in the Macro Name column.

4. Add actions, arguments, and comments for the macro.

5. Repeat steps 3 and 4 for each macro in the group.

6. Save and name the group.

Creating an AutoKeys Macro

1. Create a new macro.

2. Turn on the Macro Name column.

3. Type the key or key combination into the Macro Names column.

4. On the same row, select an action and its appropriate arguments.

5. Repeat steps 3 and 4 for any other keystroke assignments.

6. Save the macro group with the name AutoKeys.

Adding a Command Button with an Embedded Macro

1. Open an existing form in Design view.

2. Be sure that the Control Wizard button is pressed, and click the Command Button button in the Controls group on the ribbon Design tab.

Adding a Command Button to Run a Macro Using the Wizard

1. Open a form you previously saved, or create a new form. Display the form in Design view.

2. Click the Command Button button on the ribbon.

3. Click on the form or click and drag for a custom-sized frame for the command button. The Command Button wizard begins.

4. Choose the Miscellaneous category, and the Run Macro action.

5. Click the Next button to move to the next screen.

6. Choose the macro from the list of macro names.

7. Click the Next button to move to the next screen.

8. Choose the Text option button to display text on the face of the command button, and retype the caption for the command button.

9. Click the Next button to move to the next screen.

10. Choose a name for the command button. This name will be used to refer to the command button in other macros or modules.

11. Click the Finish button to complete the process.

Adding a Command Button and Embedded Macro Without the Wizard

1. Open the form in Design view or create a new form.

2. Click the Command Button icon on the Toolbox.

3. Click on the form, or draw a frame for a custom-sized command button. Click on the Cancel button to cancel the Command Button wizard, if it starts.

4. Click the right mouse button while pointing at the command button to display the shortcut menu, and select the Build Event command. The Choose Builder dialog box will appear.

5. Select the Macro Builder command.

6. Click the OK button. The Macro Builder window opens.

Attaching an Existing Macro to a Command Button

1. Open the command button property sheet.

2. Click on the Event tab.

3. Click on the On Click row and select the macro from the drop-down list of names.

Adding an Icon to a Command Button Caption

1. Select the command button and use the right mouse button to display the shortcut menu.

2. Select the Properties command. The property sheet for the command button will be displayed.

3. Click on the Format tab of the property sheet.

4. Delete the text on the Caption property line.

5. Click on the ellipsis button on the Picture property line. The Picture Builder dialog box will be displayed.

6. Scroll through the Available Pictures list box and make an appropriate selection.

7. Click the OK button. The chosen picture will be displayed on the face of the command button.

8. Close the property sheet for the command button.

Editing an Embedded Macro

1. Open the property sheet of the command button or other object containing the macro.

2. Click on the Event tab. The On Click property line should contain the value [Embedded Macro].

3. Click in the ellipsis button on the On Click property line. The Macro Builder window opens.

4. Edit the macro as needed and save.

Review Questions

1. What is a macro?
2. (T/F) All macros are attached to objects.
3. (T/F) A common event is clicking on a command button.
4. What are the commands in a macro called?
5. (T/F) An argument is an error message generated by a macro.
6. What are the two panes in the Macro Builder window?
7. Which section of the Action pane is optional?
8. Why are arguments necessary when creating a macro?
9. Does each action have an argument?
10. What information should you know before you begin to create the macro?
11. Describe at least two methods for entering actions.
12. Can you run a macro without saving it?
13. (T/F) The MsgBox action can display a message box containing Yes and No buttons.
14. Describe a method for deleting a macro action.
15. How does the Single Step mode help you debug your macro?
16. What is a conditional expression?
17. What will the macro do if the condition proves false?
18. How do you display the Condition column?
19. When are AutoExec macros are executed?
20. (T/F) You should add the prefix "mcr" to the name AutoExec when saving an AutoExec macro.
21. How many seconds is represented by a Timer Interval property of 2000?
22. How would you refer to a macro called *NewRecord* in a group named *mcrInventory*?
23. What is an embedded macro?
24. What does a command button do on a form?
25. What is an event?
26. How do you associate a macro with an event on a command button?
27. What are two types of captions that you can have on the command button?

Exercises

ACTIVITY   ## Exercise 1—Review and Guided Practice
Use the *SDAL_Ch11* database.

Exercise 1A: Displaying the Sir-Dance-A-Lot Splash Screen
1. Write an AutoExec macro that displays the splash screen named *frmSplash*.
2. Add a command button to the footer of *frmSplash* that closes *frmSplash* when clicked.

3. Save *frmSplash*.

4. Close the *SDAL_Ch11* database and open again to verify that the splash screen displays and is closed by clicking the Close button.

Exercise 1B: Reordering Inventory

1. Run the query *qryReOrders*, and then open it in Design view. The query displays all recordings that have two or fewer copies in inventory.

2. Add a new column to the query that calculates the reorder quantity. You should order enough copies to bring the quantity on hand up to five copies. Save the query.

3. Edit the form *frmReOrdersSubform*. Remove the field *QuantityOnHand* and replace it with the new field *ReOrderQuantity*.

4. Add a command button to the footer area of *frmReOrders* that prints the form showing the current data. Put an icon on the button.

5. Write a macro called *mcrReOrderEmail* that sends an email to the address shown on *frmReOrders*. The subject line of the email should say "Reorders" and the body of the message should say that the attachment contains the reorder list for Sir-Dance-A-Lot.

    a. Use the SendObject macro action.

    b. The Object Name argument should be *qryReOrders*.

    c. For the Output Format argument, choose "Excel 97–Excel 2003 Workbook." This will send the query as an Excel spreadsheet.

    d. The To argument should be "= Forms![frmReOrders]![EmailAddress]." (Type everything inside the quotes).

6. Add another command button to the footer area of *frmReOrders* that runs the macro *mcrReOrderEmail* when clicked.

7. Test the email button. It should create an email message to the address shown on the form. The subject and message body should be the text you designated, and the email should have an attachment called *qryReorder.xls*.

Exercise 1C: Updating Inventory

1. Create an update query called *qryUpdateInventory* that will add the quantity received to the quantity on hand in inventory.

    a. Use the tables *tblInventory* and *tblNewInventory*, and join them on the field *InventoryID*.

    b. Update the field *QuantityOnHand* in *tblInventory* to *QuantityOnHand* + *QuantityReceived*. The field *QuantityReceived* is in *tblNewInventory*.

    c. Save the query and close it.

2. Create a macro called *mcrUpdateInventory* that sets system warnings off and runs the query *qryUpdateInventory*. After the query is run, display a message saying that inventory has been updated. Save the macro and close it.

3. Make a copy of *tblInventory*.

4. Open the form *frmNewInventory*. Add a command button that runs the macro *mcrUpdateInventory*. Use the caption "Update Inventory" on the button. Save the form and close it.

5. Open the form *frmNewInventory*. Click on the Update Inventory command button.

6. To verify the query worked, open *tblInventory* and the copy you made in step 3. Compare the field *QuantityOnHand* in both tables.

Exercise 2—Practicing New Procedures

Open the *Personnel_Ch11* database. Your instructor will tell you whether to print the macro, or turn in the database.

Exercise 2A: Checking Data Spelling

1. Write a macro called *mcrCheckSpelling*. The macro should open the *tblInventory* table, check the spelling, and close the table.

2. Check the spelling by using the macro action Run Command, which allows you to run any menu command found on any Access menu. Be sure to fill out the necessary arguments.

3. Save and test the macro.

Exercise 2B: Backing Up a Table

1. Write a macro called *mcrBackupInventory*. The macro should make a copy of the *tblInventory* table and call it *tblInventoryBackup*. The table should be stored in the *Personnel_Ch11* database.

2. Copy the table by using the macro action CopyObject. Be sure to fill out the necessary arguments.

3. Save and test the macro.

Exercise 2C: Using AutoKeys Macros

1. Create an AutoKeys macro that does the following:

   a. Open *frmEmployee* when CTRL and E are pressed on the keyboard.

   b. Open *frmVendors* when CTRL and V are pressed on the keyboard.

   c. Close *frmEmployee* when CTRL and D are pressed on the keyboard.

   d. Close *frmVendors* when CTRL and W are pressed on the keyboard.

2. Test all the keystrokes in the AutoKeys macro.

Exercise 2D: Linking Forms with a Macro

1. Write a macro that opens the form *frmEmployeeHours*. Save it and name it *mcrDisplayHours*.

2. Add a command button to the form *frmEmployee*. The button should run the macro *mcrDisplayHours* when clicked. Put the caption "View Hours" on the button. Save *frmEmployee*.

3. Open *frmEmployee* and test the View Hours button. Does the correct data show in *frmEmployeeHours* when *frmEmployee* displays any record but the first record (Pat Appleby)? The macro only specified to open the form *frmEmployeeHours*; it didn't state to display a matching record.

4. Edit *mcrDisplayHours*. The argument Where Condition needs to be filled in. This argument should contain an equation that describes the join between the data in the two forms. Determine which matching field on each form will be used to connect the forms. The field on *frmEmployeeHours* should be to the left of the equal sign, and to the right of the equal sign should be the field on *frmEmployee*. Create the Where Condition argument based on this information. Use the expression builder, if needed. (Hint: Don't use the complete expression identifier for the field on *frmEmployeeHours*.) Save the macro.

5. Open *frmEmployee* and test the View Hours button again. The employee record shown in *frmEmployeeHours* should be the same as the one in *frmEmployee* for all employees.

Exercise 3—In-Class Group Research

ACTIVITY AND REFLECTION

This exercise requires an internet connection.

Divide into groups of two to four members as determined by your instructor. Each group is going to find an online article about Access macros, read and discuss the article, then present the information learned in the article to the other groups. Articles can be located through the Professional Tips contributors in the textbook, by visiting Microsoft's Access and Office Web pages, or by using a search engine. Some possible topics include:

- Using macros to validate fields/controls on a form during data entry
- Changing form properties with a macro
- Troubleshooting macros
- Advantages and disadvantages of using macros
- Creative ways of using AutoExec and AutoKeys macros
- Using variables in macros
- Handling errors in macros
- Macros and security issues

Exercise 4—Challenge: Writing a Conditional Macro

ACTIVITY AND REFLECTION

Open the *Personnel_Ch11* database.

1. Open the form *frmPrintLabels* in Design view and examine the controls. The purpose of this form is to allow a user to select one of two label sizes, and then initiate the printing of the correct size labels. The label size selection is made by clicking on one of the buttons in the option group named optgrpLabelSize. If "Big labels" is selected, then optgrpLabelSize equals 1, and if "Small labels" is selected, then optgrpLabelSize equals 2.

2. Write a macro named *mcrPrintLabels* that prints the correctly sized labels based on the user selection in the option group. If "Big labels" is selected, the macro should open the report *lblBigLabels* in print preview mode, and if "Small labels" is selected, the macro should open the report *lblSmallLabels* in print preview mode. Attach the macro to the cmdPrint command button on the form.

3. Save the forms and macro, and test them to make sure they work correctly.

Exercise 5—Problem Solving: Debugging a Macro

ACTIVITY AND REFLECTION

Open the *Personnel_Ch11* database.

1. Fix the macro *mcrBad Macro*. Save and print the macro when it works correctly.

Exercise 6—Discussion Questions

REFLECTION

1. You are designing a form to be used by a travel agent for booking cruises. The form displays data about one cruise on the screen, and has a command button with the caption "Book Cruise." List the steps that need to be taken in order to complete the task of booking a cruise. Think about updating data in both the tblCruise and tblPassenger tables. Should anything be printed? List the steps and write a sentence or two describing each one.

2. How might macros be used to validate data entered into a form? Give three examples.

CASE STUDY A: MRS. SUGARBAKER'S COOKIES

Use the *CSA_Ch11* database file. You can get a copy from your instructor.

Using Command Buttons

1. Open *frmCustomerDisplay*. When you select a name from the combo box, the record for that customer is displayed. However, when you use the navigation buttons to move to another record, the name in the combo box doesn't change. Mrs. Sugarbaker finds this confusing and would like to have the combo box display the name of the customer shown in the lower part of the form.

   a. Write a macro that displays the name from the lower part of the form, in the combo box (*Combo 14*). Use the Expression Builder to create the object identifiers used in the macro arguments. Name the macro *mcrUpdateComboBox*.

   b. You want the macro to run every time a new record is displayed in the form. The event that occurs when a new record is displayed is called the On Current event. This is a form event, and will be found in the form property sheet. Attach the macro to this event.

Need More Help?

If you can't get the correct data to display in the combo box, check the Bound Column property for the combo box to see what field is stored in the combo box. The data displayed in a combo box is usually not the same data as in the bound column.

2. Mrs. Sugarbaker would like to have a button on *frmCustomerDisplay* that shows a customer's orders when clicked. The form *frmOrderSummary* already shows orders, but it shows all orders, not the orders for a specific customer.

   a. Add a command button to the form footer of *frmCustomerDisplay* using the wizard. The button should open *frmOrderSummary* and show the orders for the customer displayed in *frmCustomerDisplay*.

   b. When you test the button, it probably won't work correctly. At the time this book was written, this part of the command button wizard was creating the wrong arguments for the embedded macro. Here's the way the Where Condition argument should read for an OpenForm action when you want the second form to display matching data to the first form:

   [Control Name on second form] = Forms![First form name]![Control Name on first form]

   The first form is the form with the command button. Don't use the complete identifier for the name on the left side of the equals sign. You must use it, however, for the name on the right side of the equals sign.

   Fix the macro embedded in the command button and make it work correctly.

   c. Add a command button to the footer of *frmOrderSummary* that closes *frmOrderSummary*.

Running Queries from a Macro

3. Mrs. Sugarbaker would like to expand and automate the monthly data archival process started in Chapter 8. The process of archiving consists of two steps: copying older data to another table, and removing older data from the current table. In Chapter 8, the queries were created to copy and remove data for table *tblOrders*. These queries are *qryArchiveOrdersAppend* and *qryArchiveOrdersDelete*. Mrs. Sugarbaker would also like to archive payment data.

   a. Create two new queries for archiving payment data. Create an Append query that appends data from *tblCustomerPayments* to *tblCustomerPayments11-08*. Name the query *qryArchivePaymentsAppend*. The query should allow the user to enter the month to be archived as a parameter. The month is expressed as a digit 1–12. Create a Delete query that deletes those records from *tblCustomerPayments* that were copied to *tblCustomerPayments11-08*. Again, use a parameter to allow the user to enter the month of sales to be deleted. Name the query *qryArchivePaymentsDelete*.

b. Write a macro that sets warnings off and runs all four archiving queries—*qryArchiveOrdersAppend, qryArchiveOrdersDelete, qryArchivePaymentsAppend*, and *qryArchivePaymentsDelete*. After the queries are run, the macro should display a message that archiving is complete. Name the macro *mcrArchive*.

c. Add a command button to *frmArchive* that runs *mcrArchive*. Test the button using data for the month of November. You will be prompted four times for the month.

CASE STUDY B: SANDY FEET RENTAL COMPANY

Now SFRC wants to automate some of the routine tasks that are performed with the database. The company wants everyone in the office who is working with the file to be able to use it with ease. Macros help automate these functions.

Write the macro instructions for the following requirements. Test the macros to be sure they run correctly. Debug if necessary. Note: if the objects are not in the database, you might have to create them before writing the macros or substitute similar objects.

1. Create a macro to print mailing labels for those clients who have not rented recently.

   a. Create the query. Change the join properties to display all the records form the *tblClients* and only those records from the *tblRentalTransactions* table where the records are equal. Save the query as *qry_MailingLabels*.

   b. Create the mailing label report from the query. Save the report as *lbl_MailingLabels*.

   c. Create the macro that will open the query, beep, close the query, open the report and print it. Note: Set the view to Print in the Action Arguments for the OpenReport command.

   d. Save the macro as *mcr_PrintLabels*.

2. Add a command button to the form *frmRentalInformation* that will open to a new record. Test the button to be sure it is working. Open the form *frm_ClientInformation* to make sure the new button works in the subform.

3. Add a command button to the *frm_ClientInformation* form that will print the selected form.

4. Create a macro to generate an Owner's receipt for maintenance charges.

   a. Create a new form from the *tblMaintenance*. Save the form as *frm_Maintenance*.

   b. Create a new form using Owner Information from the *tblOwners* table. Add the following fields from the *tblMaintenance* table in addition to the fields from the *tblOwners* table: *Invoice, Vendor, Date Completed, Amount, Issue,* and *Notes*. Save the form as *frm_OwnersMaintenance*.

   c. Add the *frmOwnersMaintenance* to the *frm_Maintenance* as a subform, making sure that the two forms are joined on the *Property Number* field. This field should be on both forms. Add a page break control before the subform control. The *frmOwnersMaintenance* is now on page 2.

   d. Write a macro that will move from page 1 (*frm_Maintenance*) to page 2 (*frmOwnersMaintenance*). Save the macro as *mcr_GoToPage2*. Create a button on *frm_Maintenance* that will execute this macro.

   e. Create a button on *frmOwnersMaintenance* that will print the selected record and return to page 1 of the form. Edit the macro by right-clicking on the button and choosing the Build Event command. Add a new macro action to go to page 1. Save and close the macro.

   f. Test the buttons to be sure they work.

CASE STUDY C: PENGUINS SKI CLUB

The Penguins Ski Club needs a way to process members who leave the club. Rather than deleting a member, they have chosen to flag the member as no longer active. This way, historical data is still available about the ex-member. In addition, when a member leaves before the end of the season (March 31), the member receives a prorated refund of his or her equipment rental fee. The fee is $50 per year, and a member receives a refund of $10 per month. So if a member leaves in January, he or she will receive a $20 refund for two months.

   Use the database *CSC_Ch11* for the case study. It's available from your instructor.

Flagging Inactive Members

1. Write a macro that will run from *frmMembers*. It should change the value of field *Active-Member* to No, and put today's date into the field *InActiveDate*. Save and name the macro *mcrInActiveMember*.

2. Add a command button to form *frmMembers* that runs *mcrInActiveMember* when clicked.

Need More Help?

The macro action Set Value allows you to assign a value to a field or control on a form. Be sure the Show All Actions button is pressed in so that all actions are available.
The function Date() returns today's date.

Refunding Rental Fees

3. Edit the macro *mcrInActiveMember*. Add actions to the end of the macro so that if the field *EquipmentRental* is Yes, the form *frmEquipmentRental* opens. The form should show the record from *tblEquipmentRental* that matches the member shown in form *frmMembers*, and has no data in field *ReturnDate*.

Need More Help?

Add a condition to the OpenForm action.
The function IsNull([FieldName]) tests to see if there is data in a field. If there is no data, then IsNull returns a value of true.
If you are having trouble getting the correct member to display in the *frmEquipmentRental*, read Case Study A for a description of the Where Condition argument.

4. Write another macro name *mcrRefund*. It should calculate the refund amount based on the field *InActiveDate* and the description given at the beginning of this case study. The refund amount should be placed in the field *txtRefund* on *frmEquipmentRental*. When calculating the refund amount, you can either round to the nearest $10 or pay an exact fraction based on the number of days remaining in the season.

Need More Help?

The macro action SetValue allows you to assign a value to a field or control on a form. This macro has only one action; the arguments are the hard part.
When using a date in a calculation, enclose it in #'s, such as #3/31/09#.
To express time as a fraction of months, divide it by 30.

5. Add a command button to the footer of *frmEquipmentRental* that runs *mcrRefund* when clicked.

Chapter 12

Building a Database Application

Objectives

After completing this chapter you will be able to

Use Switchboard forms:

- Understand what a Switchboard form is, how to use one, and the underlying database objects used to manage one.
- Create a Switchboard form using the Switchboard Manager Add-in.
- Edit a Switchboard form.
- Create additional pages for a Switchboard form.
- Use a Switchboard form.

Create Menu Forms without the Switchboard Manager:

- Create a menu form with command buttons and macros.
- Create a menu form with hyperlinks.

Customize the Quick Access Toolbar:

- Understand what the Quick Access Toolbar is and where it is located.
- Edit the toolbar.

Create a Modal Dialog Form:

- Understand what a Modal Dialog form is and when to use one.
- Create a Modal Dialog Form.
- Use a Modal Dialog Form.

Dictionary

AutoExec macro	A macro that automatically runs each time a database file is opened.
Command button	A button on a form that executes a command or runs a procedure in response to an event.
Database application	A complete database containing data and other objects that work together to perform a task or group of related tasks.
Event	An action that happens to an object, such as clicking the left mouse button while pointing at a command button. An event can cause a macro or Visual Basic procedure to execute.
Interface	The top layer of a piece of software—what is seen when the program runs, including tools for using the software and/or data objects. For example, a database interface consists of screens, menus, and buttons that make it easy to use database objects—reports, forms, and so forth.

Modal Dialog form	A form that requires user input before moving into the main application.
Procedure	An object that executes when triggered by an event, such as a macro or Visual Basic program.
Quick Access Toolbar	A small toolbar located next to the Office button that contacts frequently used commands and that can be customized.
Rapid prototyping	A way of performing the system design and implementation phases by building working models of the application and gathering user feedback.
Startup form	A form, usually a Switchboard form, that automatically opens when the database opens.
Switchboard form	An interactive form containing a variety of macros, buttons, menus, and toolbars that automate database functions.
Switchboard Manager	An Add-in program for Access that helps build Switchboard form automatically.
Systems Development Life Cycle (SDLC)	A way of describing the building of a computer information system as the following phases in a cycle: definition, design and development, and implementation.
Systems Development Life Cycle principles	A set of rules used to build information systems and computer applications.
Visual Basic	A programming language in which you can create procedure modules that are attached to Access databases or database objects. Modules are groups of commands, similar to macros.

12.1 Developing an Application

Q: What is the Systems Development Life Cycle?

A: The process of building an application using the systems approach.

A database application is a complete database containing data and other objects that work together to perform a task or group of related tasks. For example, data and objects pertaining to courses, degrees, and student records is a database application for managing degree programs and degree candidates. On the other hand, the databases provided with this book are used as homework and practice sets and aren't applications. Each database contains several small groups of tables and other objects that are related, but there is no overall relationship between objects, nor is there a task that they perform together.

Developing an application describes the process of creating a complete database with data, all other objects, and a usable interface. In Chapter 7 we learned how to design and create the data tables and joins needed in a database, but this is just one step in the entire process of designing, developing, and testing a database application. There are many ways to develop an application, either by following established procedures or by creating your own method. Two processes that make good starting tools are the Systems Development Life Cycle principles, and the rapid prototyping method.

Systems Development Life Cycle

The Systems Development Life Cycle (SDLC) is a popular model used to describe the process of building a computer information system. SDLC is based on systems theory and sees the process of defining, designing, and implementing a computer system as phases in a cycle. The Systems Development Life Cycle principles are a set of rules describing a methodology for building information systems and computer applications, which can easily be applied to database application development. The principles provide guidelines for the project manager to use, form planning the application through this installation and maintenance. Because some of these functions are beyond the scope of this textbook, we will focus primarily on those activities that are most closely tied to creating a database application.

There are several variations of the SDLC principles, but the differences are small and each alternative provides the same basic principles. The SDLC principles are:

1. Get the users of the application involved.

2. Use a problem-solving approach.

3. Establish phases and activities.

4. Establish standards for consistent development and documentation.

5. Justify systems as capital investments.

6. Don't be afraid to cancel or revise scope.

7. Divide and conquer.

8. Design systems for growth and change.

One of the most important ideas here is to use a problem-solving approach—apply the techniques of problem solving to the various phases of database development. In other words, think of each phase as a problem to be solved, and use the following steps in formulating a solution:

1. Identify the problem, phase, or task.

2. Understand the problem's environment—its relationship, events, and causes and effects.

3. List the requirements of an appropriate solution.

4. Identify alternative solutions.

5. Analyze alternatives and choose the solution that seems best.

6. Implement the solution.

7. Observe and evaluate the solution's impact.

8. Refine the solution accordingly.

The development phases used in SDLC vary somewhat, but overall they follow the same pattern listed in the problem-solving steps. In other words, if you apply a problem-solving approach to the task of developing a database application, you come up with the same general list of phases. These include planning, analysis, design, implementation, and support, as shown in Figure 12.1. (Prototyping is discussed later in this section.)

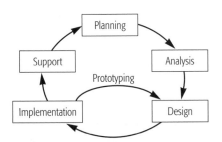

Figure 12.1 SDLC phases

Let's take a closer look at these phases. Some of them are performed by management, others are done by the database developer, and some are done by both groups. We will examine the developer's tasks in more detail than management tasks.

During the planning phase, management establishes the overall parameters for the project: scope, budget, staffing, and schedule. All team members should provide input about their availability and schedules. The database developer should take a brief look at the present system and begin considering various replacement alternatives.

The next phase is the systems analysis, which is an in-depth look at the current system. The database developer should begin interviewing the users, observing the processes, collecting input forms and other documents, and examining reports and other output documents. He or she should identify the problems with the current system, the needs of the users, and the scope of the system. The developer should prepare a written report of his or her findings for management, who then develop a project plan.

The database developer does most of the work in the design phase; however, it's during this phase that the project manager must choose an alternative for development. If there are several alternatives being considered, then the designer should provide management with the necessary information about each option. Once a choice has been made, the developer then begins to build an in-depth design.

The design phase should produce a complete list of data fields and specifications for the input, output, and processing requirements. This includes an Entity-Relationship (E-R) diagram, a list of normalized tables, a description of all input and output forms, a list of reports and other printed documents, and an explanation of any processing that needs to be done. Chapter 1 describes the method of creating lists of fields from reports and other documents, and Chapter 7 tells you how to make an E-R diagram and how to normalize tables. Have users describe and draw the forms and reports they would like to see in the new application. The processing requirements of the system will be met by creating queries, macros, and Visual Basic procedures. If appropriate, draw flow charts that represent the needed processing steps.

The implementation phase is carried out mostly by the database developer. This phase includes all aspects of creating, testing, and installing the application. The developer creates the data tables, joins, and other objects required by the application. Everything must be tested, preferably with real data from users. Begin with a small data set and test each object, then expand to a larger number of records in each table. Once the application has been reasonably tested, put it into production at the user's site. The developer should provide documentation to the users and possibly training, if management decides it's appropriate. Documentation should be assembled from the diagrams, charts, and other documents created by the developer, and from the printed reports produced by Access.

The support phase may be ongoing for some time. Its purpose is to uncover any problems with software, procedures, documentation, or training. It's probable that users will find many bugs in the application at first. Many of these are caused by miscommunication, or by the developer being unable to use actual data. Problems should occur with much less frequency over time. Users may also find that they want changes made, or they may have additional requirements for the system. It may be best to create version numbers for the application, and release updates periodically.

Table 12.1 Systems Development Life Cycle Phases

SDLC Phase	Description
Planning	Establish scope, budget, staffing, and schedule. Begin considering the alternatives to the present system.
Systems Analysis	Take an in-depth look at the current system and the alternative replacements.
Design	Select a replacement for the current system. Produce a complete list of data fields and specifications for the input, output, and processing requirements.
Implementation	Create, test, and install the application.
Support	Find and fix any problems with software, procedures, documentation, or training.

Rapid Prototyping

Rapid prototyping provides a way of performing the system design and implementation phases by building working models of the application and gathering user feedback. Advocates of prototyping say that it prevents the development of an unusable application, it speeds up the development process, it gives users experience with the software before it goes into production, and it allows users to have more input into the process.

Prototyping can be thought of as a spiral development process. The developer creates a model of the application, shows users how to operate it, gathers feedback from users, and refines the model based on the feedback. The developer creates successively more intricate models, going through the complete process as many times as are necessary.

The following steps provide a suggested sequence of database application development using the rapid prototyping method. Each step defines a working model that can be given to users for feedback. Figure 12.2 shows a graphical representation of the process.

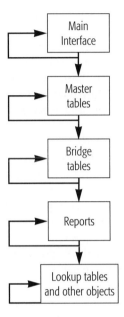

Figure 12.2 Sequence of database application implementation using prototyping

How to Implement Database Application Design

1. Develop the interface: the main screen, the look and feel of the application, the help system, and the menu and the toolbar commands for activating the objects in the application. Create a macro to display a message box for all commands on menus and toolbars. The message box should inform the user that this part of the application isn't working yet. Gradually replace the message box with working forms and reports.

2. Give the user the first version, and refine the model based on user feedback.

3. Develop the forms for editing one or two of the master tables.

4. Give the user the next version, enhance the model based on user feedback, and develop the rest of the master table editing forms.

5. Develop the forms for editing one or two of the transaction/event or bridge tables.

6. Give the user the next version, refine the model based on user feedback, and develop the rest of the transaction/event table editing forms.

7. Develop the reports and labels, give the user the next version, and improve the model based on user feedback.

8. Develop forms for editing lookup tables, give the user the next version, and refine the model based on user feedback.

9. Develop other objects needed, give the user the next version, and improve the model based on user feedback.

Q: How can I specifically apply all this to database development?

A: Read the steps listed in "How to implement Database Application Design."

12.2 / Developing an Interface

An interface is the top layer of a piece of software—what you see when you run the program. This could include tools for using the software and/or the data objects created by the software. The purpose of an interface is to make it easier to use the software or data. Access has an interface that you use to create and manipulate database objects. It consists of the windows, menus, toolbar buttons, and help screens that you use with tables, reports, forms, and so forth. Many parts of this book have been about learning to read and use the Access interface.

A database interface consists of screens, menus, and buttons that make it easy to use database objects—reports, forms, and so forth—in a specific database. For example, Figure 12.3 shows what an interface might look like for a College database that provides information about courses, class schedules, and instructors. The main screen in the interface is a form containing command buttons that activate other forms and reports in the database.

The purpose of developing an interface is to provide all users with easy access to a database and its objects, regardless of their skill level with the underlying software (in this case Access). An interface also gives the database designer/developer more control over the actions and objects available to users.

In the example shown in Figure 12.3, this screen is the main interface for a database user who has data update privileges; in other words, a college administrator who is allowed to add, update, and delete classes in the schedule and other tables. A completely different interface would be developed for putting the database on a World Wide Web page for public use. The database developer would only want to allow these users to view the data, not update it; and not all of the data would be available. For example, instructors' personal information would not be accessible from this interface.

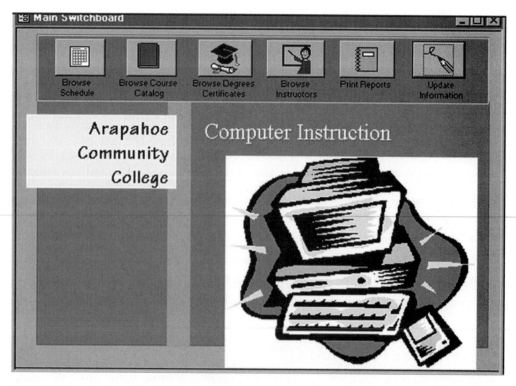

Figure 12.3 Sample database interface main screen

Planning an Interface

A little planning helps ensure that the interface will run smoothly. You should keep the interface simple for the user, yet attractive. Consider the following design questions when planning an interface.

- Who will use the interface?
- How familiar is the user with Access?
- How much control do you want to give the user?
- What actions does this user require (see Table 12.2)?
- Are macros necessary to run any of these actions? Are these macros already saved or do they need to be created?
- Are there any frequently used tasks you want to include on a custom toolbar?
- What type of look do you want your interface to have?
- How will the user open and exit this interface?
- Are there any security features that need to be included in the interface?

Table 12.2   Common Database Tasks

Task	Definition
Data updates	Adding, editing, and deleting records displayed in forms.
Printing reports	Printing reports on a regular basis.
Viewing information	Displaying query dynasets, filtered tables, sorted tables, and so forth, in forms.
Table updates	Adding, changing, and deleting fields and field properties.
Database administration	Checking referential integrity, creating and monitoring table relationships, changing table structures, backing up data, and so forth.
Database maintenance	Adding, changing, and deleting database objects, including table data, queries, reports, forms, macros, and modules.

Common Database Tasks

There's a set of actions that is shared by most databases. All tables need to be maintained, which means adding, changing, and deleting fields and field properties. All data requires updating, which includes adding, changing, and deleting records. Data updates are usually done on forms, so forms need to be opened and closed. Data retrieval tasks will need to be done also, including viewing dynasets and tables displayed in forms and printed in reports. Other maintenance tasks need to be performed on the database, such as checking referential integrity, creating and monitoring table relationships, backing up data, and so forth.

Not every interface has to include all these actions; an appropriate subset should be selected for each group of users. The tools to do these actions are often provided as objects on a Switchboard form.

Interface Objects

Several different objects can be created in Access for building an interface—Switchboard forms, menus, toolbars, startup forms, and AutoExec macros. They're described in Table 12.3 on the next page.

You can also create an icon for a database that can be placed on the Windows desktop. When the user clicks on the icon, the main screen of the database interface opens. A Switchboard form, described in Section 12.3, is often used as the main screen in a database interface.

Table 12.3   Interface Objects

Object	Description
Switchboard form	An interactive form containing a variety of macros, buttons, and other objects used to automate database functions.
Startup form	A form, commonly a Switchboard, that automatically opens when the database opens.
Modal Dialog form	A form that requires user input before moving into the database.
AutoExec macro	A macro that automatically runs each time a database file is opened.
Quick Access Toolbar	A small toolbar that contains frequently used commands and that can be customized.

Interface Design Tips

The interface is a very important part of the application and should be robust, clear, and easy to use. There are a number of tips taken from studying the human-computer interface and from practical experience that can assist you in interface design.

1. Anticipate errors.

   - If searches or queries produce no values, display a message indicating this.
   - If data is entered incorrectly, display a message describing valid data values or showing an example.
   - Use default values for fields whenever possible.
   - Verify all deletions and major changes.

2. Be clear.

   - Make the user aware of the available options on any form.
   - Label buttons clearly or assign them obvious icons.
   - Give instructions if a procedure is not obvious.
   - Use tooltips for all buttons, and for any form controls that need explanation.
   - Avoid most abbreviations and use simple but descriptive terms.
   - If there is a delay in processing, display a message giving the reason or show a progress meter.

3. Be consistent.

   - Use the same terms and language throughout the application when you mean the same thing.
   - Put command buttons and toolbars in the same place on all forms.
   - Use the same fonts, colors, and types of graphics for all forms.

4. Design forms carefully.

   - Use light backgrounds and dark text as much as possible. Always have enough contrast between the text and the background to make text easy to read.
   - Use colors tastefully. Too many colors are confusing and too many bright colors can be overwhelming.
   - Align objects with each other as much as possible, both vertically and horizontally. Don't mix centering, right, and left alignment on one page.
   - Group similar objects together. Separate groups with horizontal rules to provide a visual break on the screen.
   - Use white space on the screen to provide a rest for the eyes.

12.3 Creating and Using Switchboards

A Switchboard is an interactive form containing a variety of macros, buttons, menus, and toolbars that automate database functions. You can design and use a Switchboard for any Access database file. It is used as an interface between the user and various database objects—tables, queries, reports, and so forth. Using macros attached to command buttons, menus, and the toolbar can provide user access to available database objects and actions.

The Switchboard should provide users with easy access for performing table updates, data retrieval, and database maintenance tasks. Multiple Switchboard pages or additional Switchboard forms should be used if there are many possible tasks to select from, so that no form is too cluttered with choices. Multiple pages create a menu/submenu structure that organizes selections into groups. Switchboards are an excellent way to maintain control by limiting user choices, especially if there are multiple user groups with differing levels of familiarity with Access or differing data needs. Several groups of Switchboard forms can be created so that different groups of users have separate interfaces. Figure 12.3 shows a Switchboard form as the main screen in a College database interface.

Creating a Switchboard

A Switchboard is a form containing a series of command buttons. They are associated with a macro to an event, such as the click of the mouse button.

There are two different methods for creating a Switchboard form. You can use the Switchboard Manager, an application similar to a wizard, or you can create the Switchboard using the tools in the Form Design view.

The first method guides you through the process using the Switchboard Manager, a Database Tools command. The Switchboard Manager will automatically create the Switchboard form and all associated commands without you having to write any macros. The command actions attached to the command buttons will be generated by Access using Access Visual Basic code.

The second method of creating a Switchboard is to design the application "from scratch" in the Form Design view. With this technique, you design and create the form and the command buttons, as well as any macros associated with the buttons.

Using the Switchboard Manager

The Switchboard Manager is one of the database tools found on the Database Tools ribbon. When starting the Switchboard Manager, if there are available Switchboard forms, those will be displayed. If there are no Switchboard forms, Access will ask if you would like to create one.

When a new Switchboard is created, two new Access objects are made—the Switchboard form and the *Switchboard Items* table. This table holds information about the commands available for the Switchboard. Do not change the name of the form or the table created by the Switchboard Manager or the Switchboard will not run properly.

How to Create a Switchboard Form with the Switchboard Manager

1. Click on the Database Tools tab to display the Tools ribbon.

2. Click on Switchboard Manager in the Database Tools group (see Figure 12.4).

3. The Switchboard Manager dialog box opens indicating that there are no available Switchboards in this database. Click Yes to create a new one.

Figure 12.4 Starting the Switchboard Manager

The Switchboard Pages dialog box opens showing the name of the new page as the Default name, Main Switchboard (see Figure 12.5). The name of this Switchboard page can be changed by editing the page. New Switchboard forms can be created by clicking the New button. The Delete button will delete Switchboard pages that are not the Default page. To make a new page the Default, click the Make Default button.

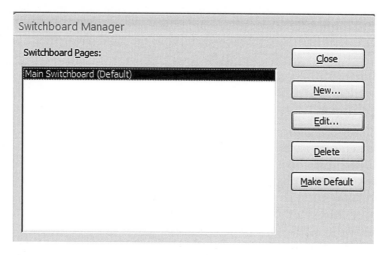

Figure 12.5 Switchboard Pages dialog box

4. Click the Edit button to make changes to the page. The Edit Switchboard Page dialog box appears (see Figure 12.6).

5. Change the name of the page (optional) by selecting the current Switchboard name and overtyping a more descriptive name.

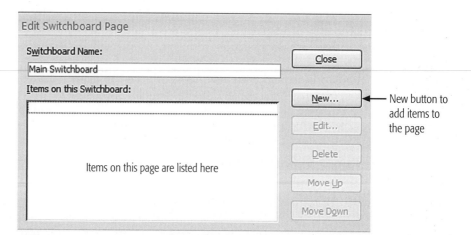

Figure 12.6 Edit Switchboard Page dialog box

6. Click the New button to add items to the Switchboard (see Figure 12.6). The Edit Switchboard Item dialog box opens with three List boxes available for editing the items (or buttons) on the Switchboard (see Figure 12.7).

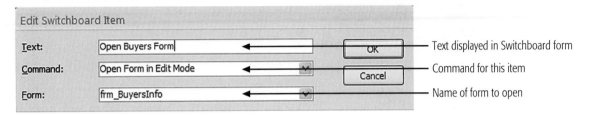

Figure 12.7 Edit Switchboard Item dialog box

7. Enter the text in the Text box (see Figure 12.7). This will be the text on the face of the command button.

8. Click the drop-down arrow in the Command text box (see Figure 12.7). The drop-down list shows several actions that can be associated with a button. Access Visual Basic code will be generated to complete these actions—you will not need to write any macros.

9. Select the action.

10. Select the appropriate data to complete the Form text box.

11. Click the OK button to return to the Edit Switchboard Page dialog box (see Figure 12.8).

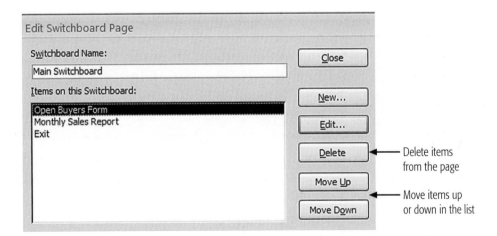

Figure 12.8 Edit Switchboard Page dialog box showing items on the page

12. Continue adding items to the Switchboard until all items are shown in the Items on this Switchboard window. Each item will result in a command button on the Switchboard form.

13. Click the Close button to close the Edit Switchboard Page dialog box. The Switchboard Manager dialog box reappears as shown in Figure 12.5.

14. Close the Switchboard Manager dialog box. You should see a new table named *Switchboard Items* and a new form named *Switchboard* (see Figure 12.9).

Open the Switchboard form to view the main interface screen, evaluate its format and test each of the commands. This form can be edited in Design view to make formatting changes. Note that the Switchboard items do not appear in Design view but they are stored in the *Switchboard Items* table.

TRY IT YOURSELF 12.3.1

Using the *G3_Ch12.accdb* file:

A. Create a new Switchboard form using the Switchboard Manager.

B. Use Figures 12.4 through 12.9 as a guide.

- Add the *frm_BuyersInfo* form to open in Edit mode.
- Add the *rpt_MonthlySales Report*.
- Add a command to Exit the application.

C. Save the form. View and test the form to be sure it links to the appropriate items (see Figure 12.9).

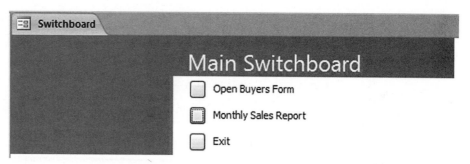

Figure 12.9 Completed Switchboard form

Editing a Switchboard

Q: Why can't I see any items when I open a Switchboard form in Design view?

A: Because the items are stored in the Switchboard Items table and managed with Visual Basic procedures.

Every Switchboard form is composed of two parts—the Switchboard form and the *Switchboard Items* table. To make formatting changes to the form, such as adding a graphic to the background or adding bold to a title, edit the Switchboard form. To change the way the Switchboard works, such as adding a new command button or new page (submenu), edit the *Switchboard Items* table or use the Switchboard Manager.

You can edit the Switchboard form the same way as any other form, by opening the form in the Design view; however, you cannot edit the menu-items text here. You can edit labels, move controls, add graphics, change colors, format controls, and so forth. There may be more command buttons showing on the form in Design view than there are when the form is in use. The extra buttons are there in case you add more action items to the *Switchboard Items* table, so don't remove them.

TRY IT YOURSELF 12.3.2

A. Edit the G3 Switchboard form.
B. Add the G3 logo (found in the Chapter 12 data set).
C. Change the title to G3 Database Interface. (The easiest way to do this is to change the name of the Main Switchboard page through the Switchboard Manager.)
D. Add a rectangle around the Switchboard items in the Detail section. Set a light background color for the rectangle. Make sure the rectangle is in the background so the items appear.
E. Enlarge the text size for the Switchboard items.
F. Save the changes.
G. View and test the form (see Figure 12.10).

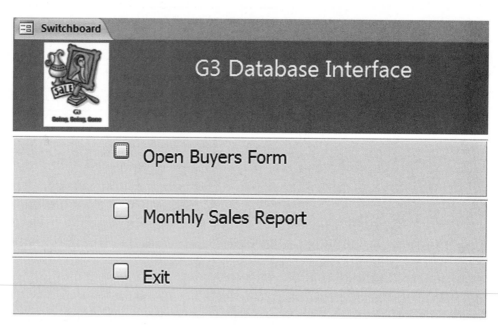

Figure 12.10 Edited G3 Switchboard

To change the actual choices on the Switchboard form, you will have to use either the Switchboard Manager or open the *Switchboard Items* table in Datasheet view and edit the data. The Music Switchboard is shown in Figure 12.11.

There are five fields in the *Switchboard Items* table—*SwitchboardID, ItemNumber, ItemText, Command,* and *Argument*. Table 12.4 shows the data type and function of these fields, and whether or not they are part of the primary key.

SwitchboardID	ItemNumbe	ItemText	Command	Argument	Add New Field
1	0	G3 Database Interface		Default	
1	1	Open Buyers Form	3	frm_BuyersInfo	
1	2	Monthly Sales Report	4	rpt_MonthlySalesRepo	
1	3	Exit	6		

Figure 12.11 *Switchboard Items* table

Table 12.4 *Switchboard Items* Table Fields

Field Name	Data Type	Primary Key	Function
SwitchboardID	Number	Yes	Switchboard page number.
ItemNumber	Number	Yes	Selection number, with 0 being the page name and 1-8 being the number of the command button from top to bottom (generally).
ItemText	Text	No	Label displayed next to the command button.
Command	Number	No	One of the commands from the list shown in Table 12.5.
Argument	Text	No	Additional data for command.

Q: What happens if I remove some of the empty text boxes on the Switchboard form in Design view?

A: Don't delete them. You may delete the space needed to display a current or future menu item.

The *SwitchboardID* and *ItemNumber* fields together form the primary key for this table. This means that for each record, the combination of these two fields is unique. It also means that these fields can't be left blank in any record.

There are nine commands that are valid in the *Command* field. These command numbers and their corresponding actions are listed in Table 12.5.

Table 12.5 *Switchboard Items* Commands

Command Number	Action
0	Define the Switchboard name (appears in the Window title).
1	Go to Switchboard.
2	Open form in Add mode (blank form only).
3	Open form in Edit mode (browse and change records).
4	Open report.
5	Design application (starts Switchboard Manager).
6	Exit application (closes the database).
7	Run macro.
8	Run code (Visual Basic module).

For example, in Figure 12.11 all items have a *SwitchboardID* of 1 (meaning they all appear on the same page). Each item is numbered sequentially from 0 to 4 and has *ItemText* that corresponds to the selection labels that appear on the form (see Figure 12.10). The first record contains G3 Database Switchboard as the *ItemText*—this is the text that appears as the Window title (see Figure 12.10). If you compare the numbers in the *Command* field of each record to those in Table 12.5, you'll see which command is being activated. The *Argument* field in each record contains the name of a form, report, or macro being opened.

The fields in the *Switchboard Items* table correlate to the objects you select in the Switchboard Manager. Compare Figure 12.11 with Figures 12.7 and 12.8 to see the item order, commands, and arguments.

Q: Is there anything else I should know about switchboards?

A: Yes. The Switchboard Manager generates Visual Basic code, which can be difficult to edit unless you have Visual Basic programming experience.

How to Edit a Switchboard Form

Formatting Changes

1. Open the Switchboard form in Design view and edit. You can add or change any control, but don't remove the command buttons on the form, even any extra ones.

Structural Changes

1. Run the Switchboard Manager.
2. Select the Switchboard that you want to edit.
3. Click the Edit button. The Edit Switchboard Item dialog box opens (see Figure 12.7).
4. Make changes to the selections and text in the Text box, the Command text box, and the Form text box as appropriate.
5. Click the OK button to return to the Edit Switchboard Page dialog box (see Figure 12.8).
6. Make changes to the selection sequence by clicking on the Move Up and Move Down buttons in the lower right corner of the window.
7. Click the Close button to close the Edit Switchboard Page dialog box. The Switchboard Manager dialog box reappears as shown in Figure 12.5.
8. Close the Switchboard Manager dialog box.

In addition to commands which open and close forms or reports, run code or macros, and exit the application, the active Switchboard can also open other Switchboard pages. Creating several secondary (not the default) Switchboard pages that contain many similar objects (such as forms or reports) is a way to organize the database application for the end user. To open tables or run queries, macros must be created with these actions. Although the command on the Switchboard would be to run the macro, these macros can be grouped together on a separate Switchboard page for queries or tables for easier use. A navigation command can also be added to each page to return to the main Switchboard page.

How to Add Another Switchboard Page (Submenu)

1. Run the Switchboard Manager and click the New button to create a new page. Enter a name for the new page. This will be the page that contains a subgroup or submenu of selections. Be sure that this new page is selected (see Figure 12.12).

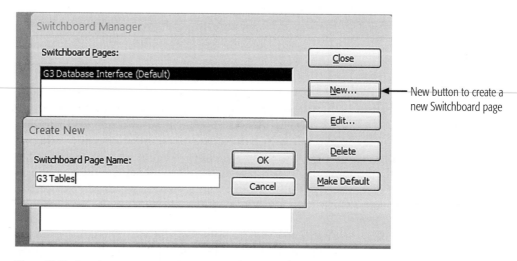

Figure 12.12 Creating a new Switchboard Page

2. Click the Edit button. Add the items, commands, arguments, and text to this new page. Make the last item a selection that opens the main Switchboard page.

3. Select the Go to Switchboard command, put the name of the main Switchboard form in the Switchboard text box, and add an appropriate text label (see Figure 12.13).

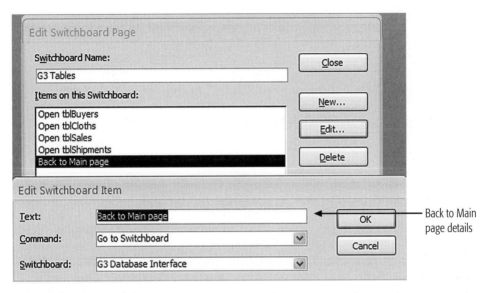

Figure 12.13 Adding Items to the new Switchboard page

4. Close the Switchboard page.

5. Edit the main Switchboard page using the Switchboard Manager.

6. Add a new item that opens the new page using the Go to Switchboard command and the page name created in step 1. You may need to move the new item up above any Exit command, as new items are added at the end of the list (see Figure 12.14).

7. Close the Switchboard Manager dialog box.

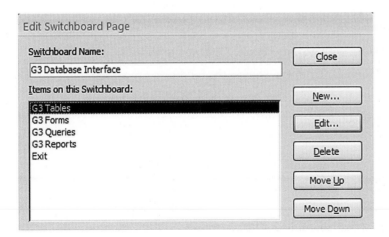

Figure 12.14 New pages on main Switchboard page

Q: Is there a faster way to change the items on a switchboard?

A: You can make changes to the Switchboard structure by editing the *Switchboard Items* table in Datasheet view.

TRY IT YOURSELF 12.3.3

Using the Switchboard Manager, make the following changes to the G3 Switchboard:

A. Add individual pages for G3 Tables, Queries, Forms, and Reports.

B. Delete the individual items on the main page for the form and report.

C. Add the following tables to the Tables page using the macros that open each table. Add a command to return to the main page.
- *tblBuyers*
- *tblCloths*
- *tblSales*
- *tblShipments*

D. Add the following forms to the Forms page. Add a command to return to the main page.
- *frm_BuyersInfo*
- *frm_Sales*

E. Add the following reports to the Reports page. Add a command to return to the main page.
- *rpt_Buyers*
- *rpt_MonthlySales*
- *rpt_Chart*
- *rptInvoice*

F. Add the following query to the Queries page using the macros that open it. Add a command to return to the main page.
- *qry_SalesReport*

G. Save the changes. View and test the modified Switchboard (see Figure 12.15).

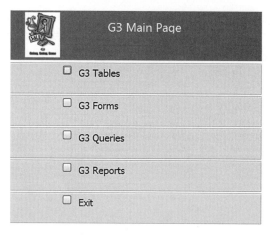

Figure 12.15 G3 Switchboard with changes

12.4 / Developing an Interface Without a Switchboard

A Switchboard is easy to create, but it can be quite cumbersome to make changes. You must be careful about changing the Switchboard form in Design view, as removing controls may prevent menu items from displaying. You must use the Switchboard Manager to add, change, or delete items from the menu, or edit the *Switchboard Items* table. If you find that a Switchboard form doesn't meet your needs, there are some alternatives for creating a way to control your application.

Creating Your Own Menu Form

The easiest way to substitute for a Switchboard form is to create your own menu form. Making your own menu eliminates the difficulties in editing described above. A menu form is just an unbound form containing a series of command buttons and descriptive labels. The labels describe the menu choices, and the command buttons are clicked to activate these choices. You can either create the command buttons using the Command Button Wizard, or you can write Visual Basic procedures that execute when a button is clicked.

Before creating the menu form, be sure that all the objects referred to by the menu have already been made. For example, if one of the menu selections is to open a form for editing data, then that form must exist prior to that menu selection being added to the form.

How to Create a Menu Form

1. Create a Blank form with no data source. Open in Design view.
2. In the Property Sheet for the form, change the following properties:
   a. Record Selectors and Navigation Button properties to No.
   b. Default View is Single Form.
3. Add a title to the form.
4. Be sure the Use Control Wizards button is selected (found on the Design ribbon). For each menu option:
   a. Click the Button command.
   b. Click on the form to place the button.
   c. Make the selections in the Command Button Wizard to activate the menu choice.

TRY IT YOURSELF 12.4.1

Using the *G3_Ch12.accdb* file:
A. Create a menu form similar to the Switchboard form that was created previously.
B. Save the form as *frm_MainMenu*. Test the command buttons.

Q: How would I get different pages in my Menu form similar to the other Switchboard pages?

A: Create other blank forms which have all similar objects grouped together (all reports together for example).

5. Add an Exit or Close button so users can leave the menu.

6. Save the form and test the buttons.

You can create the menu selections a number of ways. Figure 12.16 shows a menu in which the choices are shown as captions on command buttons. Figure 12.17 shows a menu with blank-captioned buttons and labels containing the menu choices. You can add any graphics, lines, and so forth you want.

Q: How do you make a second line in a label?

A: Go to the end of the first line, hold down the CTRL key, and press ENTER.

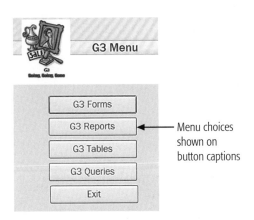

Figure 12.16 G3 menu using a Blank form

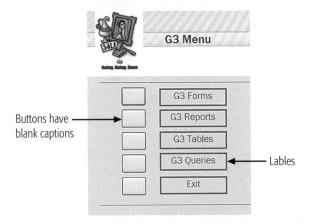

Figure 12.17 Alternative menu using a blank form

You can make a submenu quite easily using the same method. Create another unbound form for the submenu, and add an option to the main menu to activate the submenu. For example, create a menu of reports on a form, and add a command button to the main menu form with a caption such as "Print Reports."

Using Hyperlinks for Navigation

Another method for creating an application menu without the Switchboard Manager is through the use of a blank form with hyperlinks. The hyperlinks are used to open other objects in the database rather than buttons or menu items. Hyperlinks can also be used to open Web pages or send email. Figure 12.18 show an example of a main form using hyperlinks.

Creating an interface using hyperlinks is very easy. They can be placed anywhere on a form and opening a database object using a hyperlink is faster than using a button.

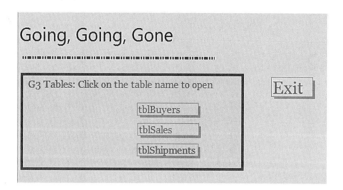

Figure 12.18 G3 Main form with hyperlinks

TRY IT YOURSELF 12.4.2

Using the *G3_Ch12.accdb* file:
A. Create a hyperlink menu form.
B. Add a hyperlink to a table, query, form, and report.
C. Add a hyperlink to the *mcr_CloseHyperlink* macro.
D. Optional: Include a graphic and add a hyperlink to that image.
E. Save the form as *frm_HyperlinkedMenu*.
F. Test the hyperlinks.

How to Create a Hyperlink Menu Interface

1. Create a blank form with no data source.
2. Click the hyperlink command on the Form Design tools ribbon, Controls group.
3. The Insert Hyperlink dialog box opens (see Figure 12.19).

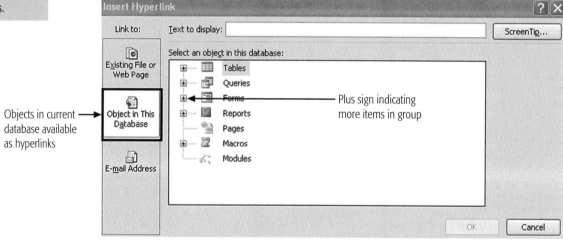

Figure 12.19 Insert Hyperlink dialog box

4. Select Object in this Database button from the Link to: list.
5. Select the object to link. If a plus (+) sign appears in front of an object, click the plus sign to view items in that object group. Select an object from that group.
6. Type the hyperlink text into the "Text to display" text box. This text will appear on the form.
7. Click on the Screen Tip button to add text that will appear when a user places the mouse over the hyperlink. (This is optional.)
8. Click OK.

    The hyperlink can be moved and formatted as any other control on a form. To change the hyperlink text, open the property sheet for the hyperlink control and change the value in the Caption property line. A hyperlink can also be attached to an image control where the image is clicked rather than text. Add the image control to the form. Open the property sheet for the image and click the Hyperlink Address property line. This will display an ellipsis to the right of the line. Click on the ellipsis and the Insert Hyperlink dialog box opens as shown in Figure 12.19. Add the hyperlink to the image and close the property sheet for that control.

12.5 / Modal Dialog Forms

A Modal Dialog form is another object that can be created as part of the database user interface. The modal form does not permit a user to switch focus to another window while it is open. It essentially locks the user to the modal form until it closes, although the user may switch to windows in applications other than Access.

An example use of this type of form would be to select a specific customer, order, or product from a list on a form, or a date which is entered to limit information viewed in a report. When further information needs to be collected from a user, a dialog box is displayed so that the data can be entered or selected. When the data is entered or selected, the user can then enter the database.

In some cases, it is important for the user to not continue in the database or switch the focus to another window until this modal dialog box is closed. For example, a form used to log users into a database should not close until a correct user name and password have been entered. The user would not be able to use another database object until the dialog box closes.

These types of forms can either be bound to a data source or unbound. Data is usually entered into a text box or selected from a combo or list box on the form. Dialog boxes have a command button that is clicked once data has been entered into the form, so the database process can continue.

There are two ways to create a Modal form. One is to use an existing form and change the Modal property on the form's property sheet to Yes. Another method is to use the Modal Form command on the Create ribbon, Forms group, More Forms command. This will create a blank form with two command buttons, one to complete the input and another to cancel.

How to Create a Modal Form

1. On the Create ribbon, click the More Forms command.
2. Choose Modal Dialog (see Figure 12.20).
3. Enter the controls for the form. These could include combo boxes, text boxes, and others.
4. Write the macro which attaches to the "OK" button.
5. Format and save the form. Test it to be sure it works properly (see Figure 12.21).

How to Change an Existing Form into a Modal Form

1. Open a form in Design view.
2. Open the property sheet for the form.
3. Click the Other tab of the property sheet.
4. Locate the Modal property and change its value to Yes.

TRY IT YOURSELF 12.5.1

A. Using the *G3_Ch12* database, open the form called *frmUserLogin*.
B. Add a command button to the form that runs the *mcrLogin* macro when clicked.
C. Change the form's Modal property to Yes, and save the form.
D. There are two valid users of this form: Guidebook (password = cookie) and Instructor (password = class). Open the form and log in as one of these users, using the correct password.
E. Open the form and log in again, this time using an incorrect password. Notice that the Navigation Pane is unavailable, and if any other objects are open, they are also unavailable.
F. Close the form.

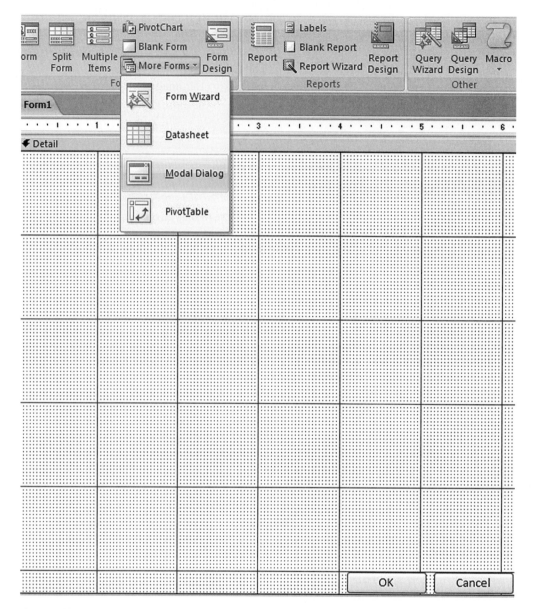

Figure 12.20 Access options

User ID

UserName

Enter Password

OK   Cancel

Figure 12.21 Setting start up options with a Modal dialog form

12.6 / Customizing the Quick Access Toolbar

The Quick Access toolbar holds frequently used commands that can also be customized for the user. This toolbar can be moved either above or below the ribbon to further customize the user interface. The Quick Access toolbar is located directly to the right of the Office button.

How to Add Commands to the Quick Access Toolbar

1. Click the Customize Quick Access Toolbar button (see Figure 12.22).

2. Choose any of the commands to enter on the toolbar.

TRY IT YOURSELF 12.6.1

A. Add the Open command to the Quick Access toolbar as a part of the default toolbar.

Figure 12.22 Customize the Quick Access Toolbar

3. If additional commands are needed, click More Commands (see Figure 12.23).

4. Choose from commands listed or use the Choose commands from: drop-down list.

5. Commands can also be added to the Default toolbar.

6. Click OK.

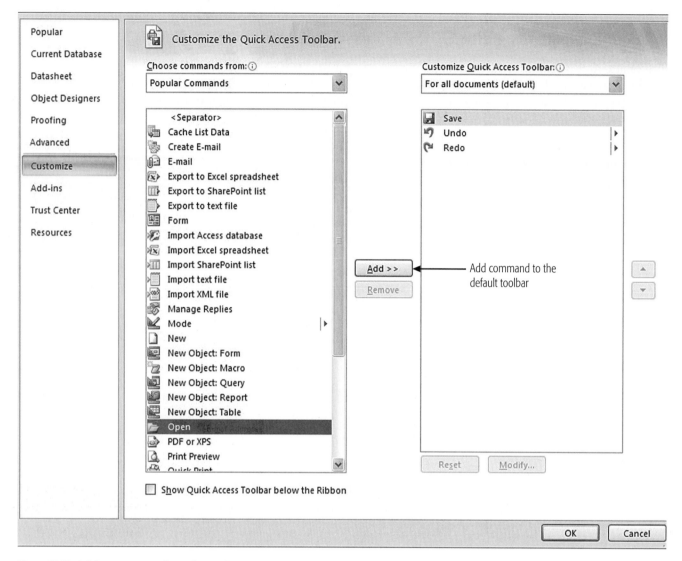

Figure 12.23 Adding commands to the toolbar

12.7 / Controlling Startup Functions

With any of the menu forms, it is quite easy to make the form display when the database is opened. The database screen can be further customized by removing the Navigation pane from view. This screen arrangement provides further security by making available only the objects on the menu form.

How to Set a Menu Form as the Startup Form

1. Open the database.

2. Click the Office button.

3. Click Access Options (see Figure 12.24).

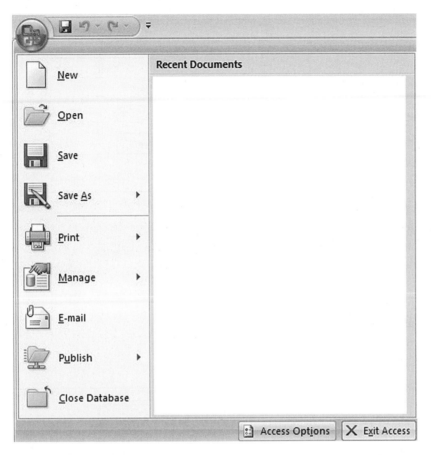

Figure 12.24 Access Options

4. Click Current Database.

5. Choose the form for startup from the Display Form: drop-down list (see Figure 12.25).

6. To remove the Navigation pane from view, uncheck the check box in front of Display Navigation Pane.

7. Click OK. The new start up properties will take effect when the database is closed and then reopened.

Using an AutoExec Macro

A special macro, called an AutoExec macro, can be set up to run automatically each time the database file is opened. An AutoExec macro can open a Switchboard form or any other form, plus perform any other function that runs from a macro. For example, in addition to opening a Switchboard or menu form, a Beep can be added when the form has opened. If you want to bypass the AutoExec macro, hold down the SHIFT key while opening the database file. The AutoExec macro is created and edited just as other macros. The macro must be named *AutoExec* for it to run automatically. For more information about AutoExec macros, see Chapter 11.

Placing a Database Shortcut Icon on the Desktop

To make it easier still to open the database, you can create a shortcut icon for the database and place it on the Windows desktop. You can also change its name to make it more descriptive and easier to find.

TRY IT YOURSELF 12.7.1

A. Set the startup properties to display any one of the menu forms that have been created.

B. Optional: Remove the Navigation Pane from the database screen.

C. Save the changes. Close the database. Reopen the database and use the menu options to access database objects.

Popular
Current Database
Datasheet
Object Designers
Proofing
Advanced
Customize
Add-ins
Trust Center
Resources

Options for the current database.

Application Options

Application Title: _____

Application Icon: _____   Browse...

☐ Use as Form and Report Icon

Display Form: [frm_MainMenu ▼] ← Choose the startup form

☑ Display Status Bar

Document Window Options
  ○ Overlapping Windows
  ◉ Tabbed Documents
  ☑ Display Document Tabs
☑ Use Access Special Keys ⓘ
☐ Compact on Close
☐ Remove personal information from file properties on save
☑ Use Windows-themed Controls on Forms
☑ Enable Layout View for this database
☑ Enable design changes for tables in Datasheet view (for this database)
☑ Check for truncated number fields

Picture Property Storage Format
  ◉ Preserve source image format (smaller file size)
  ○ Convert all picture data to bitmaps (compatible with Access 2003 and earlier)

Navigation

☐ Display Navigation Pane ← Uncheck to not display the Navigation Pane

[Navigation Options...]

Figure 12.25 Setting the Startup form

How to Create a Database Shortcut Icon

1. Click the right mouse button while pointing to the desktop. Select New, Shortcut from the menu. The Create Shortcut dialog box appears (see Figure 12.26).

2. Click the Browse button and locate the name of the database file. Be sure that All Files appears in the File Type box in the Browse window.

3. Click the Next button.

4. Type an appropriate name for the shortcut. The name of the database is usually adequate.

5. Click the Finish button. The dialog box closes and the new icon appears on the desktop.

You can test the shortcut icon by double-clicking on the icon. If you create shortcuts on your classroom or lab computer, they may not be saved permanently. Check with your instructor before making shortcuts on the computers in your classroom or lab.

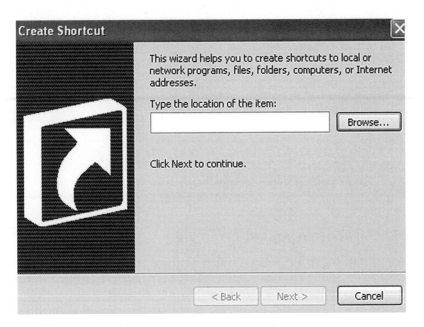

Figure 12.26 Create a Shortcut

Professional Tip: **Customizing a Startup Shortcut**

You can change the icon used to represent any shortcut on the desktop. Just right-click on the icon and select Properties from the shortcut menu. Click the Change Icon button and choose a new icon. If you have other icon files on your computer, click the Browse button to locate and select one. Once an icon is selected, click the OK button, and then click the OK button to close the Properties dialog box. The icon will change to the selection.

You can also customize the way a database opens from a shortcut icon, but you must first create a shortcut that points to Access itself (not to a specific database file). Create the shortcut using the method described above (How to Create a Database Shortcut Icon), but in step 2, browse for the file *msaccess.exe*. It will probably be found in the *Program Files* folder. Once the shortcut has been created, open the property sheet as described in the paragraph above. You can add optional information to the Target line as follows:

Option	Outcome
Database name	Opens the specified database (include path)
/ro	Opens the specified database for read only
/x Macro name	Opens the specified database and runs the named macro

For example, to open a database named *Practice12* located in C:\AccessGB\Chapter12, the Target line should contain the following:

"C:\Program Files\...\MSACCESS.EXE" c:\AccessGB\Chapter12\Practice12.mdb

To open the same as read only:

"C:\Program Files\...\MSACCESS.EXE" c:\AccessGB\Chapter12\Practice12.mdb /ro

And to run the macro named *Print Music Titles Report* when the database is opened:

"C:\Program Files\...\MSACCESS.EXE" c:\AccessGB\Chapter12\Practice12.mdb /x Print Music Titles Report

In the examples above, the ... (in Program Files\...\) represents the folder or folders in *Program Files*. These may vary on different computers. Don't type ..., type the actual folder names.

To run a Visual Basic procedure upon startup, specify a macro name containing a RunCode action that runs the procedure.

There are several other options that can be added to the Target line. Use the Help feature in Access for more information.

Fast Track   **A quick guide to procedures learned in this chapter**

Implementing Database Application Design

1. Develop the interface: the main screen, the look and feel of the application, the help system, and the menu and the toolbar commands for activating the objects in the application. Create a macro to display a message box for all commands on menus and toolbars. The message box should inform the user that this part of the application isn't working yet. Gradually replace the message box with working forms and reports.

2. Give the user the first version, and refine the model based on user feedback.

3. Develop the forms for editing one or two of the master tables.

4. Give the user the next version, enhance the model based on user feedback, and develop the rest of the master table editing forms.

5. Develop the forms for editing one or two of the transaction/event or bridge tables.

6. Give the user the next version, refine the model based on user feedback, and develop the rest of the transaction/event table editing forms.

7. Develop the reports and labels, give the user the next version, and improve the model based on user feedback.

8. Develop forms for editing lookup tables, give the user the next version, and refine the model based on user feedback.

9. Develop other objects needed, give the user the next version, and improve the model based on user feedback.

Creating a Switchboard Form with the Switchboard Manager

1. Click on the Database Tools tab to display the Tools ribbon.

2. Click on Switchboard Manager in the Database Tools group.

3. The Switchboard Manager dialog box opens indicating that there are no available Switchboards in this database. Click Yes to create a new one.

4. Click the Edit button to make changes to the page. The Edit Switchboard Page dialog box appears.

5. Change the name of the page (optional) by selecting the current Switchboard name and overtyping a more descriptive name.

6. Click the New button to add items to the Switchboard. The Edit Switchboard Item dialog box opens with three List boxes available for editing the items (or buttons) on the Switchboard.

7. Enter the text in the Text box. This will be the text on the face of the command button.

8. Click the drop-down arrow in the Command text box. The drop-down list shows several actions that can be associated with a button. Access Visual Basic code will be generated to complete these actions—you will not need to write any macros.

9. Select the action.

10. Select the appropriate data to complete the Form text box.

11. Click the OK button to return to the Edit Switchboard Page dialog box.

12. Continue adding items to the Switchboard until all items are shown in the Items on this Switchboard window. Each item will result in a command button on the Switchboard form.

13. Click the Close button to close the Edit Switchboard Page dialog box. The Switchboard Manager dialog box reappears.

14. Close the Switchboard Manager dialog box. You should see a new table named *Switchboard Items* and a new form named *Switchboard*.

Editing a Switchboard Form

Formatting Changes

1. Open the Switchboard form in Design view and edit. You can add or change any control, but don't remove the command buttons on the form, even any extra ones.

Structural Changes

1. Run the Switchboard Manager.

2. Select the Switchboard that you want to edit.

3. Click the Edit button. The Edit Switchboard Item dialog box opens.

4. Make changes to the selections and text in the Text box, the Command text box, and the Form text box as appropriate.

5. Click the OK button to return to the Edit Switchboard Page dialog box.

6. Make changes to the selection sequence by clicking on the Move Up and Move Down buttons in the lower right corner of the window.

7. Click the Close button to close the Edit Switchboard Page dialog box. The Switchboard Manager dialog box reappears.

8. Close the Switchboard Manager dialog box.

Adding Another Switchboard Page (Submenu)

1. Run the Switchboard Manager. Click the New button to create a new page. Enter a name for the new page. This will be the page that contains a subgroup or submenu of selections. Be sure that this new page is selected.

2. Click the Edit button. Add the items, commands, arguments, and text to this new page. Make the last item a selection that opens the main Switchboard page.

3. Select the Go to Switchboard command, put the name of the main Switchboard form in the Switchboard text box, and add an appropraite text label.

4. Close the Switchboard page.

5. Edit the main Switchboard page using the Switchboard Manager.

6. Add a new item that opens the new page using the Go to Switchboard command and the page name created in step 1. You may need to move the new item up above any Exit command, as new items are added at the end of the list.

7. Close the Switchboard Manager dialog box.

Creating a Menu Form

1. Create a Blank form with no data source. Open in Design view.

2. In the Property Sheet for the form, change the following properties:

    a. Record Selectors and Navigation Button properties to No.

    b. Default view is Single Form.

3. Add a title to the form.

4. Be sure the Use Control Wizard button is selected (found on the Design ribbon). For each menu option:

    a. Click the Button command.

    b. Click on the form to place the button.

    c. Make the selections in the Command Button Wizard to activate the menu choice.

5. Add an Exit or Close button so users can leave the menu.

6. Save the form and test the buttons.

Creating a Hyperlink Menu Interface

1. Create a blank form with no data source.

2. Click the hyperlink command on the Form Design tools ribbon, Controls group.

3. The Insert Hyperlink dialog box opens.

4. Select Object in this Database button from the Link to: list.

5. Select the object to link. If a plus (+) sign appears in front of an object, click the plus sign to view items in that object group. Select an object from that group.

6. Type the hyperlink text into the "Text to display" text box. This text will appear on the form.

7. Click on the Screen Tip button to add text that will appear when a user places the mouse over the hyperlink. (This is optional.)

8. Click OK.

Setting a Menu Form as the Startup Form

1. Open the database.

2. Click the Office button.

3. Click Access Options.

4. Click Current Database.

5. Choose the form for start up from the Display Form: drop-down list.

6. To remove the Navigation pane from view, uncheck the check box in front of Display Navigation Pane.

7. Click OK. The new startup properties will take effect when the database is closed and then reopened.

Creating a Modal Form

1. On the Create ribbon, click the More Forms command.
2. Choose Modal Dialog.
3. Enter the controls for the form. These could include combo boxes, text boxes, and others.
4. Write the macro which attaches to the OK button.
5. Format and save the form. Test it to be sure it works properly.

Changing an Existing Form into a Modal Form

1. Open a form in Design view.
2. Open the property sheet for the form.
3. Click the Other tab of the property sheet.
4. Locate the Modal property and change its value to Yes.

Adding Commands to the Quick Access Toolbar

1. Click the Customize Quick Access Toolbar button.
2. Choose any of the commands to enter on the toolbar.
3. If additional commands are needed, click More Commands.
4. Choose from commands listed or use the Choose commands from: drop-down list.
5. Commands can also be added to the Default toolbar.
6. Click OK.

Creating a Database Shortcut Icon

1. Click the right mouse button while pointing to the desktop. Select New, Shortcut from the menu. The Create Shortcut dialog box appears.
2. Click the Browse button and locate the name of the database file. Be sure that All Files appears in the File Type box in the Browse window.
3. Click the Next button.
4. Type an appropriate name for the shortcut. The name of the database is usually adequate, such as Music.
5. Click the Finish button. The dialog box closes and the new icon appears on the desktop.

Review Questions

1. Do the SDLC principles describe a step-by-step development process or a general approach to developing an application?
2. (T/F) SDLC emphasizes using a problem solving approach for application development.
3. (T/F) The database developer is involved in all phases of application development.
4. During which phase of development are the Entity-Relationship diagram and the list of normalized tables produced?
5. What are some of the advantages of rapid prototyping?
6. What is a database interface?

7. List five design questions that should be answered before creating the interface.

8. What is the difference between an AutoExec macro and a startup form?

9. Which object is usually used as the main screen of the database interface?

10. What is a Switchboard form?

11. What is the Switchboard Manager?

12. Which controls on the form activate each item created by the Switchboard Manager?

13. Name the two database objects that make up the Switchboard?

14. What should the last selection on most Switchboard item lists be?

15. Can you edit the Switchboard Items table?

16. Can you edit the Switchboard form?

17. Name two other methods for creating a menu interface for a database application.

18. How do you add a form as a startup form?

19. (T/F) The Navigation pane must always be displayed when a database is open.

20. What is a Modal Dialog form?

21. Give an example for using a Modal form.

22. What are two ways to create a Modal form?

23. Where is the Quick Access Toolbar located?

24. Why would you want to add commands to this toolbar?

25. What is a startup form?

26. Which form is usually used as a startup form?

27. What is an AutoExec macro?

28. For what purpose would you use an AutoExec macro?

29. How do you bypass the AutoExec macro?

30. What is the purpose of putting a shortcut icon on the desktop?

Exercises

ACTIVITY

Exercise 1—Practicing New Procedures

Exercise 1A: Using the Switchboard Manager

Using the *SDAL_Ch12.accdb* file:

1. Create a Switchboard form using the Switchboard Manager.

2. Add at least two additional pages to the main Switchboard form with submenus. Use objects already created in the database file.

   a. Group like objects together, such as reports, forms, etc.

   b. One page should have links to a table and a query. (Hint: Create macros to open these objects.)

3. Add commands to Return to Main Page on each of the additional pages.

4. Add a command to exit the application on the Main Page.

5. Test the form to be sure all commands work.

Exercise 1B: Creating a Menu Form

1. Create a Main Menu form with at least two additional pages (forms). Do not use the Switchboard Manager.

2. Link the forms using command buttons.

   a. Add a title to the main form and the additional forms.

   b. Add a graphic to the main form.

3. Add buttons to Return to Main Page on the additional forms and a button to exit the application.

4. Save the form as *frm_Ex1B_MainMenu*. Test the buttons to be sure they work properly.

Exercise 1C: Adding a Startup Form

1. Choose either the Switchboard form or the Main Menu form as the startup form.

2. Enter that form as the Startup form in Access Options.

3. Close the database and open it again to be sure the form displays when the database opens.

Exercise 2—In-Class Group Practice

Compare different methods of creating a user interface: Switchboard Manager, forms with command buttons, and forms with hyperlinks. Consider the ease of creating and editing this interface. Review the interface from the end-user perspective.

Group 1:

1. Using the *Practice_Ch12.accdb* file, use the Switchboard Manager to create a main Switchboard page.

2. Add at least two additional pages and link these to the main page.

3. Add objects found in the *Practice_Ch12.accdb* file.

4. Edit the Switchboard forms to add color, visual interest, and graphics.

5. Add navigation commands to return to the main page and to exit the application.

6. Test the Switchboard to be sure it runs properly.

7. Set it as the Startup form. Close and reopen the database file to make sure the form displays.

8. Answer the following questions:

   a. Did you encounter any problems creating this startup form with the Switchboard Manager? Identify them.

   b. How easy was it to edit any of the Switchboard forms?

   c. Did the form run properly? If not, how did you fix the problems?

   d. What is your evaluation of using the Switchboard Manager?

9. Switch files with another group and use their interface. Answer the following questions from the user's perspective:

   a. Was the interface easy to use?

   b. Did it provide clear directions and navigation?

   c. Did it run properly?

    d. Was there a way to exit the application?

    e. What suggestions do you have for the designers?

Group 2:

1. Using the *Practice_Ch12.accdb* file, create a Main Menu form using the Blank form command.

2. Add at least two additional pages and link these to the main page.

3. Add objects found in the *Practice_Ch12.accdb* file.

4. Edit the menu forms to add color, visual interest, and graphics.

5. Add navigation commands to return to the main page and to exit the application.

6. Test the Menu to be sure it runs properly.

7. Set it as the Startup form. Close and reopen the database file to make sure the form displays.

8. Answer the following questions:

    a. Did you encounter any problems creating this startup form? Identify them.

    b. How easy was it to edit any of the menu forms?

    c. Did the form run properly? If not, how did you fix the problems?

    d. What is your evaluation of using a Blank form to create a Main Menu?

9. Switch files with another group and use their interface. Answer the following questions from the user's perspective:

    a. Was the interface easy to use?

    b. Did it provide clear directions and navigation?

    c. Did it run properly?

    d. Was there a way to exit the application?

    e. What suggestions do you have for the designers?

Group 3:

1. Using the *Practice_Ch12.accdb* file, create a Main Menu form using the Blank form command.

2. Add at least two additional pages and link these to the main page.

3. Add hyperlinks to objects found in the *Practice_Ch12.accdb* file.

4. Edit the menu forms to add color, visual interest, and graphics.

5. Add navigation commands to return to the main page and to exit the application.

6. Test the Menu to be sure it runs properly.

7. Set it as the Startup form. Close and reopen the database file to make sure the form displays.

8. Answer the following questions:

    a. Did you encounter any problems creating this startup form? Identify them.

    b. How easy was it to edit any of the menu forms?

    c. Did the form run properly? If not, how did you fix the problems?

d. What is your evaluation of using hyperlinks on a Blank form to create a Main Menu?

9. Switch files with another group and use their interface. Answer the following questions from the user's perspective:

   a. Was the interface easy to use?

   b. Did it provide clear directions and navigation?

   c. Did it run properly?

   d. Was there a way to exit the application?

   e. What suggestions do you have for the designers?

Share your findings with the class.

Exercise 3—Challenge: Creating a Hyperlinked Menu Form

ACTIVITY AND REFLECTION

Use the *SDAL_Ch12.accdb* file.

1. Create a Main Menu form with at least two additional pages (forms). Link the objects and forms through hyperlinks.

2. Add a title to the main form and the additional forms.

   a. Add a graphic to the main form.

3. Add links to Return to Main Page on the additional forms and a link to exit the application. (Hint: Create any needed macros.)

4. Save the form as *frm_Ex3_HyperlinkMenu*. Test the links to be sure they work properly.

5. Write an AutoExec macro that opens this form at startup. Include a Beep command when the form opens.

Exercise 4—Problem Solving: Creating a Database Interface

ACTIVITY AND REFLECTION

Use the *Exercise12-3.accdb* file.

1. Design and create a Switchboard or Main Menu interface that opens the tables, queries, forms, and reports in the database. Use all of the objects in the database file and create any that you feel are necessary to make the menu or Switchboard run smoothly.

2. Set up this form so that it automatically opens when the database opens.

3. Test the form to be sure it runs properly.

Exercise 5—Challenge: Creating a Modal Dialog Form

ACTIVITY AND REFLECTION

Use the *SDAL_Ch12.accdb* file.

1. Create a Modal Dialog form that requires user input before moving into the database.

   a. Design the form using either the Modal Dialog command or use an existing form and change the properties.

2. You must include controls that require user input.

3. Design the macros to execute the command and control the input.

4. Set this form as the Startup form.

Exercise 6—Discussion Questions

1. Examine Figure 12.3. Note the icons that are used on the buttons, the text labels below them, the layout of the form with the buttons across the top, and so forth. Write a half-page critique of these design issues.

2. Examine Figures 12.10 and 12.15. Note that the layouts, graphics, and so forth are the same. Why? Is this desirable or not?

3. Examine the main application screens shown in Figures 12.10, 12.16, 12.17, and 12.18. Which of these screens do you like best, and why? What are some of the advantages and disadvantages of using each form style?

4. What are some of the drawbacks of rapid prototyping? The alternative to rapid prototyping is to develop the entire application and then give it to users. What are some of the drawbacks of this method? Which method seems better to you?

CASE STUDY A: MRS. SUGARBAKER'S COOKIES

Mrs. Sugarbaker wants to be able to control access to certain parts of her database, as well as make it easier to access the objects they regularly use. She has requested a user interface that would display commonly used parts of the database and provide clear navigation and directions.

1. Create a user interface to run objects in the Mrs. Sugarbaker's Cookies database.

2. Include at least three tables, queries, reports, and forms. Create any macros or other objects that would be necessary.

3. Group them by objects, putting all forms together, and so forth. Or create groups by data, putting all customer information together, all product information together, and so forth.

4. Design the forms to include graphics, instructions to the user, page titles, and navigation.

5. Make the main page of this interface the Startup form.

6. Test the interface to be sure it runs properly.

CASE STUDY B: SANDY FEET RENTAL COMPANY

Because Sandy Feet has a lot of data in their database and not all the users need access to the same data, Sandy Feet requires a user interface that will organize their data by user need. One group at SFRC works specifically with owners and another works with clients.

1. Create an interface that groups the database objects by their use, either by client or by owner.

2. Organize all tables, forms, queries, and reports on the interface pages by client or owner. Some database objects might be included in both groups.

3. Design the forms to include graphics, instructions to the user, page titles, and navigation.

4. Create any macros or other objects that would be necessary.

5. Make the main page of this interface the Startup form.

6. Test the interface to be sure it runs properly.

CASE STUDY C: PENGUINS SKI CLUB

The Penguins Ski Club would like to have everything tied together with a user interface. They would like it to be easy to use, have clear navigation, and allow access to certain objects in their database.

1. Create a user interface to run objects in the Penguins Ski Club database. Use a switchboard; or a form with a custom menu, hyperlinks, or command buttons to open and use the various database objects.

2. Include the following objects. Create any macros or other objects that would be necessary.

   - *frmMembers*
   - *frmEvents*
   - *frmTabbedInfo*
   - *frmMemberAttendance*
   - *frmEquipmentRental*
   - *rptCalendar*
   - *rptMemberDirectory*
   - *rptLabels*
   - *rptEventAttendance*
   - *rptAbilityLevels*

3. Group any items together, or create sub-menus, as needed. Be sure to use descriptive text for the menu items, hyperlinks, or command buttons. Include any instructions you think are necessary for the user.

4. Design the forms to include graphics, instructions to the user, page titles, and navigation.

5. The switchboard or main form should open automatically when the database is opened.

6. Test the interface to be sure it runs properly.

Answers to Selected Exercises

This appendix contains the answers to all the review questions and most of the questions in the first exercise set at the end of each chapter. If an answer is not given here, it is either a lengthy solution or a computer printout. Your instructor will be able to give you additional help.

Chapter 1

Review Questions

1. Data is raw facts. Information is useful processed data.
2. A database is a large collection of related data files including tables, queries, reports, and so forth.
3. A row.
4. Size, number of seats/capacity, equipment, building name, and so forth.
5. Table, query, report, form, macro, module.
6. To automate sequences of commands.
7. A student application, a student registration form, a schedule request, a new course form, an add/drop form, a course withdrawal form, and so forth.
8. A report is better because all records will be printed, whereas a query limits the number of records.
9. Click on the Explorer window *OR* click on the Access icon or the Windows Start menu.
10. A key on a piece of paper.
11. The Navigation Pane. It's on.
12. Upper. The tabs are for locating groups of commands.
13. Database objects are opened by double-clicking on the object name.
14. An object can be edited in the Design view. A subdatasheet displays related data that is stored in another table in the database.
15. Click on the ⊠ or Close button in the upper right corner of the window, or click on the Office button then click the Exit button.
16. A type of database that stores groups of information in tables that can be related.
17. It eliminates data redundancy and ensures data integrity.

18. There are many examples. A table used by a video rental company containing your name and address and so forth would have a repeating group containing the videotapes you have rented, if all the data was stored in one table.

19. A key is a field or fields that are distinct in every record and have data filled in for every record.

20. The easiest way to start planning a database is to look at the output from the existing manual or computerized system. Reports list the fields needed in the database.

21. True. Queries can include calculated fields based on data stored in a table or another query.

22. True. Forms are used for both input and output.

23. False. Forms are edited similarly to reports.

24. False. Most macros are run from forms and reports.

25. False. They can be listed in order by object, or grouped by dependency too.

26. The title of the piece would be the best key because it is the only unique field. A better choice would be to create another field called *Art ID* and create an ID number for each piece.

27. The problem with the database depicted in Table 1.2 is that each customer can rent skis multiple times, so the rental date repeats in the table. A separate table should be made for rental date and customer ID or name.

Exercise 1

Solutions are given within the exercise at the end of chapter 1.

Chapter 2

Review Questions

1. The database file stores all the database objects.

2. Tables, queries, reports, forms, macros, and modules.

3. Use a Database template, or design it yourself.

4. A lookup field is used to display data from another table or a typed list.

5. There is a key icon in front of the file name, and it has an .accdb extension.

6. To open the Field Templates pane, click on the Datasheet tab on the ribbon and click on the New Field button.

7. Switch to Design view from Datasheet view by right-clicking on the table tab name and choosing Design view. Open a table in Design view by right-clicking on its name and choosing Design view.

8. You can calculate a sum, average, count, maximum, minimum, standard deviation, or variance on the Total row.

9. Only numeric data—a number or currency type—can have an entry on the Total row.

10. You have more control over the fields that are included.

11. The top part of the window contains the field entry area where you enter the field name, type, and description. The field property area is in the lower part of the window.

12. Text, numbers, currency, dates, memo, yes/no, Auto number, OLE object, and Attachment.

13. They are used to control the validity and accuracy of data.

14. The field properties are Field Size (which determines length), Format, Input Mask, Caption, Default Value (which is the value that will be automatically assigned to the field), Validation Rule and Validation Text (which determine what is entered into the field), Required, Allow Zero Length, and Indexed.

15. The key must exist in every record and be unique in every record.

16. A key.

17. The data is deleted also.

18. No, a primary key cannot be deleted without impact to data.

19. Yes, field properties can be changed anytime.

20. Printing the table design is started by clicking on the Database Tools tab.

21. Datasheet view.

22. To format the Datasheet view, click on the Home tab.

23. No.

24. No.

25. The bottom row.

26. Hiding a column makes it disappear from the display, while freezing a column keeps it on the screen at all times.

27. Use the Quick Print button on the Quick Access toolbar, or click on the Office button and select Print.

Exercise 1

3. The primary keys for the tables are as follows:

Table Name	Primary Key
tblRecordings	Music ID—autonumber
tblInventory	Inventory ID—autonumber
tblArtists	Artist ID—autonumber
tblCategory	Category ID—text or autonumber
tblRecordLabels	Label ID—autonumber
tblMedia	Media ID—text or autonumber

5. The table definitions are as follows:

tblArtists

Name	Type	Size
Artist ID	Long Integer	4
LastNameOrBandname	Text	255
FirstName	Text	255

tblCategory

Name	Type	Size
CategoryID	Text	255
CategoryName	Text	255

tblInventory

Name	Type	Size
InventoryID	Long Integer	4
MusicID	Long Integer	4
MediaType	Text	50
QuantityOnHand	Long Integer	4
Price	Currency	8

tblMedia

Name	Type	Size
Type	Text	50
Description	Text	50

tblRecordings

Name	Type	Size
MusicID	Long Integer	4
Artist	Long Integer	4
Title	Text	50
Category	Text	255
Label	Long Integer	4

tblRecordLabels

Name	Type	Size
LabelNumber	Long Integer	4
LabelName	Text	255

Chapter 3

Review Questions

1. At the end of the table.
2. You can replace all the occurrences of a data value in one cómmand.
3. No, once a record is deleted it's gone forever.
4. The Cut, Copy, and Paste buttons. They are in the Clipboard group on the Home tab.
5. Edit, Undo.
6. Because a primary key is the main index on a table—it's used to look up a specific record. If multiple records have the same key, then it becomes impossible to find a specific record.
7. Yes.
8. An imported table is placed inside the database, while a linked table remains in its original location and a pointer to this location is placed in the database.
9. Descending.
10. Datasheet.
11. Only records that match the criteria in the filter.
12. Yes, you can apply both a sort and a filter at the same time.

13. Add a new field, delete a field, change a field, switch a primary key, and change field properties.

14. No, a caption doesn't change the name of a field.

15. The one-to-many relationship.

16. No, each table in a database must have a different name.

17. No, the two fields can have different names.

18. A window opens showing all tables and all relationships.

19. Yes, a deleted table can be restored to a database.

20. Rich text is text with a limited amount of formatting. Change a memo field's Text Format property to "Rich Text" to allow rich text.

21. The easiest way to enter a date value into a field is to click on the calendar icon that pops up to the right of the field, and choose a date from the calendar.

22. The refresh button updates data in the tables that are currently open, so they display the newest changes that have been made to the data in those tables.

23. A delimited text file is a text file containing a character separator between fields such as a comma.

24. It is easiest to import data from Excel.

Exercise 1
Exercise 1A

tblArtists—36 records

tblCategory—6 records

tblInventory—58 records

tblMedia—4 records

tblRecordings—47 records

tblRecordLabels—5 records

Exercise 1B

2. When the lookup field from *tblRecordings* to *tblRecordLabels* was created, the join between the two tables was created.

Exercise 1C

2. The average price is $12.52.

3. The first item is a cassette of "A Date with Elvis."

4. There are 11 items in the list. The average price is $12.44.

5. $13.72 is the average price of LPs.

6. There are 20 LPs in the store.

8. There are four disco albums.

9. There are nine copies of "Best of the Monkees" and the average price is $15.49.

10. There are 10 copies of "At Folsom Prison" and 7 of them are CDs. The average price of all copies is $9.32.

Chapter 4

Review Questions

1. Queries are questions asked of a table, multiple tables, or other queries to obtain specific information that can be saved as a database object

2. Tables, multiple tables, or other queries can be used as data sources for queries.

3. The resulting records when a query is run is called a dynaset.

4. Criteria are conditions set by the user to limit the records produced in the query result.

5. The two sections of the query design window are the Table pane and the Design grid.

6. Drag the field from the field list to the Design grid. Use the drop down arrows in the field cells and choose the field. Double-click on the field in the field listing.

7. * The asterisk puts all the fields from the table into the Design grid.

8. Fields are displayed in Datasheet view in the order they are entered in the Design grid.

9. Criteria are conditions set on field data in the Design grid.

10. No, only fields in the Design grid can have criteria.

11. If no other operators are entered in the Criteria cell, Access considers the default operator as "equal to." The criteria must be matched exactly for the results to be displayed in the dynaset.

12. In the OR row of the field.

13. The Not option excludes records matching the criteria.

14. Relational operators include equal to (=), greather than (>), less than (<), not equal to (<>), and combinations thereof.

15. The Like operator finds any record containing a specific word or phrase anywhere in a field. The Between...And operator finds any record containing a value within a specified range of numbers. The In operator provides an easy way to specify multiple OR criteria.

16. A Total query is a query that performs summary calculations or aggregate functions on groups of data.

17. On the Design tab, in the Show/Hide group, click Totals.

18. Group By allows the user to specify a field as a grouping field. Data will be organized and displayed into groups based on the values in that field.

19. Other options found in the Total row drop-down list include Count, Sum, Avg, Max, Min, StDev, Var, First, Last, Group By, Exp, and Where.

20. The Count option counts all non-null values in a field. If there is no data in a field, that record will not be included.

21. True.

22. False.

23. True.

24. True.

25. Use Show Table.

26. A line will be drawn between the two tables on the common field.

27. Fields from all related data sources can be used in a query.

Example 1

Example 1A:

1. *qry1A1_Rock.*

Music ▾	Artist	Title	Category	Label
1	Champs	Super Party Hits	Rock	Decca
2	BeeGees	The Very Best Of	Rock	Decca
5	Lewis	Whole Lot of Shakin'	Rock	A & M
8	Rolling Stones	Hot Rocks	Rock	Decca
9	Turtles	Happy Together	Rock	Island
10	Monkees	Best of the Monkees	Rock	Island
11	Sly and The Family Stone	Essential Sly	Rock	A & M
13	Rolling Stones	Through the Past Darkly	Rock	Interscope
14	Beatles	Rubber Soul	Rock	Columbia
15	Beatles	Abbey Road	Rock	Columbia
19	Bruce Springsteen	September	Rock	A & M
20	Bruce Springsteen	Greeting From Asbury Park	Rock	A & M
22	Money	Two Tickets	Rock	Island
23	Clash	London Calling	Rock	A & M
24	Ramones	The Ramones	Rock	Decca
28	Presley	A Date With Elvis	Rock	A & M
29	Presley	King Creole	Rock	Decca
35	Dylan	Highway 61 Revisited	Rock	A & M
36	Beatles	Revolver	Rock	Decca
37	Dylan	Blonde on Blonde	Rock	A & M
38	Morrison	Astral Weeks	Rock	Columbia
40	Morrison	Moondance	Rock	Interscope
41	Bowie	Hunky Dory	Rock	Columbia
42	Bowie	The Rise And Fall Of Ziggy Stardust	Rock	A & M
44	Eagles	Hotel California	Rock	A & M
46	Wonder	Original Musiquarium	Rock	Interscope

2. *qry1A2_Rock_Decca.*

Music ▾	Artist	Title	Category	Label
1	Champs	Super Party Hits	Rock	Decca
2	BeeGees	The Very Best Of	Rock	Decca
8	Rolling Stones	Hot Rocks	Rock	Decca
24	Ramones	The Ramones	Rock	Decca
29	Presley	King Creole	Rock	Decca
36	Beatles	Revolver	Rock	Decca

3. *qry1A3_Hits.*

Music ▾	Artist ▾	Title ▾	Category ▾	Label ▾
1	Champs	Super Party Hits	Rock	Decca
12	Lynn	Greatest Hits	Country	Decca
26	Platters	Greatest Hits	DooWop	Interscope
27	Everly Brothers	Greatest Hits	Easy Listening	Columbia
48	Patsy Cline	Greatest Hits	Country	Columbia

Example 1B:

1. *qry1B1_BeeGees.*

LastNameOrBandname ▾	Title ▾	Category ▾
BeeGees	The Very Best Of	Rock
BeeGees	Saturday Night Fever	Disco

2. *qry1B2_BeeGeesInventory.*

LastNameOrBandname ▾	Title ▾	Category ▾	QuantityOnHand ▾	Type ▾
BeeGees	The Very Best Of	Rock	4	Compact Disk
BeeGees	The Very Best Of	Rock	1	Long Playing Vinyl
BeeGees	Saturday Night Fever	Disco	2	Long Playing Vinyl
BeeGees	Saturday Night Fever	Disco	5	Compact Disk
BeeGees	Saturday Night Fever	Disco	5	Compact Disk

3. *qry1B3_Inventory>5.*

LastNameOrBandname ▾	Title ▾	Category ▾	Quantity ▾	Type ▾
Presley	A Date With Elvis	Rock	6	Compact Disk
Monkees	Best of the Monkees	Rock	8	Compact Disk
Beatles	Revolver	Rock	9	Compact Disk
Eagles	Hotel California	Rock	6	Compact Disk
Cash	At Folsom Prison	Country	7	Compact Disk
Clash	London Calling	Rock	6	Compact Disk

Example 1C:

1. *qry1C1_Decca_NotRock.*

Artist ▾	Title ▾	LabelName ▾	CategoryNa ▾
Lynn	Greatest Hits	Decca	Country
Bridges	Wild Cherry	Decca	Disco
Perry Como	Catch a Falling Star	Decca	Easy Listening

2. *qry1C2_Country<10.*

LastNameOrBandname	FirstName	Title	Type	Price	CategoryNar
Cash	Johnny	The Songs That Made Him Famous	Eight Track	$8.99	Country
Cash	Johnny	At Folsom Prison	Cassette	$5.99	Country
Cash	Johnny	At Folsom Prison	Long Playing Vinyl	$9.99	Country

3. *qry1C3_EasyListeningSale.*

Artist	Title	Price	SalePrice
Darin	The Ultimate Bobby Darin	$11.99	$10.79
Everly Brothers	Greatest Hits	$12.99	$11.69
Sinatra	In the Wee Small Hours	$11.99	$10.79
Sinatra	Songs for Swingin' Lovers	$18.99	$17.09
Perry Como	Catch a Falling Star	$11.99	$10.79

Example 1D:

1. *qry1D1_Categoryinventory.*

CategoryNar	SumOfQuan
Country	26
Disco	16
DooWop	1
Easy Listening	13
Jazz	9
Rock	95

2. *qry1D2_InventorybyType.*

Type	SumOfQuan
Eight Track	5
Compact Disk	130
Cassette	5
Long Playing Vinyl	20

3. *qry1D3_MostExpensive.*

MaxOfPrice	Title
$18.99	Songs for Swingin' Lovers

Chapter 5

Review Questions

1. Forms can be used for both inputting data into a table or displaying data as output.

2. Form tool, Split View, Multiple Items, Pivot Chart, Pivot Form, Forms Wizard, Datasheet, Blank Form.

3. Forms that are not tied to any data are called unbound forms. Forms that are tied to a data source (either a table or query) are called bound forms.

4. Unbound forms can be used to display user selections such as menus, or to display messages and information.

5. Select the table and then click the Form tool. A form using all the fields from the table will be created.

6. Data and some controls in the the form design editing tools can be edited in Layout view.

7. Data from the data source and all the controls in the form design are displayed. There are no form editing tools available. Only data can be added and edited.

8. False.

9. True.

10. Tab key, Enter key, mouse click.

11. Use the Navigation bar at the bottom of the form to go to the first record, next, previous, and last records.

12. Use the New Record command from the Records group or the New Record button on the form navigation bar.

13. Create tab, More Forms drop-down list, Form Wizard command.

14. >>.

15. Columnar, Tabular, Datasheet, and Justified.

16. When a form is opened in Form view, data can be entered and modified. When the form is opened in Design view, changes to the form's structure and design can be made.

17. Datasheet and Layout views.

18. False.

19. A Property Sheet is the list of object characteristics.

20. frm.

21. False.

22. 1:Many relationship.

23. True.

24. False.

25. False.

Exercise 1

Example 1A: *frmArtists*

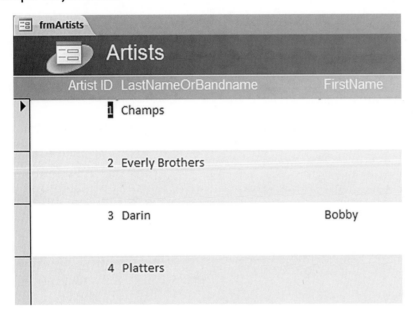

Example 1B: *frmRecordLabels*

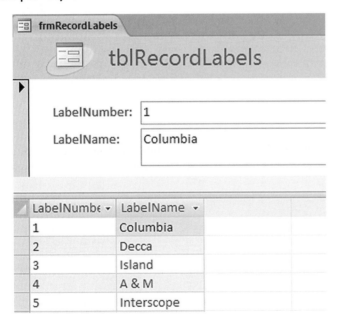

Example 1C: *frmRecordings*

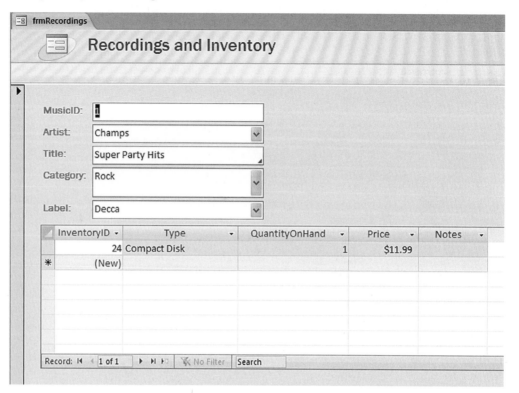

Chapter 6

Review Questions

1. Tables and queries.
2. Joined/related.
3. Many.
4. Report tool, Labels, Report Wizard.
5. Yes.
6. Sorting orders records on the sort field either in ascending or descending order.
7. The purpose of setting Grouping fields is to organize records in a report on a like field.
8. Sum, count.
9. Print Preview.
10. No, spaces, commas and other characters must be inserted when creating the label prototype.
11. Yes.
12. No.
13. Sum, Avg, Min, Max.
14. The grouping field is identified in a group header and all related records based on that group are listed together.
15. Word, HTML, XML, Text, Snapshot Preview, another Access database.
16. The purpose of a Mail Merge is to join Access data with a Word document.

17. Table or query.

18. Word.

Exercise 1

Example 1A: *rptRecordings*

Recordings by Your Name

MusicID	Artist	Title	Category	Label
1	Champs	Super Party Hits	Rock	Decca
2	BeeGees	The Very Best Of	Rock	Decca
3	Darin	The Ultimate Bobby Darin	Easy Listening	Interscope
4	Del Vikings	That Magic Touch	DooWop	Island
5	Lewis	Whole Lot of Shakin'	Rock	A & M

Example 1B: *lblArtists_Recordings_Labels*

Eagles
Hotel California
RK
A & M

Bob Dylan
Highway 61 Revisited
RK
A & M

Example 1C: *rpt_Recordingsinformation*

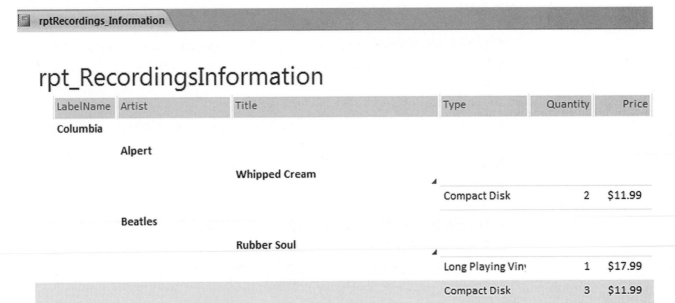

rptRecordings_Information

rpt_RecordingsInformation

LabelName	Artist	Title	Type	Quantity	Price
Columbia					
	Alpert				
		Whipped Cream			
			Compact Disk	2	$11.99
	Beatles				
		Rubber Soul			
			Long Playing Vin	1	$17.99
			Compact Disk	3	$11.99

Chapter 7

Try It Yourself 7.1.1

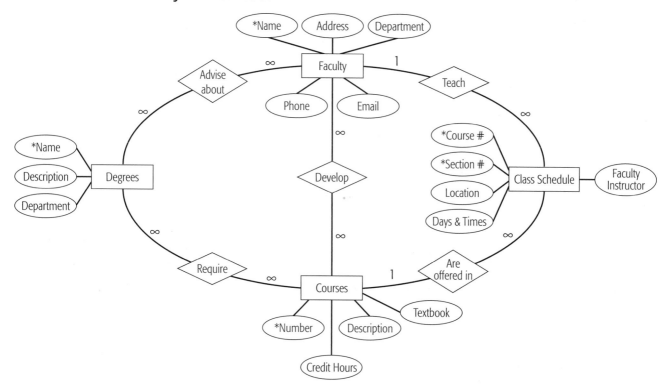

Figure A.7 E-R diagram for College Database

Try It Yourself 7.1.2

FACULTY (Name, Address, Department Name, Department Office, Department Secretary, Phone, Email Address, Courses Developed, Degrees Advised)

COURSES (CourseID, Course Title, Description, Credit Hours, Textbook, Degrees Required By)

DEGREES (DegreeID, Degree Name, Department Name, Degree Description, Faculty Advisors)

CLASS SCHEDULES CourseID, Section#, Course Title, Location, Instructor, Days Scheduled, Times Scheduled)

Review Questions

1. The two main functions of a database are to update data and retrieve data.

2. An entity-relationship diagram is a tool that helps you analyze and organize the data you need to capture in a database.

3. True. Attributes of an entity class determine the fields in the corresponding table.

4. A lookup table holds data about groups or categories of information. Other tables use them to look up data values.

5. Bridge tables hold data from two tables having a many-to-many relationship.

6. A transaction/event table is most dynamic.

7. Normalization is the process of making a table match a relational database design standard called a normal form. It eliminates data redundancy and errors.

8. Relational algebra forms the basis for relational database theory.

9. False. The field *Name* is functionally dependent on *SSN*.

10. True. If a field in a table can be broken down into smaller fields, the table is not in 1NF.

11. False. A partial dependency is when the non-key fields are functionally dependent on only part of the primary key.

12. False. A table containing a calculated field is not in 3NF.

13. True. Data anomalies occur when data is stored in multiple tables, when a transitive dependency exists, or when a partial dependency exists. All these conditions are corrected by normalization.

14. True. A lookup field in a table is the primary key in another table.

15. You change the sort order of a lookup field drop-down list by editing the underlying query and adding an ascending sort order on the non-key field.

16. True. A multiple-field primary key can be made up of four different fields.

17. True. You can create a multiple-field primary key on a table that already has data in it.

18. You index a field to speed up record searches and sorts.

19. Inner join.

20. Run the Find Duplicates query when you are changing the primary key in a table containing data. The new key will not allow duplicates.

21. The Find Unmatched Records query locates records in related tables that have no related (or unmatched) records.

22. When Cascade Delete is turned on and a record is deleted from the "one" table, all the records in the "many" table with corresponding values will also be deleted.

23. True. Databases created by earlier versions of Access can be opened in Access 2007 without converting.

24. Compacting the database rearranges how the file is stored on your disk so that it takes up less space.

25. The front-end database contains all the database objects.

26. Optimizing the database potentially reduces the time it takes to perform database tasks.

Exercise 1

A.

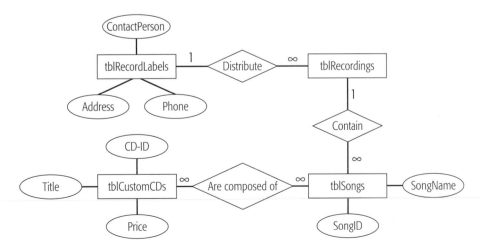

B. tblRecordLabels(ContactPerson, Address, City, State, Zip, Phone) add to existing table

tblSongs(<u>SongID</u>, SongName, RecordingID)

tblCustomCDs(<u>CD-ID</u>, CDTitle, CDPrice)

tblCDSongs(<u>CD-ID, SongID</u>)

C. To add the album covers to *frmRecordings,* display the field list and drag the field *AlbumCover* onto the form. The two jpgs should display on the form when those records are displayed.

D. The recording name and the artist's name are visible in the drop-down list, but only the recording name is seen in the field when the list is closed. Only one piece of data can be displayed in the field.

E. Two records:

tblArtists Without Matching tblRecordings
LastNameOrBandname
Dave Clark Five
Pink Floyd

F. Six records, three duplications:

Find duplicates for tblRecordings	
Artist	Title
Turtles	Happy Together
Turtles	Happy Together
Eagles	Hotel California
Eagles	Hotel California
Dylan	Blonde on Blonde
Dylan	Blonde on Blonde

G. The Performance Analyzer recommends you index *tblRecordings* on *Category, Label,* and *Artist.* These are all foreign keys in the table, and will probably be used a lot for sorting and searching.

Chapter 8

Review Questions

1. A Parameter query is an interactive query that prompts the user for criterion as the basis for running the query.

2. It is used when a different criterion is needed each time a query is run. The design of the query stays the same.

3. Yes.

4. Forms![frmCustomer]![txtLastName].

5. An Action query is a type of query that performs specific changes (some action) to table data.

6. Because Action queries make permanent changes to original table data.

7. To delete any unnecessary records from one or more related tables.

8. It adds (appends or copies) records from one table to another.

9. To see the selected records before actually creating a new table with perhaps incorrect data.

10. Only all records matching certain criteria will be changed to new values.

11. No, you cannot reverse the append process with the Undo command.

12. The purpose of a Crosstab query is to display summary data in rows and columns.

13. Row headings, column headings, and value data (numeric).

14. True. However, a field that does not represent a group or category of data will produce one record in the dynaset for every record in the data source.

15. True. The Crosstab Query Wizard adds totals automatically.

16. A function is a prewritten miniprogram that produces a result from a calculation, comparison or other evaluation.

17. An expression is a set of symbols used to define an operation.

18. Right-click and select Build command, or Builder button on the ribbon.

19. An operator is a symbol or word that lets you perform a specific action.

20. The order of precedence is the prescribed order in which Access evaluates operators and then performs their actions.

21. A new field that combines fields together to make a new field.

22. You can combine two text fields (concatenating) using an ampersand (&) between the two fields.

23. A property sheet is a dialog box that allows you to change the properties, or attributes, of an object.

24. You select a query (to open the query property sheet) by clicking anywhere on the background in the upper area of the screen. Right-click and select Properties from the menu.

25. When the Unique Records property is set, the query will return only unique records in the dynaset. All of the fields in the data source are compared, not just those fields included in the query. When the Unique Values property is set, the query will select only records with unique values in the fields included in the query.

26. SQL stands for Structured Query Language.

27. True. Access creates an SQL statement for every query.

28. False. All SQL statements do not start with the word SELECT.

29. The SELECT statement is the most frequently used SQL command.

30. The table name and dot can be omitted when identifying a field in a query using only one table.

31. The WHERE keyword allows criteria to be added to restrict the number of records retrieved.

32. Like '*Elm Street*' retrieves all addresses on Elm Street.

33. ANDs are evaluated first.

34. False. Using the GROUP BY keywords in a SELECT statement is the equivalent of creating a Total query.

Exercise 1
Exercise 1A

1.

Field:	Artist	Title	CategoryName
Table:	tblRecordings	tblRecordings	tblCategory
Sort:			
Show:	☑	☑	☑
Criteria:			[Enter Category]
or:			

2.

Field:	Title	Type	QuantityOnHand	Price	LastNameOrBandnam
Table:	tblRecordings	tblInventory	tblInventory	tblInventory	tblArtists
Sort:					
Show:	☑	☑	☑	☑	☐
Criteria:					[Enter Artist]
or:					

Exercise 1B

1.

Field:	LabelName	LastNameOrBandnam	Title	QuantityOnHand	Price	Category
Table:	tblRecordLabels	tblArtists	tblRecordings	tblInventory	tblInventory	tblRecordings
Sort:	Ascending	Ascending				
Show:	☑	☑	☑	☑	☑	☑
Criteria:				<=2		"RK" Or "CN"
or:						

2.

Field:	Price
Table:	tblInventory
Update To:	[Price]*1.1
Criteria:	<10
or:	

Exercise 1C

1.

Field:	CategoryName	Description	QuantityOnHand
Table:	tblCategory	tblMedia	tblInventory
Total:	Group By	Group By	Sum
Crosstab:	Row Heading	Column Heading	Value

RESULT

qryInventoryCount				
CategoryName	Cassette	Compact Disk	Eight Track	Long Playing Vinyl
Country	1	22	1	2
Disco		11	1	4
DooWop			1	
Easy Listening		12		1
Jazz		9		
Rock	6	81	6	13
Soul R&B				5

2.

Field:	CategoryName	Description	Price
Table:	tblCategory	tblMedia	tblInventory
Total:	Group By	Group By	Avg
Crosstab:	Row Heading	Column Heading	Value

RESULT

qryInventoryPriceAverage				
CategoryName	Cassette	Compact Disk	Eight Track	Long Playing Vinyl
Country	$6.59	$12.66	$9.89	$10.99
Disco		$11.99	$10.99	$14.32
DooWop			$12.99	
Easy Listening		$12.24		$18.99
Jazz		$11.99		
Rock	$11.28	$12.99	$13.64	$13.66
Soul R&B				$15.95

3.

Field:	MusicID	Type	QuantityOnHand	Price	InventoryValue: [QuantityOnHand]*[Price]
Table:	tblInventory	tblInventory	tblInventory	tblInventory	
Sort:					
Show:	☑	☑	☑	☑	☑
Criteria:					

TOTAL ROW

qryInventoryValue				
MusicID	Type	QuantityOnHand	Price	InventoryValuel
		176		$2,246.43

Chapter 9

Review Questions

1. A control is an object used in reports and forms. Controls can be labels, text boxes, lines, rectangles, etc.

2. Bound control is tied to a field in an Access table. Unbound control does not have a field associated with it.

3. Label (displays descriptive text); Line (a drawn line for enhancement); Logo (image used as logo).

4. Can be used to provide information for users or allow users to make selections.

5. Click the Add Existing fields command in the Tools Group. Click on the data source. Drag and drop the fields into the form.

6. Detail section.

7. Header section.

8. Title.

9. Select it. Click and drag on the resizing handles.

10. False.

11. Title puts the text in the Header section. Label adds text to any section of the form.

12. Color, font size, font style.

13. Image inserts a graphic file into the form. Unbound Object Frame inserts a variety of file types which can be edited in their original application.

14. False.

15. A property sheet is list of object properties.

16. False. All parts of the form and all the controls have property sheets.

17. cbo.

18. For organization and functionality reasons.

19. Hold the [SHIFT] key down while clicking on each individual control.

20. To provide limited data choices for data entry.

21. False.

22. T/F or Y/N.

23. Puts each record on a separate page.

24. A Combo box provides limited choices for data entry.

25. Numeric.

26. Form footer usually in a subform.

27. For emphasis. If a value reaches a certain value, the formatting will provide the emphasis.

28. In Design view, select all the controls. Click the Arrange tab and use the Remove command.

29. True.

30. The Tab Order is the way the cursor moves around the form when the Tab key is used.

31. If the form was modified, the order of the controls would need to be modified.

32. Changes the tab order to the order of the controls on the form.

33. For organization of related pieces of data.

34. Row Headings, Column Headings, Data.

35. If the form has data for a report, then you won't have to recreate it.

Exercise 1

Exercise 1A: *frmRecordings*

Exercise 1B: *frmRecordings with subform*

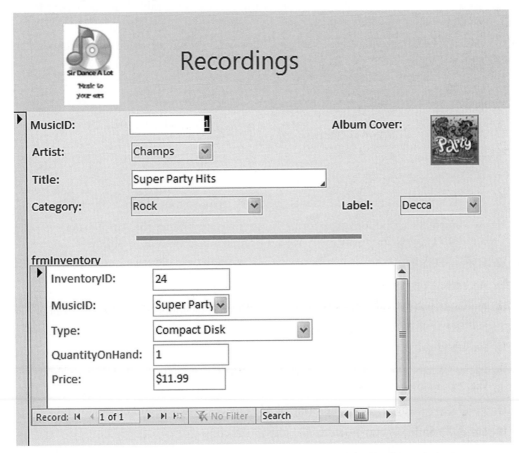

Exercise 1C: *frmRecordings_tabbed*

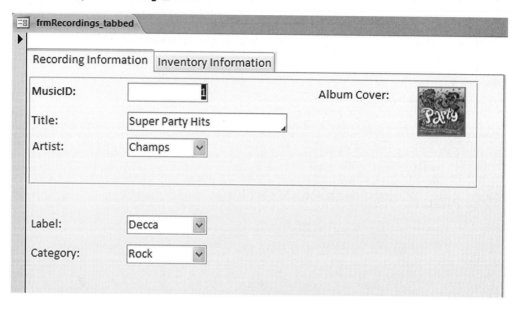

Chapter 10

Review Questions

1. To print results of table or query summaries.

2. Forms have very similar design elements and tools and the table Datasheet view looks similar to a tabular style report.

3. Data can be grouped to provide summary information about the group (subtotals, counts).

4. Page header.

5. Detail.

6. To be able to include all necessary data.

7. Make sure it all fits on the paper/page.

8. All can be resized.

9. Visual interest.

10. The rectangle covers the text so it is necessary to move that object to the background.

11. AutoFormat is good for quick formatting for a report. Since the AutoFormats are the same for reports and forms, they would bring continuity to both objects.

12. Report Header.

13. Ascending or Descending order.

14. For summarizing data about the group which could be counting the records or creating subtotals for the group.

15. Group Header.

16. In the Group, Sort and Total pane. Click on the Group name and choose to show the Footer section.

17. From the Arrange ribbon, the Control Alignment group, Align Left command.

18. Hold the Shift key down while clicking on the controls.

19. The running sum shows how each item in the group contributes to the total for the group.

20. In the Detail section.

21. On the Property Sheet for the Group Header.

22. Prints the section on the current page and then goes to the top of a new page to print the next section.

23. Create a separate title page or create a standalone chart report.

24. Design ribbon, Controls group.

Exercise 1

Exercise 1A: *rpt_Ex1A_InventoryReport*

Inventory Report

Champs

Title: Super Party Hits

    Type: Compact Disk   Category: Rock

    QuantityOnHand: 1   Label: Decca

    Price: $11.99

Everly Brothers

Title: Greatest Hits

    Type: Compact Disk   Category: Easy Listening

    QuantityOnHand: 5   Label: Columbia

    Price: $12.99

Exercise 1B: *rpt_Ex1B_InventoryReport*

Inventory Report

By Your Name

Champs

Title: Super Party Hits

    Type: Compact Disk   Category: Rock

    QuantityOnHand: 1   Label: Decca

    Price: $11.99

Exercise 1B: *rpt_Ex1C_InventoryReport*

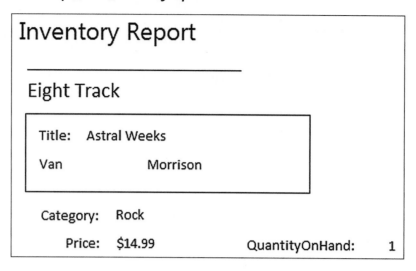

Chapter 11

Review Questions

1. A macro is a database object containing a series of actions that are run to complete a specific task.

2. False. Not all macros are attached to objects. AutoExec and AutoKeys are just two examples.

3. True. One of the most common events is clicking a command button.

4. The commands in a macro are called actions.

5. False. An argument is additional information provided to the macro action.

6. The Action pane and the Argument pane.

7. The Comments column is optional, but desirable for documentation purposes.

8. Arguments supply additional information (details) for the action to work with.

9. Just about every action has at least one argument associated with it. There are but one or two actions that have no arguments.

10. You should be able to identify the individual tasks that you want the macro to perform and also the names of the objects on which to perform these tasks.

11. a) Click into the Action cell. Click on the pull-down list and choose the appropriate action; b) Type the actual action in the Action cell; c) Use the drag and drop method for entering actions.

12. No, you can't run a macro without saving it.

13. False. The Msgbox action can only display an OK button.

14. Select the action to delete. Press the DELETE key.

15. It allows you to work through each individual action of the macro to verify its accuracy.

16. A conditional expression is a true/false expression that controls the execution of the macro.

17. If the condition is false, the macro will ignore the action and execute the next available action.

18. Click on the Condition button on the ribbon to display the Conditions column.

19. AutoExec macros are executed when a database first opens.

20. False. You should *not* add the prefix "mcr" to the name AutoExec when saving an AutoExec macro.

21. A Timer Interval property of 2000 is equal to 2 seconds.

22. You would refer to a macro called *NewRecord* in a group named *mcrInventory* as *mcrInventory.NewRecord*.

23. An embedded macro is one that is attached to an object, and can only be edited through that object. Its name does not appear in the Navigation pane.

24. A command button can execute a macro when clicked.

25. An event is a response to some action.

26. Through the Events tab on the button's property sheet.

27. Caption text or picture.

Exercise 1

Exercise 1A

1. Autexec macro is one row:

Action	Arguments
OpenForm	frmSplash,Form,,,Read Only,Normal

2. Use the Command Button wizard to add the button, choose category (form operations and action), and close form.

Exercise 1B

2. New column in query: ReOrderQuantity: 5 - [QuantityOnHand]

4. Use the Command Button wizard to add the button, choose category (form operations and action), and print current form.

5. *mcrReOrderEmail*

Action: SendObject

Arguments: Query, qryReOrders, Excel 97 - Excel 2003 Workbook (*.xls),
            = [Forms]![frmReOrders]![EmailAddress],,, Reorders, The attachment
            contains the reorder list for Sir Dance-A-Lot Music store. Thank you., Yes,

6. Use the Command Button wizard to add the button, choose category (miscellaneous and action), and run macro.

Exercise 1C

1. *qryUpdateInventory*—tables *tblInventory* and *tblNewInventory* joined on *InventoryID*

Field: QuantityOnHand

Table: tblInventory

UpdateTo: [QuantityOnHand]+[QuantityReceived]

2. *mcrUpdateInventory*

Action	Arguments
SetWarnings	No
OpenQuery	qryUpdateInventory, Datasheet, Edit
MsgBox	Inventory has been updated., Yes, None,

4. Use the Command Button wizard to add the button, choose category (miscellaneous and action), and run macro.

6. Table *tblInventory*, first eight records:

Before running macro:

InventoryID	MusicID	Type	QuantityOnHand	Price
1	I Love the Nightlife	Long Playing Vinyl	1	$15.99
2	I Love the Nightlife	Eight Track	1	$10.99
3	Saturday Night Fever	Long Playing Vinyl	2	$14.99
4	Saturday Night Fever	Compact Disk	5	$11.99
5	A Date With Elvis	Compact Disk	6	$11.99
6	Country Classics	Compact Disk	2	$11.99
7	Essential Sly	Compact Disk	2	$10.99
8	Greatest Hits	Compact Disk	3	$15.99

After running macro:

InventoryID	MusicID	Type	QuantityOnHand	Price
1	I Love the Nightlife	Long Playing Vinyl	5	$15.99
2	I Love the Nightlife	Eight Track	5	$10.99
3	Saturday Night Fever	Long Playing Vinyl	5	$14.99
4	Saturday Night Fever	Compact Disk	5	$11.99
5	A Date With Elvis	Compact Disk	6	$11.99
6	Country Classics	Compact Disk	5	$11.99
7	Essential Sly	Compact Disk	5	$10.99
8	Greatest Hits	Compact Disk	5	$15.99

Chapter 12

Review Questions

1. General approach.

2. True.

3. False.

4. During the Design phase.

5. The advantages of rapid prototyping are that it speeds the development process, gives users more experience before production, allows for more user input, and prevents development of an unusable application.

6. A database interface is the top layer of software when the program is run.

7. ■ Who will use it?
   ■ How familiar is the user with Access? How much control should the user have?
   ■ What actions does the user require?
   ■ Are macros necessary to run these actions?
   ■ Are there frequently used tasks to including in a custom toolbar?
   ■ What type of look should the interface have?
   ■ How will the user open and exit the interface?
   ■ Is there any security feature that needs to be built into the interface?

8. An AutoExcec macro is a macro that initially runs when the program is started. A startup form is a form that open with the program.

9. A Switchboard form is usually used as the main screen of the database interface.

10. A Switchboard form is an interactive form containing a variety of macros, buttons, and toolbars that automate database functions.

11. The Switchboard Manager is a command on the Database Tools ribbon that automates the process of creating a Switchboard.

12. Clicking on the buttons activates the commands for each item.

13. The two database objects that make up the Switchboard are the Switchboard items table and the Switchboard form.

14. The last selection on most Switchboard item lists should be Exit or return to Main page command.

15. Yes, you can edit the Switchboard items table in Datasheet view.

16. Yes, you can edit the Switchboard form in Design view and through the Switchboard Manager.

17. (1) Form with hyperlinks to other database objects; and (2) Form with command buttons to open other forms or database objects.

18. Go to Access Options from the Office button. Enter the name of the form to use upon startup.

19. False. The Navigation Pane can be hidden.

20. A Modal Dialog form is a form that requires user input before moving into the other database objects.

21. A form that would ask for user ID or password to progress further into the database.

22. (1) With an existing form, change the Modal property to Yes. (2) Use the Modal Dialog command to create the form.

23. The Quick Access Toolbar is located to the right of the Office button in the top left part of the screen.

24. For quick access to frequently used commands.

25. A startup form is a form that appears when the database is opened.

26. The Switchboard form or any other form that is designated to be a startup form.

27. An AutoExec macro is a macro that starts automatically when the database is opened.

28. To run a specific part of the database when the file is opened.

29. To bypass the AutoExec macro, hold the SHIFT key down while opening the database file.

30. A desktop shortcut icon on the desktop is used for easy and quick access to the database file.

Exercise 1A: SDAL Sample Switchboard

Exercise 1B: *frm_EX1B_MainMenu*

Exercise 1C: Choosing a Startup form

Access Functions

This appendix is divided into two sections. The first section is an alphabetically arranged list containing all Access, Access/Visual Basic, and Data Access Object functions. In the section following this list, you will find the most frequently used functions listed and defined according to their types. To find out more about a specific function, use the Help menu item in Access and look the function name up in the Help Index.

Functions are prewritten programs that transform or retrieve data. Functions usually require arguments or input data in order to run, and these arguments are enclosed in parentheses. Even if a function doesn't require an argument, it still requires empty parentheses following the function name. In the following example, the name of the function is *Right* and the arguments are ZipCode and 4:

Right(ZipCode, 4)

The date function doesn't require an argument; it returns the current date and is used as follows:

Date()

Functions process the arguments (or run without them) and return a piece of data. They can be used within expressions in queries, in form and report controls, and so forth.

ALPHABETICAL LIST OF ALL FUNCTIONS

Abs	CreateControl	DateValue
Array	CreateForm	DAvg
Asc	CreateGroupLevel	Day
Atn	CreateObject	DCount
Avg	CreateReport	DDB
CBool	CreateReportControl	DDE
CByte	CSng	DDEInitiate
CCur	CStr	DDERequest
CDate	CurDir	DDESend
CDbl	CurrentDb	DFirst
CDec	CurrentUser	Dir
Choose	CVar	DLast
Chr	CVDate	DLookup
CInt	CVErr	DMax
CLng	Date	DMin
CodeDb	DateAdd	DoEvents
Command	DateDiff	DStDev
Cos	DatePart	DStDevP
Count	DateSerial	DSum

DVar	IsNull	Seek
DVarP	IsNumeric	Sgn
Environ	IsObject	Shell
EOF	Last	Sin
Error	LBound	SLN
Eval	LCase	Space
Exp	Left	Spc
FileAttr	Len	Sqr
FileDateTime	LoadPicture	StDev
FileLen	Loc	StDevP
First	LOF	Str
Fix	Log	StrComp
Format	LTrim	StrConv
FreeFile	Max	String
FV	Mid	StringFromGUID
GetAllSettings	Min	Sum
GetAttr	Minute	Switch
GetObject	MIRR	SYD
GetSetting	Month	SysCmd
GUIDFromString	MsgBox	Tab
Hex	Now	Tan
Hour	NPer	Time
HyperlinkPart	NPV	Timer
IIf	Nz	TimeSerial
IMEStatus	Oct	TimeValue
Input	Partition	Trim
InputBox	Pmt	TypeName
InStr	PPmt	UBound
Int	PV	UCase
IPmt	QBColor	Val
IRR	Rate	Var
IsArray	RGB	VarP
IsDate	Right	VarType
IsEmpty	Rnd	Weekday
IsError	RTrim	Year
IsMissing	Second	

DEFINITIONS AND EXAMPLES OF SELECTED FUNCTIONS

Conversion

These functions convert data from one type to another. They're useful for creating expressions using mixed data types.

Function	Description	Syntax	Example
CCur	Converts an expression to Currency data.	CCur(Any expression)	CCur(100/4 + 5) Returns: $30.00
CDate	Converts an expression to Date data.	CDate(Any expression)	CDate("4/1/99") Returns: 4/1/99 as a date
CDbl	Converts an expression to Double Precision data (large real number).	CDbl(Any expression)	CDbl(3 * 8) Returns: 24.0

CInt	Converts an expression to Integer data.	CInt(Any expression)	CInt(47.8)
			Returns: 48 (Rounds)
CLng	Converts an expression to Long Integer data.	CLng(Any expression)	CLng(47.8)
			Returns: 48 (Rounds)
CSng	Converts an expression to Single Precision data (small real number).	CSng(Any expression)	CSng(3*8)
			Returns: 24.0
CStr	Converts an expression to String data.	CStr(Any expression)	CStr(90 + 17.32)
			Returns: "107.32"
Str	Converts a number to a string (text). Adds a leading space to the string.	Str(Any number)	Str(52.3)
			Returns: "52.3"
Val	Converts string (text) data to a numeric value.	Val("string")	Val("123")
			Returns: 123

Date and Time

These functions are used with date type data. They're useful for displaying specific data in a form or report. Note that all functions having a date argument will accept that date in any valid date format, such as: September 12, 1998; 9/12/98; and so forth.

Function	Description	Syntax	Example
Date	Displays current system date (doesn't include time, see Time function).	Date()	Returns: The current system date in short date format.
Day	Displays day as an integer from 1 to 31.	Day(date) Date can be expressed as string, number, or date literal.	Day(#September 12, 1998#) Returns: 12
Hour	Displays hour from specified time using 24-hour clock, or military time.	Hour(time)	Hour(2:05:10 pm) Returns: 14 (based on 24-hour clock)
Minute	Displays minute as an integer.	Minute(time)	Minute(6:22:01 pm) Returns: 22
Month	Displays the month as an integer.	Month(date) Date can be expressed as a string, number, or date literal.	Month("September 21, 1998") Returns: 9 (for September, the ninth month).
Now	Displays current date and time.	Now()	Returns: Today's date and current time.
Second	Displays second as an integer.	Second(time)	Second(3:12:35 pm) Returns: 35
Time	Displays current system time.	Time()	Returns: current time
TimeSerial	Displays hour, minute, and second from integers.	TimeSerial(hour, minute, second)	TimeSerial(13, 34, 55) Returns: 1:34:55 pm
Weekday	Displays the day of the week as an integer (Sunday is 1).	Weekday(date) Date can be expressed as a string, number, or date literal.	Weekday(#September 9, 1998#) Returns: 4 (which represents Wednesday).
Year	Displays year as an integer.	Year(date) Date can be expressed as a string, number, or date literal.	Year("September 9, 1998") Returns: 1998

Domain Aggregate

These functions can be used to calculate a statistic about a field in a table. They're useful for summarizing data in a subform or subreport. Note that all arguments used with these functions must be enclosed in quotes.

Function	Description	Syntax	Example
DAvg	Averages the numbers in a field.	DAvg(field name, table/query name, criteria) Criteria are optional.	DAvg("Amount", "Invoices", "InvoiceDate < #1/1/99#") Returns the average of the field *Amount* in the table *Invoices* where the *InvoiceDate* field is before 1/1/99.
DCount	Counts the numbers in a field.	DCount(field name, table/query name, criteria) Criteria are optional.	DCount("Name", "Customers") Returns the count of the field *Name* in the table *Customers* (the number of customers.)
DLookup	Looks up the value of a particular field in a table that's not open. This can be used in a form control to display data from another table or query.	DLookup(field name, table/query name, criteria) Criteria are optional; however, if you don't use criteria, the DLookup function returns data from a random record in the table.	DLookup("Name", "Customers", "Acct = 12") Returns the value in the field *Name* in the table *Customers* where the field *Acct* = 12.
DMax	Finds the largest number in a field.	DMax(field name, table/query name, criteria) Criteria are optional.	DMax("Amount", "Invoices") Returns the largest number in the field *Amount* in the *Invoices* table.
DMin	Finds the smallest number in a field.	DMin(field name, table/query name, criteria) Criteria are optional.	DMin("Amount", "Invoices") Returns the smallest number in the field *Amount* in the *Invoices* table.
DStDev	Finds the standard deviation of the values in a numeric field.	DStDev(field name, table/query name, criteria) Criteria are optional.	DStDev("Amount", "Invoices") Returns the standard deviation of the field *Amount* in the *Invoices* table.
DSum	Totals the numbers in a field.	DSum(field name, table/query name, criteria) Criteria are optional.	DSum("Amount", "Invoices") Returns the total of the numbers in the field *Amount* in the *Invoices* table.
Dvar	Finds the variance of the values in a numeric field.	DVar(field name, table/query name, criteria) Criteria are optional.	DVar("Amount", "Invoices") Returns the variance of the field *Amount* in the *Invoices* table.

Text Or String

These functions are used with text or string type data. They're useful for working with units of text that are smaller than whole fields and for formatting text.

Function	Description	Syntax	Example
InStr	Locates a text string that's embedded in another string. The function returns an integer containing the position of the string in the larger string.	Instr(start position,"string to look in, " "string to look for") Start position is optional—if you omit it, the function looks at the beginning of the string.	InStr("Black and blue", "and") Returns: 7, because the word "and" starts in the 7th position from the left.
LCase	Displays string in lowercase letters.	LCase("string")	LCase("USA") Returns: usa
Left	Displays leftmost characters in a string.	Left("string", number of characters)	Left("wxyz"2) Returns: wx
Len	Finds the length of a text string.	Len("string")	Len("Smith") Returns: 5
LTrim	Trims or cuts the leading blanks from the left end of a text string.	Ltrim("string")	Ltrim(" Smith") Returns: "Smith"
Mid	Displays characters from the middle of a string.	Mid("string", start position, length) Length is optional—if you omit it, the function returns all characters to the end of the string.	Mid("(303)-444-1829", 7) Returns: "444-1829"
Right	Displays rightmost characters of a string.	Right("string", number of characters)	Right(wxyz, 2) Returns: yz

RTrim	Trims or cuts the trailing blanks from the right end of a text string.	Rtrim("string")	Rtrim(" Smith ") Returns: "Smith"
Space	Creates a string of spaces.	Space(number) Number is an integer that defines how many spaces will be in the string.	Space(4) Returns: " "
String	Creates a string of a specified length containing a repeating character.	String(number, character)	String(5, "*") Returns: "*****"
Trim	Trims or cuts all blanks from both the right and left ends of a text string.	Trim("string")	Trim(" Smith ") Returns: "Smith"
Ucase	Displays string in uppercase.	UCase("string")	UCase("abc") Returns: ABC

Miscellaneous

These functions are helpful in creating criteria for queries, or for beginning programming needs.

Function	Description	Syntax	Example
Choose	Selects a value from a list. Lets you substitute more descriptive data for code or ID numbers.	Choose(value, choice-1, choice-2, etc.) Value is any number or numeric field. Choice-2 and greater are optional.	Choose(3, "Tom", "Dick", "Harry") Returns: "Harry" (the 3rd choice in the list).
CurDir	Finds the current path (folder name) you are using.	CurDir(Disk drive letter) If you omit the drive letter, it assumes the current disk drive.	CurDir("C") Returns: "Programs/Access/" (If this is the current folder.)
Fix, Int	Displays correct integer for numbers. Fix and Int are the same except for the way they handle negative numbers. If the number is negative, Int rounds down to the first negative integer less than or equal to number, and Fix rounds up.	Fix(number)	Fix(12.3) Returns: 12
IIf	Allows one of two values to be used depending on whether an expression is true or false.	IIf(expression, true value, false value)	IIf(InvoiceAge > 60, 10, 0) Returns: 10 if the field *InvoiceAge* is greater than 60, and 0 if it's not.
InputBox	Displays a prompt and a text box and waits for the user to input text or click a button. It returns a string containing what the user typed into the text box.	InputBox(prompt) Prompt is the text that appears next to the text box. There are many other optional arguments for InputBox, see Access Help.	InputBox("Enter Your UserName") Returns: A string containing the user name typed in (after a text box is displayed).
IsNull	Returns either True or False, indicating whether or not an expression contains any valid data. No valid data is called Null.	IsNull(expression) The expression can be any text string or number. It's probably most useful to use a field or control name as the expression.	IsNull(Middle Name) Returns: True if there is data in the field *Middle Name*, and returns False if there isn't.
MsgBox	Displays a prompt and waits for the user to click a button, and returns an integer representing the button clicked by the user.	MsgBox(prompt) Prompt is the text that appears next to the text box. There are many other optional arguments for MsgBox, see Access Help.	MsgBox("Do you want to print labels?") Returns: A number corresponding to the button clicked by the user (after a box is displayed that says "Do you want to print labels?").
RGB	Displays a color based on a combination of red, green, and blue. RGB is often used to assign colors to form controls.	RGB(red, green, blue) Red is an integer between 0 and 255 that quantifies the amount of red in the color, Blue quantifies the amount of blue and green quantifies the amount of green.	RGB(255, 0, 0) Returns: The color red.

Glossary

A

Action.   One step of a task performed by a macro.

Action pane.   The upper part of the Macro Design screen used for entering actions, conditions, names, and comments.

Action query.   A type of query that performs an operation on a table, such as deleting specified records.

ActiveX controls.   A set of additional custom controls for use in reports and forms.

Add-in.   A program that is optionally installed when Access is installed.

Aggregate data.   One piece of data that summarizes a value for an entire group.

Aggregate function.   A function that returns a summary value for a group of data, such as sum or avg.

Anomaly.   An instance of incorrect or inconsistent data.

Append query.   A query that adds records from one table to another.

Application software.   A group of files that, when running, can focus the computer on a specific task or set of tasks.

Archiving.   Moving outdated or unused data to another table for storage.

Argument.   Additional information needed by a macro or a data value passed to a function in Visual Basic. Arguments determine the object or objects involved in the action, the conditions placed on an object, text to be displayed, and other important specifics.

Argument pane.   The lower part of the Macro Design screen used for entering arguments.

Attribute.   A characteristic of an entity class.

AutoExec macro.   A macro that automatically runs each time a database file is opened.

AutoFormat.   A form/report design command that automatically formats a form.

AutoKeys macro.   A special macro that is assigned to run when a specified key or combination of keys is pressed.

B

Bit.   The smallest unit of data on a computer—a one or a zero.

Bound control.   An object in a form/report that is tied directly to a field in the data source.

Bound form.   A form that is tied to a data source, such as a table or query.

Bridge table.   A table created to simplify a many-to-many relationship between tables.

Browser.   A software application that reads and displays HTML files, which are Web page files.

Byte.   A string of eight bits representing one character.

C

Calculated control.   A control based on an expression.

Calculated field.   A new query field that uses one or more fields in a calculation.

Caption.   An alternate heading used to identify a field.

Chart.   A type of report that shows numeric data in a graphical format, such as a pie, bar, or line graph.

Chart Wizard.   A wizard that aids in creating charts and graphs.

Check Box.   A control representing a Yes/No field that appears as a box with a check mark inside.

Client file.   The file requiring data from an external source. In this case, it is an Access field.

Column.   The vertical strip of data representing a field in Datasheet view. Each column shows all the data in one field.

Columnar form.   A form layout that displays all field names in a single column down the left side of the form. One record is displayed at a time.

Columnar report.   A report that presents the data vertically in a column, one record at a time.

Combo Box.   A control that enables the user to select data from a drop-down list displayed on the form.

Command button.   A button on a form that executes a command or runs a procedure or macro in response to an event.

Comment.   The optional documentation of the macro action.

Composite, complex, or compound key.   A multiple-field primary key.

Concatenate.   Joining two string fields together to make a new field.

Condition.   An expression, evaluated as either true or false, that is used to control the actions of a macro. If the expression is true, the action will be performed.

Conditional formatting.   Formatting placed on a control based on a condition.

Control.   An object in a form or report.

Control name.   A field or other object name included in the Condition column of a macro.

Control tip.   Helpful information that appears when you rest the mouse pointer on a control.

Criteria.   Limiting descriptors or conditions placed on fields that define the records to be included in the query.

Crosstab query.   A type of query that displays summarized data in row and column format.

D

Data.   Raw facts, numbers, or names that are input into the computer for processing.

Data Definition query.   A query that creates a table or changes the structure of a table.

Data integrity.   The reliability and accuracy of the data.

Data Manipulation query.   A query that retrieves, organizes, or updates data.

Data organization.   Method of arranging data in the computer—from bits to a database.

Data type.   The kind of data contained in a field, such as numeric or text. There are eight basic data types.

Database.   A large collection of related data files, forms, queries, reports, and so forth.

Database application.   A complete database containing data and other objects that work together to perform a task or group of related tasks.

Database file.   Stored file that includes all related objects in a database.

Database management system (DBMS).   A computerized method for managing, organizing, and using a database.

Database Object.   Individual parts of a database file, such as tables, queries, reports, forms, or macros.

Database template.   A predesigned Access database file.

Database window.   The main screen for Access. It displays all objects created for a particular database file.

Datasheet form.   A type of form that displays all records in Datasheet view.

Datasheet view.   The view that displays the results of the query (dynaset).

Debug.   The act of finding and correcting the bugs, or errors, in a macro or other program.

Delete query.   A query that deletes records from a table.

Deletion anomaly.   An anomaly that happens when data is deleted from a relation.

Delimited text file.   A file with commas, tabs, or other characters separating data items from each other.

Design grid.   The lower pane of the query design window which displays the fields, criteria and other elements of the design.

Domain integrity.   When the values in any given field are within an accepted range.

Dynaset.   The set of records produced by the query.

E

Edit.   To make basic changes to a record.

Embedded object.   An OLE object that is copied into a client file and stored.

Entity.   One specific member of an entity class.

Entity class.   A group of like items (or entities).

Entity integrity.   When a database has no duplicate records in any table.

Event.   Any change in the state of an object or an action that happens to an object, such as clicking the left mouse button while pointing at a command button. An event can cause a macro or Visual Basic procedure to execute.

Event procedure.   An object, such as a macro or module, that executes when triggered by an event.

Excel.   The spreadsheet software component of the MS Office suite.

Export.   Copy data from an Access table to another type of file, including another Access database file and other applications.

Expression.   A set of symbols used to define a calculation or other operation.

Expression Builder.   A tool used to create expressions and object identifiers.

External source.   A file outside of the open Access database that contains data or other objects that can be imported into the database.

F

Field.   The smallest unit of data, such as someone's last name or phone number. One column in the table.

Field properties. The descriptive attributes of fields, such as a size specification or an automatically assigned value (default value).

File. Data or programs stored on a disk.

Filter. A command to selectively choose records based on certain criteria.

Find. A command to locate certain records.

First Normal Form. A standard for a table that requires that all the fields describe the entity represented by the table, the candidate for primary key be defined, and all fields contain the simplest possible values.

Focus. An event that occurs when a control contains the blinking cursor because it has been tabbed to or clicked on.

Footer. Text that is printed at the bottom of each page of a report.

Forced page break. A page break placed in a specific location by the report designer.

Foreign key. Field(s) containing the same values as those in the primary key of another table.

Form. A database object that displays table or query data, and is used instead of the Datasheet view to enter, view, and edit data.

Form Design view. The view that allows manual creation or editing of a form. It comes with its own set of form design tools.

Form tool. A tool that creates a form from a selected data source that displays one record at a time.

Form view. A view of the form which displays the data from the data source and allows for data entry and editing.

Form Wizard. A tool that asks the user for input to create the form.

Function. A miniprogram within Access that performs a special operation, such as rounding a number.

Functional dependency. When the value of one attribute determines the value of another attribute.

G

Grouping. A method of organizing fields based on the data values in a descriptive field.

H

Handle. A rectangle that appears on a form object when it's selected. You can drag an object by its handles to change its size and shape.

Header. Text that is printed at the top of each page of a report.

HTML. Hyper Text Markup Language, the common code for publishing documents on the Internet.

Hyperlink. Electronic links that connect to other documents or files.

Hyperlink control. A control that contains a URL, email address or internal link to another document.

I

Identifier. The complete name and location of a field, control, or property used in an expression.

Image Control. A control to add a picture or saved graphic.

Import. A command to bring in data from an external source.

Index. A field property that speeds up searches, joins, sorts, and filters associated with the field when the property is set.

Information. Useful processed data.

Inner join. Join type containing only the records from both tables having at least one corresponding record in the other table.

Input mask. A control that restricts data entry to specified characters, such as only numbers or capital letters.

Insertion anomaly. An anomaly that happens when data is added to a relation.

Interface. The top layer of a piece of software—what is seen when the program runs, including tools for using the software and/or data objects.

Internet Worldwide network of computer systems.

Intranet. Local network that behaves like a small version of the Internet, usually within a corporate or institutional structure.

J

Join. A relationship between tables based on a common field or fields.

L

Label. A control that holds descriptive text data.

Label Wizard. A wizard that aids in creating various types of labels (mailing labels, etc.).

Layout Tools ribbon. The ribbon which contains Layout Tools for editing the form.

Layout view. A view of the form which allows for certain editing changes to the structure of the form as well as data entry and editing.

Left outer join. A one-to-many join type containing all the records in the "one" table, and only those records in the "many" table containing a data value in the foreign key that matches one in the primary key of the "one" table.

Linked object. An OLE object that is used by, but not stored in, the client file. The client file knows where to find the object, and is dynamically linked to it so the client file reflects any changes made to the server file.

Linked table.   A pointer to another table in a different database.

List box.   A control that displays a list of data values and allows the user to select from the list.

Literal value.   A data value that is constant—it doesn't change. For example, "12" or "Smith" are literal values.

Logo.   An image used as a logo usually placed in the header section of a form or report.

Lookup field.   A special type of field that displays a value from another table.

Lookup table.   A table that holds data about groups or categories of information, and is used by other tables for looking up data values.

M

Macro.   A database object containing a series of steps or actions that are run to complete a specific task.

Macro Builder.   A feature that assists you in creating a macro in the Form Design view.

Macro group.   One macro containing several related macros.

Mail Merge.   A feature in Word that allows for merging a data table with a document to produce a customized copy of the document for each record in the table.

Main form.   The form used to display data from the main or "one" table in a one-to-many relationship. Data is displayed in a columnar layout.

Main/subform.   A type of form that combines two or more tables/queries into a single form with the tables having different layouts.

Make Table query.   An action query that creates a new table with selected records from another table.

Many-to-many join.   A join where many records in both tables relate to many records in another table.

Master table.   A fairly static (mostly unchanging) table that holds data about people and things.

Modal form (or Modal Dialog form).   A form that does not permit a user to switch focus to another window while the modal form is open.

Multiple-field primary key.   A primary key made up of more than one field.

Multiple Items form.   A type of form that displays multiple records in a columns and rows format.

N

Naming conventions.   Accepted standards for naming database objects using a three-letter prefix.

Navigation pane.   The left side of the Access window containing a list of database objects.

Non-key attribute.   An attribute that is not a primary key, nor part of a key.

Normal form.   A representation of a table that meets a set of rules intended to eliminate data redundancy and errors.

Normalization.   The process of making a table match a relational database design standard called a normal form.

Null.   The condition of having no data in a control or field.

O

Object.   Any item in a database object collection, such as a control on a form or a field in a table.

Object identifier.   The complete name and location of an Access object.

Office button.   A button in the upper left corner that opens the Office menu which contains database level commands.

OLE objects.   Objects that are linked or embedded in any Windows application. They can be graphics, clip art, sound, text, or video files.

One-to-many join.   A join where one record in the first table relates to many records in the second table.

One-to-one join.   A join where one record in the first table relates to one record in the second table.

Operator.   A symbol representing the action to be performed in an expression, such as mathematical, relational, logical, and string commands used to extend or limit the criteria.

Option button.   A control representing a Yes/No field that appears as a circle with a dot inside.

Overnormalization.   The process of normalizing data to the point where work becomes difficult.

P

Parameter query.   A type of query that allows the user to specify the criteria each time the query is run.

Partial dependency.   When a non-key attribute is determined by only one of the attributes in the key.

Pivot Chart.   A chart that summarizes data which can be switched or pivoted to provide different views.

Pivot Table.   A form that summarizes numeric data in rows and columns which can be switched or pivoted for different views of the data.

PowerPoint.   The presentation graphics software component of the MS Office suite.

Primary key.   A field or group of fields that uniquely identifies a record.

Prompt.   A message to the user displayed on the screen.

Property.   A characteristic or attribute of an object or control.

Property sheet.   A list of attributes of a control or object.

Q

QBE.   Query By Example method for designing queries.

QBE grid.   The grid used to define a QBE that has columns for query fields and rows for query criteria.

Query.   Questions asked of a table (or tables) to obtain specific information. A query limits information to records that match specific criteria and can be used as input for other database objects.

Query Datasheet view.   The window that displays the results of the query (the dynaset).

Query Design window.   The view that allows the user to create the query.

Query Wizard.   A feature of Access that helps the user create several different types of queries.

Quick Access toolbar.   A small customizable toolbar for frequently used commands.

R

Rapid prototyping.   A way of performing the system design and implementation phases by building working models of the application, and gathering user feedback.

Record.   A collection of related fields that describes one member of the group represented by a table.

Referential integrity.   A set of rules that ensures that data in joined tables remains accurate.

Refresh all.   A command that refreshes the data in all open database objects when clicked.

Relation.   A table in a relational database.

Relational database.   A type of database (such as Access) that stores groups of information in tables that can be related, or cross-referenced.

Relationship.   Joining of tables on related fields.

Replace.   Command to assist in editing records by locating and replacing data in fields.

Report.   An Access object that summarizes data from tables or queries into a concise, readable, organized format.

Report sections.   Parts of a report, such as the Report Header/Footer, Page Header/Footer, Detail, or Group Header/Footer.

Report Wizard.   A wizard that aids in report creation.

Restructuring.   Changing the structure of the table by adding, removing, or changing a field, or by altering the properties of a field.

Ribbon.   An area in the upper part of the window containing buttons for database commands.

Rich-text file.   A standard file format for many software applications. Access objects can be saved in this format for exporting to other applications with some formatting features preserved.

Right outer join.   A one-to-many join type containing all the records in the "many" table, and only those records in the "one" table containing a data value in the foreign key that matches one in the primary key of the "many" table.

Row.   The horizontal strip of data representing a record in Datasheet view.

S

Second Normal Form.   A standard for a table that requires it to be in First Normal Form and have no partial dependencies.

Select query.   A type of query that selects records based on certain criteria. This is the default query type.

Server.   A host computer containing Web page files.

Server application.   The application in which the OLE object was made.

Smart Tags.   Links to actions that can be performed in other programs. Can be attached to tables, queries, and controls on forms, reports, and data access pages.

Sorting.   A method of organizing records based on ascending or descending order of values in a field or fields.

Split View form.   A type of form that combines all fields from a data source in two distinct views: Layout view and Datasheet view.

Structured Query Language (SQL).   A set of commands used to define a query.

Startup form.   A form, usually a Switchboard form that automatically opens when the database opens.

Subdata sheet.   A datasheet that displays data from a joined table.

Subform.   The form used to display data from the sub or "many" table in a one-to-many relationship.

Subreport.   A report that is inserted in another report.

Switchboard form.   An interactive form containing a variety of macros, buttons, menus, and toolbars that automate database functions.

Switchboard Manager.   An Add-in program for Access that helps build Switchboard forms automatically.

Syntax.   The structure of an expression or statement.

Systems Development Life Cycle.   A way of describing the building of a computer information system as the following phases in a cycle: definition, design and development, and implementation.

T

Tab order.   The order in which the cursor moves between the fields in a form.

Tabbed form.   A control that displays multiple pages (tabs) on a form.

Table.   Access object that contains data about a specific group or entity of related items.

Table Datasheet view.   A view of the table data organized into columns and rows.

Table Design view.   A view of the structure or organization of the table, showing all field properties.

Table pane.   The upper pane of the query design window that displays the data source(s) for the query (tables and/or queries).

Tabular.   A form layout that has several fields and records displayed on the screen in a tablelike design.

Tabular Report.   A report that presents the data in rows and columns, showing several fields and records at a time.

Templates.   A group of prewritten files containing formatting for HTML documents.

Text Box or control.   A box where field data or calculated data is displayed.

Third Normal Form.   A standard for a table that requires it to be in Second Normal Form and have no transitive dependencies.

Toggle button.   A control representing a Yes/No field that appears as a raised or sunken box.

Top(N).   Used with queries to limit the records displayed to a specified number or percentage.

Total query.   A query that produces totals and other summary information for defined groups of records.

Total row.   A row that can be added to the bottom of a table or query displayed in Datasheet view. Simple statistical calculations can be shown in this row.

Transaction/event table.   A table that contains data about transactions or about events that occur to the data in tables.

Transitive dependency.   When a non-key attribute determines the value of another attribute.

Tuple.   A record in a table.

U

Unbound control.   An object in a form/report that is not directly tied to a field in the data source.

Unbound form.   A form that is not tied to a data source.

Undo.   A command to cancel a previous operation.

Union query.   A query that displays data from multiple tables even if the tables have no common fields.

Unique Records.   A query property that returns only unique records in the dynaset.

Unique Values.   A query property that selects only records with unique values in the fields included in the query.

Update anomaly.   An anomaly that happens when data is changed in a relation.

Update query.   An action query that makes global changes to table data.

URL.   Uniform Resource Locator, or the address of a specific Web site.

User-defined integrity.   When the data in a database complies with specific business and user rules.

V

Validation.   A control that restricts data entry to specified values, such as data with a value of either 1 or 2.

W

Web page.   A file containing text, graphics, or other media that can be displayed on computers connected to the Internet.

Wildcards.   Used in searching to represent specific characters in the search string.

Wizard.   A feature in Access to assist in database and object creation.

Word.   The word processing software component of the MS Office suite.

World Wide Web.   A set of connected files, or Web pages, that are stored on computers connected to the Internet.

Z

Zoom.   A feature in query design that enlarges the screen display of a cell.

Index